Fern Grower's Manual

Fern Grower's Manual

Revised and Expanded Edition

Barbara Joe Hoshizaki and
Robbin C. Moran

TIMBER PRESS
Portland, Oregon

The in-text *Adiantum* line drawings are by Lynn Vander Velde; unless otherwise credited in the captions, all other line drawings are by Barbara Joe Hoshizaki.

Unless otherwise credited in the captions, the in-text black-and-white photographs are by Arthur Takayama.

Unless otherwise credited in the captions, the color plates are by Barbara Joe Hoshizaki.

Published in 2001 by
Timber Press, Inc.
The Haseltine Building
133 S.W. Second Avenue, Suite 450
Portland, Oregon 97204, U.S.A.

Printed in Hong Kong

Library of Congress Cataloging-in-Publication Data

Hoshizaki, Barbara Joe.
    Fern grower's manual / Barbara Joe Hoshizaki and Robbin C. Moran.—
Rev. and expanded ed.
        p.   cm.
    Includes bibliographical references (p.   ).
    ISBN 0-88192-495-4
    1. Ferns, Ornamental. I. Moran, Robbin Craig, 1956– II. Title.

SB429. H64 2001
635.9′373—dc21
                                                                00-059999

Contents

Color plates, including USDA Plant Hardiness Zone Map, follow page 240

Preface

Ferns continue to hold the interest of gardeners as we enter a new millennium. After the Victorian fern craze, interest in ferns focused mainly on the native species and some of those common in the trade. After World War II, interest in exotic ferns gradually took hold, and this fostered the formation of new fern societies and the offering of a greater selection in the trade.

It has been more than 25 years since the first edition of *Fern Grower's Manual* was published (Hoshizaki 1975). At the time, the author thought it would interest the horticultural public for only a few years before ferns would fall out of vogue. She was wrong. A strong interest in ferns continues today as evidenced by the great increase in fern societies all over the world for both amateurs and professional botanists. Also, the number of fern species in cultivation has increased tremendously. The contributions of fern botanists in writing floras and monographs, clarifying species, and supporting amateur interest are important factors in this growth. The horticultural area has also made great contributions, particularly in pest control, tissue culture, plug culture, new products, and determining the growing needs of certain ferns.

All this interest in ferns has created a need for a revised edition of *Fern Grower's Manual*—one that updates the information on pest control, propagation, new materials and products, cultural requirements, and many other topics. But unlike other recent fern books, this revised edition emphasizes identifying cultivated ferns by way of the text and illustrations for the 124 genera and more than 700 species treated (each species is illustrated). Because diagnostic features are often unclear in photographs, this edition relies heavily on silhouettes and line drawings. With additional help from the book's glossary and a good hand lens, the reader should be able to identify most of the cultivated species.

This revised edition treats all the commonly cultivated (and some rarely cultivated) fern species, varieties, and many cultivars in the United States. Besides identification, this new edition will help readers learn more about a particular fern by including its geographical distribution and author citations after the species names. This information enables readers to have a better idea of which floras, texts, or journals to consult for further information about a fern. An expanded bibliography also points to other literature sources.

This book is mainly written for people seriously interested in growing ferns, knowing their names and what makes them similar or different, and appreciating their diversity. It is not a coffee-table book, nor a chatty type of garden book meant for light reading. Beginning fern amateurs may find more information than they need, but they will also find information useful at their level. Although this book primarily is a reference, it is also for browsing and gleaning bits of information not readily found elsewhere.

The core information in this book will be particularly helpful to plant people who want to grow or identify different ferns and fern allies. Gardeners, nursery people, commercial growers, plant inspectors, botanical garden staff, horticulturists, botanists, biology teachers, and others will find the information they need in this one volume. The alternative would be to have a library of horticultural books and floras from the world over and/or access to a fern botanist with a large herbarium. Botanists needing to grow ferns for their research will find specific information on growing genera of ferns as well as general cultural information.

Students in horticulture, botany, and biology will find that this book gives an overview of fern information that is basic and up-to-date, but they also should note that much remains to be discovered. In addition to examining the growth response of ferns to various environmental conditions, there is also much to clarify on the relationships of genera and species. It is hoped that this book will stimulate students to study horticultural and botanical problems of ferns or use them in their research. Although this type of problem solving has been traditionally left to the scientist, observant, thoughtful, and innovative growers have made and will continue to make valuable contributions to studying ferns (pteridology). Gardeners without scientific training have introduced new species to horticulture, produced new cultivars and hybrids, and found the right combination of conditions to grow difficult species. Much is unknown about temperature tolerances of ferns, and this too is information that may be observed by growers and added to the store of knowledge about ferns. Commercial growers have worked out detailed cultural information on growing Boston ferns and leather ferns. Cultural details for other important trade groups have yet to be fully reported.

Keeping an accurate list of the species in cultivation has become increasingly difficult, if not impossible. Many name changes since the first edition of this book have greatly complicated the task. Moreover, new ferns are constantly being introduced to horticulture. There are about 10 fern societies in the world whose members often bring new ferns into cultivation, and the number of species that can still be introduced is sizable. An annual list recently offered by a fern society listed 775 packets of spores for exchange. With so many possible species to list, it was thought better to err on the side of including too many instead of too few. Several new and promising introductions came to our attention too late to be fully treated. Several species listed as cultivated could not be verified, and others may have been overlooked. Since few monographs have been written about problem ferns, identification was sometimes difficult and often complicated by not knowing the country of origin.

Acknowledgments

Writing this book has been a prolonged and immense undertaking, and many people have helped and encouraged us to reach the finish line. We especially wish to thank those people who read portions of the manuscript for accuracy and gave helpful suggestions. They are Dr. Wade L. Berry, a plant physiologist and soil scientist of the University of California, Los Angeles, who edited the cultural information; Dr. A. James Downer, Farm Advisor, of the University of California Extension, Ventura, who edited the section on insect pests and diseases; Dr. Ole Becker, of the University of California, Riverside, who edited the section on nematodes; and botanist Sharon Ishikawa, of the United States Department of Agricultural, Animal and Plant Health Inspection Service, who edited the section on importing plants.

We are indebted to the kindness of Dr. Alan R. Smith, of the University of California, Berkeley, and Dr. John T. Mickel, of The New York Botanical Garden, for their assistance and time while we worked at their herbaria. We also thank Dr. Art Gibson, of the University of California herbarium, for use of their facilities. For identifying difficult ferns, we wish to thank the following people: Dr. Christopher R. Fraser-Jenkins for *Dryopteris;* Dr. Richard Hauke for *Equisetum;* Dr. Blanca León for *Campyloneurum;* Dr. John T. Mickel for *Elaphoglossum* and hardy ferns; Dr. Alan R. Smith for *Thelypteris* and other genera; Dr. Rolla M. Tryon for cheilanthoids and suggestions on genera designations; and Dr. Iván Valdespino for *Selaginella.*

We were fortunate to have the help of other pteridologists from around the world. For Asian ferns we were helped by many Japanese botanists. We are particularly grateful for identifications from Dr. Toshiyuki Nakaike, Prof. Keisuke Yasuda, and Prof. Norio Sahashi. Also of assistance were Prof. Masahiro Kato,

Prof. Reiko Yoroi, Prof. Ryoko Imaichi, Dr. Haruki Hirabayashi, Dr. Mitsuyasu Hasebe, and Dr. Noriaki Murakami. The late Dr. Warren H. Wagner Jr., Dr. Dan Palmer, and Dr. Barbara Parris were valuable sources of information on Pacific Island ferns. Dr. David B. Lellinger supplied information about Costa Rican ferns, Dr. Lynn Raulerston about Guam and Palau ferns, Martin Rickard about English ferns, Michael Price about Philippine and Malaysian ferns, and Dr. Peter Bostock and Chris Goudey about Australian ferns. Yolanda Orta and Martin Grantham shared their expertise about fern propagation. For keeping us informed of ferns in their area and for generous assistance in other ways, we are indebted to Marilyn Johnson of Florida, Judith Jones of Washington, John and Carol Mickel of New York, and Nancy Swell of Virginia.

We also thank the following for obtaining specimens and answering specific questions: the late Virginia Ault, Ed and Phyllis Bates, Betsy Feuerstein, Robin Halley, the late Gerda Isenberg, Hildegard and Bruce Jackson, Al and Marilyn Johnson, Judith Jones, Miriam Leefe, Robert Manthorne, Dr. Bruce McAlpin, Duane Petersen, Milton Piedra, Ruth Radcliffe, Martin Rickard, the late Dorothy Skula, Nancy Swell, Roy Vail, Helen Woodley, and Reggie Whitehead. In addition, we learned much from interacting with many members of the South Florida Fern Society, the Tampa Fern Society, the New York Chapter of the American Fern Society, the Los Angeles International Fern Society, the San Diego Fern Society, the Hardy Fern Society, and the Southwestern Fern Society.

Many commercial growers were generous with their help and information. We thank Ades and Gish Nursery, Barford's Hardy Ferns, California Ferns, Casa de Flora, Clark's Nursery, Charles Alford Plants, Daisy Plant Farm, Eisenbraun Ferns, Fancy Fronds, Fender's Nursery, Fern Farm, Foliage Gardens, Frank and Dorothy Skula, Freshwater Fauna and Flora, Glasshouse Works, H. Marugame, Half-moon Bay Nursery, Henry's Plant Farm, Huntley Greens, Jerry Horne, Lyndon Horticultural Enterprises, Marilyn Johnson, Monrovia Nursery, MSK Rare Plant Nursery, Plants Unlimited, Santa Rosa Tropicals, Siskiyou Rare Plant Nursery, Swell's Nursery, Talnadge Fern Gardens, Tropical Gardens, Varga's Nursery, Weatherwood Nursery, Wedel's Nursery, Weeks Nursery, Yerba Buena Nursery, and Yolanda's Ferns.

For helping with computers, locating citations, assisting with the illustrations, and just making things work smoother, we would like to acknowledge the help of Joan DeFato, Carol Brooks-Hoshizaki, Jon and Madeleine Hoshizaki, Janet Keyes, Harry Le Vine Jr., Alvin Lee, Sylvia Louie, Vickie Milane, Mamie Moy, Damon Woods, and Leo Yamanaka. We wish to acknowledge Arthur Takayama for taking and preparing most of the black-and-white photographs and Lynn Vander Velde for the *Adiantum* line drawings. When the senior author desperately needed editing assistance, Ed and Phyllis Bates, Ann Herrington, Marilyn Johnson, and Susan MacQueen came to her rescue. Dr. Kenneth Wilson has been a source of unflagging help, ranging from providing botanical expertise to trouble-shooting computer problems. The senior author's husband, Dr. Takashi Hoshizaki, a plant physiologist, suggested doing this revision more than 15 years ago. He helped with the editing and artwork, but most importantly gave cheerful support and encouragement over the years.

The authors apologize for any oversights in our acknowledgments and wish to assure all that their contributions are nevertheless deeply appreciated.

The senior author also expresses her gratitude and deepest thanks to the junior author, Dr. Robbin C. Moran, for consenting to join in producing this book. Not only is he one of today's leading fern scientists, he has also demonstrated his interest and ability in writing for general fern audiences. He has added valuable information to the text, clarified complicated topics, and improved the book in many ways. Without his broad knowledge of ferns, his patience, and his energy to check on innumerable details, make the required changes, do the editing, and work with Timber Press, this book would have languished much longer in manuscript form.

We wish to especially acknowledge and thank our editor, Josh Leventhal. He made our work so much easier and the book so much better with his careful editing and good judgment.

Although we relied heavily on the counsel of many people and are greatly indebted to their contributions, any discrepancies or errors in this publication are entirely our own. The information and advice contained in this work have been brought together with care, but because of the large number of variables we cannot guarantee complete accuracy or results. The reader acts on his or her own responsibility.

Barbara Joe Hoshizaki
Los Angeles, California

Robbin C. Moran
The New York Botanical Garden

1 About Ferns

Ferns bring to mind pleasant, cool glens and shaded forests. We recall such things when we use ferns in our gardens and homes. The ferny look is well known and loved, and some of us are content to sit back and relax as we enjoy the soft green array of patterns and textures in ferns. But there is more to appreciate about ferns than their mere appearance.

Ferns are usually recognized by their finely divided leaves, a type of leaf so characteristic that it is called a "ferny leaf." There are, however, many plants with ferny leaves that aren't ferns, and many ferns that don't have typical ferny leaves. What, then, makes a fern a fern?

Ferns are spore-bearing plants; they lack flowers, fruits, and seeds. The so-called asparagus fern (*Asparagus setaceus*) is not a fern despite its finely divided appearance because it bears flowers and seeds (it is actually a member of the lily family; its fruits are the orange berries often seen on the plant). Spores and seeds greatly differ. Spores are simple one-celled microscopic structures, whereas seeds are complex, many-celled structures usually visible to the unaided eye. Although plants such as algae, liverworts, and mosses produce spores, they differ from ferns by lacking the large, thin, true leaves. Ferns further differ from these spore-bearers by their development of specialized tissue (xylem and phloem) to conduct food and water. These tissues also strengthen the stem and enable ferns to grow taller than other spore-bearing plants.

Unlike seed plants, ferns depend on water to complete their typical life cycle. They grow in places where, when the time comes to reproduce, enough water is available for the sperm to swim to the egg. Seed plants, such as pines and flowering plants, produce cones or flowers that use wind or insects to complete their life cycle. They do not need water in the external environment for fertilization, and therefore they can grow in drier conditions and dominate more of the landscape.

Nevertheless, some ferns have the surprising ability to thrive in extreme climates. Desert ferns, of which there are few, often grow in the shade of rocks and boulders, using every bit of available water. Their roots grow deep in the soil between the cool rocks, and their fronds are often covered with woolly hairs or scales to protect them from water loss. When water is insufficient for new growth, many desert ferns curl their leaves or shed their leaflets and suspend growth until the next rain.

Like desert ferns, alpine ferns are also adapted to climatic extremes. They tend to be small and have hard-textured fronds that can endure the cold, dry winds. They grow only during the short summers as weather permits.

Most ferns of temperate regions grow in the ground or on rocks, and only a few species grow on trees. Approximately 200 species of ferns are native to the temperate areas of the United States. Temperate to subtropical areas noted for their abundance of ferns include parts of the Himalayas, Australia, New Zealand, and Japan. The tropics, however, harbor the largest number of fern species, particularly at middle elevations in the mountains. Here the mountain fog encourages an abundance of ferns.

New ferns are still being discovered in well-known parts of the world, and in the lesser known parts many more remain to be discovered. There are about 12,000 named species, and many of these have never been introduced into horticulture. Temperate places like Japan and the cool, mountain slopes of the tropics have many ferns suitable as new introductions for temperate gardens in the United States.

Compared to other plants, ferns have few economic uses. Nevertheless several are important. Ferns and fern allies dominated the extensive coal-forming swamps of the Carboniferous period 280 to 345 million years ago. Coal, therefore, is often composed of the compressed remains of ancient ferns and fern allies. If you are reading this book by electric light and your local power plant is fueled by coal, chances are that the energy used to generate the electricity for your bulb was captured millions of years ago by a fern or fern ally!

An important economic fern is *Azolla,* the mosquito fern. It is a rich source of nitrogen, a nutrient usually limiting to plant growth. *Azolla* is often used as an organic fertilizer in the rice paddies of southeastern Asia. Considering how many people rice feeds in that part of the world, *Azolla* must rank among the world's most important economic ferns. It is also used to a lesser extent to supplement the diet of chickens, pigs, and fish.

Perhaps the best-known use of ferns is the edible fiddleheads of species such as the ostrich fern of the eastern United States and the bracken fern of Asia. (An early Oregon agricultural bulletin gave recipes on how to cook bracken, including one on making "creamed bracken." Subsequent research, however, has shown that bracken contains carcinogens and should not be eaten.) The foliage of the water fern (*Ceratopteris*) and *Diplazium esculentum* are eaten in the tropics.

Various ferns with fibrous stems have been used as a substrate to cultivate epiphytic plants. The fibrous stems of *Osmunda* and tree ferns have been shredded to make a planting medium for orchids. More recently, tree-fern trunks have been cut and shaped to make containers for hanging-basket ferns. Because of conservation concerns, however, the export of tree ferns and tree-fern products is restricted. In areas where they abound, tree ferns have also been used to line roads and to construct small buildings because their trunks are resistant to rot.

Other uses of ferns include thatching roofs and making tea and dyes. Some fern rhizomes and rachises, such as those of the Gleicheniaceae and *Lygodium,* are flexible and tough enough to be used in basketry. Folklore ascribes many dubious uses to ferns, such as restoring hair, making oneself invisible, and providing lucky amulets. The use of the male fern to treat worm infections, however, is an example of one such tale being true. Some ferns, such as the bracken fern, gleichenias, and the hay-scented ferns, are considered weeds. Ferns have also been used to investigate basic problems in plant biology, such as organ development, hormones, genetics, evolution, and responses to light. But of all their uses, ferns are by far most important for their ornamental value.

2 The Structure of Ferns

Like sunflowers, oaks, pines, and other familiar plants in the landscape, the ferns have stems, roots, and leaves. Although these parts are familiar to most of us, their character and function are sometimes unusual. Much of this chapter might seem complicated, but you will find that a basic understanding of fern structure is extremely useful in making use of the rest of this book. Figure 2.1 illustrates the parts of a fern.

Stems

The stems of ferns can become tree-like and conspicuous, or they may be horizontal and go unnoticed. Inconspicuous stems might be short, partly buried in the soil, or densely covered with leaf bases, hairs, or scales. If the stem is erect and stout, it may be called a rootstock (Figure 2.2a). If it lies horizontally on the ground and is anchored to the soil by roots, it is called a rhizome (Figure 2.2b–e). Some rhizomes are long, freely branched, and climbing or scrambling over soil, rocks, or trees. They can bear fronds close together or far apart. Some rhizomes may grow into the soil and send out new fronds in unexpected places. Others branch frequently and form dense clumps. These clumps usually produce fronds in whorls, in irregular clusters, or arranged in two ranks. Erect stems generally produce fronds in a whorl or vase-like cluster. Semi-erect stems may have less perfect whorls. The slender, long stems on Boston ferns (*Nephrolepis exaltata*) and other species are called stolons (Figure 2.2f). These spring from the main stem or rootstock and produce new plantlets at their tips or from side buds. The stems of tree ferns are so large and wide that they are rightly called trunks (Figure 2.2g). Some grow up to 18 m (60 ft.) tall. Where abundant, tree ferns have been used to construct small buildings, and the starch in their stems has been used for food. Some ferns have thick, hollow stems that house ants. The ants protect the fern and provide some nutrients to the fern in exchange for shelter.

Stems serve the plant in several ways. First, the stem tip produces new stems, leaves, and roots. If this tip is damaged, it might kill the fern, particularly if the stem does not branch laterally. Given its importance, the stem tip is often protected by a covering of hairs or scales (Figure 2.2j, k). Second, the stem supports the leaves. Leaves can be supported in large clusters at great heights, as in tree ferns, but most ferns have their leaves supported on short- to long-creeping stems. Whatever the pattern of support, the leaves are always held up to the light and air. Third, stems conduct water and nutrients between the roots and leaves. For this purpose they are equipped with strands or bundles of special tissue known as xylem and phloem or, collectively, as vascular or conducting tissue. The vascular tissue can have different patterns depending on the species or taxonomic group to which the fern belongs (Figure 2.2h, i). Fourth, stems store food and water,

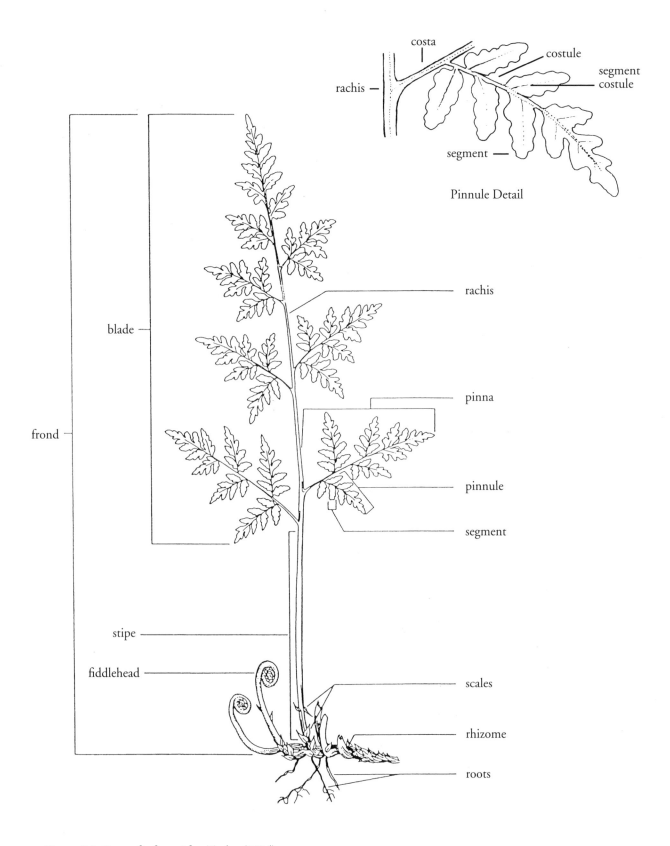

costa

costule

rachis

segment
costule

segment

Pinnule Detail

rachis

blade

pinna

pinnule

segment

frond

stipe

fiddlehead

scales

rhizome

roots

Figure 2.1. Parts of a fern. After Taylor (1984).

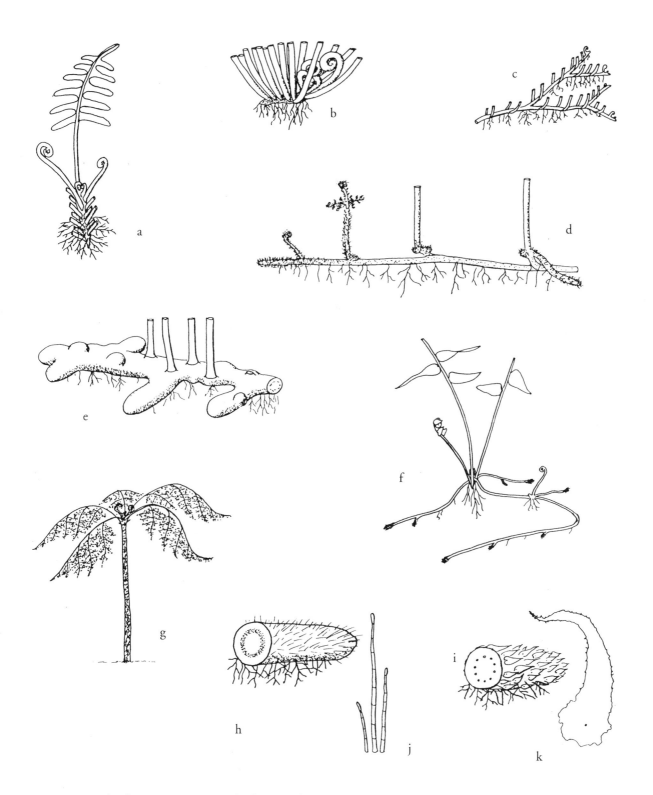

Figure 2.2. Kinds of stems: a. erect stem; b. rhizome, short-creeping (*Asplenium bulbiferum*); c. rhizome, wide-creeping and branching (*Gymnocarpium dryopteris*); d. rhizome, wide-creeping and branching from stipe base (*Hypolepis tenuifolia*); e. rhizome creeping, branching and fleshy (*Phlebodium*); f. stolons (*Nephrolepis exaltata*); g. trunk of a tree fern; h. vascular or conducting tissue within rhizome (*Hypolepis*); i. vascular or conducting tissue within rhizome (*Polypodium*); j. hairs covering the rhizome of h; k. scales covering the rhizome of i.

particularly if they are thick and fleshy (Figure 2.2e). Some stems, such as stolons and branching rhizomes, reproduce plants or increase the size of the colony.

Roots

The roots of adult ferns grow from the stem. There is never a main root system consisting of a taproot and lateral branch-roots. Fern roots are mostly fine, fibrous, densely branched, thick masses; rarely are they thick and fleshy. They grow close to the soil surface and are easily injured when the soil is tilled or disturbed. Young, actively growing roots have whitish or yellowish tips. Older portions of the roots are dark brown or black. The presence of a large number of young roots is a good sign of active growth.

Creeping or reclining rhizomes produce new roots as they grow forward. These roots are usually located on the underside of the rhizome just behind the tip. Ferns with erect stems produce new roots from the stem base. Erect-stemmed ferns may have their bases covered with old leaf bases, making it hard for the emerging roots to establish themselves into the soil (Figure 2.2a). If, however, the old fronds decay and a fine layer of forest litter accumulates around the stem, emerging roots will find a rooting medium. In cultivation it may be necessary to remove the old leaf bases of erect stems and replant the fern deeper into the soil to give the emerging roots a better chance to establish themselves and prolong the life of the fern.

Old tree ferns often have masses of roots on their stems. These roots are called aerial roots and form a fibrous outer layer around the stem. They absorb water and add strength and rigidity to the stem, which is necessary to support the heavy crown of fronds. The trunks of some tree ferns—for example, the Hawaiian tree fern *Cibotium glaucum*—readily send out new roots when planted.

The roots of some ferns house fungi in a symbiotic relationship. The fungi (mycorrhizae) help gather mineral nutrients for the fern in exchange for food. The fungi reside in the cells of the root or the root hairs that often become swollen and mucilaginous at their tips. The mycorrhizae that have been studied on ferns are reported to be cup fungi (*Ascomycetes*) and *Glomales* (Moteetee et al. 1996). Mycorrhizae of agricultural crops studied have been found to enhance growth when soil nutrients are low and not when sufficient or high. Whether these findings apply to ferns is not known.

The primary function of roots is to absorb water and minerals as well as hold the plant in place. Some ferns have roots with other functions, such as producing new plants or storing food and water.

Leaves

The leaves of ferns are called fronds and are produced at the stem tip. They develop by uncoiling and while doing so are called fiddleheads or monkey tails (see Figure 2.1). Technically, they are called croziers, from the term for a shepherd's crook. Croziers are tender and vulnerable to drying and damage. They are often protected by a covering of hairs or scales. A few ferns have emerging fronds that are hook-shaped or straight rather than coiled.

When a crozier uncoils, it produces a frond that typically has two parts: the stipe (petiole) and blade (see Figure 2.1). The stipe is the stalk, and the thin leafy part it supports is the blade. The stipe commonly bears hairs or scales that are often important in identification of a fern. In some ferns the stipes may be dark and highly polished, as in the maidenhair ferns (*Adiantum*). The stipes may also be long, short, or entirely absent (sessile). If the stipe naturally breaks or separates from the stem along a predetermined line or joint, it is said to be jointed or articulate. The tissue found in or near the middle of the stipe is called the vascular or conducting tissue (stipe bundles), which can be seen if you cut through the stipe with a razor blade. Many fern genera can be identified by the patterns of this tissue.

Blades come in many shapes and may be undivided, little divided, or much divided into smaller parts. Names are given to all these shapes, states of division, and their parts. The undivided state is called simple (Figure 2.3). If the blade is divided to the central vein or midrib, the frond is said to be compound (Figure 2.4). If each resulting leaflet is again divided to its midrib, the frond is twice compound. Tree ferns are often two- or four-times compound. If the blade is cut so that the leaflets form along the midrib, the frond is said to be pinnately compound or pinnate. If the blade is cut so the leaflets join at the same point on the stipe, the frond is said to be palmately compound or palmate. If the lateral leaflets on a palmate frond are cleft into two or more segments the frond is called pedate. Most ferns are pinnately compound.

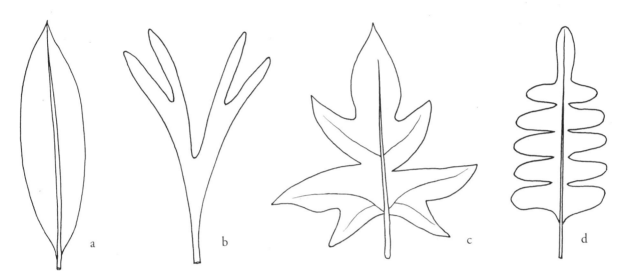

Figure 2.3. Simple fronds: a. simple and entire; b. bifurcate; c. pinnatifid, with pedate base; d. pinnatifid.

Whether the blade is pinnate, palmate, or pedately compound, the leaflet of the first division is called a pinna (pinnae is the plural). If the pinna is divided, its divisions are called pinnules or secondary pinnae, and the frond is two-pinnate (bipinnate). If the secondary pinnae are divided, their divisions are called tertiary pinnae, and the frond is three-pinnate (tripinnate). A general name for these parts, whether primary, secondary, or tertiary in rank, is leaflet. If a frond is pinnately compound, its midrib appears like a continuation of the stipe and is then called a rachis. The margins of the blade or its leaflets may be variously modified (Figure 2.5).

Venation patterns differ greatly among ferns (Figure 2.6). Veins may be unforked (simple) or forked. If forked, they can be branched distinctively. Their ends may be free or joined with others to form meshes, in which case they are said to be netted (or areolate or anastomosed). Sometimes free veins are enclosed in a mesh, and the ferns are said to have included veinlets. Some ferns have veins that are deeply immersed in the blade and hardly visible.

The great variety in frond shape, size, and venation does not affect the ability of the frond to fulfill its main function—to make food for the plant with the help of sunlight.

Fruiting Bodies

The lower surface of the frond may bear rusty patches or black dots or lines known as sori (sorus is the singular). These are clusters of spore cases or sporangia. The sori may be round, oblong, linear, or of some other

Figure 2.4. Compound fronds (r = rachis; p = pinna; sp = secondary pinnule; tp = tertiary pinnule): a. pinnatifid above to pinnate below; b. pinnate; c. pinnate-pinnatifid; d. bipinnate; e. tripinnate; f. pedate, the pinnae pinnate; g. palmate or radiate, the pinnae pinnate.

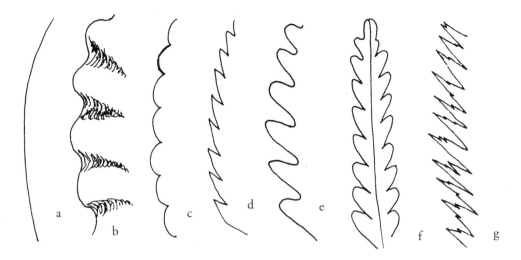

Figure 2.5. Leaf margins: a. entire; b. undulate; c. crenate; d. serrate; e. lobed; f. pinnatifid; g. incised.

shape (Figure 2.7). Some ferns have loosely arranged sori, not definite clusters. The sporangia may be scattered along the main veins, or they may completely cover the lower surface of the frond. The sori of some ferns are protected by an indusium, a bit of tissue that, depending on the species, is formed in various ways from various parts of the blade (Figure 2.8). In some ferns it consists only of the margin of the leaf rolled over the sori (Figure 2.8c). Such an enrolled leaf margin is called a false indusium. The shape and location of the sorus and the kind of indusium (if present) are important in identifying ferns.

The spore cases or sporangia are easily seen with a ten-power (10×) magnifying glass, but to see their finer details requires a microscope. They will be seen as stalked capsules or cases containing spores. If the sporangia have already shed their spores, they will appear frayed or cracked (Figure 2.9). If the sporangia still contain spores, the case will be round and intact. In this condition you may be able to see a slightly raised dark ring of cells around the case. This ring is called the annulus and acts like a catapult to open the case and hurl out the spores. The annulus may vary in position on the spore case, and in some genera it is only a patch of slightly thickened cells instead of a well-defined ring (Figure 2.10). In some species all the sporangia in a sorus open at about the same time, but in most ferns the sporangia open at different times over an extended period.

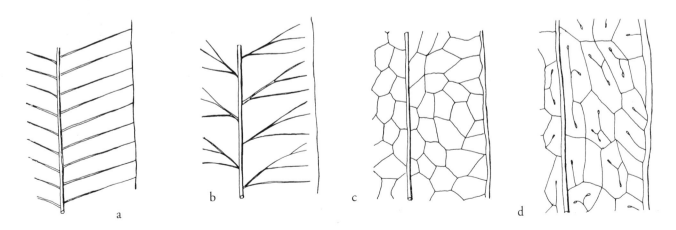

Figure 2.6. Veins: a. simple; b. forked with free vein endings; c. netted or areolate; d. netted with included veinlets.

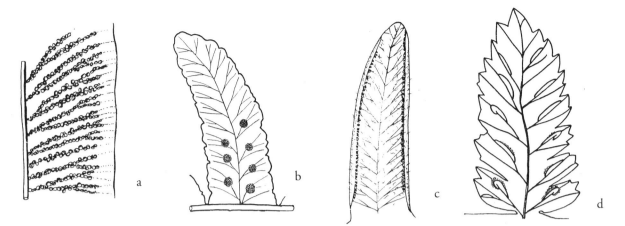

Figure 2.7. Sori: a. along the veins (*Coniogramme*); b. round (*Macrothelypteris*); c. linear and marginal (*Pteridium*); d. linear and medial (*Athyrium*).

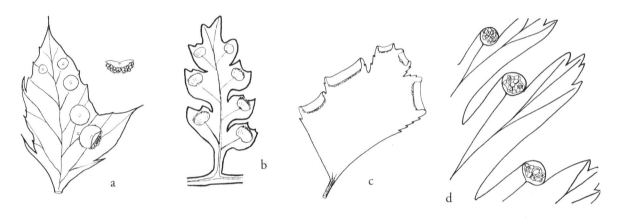

Figure 2.8. Indusia: a. peltate or umbrella-shaped (*Polystichum*); b. scale-like (*Davallia*); c. false indusium, formed from an enrolled leaf margin (*Adiantum*); d. cup-shaped (*Dennstaedtia*).

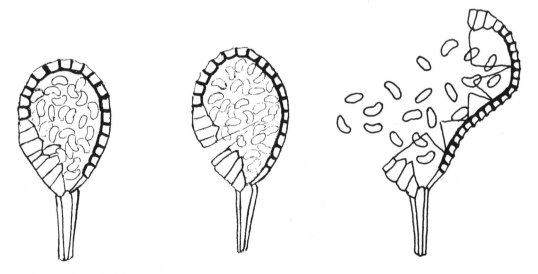

Figure 2.9. Sporangium shedding spores.

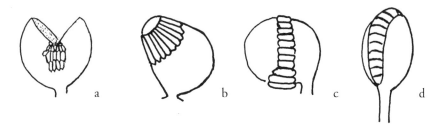

Figure 2.10. Annulus positions: a. lateral (*Todea*); b. apical (*Lygodium*); c. oblique (*Gleichenia*); d. vertical (*Polypodium*).

A single frond may produce hundreds of thousands of spores. To the unaided eye, spores appear as a fine dust. Under the microscope, they can be seen to have two basic shapes, depending on the species (Figure 2.11). Some have bean-shaped spores (monolete), whereas others have more or less pyramidal or slightly three-angled globose spores (trilete). Both shapes usually have patterns or embellishments on their surfaces, and these markings often characterize certain families or genera. The spores of most ferns are brown or black, but yellow spores are characteristic of the polypods, and green spores are found in some groups. Green spores are short-lived, usually lasting only one or two weeks. In contrast, nongreen spores usually remain viable for several years, but with age they germinate more slowly and less dependably.

Figure 2.11. Kinds of spores: a–c. monolete; d–e. trilete.

The life cycle of ferns is complex but of great importance to growers. It is discussed further in Chapter 8 in connection with propagation techniques.

3 Obtaining Ferns

Fern Nurseries and Fern Organizations

Most plant nurseries carry at least a few ferns and usually can direct you to specialty nurseries or mail-order businesses that carry a wider variety. Local newspapers announce garden club meetings and flower shows. These activities will give you the opportunity to meet local botanists and gardeners who can help you to locate ferns. Botanical gardens usually know what plant societies exist in your area and whom to contact for information. They may also have a file of more distant and foreign nurseries that might ship ferns. Fern societies have been organized in various parts of the world. These organizations mail newsletters, print journals, sponsor spore exchanges, conduct field trips, provide programs, and maintain a fern library or Web sites for their members. For information on contacting these fern groups, see Appendix II, "Fern Societies."

Purchasing Ferns

Before you buy a fern, check its climatic needs to determine whether you can provide it with the proper temperature, shade, and humidity. Also determine whether it will produce the desired landscape effect, especially given its size when fully grown. Some ferns take up more space than you intended.

Once at the nursery, purchase the fern in a 10 cm (4 in.) to 3.8 liter (1 gal.) size container, unless you are in a hurry to have a larger plant. Leave the smaller sizes for a time when you have gained more experience in growing them. Plants larger than the 3.8 liter (1 gal.) size are more expensive, and some may have passed the stage of rapid growth.

Examine the growing tip. Select a fern that has a firm, large, growing tip. Avoid any that seem discolored, shriveled, or undersized. If the fern is actively growing, see that the tip is forming healthy new fronds. Avoid ferns with shriveled or deformed growth. If you do not want to repot the fern in the near future, pick one that has not already overgrown its pot. The growing tip should not be pushing against the edge of the pot. If you are obtaining a fern that forms clumps of rhizomes, select the one that has the largest number of healthy rhizome tips.

Nurseries use different soil mixes. Be aware that some mixes require more watering than others. Also, the smaller the pot and the larger the fern, the more water it will require. If the fern is accustomed to growing in high humidity at the nursery, it may wilt when you get it home. If you give it just enough humidity to keep it from wilting, new fronds should adapt to the drier conditions without difficulty. Otherwise, see the section in Chapter 4 entitled "Air Circulation and Humidity."

Collecting Ferns

Certain parts of the world are particularly rich in ferns, and it is tempting for you or your friends to collect some exotic ferns during travels to these areas. But given the concern about the environment and rare or endangered species, collecting wild plants is discouraged. Collecting wild plants is forbidden in nearly all countries unless special collecting permits are obtained. In addition, export permits are also required, and customs or agricultural inspectors may want to see those permits when you exit a country or re-enter your country. See Appendix III for more information on permits and restrictions.

If collecting ferns from private property, seek out the owner's permission. Before collecting wild plants, be sure to have the proper permits and check that the plants are not on the rare, threatened, or endangered list. Plants so listed are protected by law (see Appendix III for details). Some plants, such as certain species of *Azolla* and *Salvinia,* are deemed potential pests and are barred from entry into the United States and within the country cannot be transported without a permit. Even with nonthreatened species, resist the temptation to collect indiscriminately, wastefully, and without regard for the environment. Thoughtless collectors have given all collectors a bad reputation. Take only the number of plants that you can grow.

If you live in an area where native ferns abound, you will have access to species suited for the climate but not necessarily for garden culture. Temperate, deciduous ferns are usually collected in the late fall or early spring, and other ferns just before the growing season, usually in early or mid-spring. Although ferns may be collected at any time, their chances of survival are best when they are transplanted just before their active growing period so that they have a full season to grow and establish themselves. Recently matured ferns (as opposed to older or long-mature plants) have the best chance of re-establishing themselves. Also, plants with thick rhizomes generally have a better chance of survival than those with thinner ones. If the fern is branched or clumped, one piece of the branch or clump is enough to start a new plant. When collecting a rhizome, take as many of the roots as possible and try not to disturb the soil attached to them. Firm the soil around the exposed roots of the remaining plants. While transporting the plant, keep the soil and foliage cool and moist, and replant the fern as soon as possible.

By visiting local nurseries, gardens, and members of plant societies, you might be able to obtain interesting species and establish valuable contacts as well. Above all, keep in mind that spores usually do not require permits for import and are easier to collect, pack, and mail. Also, spore-grown plants tend to adapt more readily to cultivation.

Holding Ferns until Departure Time

If you have collected ferns and will not return home for a week or so, be sure to remove the plants with as little disturbance to the roots as possible and put them into a plastic bag kept open for ventilation. Water the fern sparingly, and provide drainage in the bag if needed. Find a cool, shady place to store the plants as you travel. Prior to departure, prepare and package the plants as discussed in the following section.

Packing Ferns

Water the ferns a day before packing so that excess water has time to drain away. Ferns to be transported with soil on their roots need only be wrapped in newspaper. If the ferns are in pots, they may be tapped out of the pots to reduce the weight. When bringing plants into the United States, all soil must be removed from the plant. Dip the roots into a bucket of water so the soil will fall away, but try to leave intact as many of the roots as possible. A number of dips and a gentle agitation in the water should get the soil off. Remove all dead and broken fronds. Double-check to see that all insects are removed. The tip of the stem or rhizome is the most important part of the fern and must be well protected. If fronds must be removed for packing, do so, but keep the roots and particularly the rhizome or crown intact. Protect the rhizome and roots from being crushed by surrounding them with packing material. If packing material other than newspaper is used and ferns are to be sent into the United States, make certain that the material is on the approved list issued by the Plant Import Permit Station. If you are going to remote areas, bring your own packaging and wrapping supplies. Stringed tags are useful labels, as are gummed labels that will stick on plastic. Write the name and place of collection on the labels in pencil or permanent ink.

Some plants can be wrapped for protection in newspaper rolled into a cylinder or a cone and placed in a plastic bag to retain moisture. Make certain that the plants are not too wet, especially if they are put into plastic bags without any newspaper to cushion the plant and absorb extra water. Plants that are too wet will rot readily in plastic bags, especially in warm climates. Air may be blown into plastic bags and sealed to serve as a cushion. Plants sent to the United States should be in sealed bags. If pests are found in any one open bag, then all the other open bags in the shipment might be considered infested and would be quarantined by agricultural inspectors.

Empty plastic water bottles can be made into excellent containers for transporting plants. Cut the bottle in half around the middle. One piece will fit snugly inside the other piece with a slight squeeze when you wish to close the container.

Cardboard cartons lined with wax paper or plastic can be used to ship ferns. In some areas, woven baskets are easier to obtain and can be used, unless they are made of willow or other wood likely to carry boring insects. Such baskets are barred from entry into the United States. Secure the individually wrapped ferns so they will not slip or slide in the box.

Commercial growers have reported that potted, established plants may show stress after 7 to 10 days if left in the dark, even when other conditions were favorable.

Interstate Transport of Ferns

Regulations about the interstate movement of plants vary between states and even between counties within a state. Check with your local state and county agricultural offices before shipping plants. Many states regulate interstate commercial activities involving legally acquired protected species. States that have large agricultural businesses also have many restrictions. Contact the appropriate state fish and wildlife agency for further information.

4 Cultural Needs

Understanding Fern Needs

Ferns have the same basic growing requirements as other plants and will thrive when these are met. There is nothing mysterious about the requirements—they are not something known only to people with green thumbs—but the best gardeners are those who understand plant requirements and are careful about satisfying them. What, then, does a fern need?

All plants need water. Water in the soil prevents roots from drying, and all mineral nutrients taken up by the roots must be dissolved in the soil water. Besides water in the soil, most plants need water in the air. Adequate humidity keeps the plant from drying out. Leaves need water for photosynthesis and to keep from wilting.

All green plants need light to manufacture food (sugars) by photosynthesis. Some plants need more light than others, and some can flourish in sun or shade. Most ferns, however, prefer some amount of shade.

For photosynthesis, plants require carbon dioxide, a gas that is exhaled by animals as waste. Carbon dioxide diffuses into plants through tiny pores, called stomata, that abound on the lower surface of the leaves. In the leaf, carbon dioxide is combined with the hydrogen from water to form carbohydrates, the plant's food. This process takes place only in the presence of light and chlorophyll, a green pigment found in plant cells. To enhance plant growth, some commercial growers increase the carbon dioxide level in their greenhouses to 600 ppm (parts per million), or twice the amount typically found in the air.

Plants need oxygen. The green parts of a plant do not require much oxygen from the air because plants produce more oxygen by photosynthesis than they use. The excess oxygen liberated from the plants is used by all animals, including humans. What do plants do with oxygen? They use it just as we do, to release the energy stored in food. We use energy to move about, to talk, to grow, to think—in fact, for all our life processes. Although plants don't talk or move much, they do grow and metabolize and must carry on all their life processes using oxygen to release the stored energy in their food.

Roots need air all the time. They get it from the air spaces between the soil particles. Overwatering displaces the air between soil particles with water, thereby removing the oxygen needed by the roots. This reduces the root's ability to absorb mineral nutrients and can foster root-rot.

Plants need minerals to grow properly. The minerals are mined from the soil by the plant's root system. If a certain mineral is missing, such as the calcium needed for developing cell walls, then the plant will be stunted, discolored, or deformed.

Some plants tolerate a wide range of temperatures, whereas others are fussy. If the temperature is too high or too low, the machinery of the plant will not operate satisfactorily or will cease entirely.

The basic needs of plants are not hard to supply, but growing success depends on attending to these needs with care and exactitude. The remainder of this chapter is devoted to a discussion of these requirements, with the exception of mineral needs, which are discussed in Chapter 5.

Temperature

Ferns vary greatly in their temperature requirements. Most grow best at daytime temperatures of 18 to 27°C (65–80°F). Tropical ferns generally prefer ranges from 21 to 27°C (70–80°F) during the day, and some may even tolerate similar nighttime temperatures. Most ferns grow best when the nighttime temperature is about 5°C (10°F) cooler than the daytime temperature. Some ferns need seasonal periods of cooler temperatures to grow well. You cannot predict a fern's temperature tolerance simply by the looks of the plant. Knowledge of its native habitat and the temperature tolerances of its relatives will help, but there are sometimes surprising exceptions. When the hardiness of a species is unknown, it is best to use larger individuals because they generally withstand temperature extremes better than small plants. Since the minimum temperature tolerance is not known for many ferns, gardeners can make useful contributions to horticulture by reporting such data from their garden to appropriate fern societies and journals.

Floras, which are books for identifying the plants of a particular region, sometimes provide information on determining the temperature tolerance of ferns in a given area. Some relatively recent fern floras helpful to gardeners have been written for Australia (ABRS/CSIRO 1998; Andrews 1990; Jones and Clemesha 1981), New Zealand (Brownsey and Smith-Dodsworth 1989), South Africa (Burrows 1990; Jacobsen 1983), and Japan (Iwatsuki et al. 1995; Kurata and Nakaike 1964–1997, fully illustrated with maps). North America and Canada have a flora (Flora of North America Editorial Committee 1993) and there are many smaller ones. In tropical America, fern floras have been written for the West Indies (Proctor 1977, 1985, 1989), Chihuahua, Mexico (Knobloch and Correll 1962), Oaxaca, Mexico (Mickel and Beitel 1988), Chiapas, Mexico (Smith 1981), Central America (Moran and Riba 1995), Costa Rica and Panama (Lellinger 1989), the Venezuelan Guayana (Smith 1995), Peru (Tryon and Stolze 1989–1994), and Chile (Marticorena and Rodríguez 1995). Except for Taiwan (Huang 1994) and Hong Kong (Edie 1978), China and Korea have not been adequately covered (at least not in English). The ferns of the western Himalayas have been treated (Khullar 1994) as well as those of Thailand (Tagawa and Iwatsuki 1979–1989), and western Malaysia (Piggott 1988). Many of the Pacific Islands have floras, but noticeably lacking are floras for eastern Malaysia, Indonesia, and New Guinea. The British Isles have many recent floras, but those for Continental Europe in English are not updated.

Ferns may be classified as hardy, semi-hardy, semi-tender, or tender. This classification refers to the coolest temperature range that a fern can tolerate. It is somewhat arbitrary, since many ferns fall on the borderline between categories or can endure short periods of lower temperatures. The classification, however, ensures that the temperature preferences of ferns can be more easily known. See the section "Outdoor Ferns" in Chapter 9 and the individual entries in Chapter 13 for temperature requirements of particular species.

HARDY FERNS

Hardy ferns can be grown outdoors in temperate or colder areas of the United States. They tolerate winter temperatures well below freezing. Also belonging to this group are alpine species that can endure very cold temperatures for a long time.

Hardy garden species are mostly native to northern and central Europe, North America, and northern Asia. Many ferns native to the eastern United States are suitable for cultivation. Some adapt to gardens in warmer climates, but others do not. The cultivation of hardy ferns is treated in several references, including those by Dyce (1991), Foster (1993), Grounds (1974), Kaye (1968), Mickel (1994), Rush (1984a), and Rickard (2000).

SEMI-HARDY FERNS

Semi-hardy ferns usually tolerate nighttime temperatures above 4°C (40°F) during the cool season. They survive periods of freezing temperatures that are short and not too severe. These ferns come from many parts of the world, mostly where warm-temperate climates prevail, such as Japan, Korea, and China. Semi-hardy ferns grow outdoors in the southeastern United States and warmer northern areas. They are good choices for inland valleys along warmer coastal regions.

SEMI-TENDER FERNS

Semi-tender ferns grow well where nighttime temperatures are mostly above 10°C (50°F) during the cool season and where freezing temperatures are rare. Frost may burn the foliage or kill the plant, although some species can survive near-freezing temperatures for a few hours. The semi-tender ferns are native to subtropical and warmer areas with typical daytime temperatures of about 18°C (65°F). Many come from Latin America, Australia, and New Zealand. Coastal southern California is particularly well suited for semi-tender ferns, whereas those that tolerate cooler temperatures can be grown inland or farther north along the coast.

TENDER FERNS

Tender ferns (also known as warm or "stove" species) usually grow poorly when temperatures drop to 16°C (60°F) or below for successive nights. These ferns are mostly native to the lowland tropics where year-round warmth and humidity prevail. Southern Florida and the Hawaiian lowlands are particularly favorable places to grow tender ferns outdoors. Here, nighttime temperatures are closer to 21°C (70°F) or above for most of the year, and daytime temperatures are near 24°C (75°F) or above. In other areas of the United States, most lowland tropical species must be grown under glass, at least during the cool months, especially the very tender species that do not like successive nights of temperatures below 21°C (70°F).

Some semi-tender and tender ferns prefer cooler temperatures at night and do not do well in areas with warm nighttime temperatures. These ferns are usually native to the cooler upland areas of the tropics and include most of the tree ferns. Conversely, some lowland tropical ferns may not grow in places where the nighttime temperatures are consistently much lower than the daytime temperatures.

LOCAL TEMPERATURE VARIANCE

In coastal areas where the temperatures are ameliorated by the sea, a diversity of climates will be found within a few miles, especially if the area is hilly or mountainous. In these places it is especially important to know the temperature conditions of your specific locale. In southern California, for example, climates ranging from subalpine to subtropical occur within a distance of 64 kilometers (40 miles). Many noncoastal areas also may have microclimates due to local geography. For information on your local climate, write the United States Department of Commerce, National Climatic Data Center, Federal Building, Asheville, North Carolina 28801, or call 704-CLIMATE (254-6283). Also consult the U.S. Department of Agriculture's map of hardiness zones, which gives minimum winter temperatures throughout the United States and Canada (last page of the color plates section).

LOW-TEMPERATURE DAMAGE

Low temperatures (but above freezing) can damage plants. In such instances the plant usually turns yellow, produces little growth, and wastes away. But before you dig up a fern to move it to a warmer place, be sure it is not merely taking its normal rest period. Many ferns take a rest period, especially during the cooler winter months, when they normally turn yellow and produce little growth. They vigorously renew growth usually in spring, whereas those that have suffered from low temperatures slowly recover and often have stunted, undersized rootstocks or rhizomes.

Semi-tender and tender ferns growing in marginally favorable temperatures need to be watered lightly during the cooler months. At this time growth is slow, and overwatering can often result in root-rot. All ferns, tender or hardy, are more vulnerable to low temperatures if they are young, weak, recently transplanted, or have much new growth.

Various steps can be taken to prevent or reduce damage when temperatures drop, but success will ultimately depend on the fern's sensitivity to cold and the severity and duration of the low temperatures. Harden the plants for several weeks or more by giving them less water and exposing them to low but not injurious temperatures prior to winter weather. Some plants are easier to harden than others. Avoid heavy pruning or fertilizing late in the season to discourage vulnerable, tender new growth. Keep withered fronds on the plant to provide some protection through the winter. Transplant ferns early in the growing season so they will be well established by fall. Protect weak, young, or susceptible plants by moving them to warmer places such as against buildings, under eaves or trees, or on slopes where the cold air drains away. Temporary coverings of burlap, straw, leaves, or newspaper will provide some protection during cold spells. Various foams are available that are nontoxic and work by insulating the plant. Commercial sprays that protect foliage from frost are also available, but their effectiveness on ferns is unknown.

Once frost or freezing is imminent, increase heat and reduce heat loss from the ground, plant, and surroundings. On clear, still nights the coldest temperatures are likely to come an hour or so before sunrise, and that is when protective measures may be needed. Shortening the time a plant is exposed to lethal low temperatures from hours to minutes can prevent injury or death. When adding heat with various heaters, be sure to guard against dehydration, especially from electric heaters in small enclosures. Air movement by means of fans may bring in warmer air if a low inversion layer is present (that is, a low-lying layer of warm air above the cold). Inversion layers can be expected when the night is calm and clear but the preceding day was warm and sunny. This causes the warm air of the day to rise during the night and the heavier colder air to move downward and settle around the plants.

Fog can be used to protect crops during cold spells with temperatures as low as −2°C (28°F). Farmers place fog-producing nozzles about 1 m (3 ft.) apart and 2 to 3 m (6.5–10 ft.) above the ground over the aisle to prevent any dripping water from damaging the plants. The dense fog is confined by a roof of shade cloth and plastic curtains. The cold temperature is absorbed by the fog, leaving less to damage the plants. True fog differs from mist in that fog droplets are so small that they do not settle out of the air, whereas mist droplets are larger and settle out. These larger droplets are less efficient than true fog. Fogging or misting should be started as soon as temperatures drop below 2°C (35°F), and then maintained continuously or at regular intervals. It should be continued until the sun has warmed the air above 0°C (32°F). Stopping the treatment too early may cause the lethal temperature of the plant to be reached.

The formation of frost or ice gives off heat. The layer of frost or ice covering or encasing the plant also confers some insulation advantage, but the weight of the ice might damage or discolor the plant. Furrow irrigation is another means of increasing the temperature, when the water in the furrow freezes, but plants can become overwatered by this method, and the rise in temperature may be insufficient to protect the plant.

Plants that have been super-cooled (that is, cooled so quickly that damaging ice crystals have not formed on the plant tissue) should not be moved or disturbed because the movement will cause the sudden formation of ice crystals that, as they grow, pierce and kill the cells of the plant. Super-cooling is apt to occur when plant surfaces are dry. Allow super-cooled plants to warm slowly.

If plants are frozen, allow them to thaw gradually. This can be done by placing newspaper over the plant to insulate and shade it from the sun, the warmth of which would otherwise melt the ice crystals within the plant too rapidly.

Ferns damaged by frost or freezing generally wilt (unless hard tissue is present) and turn black. Less severely damaged fronds have spots or areas that appear scorched or burned, especially on the more exposed parts. Damage from desiccation can also occur. For tree ferns and species with woody tissue, particularly subtropical species, a common practice is to keep the damaged parts on the plant until there are signs of new growth. Herbaceous ferns that collapse and have completely black fronds may recover if the rhizome is still firm. Damaged stems or rhizomes often produce distorted, weak growth and will recover slowly, if at all. Any cold-damaged plants should be watered sparingly because the loss of foliage reduces their water needs. Assessing the extent of damage may take as long as one growing season on tree ferns. For more details, see Reasoner (1982).

High-Temperature Damage

In arid areas, high-temperature damage is difficult to distinguish from damage caused by dry air. Even with sufficient humidity, high temperatures can scorch or wilt fronds. If the wilted parts do not recover, they turn brown and brittle. On thicker fronds the scorched areas are usually near the margin or exposed places. During heat waves, shade the ferns and keep the air humid and the soil moist. In greenhouses, open the vents and keep the mist nozzle operating. Water sprayed on the roof of the greenhouse will reduce the temperature appreciably. Never keep plants in a closed car or its trunk on hot days.

Cold Requirements

Certain temperate and alpine ferns need cold temperatures during the winter to grow well. Without a cold period these ferns will not renew growth in the spring, or if new growth is produced, it is weak and ultimately wastes away. Growers have established the specific cold requirements of several ferns (see the section "Forcing Ferns" in Chapter 10). Not all temperate ferns, however, have chilling requirements, and species that have populations in the southern parts of their ranges may not require cold. Growers in warm climates should be aware of the difficulties of growing species that require a cold period. Even tropical ferns taken from higher elevations can prove difficult to grow in hot, lowland tropical climates because of this requirement.

Experiments on Michigan ferns (Hill 1976) showed that different species require different cold periods, if at all, to renew growth in the spring. *Osmunda claytoniana,* for example, needs 8 to 12 weeks at 4°C (40°F) in the dark to achieve 100% bud-break or renewed growth. If the plants are removed from the cold and dark and placed in a warm, sunny greenhouse (at 20 to 30°C [68–86°F] with 24 hours of light), those that received the longest cold treatment emerge the fastest (plants with 12 weeks of cold treatment emerged within 10 days once in the greenhouse). In contrast, bud-break in *Adiantum pedatum* and *Thelypteris palustris* was less influenced by the length of the cold treatment, and in *Cystopteris fragilis, Onoclea sensibilis, Deparia acrostichoides,* and *Diplazium pycnocarpon,* no cold treatment was required for bud-break. The latter species began growth without cold treatment soon after they were brought into the greenhouse. These experiments explain why it is difficult to grow *Osmunda claytoniana* in warm climates whereas it is easy to grow *Diplazium pycnocarpon.*

Light

HOW MUCH LIGHT?

Most ferns grow best in shade or filtered light. The optimal amount of light for most ferns is that provided by the sun on a dim, overcast day. This measures between 200 and 600 foot-candles. Foot-candles (f.c.) is a unit for measuring light intensity; another more recent system uses micromole (μmol) units. (See Appendix I, which describes a method for measuring light intensity with a photographic light meter.) Adult ferns prefer more light than younger ones, and most spores germinate and grow best in low light. Contrary to what many people believe, dense shade is unsuitable for most ferns. In dense shade, fronds grow spindly, are less frequently produced, and tend to yellow and die early.

Ferns growing in low but adequate light are usually large and luxuriant. Under high light, the fronds become firmer, thicker, more soriferous, and more tolerant of environmental changes. Ferns suffering from too much light are smaller, less luxuriant, yellowish green, and may have brown margins.

In coastal areas with typically overcast weather, ferns can be planted in full sun. Inland areas may have brighter days, and the ferns will require more shade. When planting ferns, do not overlook the added light reflected from walks and buildings. This light can become intense at certain times of the year as the sun's angle changes with the seasons.

SHADING FERNS

Trees, laths, painted glass, fiberglass, and plastic cloth all may be used to shade ferns. Plastic cloths made of polypropylene (sold as Prop-a-Lite, which superseded Saran or Lumite) are much used by the nursery trade. Different grades give from 30 to 90% shade. In sunny areas such as southern California, 73% shade cloth (giving 73% shade) has been used with good results. If ferns must be grown in direct sun, they should be shielded from the sun between noon and 3 P.M., the brightest and hottest hours of the day.

LIGHT QUALITY

Sunlight is composed of a variety of colored lights. These colors are seen separately in a rainbow or through a glass prism. The red and blue parts of this color spectrum are absorbed by the plant's pigments and are used in photosynthesis. Most of the remaining colors in the spectrum are not used by plants and are passed through the leaf or are reflected. Green light in particular is reflected, which explains why leaves appear green. Light intensity (discussed earlier under "How Much Light") should not be confused with light quality. Light intensity refers to how strong the emitted light is, whereas light quality refers to the kinds of colored light present. Gardeners who grow plants in sunlight need not be concerned about whether their plants get enough red and blue light, as they can do little to modify the sunlight's quality or spectrum. However, gardeners who grow plants under artificial light to increase the light intensity may also want to know whether the lamps they are using gives the proper light quality or light spectrum.

ARTIFICIAL LIGHT

Ferns grown indoors, especially in more northerly areas, often suffer from too little light. Supplemental or full artificial light must be given. Although fluorescent (cool-white) lamps are the usual choice, they are deficient in red light. Fluorescent lights can be used alone, though they are often used in combination with incandescent lights (ordinary light bulbs) to supplement the red light. Incandescent lights may also be used alone, but they produce more heat that can injure plants and are very low in blue light. Gro-Lux lights give a slightly better light quality than cool-white fluorescent but are twice as expensive. High-intensity lights have a good light spectrum and are more energy efficient. They are increasingly easier to install and more economical. Because they have higher light intensity than other lamps, they can be hung farther away from the plants. Of the two types of high-intensity lights, the metal halide lamps provide a better spectrum for plants and a more pleasing light to the human eye. High-pressure sodium lamps produce a yellowish cast that some people find objectionable. Old lamps may need to be replaced as their intensity diminishes. Light intensity can be increased by 20 to 50% by walls and benches with reflecting surfaces, such as by lining them with aluminum foil.

Table 4.1 shows light intensities from two 4-foot fluorescent tubes of 40 watts placed at various heights above the plants. Light intensity is given at 15 cm (6 in.), 30 cm (12 in.), 45 cm (18 in.), and 60 cm (24 in.) below the light source. High-intensity lamps will give approximately twice the foot-candle readings shown in Table 4.1. Use of a reflector will also increase the intensity of light. Most ferns grow best at 200 to 600 foot-candles. Light intensity is measured at the top of the plant. (Also see Appendix I.)

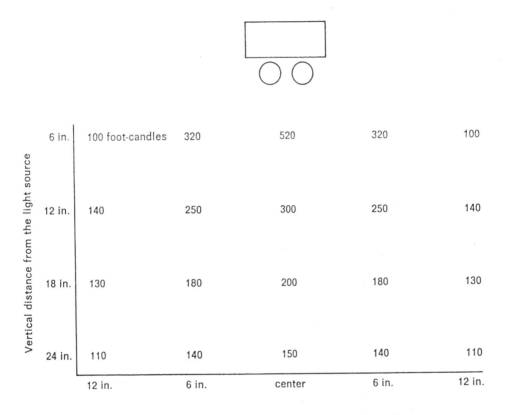

Vertical distance from the light source					
6 in.	100 foot-candles	320	520	320	100
12 in.	140	250	300	250	140
18 in.	130	180	200	180	130
24 in.	110	140	150	140	110
	12 in.	6 in.	center	6 in.	12 in.

Horizontal distance from the center of the lighted area

Table 4.1. Light intensity, in foot-candles (f.c.), below two 4-foot, 40-watt cool-white fluorescent tubes at various distances above the plant material. The light intensity was measured on a horizontal surface with a light meter (Weston illumination meter model 756).

PHOTOPERIODIC RESPONSES

Little has been reported about the photoperiodic responses of ferns—that is, how they respond to changes in day length. Such changes can affect growth and the ability to form spores (Patterson and Freeman 1963). Some ferns seem to become deciduous, resume growth, or produce dimorphic fronds in response to different day lengths.

Watering

HOW MUCH WATER?

Most cultivated ferns prefer moist—not soggy—soil. Continuously saturated soil should be avoided as much as dry soil. A few cultivated ferns might prefer soil that is drier or moister than the average, but these are exceptions. Ferns should receive less water during cool weather, especially when they are not actively growing. Chapter 13 gives the water requirements for specific ferns.

HOW OFTEN?

There is no precise answer to the question of how often to water ferns. Average conditions require watering every two or three days, less during cool weather and more during warm. Plants in small pots dry faster and need to be watered more frequently than those in larger pots. Plants in clay pots need to be watered more frequently than those in plastic or glazed pots. Because water drains faster through sandy or coarse soil mixes, plants growing in such soils will need to be watered more frequently than those in silt- or clay-soil mixes. It is wisest to water a plant when it needs it rather than on a regular time schedule.

DETERMINING WHEN WATER IS NEEDED

Do not wait for the plant to wilt. Feel the soil surface. If it is dry or starting to dry, it is time to water. Another indication that the plant needs water is if the pot feels lighter than usual. A useful test for ferns in clay pots is to tap the pot: if it is very dry, there will be a ringing sound. If you still are unable to decide whether more water is needed, probe the soil to a depth of about 4 cm (1.5 in.) below the surface in a spot where you will not injure the plant, and feel if the soil is dry. Peat-based soil mixes become lighter in color when dry. In any case, water before the soil shrinks and pulls away from the sides of the pot.

HOW TO WATER

Once you have determined that water is needed, thoroughly water the plant with a gentle sprinkle or flow. Avoid forceful streams because large droplets will compact the soil or wash the soil away from the roots. Stop when you see water coming through the pot's drainage hole. If the plant is in the ground, be sure that the water has reached the soil around the roots. Overhead watering, which wets the foliage, is not recommended for some ferns, particularly xerophytic species or those with finely divided leaves. These ferns should be watered at soil level. In areas with high humidity and poor air circulation, you should water plants in the early part of the day so that the foliage does not remain wet for long. This helps discourage certain diseases. Scant sprinklings of water will increase the humidity but are seldom sufficient for medium-sized or larger ferns. Such sprinklings can also cause an accumulation of salts that are injurious to plants.

TREATING A WILTED PLANT

A wilted plant needs water immediately. As you water, be sure that the water reaches the roots and is not running down between the pot wall and the ball of dry soil. If this happens, submerge the pot in water and soak it until it is thoroughly wet. Then remove it and drain. Thereafter water only to keep the soil moist. Do not overwater. Wilted fronds that do not recover will turn brown in a few days and should be removed. Keep as many green fronds on the plant as possible. Recovery of a wilted plant will depend on the extent of damage to the roots and the plant's innate vigor. Generally, the thicker the rhizome, the greater the chances of recovery. Thicker rhizomes contain more stored food, and this fosters new growth to replace the damaged tissue.

TREATING AN OVERWATERED PLANT

Sometimes a plant wilts even though you have been watering it. The most common cause of this is overwatering, which will damage the roots. Soil that feels wet even two or three days after watering may be too wet for the plant. With extreme overwatering, the soil will feel soggy wet and may smell bad. When lifted, the pot will feel heavy for its size because of the waterlogged soil. When tapped, it gives a dull thud.

Damage to the plant may be gradual or sudden. If gradual, the fronds will first yellow and then grow poorly. The fronds might wilt, at which point examination of the roots usually reveals that they have rotted away. If the plant hasn't yet wilted, reduce the watering. If it has wilted, determine how badly the roots and rhizomes are damaged. If most of the roots are rotted and the rhizome is soft and discolored, the plant will probably not survive and should be discarded. Otherwise, trim off the rotted parts and replant the healthy part in fresh, well-aerated soil. Keep the soil moist and hope for the best. Be careful not to overwater again. The cut ends of rhizome and roots may be dusted with a fungicide, such as Captan, to discourage further rotting.

HOW OVERWATERING CAUSES DAMAGE

Roots need air. The oxygen contained in the air is used by the roots to metabolize their stored-food energy, and this energy is essential to the life processes within the roots. Overwatering displaces the air within the soil and replaces it with water. As a result, the roots suffocate. In addition, the excess water promotes the growth of bacteria and fungi that can attack the plant. (Aquatic plants avoid suffocation by having internal air canals that supply their underwater parts with oxygen.)

WATER QUALITY AND SALT INJURY

Water your plants with a water temperature that feels comfortable to your hands, generally between 19 and 27°C (66–80°F). Be careful not to use hot water from garden hoses or pipes left in the sun; let the water run and cool down first. Very cold water also should be avoided because it slows the uptake of nutrients.

Fluoride and chlorine are commonly added to tap water but not in amounts harmful to ferns. You should not, however, water your plants with water from swimming pools. Its chlorine content and other additives kills plants.

Salts in fertilizers provide the minerals plants need, but too much salt can slow growth or even kill plants. Excess salts accumulate in the soil from repeated watering with water that is high in salts. If the salt in the soil becomes too concentrated, the roots cannot absorb water, and in extreme cases water will move out of the roots and back into the soil. When this happens, the result is known as root burn.

To reduce the risk of root burn, do not use water containing softeners because it contains sodium. Excess sodium not only burns the roots but also harms soil structure and replaces desirable nutrients. Perhaps the most common cause of root burn is overfertilizing. Do not add too much manure, ashes, or compost of sedge peat, which may have a high salt content. When salt becomes excessive, a crust of salt, usually whitish gray, accumulates on the soil surface or flowerpot. Salt damage is common in arid areas, where the soil is high in salts because there is insufficient rain to wash it away. Water supplies coming from arid areas may also contain undesirable levels of salt.

Salt injury can be reduced by proper watering. Water ferns thoroughly until the amount of water equal to about 20% of the pot's volume passes through the pot. Provide good drainage to allow for adequate leaching. Salt-encrusted pots should be cleaned or discarded (see the section in Chapter 7 on "Planting in Pots"). Remember, light sprinklings of water will add salt to the soil, not leach it out.

ADDITIONAL TIPS ON WATERING

Sometimes watering a hanging-basket fern will damage the ferns planted below it because the water draining from above batters the plants below. The plants underneath might also become overwatered. To avoid this, the basket can be taken down and watered, or the plants underneath can be removed while the baskets above are watered. Another alternative is to provide catch basins in the basket by building a substantial rim of moss around the upper edge of the baskets. This will hold more of the water and reduce the spillage. Also, before planting, you can place a saucer at the bottom of the basket on top of the moss lining to act as a hidden catch basin (see "Planting in Baskets" and "Special Care" in Chapter 7). Watering with a fine gentle spray takes longer but will result in a better soaking of the basket and less runoff.

To prevent potted ferns from drying too quickly, plant the smaller pot into a bigger one. Fill the spaces between the pots with sand, planting mix, or coarse sphagnum moss. This method is known as double potting (see Figure 4.1f). Placing a watered plant in a clear plastic bag will keep it moist for a week or more depending on how wide the bag is left open. If closed, the bag should have some ventilation holes, unless ample air space surrounds the fern inside the bag. This is a handy way to care for ferns when you are away for a week or so.

Air Circulation and Humidity

AIR MOVEMENT

Ferns need protection from drafts and hot, dry, battering winds. Although some ferns tolerate wind, their fronds usually look ragged. A small amount of air circulation and ventilation is desirable in greenhouses or similar enclosures. Air circulation discourages fungi and distributes humidity and temperature evenly. Small fans, partially open windows, and vents circulate air adequately in the average home greenhouse. Some outside air flowing into the greenhouse also can be beneficial, as it replenishes the carbon dioxide necessary for plant growth. Incoming air is detrimental, however, when it is extremely dry, hot, cold, smoggy, or apt to bring in insect pests.

HOW MUCH HUMIDITY?

Most ferns prefer conditions of 60 to 80% relative humidity during the day. Too much humidity will cause condensation that promotes bacterial and fungal disease on the foliage. Older and more robust ferns can tolerate less humidity, whereas more delicate or younger ones prefer higher levels. Most epiphytes and all xerophytes can tolerate less humidity than other ferns.

LOW-HUMIDITY DAMAGE

Low humidity is one of the most common causes of poor indoor growth. During the winter, the relative humidity in a typical, centrally heated living room is 40 to 50%—much lower than what most ferns prefer. Increasing the air temperature worsens the problem because it lowers the relative humidity. Low humidity can damage ferns in several ways. Emerging fronds tend to shrivel and older fronds yellow more quickly. Typically, the fronds wilt or the margins become scorched. Barely adequate humidity can result in

Figure 4.1. Increasing the humidity: a. mister or humidifier; b. grouping plants; c. placing pots just above the water level on pebbles in a tray or pot; d. and e. enclosing plants in plastic frames or glass; f. double potting.

thicker, smaller, harder-textured fronds that may be heavier spore-bearers. An indirect problem of insufficient humidity is increased infestations of red spider mite.

INCREASING THE HUMIDITY

Humidity can be increased several ways (Figure 4.1). Mechanical devices for increasing humidity indoors and in greenhouses are available on the market. Indoor units are controlled by electricity; greenhouse and outdoor units are generally attached to the water line. All units produce a fine mist. In these mechanical devices, the minute openings in the valve frequently become plugged and must be cleared regularly. Intermittent spraying of the air, foliage, and walkways with a fine mist from a garden hose is effective in increasing the humidity outdoors. A single misting is inadequate during hot, dry days because the moisture evaporates quickly. Depending on the amount of dryness, misting might be needed several times during the driest part of the day. Venting the household clothes drier into an adjacent greenhouse makes good use of the warm humid air on days when it is needed. Grouping potted plants together or planting them in the ground will keep them in more humid conditions. Increasing the humidity is desirable, but always avoid overwatering.

A simple procedure to increase the humidity indoors is to place potted plants on pebbles spread out in a shallow tray containing water. The bottom of the pot should not touch the water. Planting smaller plants in glass or plastic containers or enclosing larger plants on the sides with plastic sheets or glass frames will also help retain the moisture and humidity. The foliage can be misted during the hotter, drier part of the day. Double potting (see "Additional Tips on Watering," earlier in this chapter) will also increase the humidity around plants. Kitchens and bathrooms are usually the most humid areas in the home, and if light is sufficient, they are good places to grow plants.

HIGH-HUMIDITY DAMAGE

Excessive humidity, especially accompanied by condensation, is harmful for most ferns and should be controlled, particularly during the night when the temperature may drop quickly. Control can be accomplished by watering or misting early in the day or by opening vents to increase air circulation. Excessive humidity encourages fungal diseases and algae and results in the plants growing soft, weak, and succulent, making them vulnerable to sudden climatic changes. Under high humidity and warm temperatures, some ferns with firm, smooth fronds (such as polypodiums) develop brownish-purplish areas, particularly where the fronds arch or bend. Finely divided fronds, as in some cultivars of *Nephrolepis exaltata,* might yellow and shed their leaflets if the humidity is too high.

SMOG AND OTHER HARMFUL GASES

Heavy smog is known to damage young plants of *Blechnum gibbum* and *Microlepia platyphylla* (and it probably damages others). The damage appears in about one day. The first signs are tan or purple spots near the smaller veins on the fronds. These spots then dry and turn brown in about two days. Parts of the frond or the whole frond may die. Installing anti-smog devices is impractical for home growers, and the only corrective measure is to close outside air vents during periods of heavy smog or avoid planting smog-sensitive species.

Other air pollutants such as ethylene, carbon monoxide, sulfur dioxide, and natural and manufactured gas can injure ferns and other plants. Fern foliage suffering from toxic gases tends to curl under and/or turn yellow. Typical symptoms in flowering plants are curling of parts, growth of dormant buds, and early petal drop or closure. A sensitive test for the presence of ethylene is the early folding of carnation petals.

5 Soils and Fertilizers

Soils

There are probably as many soil mixes as there are growers. Experienced growers prepare their own mixes to best suit their particular style of gardening. If the grower waters frequently, a coarser mix will be used; if less frequently, a finer mix. If the grower fertilizes regularly, a soil mix without fertilizer will be used. If fertilizers are applied irregularly, the grower will add fertilizer to the mix or use a mix that contains rich garden soil. Whatever mix is used, however, ferns need a growing medium that will hold moisture, provide aeration, support the roots, and provide nutrients or retain added ones.

Soil for Potting

Beginners and even commercial growers may find it easier to purchase commercially prepared planter mixes. Most of these contain 50 to 75% organic matter (peat moss, leaf mold, wood shavings, bark chips, or various combinations of these), with the balance being inorganic matter (sand, perlite, vermiculite, soil, or various combinations of these). Some potting mixes might also contain additional nutrients and wetting agents. Soilless mixes are favored by most commercial growers because the mixes with soil are heavier and can vary in quality depending on the type of soil used. Some standard mixes for ferns (with or without soil) are given in Table 5.1.

A simple mix consists of one part peat moss and one part fine sand, to which is added 10 to 15 g per 3.8 liters (2–3 tsp. per gal.) of a 10-10-10 general fertilizer. The mix may need to be sieved with a screen to get fine-textured soil for very young or small ferns. For basket ferns and terrestrial ferns requiring good drainage, add another part or two of coarse material, such as chipped or ground bark, coarse leaf mold, or perlite. (Also see the Cornell epiphytic mix in Table 5.1.)

Soil for Outdoor Planting Beds

Consider yourself fortunate if the soil in your planting bed is loam and at least half organic matter. From time to time the organic matter might need to be replaced, but such a soil is ideal and easy to work for outdoor plantings. If the soil is on the sandy side, it can be improved by adding water-holding materials such as peat moss. Sandy soils require more watering and fertilizing than other soils, but they are easy to work, provide excellent aeration, and do not accumulate salts. Plants grown in sandy soils respond quickly to fertilizer.

Table 5.1. Commonly Used Planting Mixes

Planting Mixes with Soil

GARDEN SOIL MIX

Leaf mold	4 parts
Garden loam	1 part
Sand	1 part

GARDEN SOIL MIX FOR LIME-LOVING FERNS

Leaf mold	3 parts
Garden loam	1½ parts
Sand	1½ parts
Calcium carbonate (ground limestone)	1 gram per liter of mix (or 1 ounce per cubic foot) or more to bring pH to 7–8

Soilless Planting Mixes

UNIVERSITY OF CALIFORNIA SOIL MIX C (Matkin and Chandler 1957)

Peat moss (Canadian or German sphagnum or California hypnum)	0.14 cubic meter (5 cubic feet)
Sand, fine	0.14 cubic meter (5 cubic feet)
Potassium nitrate	43 grams (1.5 ounces)
Potassium sulfate	43 grams (1.5 ounces)
20% superphosphate	397 grams (14 ounces)
Dolomite lime	78 grams (2.75 ounces)
Calcium carbonate (ground limestone)	397 grams (14 ounces)

If a moderate amount of reserve nitrogen is desired, add 397 grams (14 oz.) of hoof and horn or blood meal to the above, but use the mixture within a week of preparation.

For limestone-loving plants, add more limestone, up to 397 grams (14 oz.).

Silty soils hold more water and nutrients than sandy soils, but they might need improved aeration for good fern growth. Adding organic matter, sand, or perlite will improve the aeration.

Partial or light clay soils need additional coarse and resilient material to improve aeration and to keep the clay from packing and becoming hard. Add coarse-textured organic matter until it makes up about half or more of the soil. Perlite or gypsum (calcium sulfate) will also be helpful additives to reduce packing of the clay. Be cautious about adding sand to certain clays, as binding reactions may occur.

If the soil is primarily dense clay, replace it with potting mix. The replacement is only needed in pockets where the ferns are to be planted. Clay soils are difficult to dilute. Even if an equal amount of organic matter is added to heavy clay soils, the soil will be suitable for ferns for only about three years. As the added organic matter gradually decays, clays predominate more and more, and the result is poor aeration and drainage. These conditions slow plant growth and promote rot, particularly during cool weather. Top applications of mulch are usually too thin to improve a clay soil, and thicker mulch layers may bury the ferns. In either case, little organic matter will reach the roots. If the soil has reverted to heavy clay, dig out the ferns in spring, add organic matter, perlite, or gypsum, and replant. Tree ferns and large ferns are difficult to replant, so be certain that the soil is suitable before planting in the first place.

Table 5.1. Continued

CORNELL FOLIAGE PLANT MIX (Boodley 1972)

Peat moss (Canadian or German sphagnum)	0.14 cubic meter (5 cubic feet)
Vermiculte, #2 grade	0.07 cubic meter (2.5 cubic feet)
Perlite, medium-fine grade	0.07 cubic meter (2.5 cubic feet)
Dolomite lime	1.4 kilograms (3 pounds)
20% superphosphate	340 grams (12 ounces)
10-10-10 fertilizer, inorganic	0.45 kilogram (1 pound)
Iron sulfate	113 grams (4 ounces)
Potassium nitrate	170 grams (6 ounces)
Peter's Soluble Trace Element Mix	5 grams (1 teaspoon)

For limestone-loving plants, add 1.4 kilograms (3 lbs.) of dolomite lime.

CORNELL EPIPHYTIC MIX (Boodley 1972)

Peat moss (Canadian or German sphagnum), shredded or screened through 6 mm (0.2 in.) mesh	0.14 cubic meter (5 cubic feet)
Douglas fir bark, screened through 3–6 mm (⅛–¼ in.) mesh	0.14 cubic meter (5 cubic feet)
Perlite, medium-fine grade	0.14 cubic meter (5 cubic feet)
Dolomite lime	1.4 kilograms (3 pounds)
20% superphosphate	1.2 kilograms (2.7 pounds)
10-10-10 fertilizer, inorganic	0.6 kilogram (1.3 pounds)
Iron sulfate	170 grams (6 ounces)
Potassium nitrate	227 grams (8 ounces)
Peter's Soluble Trace Element Mix	15 grams (1 tablespoon)

Commercially Prepared Mixes

A number of commercially prepared mixes are available on the market. Some may need additions of perlite or sand for better drainage.

Clay soils hold more nutrients and water than sandy soils. The main problems with clay soils are their harsh texture, tendency to expand when wet and shrink when dry, and lack of aeration. Although tropical ferns grow on clay, they are usually located on slopes with good drainage and in a climate where the clay seldom dries and shrinks.

Coarse granitic soils or decomposed granite formed from the breakdown of granite are unsuitable for growing ferns. They contain little or no organic matter and the main particles are coarse, resembling crumbly gravel. Although granitic soils contain some nutrients, water drains through them so quickly (due to the coarse particle size) that the roots have little time to absorb the water. The fine roots of ferns will dry rapidly in such soil. For most ferns, growing on granitic soil requires incorporating large amounts of water-holding, humus-forming material such as peat moss and compost.

Raised Planting Beds

Where appropriate, raised planting beds can be a good solution for poor soil or a lack of topsoil. Raised beds may be erected over poor soil and filled with planter mix. If commercial planter boxes cannot be used, redwood planks or rocks are suitable as retaining walls. Be certain that the soil is well drained, and if not, provide drain holes to the sides and add a layer of pot shards, gravel, or coarse sand to the bottom of the planting bed.

Mulches

Mulches are loose materials placed over the soil, such as peat moss, leaf mold, and wood or bark products. Mulches serve several functions. They reduce evaporation from the soil, prevent mud from splattering on the foliage, discourage weeds and some pests, protect exposed roots, and impart a neater appearance to the garden. On foot paths, medium-sized bark or wood chips reduce soil compaction. Ferns benefit from mulching, and spring is a good time to do so. The major precaution is to avoid burying the crown of the fern.

Soil Additives

Soil additives are incorporated into the soil to improve its quality or suitability for plants. New additives are constantly being developed. Some are made from recycled products such as rubber or Styrofoam, and others are old materials that have had their character changed, such as baked clay. Some are products that are given a new use, such as lichen (reindeer moss). The following are common soil additives used for growing ferns.

Bark products. Bark can be shredded, ground, or chipped. Bark products decay more slowly than wood by-products or peat and are used when a well-drained, long-lasting organic material is needed. Composted bark (partly decayed) is often used in commercial planting mixes. Nursery growers favor using bark products from fir trees.

Charcoal. Charcoal is added to mixes that might become waterlogged. It absorbs toxic materials produced when the soil is poorly aerated. There is, however, a limit to what charcoal can do for a soil, and it is best to avoid waterlogged soils from the start.

Fertilizers. Fertilizers contain minerals needed by the plant. Fish emulsion, blood meal, hooves, and horns are examples of organic fertilizers often used in soil mixes for ferns. Planting mixes with added organic fertilizers should be used within a week after being prepared. Inorganic fertilizers that can be added to planting mixes include potassium nitrate, potassium sulfate, superphosphate, dolomite lime, and calcium carbonate. Mixes containing inorganic fertilizers can usually be stored for a long time.

Humus. Humus is the dark, resilient, water-holding material that results from the partial decay of plants. A "humusy" soil is one that contains much partially decayed plant material. Any plant material can be made into humus. Compost, of course, is very high in humus.

Inorganic matter. Inorganic matter lacks substances derived directly from plants or animals. Inorganic matter commonly used in planting mixes for ferns includes perlite, vermiculite, sand, and silt.

Leaf mold. Next to peat moss, leaf mold (or partly decayed leaves) is the most popular substance used in soil mixes for ferns. Quality oak-leaf mold is increasingly difficult to obtain. In California it is illegal to remove leaf mold from many areas, and if taken from lowland areas it may be infected with *Armillaria* or oak root-rot fungus.

Lime. See the discussion under "Acidic and Basic Soils" later in this chapter.

Loam. Loam is a soil that has a mixture of different grades of sand, silt, and clay in such proportions that the characteristics of no one component predominate. An average loam soil contains about 1 part sand, ⅔ part silt, and 1 part clay, although the proportions can vary considerably depending on the grade (size) of the sand, silt, and clay. Loam is an ideal general garden soil with sufficient drainage, aeration, water-holding capacity, workability, and nutrient-holding capacity.

Organic matter. Organic matter is anything derived from plants or animals or their remains. It adds nutrients and humus to the soil. Organic matter commonly used in planting mixes for ferns includes peat moss, leaf mold, sawdust, wood shavings, ground or shredded bark, compost, and manure. Manure and compost are not favored for commercial planting mixes because of their variable quality and possible contamination with plant diseases.

Oyster shell. See the discussion under "Acidic and Basic Soils " later in this chapter.

Peat moss. Peat moss is partly or wholly decomposed moss that provides resilience and aeration to the soil as well as water-holding capabilities. It may be composed of a mixture of moss species or of individual species such as sphagnum moss or hypnum moss. Sedge or black peat does not contain moss and is not recommended for use with ferns because it might contain excessive salts. Milled peat moss is the common form used in planting mixes.

Peat moss can be difficult to wet. Try moistening it a day or two before use. It will absorb warm water faster than cold water, and adding a wetting agent to the water also speeds absorption. Milled peat moss may need to be mixed and squeezed to ensure an even distribution of moisture. Certain brands of milled peat moss come in a coarser grade suitable in soil mixes for growing larger ferns and epiphytes. Fine-textured, milled peat moss breaks down more rapidly but is suitable in mixes used for growing spores or small plants.

Uncut moss consists of intact strands or clumps that have been harvested and dried. It is coarse and stringy and is often used to line hanging baskets or to plant epiphytes. The best kind comes from various species of sphagnum moss. Other uncut moss, usually taken from tree trunks, is a mixture of various moss species and has a harsher texture and holds water less evenly. This kind is sometimes sold as green moss and should not be confused with the live sphagnum moss used to grow insectivorous plants. Uncut moss holds moisture yet provides excellent aeration if not kept too wet. When used for epiphytes mounted on boards or tree trunks, pads of uncut moss are placed around the roots and rhizomes. When used in pots, the moss should not be packed too tightly because it might hold too much water. The purity of commercially available uncut moss has deteriorated over the years, and nowadays it often contains twigs, grass, and leaves or is very fragmented. Uncut sphagnum moss from New Zealand is expensive but of excellent quality. Spanish moss (*Tillandsia usneoides*) should not be confused with the uncut sphagnum moss of horticultural use.

Uncut moss that is soaked and drained before use is easier to work. Use gloves when handling wet uncut moss. Cuts in the skin occasionally become infected by a fungus that lives in the moss. Coconut fiber and tree-fern trunk fibers are sometimes substituted for uncut moss in lining baskets, but they are stiffer and retain less water than peat moss.

Perlite. The drainage and aeration of soil can be improved by adding perlite, which is also known by the brand name Sponge Rok. Perlite is a sterile inorganic material derived by heating and expanding siliceous rock. It is light, porous, loose, and firm. The particles come in various sizes.

Rockwool (Gordan). Rockwool is a sterile substance made from coal, carbonate, and basalt heated and blown into fibers. It is 97% air, chemically inert, and does not decompose. Rockwool is used in soilless mixes. Compressed forms come in blocks, mats, or tubes for special horticultural or floral use. Do not reuse rockwool that is designed for floral use because it might contain formaldehyde.

Sand. Sand refers to rock particles in a particular size range. The fine grade, commercially designated as United States Screen Mesh size #30 (approximately 0.5 mm in diameter), is recommended for potting mixes, although finer sizes to #270 (0.05 mm in diameter) may be used. Coarser grades of size #12, #16, or #20 (1.6 mm, 1.2 mm, and 0.85 mm in diameter, respectively) are added to soil to increase aeration and drainage. Size #8 (2.5 mm in diameter) and lower number sizes are designated as gravel. Quartz sand and washed builder's sand are suitable for gardening. Do not use sand from ocean beaches or other saline areas unless it is washed to remove excess salts that might otherwise burn roots.

Sawdust and other wood by-products. Adding wood by-products such as sawdust, shavings, or chips increases the humus content and improves the soil structure. Wood by-products, however, contain few mineral nutrients.

Fresh or partly decayed sawdust (or other wood waste) may be used. Most fresh sawdust and wood waste contain no appreciable amounts of toxic substances, and those toxins that might be present will decompose within a few weeks after incorporation into the soil. Reports of toxicity are associated with finely ground sawdust that rots under conditions of low oxygen, producing toxins in the process. Sawdust is converted to humus by microorganisms that need air and mineral nutrients to grow. Therefore it is best to aerate the compost and provide additional minerals for the microorganisms. Add 5.4 kg (12 lbs.) of 10-6-4 fertilizer for every 45.4 kg (100 lbs.) of sawdust. Other fertilizers rich in nitrogen and phosphorous may be used. Nitrogen is the most important mineral, and calculations are based on supplying 0.5 kg (1.1 lbs.) of nitrogen per 45.4 kg (100 lbs.) of sawdust. Apply the minerals at intervals throughout the composting period. Nitrified sawdust has nitrogen added, sometimes in forms or amounts that can burn fern roots.

Soil. Typically, soil is decomposed, finely divided rock material with a small amount of organic matter. Sand, silt, and clay (listed from largest to smallest size) are the most important rock particles in garden soil. Sand provides excellent drainage, aeration, and workability, but retains little water or nutrients. Clay, the finest textured particle, has poor drainage, poor aeration, and difficult workability, but retains water and adsorbs and retains nutrients. Silt, being intermediate in size to sand and clay, has essentially intermediate properties but lacks clay's chemical ability to attract and retain nutrients.

Vermiculite. Vermiculite is a sterile inorganic material produced by heating bits of mica and causing them to expand. It comes in various particle sizes and contains some potassium and calcium. Vermiculite adsorbs minerals and makes them available to plant roots. It also retains water but tends to collapse in a relatively short time. Wet vermiculite should not be pressed or compacted because its pore structure will be ruined.

ACIDIC AND BASIC SOILS

Growers place much importance on whether a soil is acidic or basic (alkaline). The importance is not in the degree of acidity itself, but in the acidity's effect on the availability of soil nutrients to plants. If your plants are growing well, do not worry about soil acidity. If they are languishing and unresponsive to balanced fertilizers, check first for unfavorable growing conditions, then check for acidity. In general, regions with arid climates have basic soils and ones with rainy climates tend to have acidic soils.

Determining acidic or basic soil. The range from an acid to base condition is known as the pH range and is measured on a logarithmic scale from 1 to 14. A pH of 7 is neutral, less than 7 is acidic, and more than 7 is basic. The greatest amount and variety of nutrients are available to plants at pH values between 5.5 and 7. Therefore, most plants grow best somewhere in this range. Most ferns flourish between pH 6 and 7. Many plants show iron deficiency (yellowing of the leaves) at pH levels of 5.5 to 6, although this has not been reported for ferns. An inexpensive way to determine soil pH is with pH paper, which turns a color corresponding to a particular pH value.

Limestone-loving ferns or ferns of basic soil (pH 7–8). Ferns native to basic soils or limestone need more calcium than other ferns. Chapter 9 includes a list of ferns for such soil. To grow these ferns it might be necessary to add calcium, usually dolomite ($CaCO_3 \cdot MgCO_3$), ground limestone ($CaCO_3$), or oyster shells. Burned or quick lime (CaO) and hydrated or slaked lime ($Ca[OH]_2$) should be used sparingly because small amounts can greatly increase the pH and harm the plants. Where limestone is available, ferns can be grown in soil pockets between these rocks, or crushed limestone may be added to the soil. Some growers have had success using pieces of concrete instead of limestone.

Testing for calcium in the soil is easy. Obtain a teaspoon of a strong acid, such as sulfuric acid or muriatic acid (hydrochloric acid or hydrogen chloride). Sulfuric acid may be obtained from a car battery. Muriatic acid may be obtained from some toilet bowl cleaners. Place 5 ml (1 tsp.) of the acid on a cup or less of soil and watch for bubbling. Bubbling indicates the presence of calcium in the form of lime (calcium carbonate). If no bubbling occurs, you may not have enough calcium in the soil, or you may have one of the few soils that has calcium but does not respond to this test, in which case you might have to have the soil tested commercially.

Acid-loving ferns (pH 4–7). Some acid-loving ferns grow in wet, marshy areas where decaying organic matter produces carbonic acid. Other acid-loving ferns may grow in well-drained soil that is acidic because its calcium and basic salts have been leached away. A peaty or highly organic soil will provide acidic conditions for ferns. Also, soils can be acidified by adding aluminum sulfate, ammonium sulfate, ammonium nitrate, or finely ground sulfur. The latter is the most economical and efficient additive. Chapter 9 includes a list of ferns for acid soils.

STERILIZING SOILS

In the strict sense, soil sterilization means killing all microorganisms, but in general horticulture it usually refers to destroying disease organisms, insects, and weeds. It will here be referred to as soil "treatment" to distinguish it from true sterilization.

Except for commercial growers, planting mixes for ferns are usually not given soil treatment unless diseases are present or the mix is used for growing fern spores or young ferns. The use of compost, manure, soils, or leaf mold in soil mixes increases the need for treatment. Soil mixes can be treated using chemicals or heat (complete soil sterilization is usually done in an autoclave or oven). For information regarding soil treatments, the commercial grower will find the publication by Matkin and Chandler (1957) particularly helpful.

Chemical treatments. Chemicals such as methyl bromide and formaldehyde can be used to treat soil but not, of course, around living plants. However, such chemicals are restricted or no longer available or have been discontinued for health and environmental reasons. Home growers might find it easier, although not as effective, to use fungicide drenches such as pentachloronitrobenzene or PCNB (Terraclor), thiram (Arasan), captan, or quaternary ammonium compounds such as Consan or Physan 20. (See Chapter 11 and Appendix IV.) These products can be used around live plants.

Steam treatment. Most commercial growers use steam to treat the soil. The steam is applied through various types of equipment until all parts of the soil have been heated to 71°C (160°F) for 30 minutes. For a better margin of safety, heat at 82°C (180°F) for 30 minutes. High heat, however, might produce toxic conditions. If this happens, let the soil stand for a few weeks or leach it thoroughly with water.

For small amounts of soil, a homemade steam sterilizer can be devised for treatment. Get a large cooking pot or roasting pan and fill with about 1 cm (0.5 in.) or more of water. Place a rack in the pan to raise the soil (or to raise pots containing the soil) above the water level. Cover and heat this over the stove or in the oven at about 120°C (250°F), or high enough to produce steam. Be sure that the steam penetrates all parts of the soil for at least 30 minutes. This might require placing the oven controls at about 150°C (300°F) for half an hour if there is much mass to be penetrated. Very moist soil wrapped in aluminum foil can also be heated in this manner.

Since most plastic pots or boxes cannot be treated with high heat, they have to be disinfected separately by soaking for 30 minutes in a 10% bleach solution, after which they are rinsed with previously boiled water and then filled with the treated soil.

Microwave treatment. Treatment in a microwave oven is suitable for small amounts of soil. Add generously moistened soil to a 2 liter (2 quart) casserole dish, cover, and set the oven on high for 5 to 15 minutes, or until the steam thoroughly penetrates all the soil. Keep it covered while cooling.

Boiling water treatment. Many growers find that gently pouring boiling water over pots filled with small amounts of soil and provided with good drainage is a satisfactory treatment, especially if the soil will be used for growing spores. For a given amount of soil, pour at least twice as much boiling water gently through it. By placing a clean paper towel over the moist soil before pouring, you can prevent much of the lighter material in the mix from floating up to the surface.

Direct boiling treatment. Although it kills soil pathogens, boiling soil in a cooking pot is not recommended. This treatment ruins the soil's structure, reducing it to a soggy mush that takes a long time to drain and, upon drying, lacks aeration.

Steam sterilization. Complete sterilization kills all organisms including their spores. Except for scientific work, such as growing ferns in agar, full sterilization is unnecessary. In steam sterilization, the material to be sterilized is placed in an autoclave at a pressure of 1 kilogram per square centimeter (15 lbs. per sq. in.) for 15 minutes or longer (depending on the amount) at a temperature of 121 to 123°C (250–254°F). Small amounts of soil, pots, dishes, or other items can be sterilized in a home pressure-cooker at 1 kilogram per square centimeter (15 lbs. per sq. in.) for 20 to 30 minutes.

Dry heat sterilization. In dry heat sterilization, soil is placed in an oven at 160°C (320°F) for two hours or longer, depending on the amount of soil. This method has the disadvantage of making the soil difficult to wet; however, it is useful for sterilizing paper envelopes used to store sterilized spores. To sterilize envelopes, put them in a heavier box before heating them to the oven temperature given above.

Fertilizers

Ferns growing in rich soils are well supplied with mineral nutrients and do not need fertilizers or other supplements. Although most gardeners do not have such fertile soils, they want the best-looking plants possible. Ferns that receive ample fertilizers or mineral nutrients grow faster and bigger and more luxuriant. Ferns, however, are extremely sensitive to overfertilizing, and the novice grower, being aware of this fact, is often hesitant to fertilize. It is therefore important to learn how to select the proper fertilizers and apply them correctly.

WHEN FERNS NEED FERTILIZER

You can tell when a fern needs fertilizer because it grows slowly, is smaller than normal, and produces poor-quality foliage. Ferns producing healthy green fronds do not need fertilizers. If you do not want a fern to grow large or quickly, do not fertilize unless it shows poor foliage color. In that case, light applications of fertilizer will improve the color.

Choosing a Fertilizer

Beginners are advised to select fertilizers that have a reputation for "low burn." These contain a low percentage of highly soluble salts (that is, salts that dissolve quickly in water). Liquid fertilizers with a low-burn reputation include fish emulsion and those containing urea. Dry fertilizers with low-burn properties include fish meal, cottonseed meal, castor-bean oil, and activated sewage sludge.

Liquid Versus Dry Fertilizers

Liquid fertilizers are probably safer and easier to use for the beginning grower. They can be applied while watering, and this saves labor. Also, there is less likelihood of accidental overdose as a fertilizer is diluted for application. A disadvantage of liquid fertilizer is that some of it quickly passes beyond the root zone and is wasted. That which remains will also leach out of the soil more rapidly than dry fertilizers, and so liquid fertilizers need to be applied more often. With dry fertilizers, you must spread the powder or granules thinly and evenly over the soil surface. If the dry fertilizer contains much soluble salt and is accidentally concentrated in one spot, it will injure the plant.

Fertilizers have been developed that slowly release soluble salts for three to nine months. Some release a bit of their salts each time the plant is watered. Because ferns require more frequent watering than other plants, be careful not to overfertilize when using these fertilizers. New fertilizers (such as Nutricote) release nutrients at certain temperatures, making frequent watering less of a problem. Dry and slow-release fertilizers are not recommended for staghorn ferns (*Platycerium*) because the granules can get caught behind the base fronds and injure the tissue.

Organic Versus Inorganic Fertilizers

Organic fertilizers are derived from organic substances, whereas inorganic fertilizers are mostly derived from chemicals or mining processes. Fertilizers such as fish emulsion, bone meal, or castor-bean meal are organic; ammonium sulfate and superphosphate, among others, are inorganic fertilizers.

Beginners are advised to use organic fertilizers with low-burn reputations and defer use of inorganic types unless they also have a low-burn reputation. Generally, organic types contain fewer soluble salts than inorganic types and result in less burn. They also release their nutrients more slowly than inorganic types and tend to last longer in the soil. Inorganic fertilizers, however, produce quicker plant responses. Exceptions occur in both categories of fertilizer in regard to soluble salt content. Blood meal, an organic fertilizer, contains a high amount of soluble salt and may readily burn plants if applied carelessly. Some inorganic fertilizers have salts that dissolve slowly in water and therefore burn plants less readily. Do not use manures in places such as greenhouses where warmth and high humidity prevail. Their use encourages bacteria and molds.

Complete or Incomplete Fertilizers

Beginners should use complete fertilizers, which contain the three most important elements needed by a plant: nitrogen (N), phosphorus (P), and potassium (K). Incomplete fertilizers have only one or two of these elements. Complete fertilizers are generally preferred over incomplete ones, although results vary according to the plant, soil, and cultural conditions.

The approximate percentages of each of the three main elements contained in a fertilizer is cited on the package as a series of three numbers. The first number refers to nitrogen, the second to phosphorus, and the third to potassium. Most fish emulsions have percentages of 5-2-2, while hoof and horn is listed as 15-0-0. Fish emulsion is a balanced fertilizer whereas hoof and horn is not.

Plants require several elements, but nitrogen is the most important. Trace elements (those needed by plants in minute amounts) are usually abundant enough in the soil or in fertilizers as impurities. An exception is calcium. Non-limestone-derived soils in areas of high rainfall often must have calcium added, usually in the form of dolomite or ground limestone. The amount of calcium in a fertilizer is usually indicated by percent on the label.

FERTILIZER APPLICATION

Always follow the manufacturer's directions for application of a fertilizer. Never give more than the recommended dosage. If you are uncertain about the fern's sensitivity to the fertilizer, there is no harm in reducing the concentration. Some growers regularly use only half the recommended dosage. It is more beneficial to give smaller amounts over several applications than to give the full dosage all at once. Although this involves more work, the plant makes better use of the fertilizer.

Fertilizers that must be diluted should be diluted accurately. Dissolve as much of the fertilizer as possible before application. For watering large numbers of plants, a range of mechanical devices are available. Great time-savers are those that mix the fertilizer with the water as it flows through the hose. Watering devices that operate only with a strong stream of water are not desirable, as the force of the water may damage the fronds and wash the soil from the roots.

Powders or granular forms must be sprinkled evenly and thinly over the moist soil surface. Do not mix these fertilizers into the soil by tilling. Fern roots are fine and fibrous and grow close to the surface. Tilling will injure the roots. Water thoroughly immediately after applying the fertilizer powder or granules. Any fertilizer accidentally spilled on the foliage should be washed off immediately. If too much fertilizer has been accidentally applied to one spot, particularly if near the crown of the fern, remove it or spread it out thinly to reduce the possibility of burning the fern and encouraging undesirable mold growth. Although organic fertilizers require microorganisms such as molds to decompose them and release their nutrients, a high concentration of mold may damage the fern.

FREQUENCY OF APPLICATIONS

The frequency of fertilizer application depends on the manufacturer's recommendations. On the average, one application every three weeks is needed for liquid fertilizers and longer intervals for dry fertilizers. Fertilize infrequently if you do not want the fern to grow too large. Ferns that do not enter any noticeable rest period but continue to grow actively throughout the year benefit from fertilizers applied at any time. If you want to discourage new growth prior to winter or for fear of frost damage, do not fertilize late in the season. Also, do not fertilize ferns during their periods of rest or dormancy because there is little intake of nutrients at that time.

Where there is heavy watering or frequent rainfall on porous soils, the water will leach the fertilizer. Ferns growing in such areas should be fertilized more often. On the other hand, soils that do not drain readily retain fertilizer and can be fertilized less frequently. For commercial growers, the recommended nitrogen level for maintaining the best fern foliage color is about 150 ppm, which amounts to about 2.5 ml (½ tsp.) of a fertilizer in 3.8 liters (1 gal.) of water if the fertilizer contains a 20% nitrogen content. This should be applied as needed.

TREATING OVERFERTILIZED FERNS

Overfertilization results in burned or wilted foliage. Damage to roots and rhizomes may also occur. If you have accidentally overfertilized, immediately remove all fertilizer that might be on the surface and make sure that the soil is well drained. Then water heavily to leach out any remaining fertilizer. Later watering should be sparing so that the soil becomes well aerated. Increase the humidity and remove badly burned and wilted, dead fronds. Recovery of the plant usually depends on how badly the roots and rhizomes have been damaged. Young ferns or those with thin, nonfleshy rhizomes are more difficult to save than older ferns or those with fleshy rhizomes.

Successful fertilization works on the principle that a little soluble fertilizer salt is good but too much is bad. Damage from overfertilization is caused by the release of too much soluble salt. This causes water to flow out of the roots and into the soil, thus dehydrating, wilting, and eventually killing the plant. If only some of the roots are injured, there may be a partial wilting and/or the characteristic leaf scorch or burned appearance. The partial loss of roots or foliage sets the plant back, and it may be stunted for some time. Fertilizer salts on the leaf can also dehydrate and burn the tissue. (See "Water Quality and Salt Injury," in Chapter 4.)

Ferns and Plant Hormones

The effects of plant hormones, such as auxin and gibberellic acid, on ferns are complex and reported in scientific journals. Gibberellic acid has been shown to increase the growth rate of young walking ferns (*Camptosorus rhizophyllus*). Other hormones are known to interact in complex ways on the germination of spores and the early development of prothalli (gametophytes) and sporelings. The quality of light and various chemicals also interact with plant hormones to affect spore germination and prothallial development.

6 Through the Year with Ferns

Year-round Needs

Where ferns grow throughout the year, it is necessary to water, fertilize, and groom year-round. Elsewhere, for best growth, fertilize more frequently during the growing seasons and less so or not at all during the cool months. Watch for slugs and snails as well as other pests and for sudden and damaging changes in the weather.

Remove old or badly damaged fronds from vigorously growing plants. Cut them off at the base of the stipe. Removing these fronds maintains a neat appearance and reduces hiding places for pests. If the plant is growing poorly and has only a few fronds, avoid removing any fronds except those that are totally brown or yellow. Sometimes only the tip or margin of an otherwise lovely frond is disfigured. Instead of removing the whole frond, the disfigurement may be trimmed away with scissors and the remaining part cut into a shape that is close to the natural one.

There are advantages and disadvantages to the grooming practice of cutting off all the tattered, leggy, misshapen fronds along with the undamaged fronds. The advantages are

1. In dense frond clusters it is easier to cut off all the fronds than to single out only the damaged ones.
2. In a few weeks, fresh new compact growth will appear.
3. The frond shapes will be symmetrical due to greater space for development.

The disadvantages are

1. Certain species are harmed by having all their fronds removed at the same time.
2. Encouraging vulnerable new growth just before a frost or cool weather may bring about the demise of non-deciduous ferns.
3. The bare look, even if temporary, is unattractive to some gardeners.

If the advantages outweigh the disadvantages, then be sure that the plant is a vigorous grower that ordinarily produces many fronds during the growing season (as are the common species of *Adiantum, Pteris,* and *Microlepia*). Also, make sure that the fronds are removed when plenty of growing season lies ahead. In areas with short growing seasons, cutting back all the old fronds is best done in early spring before the fiddleheads have emerged. In areas with longer growing seasons, this may be done later. In areas with year-round growing conditions, the time to cut back fronds is not critical for most non-deciduous ferns.

Ferns benefit from an occasional fine spray to remove dust, dirt, and lurking insects. Fronds with hairy surfaces tend to catch debris that does not wash off easily. Usually the debris can be loosened with a soft brush.

Leaf spots left by salts in the water are harmless if not too numerous. If conspicuous and unattractive, the spots can be removed by misting them gently with a liberal amount of water to wash off the salts. About half a tablespoon of mild household detergent added to a quart of water (about 15 grams per liter) helps dissolve the salt faster. This treatment must be followed with a thorough water rinse. When applying the detergent solution and rinse, tilt the pot to prevent the detergent from dripping on the soil. Spots can be avoided if rain or de-ionized water is used instead of tap water. Remember that liquid fertilizers applied on the leaves will also produce water spots. Commercial leaf polishes can be used on thick, leathery ferns to remove spots and to shine the surface, but the shine does not necessarily help the plant.

Winter Care

If you live in a temperate area, your outdoor ferns will be dormant during the winter and require little care other than checking that their protective coverings or shelters are not disrupted. Outdoor ferns in subtropical climates grow slowly during the winter, and there is little to be done besides watering, removing withered fronds, and fertilizing once or twice a month (or not at all). Winter is the low point in an outdoor subtropical fern garden, but if the fronds are taken care of in late summer and fall, they will grace the garden throughout the winter. Watch for early spring growth and remove old fronds before the emerging fiddleheads become hopelessly entangled in them. Indoor ferns, greenhouse ferns, and those in tropical gardens require their usual care, although species with a rest period should be watered and fertilized less.

Spring Care

In temperate and subtropical areas, ferns grow vigorously in the spring as new fiddleheads emerge and uncoil. In temperate areas, the winter shelters can be removed in spring. In all areas, dead and old fronds should be removed before the new fiddleheads emerge. This minimizes injury to the new fiddleheads and gives them room to develop. Aphids commonly appear on ferns in early spring, so watch for them as well as other pests. If the winter rains have washed some of the soil away from the roots, replace this soil or cover with mulch, particularly the area around the tip of the rhizome where new roots emerge. Resume fertilizing every two or three weeks if maximum growth is desired. All ferns must be protected from early heat waves, particularly while new fronds are uncoiling since they are soft and easily dehydrated. Spring is a good time to divide, transplant, or repot ferns, and this should be done before the fiddleheads uncoil.

Some ferns will shed all or most of their fronds just before putting forth new ones. The squirrel's-foot fern (*Davallia mariesii* var. *stenolepis*) drops its fronds in late winter or early spring; the Canary Island davallia (*D. canariensis*) drops its fronds in spring or early summer; and the knight's polypody (*Goniophlebium subauriculatum* 'Knightiae') drops its fronds in late spring. These ferns look forlorn with their withered fronds, but new fronds will soon clothe the basket again. Remove any lingering old fronds to make way for the new.

Summer Care

Most ferns produce new fronds well into the summer. Their older fronds that turn yellow or brown should be removed. Fertilization should be continued for maximum growth. Watering and keeping the air humid will be the major problem in some areas, especially for hanging baskets and pots. Watch for thrips and scale insects that usually appear at this time. Snails, slugs, and other pests will also be active. In many parts of the country that have a long growing season, it is still possible to divide, replant, and repot in summer. Trim the more robust ferns when they threaten to shade the smaller and slower growing species. Be ready to mist your ferns when the weather gets too hot. Avoid overwatering the soil when increasing the humidity; sprinkle the walkways instead of saturating the soil. Fern spores are most frequently formed at this time and in the fall.

Fall Care

From late summer into fall, fern growth wanes and less water is required. Fertilizers should be reduced or withheld. Deciduous ferns will yellow and brown, and new growth stops until spring. Leave the old fronds on the plant to protect them through the winter in areas where frost and freezes occur. In very cold climates, some ferns need mulches and even screens or frames built over them. It is important to mark or remember where deciduous species are planted so that they will not be accidentally dug up or injured during winter garden activities.

In subtropical gardens with a long growing period, the ferns will still need to be groomed and watered. Where there is danger of frost, do not remove green fronds, even if they are tattered, because removing them will encourage new growth that could be damaged by frost. Resist the urge to trim until the danger from frost has passed. Also reduce fertilizers to discourage new growth before winter. As the weather cools, ferns need less fertilizer and water. Most of the fronds that remain on the plant in late summer and fall will stay on the plant throughout the winter; however, if temperatures are mild, some ferns will continue to produce a few smaller fronds in the months ahead. If the temperature drops very much, the fronds will yellow.

7 Planting

Planting Time

Spring is generally the best time to plant, replant, transplant, or propagate ferns. It allows for a long growing period so that the fern can establish itself before cool weather. Ferns that form only one set of fronds per year—for instance, some osmundas—are best moved in early spring before the new fronds have appeared, or in fall after the old ones have died. If they must be moved in leafy condition, preserve as much of the foliage as possible to ensure good growth the following year. Ferns that produce new fronds throughout a long growing season can be safely moved while in leaf. Avoid moving ferns with soft, newly formed fronds because they wilt and damage easily. If a fern must be moved at this time, avoid disturbing the roots and keep the root ball intact (as is done for all transplants). After replanting, water well and keep the plant shaded and the air humid.

Beds, Pots, or Baskets?

Deciding whether to plant ferns in the ground, in pots, or in hanging containers is determined by the climate, setting, personal preference, and species being planted. Ferns planted in the ground usually require less care than those in pots or baskets. They do not dry out as fast, and the soil acts as a buffer to absorb extra moisture, excess fertilizer, temperature extremes, and other unfavorable conditions. Also, ferns planted in the ground do not have to be replanted as frequently as those grown in pots. Hanging containers, however, show cascading or drooping fronds to best advantage. Trough gardens (discussed in Chapter 10) may be large enough to have conditions between those of ground plantings and container plantings.

If you want to move your plants around for decorative purposes or winter protection, plant them in containers. If you want to keep a natural effect with potted plants, sink the pots in the ground to hide them. Many ferns that grow naturally in the ground (terrestrial ferns) can be planted in baskets or in pots subsequently placed in a basket. Terrestrial ferns in baskets or pots need to be kept moist. Ferns that naturally grow on trees (epiphytic ferns) or on rocks (epilithic or saxicolous ferns) are generally planted in pots or baskets with a loose soil mix, but they can also be planted in the ground if the drainage is good.

Terrestrial or epiphytic ferns with long-creeping rhizomes bearing fronds that grow far apart are generally unattractive in pots. They soon grow to the edge of the pot and can die from salt burn if salt has accumulated around the edge, or if the plant grows beyond the edge of the pot it might die from drying. Sometimes the rhizome will grow down into the pot and become trapped at the bottom. In any case, the old portions of the rhizomes are left exposed and in full view at the top of the pot. With age they become unattractive. For these reasons, ferns with long-creeping rhizomes should be planted in beds or moss-lined baskets where they can root over a broader surface. Nevertheless, they are usually planted to best effect in the ground where they have ample space to grow and are free to climb up trees or moss-covered posts.

Ferns with closely spaced fronds, erect or semi-erect stems, or short-creeping rhizomes are best for planting in pots where they can display their foliage patterns. Ferns native to dry or seasonal climates are best planted in pots or isolated places in the garden where their particular watering needs may be more easily met. Trough gardens are especially suitable for such purposes (see Chapter 10). Bottle gardens or terrariums are used to grow ferns and selaginellas requiring high humidity.

Planting in Beds

SELECTING THE SITE

Before planting in the ground, check the site for proper light, wind exposure, and soil conditions. Anticipate the full size of the fern you are planting. Will it fit your landscape needs? It is easier to consider these factors now rather than later. If possible, start with hardened plants—that is, ones acclimated to exposed conditions. Greenhouse plants moved outdoors can wilt, especially if they have soft succulent growth. These plants should be gradually exposed to drier air over a week or more.

PREPARING THE BED

Prepare the soil so that it is moist and loose (friable). Use soil that contains at least half organic matter (see Chapter 5). Soil in the planting bed does not have to be deep because fern roots generally grow near the surface. About 20 to 45 cm (8–18 in.) of soil is sufficient for small to medium ferns. Tree ferns grow best with 60 cm (24 in.) of soil or more. These requirements do not mean the entire bed needs to be deepened. If the soil is unsuitable for ferns and you do not want to change the whole bed, plant the ferns in pockets of suitable soil and provide good drainage, especially in heavy clay soils, by adding coarse gravel or shards to the bottom of the planting hole. An area of suitable soil for ferns should be large enough to accommodate the expected spread of roots. Usually this equals about one-third to one-half of the spread of the fronds. Once the soil has been prepared, dig the hole to the depth and width of the container. Gently compress the soil at the bottom of the hole so it will not settle too much after planting. Then proceed as follows.

BASIC PLANTING PROCEDURES

Getting the plant out of the container. If the soil in the container is dry, water it. If possible, do this a day before removal so that the soil will not be muddy. Moist soil will not fall away from the roots as easily as dry soil and is less likely to stick to the inside walls of the pot. If the fern is in a can, have the nurseryman cut the can. Ferns in small pots are easily tapped out. You can do this by supporting the top of the soil with one hand, turning the pot over, and giving the rim a sharp tap on the edge of a bench (Figure 7.1). The ball of soil and the fern should slide out intact. Lay larger pots on their side, protect the edges with padding, and then tap with a mallet until the mass of soil slides away from the pot. Applying water pressure from a hose into the drain hole can float out stubborn soil masses.

Digging ferns from the ground for transplanting. If a fern must be taken out of the ground and replanted, the best time to do this is in early spring. Water the plant a day or two before transplanting so that the soil will be moist enough to cling to the roots (but not muddy) when the plant is moved. The diameter of the root ball and soil should be about half the spread of the fronds. The depth will depend on the size of the fern.

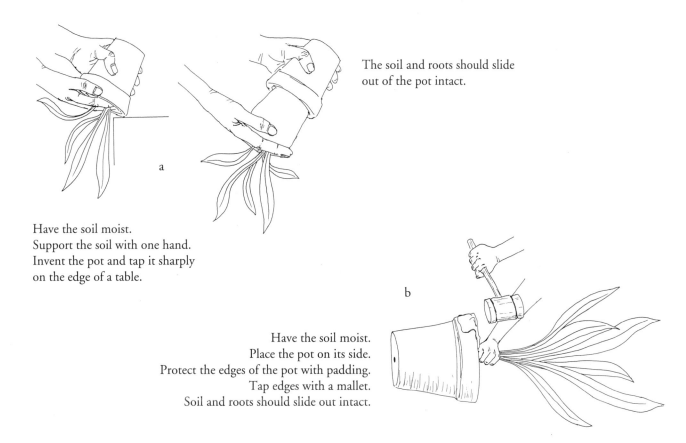

The soil and roots should slide
out of the pot intact.

a

Have the soil moist.
Support the soil with one hand.
Invent the pot and tap it sharply
on the edge of a table.

b

Have the soil moist.
Place the pot on its side.
Protect the edges of the pot with padding.
Tap edges with a mallet.
Soil and roots should slide out intact.

Figure 7.1. Removing plants from pots: a. from a small pot; b. from a large pot.

Positioning and planting the fern. Normally, note the soil level of the fern you are moving and replant it at the same level (Figure 7.2). If an erect or semi-erect fern has been tipping over, remove the old stipe bases and bury the rootstock or rhizome deeper in the soil, leaving its crown or growing tip uncovered, not buried (Figure 7.3). Measure the height of the soil ball. Add or remove soil from the hole (or pot) to bring the crown to the proper level when set in place. For pots, the level of the soil should be about 1 cm (0.5 in.) or more below the top edge to provide a catch basin for water (Figure 7.4). All added soil should be gently firmed in place.

If the soil attached to the roots is poor, gently shake most of it loose before replanting. Remove dead, old, and inactive roots. Cut old broken fronds and stipe bases at the rhizome. If the fern is badly root-bound, gently loosen some of the surface roots and spread them out.

For creeping ferns, position the growing tip of the rhizome to face the direction in which you wish it to grow. If rhizomes creeping over the soil surface refuse to stay in place after planting, anchor them with pieces of bent wire or small rocks. When planting in pots, place the growing tip as far from the edge as possible (Figure 7.5). This might place the foliage at the edge of the pot instead of the center, but it will provide maximum room for future growth.

Once the plant is positioned, fill in the spaces around the roots. Gently press the soil into place (but do not compact it) as it is added until you reach the desired level. Do not cover the crown or growing point if it was growing exposed before. Water the plant well with a gentle sprinkle. A strong stream of water will flatten the plants, wash soil from the roots, and compact the soil, destroying its aeration. Some growers recommend commercial vitamin B_1 preparations for stimulating root growth of transplanted ferns, but this treatment generally has no effect on intact plants. The leaves make enough of this vitamin, and it can be

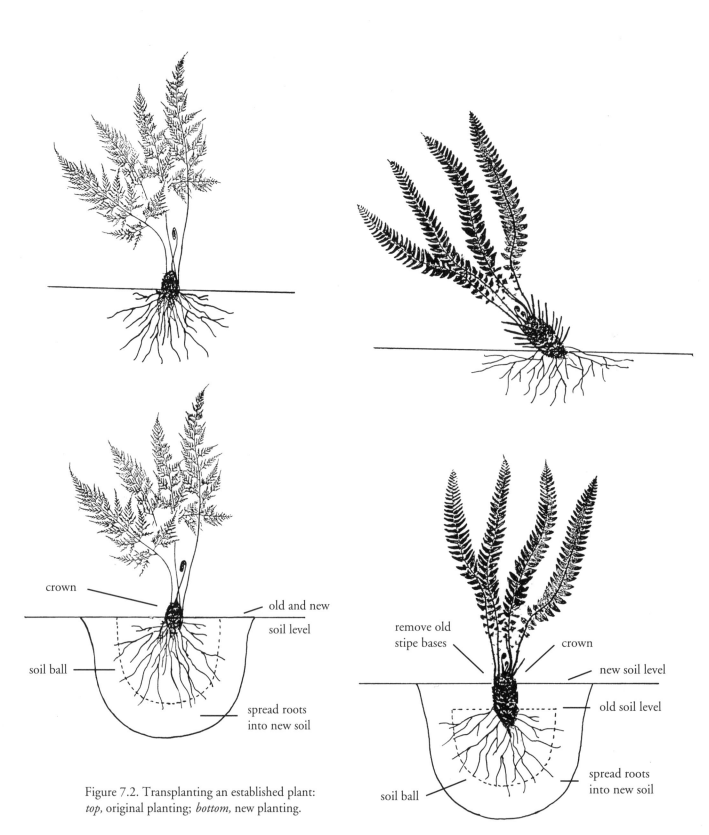

crown

old and new
soil level

soil ball

spread roots
into new soil

Figure 7.2. Transplanting an established plant:
top, original planting; *bottom,* new planting.

remove old
stipe bases

crown

new soil level

old soil level

soil ball

spread roots
into new soil

Figure 7.3. Replanting a toppled plant: *top,* toppled
plant; *bottom,* replanted fern, with old stipe bases
removed and rootstock planted deeper, but without
covering the crown.

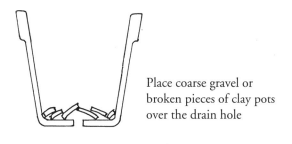

Place coarse gravel or broken pieces of clay pots over the drain hole

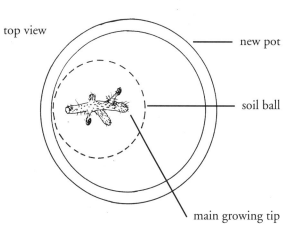

top view

new pot

soil ball

main growing tip

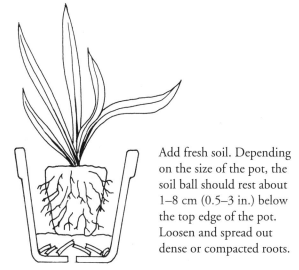

Add fresh soil. Depending on the size of the pot, the soil ball should rest about 1–8 cm (0.5–3 in.) below the top edge of the pot. Loosen and spread out dense or compacted roots.

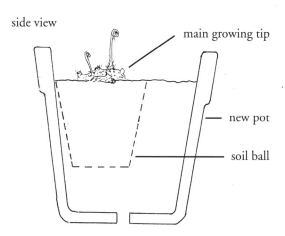

side view

main growing tip

new pot

soil ball

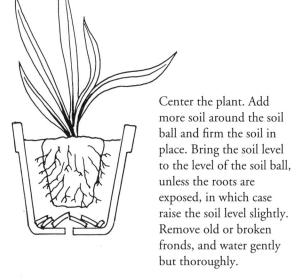

Center the plant. Add more soil around the soil ball and firm the soil in place. Bring the soil level to the level of the soil ball, unless the roots are exposed, in which case raise the soil level slightly. Remove old or broken fronds, and water gently but thoroughly.

Figure 7.4. Repotting.

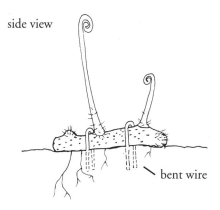

side view

bent wire

Figure 7.5. Potting ferns with creeping rhizomes, with the growing tip placed as far from the edge of the pot as possible.

stored in the stem or passed to the roots. A temporary shade placed over recently transplanted plants will help them recover and may reduce frond loss. Slug and snail control may also be in order. Within the first few days after planting, some of the softer fronds might wilt, and if they do not recover should be removed. New fronds will soon grow to replace them.

SPECIAL CARE

Remove dead and damaged fronds. Rake leaves away from the crowns, particularly if slugs and snails are a problem. Keep alert about trimming fast-growing plants that shade the slower growing ferns. Promptly replace soil that has been washed away by rain or watering. Apply mulches if desired (see Chapter 5). Some beds may need to be reworked every few years. Slower growth and packed soil indicate that replanting is needed.

Planting in Pots

SELECTING THE POT

A well-selected pot will provide the best growing conditions possible and display the fern to its best advantage. Some growers routinely repot in early spring to provide fresh soil and larger pots. If ferns are growing well and not root-bound, they do not need to be repotted. A fern collection containing pots of many shapes and sizes and variable soil mixes will need more attention during watering.

Pot size. In general, the diameter of the pot should be about one-third the height of the fern as measured from the soil level. Repotting will generally require the next size up. For best appearance and growth, avoid planting ferns in pots that are too big. Many ferns, especially the maidenhairs (*Adiantum*), grow poorly when over-potted because the soil holds too much moisture in proportion to the active roots. The roots cannot use up enough of the surrounding moisture to keep the soil well aerated.

Clay versus plastic pots. If proper adjustments are made, ferns do equally well in plastic or clay pots. Remember that plastic or glazed pots retain more moisture than porous clay pots or wooden tubs. Thus, water the plastic or glazed pots less or use a coarser, quicker-draining soil mix than you would with clay pots.

If the soil in a plastic pot has dried and pulled away from the sides, wet the soil thoroughly so that it expands and the water will not trickle between the soil and the pot without penetrating to the roots. Unlike clay pots, plastic ones are not as likely to support algae or become heavily encrusted with salt. Plastic pots also have the advantage of weighing less, and holes for extra drainage are easily made with a hot ice pick or awl.

Pots without drainage holes. Beginners should use pots with drainage holes and avoid those without. If pots without holes must be used, however, there are two ways to provide drainage. The first is to place one to two inches of coarse material at the bottom of the pot before planting. Water the plant with distilled water just enough to moisten (not wet) the soil—do not overwater. The second method is to find a clay or plastic pot that has drainage holes and will fit inside the undrained pot. Plant the fern in the pot with the drainage hole and place it within the undrained one. The fern can be removed as needed for watering, permitted to drain, and then slipped back into the pot lacking the hole. Some gravel or drainage material may be placed at the bottom of the hole-less pot to prevent the fern from standing in water that may have accumulated at the bottom.

Pot shape. Most ferns do well in standard pot shapes, particularly the stout pots known in the trade as fern or bulb pots. If drainage, aeration, and room for soil are adequate, the shape of the pot should not affect the growth of the plant. Also consider the aesthetic aspects of the pot. It should highlight the plant, not detract from it. Bright colors and bold designs draw attention to the pot, not the plant.

When purchasing pots, look inside them to see that the drainage hole is large enough and is either flush with the bottom or depressed to allow the water to drain freely. Pots with flat, broad bottoms tend to drain slowly. Add extra gravel or other drainage material if more or larger holes cannot be made. Some novelty containers have such a small capacity that frequent watering may be necessary to keep the plant from wilting, and roots may fill the space too soon.

PLANTING IN THE POT

Providing drainage. Small pots 6.5 cm (2.5 in.) wide do not need anything to cover the drainage hole. Larger pots 10 to 20 cm (4–8 in.) wide, however, need at least a piece of broken clay pot, gravel, or coarse moss over the drainage hole. This lets the water drain and keeps the soil in the pot. Deep pots and those over 25 cm (10 in.) wide need a layer of drainage material at the bottom. Pot shards, gravel, or perlite can be used. The amount of drainage material will depend on the pot size, frequency of watering, and soil mix. Hanging pots that drain poorly in spite of sufficient drainage material can be induced to drain by inserting a cotton wick through the drainage hole. Where slugs are a problem, a fine screen or plastic mesh placed over the drainage hole before planting prevents slugs from entering the pot.

Cleanliness. Pots should be clean. Those previously used should be scrubbed thoroughly before reusing.

Basic planting procedures. After providing proper drainage, follow the "Basic Planting Procedures" discussed under "Planting in Beds" earlier in this chapter.

SPECIAL CARE

Potted plants need to be watched for drying or excessive water.

Poor drainage. Never let a pot stand in water unless it contains a fern that grows naturally in swamps or aquatic habitats. If the saucer below a pot accumulates water long after watering, it should be emptied. Pots can be raised on pebbles above the water level to avoid becoming waterlogged. If your plant wilts without standing in water, it probably needs repotting.

Poor drainage in small- to medium-sized pots can be detected by tapping the soil ball out of the pot a day or two after watering. Examine the soil to see whether it is waterlogged. Replace the soil ball, and examine it again the next day. If the soil is still soggy and the plant is not growing well, water it less frequently or improve the drainage. Poor drainage can also be detected by the presence of soft decaying roots and a strong odor of decaying vegetation (see "Watering," in Chapter 4). In flower beds or large containers it may be necessary to check the drainage by digging a narrow hole into the soil to determine whether it is waterlogged.

Root-bound ferns. A fern that is too big for its pot and becomes root-bound (filling the pot with roots) will grow slowly, produce small fronds, and have leaves that rapidly turn yellow. Such plants need frequent watering. If the rhizome branches or clumps, the center may be inactive or dead while the younger parts may be growing over each other at the periphery of the pot. Such a plant can be kept growing for a time with careful watering and fertilizing, but its vigor will gradually decline.

Root-bound ferns should be replanted or divided and replanted. If you want to increase the size of the plant, cut off its dead parts and replant it into a next larger size pot. If you want to keep the fern in the same size pot, it can be divided if it has many growing tips, and thin it to size by removing the smaller and weaker rhizome branches and other dead parts. Keep several large rhizomes with their growing tips intact, and replant in the same size pot. Root-bound tree ferns and ferns with unbranched rhizomes cannot be divided and usually must be transplanted into larger pots. If there are many old and inactive roots, they can be trimmed so that the root ball can be replanted in the same pot.

Salt crust on pots. A whitish salt crust on pots is unsightly and injurious to ferns. Unfortunately, it is hard to dissolve. If possible, change the pot or soak and wash it. For soaking, add Physan (Consan) to the water because it facilitates scrubbing. For badly encrusted pots, chip or scrape off as much of the crust as possible, then soak the pot and flush it with water. Vinegar dissolves some of the salt crust, but avoid getting vinegar on the soil or plant. If the pot is so heavily encrusted that it cannot be cleaned, then it should be discarded. Remember that salt build-up on pots can be reduced by watering thoroughly (rather than sprinkling), or by using rainwater, or by using plastic pots or cans instead of clay pots (see Chapter 4).

Planting in Baskets

Ferns that grow on trees are called epiphytes. They are not parasites but merely use the tree for support. Because soil is absent from tree trunks and branches, epiphytic ferns secure nutrients and moisture by sending their roots into the bark or the accumulated debris of leaves, mosses, and lichens. Epiphytic ferns are adapted to rapid drainage and drier air than terrestrial ferns. Most ferns used in hanging containers are epiphytes, although some terrestrial ferns also grow well in baskets. Ferns with drooping or cascading fronds look particularly attractive in hanging baskets.

Selecting the Basket

To simulate the native habitat of epiphytic ferns, plant them in open baskets that provide good drainage and have openings where creeping rhizomes can take root. Terrestrial ferns may be planted in open-structured baskets but do better in more tightly woven ones that drain more slowly. Baskets may be made of wire, wood, tree-fern trunks, ceramic, or plastic. Although clay or plastic pots can be used, they have to be planted with a looser soil mix or watered less frequently. Also, ferns with creeping rhizomes might grow into the pot and become trapped, or the rhizomes may grow over the edge of the pot where they are in danger of drying because there is no moist surface in which they can root.

Wire baskets. Commercially made wire baskets are inexpensive and readily available. There are, however, drawbacks to their use. Their open structure requires a lot of lining material, and the wire rusts away in a relatively short time, though commercial anti-rust compounds can be used to protect galvanized wire. Epiphytes with long-creeping rhizomes, especially those that tend to grow down the sides of a container, do best in wire baskets that provide numerous places for the rhizomes to root. Never use copper wire for baskets because it is toxic to plants.

Wood baskets. Wood baskets come in many designs and are generally less open and therefore require less lining material. Redwood baskets are favored because they resist rot. Epiphytes that prefer moister conditions and have short-creeping or clumped rhizomes grow best in wood baskets.

Tree-fern fiber baskets. Baskets made from tree-fern fibers are good for epiphytes because they drain well yet retain sufficient moisture. They do not need lining material. Baskets made from Central American tree ferns are more durable than those from the Hawaiian Islands. Because of environmental concerns, the importing of tree fern products is restricted or prohibited by law.

Ceramic and plastic baskets. Ceramic baskets come in a variety of styles. The open-structured ones provide excellent drainage and are well suited for ferns with long-creeping rhizomes. Keep in mind that cascading fronds will obscure the design of a basket. Plastic baskets are inexpensive and usually have large enough meshes to allow thick rhizomes to emerge. Plastic baskets need less moss than wire baskets to line their inner surfaces, and their meshes are just small enough that the moss does not fall out easily.

Planting the Basket

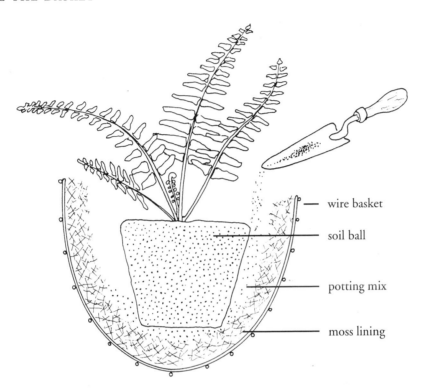

Figure 7.6. Planting basket ferns.

1. Line the basket with about 5 cm (2 in.) of moist, coarse or uncut moss (green moss or uncut sphagnum moss), coarsely shredded tree-fern fiber (hapu), or coconut fiber. Shredded redwood bark also works but is not commonly sold.
2. Add the potting mix to the basket and place the soil ball about 5 to 8 cm (2–3 in.) below the rim of the basket (Figure 7.6).
    If the fern is an epiphyte, plant it in the cavity with uncut or shredded sphagnum moss or a very friable potting mix high in organic matter, such as coarse peat, or composted bark. For terrestrial species, use ordinary potting mix in the cavity (see "Basic Planting Procedures," earlier in the chapter).
3. Press the soil firmly in place around the soil ball.
4. Cover the potting mix and the exposed part of the soil ball with about 2.5 cm (1 in.) of lining material. This will prevent subsequent watering from dislodging the loose soil mix. Extra pieces of rhizomes may be poked through the sides of the basket into the moss. Rhizomes that will not stay in place can be anchored with bent wires.
5. Water the newly planted basket with a gentle but thorough spray or soak it for a few minutes in a tub. Check for large leaks, which should be plugged up with additional moss.

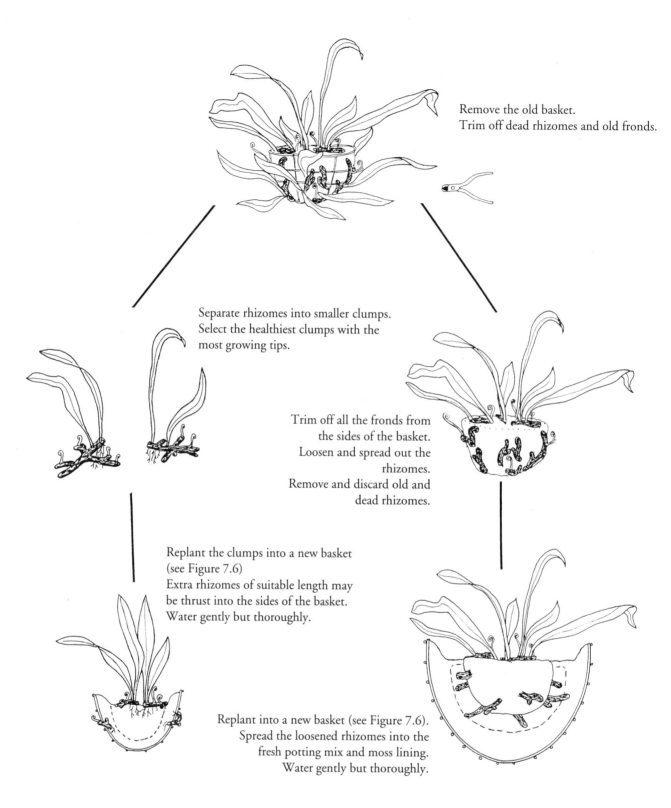

Remove the old basket.
Trim off dead rhizomes and old fronds.

Separate rhizomes into smaller clumps.
Select the healthiest clumps with the
most growing tips.

Trim off all the fronds from
the sides of the basket.
Loosen and spread out the
rhizomes.
Remove and discard old and
dead rhizomes.

Replant the clumps into a new basket
(see Figure 7.6)
Extra rhizomes of suitable length may
be thrust into the sides of the basket.
Water gently but thoroughly.

Replant into a new basket (see Figure 7.6).
Spread the loosened rhizomes into the
fresh potting mix and moss lining.
Water gently but thoroughly.

Figure 7.7. Replanting overgrown basket ferns.

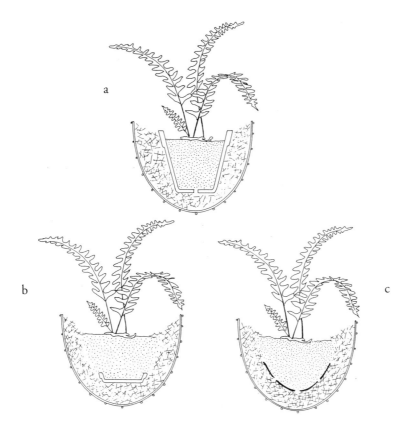

Figure 7.8. Keeping basket ferns moist: a. plant a potted fern in a basket lined with moss; b. place a shallow clay saucer over the moss lining before planting; c. place a piece of plastic sheet, with drainage holes punched into the plastic, over the moss lining before planting.

REPLANTING BASKET FERNS

It is time to replant a basket fern when the basket rusts or rots away or when the rhizomes begin to grow over one another and become weak and thin (Figure 7.7). If the fern is growing out of the top of the basket only (not out of the sides or bottom), then it can be merely freed from the basket, cleaned of dead tissue and old soil, and planted into a new basket as described above.

If the fern is growing out of the top, sides, and bottom of the basket, replanting is a bit more involved, but it can be accomplished in several ways. One method is to cut away the basket and remove the rhizomes in big pieces. The biggest and healthiest pieces can be replanted in a new basket as previously described. Alternatively, you can remove the fronds from the sides and bottom of the basket, lift out the plant, and drop it into a new basket lined with fresh moss. Any intervening spaces should be filled with loose planting mix or moss. In time, new rhizomes will grow through the moss layer. Another way to revitalize an old basket fern covered with rhizomes is to cut out the center of the basket from the top, without disturbing the growth at the sides and bottom. Fill the hole with fresh potting mix and then cover with uncut sphagnum or green moss. If the outer part of the wire basket has rusted away, mend it with wire or fashion a wire sling to support the basket. (Remember: do not use copper wire.)

Some growers prefer to build a new basket around the old one. This requires suitable wire, much patience, and care to minimize the damage to fronds and rhizomes on the sides and bottom of the basket. Cut galvanized wire of suitable strength to form the rings of the new basket. Join each of the rings around the old basket. To hold the rings in place, tie them with cross-wires or solder on cross-wires. Moss is then stuffed into the space between the old and new baskets.

SPECIAL CARE

If properly planted, a basket fern will last a few years. If it is an epiphyte, the fern must have good drainage. Terrestrial ferns planted in baskets have a tendency to dry too quickly, and their fronds are susceptible to dryness, particularly if hung indoors. These plants should be substituted with more adaptable plants or rotated with fresh ones. If you keep them in pots, they can be lifted out of the moss-lined baskets and easily replaced (Figure 7.8). In arid climates, hanging baskets tend to dry quickly and can be difficult to wet again without soaking. To slow the drying, place a small sheet of plastic over the moss lining at the time of planting. A shallow clay saucer can also be used, but holes for better drainage are punched more easily into the plastic. A flowerpot may be sunk at the top of the basket, to one side of the fern, to act as a catch basin for water. The rim of the basket can be built up to act as a catch basin as well. Keep alert for weak or rusting wires and replace them immediately. As moss or lining material decays or falls away, replace it by stuffing fresh lining material into the cavities.

8 Propagation

Ferns can be propagated two basic ways: from pieces of the parent plant or from spores. The first involves vegetative reproduction and gives rise to offspring genetically identical to the parent. The second method involves sexual reproduction and gives rise to offspring genetically different from the parent and among themselves. Before learning to propagate ferns by spores, you need to understand the fern life cycle.

Typical Life Cycle

Fern spores grow into new ferns indirectly (Figure 8.1). If a spore lands on a moist place with sufficient light, it germinates. Several days or weeks later, it sends out a slender cell (a rhizoid) that anchors the spore in place. It then produces a green cell that divides repeatedly in one direction to form a thread of cells. Eventually the cells at the tip of the thread divide laterally to widen the structure, and in about three months the thread grows into a flat, heart-shaped piece of tissue about 5 mm (0.2 in.) wide. This small plant is called the gametophyte or prothallus (plural, prothalli). On the underside of this tiny plant are male sex organs (antheridia) containing sperm and the female sex organs (archegonia) each containing an egg. Mixed among these are numerous rhizoids that secure the gametophyte to its substrate. When enough water is present in the environment, the antheridia burst and release the sperm. The sperm swim to an egg and fertilizes it. The egg can be on the same or a different prothallus. A film of water must be present in the environment to allow the sperm to swim to the egg, which explains why ferns are most abundant in wet habitats.

The union of a sperm and egg is known as fertilization. It marks the start of the sporophyte—the familiar fern that eventually bears the spores. The fertilized egg (zygote) divides and forms an embryo or young sporophyte that develops roots, stems, and leaves. As the roots grow and anchor the sporophyte in the soil, the prothallus withers, leaving the sporophyte on its own. If fertilization does not occur, the prothallus continues to live, sometimes for many years.

The first series of leaves produced by the young sporophyte do not resemble those of the adult plant. The successive leaves that are produced gradually assume the typical adult leaf form (Figure 8.2). About five months to a year after the spores have germinated, a small but well-formed fern is developed. Some ferns grow faster and can produce spore-bearing fronds in six or seven months. The fastest growing is the water fern (*Ceratopteris*), which can grow from spore to mature spore-bearing fronds in only one month. Most ferns, however, take two years or more to complete their life cycle. Normally once the sporophyte is established, the spore-bearing fronds are produced year after year.

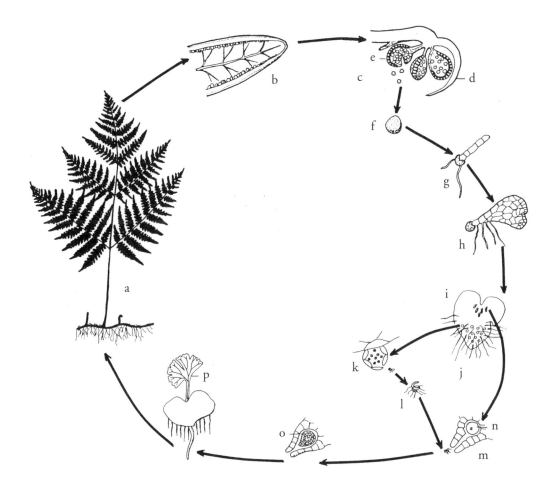

Figure 8.1. Fern life cycle: a. familiar fern plant or sporophyte; b. pinna bearing sori; c. sorus; d. indusium; e. sporangia; f. spore; g. spore germinating; h. young prothallus or gametophyte; i. underside of mature prothallus or gametophyte; j. rhizoids; k. antheridium; l. sperm; m. archegonium; n. egg; o. embryo; p. young sporophyte.

Variations of the Life Cycle

Ferns reproduce by other means as well. They can multiply directly from parts of the sporophyte such as the root, rhizome, or frond. Taking branches from the rhizome is a common way to propagate ferns. On some ferns, clumps of tissue known as buds or bulblets form and grow into new plants. Depending on the species, these buds develop on the roots, blades, veins, or rachises (Figure 8.3). Less commonly, pieces of the stipe base may be induced to form buds, such as in *Cystopteris, Dryopteris carthusiana, Dryopteris filix-mas, Matteuccia struthiopteris, Phyllitis scolopendrium, Pteridium aquilinum.* The stipules at the stipe bases of marattiaceous ferns (*Angiopteris* and *Marattia*) also produce buds if properly planted. Fronds from young plants of some ferns can also be induced to form buds. In rare cases, prothalli grow directly from fronds of young sporophytes (*Osmunda regalis* var. *regalis* 'Cristata', *Polystichum setiferum,* and others). This is known as apospory, which means "without spores" (Figure 8.4).

Some ferns (especially those of dry habitats) produce spores but reproduce asexually by proliferating a new plant directly from the prothallus instead of through the union of egg and sperm (Figure 8.5). This process, called apogamy (without sex cells), produces ferns faster than the sexual method. Apogamous ferns, such as many cheilanthoids, can produce sporophytes in six weeks after sowing (under 18 hours of

Figure 8.2. Age variation in fronds, showing fronds produced from a progressively (left to right) older plant of *Doryopteris nobilis*.

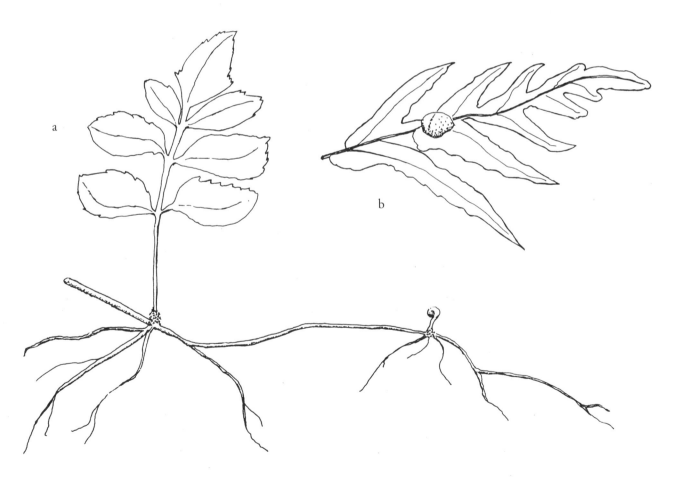

Figure 8.3. Proliferous buds: a. root bud and a young plant established from *Asplenium auritum* roots; b. leaf bud on the underside of a frond tip of *Woodwardia radicans*.

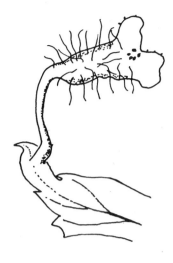

Figure 8.4. Apospory: prothallus developing from the tip of a pinnule in *Polystichum setiferum*.

artificial light). *Pteris cretica* produced sporophytes in two and a half months after sowing without artificial light. In a sowing of spores, the sporophytes of apogamous prothalli tend to appear at the same time, whereas the sporophytes of sexual prothalli appear at different times. Ferns that develop apogamously also tend to produce leaves before the roots, whereas ferns going through the sexual life cycle tend to produce roots before the leaves. The leaves appear just below the notch of the prothallus. Ferns that reproduce entirely by apogamy (those in which no sexual cycle is known) include such familiar cultivated species as *Cyrtomium falcatum*, *C. fortunei*, *Dryopteris cycadina*, and *Pteris cretica*. Some ferns reproduce by apogamous and sexual means.

A single prothallus can produce more prothalli. New ones may form along the margins of the old ones (Figure 8.6a). If conditions are favorable and if fertilization does not occur, growth continues for years. If

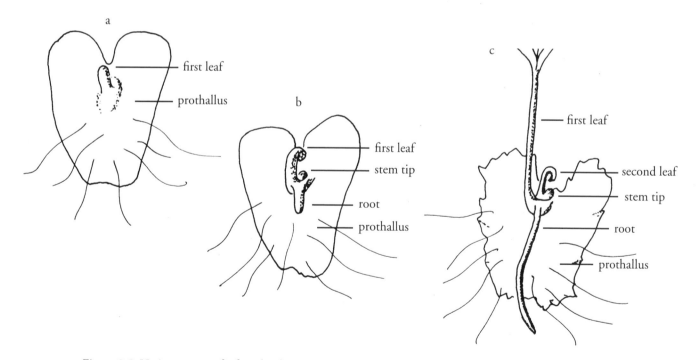

Figure 8.5. Various stages of a fern developing apogamously: a. the first leaf emerging from the prothallus; b. stem tip and root formation; c. the first leaf and roots expanding, as the second leaf emerges. The new fern is formed directly from the surface of the prothallus, not from within an archegonium as in sexually reproducing ferns.

fertilization does occur, the prothallus dies as the sporophyte develops. In filmy ferns, shoestring ferns, grammitids, and some polypodiums, new prothalli are produced from spindle-shaped or rod-shaped structures (gemmae) borne on short stalks along the margin of the prothalli (Figure 8.6b).

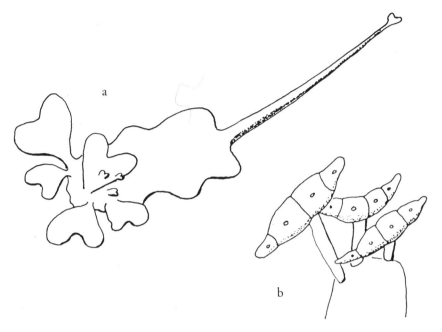

Figure 8.6. Prothallus proliferation: a. an old prothallus forming eight new prothalli and one on the tip of a tapered process, as shown on *Platycerium quadridichotomum*; b. gemmae borne on stalks growing from the edge of the prothallus in *Trichomanes,* each gemma grows into a new prothallus.

Vegetative Propagation

Plant parts that reproduce new plants are the rhizome, root, and frond. The branching rhizome is requently used in vegetative propagation. Ferns without branching rhizomes or buds generally cannot be vegetatively propagated and must be grown from spore (this is true for most tree ferns). Success in vegetative propagation is greatest when moist soil and sufficient humidity are maintained with as little watering as possible.

DIVISIONS

To divide a rhizome, look for the growing tips where new fronds arise. Before making the division, you can stimulate new side buds to form on a thick rhizome by partly cutting through it and waiting for the side buds to develop. Before you remove a tip or a clump of tips for dividing, be certain that enough growing tips are left on the parent plant to keep it alive. Look for a joint or naturally weak spot to make the cut from the parent plant (Figure 8.7a). The larger the rhizome or clump taken, the better the chances of a successful division. Use a clean, sharp knife to make the cut. With a trowel, dig up the division. Avoid injuring the growing tips, and keep as much of the soil around the roots of the division as possible. Cut off old or broken fronds and remove parts of the larger fronds to reduce water loss, particularly if the air is dry. Cut the bladeless and withered stipes as close to the rhizome as possible and remove any old or broken roots.

Before planting the division, dust its cut ends with a fungicide such as Captan. Select a rooting medium that is well-drained, such as a mixture of one part peat moss and one part perlite. Epiphytes often root well

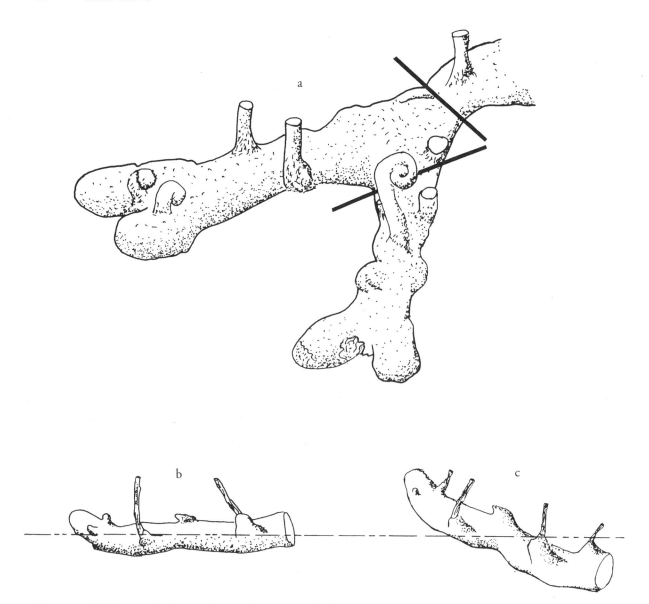

Figure 8.7. Dividing and planting rhizome divisions: a. dividing the rhizome (roots not shown) (*Polypodium*); b. planting the rhizome at half its thickness (*Davallia*); c. planting the rhizome diagonally (*Davallia*).

in moist uncut sphagnum moss. Avoid using soil, manure, compost, or other substances that harbor a lot of bacteria and fungi. Provide the box, flat, or pot with good drainage.

Replant the division at its former soil level. If its roots were previously exposed, set the division slightly deeper so that the roots are covered. Firm the medium in place and water well. Keep the plant lightly shaded for a few days.

Pieces of creeping rhizomes without roots should be secured to the rooting medium to keep them from drying out. Plant these at half their thickness into the medium (Figure 8.7b); bent wire can be used to hold them in place. If the rhizome pieces are a few inches long, thrust their cut ends diagonally into the soil to about one-third their length, leaving the growing tip exposed (Figure 8.7c).

After planting, the divisions still need to be cared for. Keep them in a humid, shaded, warm place until rooted enough to be transplanted. Guard against fungus gnats and other pests that feed on exposed tissue or new roots. Above all, avoid overwatering that might foster mold or decay. If this develops, increase ventilation, stop overhead watering, and apply a fungicide drench or Physan. Apply inorganic fertilizer two to three weeks after dividing.

Plants can be easily propagated by air-layering if they have rhizomes that are long and tend to grow away from basket or soil. Wrap damp uncut sphagnum moss around the rhizome of the mother plant. Tie the moss into place with string or strips of plastic. The moss may also be wrapped with a small sheet of plastic before tying. When roots have developed in the moss, the rhizome can be separated from the mother plant and planted.

BUDS

Some ferns produce new plantlets from buds on their fronds or, more rarely, roots. Bud-producing fronds can be anchored to the soil while still attached to the mother plant, or they may be detached and planted (Figure 8.8). The benefit of leaving the bud on the mother plant is that it will have an adequate supply of water and food while taking root. The bud can be anchored to the soil with a bit of soil or clean sand. If detached from the mother plant, bud-bearing fronds may be planted whole or in pieces. These are anchored to the soil surface with a planting mix or clean sand, watered, and then covered to provide adequate humidity. Once the buds have rooted, cut the mother frond to separate the plantlets. Some species root more readily if the bud is left attached to the mother plant (this is particularly true for *Adiantum caudatum*).

A detached bud should be planted at half its thickness in a rooting medium. Water gently but thoroughly and then cover with a piece of glass or plastic. Keep the air humid, but avoid excess humidity and overwatering.

Detached buds may also be grown conveniently in clear plastic shoeboxes or refrigerator boxes, preferably with holes for drainage. Line the bottom of the box with an inch of perlite. Place the planting medium (usually half sand and half peat) over the perlite, then plant the buds. The lid might need to be opened to control excessively high humidity.

Plants that can be propagated from detached buds include *Asplenium bulbiferum*, *A. daucifolium*, *Polystichum setiferum* Divisilobum Group, *Tectaria gemmifera*, *Woodwardia orientalis*, and *W. radicans*. For these species, apply a weak solution of inorganic fertilizer every two to three weeks, and gradually remove the covering over the planting as the buds grow. Transplant the larger individuals to avoid overcrowding. If mold develops, increase the air circulation and use a fungicide drench.

Root buds develop on ferns such as *Ophioglossum*, some *Platycerium*, *Diplazium esculentum*, and *Asplenium auritum*. They are usually unnoticed until the new plantlets emerge from the soil. When these plants are several inches tall they can be separated from the mother plant and transplanted.

PROPAGATION FROM THE STIPE

The leaf stalk or stipe can be used to propagate the hart's-tongue fern (*Phyllitis scolopendrium*), lemon-scented fern (*Thelypteris limbosperma*), lady fern (*Athyrium filix-femina*), and soft shield fern (*Polystichum setiferum*). Probably many other ferns can be propagated by this method, but they have yet to be tried.

The stipes of the hart's-tongue can be induced to form buds by sowing small green, plump, healthy pieces over a sterilized planting mix and covered to raise the humidity. Another method is to select older leaves with stipes that are still plump and green and snap them off near the rhizome. Wash the frond and cut the stipe into 2.5 cm (1 in.) lengths. (The base of the frond with stipe attached may also be used.) The pieces are planted upside down with the stipe about 3–6 mm (0.1–0.2 in.) above the soil. To prevent drying, cover the container with plastic, and mist as necessary. The appearance of small green blisters on the stipe indicates bud formation. When the buds develop into plants about 1 cm (0.5 in.) tall, they can be carefully removed and treated as young ferns. The development of a bud into a plantlet takes about three

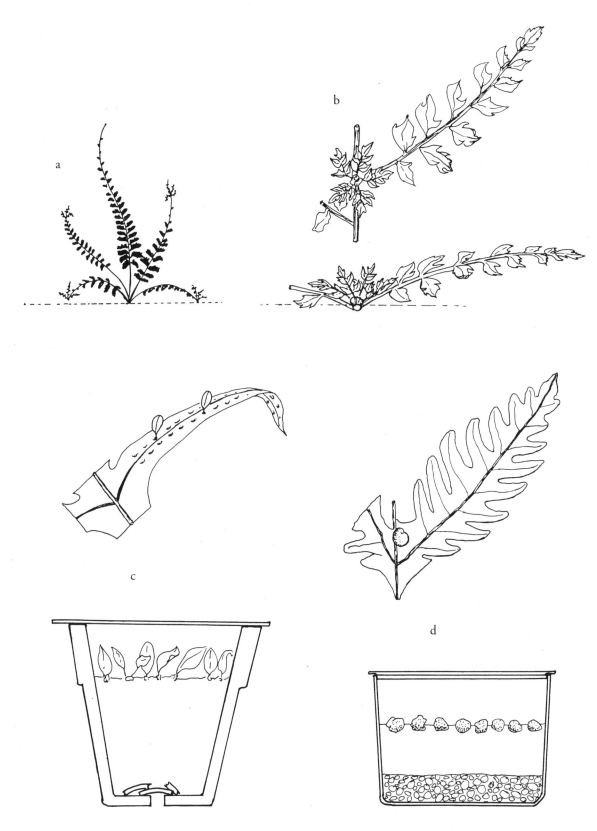

Figure 8.8. Planting buds: a. layering or rooting a bud still attached to the mother plant (*Adiantum caudatum*); b. rooting a bud attached to a section of a frond, top and side view (*Polystichum setiferum*, a proliferous variant); c. rooting detached buds in a pot (*Woodwardia orientalis*); d. rooting detached buds in a plastic container (*Tectaria gemmifera*).

months. For the lady fern, a portion of the rhizome tissue should be left on the stipe. To prevent mold or rot, treat the stipe pieces with Physan 20 or a similar fungicide. For more details see Dyce (1985) and Rickard (1986).

PROPAGATION FROM THE STIPULE

Stipules are the somewhat fleshy, flap-like outgrowths that clasp each side of the stipe base in *Angiopteris* and *Marattia*. A stipule may be cut and planted, usually upright, one-half to two-thirds its length in perlite or other clean, well-drained medium. Young plants will develop from the edges in a few months. Once its roots develop, the young plant may be separated from the stipule and planted. If the stipule is still firm, it can be induced to form additional plantlets. Maintaining humidity and controlling mold is the same as that explained under "Propagation from the Stipe."

TISSUE CULTURE

Tissue culture is the process of growing entire plants from bits of tissue by planting them in a growth medium of nutrients and hormones. Aseptic conditions must be maintained throughout the procedure, which involves transferring the tissue from one formulation to another at certain stages. Most Boston ferns and many other species are commercially propagated by tissue culture. The advantage of growing ferns by tissue culture is that large numbers of genetically uniform, disease-free plants can be produced in a small area. Ferns for which there is limited vegetative propagating material, or those that do not produce viable spores, are especially suitable for tissue culture.

Some ferns propagated by tissue culture are more attractive than those grown from spores. They tend to be fuller and more compact due to greater branching of the rhizome. Shorter production time is not always achieved through tissue culture—it depends on the species and growing conditions. It may take as long to grow maidenhair (*Adiantum*) from tissue culture as it does from spores; however, staghorn ferns (*Platycerium*) usually take less time. Ferns that have been divided and replanted in tissue cultures for three or more generations tend to produce many mutations, most of which are misshapen and unattractive. The more troublesome problems in tissue culture include obtaining uncontaminated tissue (explants) and getting young plants acclimated to greenhouse conditions.

Tissue culture involves three basic stages. In the first or establishment phase, the explants are disinfected and planted in a growth-inducing medium. Fern explants are usually taken from leaves or young stems (or stolons in Boston ferns). In the second stage, called the multiplication phase, the explants are planted on a medium that induces shoot proliferations. Growth at this stage can be subcultured to increase the number of plantlets. In the final stage, or pre-transplant stage, the clumps of shoots are divided and transferred to a medium that stimulates further development, particularly of the roots. Growth at this stage can also be subcultured to increase the number of plantlets. After the plantlets have developed roots, stems, and leaves, they are transplanted into a soil mix and placed in a greenhouse. The tubes or bottles containing the various stages of growth are usually kept at 27°C (81°F) and given 16 hours of artificial light at 300 foot-candles, although some growers use lower temperatures (to 16°C or 60°F) and lower light (100 foot-candles).

The main ingredients in the various culture media are water, inorganic nutrients, sugar, vitamins, and plant hormones called auxins (which stimulate root growth) and cytokinins (which stimulate shoot growth). Ferns grow best on a solid rather than liquid medium, which is why agar or agar substitutes are also added. The recipes for growth media vary from stage to stage and from one species to another. Most ferns grow well on only two formulations, with the same formulation used for the first and second stages. Murashige's formulations for *in vitro* propagation are satisfactory for a wide variety of plants and can be bought premixed. For the beginner at tissue culture, it is easiest to buy a tissue-culture kit from a scientific or biological supply house. Occasionally, plant societies, colleges, and universities offer workshops or classes on tissue culture, and much literature is available for all levels of interest.

Spore Propagation

Although not difficult, growing ferns from spores takes time and patience, but the fascination and pleasure derived from this activity is a reward in itself. The space and equipment needed are minimal. Most ferns grown commercially from spore take about 6 to 10 months until they are large enough to be planted into 5-cm (2-in.) pots. Other ferns take longer, such as filmy ferns, which take a few years to develop sporelings. For raising fern allies from spores, see "Fern Allies" in Chapter 10. To grow gametophytes for experimental purposes, see Dyer (1979).

COLLECTING SPORES

To collect spores you need to find the sporangia (spore cases). These are usually grouped in clusters, called sori, on the underside of the frond. The sori are mostly 2 to 5 mm (about 0.1–0.2 in.) wide and may be round, oblong, or linear. Less frequently, the sporangia are scattered over the entire lower surface of the frond or borne on modified portions of the leaf.

When collecting spores, it is important to recognize whether the sporangia are ripe or have already shed their spores. Immature sporangia usually appear whitish green. As they mature, they turn light brown and finally medium or dark shiny brown, or in some species blackish (Figure 8.9). (In some ferns, such as *Polypodium*, the mature sporangia are yellowish due to the color of the spores within.) The sporangia appear dull brown and frayed after the spores are shed. Another clue to the ripeness of spores is the appearance of the indusium. Green or whitish indusia indicate unripe spores; light brown, yellow, or nearly black indusia indicate mature spores. Shed or shriveled indusia usually indicate that the spores have been shed. Ripeness of the sporangia may be more accurately determined with a 10× hand lens (or jeweler's loop). Plump sporangia without a cracked wall contain spores, whereas sporangia frayed or with cracks or slits have shed their spores. Shriveled sporangia will not produce viable spores. Pick fronds when most of the sporangia are still plump and shiny.

To gather spores for sowing, place the picked frond in an envelope or over a clean piece of smooth paper with the sporangia side down. Cover the frond to prevent the shed spores from blowing away or other spores from contaminating your collection. Usually the spores will be shed on the paper within minutes, but wait a day or two if you want to collect the maximum number of spores. They will resemble fine dust. Some fronds produce large quantities of spores whereas others do not. The spores are often brownish but may also be green, yellow, or black, depending on the species. Also shed are whole or fragmented sporangia, bits of hair, scales, or other tissue. Tree ferns of the *Cyathea* group tend to shed whole sporangia that later open to shed the spores. Examine the paper with a hand lens to be certain that spores are present. Store the spores in an envelope or folded paper packet. For reference, write the name of the species, the source, and the date on the outside of the packet.

Contamination by other fern spores can be a problem during collection. To reduce the risk of contamination, pick only clean fronds, or if these are not available, brush or rinse away dirt and debris. Collecting the spores on a cool or dim day reduces spore loss and contamination from other spores.

Another way to collect spores is to place leaflets bearing ripe sporangia in a plastic bag to keep them from drying in transit. Then follow the directions given later in this chapter under "Sterilization of spores within sporangia."

Figure 8.9. Determining when to collect spores (*Thelypteris puberula*): *left,* too young; *middle,* ripe; *right,* too old.

Spore envelopes. The best way to collect and store spores is in folded paper packets (Figure 8.10). These are easy to make and are leak-proof. The problem with using ordinary envelopes is that the spores tend to leak out, and if the leaks are covered with cellophane tape, many spores can be lost because they stick to the tape. Plastic bags seem like an obvious alternative, but they have the disadvantage of the spores sticking to the bag and being hard to remove. Fertile leaf material dries more quickly in paper packets, averting mold problems.

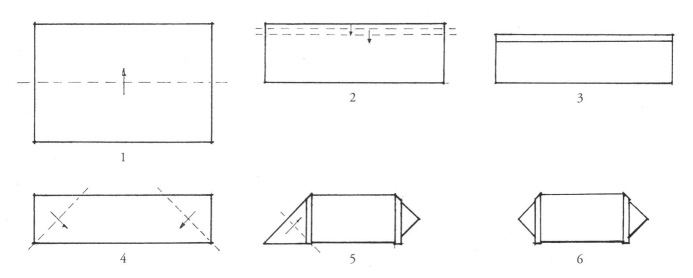

Figure 8.10. Making a spore envelope: 1. Fold thin paper in half lengthwise (along the dotted line). 2. Double fold the upper open edges. 3. The folded and sealed upper edge. 4. Turn the envelope over (keep folded edge on top) and fold diagonally along the dotted lines. 5. Tuck the folded right corner under the band as shown. 6. To seal the envelope, tuck the left corner under the band. Label with name, date, and source. Leaflets or spores are best enclosed at step 1 or 5.

CLEANING SPORES

Removal of nonspore material (sporangia, scales, hairs) reduces contamination by algae, bacteria, fungi, and mosses. The larger nonspore material can be picked out with forceps or brushed away with a fine brush. If pure or nearly pure spores are desired, separate the nonspore material by slightly tilting the paper upon which spores were collected and gently tapping it. The spores are left behind as the fluffier nonspore material tumbles ahead and can be brushed away. The spores can then be stored until use.

Small bottles with a very fine (about 0.05 mm) screened mesh in place of the top can be used to separate spore from nonspore material and to evenly sow the spores. The finest tea screen available, lens paper, and even cheesecloth have been used as satisfactory screening material. Check the material with a hand lens to be sure that the separation is adequate.

STERILIZING SPORES

Most hobbyists and commercial growers do not sterilize (disinfect) spores before sowing. Scientific work, however, requires it. Most methods use bleach diluted with water and a wetting agent such as Tween 20, Aerosol OT, Alconox, or a mild household detergent, which will prevent the spores from sticking together. The following methods of disinfecting spores are representative of the many kinds used. For more details, see Ford and Fay (1990).

Sterilization of spores freed from the sporangia. Clean the spores to remove the larger nonspore material. Place the spores in a 5 to 10% bleach solution and add a fraction of a drop of wetting agent (1 part Tween 20 to 2000 parts bleach solution). Soak the spores for one minute. Collect the spores on filter paper. Rinse two to four times with sterile water. Sow from the water solution or dry and store until needed. Some species are sensitive to bleach and may require a weaker solution and less soaking time. For such species, reduce the concentration of bleach solution to 2% and soak for about 5 to 10 seconds. Researchers report that soaking green spores in 2% bleach solution for two to four minutes gives satisfactory results.

Sterilization of spores within sporangia. Select leaflets or fronds with ripe but unopened sporangia. Soak in a 5 to 10% (rarely 20%) bleach solution to which a wetting agent has been added as above. Remove all air bubbles with a small brush, and keep the leaflets immersed 5 to 10 seconds. Do not rinse. Place in a clean envelope. (Envelopes can be disinfected by placing them in a box and baking in an oven at 160°C [320°F] for about two hours. *Never* heat the spores.) The envelopes containing the disinfected leaflets can be placed between layers of clean paper to absorb the moisture. With regular changing of the absorbing paper, the spores should be shed and ready for use or storage in about three days.

VIABILITY OF SPORES

The fresher the spores, the greater and faster the germination. Depending on the species, fern spores can remain viable from 2 days to 130 years. Storing nongreen spores under cool conditions, including refrigeration, prolongs their viability. Variation exists in the percent germination from spores taken at different times from the same plant and from different plants of the same species. Spores collected from vigorously growing plants usually have the highest germination rate. The spores of some species require dormancy before germination. The dormancy can range from two weeks to one year. For more information, see Rush (1984a, b).

Green spores, such as those in *Osmunda, Todea, Equisetum,* and *Grammitis,* generally have the shortest viability, averaging about two months (the shortest recorded is two days, and the longest about one year). Because of their short viability, green spores should be sown soon after collecting. For *Osmunda* (and probably other genera with green spores), viability can be prolonged by refrigeration at 4°C (40°F). *Osmunda* spores stored in a freezer at −20°C (−4°F) for 2 to 3 years retained their viability (Rush 1984b).

Nongreen spores remain viable longer than green ones, generally from 1 to 48 years, with the extremes being a few weeks (*Cyathea*) to 130 years (*Marsilea*). See Lloyd and Klekowski (1970) for a discussion of viability and germination times in green versus nongreen spores.

SOWING METHODS

There are many ways to grow ferns from spores, but only the most common methods are discussed here (Figure 8.11). Before sowing it is helpful to sterilize or treat the soil. This discourages algae, mosses, bacteria, fungi, and other pests that can crowd or attack the spores and prothalli (see "Sterilizing Soils" in Chapter 5). Because fern spores are easily airborne and may contaminate other sowings, avoid successive sowings of different species on the same day. Several methods have been developed to control the amount of spores sown, such as mixing the spores with inert, dry material, spraying them through an atomizer, or delivering aliquot amounts through a syringe (Basile 1973). For sowing small amounts, a cotton swab dipped in the spore and tapped over the container gives better control than merely tapping the spores out from an envelope. For more details, see Basile (1973).

Growing a few plants. The following methods are suitable for a hobbyist who wants to raise only a few plants. Milled sphagnum moss is good for beginners, but any of the soil mixes listed under the commercial

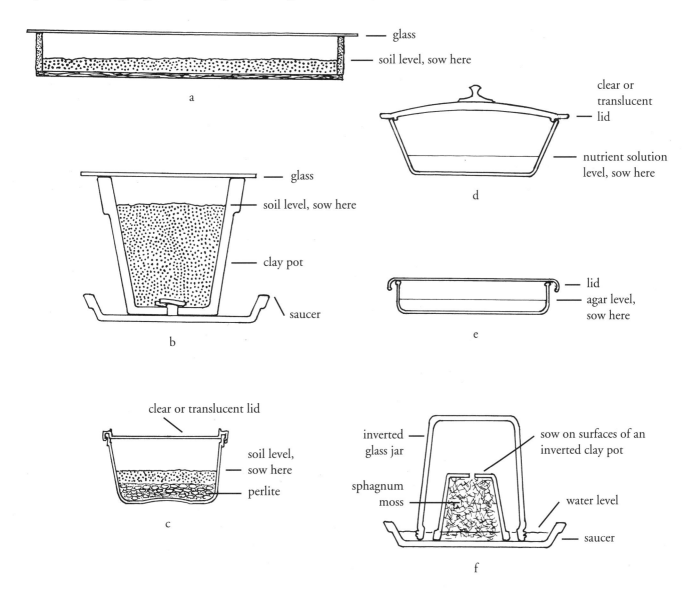

Figure 8.11. Common methods of planting spores: a. in a flat; b. in a pot; c. in a plastic container; d. on a nutrient solution; e. on an agar plate; f. on an inverted pot.

method can be used as a planting medium. For small sowings, adequate space is any small, clear container that is wide enough to allow fingers or forceps to easily remove the prothalli or sporelings and is deep enough to hold 5 cm (2 in.) of soil and provide 2.5 to 5 cm (1–2 in.) of overhead space. The container will need a cover, and transparent lids are best, but plastic wrap or glass can also be used. If the soil is disinfected by pouring boiling water through it, drain holes will be necessary in the container. Allow enough overhead space for growth; avoid filling pots too close to the top. If overhead space for the sporelings becomes inadequate, an inverted clear-plastic cup placed over the pot will provide more room and retain humidity. Containers without drain holes may be layered on the bottom with 1.5 to 2.5 cm (0.5–1 in.) of perlite (Sponge Rok) to drain excess water from the soil above. Because additional watering after sowing is infrequently needed, many growers use cups or containers without drain holes or omit the layer of perlite. The container should have about a 5 cm (2 in.) layer of planting medium.

If microwaveable planting containers are used, they can be disinfected along with the soil mix in a microwave oven. Before microwaving, generously moisten the soil, gently firm it in place, loosely cover with a lid or wax paper, and cook for about five minutes on high. Upon removal, the soil mix should be steamed through and moist. Remoisten with boiled water if necessary. Keep these disinfected containers covered until sowing time. With plastic containers that distort in heat, the soil will need to be disinfected previously in heat-resistant containers and then spooned into the plastic container when cool. The containers can be previously disinfected with a 10% solution of bleach or Physan 20 and rinsed with boiled water.

A simpler procedure, but one with greater risk of contamination, is to lightly pasteurize a soil mix in a clean, undrained plastic cup. To do this, add just enough boiling water to moisten the soil for planting (plastic cups generally do not distort with only this amount of boiling water). A novel use of the pressed-peat pots (Jiffy-pot pellets, with mesh removed if present) is to place a pellet in a small (180–240 ml or 6–8 oz.) plastic tumbler and moisten with about 120 ml (4 oz.) of boiling water. When the peat has expanded, loosen it, gently firm it down, cover the tumbler, and let cool. Sow the spores thinly to avoid spindly, tangled prothalli, and minimize crowding. A cotton swab dipped in the spores and gently tapped over the medium helps to control the amount of spores sown. Although dense sowings can be thinned, the thinning process tends to disrupt and damage growth. Therefore thin sowings are best. After sowing, the containers are covered with clear lids or glass or plastic wrap held in place with a rubber band.

Commercial method. The spore-planting media vary from grower to grower. Most growers use a mixture of one to two parts peat moss and one part fine sand. Some growers add loamy soil, fine perlite, or other additives to this mix. Commercial planting mixes formulated for growing seeds can also be used for spores. Finely milled sphagnum moss used alone provides good results but might not be suitable for all ferns. Whatever soil medium is used, it should be able to pass through a 3 mm (0.1 in.) mesh. Fine texture is important because it ensures good contact with the prothalli and facilitates transplanting. Some growers use a fine-textured mix on top of a coarser mix to promote drainage.

Glass or plastic containers may be used as previously discussed. New wood flats and larger clay pots with drainage holes are traditionally used because they can be sterilized or disinfected easily.

Commercial growers have devised several ways of sowing spores as evenly as possible over a broad surface. Salt shakers and spray bottles (atomizers) with spores suspended in water have been used. Depending on the species and the transplanting procedures, some growers sow spores densely so that the growth soon after germination is a solid green mat, which will need early separation. By sowing a small amount of spores into each plug (a depression in a special plastic growing tray; see "Growing in Plugs" later in this chapter), growers save labor in transplanting. After sowing, the containers are covered with clean plate glass. Plate glass is better than plastic wrap, which will sag when stretched over a wide container and cause condensation to collect and drip on one spot. The resulting wet spots promote the growth of fungi, bacteria, and algae.

Nutrient solution method. Many different types of nutrient solutions are used commercially and are of interest to amateurs. Some growers use distilled or tap water or dilute solutions of balanced inorganic fertilizers (at one-quarter strength), though the more common nutrient solutions are not diluted (Table 8.1). Other solutions include Beyerincks (Brown 1920) and Knudson C without the sugar and agar (Knudson 1946). The measures given in Table 8.1 are given in the metric and English systems to avoid the need for special measuring equipment. However, since fractions of ounces or tablespoons are difficult to measure, the formulation makes 95 liters (25 gal.) of solution—the surplus can be used as a liquid fertilizer. If smaller amounts are desired, the measurements given in grams make one liter or approximately one quart of solution. The ingredients are inexpensive and can be obtained from local chemical supply houses, firms selling fertilizers, and drugstores. Prepare the solution by adding the salts to the water in the order given. Impurities in the chemicals and from the water (tap water) will probably provide the trace elements needed. If you want to add trace elements, however, use the formulation in Table 8.1. If the solution is to be stored for a long time, add the iron or trace elements just before use.

These solutions will have a pH of about 6 if distilled water is used. A pH of 6 is optimum for germinating most fern spores. In general, the pH range for germinating spores is 5–7. A more acidic solution can be obtained by omitting calcium compounds. Some ferns of limestone habitats have spores that can germinate at pH 7–9.

The nutrient solution can be sterilized by placing it in a pressure cooker for 15 minutes at 1 kilogram per square centimeter (15 lbs. per sq. in.) or by boiling it for a few minutes. The solution is poured into previously sterilized dishes or plastic containers (which may be sterilized by boiling or washing with a 10% bleach solution and rinsed). The depth of the solution may vary, but 6 mm (0.2 in.) is enough for germination. Cover the solution and allow it to cool. Then sow the spores and replace the cover. To keep the spores floating on the solution, avoid moving the dish after sowing. Tilt the lid slightly to prevent condensation from dripping on the spores.

Nutrient agar solution. This method provides a solid nutrient medium for growing spores. It has no advantage over other methods, and ferns are reported to grow slower by this method. It is used mainly for scientific research or when the spore material is extremely valuable and sterile techniques are necessary to ensure survival. Agar, the solidifying substance, can be obtained from scientific supply companies. Less expensive substitutes are now available.

The medium is made by adding 14 g (approximately ½ oz.) of agar to 1 liter (approximately 1 quart) of any suitable nutrient solution. (Seven drops of a general-purpose, water-soluble fertilizer to one liter of water makes a convenient nutrient solution.) Dissolve the agar by heating it in the nutrient solution, stirring occasionally. Then pour the dissolved solution 6 to 9 mm (0.2–0.4 in.) deep into shallow dishes, cover loosely, and sterilize immediately in a pressure cooker for 15 minutes at 1 kilogram per square centimeter (15 lbs. per sq. in.) pressure. After the dishes have been removed from the pressure cooker and the agar has cooled and solidified, they are ready to be planted, preferably with disinfected spores. Before and after planting, keep the dishes covered to avoid airborne contamination and moisture loss. Ordinarily the agar will remain moist enough to support growth into the mature prothalli stage. Vaseline petroleum jelly can be used to seal the edges to prevent drying. If the agar should dry or crack, transfer the growth to a fresh medium as soon as possible. A nutrient solution originally used to grow orchid seeds and containing sugar (sucrose) has been reported as good for growing fern spores. It works best at pH 5 (Knudson 1946).

Inverted pot method. The inverted pot method is ideal for exhibiting the growth of prothalli and young ferns. It is inefficient for growing ferns commercially because scraping prothalli off the pot is tedious and awkward.

Fill a small, clean, porous clay flower pot with uncut sphagnum or peat moss, then invert it into a saucer or shallow dish. Sterilize the unit with steam or by pouring boiling water over it, or place the whole

Table 8.1. Nutrient Solutions

Salt	Formula	Grade of salt	Grams per 1 liter of water	Ounces per 25 gallons of water	Tablespoons per 25 gallons of water
BEYERINCK'S SOLUTION					
Ammonium nitrate	NH_4NO_3	Technical	0.5	2	4
Potassium phosphate	KH_2PO_4	Technical	0.2	¾	1½
Magnesium sulfate	$MgSO_4 \cdot 7H_2O$	Technical	0.2	¾	2
Calcium chloride	$CaCl_2$	Technical	0.1	½	1
Ferric chloride	$FeCl_3$	Technical	trace	trace	trace
KNUDSON'S C SOLUTION (after Knudson 1946)					
Calcium nitrate	$Ca(NO_3)_2 \cdot 4H_2O$	Fertilizer	1.0	4	8
Ammonium sulfate	$(NH_4)_2SO_4$	Fertilizer	0.5	2	4
Magnesium sulfate	$MgSO_4 \cdot 7H_2O$	Technical	0.25	1	2
Ferric sulfate	$FeSO_4 \cdot 7H_2O$	Technical	0.025	1/10	1/5
Manganese sulfate	$MnSO_4 \cdot 4H_2O$	Technical	0.0075	1/30	1/15
Potassium phosphate	KH_2PO_4	Technical	0.25	1	2
KNOP'S SOLUTION					
Potassium phosphate	KH_2PO_4	Technical	0.2	¾	1½
Potassium nitrate	KNO_3	Fertilizer	0.2	¾	1½
Calcium nitrate	$Ca(NO_3)_2 \cdot 4H_2O$	Fertilizer	0.8	3	7
Magnesium sulfate	$MgSO_4 \cdot 7H_2O$	Technical	0.2	¾	2
Ferric phosphate	$FePO_4$	Technical	trace	trace	trace
HOAGLAND'S SOLUTION #2 (after Hoagland and Aron 1950, except iron chelate replaces ferrous tartrate)					
Ammonium phosphate	$NH_4H_2PO_4$	Technical	0.12	½	2
Potassium nitrate	KNO_3	Fertilizer	0.62	2½	5
Calcium nitrate	$Ca(NO_3)_2 \cdot 4H_2O$	Fertilizer	0.62	2½	6
Magnesium sulfate	$MgSO_4 \cdot 7H_2O$	Technical	0.38	1½	4
Chelates of iron as Versene or Sequestrene		Commercial	trace or 2 ppm to the nutrient solution		

Trace elements (after Hoagland and Aron 1950). A stock solution is made by adding the following to 1 liter (1 qt.) of water. Use 1 ml (12 drops or 0.034 oz) of the stock solution to 1 liter (1 qt.) of any of the nutrient solutions given above. If tap water is used, the addition of trace elements is generally not necessary.

Salt	Formula	Amount
Boric acid	H_3BO_3	2.86 g
Manganese chloride	$MnCl_2 \cdot 4H_2O$	1.81 g
Zinc sulfate	$ZnSO_4 \cdot 7H_2O$	0.22 g
Copper sulfate	$CuSO_4 \cdot 5H_2O$	0.08 g
Molybdic acid	$H_2MoO_4 \cdot H_2O$	0.02 g

unit in boiling water. When drained and cooled, sow it with spores and cover with a larger glass or jar. Replace water in the saucer as needed. There is less likelihood of overwatering by this method, and if the spores are not too densely sown, nicely formed heart-shaped prothalli will develop, free from bits of planting medium. A dilute solution of fertilizer applied in the saucer will hasten growth. Young ferns may be loosened and lifted off the clay pot with forceps or a thin, flat blade and planted in potting mix.

Miscellaneous methods. Other media and methods are used to sow fern spores, such as plaster of Paris blocks, broken clay pots, moistened bricks, tree-fern-trunk fibers, soil, peat moss, and uncut sphagnum moss. Milled sphagnum is particularly good. The soil and container should be sterilized or treated with steam or boiling water as a precautionary measure.

After-Sowing Care

After sowing, the planting should be placed in the proper light and temperature. The first sign of growth is the appearance of a very thin green mat about 14 days after sowing. In the early stages of germination, the emerging green cells are too small to be seen without magnification. Germination usually starts in 4 to 14 days but may take as long as a year. Ferns grown for the trade usually form mature prothalli in several months. Others take more than a year to mature.

Light. Place the sown spores in filtered sunlight of low to medium intensity (150 to 500 foot-candles). If artificial (cool-white fluorescent) light is used, it may be left on continuously or for 8 to 16 hours per day as desired. Research indicates different cellular responses with blue, red, and far-red light, but these responses are unimportant to the general growing of spores. Several weeks in total darkness are required for spore germination in *Botrychium dissectum* and *Ophioglossum,* and they may need mycorrhizal fungi to develop further unless grown in a nutrient medium.

Temperature. The optimal temperature for spores to germinate and grow is 20 to 28°C (68–86°F). Most growers keep the temperature near 25°C (77°F) and lower it as the plants mature. Uniform temperatures reduce problems associated with water condensation.

Watering. Watering is unnecessary after sowing if the medium was thoroughly moistened and the planting covered. The edges of the containers may be sealed with Vaseline petroleum jelly to retain moisture. If water must be added, set the pots in a saucer of water. Flats and plastic boxes may be watered with a fine mist or spray. Distilled or cooled boiled water is best during these early stages. Tap water can be an unwanted source of algae.

Fertilizers. Two to three weeks after the green mat of germinated spores appears, weak solutions of fertilizer (about half the recommended strength) can be applied. Commercial growers differ on the concentration and timing of these applications. Concentrations vary from 100 to 200 ppm, given at every watering or every other watering. Although researchers have applied sugar (2.5% sucrose) under sterile conditions to hasten growth, this is not recommended for ordinary purposes because it encourages mold.

Transplanting. Where only a few plants are desired and the prothalli are healthy, transplanting may be delayed until the sporelings have developed about three leaves. They are then picked out and transplanted, usually to 6.5 cm (2.5 in.) pots containing a fine-textured potting mix.

In commercial operations, transplanting starts when the green mat of prothalli have formed, about two months after sowing. Some growers transplant at an early stage when the mat is thick enough to lift off. Small pieces of the mat 6 to 12 mm (0.2–0.5 in.) across are lifted off with forceps (or the tip of a spoon if a liquid medium is used). Waiting longer with a liquid medium can result in tangled growth and make it difficult to get the prothalli to drop off the spoon during transplanting.

The clumps of prothalli are spaced about 12 mm (0.5 in.) apart and firmed onto a moist, finely screened potting mix of half peat and sand, or whatever mix is desired. Be certain the clumps are in good contact with the planting medium, otherwise they will dry out. Keep a spray bottle of distilled or boiled cool water handy, and use it while transplanting. Although not always done, the planting mix should be sterilized or disinfected. Some growers treat the soil at 88°C (190°F) for three hours before use, and all subsequent watering is done with cooled boiled water (until the covers are removed from over the planting). Some growers use fungicide drenches on the transplants at this stage. After they are in place, the transplants should be watered with a fine spray, preferably of cooled boiled water. Cover the planting with glass or plastic.

The second transplant is done when the prothalli have enlarged to about 4 mm (0.2 in.) in diameter for most species. For commercial ferns this is usually about three to four months after sowing. Clumps of prothalli about 10 mm (0.4 in.) or more wide are firmed onto the soil mix and watered as on the first transplant. Some commercial growers start the second transplant when sporelings appear, at which point a clump of prothalli along with one or more sporelings is then transplanted, sometimes directly into cell packs or plug trays, which are plastic trays with small depressions in which the plants are grown and eventually marketed. Keeping the prothalli in small clumps seems to result in better growth than separating them too finely.

Growers who prefer to sell larger plants usually do a third transplant. This is done when the ferns are about 1.5 to 2.5 cm (0.5–1 in.) tall or have three well-developed leaves, which in commercial ferns is about five to seven months after sowing. Sporelings may be planted in fresh flats of soil or 6.5 cm (2.5 in.) pots, with the usual attention to firm them into place and protect them from drying.

Potted transplants are initially protected in frames under glass or plastic coverings. Once established, they must be hardened. Hardening is achieved by lifting the glass or plastic covering more and more each day to allow the foliage to adapt to drier air and higher light. Eventually a lath covering is put in place. The hardening process may take three to six weeks. Ferns hardened in 6.5 cm (2.5 in.) pots still need protection and should not be planted directly in the ground unless sheltered conditions can be provided.

During the third transplant, some growers separate the sporelings into uniform size classes before replanting them in flats or pots. If replanted into flats, the fourth transplant (about nine months after sowing) moves the sporelings into 6.5 cm (2.5 in.) pots, and they are hardened off and marketed in about a month or two.

Early transplants are almost always made as clumps of prothalli, with or without attached sporelings. No attempt is made to separate the clumps into individual prothalli because clumps produce more vigorous sporelings than isolated prothalli. This is probably due to greater opportunities for out-crossing with nearby prothalli. With apogamous ferns, clumps rather than individual prothalli are transplanted for ease of handling. Between and during transplants it is essential to maintain high humidity and soil moisture because the transplants are small and will dry quickly. Always use a fine spray of water. If sporelings are slow to appear, spray the prothalli with enough water to leave a thin film on them for a few hours. This can be repeated in a few days. Discoloration may indicate a lack of fertilizer or overwatering. Disease may develop in spite of all precautions (see "Special Care").

Growing in Plugs

Home and commercial growers sometimes cultivate ferns entirely in plugs. Plugs are plastic trays with depressions provided with drain holes. The depressions, or "plugs," come in different sizes and numbers per tray. Growing ferns in plugs instead of pots saves labor, planting media, and bench space. It also allows for holding plants in cooling chambers for a limited time until needed. Cooling chambers hold back growth to fit marketing schedules. Plug trays designed for the home propagator come with a lower tray to catch draining water and a clear plastic cover to maintain high humidity. The plug trays with small-diameter depressions (25 mm [1 in.] or less) are suited to growing young ferns and even spores.

The commercial planting mix for plugs differs from most soilless planting mixes by its finer texture and by containing a wetting agent. For the home gardener, a finer textured soilless mix suitable for planting seeds will do.

Because the soil capacity in the plug is small, problems can develop rapidly. Greater care must be taken with the amount and timing of watering. The even distribution and penetration of water are important. Avoid allowing water to remain on the foliage by watering at a time of day that allows the foliage to dry. Good air circulation is also important. Crowded wet plants and poor air circulation promote disease (especially *Botrytis* in cooler temperatures). Drying of the soil stresses plants and makes them more vulnerable to diseases as *Rhizoctonia* and *Pythium.*

Etiolation, or weak spindly growth resulting from low light, is another problem. It can be prevented by placing the trays under a strong light (but not so strong that it causes the foliage to turn yellow). Transplants that are already etiolated make poor material for plug (or small pot) plantings. They often remain leggy and do not achieve the sturdy growth required of commercial plants. Firmer tissue can also be promoted by adequate ventilation and judicious use of fertilizers. Some growers prefer to use fertilizers sparingly. They also use nitrate fertilizers, instead of ammonium ones, which they claim produce stockier plants.

Like other plants grown under protected conditions, those grown in plugs will need to be gradually hardened off. Care must be taken in deciding whether to increase or decrease exposure during the process. The ideal result among commercial growers is to have "toned plugs," or plants that are compact, sturdy, of good color, and hardened off enough to take the rigors of transport to the market.

SPECIAL CARE

Mold may develop on the soil, prothalli, and young sporophytes in spite of all precautions. If this happens, take the following steps immediately. Stop overhead watering. Water with cooled boiled water. Check that water is not dripping from condensation overhead. Remove the mold and at least 12 mm (0.5 in.) of the plant tissue beyond the infected area. Finally, drench the area with fungicide and repeat as directed on the product label (see "Fungi and Bacteria" in Chapter 11).

Water molds (*Pythium* and *Phytophthora*) usually cause the prothalli to turn dark and watery and subsequently collapse. Gray mold (*Botrytis*) appears as gray tufts on the prothalli and foliage. It flourishes under cool-moist conditions and can therefore be combated by increasing the temperature and decreasing the humidity. A cyanobacterium (*Oscillatoria*) also forms a blackish to grayish mold-like growth, and the threads form dense mats and inhibit growth (see "Algae, Mosses, and Liverworts" in Chapter 11). A pink, nonpathogenic fungus (*Pyronema*) that is very resistant to steam treatment may grow over the prothalli and crowd them out. *Rhizoctonia* appears as well-spaced threads. If persistent mold or alga infection occurs even after materials and equipment have been sterilized and the proper cultural conditions are employed, the sporing room may need to be washed down or drenched with a disinfectant such as formaldehyde, bleach, or quaternary ammonium compounds (Physan 20, Consan). In sporing rooms and growing rooms, it is important to reduce air movement from the outside because it might carry in fungus spores.

Insects are another problem (see Chapter 11). Fungus gnat larvae can attack prothalli. They can be killed by sprays, but it is best to keep the adult flies out of the cultures by tightly sealing the containers with plastic wrap, Vaseline petroleum jelly, or cotton batting placed between the pot and glass covering. Cultures grown in terrariums are said to be undamaged by fungus gnats if an insectivorous plant, such as sundew (*Drosera*), is also placed in the terrarium. Foliar nematodes can also damage prothalli.

The failure of prothalli to produce young ferns (sporophytes) long after sowing (6 to 18 months) can be due to several causes. The most common cause is insufficient water for the sperm to swim to the egg. If sporelings develop only near the edges of the container (where water condensation is greatest), this is a good indication that more water is needed. If misting does not produce sporophytes, fertilization can usually be achieved by flooding the prothalli with a thin film of water for a few hours and then letting it drain away. Other reasons for failure are more difficult to determine. Sometimes the sowing is so dense that the crowded prothalli produce only antheridia, not archegonia, in which case sporelings cannot be produced because there are no eggs to be fertilized. In other cases, ferns need a basic medium to grow healthy prothalli (as in some *Pellaea* species). Some ferns just take a long time to form sporelings (two years is not uncommon). Slow-growing cultures often become contaminated by algae and mosses (see Chapter 11).

FERNS EASY TO GROW FROM SPORES

Some ferns are easy to grow from spores whereas others (such as *Elaphoglossum* and some *Blechnum*) are difficult. *Polystichum* and many species of *Polypodium,* for example, germinate satisfactorily but produce sporelings slowly. On the other hand, the following ferns are easy and quick to grow from spores and readily form sporelings. They are highly recommended for the beginner.

Adiantum capillus-veneris	*Microlepia platyphylla*
Adiantum hispidulum	*Osmunda*, most species—fresh spores can
Adiantum raddianum	germinate in one day
Asplenium platyneuron	*Pellaea viridis*
Athyrium filix-femina	*Phlebodium aureum*
Cheilanthes bonariensis	*Phlebodium pseudoaureum*
Cheilanthes wrightii	*Pityrogramma austroamericana*
Cyrtomium falcatum	*Pteris cretica*
Doodia aspera	*Pteris multifida*
Doodia media	*Pteris tremula*
Dryopteris affinis	*Pteris vittata*
Hypolepis tenuifolia	*Thelypteris dentata*
Macrothelypteris torresiana	*Thelypteris parasitica*
Matteuccia orientalis	*Thelypteris puberula*
Microlepia strigosa	*Todea barbara*

COMING TRUE FROM SPORES

Most fern species or cultivars produce relatively uniform offspring, but occasionally they produce sporelings that appear quite different. The differences range from subtle to conspicuous (see "Variation Within Species" in Chapter 12). Some commonly cultivated species that produce variable offspring include *Adiantum raddianum, Asplenium bulbiferum* (the narrow-segment form), *Athyrium filix-femina, Phlebodium aureum, Phyllitis scolopendrium,* and *Polystichum setiferum.* With these species it is necessary to cull by hand those sporelings that vary greatly from the parents, but there is always the possibility of being rewarded with a sporeling that has highly unusual but attractive characteristics. Such sporelings are mostly the result of mutations or new hereditary combinations and might not reproduce true from spore. Rarely are they due to hybridization between different species.

Hybridizing Ferns

Ferns are famous (or infamous!) for hybridizing. They hybridize in nature, and many fern hybrids have been artificially produced in the laboratory. Some genera that hybridize frequently are *Asplenium, Dryopteris,* and *Thelypteris.*

Fern hybrids can be recognized because they are intermediate between their parents. If the parents greatly differ, the hybrids tend to be irregular and vary widely in size, shape, or number of discrete structures (pinnae, pinnules, sori, and so forth) between the extremes set by the two parents. Hybrid intermediacy can usually be seen in frond shape, vein patterns, and sorus shape. Contrary to expectation, hybrids made at different times from the same parents are not always identical.

Fern hybrids are not always superior to their parents, but some do display hybrid vigor. For example, *Adiantum×tracyi* has physiological qualities superior to both its parents (*A. jordanii* and *A. pedatum*). In cultivation, the hybrid grows more robustly than either parent and, in California, it remains green most of the year. An unfortunate feature of this hybrid (and many others like it) is that it is sterile and can only be propagated by dividing its rhizome. Only rarely are fern hybrids fertile—that is, capable of producing viable spores.

The simplest method for hybridizing ferns is sowing spores of the two parents together and hoping that cross-fertilization will occur (Figure 8.12a). The resulting sporelings have to be grown to a fairly large size to see whether they have the expected intermediate characteristics of the hybrid. This takes a lot of time and material.

Another method involves sowing the spores of the parents separately and then transplanting the prothalli close to each other in the hope that a hybrid will develop. With this method you can be certain that spores of both parents have germinated and produced prothalli. For details about this method, see Rasbach et al. (1994).

Hybrids can also be produced by planting different parts of two mature prothalli close together (Figure 8.12b). The notched end of the prothallus bears most of the archegonia that contain the eggs; the remaining part of the prothallus (the tapered end) bears most of the antheridia that contain the sperm. By cutting one-third of a prothallus at the notched end of one parent and one-third at the tapered end of the second parent, and by planting these ends together, it is possible to obtain a hybrid. Any sporophytes resulting from this method are not necessarily hybrids, however. It is possible that the sporeling resulted from self-fertilization that occurred before separation, or from a selfing after separation (sometimes antheridia are still present near the notched end of the prothallus), or from new proliferations of the prothallus. Nevertheless, the chances of producing a hybrid by this method are much better than planting complete prothalli of two species next to each other (Lovis 1968).

Hybrids can also be produced by concentrating the sperm from one parent in water and then adding prothalli of the other parent (Figure 8.12c). The spores from the species intended to be the male parent are densely sown to encourage antheridia to form. Prothalli used as the female parent are sown thinly or spaced apart by transplanting to produce more archegonia. The prothallus cultures are sparingly and carefully watered by soaking the soil from below, so as to prevent a film of water from developing between the soil and prothalli—this film of water may cause premature dispersal of the sperm and unwanted self-fertilization. Care must be taken to prevent condensation on the planting cover from falling on the prothalli. Because antheridia develop before archegonia, the spores of the intended female parent should be sown four to six weeks earlier so that both parents will be at the proper stage of development simultaneously. Because it is difficult to know when the parents are at the optimum stage of development for hybridization, it is useful to have several cultures of both parents sown on different dates. Prothalli with antheridia suitable for hybridization usually develop three to four months after sowing, whereas archegonia will develop one to two months after

a

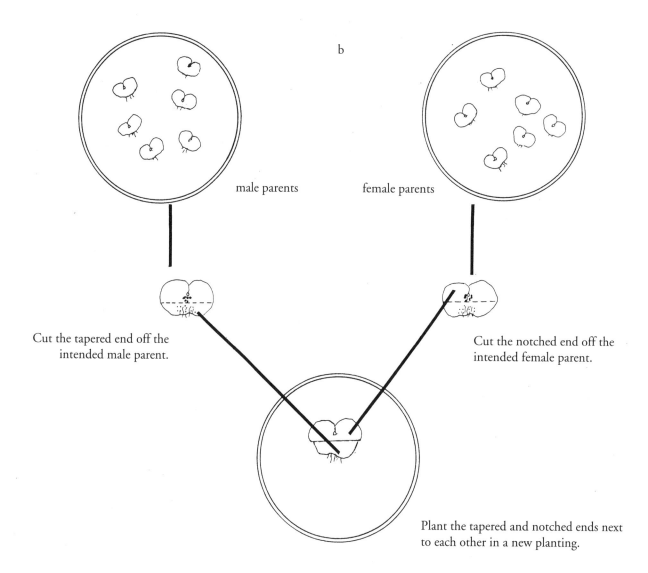

b

male parents

female parents

Cut the tapered end off the
intended male parent.

Cut the notched end off the
intended female parent.

Plant the tapered and notched ends next
to each other in a new planting.

Figure 8.12. Various methods of hybridizing ferns: a. planting spores or young prothalli of intended parents together; b. exchanging notched and tapered ends of intended parents; c. growing parents separately, mixing them, and then growing potentially fertilized prothalli separately.

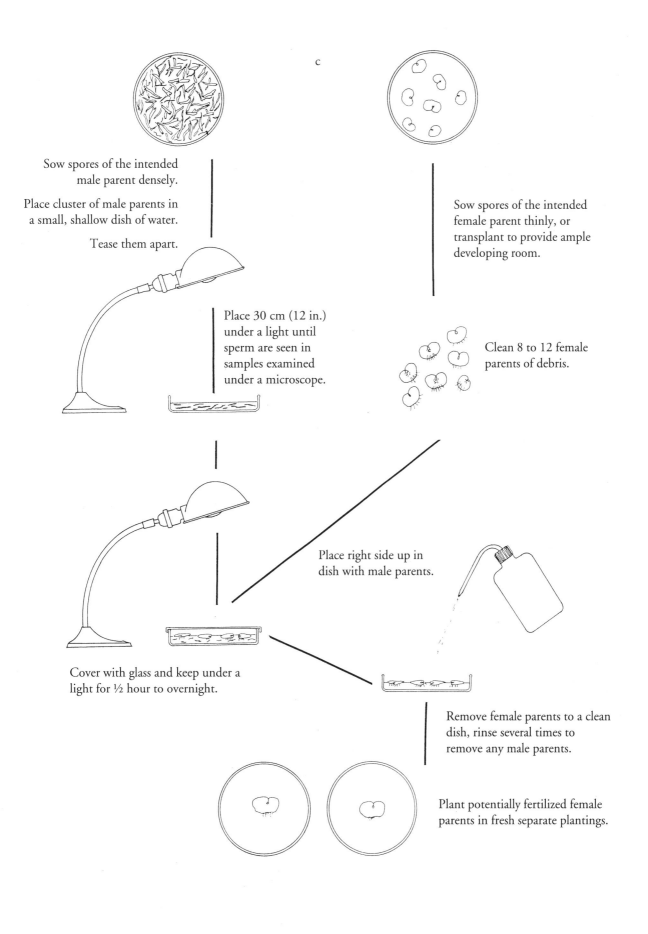

c

Sow spores of the intended male parent densely.

Place cluster of male parents in a small, shallow dish of water.

Tease them apart.

Sow spores of the intended female parent thinly, or transplant to provide ample developing room.

Place 30 cm (12 in.) under a light until sperm are seen in samples examined under a microscope.

Clean 8 to 12 female parents of debris.

Place right side up in dish with male parents.

Cover with glass and keep under a light for ½ hour to overnight.

Remove female parents to a clean dish, rinse several times to remove any male parents.

Plant potentially fertilized female parents in fresh separate plantings.

the antheridia are ready. Because unwanted self-fertilization may occur, the archegonia must be examined for signs of sporophyte development before use. This is best done under a dissecting microscope.

The hybridization technique consists of placing about 1.5 square centimeters (¼ sq. in.) of the small young prothalli bearing the antheridia in a dish (watch glass) with a small amount of warm water, about 25 to 35°C (77–95°F), and teasing the antheridia apart. The dish is then placed 30 cm (12 in.) beneath a 40-watt light bulb or in sunlight. At 20-minute intervals, the water is checked under a microscope for active sperm. Once active sperm have been found, 8 to 12 prothalli of the female parent, which have been cleaned of debris and examined for the absence of sporophytes, are immediately placed, archegonia-side down, on the water containing the sperm. The dish is covered with glass to prevent drying and returned to the light. It is left undisturbed for a half-hour to overnight. At the end of this time the female prothalli are removed, washed several times in fresh water to remove any of the small male prothalli, and planted in fresh soil.

Hybrid sporophytes usually appear four to six weeks after fertilization. Any sporophytes that appear before this time generally are the result of self-fertilization. A success rate of about 80% has been reported with this technique in producing hybrids between closely related and compatible strains. Fern sperm is known to be attracted to malic acid (0.01%) and citric acid, and this may be of use in hybridization work.

Generally, only closely related ferns hybridize. Other abnormal plants are sometimes confused with hybrids. Abnormal fronds are caused by injury, mutation, or unusual gene recombinations. If a suspected hybrid can be duplicated by artificial hybridization in the laboratory, then it probably is a true hybrid. Indirect proof can be found by comparing a suspected hybrid with its parents and looking for intermediate features. In all cases, keep records of the parents and the methods used in hybridizing because this information is scientifically important.

9 Landscaping

When landscaping with ferns, as with any plants, be sure that they receive enough warmth, sunlight, humidity, protection from wind, and proper soil conditions. Keep in mind their size when fully grown and any special problems that may arise in their upkeep. Attention to these considerations early on avoids disappointment later.

The planting design you have in mind should be visualized in relationship to its surroundings. Will the fern harmonize with its surrounding environment? Will it eventually be too shaded or crowded by surrounding trees and shrubs? Are there too many elements in the design that create a sense of "busyness" or confusion? Sometimes plants that differ greatly provide a refreshing sense of contrast; however, they can be jarring or disturbing if carelessly selected. The placement of the plants in relationship to the surroundings should provide a restful sense of balance. If unbalanced, the design can be disturbing to the eye's sense of equilibrium. These considerations are basic landscape design principles which when correctly applied provide the most pleasing aesthetic arrangement to your garden.

Solving Particular Landscaping Problems

Besides using ferns in general landscaping and for blending or contrasting with other plants, ferns can be used to solve particular problems or needs. Lists of appropriate ferns to use for some of these purposes are provided later in the chapter under "Ferns for Particular Landscape Purposes."

CENTER OF INTEREST

Plants used to create center points of interest are called accent plants. The most effective accent plants have either strong, bold, well-defined patterns to their foliage or, at the other extreme, are soft, fine, and delicate. Accent ferns should not be too small or be crowded among other plants. The general outline of the plant should have an interesting pattern rather than be just an uninteresting blob of pretty foliage.

CREATING THE ILLUSION OF DISTANCE

Use fine-textured, airy-looking plants with soft lines to give the feeling of distance. Coarse-textured plants give the feeling of closeness. Generally, soft-colored foliage gives the sense of distance, whereas bright colors give a sense of closeness.

Figure 9.1. Ferns can be useful in hiding distracting views.

Figure 9.2. Using ferns as a center of interest.

HIDING DISTRACTING VIEWS

Ferns can be used to hide unwanted views. Hanging baskets are good at blocking the top of a distracting view. The lower part can be hidden with medium-sized ferns planted in back or in front of the hanging baskets.

Figure 9.3. Creating the illusion of distance with ferns.

MAKING A CURTAIN OF FERNS

By carefully hanging baskets at different heights it is possible to produce a curtain of foliage across the side of a patio or outside a window. The climbing ferns (*Lygodium*) are well suited to producing a screen of foliage if they are provided with wires for support.

Figure 9.4. A curtain of ferns.

ADDING HEIGHT TO WALLS

Basket ferns can be placed on top of walls to give added height or to hide distracting views (such as the neighbor's clothesline). Wire fencing (2-by-1-inch mesh) can be cut, bent, and formed into a basket that will fit nicely across the top of a concrete block wall. The lower front and back edge of the basket should be extended to form a lip to secure the basket on the wall. The basket in effect straddles the wall. Wooden boxes constructed to securely straddle the wall are also suitable.

Figure 9.5. Using ferns to add height to walls.

PROVIDING FOLIAGE ABOVE EYE LEVEL

Sometimes the effect of a small palm or tree is needed inside a small room, but there is not enough space to put a large container on the floor. Hanging a basket fern from the ceiling will achieve the same effect and keep the floor space open.

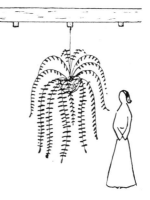

Figure 9.6. A hanging basket fern offers foliage above eye level.

ADDING INTEREST TO A BARE WALL

A bare wall can be made attractive by hanging ferns in baskets or containers or with staghorn ferns mounted on boards. A small piece of wood or a wad of aluminum foil wedged between the basket and the wall will help prevent water stains on the wall.

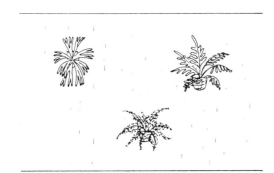

Figure 9.7. Ferns used to decorate a bare wall.

SOFTENING ROCK SURFACES

Certain ferns creep over rocks and thereby have the effect of softening hard lines. Provide pockets of soil in the rock to get these ferns started. Many species of *Davallia* and *Polypodium* are admirably suited for this use.

Figure 9.8. Softening rock surfaces with ferns.

Border and Foundation Plantings

Border ferns are useful for softening the hard lines of a concrete walk. Use small- to medium-sized ferns that will not quickly grow out of bounds. Many maidenhair ferns (*Adiantum*) are the right size for this and grow well along the concrete. *Blechnum appendiculatum* is suitable in warmer climates. Many ferns can also be planted along the base of a bare foundation or wall to break the visual monotony. Using species with short-creeping rhizomes will reduce maintenance needs. The ostrich fern (*Matteuccia struthiopteris*) is frequently used as a foundation planting around homes in the eastern United States.

Figure 9.9. Ferns can effectively soften the border along a wall or walkway.

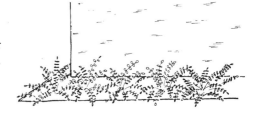

Ground Cover

Where conditions are shady or semi-shady, ferns do well as a ground cover. In such uses, ferns also help prevent erosion.

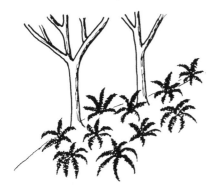

Figure 9.10. Ferns used as ground cover.

Ferns for Particular Landscape Uses

A variety of landscape situations can be served by a range of fern species, depending on the climate and the intended landscape effect. The lists presented here suggest some of the more common or adaptable ferns for specific purposes. Chapter 10 also includes information on growing ferns for certain situations and on the landscape use of specific types of ferns, such as the tree ferns. The entries in Chapter 13 provide more detailed information on the requirements and uses of these ferns.

OUTDOOR FERNS

The 10 ferns listed here for each section of the United States were selected because they are easy to grow, attractive, and readily obtainable. Native ferns are favored on these lists. Most parts of the United States require hardy to very hardy ferns. For additional outdoor species and their temperature tolerances, see Chapter 13.

Northeastern United States. Hardy to very hardy ferns are the only ones suitable for the northeastern United States, where prolonged periods of cold are common. This area includes mostly Zones 3–6. Summers are hot and humid in some areas and often difficult for ferns that prefer cooler summers.

Adiantum pedatum
Deparia acrostichoides
Dryopteris erythrosora
Dryopteris goldiana
Dryopteris marginalis

Matteuccia struthiopteris
Onoclea sensibilis
Osmunda claytoniana
Osmunda regalis
Polystichum acrostichoides

Southeastern United States. Depending on the locality, ferns for the southeastern United States may be hardy to semi-tender. This area includes mostly Zones 6–8. For the cooler areas of the Southeast, see the listing for "Northeastern United States," and for milder areas see "Southern Florida and Hawaii" and "Coastal Central and Southern California." Ferns adapted to hot, humid summers thrive in this area.

Southern Florida and Hawaii. This area includes mostly Zones 10 and 11. Tropical species are favored here, but a wide range of ferns are adapted to the climate of southern Florida and Hawaii, except those ferns that like cool summers or need cold temperatures to break dormancy. The occasional cold spells may require moving the more tender species to protected areas.

Adiantum trapeziforme
Aglaomorpha coronans
Asplenium nidus and relatives
Davallia, many species
Microsorum grossum

Microsorum punctatum
Nephrolepis falcata 'Furcans'
Platycerium bifurcatum and cultivars
Selaginella, many tropical species
Sphaeropteris cooperi

Central United States. This area includes mostly Zones 3–6. In the northern part of this area, only very hardy ferns are suitable; see "Northeastern United States." For the southern area, see the listings for southeastern and southwestern states.

Northwestern United States. This area includes mostly Zones 5–8, with a few pockets of Zone 9. Some semi-hardy ferns will grow in coastal areas, but the hardy species listed here will be more reliable on coastal and inland areas. Coastal areas have cooler summers that may not favor species adapted to hot summers.

Adiantum aleuticum	*Dryopteris dilatata*
Athyrium filix-femina	*Phyllitis scolopendrium*
Athyrium niponicum 'Pictum'	*Polypodium vulgare*
Blechnum spicant	*Polystichum andersonii*
Dryopteris affinis	*Polystichum munitum*

Southwestern United States. This area includes mostly Zones 6–9. In most areas, hardy or semi-hardy ferns will do best. Some milder areas will support semi-tender species. High aridity and summer heat are usual problems. The water or soil can be basic in certain locales, making it difficult to grow acid-loving ferns.

Adiantum capillus-veneris	*Osmunda cinnamomea*
Asplenium platyneuron	*Pellaea atropurpurea*
Athyrium filix-femina	*Polystichum setiferum*
Dryopteris filix-mas	*Woodsia obtusa*
Onoclea sensibilis	*Woodwardia virginica*

Coastal central and southern California. This area includes mostly Zones 9 and 10. In southern California and the central coastal areas, semi-hardy or semi-tender species do best. Many temperate ferns adapt to this area, but not those that need a cold winter to break dormancy. Aridity is a problem during heat waves, and the water or soil in some areas are basic, making it difficult to grow acid-loving ferns.

Adiantum raddianum and cultivars	*Microlepia strigosa*
Asplenium bulbiferum	*Polystichum polyblepharum*
Cyrtomium falcatum and cultivars	*Pteris cretica*
Davallia mariesii var. *stenolepis*	*Rumohra adiantiformis*
Dicksonia antarctica	*Sphaeropteris cooperi*

SHADE-TOLERANT FERNS

The following ferns will grow in areas that are shadier than usual, but they still must have a certain amount of light. Provide more light in climates where the weather is frequently overcast. Most of these ferns will grow in brighter light, but they may be less luxuriant.

Adiantum aleuticum	*Dryopteris goldiana*
Adiantum capillus-veneris	*Dryopteris marginalis*
Adiantum pedatum	*Gymnocarpium dryopteris*
Adiantum raddianum	*Nephrolepis cordifolia*
Arachniodes standishii	*Osmunda cinnamomea*
Asplenium bulbiferum	*Phegopteris connectilis*
Athyrium filix-femina	*Phyllitis scolopendrium*
Blechnum spicant	*Polystichum acrostichoides*
Dennstaedtia punctilobula	*Polystichum munitum*
Dryopteris dilatata	*Polystichum setiferum*
Dryopteris filix-mas	

SUN-TOLERANT FERNS

Ferns seldom look their best when growing in direct sun (if they grow at all in such intense light). The following ferns appear reasonably attractive if grown in places with direct morning or late-afternoon sun. Some tolerate full sun if the skies are often overcast. Elsewhere they need filtered light during the hottest part of the day. Those species marked with an asterisk (*) will tolerate full sun only if soil moisture and humidity are adequate.

Aglaomorpha coronans
Athyrium filix-femina
Blechnum appendiculatum
Cheilanthes, most species
*Cibotium glaucum**
Cyrtomium falcatum
*Dennstaedtia punctilobula**
Doodia media
Dryopteris erythrosora
Dryopteris ludoviciana
Lygodium japonicum
Microlepia platyphylla
Microlepia strigosa
Nephrolepis cordifolia
*Onoclea sensibilis**

Osmunda, all species*
Pellaea, most species
Phlebodium pseudoaureum
Pityrogramma, most species
Platycerium veitchii
Polystichum polyblepharum
*Pteridium aquilinum**
Pteris cretica
Pteris tremula
Rumohra adiantiformis
Sphaeropteris cooperi
Thelypteris noveboracensis
Thelypteris puberula
Todea barbara

Aquatic Ferns

Aquatic ferns are those that have their foliage submerged (or partly so) or floating on the surface. Such ferns vary considerably in form compared to bog and wet-soil ferns. Some aquatic ferns can be purchased from aquarium supply stores. For some species, water that is high in salts may stunt growth or may burn or blotch the leaves. Changing the old water completely rather than adding more helps reduce salts and increase aeration. Using a high proportion of sand and adding charcoal to the rooting medium will help keep the water free of noxious chemicals and odors.

Acrostichum aureum
Azolla, all species
Bolbitis heudelotii
Ceratopteris, all species

Marsilea, all species
Microsorum pteropus
Salvinia, all species

Bog or Wet-Soil Ferns

Bog ferns grow in soggy or poorly drained areas and only incidentally have their foliage submerged in water. Their roots tolerate submergence—though some species are more tolerant than others. In very wet soils, avoid high amounts of organic material. Sharp sand and charcoal can be added to keep the soil sweet (that is, to avoid anaerobic fermentation and the accumulation of its often toxic or unpleasant byproducts). For ferns that float or grow partly or totally submerged, see the preceding discussion of "Aquatic Ferns." Some ferns may be both aquatic and bog-adapted, such as *Ceratopteris* and *Marsilea.*

Acrostichum aureum
Acrostichum danaeifolium
Blechnum serrulatum
Ceratopteris, all species
Dryopteris ludoviciana
Equisetum, all species

Marsilea, all species
Matteuccia struthiopteris
Microsorum pteropus
Onoclea sensibilis
Osmunda regalis
Thelypteris palustris

FERNS FOR BASIC OR LIMESTONE SOILS

These ferns need more calcium than others, preferring a soil pH of 7–8. Where limestone is available, the plants can be grown in soil pockets in the rock. (See Chapter 5 for more information on limestone-loving ferns.)

Adiantum tenerum
Asplenium adiantum-nigrum
Asplenium ruta-muraria
Asplenium platyneuron
Camptosorus rhizophyllus

Ceterach officinarum
Gymnocarpium robertianum
Phyllitis scolopendrium
Polypodium cambricum
Polystichum aculeatum

FERNS FOR ACID SOILS

These ferns grow in acidic soils with pH 4–7. (See Chapter 5 for more information on acid-loving ferns.)

Blechnum penna-marina
Blechnum spicant
Dennstaedtia punctilobula
Dryopteris clintoniana
Dryopteris expansa

Dryopteris tokyoensis
Osmunda claytoniana
Phegopteris connectilis
Polystichum, various species

DRIER SOIL FERNS

The following ferns tolerate drier, more exposed areas than most ferns. They need regular watering and protection until established. These are not xerophytic ferns, which are discussed in Chapter 10.

Aglaomorpha coronans
Blechnum appendiculatum
Cyrtomium falcatum
Davallia mariesii var. *stenolepis*
Davallia tyermannii
Dennstaedtia punctilobula
Dryopteris filix-mas
Microlepia strigosa

Microsorum viellardii
Nephrolepis cordifolia
Phlebodium pseudoaureum
Pteridium aquilinum
Pteris cretica
Pteris vittata
Rumohra adiantiformis
Sphaeropteris cooperi

RAPIDLY GROWING FERNS

In optimum conditions of temperature, light, and nutrients, the following species grow relatively rapidly.

Adiantum raddianum
Anogramma chaerophylla
Athyrium filix-femina
Cibotium schiedei
Dennstaedtia punctilobula
Goniophlebium subauriculatum 'Knightiae'
Hypolepis, most species
Macrothelypteris torresiana

Matteuccia struthiopteris
Microlepia strigosa
Nephrolepis cordifolia
Onoclea sensibilis
Phegopteris connectilis
Pteridium aquilinum
Pteris cretica
Pteris tremula

Pteris vittata
Selaginella kraussiana
Sphaeropteris cooperi
Sphaeropteris excelsa

Thelypteris, most species
Woodwardia radicans
Woodwardia virginica

SLOWLY GROWING FERNS

The following greenhouse or subtropical ferns are slow growing.

Alsophila tricolor
Angiopteris, all species
Cibotium glaucum
Dicksonia antarctica
Dicksonia fibrosa

Drynaria, all cultivated species
Elaphoglossum, most species
Marattia, all cultivated species
Platycerium, all species
Pyrrosia lingua

COLOR IN FERN FRONDS

The young fronds of many species of *Adiantum* and *Blechnum* are red when they emerge and turn green with age. Other ferns are white or yellow on the underside and remain so at maturity. Variegated ferns —those with stripes or blotches of white, yellow, red, or other colors on their fronds—are mostly cultivars or forms of green species and are generally more difficult to grow.

Adiantum hispidulum—young fronds red
Adiantum macrophyllum—young fronds red
Adiantum raddianum 'Variegatum'—variegated white
Alsophila tricolor—underside white
Arachniodes simplicior—variegated white and yellow
Athyrium niponicum 'Pictum'—variegated grayish and purple
Athyrium otophorum—stipe, rachis, and costa red
Blechnum appendiculatum—young fronds red
Blechnum brasiliense—young fronds red
Cheilanthes argentea—underside yellow or white
Dryopteris erythrosora—young fronds red, indusia typically red
Microlepia platyphylla—bluish green foliage
Phlebodium aureum 'Mandaianum'—bluish green foliage
Pityrogramma austroamericana—underside yellow
Pityrogramma calomelanos—underside white or yellow
Pteris argyraea—variegated white
Pteris aspericaulis—stipe, rachis, and costa deep red
Pteris ensiformis 'Evergemiensis'—variegated white
Pteris ensiformis 'Victoriae'—variegated white
Pteris nipponica—variegated white
Selaginella, several species—red, gold, blue, iridescent, or variegated

EVERGREEN AND DECIDUOUS FERNS

The question of whether ferns are evergreen or deciduous is of varying importance to different gardeners. In climates where the garden is used year-round, evergreen ferns are preferred. Where the garden is used seasonally, deciduous species are more frequently cultivated, although some hardy evergreens might be welcomed. Where seasonal changes are eagerly anticipated, the deciduous species are symbols of spring as their crowns of beautiful fresh green fiddleheads emerge after a long winter.

One reason it is important to know whether a fern is deciduous is so that you do not think it is dying when it goes into its rest period. Growing hardy, deciduous ferns in warm climates requires selecting adaptable species (sometimes a matter of trial and error), not giving them too much water in the winter (they will rot), and remembering not to accidentally dig them up when working in the garden. Young plants of some deciduous species can retain their greenness during their first one or two years of life.

A fern that is deciduous will have all its leaves decline at about the same time. In contrast, an evergreen fern has leaves that do not decline all at the same time. Contrary to popular belief, evergreen plants do not have leaves that stay green forever—the older leaves are eventually shed. Whether plants are deciduous or evergreen, their declining leaves may be self-shedding (articulate) or they may wither in place (marcescent). These characteristics affect their landscape use and maintenance.

Deciduous ferns with self-shedding fronds have a special layer (the abscission layer) near the base of the stipe that allows a clean break at the joint with the stem. Self-shedding fronds require mostly seasonal raking for maintenance.

Deciduous ferns with fronds that wither in place are more troublesome to groom because their fronds will need to be cut from the plant to maintain neatness. Because withered, persistent fronds protect the crown from winter cold, they are usually removed in spring before the new fronds have emerged. For neatness, year-round grooming may be needed to remove any off-season, withered leaves.

Fronds of evergreen ferns generally live a few months to a few years, depending on the species and cultural conditions. Spent fronds of evergreen ferns may be self-shedding (as in *Polypodium*) or marcescent (as in *Polystichum*). Expect a light litter or light grooming problems year-round with most evergreen ferns. For more details on grooming, see Chapter 6.

The distinction between being evergreen and deciduous is not always clear. Some ferns lose all their leaves in cold climates but do so only partly in warmer climates. Reclined, marcescent fronds can still contain functional conducting tissue and may stay green and photosynthetic for weeks. Other ferns gradually reduce growth, and in the absence of new growth, the existing fronds become increasingly tattered but stay erect. In certain climates the period of dormancy in some ferns is so short that the shedding of the old fronds is simultaneous with the flush of new fronds, which makes it seem as if the plant is evergreen. Some species have a rhythm of leaf loss that does not coincide with Northern Hemisphere winters. Many tropical species grow slowly during the cool months and resume active growth as soon as warm weather returns. Given these intermediate conditions, discrepancies abound in the literature on the subject. To be clear, deciduousness or evergreenness should be stated relative to a given climate.

Deciduous ferns. The following ferns are commonly available and obligately deciduous. Their fronds are deciduous even in warm climates, although their dormancy period may be shorter. Those listed here are marcescent.

Athyrium filix-femina	*Gymnocarpium dryopteris*
Athyrium niponicum	*Matteuccia struthiopteris*
Athyrium otophorum	*Onoclea sensibilis*
Deparia acrostichoides	*Osmunda regalis*
Diplazium pycnocarpon	*Phegopteris connectilis*

Evergreen ferns. The following common ferns are evergreen even in cold-temperate climates, although their new growth may be delayed until spring. Those listed here are marcescent.

Blechnum penna-marina	*Cyrtomium falcatum*
Blechnum spicant	*Dryopteris erythrosora*

Dryopteris intermedia
Phyllitis scolopendrium
Polystichum acrostichoides
Polystichum setiferum
Polystichum tsus-simense

ACCENT FERNS

Accent ferns have distinctive lines, shapes, textures, or patterns. They can be used as center points of interest in landscaping.

Aglaomorpha coronans
Asplenium bulbiferum
Asplenium nidus
Blechnum brasiliense
Blechnum gibbum
Cyrtomium falcatum
Didymochlaena truncatula
Matteuccia struthiopteris
Microsorum punctatum 'Grandiceps'
Nephrolepis exaltata and cultivars
Osmunda, all species
Phlebodium aureum and cultivars
Platycerium, all species
Tree ferns, all species

BORDER AND FOUNDATION FERNS

The ferns listed here spread sparingly or keep their general shape when planted along a flower border or walk or foundation of a house. Ferns that are short-creeping or clumping or have erect rootstocks are good for this use. Ferns with long-creeping rhizomes are unsuitable because they outgrow their boundaries too quickly, and they are best used as ground covers.

Adiantum hispidulum
Adiantum pedatum
Adiantum raddianum
Athyrium filix-femina
Athyrium niponicum 'Pictum'
Diplazium subsinuatum
Dryopteris erythrosora
Microlepia strigosa
Pellaea rotundifolia
Phyllitis scolopendrium
Polystichum acrostichoides
Pteris cretica and cultivars
Pteris multifida and cultivars
Thelypteris, many species

FERNS FOR GROUND COVER

Ferns useful as ground covers eventually carpet the ground by means of their widely creeping rhizomes or stolons. In some cases, ferns with short-creeping rhizomes and clusters of arching fronds can produce the same effect. The following ferns spread by rhizomes or stolons.

Blechnum appendiculatum
Blechnum penna-marina
Davallia, all species
Dennstaedtia, all species
Gymnocarpium dryopteris
Hypolepis, all species
Matteuccia struthiopteris
Nephrolepis cordifolia and other species
Onoclea sensibilis
Phegopteris connectilis
Phegopteris hexagonoptera
Selaginella, several species
Thelypteris acuminata
Thelypteris palustris

BASKET FERNS

Ferns in hanging baskets or containers are commonly used in today's house and garden decor. Both epiphytes and terrestrial ferns can be used in hanging displays. Species with long fronds that droop over the edges of the container are particularly attractive. General directions on the selection, planting, and care of basket ferns are given in Chapter 7, and details on growing specific groups of ferns are provided in Chapter 10. Some of the more popular basket ferns are listed here.

Adiantum capillus-veneris   *Phlebodium aureum*
Adiantum raddianum   *Phlebodium pseudoaureum*
Aglaomorpha, all species   *Platycerium,* all species
Campyloneurum, most species   *Polypodium,* most species
Davallia, all species   *Pyrrosia lingua*
Goniophlebium, all species   *Rumohra adiantiformis*
Nephrolepis, all species

ROCK GARDEN AND WALL FERNS

Many ferns can be grown among rocks, but rock walls or rock gardens are traditionally planted with small to medium-small ferns. The rock background allows these ferns to be more easily seen yet safely tucked away to avoid being stepped on or overly shaded by rapidly growing plants.

Ideally, some of the rocks should be limestone so that lime-loving ferns can be grown. If limestone cannot be found, lime can be added to the soil mixes (see Chapter 5).

Using the proper soil before setting the rocks in place avoids future growth problems. The ferns should be firmly planted with a loam or potting mix in an area between the rocks that is a few inches wide and deep and has good drainage. Some ferns will need additions of coarse sand. Small rocks added during planting will help secure the fern and soil in place. Protect the surface soil against erosion by firming it and placing gravel or a few small stones on top of it. Generally, temperate species of rock ferns adapt poorly to warm-climate gardens. Where rainfall is moderate to sparse, xerophytic ferns do well in rock plantings (see "Xero-phytic Ferns" in Chapter 10). Also see "Trough Gardens" in Chapter 10. Kaye (1968) provides further details on planting hardy ferns in rock gardens. Some suitable ferns for rock gardens are

Adiantum aleuticum subsp. *subpumilum*   *Davallia tyermannii*
Adiantum capillus-veneris   *Dryopteris,* small species or cultivars
Adiantum hispidulum   *Gymnocarpium dryopteris*
Adiantum raddianum 'Pacottii'   *Lemmaphyllum microphyllum*
Adiantum venustum   *Nephrolepis cordifolia* 'Lemon Buttons'
Asplenium ×ebenoides   *Nephrolepis exaltata,* dwarf forms
Asplenium platyneuron   *Pellaea,* all species
Asplenium ruta-muraria   *Phyllitis scolopendrium*
Asplenium trichomanes   *Pityrogramma,* all species
Astrolepis, all species   *Polypodium,* all species of the *P. vulgare*
Athyrium filix-femina, small cultivars   complex
Camptosorus rhizophyllus   *Polystichum lemmonii*
Camptosorus sibericus   *Polystichum tsus-simense*
Ceterach aureum   *Pteris cretica* and cultivars
Cheilanthes, all species   *Pteris multifida* and cultivars
Cryptogramma crispa   *Pyrrosia,* all smaller species
Cystopteris bulbifera   *Selaginella,* many species
Cystopteris fragilis   *Woodsia obtusa*
Davallia mariesii   *Woodsia oregana*

10 Growing Special Ferns

House Ferns

Ferns add grace to a room, and if the room is not too dry and has adequate light, many species can serve as permanent decorations. Light and humidity often can be improved, but if not, it is best to use several ferns in rotation, replacing a plant with a fresh one when it shows poor growth. Plants removed from display will recover if given sufficient light, humidity, and care. Since the kitchen and bathroom are often the most humid rooms in the house, they are good places to grow ferns if the light is adequate.

Generally, robust ferns with leathery fronds, such as the house holly fern (*Cyrtomium falcatum*) and leather fern (*Rumohra adiantiformis*), grow well indoors. Most davallias are also good as house ferns, and some are attractive for their finely cut foliage (*Davallia fejeensis* and *D. mariesii* var. *stenolepis*). The most frequently used indoor ferns are the Boston ferns (*Nephrolepis exaltata* and its cultivars), which come in a variety of textures.

If possible, start with nearly mature ferns that are acclimated to drier conditions. These "hardened" plants will grow better in the drier air of a house than those recently removed from a humid greenhouse. Avoid selecting plants that appear too soft and green.

Frequency of watering depends on the relative humidity of the room, the size of the fern, the type of soil, and the kind of pot. Most indoor ferns require a thorough watering two to three times a week, more if the air is dry and less if cool. Water the pot until the water runs out of the drain hole in order to wash out the salts that accumulate in the soil. Do not permit pots to sit continually in saucers of water. If you are watering pots by setting them in saucers, remove the pots as soon as the soil has become moistened throughout. If the pots lack drain holes, use distilled water or rainwater to avoid salt accumulation, but be careful not to overwater. Be sure that a layer of coarse drainage material such as gravel, pot shards, or perlite is at the bottom of pots lacking drain holes. Charcoal added to the soil absorbs noxious chemicals produced by microorganisms that thrive in the wetness. It is better, however, to avoid overwatering than to rely on the charcoal's absorptive power. Always remember that the soil should feel moist, not soggy.

Every two weeks or so, apply a fine spray of water to the foliage to wash off dust and insects. Watch for scale insects, mealybugs, and aphids. These pests can spread quickly because they have few natural enemies indoors. Furthermore, they are not washed off the plant by rain or overhead watering, as often happens outdoors.

The main challenge in growing ferns indoors is to provide enough humidity and light. Otherwise the culture of indoor ferns is similar to that of ferns used elsewhere. The following are some favorite house ferns.

Adiantum hispidulum

Asplenium antiquum

Asplenium australasicum

Asplenium bulbiferum

Asplenium daucifolium

Asplenium nidus

Cibotium schiedei

Cyrtomium falcatum and cultivars

Davallia fejeensis

Davallia mariesii var. *stenolepis*

Microsorum grossum

Microsorum punctatum and cultivars

Nephrolepis exaltata and cultivars

Pellaea rotundifolia

Phlebodium aureum

Phlebodium pseudoaureum

Platycerium bifurcatum

Pteris cretica and cultivars

Pteris tremula

Rumohra adiantiformis

Trough Gardens

Trough gardens can be thought of as large, deep-dish gardens. Stone troughs used by farmers to water animals became much prized as planters for miniature plants. Trough and similar broad containers are ideal for displaying small ferns, confining species with long-creeping rhizomes, and serving as garden ornaments.

Handsome troughs can be made from easily obtainable materials. Hypertufa troughs are made from one part cement, one part coarse sand, and two parts shredded peat moss. These ingredients are mixed with water to the consistency of creamed cottage cheese and poured into a mold to form 5-cm (2 in.) thick walls. The mold can be fashioned from two cardboard cartons and reinforced with wire mesh. After two days, the mold is peeled away and the cast allowed to cure for seven days. Any plant toxins in the cement are neutralized by filling the trough with water and adding about 2.5 g (½ tsp.) of dissolved potassium permanganate. After two to three hours, the solution is discarded and the trough is rinsed out. Drainage holes are drilled into the trough. Troughs are allowed to cure for another two or three days. See MacPhail (1990) for details on reinforcing thin (less than 5 cm [2 in.] thick) troughs with hardware cloth, creating textural refinements, using other materials, and readying the trough for final planting. Rock garden magazines often list other ingredients and directions for building planting troughs. When preparing the soil for a trough, remember that containers with broad bottoms tend to drain slowly, so use a well-drained mix or provide ample-sized drain holes.

Terrariums or Bottle Gardens

Many fern species are suited for terrariums or glass bottles because they flourish under the high humidity within the container and the low light found indoors.

Selecting the Container

Suitable containers come in many shapes and sizes. Avoid thick, dark-colored glass containers that reduce the light. Shallow containers without covers are unsuitable for most ferns because they dry too quickly. If such containers are used, place them in a protected, humid place and frequently check for moisture. It is best to select containers that are deep enough to provide for a few inches of soil and sufficient overhead growing space for the plants. Fish aquariums, large brandy snifters, or containers with similar shapes are satisfactory. Some ferns require less humidity than others and grow well in containers with large openings. A container with a wide opening makes planting and maintaining the terrarium easier. Wide openings can always be effectively reduced by covering with plastic wrap.

Plastic containers designed as terrariums are utilitarian. They are lightweight, less likely to break compared to glass, easily opened, have a ventilation hole, and are shaped to accommodate plants. Some problems, however, are that plastic containers scratch easily and might be unsuitable in certain decors.

SELECTING THE PLANTS

Small plants in 5 to 10 cm (2–4 in.) pots are best for terrariums. Young plants of large species are easy to obtain but will soon outgrow the container. Some slower growing large species may be suitable if others are unavailable. Always start with healthy plants. Do not mix moisture-loving plants with those that like drier conditions. The following recommended plants are small to medium-small species or have small cultivars adapted for terrariums. Because some are slow growers and tender, they are not common nursery items and must be purchased in specialty shops. Many ferns of dry habitats are small and suitable for use in terrariums; see the listing under "Xerophytic Ferns" later in the chapter.

Adiantum capillus-veneris
Adiantum hispidulum
Adiantum raddianum 'Gracillimum',
    'Micropinnulum', 'Pacific Maid', or
    'Pacottii'
Anogramma chaerophylla
Asplenium cuspidatum
Asplenium daucifolium
Asplenium oligophlebium
Asplenium trichomanes
Bolbitis heteroclita Difformis Group
Camptosorus rhizophyllus
Davallia parvula
Diplazium tomitaroanum

Hemionitis, all species
Lemmaphyllum microphyllum
Microgramma vacciniifolia
Nephrolepis exaltata 'Elsevier' and
    'Mini-ruffles'
Polystichum tsus-simense
Pteris cretica 'Wilsonii'
Pteris ensiformis 'Victoriae'
Pteris multifida
Pyrrosia, small species
Selaginella, small species
Tectaria zeylanica
Vittaria lineata

PLANTING THE TERRARIUM

For a 4 to 8 liter (1–2 gal.) container, place about 2.5 to 5 cm (1–2 in.) of perlite at the bottom for drainage. If you have charcoal granules, mix some into the perlite or place a layer over the perlite. Place about 5 cm (2 in.) or more of moist potting soil over the perlite and charcoal. There is wide variety in soil preferences, ranging from sand to peat-soil mixes to uncut sphagnum. The potting soil is best disinfected to kill any algae, bacteria, or fungi and should be done a few days before use. The microwave, boiling water, a soak in Physan (Consan), or some other method is usually adequate to disinfect the soil (see "Sterilizing Soils" in Chapter 5). Let the soil drain. At planting time, use evenly moistened soil, not one that is too wet or too dry.

Plant the fern in the container at the same soil level as it was previously planted. If necessary, remove some of the soil around the roots or from the terrarium to accommodate the roots of the new fern. Tall ferns should be planted in the center or back of the terrarium with the smaller ferns, selaginellas, or mosses in front. Firm the soil around the roots with a blunt-tipped tool. Long sticks and tongs may be needed to plant ferns in narrow-mouth jars. Wire tools made from bent coat hangers are also serviceable. Long forceps are useful for picking off dead fronds.

After planting, moisten the soil mix thoroughly with distilled water, but avoid overwatering. The terrarium might need to be covered or partly covered, depending on the humidity and water needs of the plants, the size of the opening, the amount of soil moisture, and the extent of damage to the roots during planting. If too much condensation appears on the sides of a covered container, uncover it temporarily or enlarge the opening in the plastic wrap to allow evaporation. For the first few days after planting, keep the terrarium in a well-shaded place. In covered containers, a decrease in condensation is usually a signal that watering may be needed. The effects of using commercial products, usually containing silicon or glycerine, for reducing condensation is mixed. In any case, avoid getting these products on the plant or in the soil.

CARE OF PLANTED TERRARIUMS

Caring for terrariums is relatively easy, but several factors need attention. Light needs to be ample, but terrariums should never be placed in direct sunlight. Too little light can sometimes be a problem, which is revealed by the plants' developing long, thin, weak, light-green growth (etiolation). Another problem related to lighting is when the plants all lean to one side in the direction of the light. To avoid this, turn the terrarium occasionally or use overhead fluorescent lights.

The temperature must also be carefully considered. Growth will be faster in warm rooms and slower in cold ones. The best growth usually occurs between 21 and 27°C (70–80°F). Never place terrariums in hot places such as on the top of a television or beside a heater.

Water and humidity in terrariums also need to be monitored. As long as the soil stays moist (not soggy) the terrarium does not need extra water. Much of the water in a closed or nearly closed terrarium will evaporate from the soil and foliage, condense on the glass, and fall back on the soil. Expect some condensation on the glass. This recycling of water often provides sufficient moisture for the plants, and extra water might not be needed for six weeks or more. To be safe, however, check the water weekly. Open terrariums need to be watered more frequently. Apply distilled water when the soil starts to feel slightly less than moist— never let the soil dry beyond this point. Apply water as a gentle sprinkle. Very fine-textured ferns and most xerophytes should not be watered on their foliage. If you accidentally overwater, carefully tilt the terrarium and blot up the excess with paper towels or other absorbent material, or push a long eyedropper or turkey baster to the bottom and suck up the excess water. Leave the terrarium uncovered to allow the excess water to evaporate.

If growing well, terrarium ferns do not need fertilizer. If they become off-color, they can be fertilized sparingly with a dilute solution (half strength or less) of liquid fertilizer. Do not fertilize too much because the plants will grow too large for the terrarium, in which case they will need to be trimmed back or replaced. If a white crust of fertilizer salts develops on the soil, remove it and replace with fresh soil.

Maidenhair Ferns

Maidenhair ferns (*Adiantum*) have a fine billowy appearance and shiny black stalks that, because they resemble hair, give the group its name. They are found in many parts of the world but are most abundant in the American tropics. Most of the cultivated species are finely divided, and many have ruffles, fringes, crests, and other types of fancy foliage.

The common species are easy to cultivate. The three most important factors are moist soil, good drainage, and humidity. Let them go to the dry side of moist before rewatering, but not to the point of wilting. *Adiantum* is best grown outdoors or in greenhouses instead of indoors, unless a humid place is available such as the kitchen or bathroom. Shriveling of new fronds is usually a sign of low humidity, especially if the soil is moist. The other common cause of shriveling is poor root development, possibly the result of overwatering, lack of nutrients, or poor drainage. Maidenhairs are particularly sensitive to being planted in pots that are too big for them, as the roots are poorly aerated in oversized pots. Most maidenhairs slow their growth by the fall and take a rest period until spring. Water them lightly during this inactive period because too much watering causes the rhizomes to rot.

Dividing, transplanting, or repotting is best done in spring before growth is renewed. A suitable soil is one consisting of one part sand and one to two parts peat moss or leaf mold. A handful or two of coarser material (ground bark or perlite) may be added to a 15 to 20 cm (6–8 in.) pot for better drainage. The delta maidenhair (*Adiantum raddianum*), Venus's hair (*A. capillus-veneris*), and fan maidenhair (*A. tenerum*) thrive in calcium-rich soils. The use of balanced fertilizers usually satisfies this requirement, but lime, limestone, or oyster shell may also be added. Fish emulsion or other suitable fertilizers are applied every three weeks to ferns planted in sand and peat moss alone.

To maintain attractive plants, remove old or discolored fronds. Sometimes, especially with species that form dense clumps (such as *Adiantum capillus-veneris* and *A. raddianum*), the fronds in the center will die. To avoid the need for complete replanting, remove the dead part and refill the space with fresh soil. In frost-free climates, all the spent and unsightly fronds may be removed between fall and spring, but in areas with frosts, wait until spring to remove the dead fronds. In either case, damage to new growth can be avoided by trimming off all the old fronds in spring just before the new growth uncoils. Although the plant looks bare after this procedure, the alternative—having to remove the old fronds carefully without injuring the new ones—is far more tedious.

Maidenhairs are plagued by several pests that must be controlled. Slugs and snails are a constant problem in some areas, and sowbugs and pillbugs can also cause damage. Aphids usually appear in spring and can be difficult to eliminate. These pests can be controlled by applying the proper insecticide, but be extremely careful in doing so because maidenhairs are easily burned by most insecticides. If it is unknown whether an insecticide will burn the plant, apply it only on a test plant. (Also see Chapter 11 for more information on controlling pests.)

Some maidenhairs are best grown under particular horticultural conditions. The American or five-finger maidenhair (*Adiantum pedatum*) is easy to grow in cold-temperate climates but not in warm ones. The Venus's hair (*A. capillus-veneris*) and the rough maidenhair (*A. hispidulum*) are good for warm, temperate, and subtropical climates. The delta maidenhair (*A. raddianum*) is more tender than the Venus's hair but possesses the advantage of having many attractive cultivars. The delta maidenhair and Venus's hair are sometimes slow to establish, but once in place they grow rapidly, particularly among cement sidewalks and foundations where presumably more calcium is present. In tropical areas and greenhouses, you can easily grow *A. tenerum* and the coarser-leaflet forms such as the silver-dollar fern (*A. peruvianum*), diamond maidenhair (*A. trapeziforme*), two-edged maidenhair (*A. anceps*), and large-leaved maidenhair (*A. macrophyllum*). The rough maidenhair tolerates lower humidity than most and is suitable as a houseplant.

Several species of maidenhair are especially attractive but difficult to grow. The kidney-shaped fronds of *Adiantum reniforme* are handsome and eye-catching, but the plant is tender and hard to cultivate. The trailing maidenhair (*A. caudatum*) is interesting for its long fronds that produce a new plantlet at their whip-like tips. It is easy to grow in well-drained soil but must be cultivated in a warm greenhouse. *Adiantum ×tracyi*, a semi-hardy, evergreen species, is rarely cultivated because it reproduces only from divisions, not spores. Large elegant fronds are produced by *A. formosum*, but because of its wide-creeping habit this species is not grown in pots, and few people have greenhouses with beds large enough to accommodate it. It will grow outdoors in warmer subtropical gardens.

An old favorite in cultivation is the Farley maidenhair (*Adiantum tenerum* 'Farleyense'). It has gracefully arching fronds and many ruffled segments. It develops most luxuriantly when grown in warm greenhouses with daytime temperatures near 21°C (70°F). Another maidenhair that is smaller but just as lovely is green petticoats (*A. capillus-veneris* 'Imbricatum'). It is a difficult fern for beginners but needs less heat than 'Farleyense'. *Adiantum raddianum* 'Pacific Maid' has broadly overlapping segments and the light fluffy look of the preceding two selections, but it is a more erect, stiffer plant. It is good for beginners and readily available in the trade.

With a greenhouse or similar means, many of the subtropical and tropical species can be grown without difficulty. Keep in mind their particular needs for humidity and consistently moist but well-aerated soil. For more details on cultivating *Adiantum*, see Chapter 13 and also Hoshizaki (1970a).

Staghorn Ferns

Staghorn ferns (*Platycerium*) are prized for their striking appearance and usefulness as decoration on walls or tree trunks. In subtropical climates the common ones are grown outdoors year-round, and once established, they require minimum care. Because they require only moderate humidity, staghorn ferns are suitable indoors, if provided with plenty of filtered light. Plants established and properly mounted need only be hung in place and watered and fertilized occasionally.

If plants are watered with a hose, water them thoroughly. Small plants may be soaked in water for 10 to 15 minutes. Do not be tempted to water or sprinkle staghorns every time you water other ferns. Staghorns need less water. More water will be required in a hot spell, less if the weather is cool and cloudy.

Staghorns are susceptible to overwatering by beginner growers because the outer surfaces of the base fronds may feel dry even if the spongy inner layers are completely saturated with water. To test the moisture, press your fingers firmly against the brown (not green) base fronds. If they are too wet, water will ooze out. If they feel moist but no water oozes out, the moisture level is just right and the plant should not be watered. Do not press against the freshly developed green base fronds because this can cause damage. Some growers wait until the moss at the bottom of the planting is dry and crumbly before watering. Others wait until the fertile fronds start to become limp. The weight of the plant also indicates relative wetness and dryness. You should learn to determine whether a plant needs water by lifting it and judging its weight.

Inadequate watering usually results in slow or no growth. A sudden and severe lack of water causes young fronds to wilt and the older ones to become limp and take on a grayish cast. The inner layers of base fronds will be dry. Sometimes drought-like symptoms are caused by sowbugs, pillbugs, slugs, and snails eating the emerging roots. These pests are best seen at night.

When deciding where to hang a staghorn fern, be sure that it will not receive a constant drip of water from overhanging baskets or from the eaves or roof. The symptoms of overwatering include no or poor growth, absence of new base fronds, soggy base fronds, algae developing on the moss, and (at worst) purplish to blackish decay spots on the base fronds.

Beginners should start with the easily grown species, such as *Platycerium bifurcatum*, *P. hillii*, and *P. veitchii*. Slightly more difficult to grow and needing warmer conditions are *P. willinckii* and *P. alcicorne*.

Staghorn ferns can be propagated from the buds or young plantlets that form on their roots and sometimes their rhizomes. These plantlets are called "pups" by some gardeners. When the pups are big enough, they can be separated from the parent plant. There is a greater chance of success if the pups are not removed until they have several brown base fronds. Spring is a good time to remove them, or just before fresh shield fronds grow out. Use a garden fork or knife to pry or cut beneath and around the oldest shield frond of the pup (Figure 10.1). If possible, take a little of the base frond from the mother plant. Slip your fingers into the cut and lift the pup from the mother plant. Plant the pup with the growing tip on the upper side.

The pups are usually mounted on either a tree or a board (Figures 10.2, 10.3). How you mount the pup on a board depends on the total thickness of the base fronds. If more than 2.5 cm (1 in.) thick, the pup can be mounted directly on a board and secured with wire (not copper) or stout strips of plastic. If the base fronds are less than 2.5 cm (1 in.) thick, then place a 2.5 to 5 cm (1–2 in.) pad of sphagnum moss between the base fronds and the board. If you are mounting the pup on a tree, do not wrap wire around the trunk,

Figure 10.1. Removing a plantlet, or pup, from a staghorn fern.

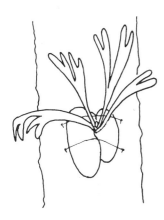

Figure 10.2. Planting a staghorn fern on a tree.

Figure 10.3. Planting a staghorn fern on a board, front and side view.

which might girdle the tree and kill it. Instead, use plastic strips, nylon fishing line, discarded hosiery, or string. If wire must be used, hammer small nails into the trunk and tie the wire to the nails.

It is also possible to grow a large staghorn in such a way that will not require remounting soon. Fill a broken clay pot, wire basket, or shallow box with a loose, coarse humusy soil, covering or lining it with sphagnum moss to keep the mixture from falling out (Figures 10.4, 10.5, 10.6). The moss can be kept in place by covering it with chicken wire in which a hole has been cut for the plantlet. The surface of the plant, particularly the buds, should be level with or slightly above the surface of the sphagnum moss. Plants so mounted will have the advantage of more rooting medium, but the disadvantage of being susceptible to overwatering. Recently mounted pups should be kept moist but well drained. When foliage no longer appears wilted, the plants can be placed in more exposed places. The wires or strips of plastic will soon be covered with new base fronds. Remounting established plants is the same as for mounting pups, except that old base fronds might need to be trimmed away. To grow large symmetrical staghorns, keep one plant and remove all the pups that appear.

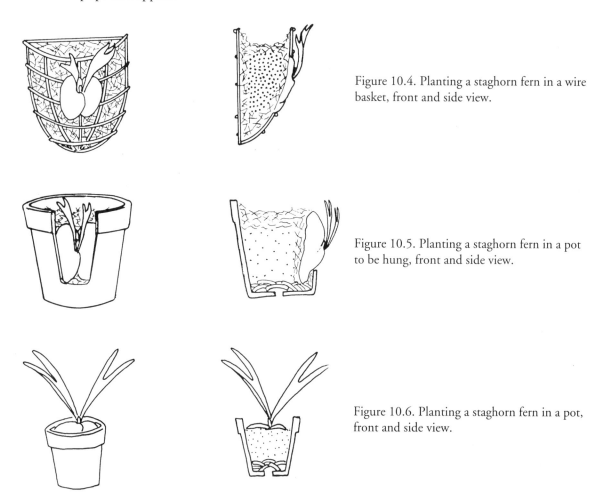

Figure 10.4. Planting a staghorn fern in a wire basket, front and side view.

Figure 10.5. Planting a staghorn fern in a pot to be hung, front and side view.

Figure 10.6. Planting a staghorn fern in a pot, front and side view.

Fertilize the plants about every three weeks, although less so during cooler months. Use liquid fertilizers because solid fertilizers, such as granules, powders, or pearl types, do not dissolve readily and, if caught between the base fronds, can burn the tissue or promote infection by mold.

Once fungi or bacteria infect a leaf they are difficult to control. Several control methods are available, but they are not always effective. Some growers report limited success by removing the decaying spot before it spreads. They cut at least 1.5 cm (0.5 in.) beyond the decayed area. Others soak the plant in fungicides (see Chapter 11). Some growers reduce the watering drastically in hope of killing the infection before killing the plant. Prevention is better than an uncertain cure. Do not overwater, and use only thoroughly dissolved fertilizer.

Aside from requiring a bright airy place and sufficient water, the common species of staghorn ferns pose no special problems and will reward you with their striking and unusual foliage. If you have experience growing the common species, the less common ones are also worth trying, although they can be more difficult. Most of these other species are large plants that require more space. See the references listed under *Platycerium* in Chapter 13 for more details.

Davallia

The squirrel's-foot fern, *Davallia mariesii* var. *stenolepis* (*D. trichomanoides* of trade), is the most commonly cultivated *Davallia*. Its finely divided triangular fronds attract attention, as do its long, chaffy rhizomes that can creep over an entire basket. Davallias are adaptable to a wide variety of situations. Although usually grown in hanging baskets or pots, they are also suitable as ground covers and even over rocks if given enough soil to secure a footing. They can also flourish indoors in sufficient light. Because they are epiphytes with firm-textured leaves, davallias can usually withstand the slightly drier air indoors better than most other ferns. They should not be kept too moist. If fertilized a few times during the growing season, *Davallia* plants will multiply readily from their creeping rhizomes.

Most davallias grow seasonally, shedding their fronds once a year between fall and spring and then entering a period of slow growth. Sometime later a flush of new growth fully refoliates the plant. The exact time of foliage shedding, and the length of time before new ones appear, varies with the species and climate. Fronds persist longer on luxuriantly growing plants. In warmer climates such as southern California and Florida, the deciduous habit of most species is hardly noticeable because new fronds appear before the old ones have withered. The fronds sometimes turn a beautiful yellow before they wither and drop. If old fronds have not fallen by the time new ones appear, they should be removed to provide room for the new ones. The self-shedding of spent fronds is a decided advantage in dealing with high-hanging baskets.

Baskets that become covered with layers of rhizomes should be replanted. In mild climates, the best time to do this is the fall or spring. Tear the clumps apart, saving those clumps with the most growing tips, and then discard the dead or old parts of the reusable clumps. Davallia baskets should be lined with uncut sphagnum moss and filled with a humusy, loose planting mix. Keep the basket moist but well drained, and set it in a humid place until the plants are established. Further details on planting in baskets are provided in Chapter 7.

The tender species *Davallia fejeensis* and *D. solida* are frequently seen in greenhouses and conservatories. In warm-temperate climates the following species will grow and withstand light frost and short periods of freezing temperatures: *D. canariensis, D. mariesii* var. *mariesii* and var. *stenolepis, D. pyxidata,* and *D. tyermannii.*

The Boston Fern and Its Relatives

The Boston fern and its relatives belong to the genus *Nephrolepis* and are among the most popular ferns for home and garden. The original Boston fern was the *Nephrolepis exaltata* cultivar 'Bostoniensis', from which numerous cultivars have been selected. Loosely speaking, the common name "Boston fern" has come to be used to describe the many cultivars of *N. exaltata*. In warm climates these ferns are particularly favored as indoor or outdoor pot or basket plants. They are mostly epiphytes and prefer bright airy places and good soil aeration. *Nephrolepis* species as a group do not like soggy soil and so should be kept on the drier side of moist, especially when they are not actively growing in cool weather. The fronds are fuller if provided with ample humidity and the plants regularly fertilized.

The most common causes of poor growth in these ferns are under-watering or overwatering, low humidity, and (for some species) cool winter temperatures. The well-known Boston fern cultivar 'Fluffy Ruffles' seems to tolerate slightly cooler temperatures than the other cultivars of *Nephrolepis exaltata*. Some of the fancy cultivars quickly succumb to poor cultural conditions and can soon yellow and shed their leaflets. Even with good growing conditions, however, a few lower leaflets on older fronds will yellow and should be trimmed off. *Nephrolepis* produces long, slender, scaly, string-like stems (stolons) from its central stem. These can be removed or wound around the plant and tucked inside the pot to keep a tidy look.

Repotting *Nephrolepis* is best done before active growth, usually in the spring. The taller, older plants may need to be set deeper into the soil than they were before, but be sure not to bury their stem tips. Cut away most of the old leaf bases from the stem. Avoid planting them in oversized pots; they tolerate being slightly root bound. Use an epiphytic soil mix or a mixture of half sand and half peat moss (see Chapter 5).

Most species of *Nephrolepis* can be propagated by sowing spores. All can be propagated by divisions or by layering the stolons, which produce new plants when they touch the soil. Planting in benches or shallow, broad containers gives the stolons room to spread in all directions and take root. The resulting plants can be separated and potted when they have two or more fronds. The Boston ferns usually do not produce spores and must be propagated by rooting the stolons or by meristem culture. Provide bright airy places for their culture. Commercial greenhouses use as much as 3000 to 3500 foot-candles of light or 73% shade cloth (see Chapter 8 for details on propagation).

The numerous cultivars of *Nephrolepis exaltata* offer a wide variety of sizes, shapes, and textures. Some cultivars produce fronds as long as 1.5 m (5 ft.), whereas others produce fronds that are extremely broad or narrow. These and other fancy-foliage forms, especially the finely divided ones, often grow slowly.

Boston fern cultivars with finely divided or congested fronds must be watered carefully. Their foliage cannot support water applied directly from above, which tends to mat and break the fronds. If allowed to remain on the leaves, the water causes the leaflets to have a dark, water-soaked appearance and can result in loss, disfigurement, or yellowing of the foliage. If water mats the foliage, gently shake it off or blot it up.

Cultivars with densely clustered leaves need to be groomed regularly. Remove the dead or declining fronds and unwanted stolons. This will allow more air and light to reach the younger growth below and give the plant a more attractive appearance.

Besides Boston fern, the tuber sword fern (*Nephrolepis cordifolia*) is easy to grow. It is probably the most cold tolerant of all sword ferns, being able to withstand short periods near 0°C (32°F). In subtropical and tropical climates it is commonly planted as an outdoor border plant—a purpose to which it is well suited because of its usually stiff, erect fronds. It can even be clipped like a hedge. The tuber sword fern has several cultivars, the most popular being 'Tesselata' ('Plumosa'), which has divided leaflets. 'Tesselata' grows more slowly than the species form. Even slower is 'Duffii', which has rounded leaflets and is best grown under glass (except in warm, humid climates where it can be grown outdoors).

The scurfy sword fern (*Nephrolepis hirsutula*) is rank and generally unattractive except in warm, humid places. It grows poorly where nighttime temperatures dip below 16°C (60°F) and has no advantage over the other species except that it grows easily from spores.

Nephrolepis species or cultivars with long, drooping fronds are difficult to find commercially because growers dislike the difficulties involved with growing and shipping them. They must be displayed in baskets or elevated containers to be attractive. Some long-frond types sold by specialty nurseries include *Nephrolepis falcata, N. pendula,* and *N. exaltata* and its cultivars 'Gretnae' and 'Rooseveltii'.

Polypodium and Relatives

The genus *Polypodium* and its relatives (the family Polypodiaceae) form a large and diverse group that varies greatly in cultural requirements. Most are epiphytes and grow best in baskets or hanging containers with good drainage and aeration. Others can be grown in the ground if provided with good drainage and not overwatered. Most cultivated species are tender or semi-tender and therefore must be grown in greenhouses in most parts of the United States. They need ample light but should never be placed in direct sun. They prefer a loose, humusy soil mix. Creeping types are best planted in a moss-lined basket so that they can root in the moss as they grow. (For a monographic treatment of the group, see Roos 1985.)

The rabbit's-foot ferns or golden polypodies (*Phlebodium*) are among the most popular polypodiums grown in the United States. *Phlebodium aureum* and *P. pseudoaureum* include several cultivars, some of which have attractive bluish gray foliage. Once established, the golden polypodies grow rapidly if given plenty of light. They should be watered when the soil is nearly dry. Some selections tolerate cold better than others. Variants with broader, thinner lobes and sori in two or more rows on each side of the segment need warmer temperatures than those with the narrower, firm lobes and sori in one to nearly two rows on each side of the segment. The bluish green *P. aureum* 'Mandaianum' has thin, ruffled lobes. If unblemished fronds are desired, grow it indoors or in sheltered places.

Knight's polypody (*Goniophlebium subauriculatum* 'Knightiae') is another favorite basket fern. The long, pinnate fronds are fringed and arch down to form a beautiful hanging plant. Established plants tolerate irregular watering. Outdoors in warm areas, the old fronds are shed in spring but are soon replaced with new ones. The cut fronds last a long time in flower arrangements.

Another polypody fern, *Microsorum pustulatum,* is not widely cultivated but should be. In England it is a hardy fern, and it should be tried in cooler areas of the United States. *Microsorum pustulatum* is medium-sized with deeply divided blades resembling those of the East Indian polypody (*M. scolopendria*).

Microsorum punctatum 'Grandiceps' makes a handsome houseplant. Its thick, glossy leaves, ruffled and irregularly forked or notched, withstand the drier air of the indoors admirably well. Because it grows slowly, it seldom needs repotting.

A coarse, large, durable member of the polypody group is *Aglaomorpha coronans.* Although it grows slowly, the species tolerates periods of dryness and aridity once established. Remove the old fronds as they start to decline, because otherwise the individual leaflets will drop and scatter about.

Most of the small polypodium relatives that have simple, entire fronds are tender species and must be grown in humid greenhouses or terrariums. Because they are small, they are not particularly showy and therefore seldom seen in collections. One of these small species, *Microgramma squamulosa,* is attractive due to its dark veins.

The temperate species of *Polypodium* vary in their cultural needs. The more common ones are planted in baskets or among rocks. The licorice fern (*Polypodium glycyrrhiza*) often volunteers in baskets lined with moss collected from western Canada and the western United States. A choice species is the leathery polypody (*P. scouleri*), which grows along the coast in the Northwest. Its fronds are small- to medium-sized, deeply lobed, thick, and glossy. It grows slowly and is suitable for pots and baskets in cool humid climates. The resurrection fern (*P. polypodioides*), a common epiphyte in the southeastern United States, is a small fern that curls its leaves during drought and unrolls them when wet weather returns; it is difficult to establish.

Tree Ferns

Whether planted individually or in groups, tree ferns are sure to be noticed. They can provide a background for other plants, and their trunks can be used to display small epiphytic orchids, tillandsias, and ferns.

Most ferns that bear fronds at the top of a tall trunk are called tree ferns by gardeners, although such growth forms are found in unrelated ferns such as *Sadleria, Blechnum,* and *Ctenitis.* Most of the ferns in the *Dicksonia* and *Cyathea* families (Dicksoniaceae and Cyatheaceae) are tree-like and are the ones typically referred to as tree ferns by botanists. They range from 1 to 15 m (3–50 ft.) tall. In many species, the girth of the trunk is increased by producing a thick layer of hard, dark, tangled roots—the root mantle. This layer forms a substrate on which epiphytic plants grow.

Ferns of the *Cyathea* and *Dicksonia* families, as well as some tree-fern-like members of *Blechnum,* are mostly native to cool, moist mountainous regions of the tropics (a few species occur in warm-temperate areas). There are about 700 species in these two families, but probably fewer than 50 have been tried in cultivation in Europe and the United States.

Temperature tolerances of the tree ferns are the first consideration in selecting them for cultivation. Some species tolerate occasional frost and mild freezes, whereas others are intolerant of prolonged periods at temperatures of 15°C (59°F). Nighttime temperatures are also an important consideration because many species prefer cooler nighttime than daytime temperatures. Those tree ferns native to lowland tropics where nighttime and daytime temperatures are relatively constant do well outdoors in tropical gardens. The many species native to Australia and New Zealand grow well outdoors in subtropical areas, and some (such as *Dicksonia antarctica*) grow in mild-temperate areas. In cold-temperate areas, tree ferns must be moved indoors during the winter.

Tree ferns should be planted in well-drained soil. Add peat and sand (or perlite) to heavy soils, or replace parts of it. Windy sites must be avoided. Although some species can grow in direct sun, they are more luxuriant in shade. Water from overhead leaves or hanging baskets should not be allowed to drip into the crowns of tree ferns. Provide plenty of overhead space for development. Tree-fern diseases continue to be reported on wild and cultivated species. *Rhizoctonia* and tip blight (see Chapter 11) infect tree ferns, and there may be other diseases as well.

Although some tree ferns can be shortened by severing their trunks and replanting them, the risk involved in doing this is high. Some species root from trunks more readily than others. The Australian tree fern of the trade, *Sphaeropteris cooperi,* does not root from severed trunks, whereas *Cibotium glaucum, C. menziesii,* and *Dicksonia antarctica* root fairly well.

Cutting the trunk is best done before the active growing period and before new fronds emerge (usually in the spring). After cutting, dust the cut ends with a fungicide to protect against rot, then plant in a pot with a well-drained soil mix, and water sparingly to discourage rotting. Avoid watering the crowns, which are fleshy and prone to rot. The number of remaining fronds can be reduced by half to prevent too much water being lost from the trunk. If the trunks are too fleshy and not in danger of drying, it might be best to wait before planting until a protective "skin" develops over the cut tissue. To encourage this, put the trunk in a cool, humid place and keep it from drying. After the skin develops, plant the trunks about one-fourth to one-third their length into moist soil, making sure to keep the trunks shaded and humid. When new fronds emerge, the plant can be watered more. A few months before cutting the trunk, wrap a layer of moist uncut sphagnum moss above the cutting point. This encourages roots to form, which then grow into the moss. The moss layer should be thick enough that it will not dry quickly. Ample humidity and warmth hasten root formation.

The Australian-native Cooper's tree fern (*Sphaeropteris cooperi*) is the most frequently grown tree fern in the United States. It grows in sun or shade in coastal, central, and southern California, in southern Florida, and in conservatories in cooler areas. It tolerates frost and short periods of freezing temperatures, but its foliage might die back. On older plants the fronds tend to spread more horizontally than on younger plants and may be 6 m (20 ft.) across. The trunks are relatively slender, and cultivated plants seldom form extensive aerial roots enveloping the stem. Because these roots are usually absent, the trunks are weak and can snap off in strong winds. Therefore Cooper's tree fern is best grown under tall trees where their crowns have room to spread but are protected from wind. The lower fronds will droop or drop several times a year. This foliage drooping is usually accompanied or preceded by a heavy discharge of spores. For the sake of neatness, drooping fronds close to the trunk can be removed, but if left on the plant they eventually dry and fall off on their own. Under optimum conditions this fern may grow 30 cm (1 ft.) per year when young, and the cultivar *S. cooperi* 'Brentwood' grows even more rapidly. The fronds and trunk of Cooper's tree fern are covered with many small scales that can irritate the skin and especially the eyes. Washing the skin removes the scales and itching. Goggles should be worn to protect the eyes when working with this fern.

The Tasmanian dicksonia (*Dicksonia antarctica*) is the second most frequently cultivated tree fern. It is semi-hardy to semi-tender and has been reported to endure −7°C (20°F), or a bit lower for short periods, as well as snow on its fronds. It prefers an average winter temperature of about 9°C (48°F). Its fronds are shorter, narrower, stiffer, harsher, and more numerous than those of *Sphaeropteris cooperi*. The crown of foliage reaches about 4 m (13 ft.) across and has a tufted appearance on the stout trunk. It grows more slowly than Cooper's tree fern—about one-third as fast. The Tasmanian dicksonia prefers climates influenced by the ocean or cool and humid conditions. *Dicksonia fibrosa* and *D. squarrosa* are seldom cultivated because they are more difficult to grow.

The Hawaiian tree fern (*Cibotium glaucum*) is seen now and then in outdoor plantings in southern California. Bare-root trunks are imported from the Hawaiian Islands, and these can be rooted by planting them about one-third their length in a well-drained soil mix. Spore-grown plants form more symmetrical crowns but are infrequently found in the trade. The fronds of the Hawaiian tree fern tend to ascend and arch more gracefully than those of Cooper's tree fern. Their leaf bases and trunks are covered with silky, yellowish tan hairs, unlike the chaffy scales of Cooper's tree fern.

Occasionally, trunks of *Cibotium menziesii* and *Sadleria cyatheoides* are found in shipments of *C. glaucum* trunks due to their similar appearance. *Cibotium menziesii* is called the "man fern" by the Hawaiians, possibly because its trunk is covered with stiff black hairs. It requires the same cultural conditions as the Hawaiian tree fern. *Sadleria cyatheoides* tends to be more difficult to grow than the other Hawaiian species and is sensitive to having its roots disturbed. Bare-root trunks of this species may be distinguished from others by the presence of scales instead of hairs. *Sadleria* and Hawaiian cibotiums tend to grow more slowly than *Sphaeropteris cooperi*.

The Mexican tree fern (*Cibotium schiedei*) was once widely sold as a houseplant, but it grows too big for the average house. It hardly forms a trunk but produces offshoots freely around its base. Its many light green fronds droop gracefully to give the plant a soft effect.

The silver tree fern (*Alsophila tricolor*) and the black tree fern (*Sphaeropteris medullaris*) need more protection from wind and sun than other tree-fern species to look their best.

Cultivated species that resemble tree ferns include *Blechnum gibbum* and *B. brasiliense*. These ferns are medium-sized and form erect trunk-like stems. They are semi-tender to tender. The plant sometimes called the American tree fern (*Ctenitis sloanei*) is native to southern Florida and might form a short, erect stem, giving it a tree-fern–like appearance. *Diplazium esculentum* could be considered a small tree fern because it produces an upright stem, but it is only 2 to 4 cm (0.75–1.5 in.) in diameter. This Asian species has become naturalized in Louisiana and Florida. It is cultivated in Florida and California.

Xerophytic Ferns

Xerophytes are plants adapted to dry climates. Many xerophytic ferns grow in the arid southwestern United States. In more humid regions of the country, they are found in exposed places such as on tree branches, rocks, or cliffs.

Many fern genera have xerophytic species. Genera that are mostly xerophytes include *Actiniopteris, Astrolepis, Cheilanthes, Doryopteris, Notholaena, Pellaea,* and *Pityrogramma*. Hairs, scales, or powder cover the foliage of many xerophytic ferns to help retain moisture. These coverings can be white, silver, or yellow and make the fern especially attractive. Ferns that are adapted to dry climates are often small and therefore suitable for rock or trough gardens. Some xerophytic species are challenging to grow and may require several attempts before the proper conditions are found.

In cultivation, xerophytic ferns grow best in bright but indirect sunlight, except along cloudy coastal areas where they may be planted in full sun. They prefer a well-drained soil kept on the drier side of moist.

Most grow well in an evenly moist soil or one that does not rapidly fluctuate between wet and dry. In general, the fronds should be kept free of water droplets resulting from condensation and overhead watering, although fog does not seem to bother some xerophytic ferns.

Soil mixes range from simple to complex, but all must be well drained. A simple mix consists of one part peat moss or leaf mold and one to two parts gravelly sand. A more complex mix consists of one to two parts decomposed granite about 6 mm (0.2 in.) in diameter, two parts compost (leaf mold or fir bark), one part perlite (#2 size), and one part sand (#20 size). Adding horticultural charcoal to the mix is optional, as is placing a top dressing of half-inch fine gravel on the soil surface after planting.

Xerophytes should be planted with their crowns slightly above the soil. If using pots, make sure that the soil level is close to the rim in order to reduce the amount of water that could be caught in the pot during watering. A process known as double potting maintains uniform soil moisture over a longer time. The fern is planted in a porous clay pot, which in turn is planted in a larger clay pot, usually 5 to 7.5 cm (2–3 in.) wider than the first. The same soil mix is used in both pots. Xerophytes can be successfully grown in terrariums if the soil moisture is carefully monitored and the humidity not excessive. Soil water evaporates slowly in a terrarium, thus maintaining a more constant moisture level. In such a protected environment fronds may develop more fully than in nature.

Outdoors, xerophytes are often planted in trough gardens (see "Trough Gardens" earlier in the chapter), among rocks, or on well-drained sites (also see "Rock Garden and Wall Ferns" in Chapter 9). Xerophytic ferns are extremely sensitive to overwatering and can die if overwatered only a few times, and so they should be planted away from plants that require more water. Whether in the ground or in pots, the plants should be watered early in the morning so that any water settling on the fronds will evaporate during the day.

Most xerophytic ferns go dormant during the summer in their native habitats. In cultivation, however, dormancy might not occur. In addition, many xerophytic ferns grow more slowly or go dormant as cool weather approaches. Dormant or slow-growing plants need less water.

Filmy Ferns

Filmy ferns have been grown successfully in botanical gardens and private collections and were popularly grown in Wardian cases in England during the Victorian era. These mostly small ferns are distinctive by their membranous leaves usually one cell thick between the veins. Because of their thinness, the plants need high humidity and shade. They also require good drainage. In nature most grow as epiphytes or terrestrially, and the group reaches its greatest development in tropical montane forests that are covered by clouds most of the day and have an abundance of mosses on tree trunks and branches. The filmy-fern family (Hymenophyllaceae) also includes the kidney fern (*Trichomanes reniforme*), an eye-catching species cultivated in New Zealand and Australia but rarely in the United States. The elegant Prince-of-Wales plume (*Leptopteris superba*) is not a filmy fern even though it has membranous leaves; however, it does require the same cultural conditions as filmy ferns. It is rarely grown in the United States but is grown in Australia, New Zealand, and England.

Filmy ferns from warm-temperate areas grow well in temperatures from 4 to 21°C (40–70°F), although they also tolerate short periods of slightly lower or higher temperatures. Climates where temperatures are consistently higher than 27°C (80°F) for days are unsuitable. Most tropical species come from cooler montane forests and grow best in temperatures ranging from 16 to 24°C (60–75°F). In favorable climates filmy ferns can be grown in terrariums or bottles provided with uncut sphagnum moss or a well-drained potting soil. In warm climates, air conditioners are needed to keep the temperature low.

Special chambers or houses, often located in a shady corner of a greenhouse, can be built to hold filmy ferns. An intermittent misting system should be installed and, depending on the climate, possibly some means of cooling. The chamber's top and one side should be made out of glass or translucent plastic. If the chamber is situated in an area with abundant light, only the top needs to be glass. Line the walls with uncut sphagnum moss held in place by nylon fishing line or chicken wire (do not use copper wire). Plant the ferns in pots or on pieces of tree-fern trunk and hang them on the moss, or plant them directly into the wall of moss. Humidity should be kept near 100% by misting several times a day or by automatic humidifiers. Chamber walls can also be made out of hollow concrete blocks filled with sphagnum moss or suitable excelsiors. The filled blocks are placed with the open end up, and a pipe set on the top of the block drips water into the moss to keep the walls moist. Ferns are hung in pots against the wall. Some means of draining the water away from the enclosure should be provided. The quality of water can also pose problems. If the salt content is high, salt-free water will have to be used. Farrar (1968) achieved good growth of filmy ferns in chambers at 100% relative humidity with temperatures between 18 and 24°C (65–75°F) and indirect natural light at or below 300 foot-candles. The ferns were given a fine mist for 15 minutes every hour.

Fern Allies

Fern allies are the whisk ferns (*Psilotum*), ground pines (*Lycopodium*), spike mosses (*Selaginella*), and horsetails (*Equisetum*). Like ferns, these plants reproduce by dispersing spores, but none has leaves like ferns. Instead, the leaves of the fern allies are small, inconspicuous, and often scale-like with only a single vein. Water clovers (*Marsilea*), mosquito ferns (*Azolla*), and water spangles (*Salvinia*) are ferns but might be mistaken for fern allies because of their unfernlike appearance.

PSILOTUMS OR WHISK FERNS

A handful of stems from a *Psilotum* plant resembles a small whisk broom, hence the name whisk fern. The green stems seem leafless but actually bear scattered, small, scale-like leaves. The upper branches may have rounded, three-lobed sporangia (spore cases). The plants grow on trees, especially in the leaf axils of old palm leaves, or in rock pockets in tropical or subtropical areas. They grow easily in greenhouses with strong light and respond well to bone meal and general fertilizers. Propagation is easy by division of the rhizome clump, although transplants are sometimes slow to establish. In greenhouses the plants volunteer readily from spores, but growing by the intentional sowing of the spores is difficult. Laboratory studies indicate that it can take as long as 3 to 18 months for spore germination. The gametophytes (comparable to the prothalli of ferns) are about 4 mm (0.2 in.) long, cylindrical, and grow beneath the soil.

LYCOPODIUMS OR GROUND PINES

Lycopodiums are terrestrial or epiphytic species with erect, creeping, trailing, or drooping stems. They range from a few inches tall to several feet long. The stems are amply covered with scale-like leaves, some of which have small roundish to bean-shaped spore cases (sporangia) at their base.

The temperate species of *Lycopodium* are particularly difficult to grow from transplants because they do not readily re-establish themselves in a new location. Transplants have been reported to establish successfully by planting in oak-leaf mold and applying aluminum sulfate to maintain acidity (amounts not specified). The plants were kept constantly moist. Transplants of *Lycopodium selago* have been successfully grown in uncut sphagnum moss watered with distilled water or water treated by reverse osmosis.

A few tropical epiphytic lycopodiums, such as *Lycopodium phlegmaria* and *L. phlegmarioides,* are grown in moss-lined hanging baskets or anchored on boards with a pad of uncut moss. Boards of tree-fern fiber are used in Florida. Warmth, humidity, and constantly moist soil with good drainage are required for most epiphytic species.

Tropical epiphytic lycopodiums are usually propagated by divisions or layering because they are difficult to start from cuttings. Species such as *Lycopodium phlegmaria* can be propagated by layering or by anchoring the stem tips in vermiculite or sand and waiting for rootlets to develop. Rooting should take place in six to eight months, after which the plantlets can be separated from the mother plant.

Besides layering, cuttings are another method of propagating, although it tends to be less successful. The usual procedure is to take 8 cm (3 in.) long pieces from the tips of stems bearing sterile leaves (that is, those not bearing sporangia). The leaves are removed from the lower third, and the cutting is rooted in clean potting soil mixed with four to five parts sand. Be careful not to overwater the potting soil, otherwise rot can easily result. Provide the cuttings with only enough moisture and humidity to prevent rotting. The temperate *Lycopodium selago* has been successfully propagated from cuttings rooted in uncut sphagnum moss and watered with distilled water. Whether propagating by layering or cutting, some bottom heat will hasten the process.

Growing lycopodiums from spores is rarely done, but the process would be essentially the same as for selaginellas, discussed in the following section.

SELAGINELLAS OR SPIKE MOSSES

Selaginellas are more widely cultivated than lycopodiums. The name spike moss refers to the spike-like cluster of fertile leaves at the branch tips. About 700 species of *Selaginella* exist worldwide, some of which are adapted to deserts (where they are often nestled between rocks) and others are found on rain-forest floors. Almost all the species are terrestrial. Some resemble lycopodiums, but the cultivated species are generally softer, mossier, or fernier compared to the stiffer, harder-textured lycopodiums. The two genera also differ by their spores: *Selaginella* produces two kinds of spores (separate male and female), whereas *Lycopodium* produces only one (bisexual).

The resurrection plant (*Selaginella lepidophylla*) is one of the few desert species that are grown. It requires excellent drainage and less humidity than other selaginellas. Most of the temperate species are small plants, moss-like in growth and useful as ground covers. *Selaginella apoda* often invades moist, shaded lawns in the eastern United States. In humid warm-temperate areas, *S. kraussiana* can also be invasive. Most tropical species thrive in warm, humid greenhouses, growing luxuriantly at temperatures of 21°C (70°F) or more. They tend not to be too fussy about their soil mix as long as it retains adequate moisture and is well drained. They respond well to regular applications of fertilizer. The erect forms (such as *S. umbrosa*) are used as taller ground covers or in pots.

Most selaginellas can be propagated by cuttings or layering (pegging the foliage to the soil and waiting for it to root). All can be propagated by dividing the clump. Species that root all along the underside of the stem are easily propagated by about 4 cm (1.5 in.) long cuttings placed in clean builder's sand and finely misted three or four times a day until rooted. Species that root only near the base of the stem are more difficult to root by cuttings. All species may be propagated sexually.

To propagate by spores, select recently matured fertile spikes or leaf clusters that have unopened sporangia—the sporangia appear as plump, rounded, yellowish structures at the base of each fertile leaf. Cut the spikes into short lengths and scatter them over a clean, firmed, well-drained mix of one part garden soil and four to five parts sand. (Other mixes such as uncut sphagnum moss have also been used.) Some of this finely screened soil should be sprinkled over the spike pieces to anchor them. The container or flat is then watered gently and covered with a piece of glass or plastic wrap and kept at 21°C (70°F). About nine months later, small plants should appear.

For this method it is important to use mature fertile branches containing male and female spores. If the maturity of the fertile branches is difficult to determine, pick and sow them at intervals to increase the probability that both kinds of spores will be present. The methods for hybridizing selaginellas are somewhat involved due to the presence of male and female spores. For details, see Webster (1979).

EQUISETUMS, HORSETAILS, OR SCOURING RUSHES

Horsetails (*Equisetum*) are reed-like plants with jointed, hollow stems that range from a few centimeters to about 6 m (20 ft.) tall. Because they grow near or in wet areas and their stems contain silica, pioneers used them for scrubbing pots, hence the name scouring rush. They are useful in wet parts of the garden such as pools, or as novelties in pots. Some species are deciduous. They are well suited to full sun or bright light and wet soil or standing water. Some species spread aggressively from underground stems, sending up isolated erect stems. The winter scouring-rush (*Equisetum hyemale*) is a particularly aggressive spreader. It is difficult to eradicate once established and should be planted in sunken containers to limit its spread.

Horsetails can be propagated by rhizome divisions, cuttings, or spores. Division works best with large rhizome pieces that have new shoots or buds attached. The divisions can be planted in various kinds of soil but do best in soil that is low in organic matter, about 25% (wet organic soils spoil or sour readily). To propagate from cuttings, cut the stem into pieces containing at least three joints. Plant the pieces upright with about one-half to two-thirds of their length in sand. Keep the cuttings moist until lateral shoots appear; if drying is a problem, pots may be placed in a shallow saucer of water. Guarding against poor aeration and sour soil is particularly important during the rooting process. Some species can be propagated by bending the stems of the mother plant and anchoring them in place in the soil or in a pot of water until well rooted.

The spores of equisetums are contained in cones at the stem tips. In some species the cones appear on green stems, and in other species they are produced only in the spring on ephemeral, nongreen, erect shoots. The hexagonal plates on the cone separate when the spores are ready to be shed, and this is the time to collect the spores for propagation. The spores are green and remain viable for only a few days. They should be sown soon after collecting. The procedures for sowing and growing are the same as for ferns (see Chapter 8). The germinated spores will develop into disk- or cushion-shaped gametophytes typically about 3 mm (0.1 in.) long. When transplanting the gametophytes, keep them in small clumps to ensure a mix of male and female gametophytes. (Gametophytes are at first either male or female, but females can later become bisexual.) Young sporelings are transplanted by the same procedures as for ferns.

Ferns for Shows and Exhibits

GROWING SHOW FERNS

The beautiful ferns seen in shows and exhibits can be grown by any gardener willing to give a little time on a regular schedule. Consistency and staying alert for sudden changes in weather or growing conditions are especially important. Large, showy plants need plenty of space to produce symmetrical growth, but small- to medium-sized plants can be grown in limited space. Although large ferns make spectacular show subjects, the smaller species are often more interesting and too frequently overlooked by amateurs. Particularly for show plants, you need to provide the following conditions:

1. Ample growing space protected from temperature extremes and wind. Crowded plants compete for light and usually produce lopsided foliage. Space lacking adequate protection from the weather is of no avail because the fronds will become disfigured or damaged.
2. Light on all sides. Evenly distributed light will help produce symmetrical growth. If the light is stronger on one side of the fern, turn the fern each week to encourage symmetrical growth. For large baskets, attaching a swivel to the wire-hang will assist in turning the plant.

3. Frequent, dilute applications of fertilizers. Make frequent applications of fertilizer at one-quarter strength rather than monthly applications at full strength. Apply weak solutions every one to two weeks during periods of active growth. If water spots (salt deposits) appear on the leaves, apply the fertilizer solution to the soil, not the foliage.

4. Groom plants as necessary. Grooming encourages the development of perfect fronds. Remove yellowed, damaged, and misshapen fronds, as well as those that crowd perfectly formed and positioned fronds.

5. Produce one large plant. Most show entries are based on one plant per container or entry, unless you enter under a multiple-plant category. Offshoots produced in close proximity to the crown of the main plant should be removed if one large plant is desired. Use a sharp knife to cut the rhizome, but pull the roots of the two plants apart with a fork or your fingers. Tearing the roots apart will leave more roots on the offshoot and the parent than cutting them will. Ferns with creeping, branched, mat-forming rhizomes are considered a single plant and need not be reduced to one creeping rhizome.

6. Be alert to unfavorable growing conditions such as pest damage, sudden dry weather, heavy rain, strong winds, or other unexpected changes. Cope with such situations immediately. Spots and blemishes are often due to plant stresses that are avoidable. Do not procrastinate!

7. Before the show, groom the plants carefully. Remove water spots and dust from the foliage. Commercial polishes may be used on coarse, leathery ferns, but they give an artificial shine that is objectionable to some judges. Before show time, clean the pots of algae and salt. If it is customary to cover the soil in the pot for entry, do so with materials that will not detract from the effect of the plant. To prevent damage during transport, wrap the plant in a cone of newspaper. Ferns with spreading fronds might need to have their fronds tied back to avoid damage. Soft strips of fabric or women's hosiery can be used to tie back the fronds. Do not transport the plants in an open vehicle unless they are well protected. Do not leave them in a closed vehicle on a hot day. Anchor them securely in place for transport.

8. Register plants carefully. Follow the registration procedures for the show and enter the plants in the proper category. Be certain the exhibitor's ticket is secured to the plants. Before you leave the plants, check that they have enough water, and make arrangements to have them watered during the show if this is not done by the show authorities.

FORCING FERNS

Some hardy deciduous ferns that are to be exhibited out of season may be forced into early growth for the show. Others, such as *Woodsia glabella* and *Polystichum braunii,* apparently do not take kindly to forcing. Some will develop deformed fronds, and others will collapse soon after producing fronds.

Thurston (1939) successfully forced many ferns from New England and mid-Atlantic states for a flower show in March. The ferns were planted in pots or flats in fall or earlier. They were placed in outdoor frames and covered with lath. As the weather cooled, the ferns were gradually covered with leaves. The ferns were permitted to freeze in November but under the protection of layers of leaves, branches, lath, glass sash, and straw so as to be easy to dig out at the end of December. Plants were then removed from the frames and placed in a dark shed to thaw for four days at temperatures between 4 and 10°C (40–50°F). Afterward they were moved to a greenhouse and given light and exposed to temperatures of 13°C (55°F) during the day and 4 to 10°C (40–50°F) during the night. After five days, the temperature was raised to 21°C (70°F) during the day and 10°C (50°F) at night. The water, heat, light, humidity, and ventilation for each species was judiciously adjusted in the greenhouse. The water given was at 21°C (70°F) and was not permitted to touch the foliage of most of the ferns; the exceptions were *Camptosorus* and others that like humidity, which were misted to create relative humidity of 80%. Hardening off of the ferns began in the second week of February, and temperatures dropped to 13 to 16°C (55–60°F) during the day and to 7 to 10°C (45–50°F) at night. The ferns were ready for the show by the first week of March. Thurston observed that forced ferns produced good growth for the show, but the continued new growth was not as vigorous as in nonforced ferns.

Most semi-hardy and more tender ferns can be kept in show condition by keeping them in warm greenhouses and protecting the fronds from damage. Little is known about forcing tender species that are deciduous.

11   Troubles with Growing Ferns

Recognizing Cultural Troubles

The earlier you detect and correct a problem, the better. As soon as your fern starts to decline, consider its basic conditions. Have you been giving it too much or too little water? Has the weather turned too cool for the fern? Have you forgotten to fertilize, or have you fertilized incorrectly? Is the light sufficient? Is the plant entering its rest period? Most troubles are caused by poor cultural conditions, unless, of course, there are pests. Common symptoms and causes of illnesses are outlined here. (See also Chapter 4 for more details on providing proper cultural conditions.)

SYMPTOM: SLOW GROWTH; FEW NEW FRONDS; THE FRONDS YELLOWISH OR ABNORMALLY LIGHT GREEN.

Common Cause	*Possible Solution*
Plant is entering its normal rest period or dormancy.	Check species for deciduous habit.
Plant is overwatered, especially if the lower leaves yellow and the soil is wet most of the time.	Decrease water and/or increase drainage. Use coarser soil mixes. Use clay instead of plastic pots. If the plant is overpotted, plant it in a smaller pot.
Temperatures are too low.	Growth improves when the plant is moved to a warmer location, or as the cool weather turns warmer.
Too much light, especially if the plant is in direct sun or very bright indirect light.	Reduce light.
Not enough fertilizer, especially if the new leaves are small and slow to grow.	Fertilize.
Plant is root-bound, especially if it wilts between waterings and roots can be seen to have filled the pot.	Repot.

Symptom: Fronds partially yellowed, browned, or burned; new growth shriveled or wilted.

Common Cause	*Possible Solution*
Air is too dry. Plant may be in draft or wind, especially if damage is along the edges of the frond and appears after a windy or dry period.	Increase humidity or move the plant to a more protected place.
Temperatures are too high. If this is the case, the damaged spots will be found where the leaf is most exposed to the heat source. The frond's margins may also be burned. Damage appears after or during a heat wave.	Provide more shade and ventilation. Lower the temperature in greenhouses.
Soil was or is too dry.	Parts of a wilted frond may recover, but other parts may be permanently damaged. Trim off dead parts, water well, then keep the plant moist, not wet.
Too much light.	Reduce light.
Insecticide, fungicide, or fertilizer burn, especially if treatment has been applied around the plant.	Trim away badly damaged parts.
Water-soaked tissue, resulting in brown spots or areas.	Trim away badly damaged parts. Do not permit water to sit on fronds.
Salt damage, especially if a thick white crust accumulates on the pot or soil and the water is known to contain high amounts of salt.	Use fertilizers sparingly. Leach the soil thoroughly. Water less frequently but more thoroughly.
Frost or freeze damage, especially if the weather has been cold.	Trim back dead parts.

Symptom: Edges of the frond cupping under; fronds distorted.

Common Cause	*Possible Solution*
Dryness when fronds were developing.	Provide more soil moisture and humidity. Damaged fronds cannot be restored.
Earlier gas, insect, or insecticide damage.	Remove toxic gas or insects; change insecticides. Damaged fronds cannot be restored.

Symptom: Fronds suddenly wilting without evidence of burn or injury.

Common Cause	*Possible Solution*
Root damage caused by drying or overfertilization.	Water well, then keep plant moist but not wet.

Root damage caused by overwatering or noxious materials. The soil may smell bad.

If roots have deteriorated, trim dead parts away, replant the rhizome into fresh soil, keep moist but not wet, and hope for the best.

SYMPTOM: FRONDS SKIMPY IN DEVELOPMENT, APPEARING STRETCHED-OUT.

Common Cause
Not enough light.

Possible Solution
Give more light.

SYMPTOM: FRONDS WITH GOOD COLOR, AMPLE IN SIZE, BUT THIN AND LACKING FIRMNESS.

Common Cause
Too much humidity.
Too much nitrogen fertilizer.

Possible Solution
Reduce humidity.
Reduce nitrogen fertilizer.

Recognizing Pests and Diseases

If you cannot find any problems with the basic cultural conditions, inspect the plant for signs of insects, fungi, bacteria, or other pests. A hand lens is helpful. Nursery growers generally find that cultural problems are uniformly distributed in nursery plots and tend to produce more regular patterns on plants, whereas pests and diseases are spotty and localized and spread in a gradient from the original infection, making more irregular patterns on the plant crop. Home growers, not having the uniformity of a large crop to check, must look at individual plants with the eyes of a detective.

For signs of pest or disease damage, check the roots for abnormalities, particularly decay. Look carefully on the undersides of the fronds for specks, dots, or unusual-looking structures—do not confuse these with the clusters of spore cases or sori. Most sori are regularly placed on the underside of the frond, whereas insects are unevenly scattered and often favor nesting in the angle of the veins. Sucking insects can cause poor growth, puckered foliage, distortion, bleached spots, and discoloration (discoloration is also caused by nematodes). The most common sucking insects on ferns are aphids, scale insects, mealybugs, and thrips. Biting insects and pests chew parts of the frond away. Some of the common examples are grasshoppers, caterpillars, cutworms, pillbugs, sowbugs, slugs, and snails. Their presence may often be indicated by frass on the foliage.

Fungal or bacterial infections usually accompany overwatering or excessive humidity. They usually produce symptoms such as tissue that is rotted, slimy, or water-soaked. Sometimes colonies of the organisms can be seen as tufts or mats of mold, sooty spots, and circular spots of dead tissue, particularly those with small dots or concentric patterns. The organisms can be found anywhere on the plant. Do not overlook the base of the stipe near the soil; infections sometimes start there. Fungi can cause sudden wilting of the plant, marginal browning of fronds, and distortion of emerging fronds. These symptoms, however, are difficult to distinguish from culturally caused troubles.

Alternatives to Chemical Controls

Some pesticides and fungicides are toxic to humans, pets, and many beneficial organisms. Alternatives to the use of these chemicals are being actively researched by scientists. Some of the alternatives are cultural and physical methods, biological control, and use of nontoxic or low-toxic controls. These methods can control a specific pest with one or more applications. Repeating the application as needed will be satisfactory for most cases. Attaining long-term control with few repeat applications and still avoiding the use of toxic chemicals requires integrating and analyzing a range of information. This approach is called Integrated Pest Management (IPM). The identity of the pest, its life cycle, the cultural conditions that can thwart them or favor their enemies, use of predators or parasites, and when, how much, and under what conditions to release these predators are types of information that must be known and assessed for each situation. In its fullest sense, IPM is a holistic approach. More information on IPM can be obtained from local libraries, county agricultural offices, and organizations or journals devoted to the subject.

BIOLOGICAL CONTROLS

Biological control uses beneficial organisms to kill pests. Familiar control organisms include the praying mantis, lady bugs, lacewings, ant lions, spiders, lizards, toads, and birds. Less well known are bacteria, fungi, nematodes, parasitic mites, and wasps. All these controls are harmless to humans and pets. New control organisms for specific pests are constantly being offered, and inquires should be made to county agricultural extension services for restrictions and suppliers.

To work effectively, control organisms must be released before infestation becomes severe and well after application of any long-lasting insecticides. Results take time, and close monitoring might be required to determine effectiveness. Several releases may be necessary. Control rather than annihilation is the objective.

If control organisms are microscopic (such as bacteria), they can be formulated as a dust or liquid solution. Insects or animals are released as eggs, juveniles, or adults, depending on the species. Severe infestations are best treated first with a quickly biodegradable pesticide before the release of the controls. Because healthy plants resist pests better than unhealthy ones, it is essential that you maintain proper fertilization and optimum cultural conditions. You can also encourage naturally occurring controls such as spiders, lizards, and toads.

To maintain beneficial organisms after they have controlled the pest might require advanced planning, unless you intend to make new releases. Ask the supplier how to provide for the control organisms until the next pest attack or season. It might require alternative food sources and suitable habitats and protection from certain pesticides.

SOAP, OIL, AND FATTY ACID SPRAYS AND ALCOHOL

Sprays of soaps, neem extracts, oils, and fatty acids are safe for humans and less harmful to the environment. Insecticidal soaps are effective on soft-bodied pests. Their main drawback is that they can damage the plant or leave behind an unsightly white residue on the leaves. It might be necessary to test spray to determine the fern's sensitivity. Plants should not be sprayed when temperatures are above 32°C (90°F). If plants are sensitive, they could wilt, spot, or burn (particularly along the margin), symptoms which may be seen within hours or days. Soft young foliage is most susceptible. If possible, delay spraying until young tissue matures. If wilting is noted within a few hours, rinse immediately with water.

Insect sprays made from liquid dishwashing detergent and water are effective on soft-bodied insects but usually must be reapplied periodically. The recommended proportion of dishwasher detergent is between

0.4 and 2.0%, or about 5 to 10 ml per 480 ml (1–2 tsp. per 2 cups) of water. The more detergent, the more effective the spray and the more risk of burning the fronds. One test using a 3% solution found no damage to maidenhair ferns (*Adiantum*). Studies indicate that soap used with acephate (Orthene), pyrethroids, and chlorohydrocarbon pesticides increases the effectiveness of the spray. Commercial insecticidal soaps are also available, but commonly used brands are not recommended for most ferns.

Alcohol also kills insects. It must be applied laboriously with a cotton swab by touching it to the insect. Generally concentrations of 35 to 40% are used.

PLANT-DERIVED INSECTICIDES

Although plant-derived insecticides are rapidly biodegradable and generally safer to use than synthetic chemicals, they are not selective and could harm beneficial insects and fish. Sprays and dusts are available, and protective gear should be used to prevent inhalation. Several new plant-derived insecticides, such as neem (Margosan), seem promising. Old standbys include rotenone, best if ingested by the pest, and pyrethrin (pyrethrum), which is best for adult insects. These pesticides kill ants, aphids, caterpillars, cutworms, leaf hoppers, mites, thrips, whiteflies, earwigs, mealybugs, millipedes, and sowbugs. They are ineffective against adult scale insects.

Nicotine compounds are also plant-derived insecticides. Although they degrade quickly, they are toxic to mammals and therefore unavailable to home growers. Commercial growers use them against pests such as aphids, young scale, mealybugs, thrips, and fungus-gnat larvae.

Several synthetic plant-derived insecticides (as pyrethroids modified from pyrethrin) are on the market. They have the advantages of being more effective on specific pests or longer lasting. Some are mentioned under the pest that they best control.

INSECT GROWTH REGULATORS

Insect growth regulators (IGR) interrupt the normal development of pests and thus prevent them from maturing or laying eggs. Most target certain insects and do not harm the beneficial ones. Kinoprene (Enstar 5E) affects aphids, mealybugs (ground and foliar), scale insects, whiteflies, and fungus gnats. It is, however, known to damage maidenhair fern. See the further discussion under aphids. Some growers reportedly have obtained satisfactory results by combining IGR and synthetic pyrethrin.

PHEROMONES

Pheromones are substances given off by plants or animals that cause specific behavioral responses in other individuals of the same or different species. Some pheromones are sex attractants used to lure insects into traps. Most pheromones available in the trade are used to control moths, flies, and beetles whose young feed on plants and may only incidentally feed on ferns. Pheromones are nontoxic to humans, pets, and the environment.

PHYSICAL CONTROLS: TRAPS AND BAITS

Sticky traps are frequently used in pest control. Flypaper, sticky paste, and sticky colored paper can be used to trap insects and detect early infestations. For sticky colored paper, blue attracts thrips, whereas yellow attracts aphids, whiteflies, leaf hoppers, moths, and fungus gnats better than white paper. Yellow plastic lids or containers coated with SAE 90 grade oil are also effective traps. Nowadays the effectiveness of traps is often enhanced by adding pheromones and baits with pest-attracting odors. Insects are also attracted by ultraviolet light, and such lights are used in "bug zappers" with electrically charged grids that kill adult flying insects on contact. Ultraviolet light can be useful to control moths that in their caterpillar or grub stage eat plants.

Mulches may help reduce surface-crawling pests, and a layer of ashes often discourages slugs and snails, but use sparingly because too many ashes could harm the soil. A commercially available diatomaceous earth dust is reportedly effective against soft-bodied insects. The microscopic needles of silica in the dust puncture the insect's guts after ingestion. It should not be applied when beneficial insects are active. Reportedly, this talc-like powder can be handled safely without gloves.

Spraying with water dislodges some pests and gives a certain measure of control. Adding a few drops of liquid detergent to the water helps loosen pests attached to stems or leaves. Picking off insects by hand or dabbing them with an alcohol- or oil-soaked cotton swab is labor intensive. The best time to look for slugs, snails, and cutworms is at night, especially when the ground is moist. Providing good sanitation will reduce hiding and breeding places of pests.

Chemical Pesticides and Fungicides

The Federal and State Environmental Protection Agencies regulate and proscribe the label contents and directives for all pesticides. In effect, the label is the law. The availability of and methods of applying pesticides are regulated by governmental agencies. In some cases the regulations restrict the sale of certain chemicals to licensed agricultural growers, in others they restrict the use of pesticides to certain regions of the United States. The following pages mention some of these restricted pesticides and fungicides along with their more widely available alternatives. Government regulations frequently change, and producers may modify their products as well. Therefore, readers should obtain updated information from their local county agricultural service.

The chemicals of choice are given under each pest discussed in this chapter. Further details on most of the insecticides may be found under "Aphids." Also see Appendix IV for cross-references to chemical and trade names and notes. No endorsement is intended by the inclusion of trade names, nor is criticism implied of products not mentioned. Although the advice contained has been carefully compiled, the authors cannot guarantee results. The reader acts on his or her own responsibility.

PREVENTING PESTICIDE AND FUNGICIDE DAMAGE

If you must use pesticides or fungicides, observe the following cautions. These will help you better control the pest or disease, avoid or reduce damage to plants, and minimize the dangers to humans, pets, and the environment.

1. Read the manufacturer's label and directions carefully. Follow recommended follow-up treatments. The label is the law!
2. New products and brands should be used with care. Note that brands vary according to the grade of the pesticides used, the percentage of active ingredient, the formulation, and whether they are used as a liquid, powder, granule, or aerosol.
3. Pesticides have a shelf life, and some lose their effectiveness in two to three years. Always buy and use fresh pesticides. Store as directed on the label.
4. Use dust or sprays made from wettable powders instead of emulsifiable concentrates, if a choice is available. Granules cause less damage than emulsions, which contain oils that damage ferns.

5. Test the products on a few plants before applying them to other plants. Damage usually appears after one day to two weeks and is evident as wilting, yellowing, spotting, marginal or surface burning, or abnormal growth.

6. Proper dosage is given on the label, but only a few fern species have been tested at the dosages listed by the manufacturer. The recommended dosage will often damage susceptible ferns. Reducing the dosage, however, violates the label law, even if a lower dosage is effective and does not damage the fern.

7. Sprays and dusts are most effective when thinly and thoroughly applied to all surfaces of the foliage. Fine mist sprays are the best. Water at the soil level after spraying or dusting so that the residue is not washed off the foliage.

8. Aerosols or smoke generators should be used only in greenhouses or tightly sealed plastic houses.

9. Spray, dust, or apply granules when the leaves are dry to avoid or minimize damage.

10. Spray early in the day so that plants can dry rapidly.

11. Spray when the air temperature will stay below 29°C (85°F) for at least two hours after spraying.

12. Move houseplants outdoors for treatment if possible.

13. The healthier the plant, the less likely the possibility of spray damage. Plants most easily damaged are those that are root bound, in need of water, or very young. Any damage that does occur might only affect the existing foliage, and any new growth may be unharmed if the roots and rhizomes have not been damaged.

14. Assume that all pesticides and fungicides are toxic. To reduce the possibility of damage to your (and others') health, proper procedures, protective clothes, and equipment must be used, and re-entry periods observed.

15. For the commercial grower, the suitability of a pesticide or fungicide for large-scale use should be checked with local county agents, state experiment stations, extension specialists, or the manufacturer's technical representatives. These specialists can determine the suitability of a specific pesticide for local soils, temperatures, moisture conditions, cultural practices, and dosage rates.

Systemic pesticides are those taken into the plant tissue and are effective in controlling the pest or disease from within the plant. A drench is a solution applied by sprinkling it over the soil.

Insect and Other Pests

ANTS

Ants feed on honeydew, a sweet secretion deposited by pests such as scale insects, aphids, and mealybugs. The ants not only protect these pests, but also disperse them!

PREVENTION AND CONTROL. If nests are found, pour enough boiling water to reach the main chambers.

Chemical controls of choice are chlorpyrifos (Dursban), diazinon, or malathion. Carbaryl (Sevin), bendiocarb (Dycarb, Turcam), and pyrethrin are other choices. Several other chemicals are used for ant control, but their availability is restricted in some states.

Aphids

Aphids are small, soft-bodied insects that are red, green, yellow, orange, or black. The fern aphid is black with whitish legs. Aphids weaken plants by sucking juices and causing distortion and stunting of foliage. They also produce a secretion called honeydew that is sipped by ants. Because the ants encourage and protect the aphids, they must also be controlled (see above). Some aphids are easy to kill but difficult to control because reinfestation often occurs from nearby areas. The fern aphid is common on new growth, particularly in the spring (Figure 11.1).

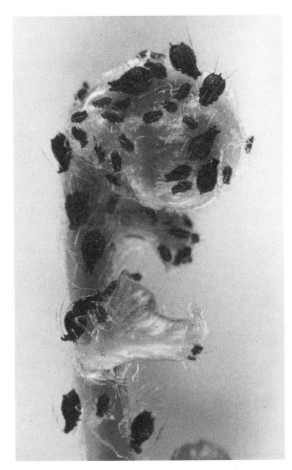

Figure 11.1. Aphids (8×).

Prevention and Control. For nonchemical control, see the various measures discussed under "Alternatives to Chemical Controls," earlier in the chapter.

Acephate (Orthene) is a systemic, broad-spectrum insecticide. Fern growers prefer the 75% soluble powder used at the manufacturer's rate of 5 ml (1 tsp.) to 3.8 liters (1 gal.) of water. Because damage has been reported on *Blechnum gibbum, Phlebodium aureum, Polystichum,* and *Pteris ensiformis,* you should do a sample test before using acephate powder on your ferns. Emulsions are more easily available and should also be tested before wider use. The manufacturer recommends an acephate emulsion of 9.4% used at 30 ml per 3.8 liters of water (2 tbsp. per gal.) for aphids and 45 ml per 3.8 liters of water (3 tbsp. per gal.) for mealybugs and scale insects on ornamentals in general. This dosage, however, could burn some ferns, so test first. Orthene aerosol might also burn some ferns.

Carbaryl (Sevin) is a broad-spectrum insecticide that can be used around edible plants. Carbaryl is registered for aphid use, but only for the apple aphid and rose aphid. For the fern aphid, other insecticides are more effective, though carbaryl is also useful for other pests that attack ferns. It is available as a dust, emulsion, or wettable powder. Emulsions burn sensitive ferns.

Diazinon is another broad-spectrum insecticide. Diazinon emulsions of 25% are recommended by the manufacturer to be used at 10 ml to 3.8 liters of water (2 tsp. per gal.) for foliage plants, but not for certain ferns. Dosages reduced one-quarter to one-half the recommended concentration gave adequate control with little damage, but such dosages violate label laws. Wettable diazinon powder of 50% at 15 ml per 3.8 liters of water (1 tbsp. per gal.) is recommended for foliage plants; however, the manufacturer also reports that maidenhairs and other ferns are burned at this concentration. In all cases, sample test on a few plants before wider use.

Dimethoate (Cygon 2E), a systemic, broad-spectrum insecticide, is effective for three weeks after application. When used as a drench to minimize foliage burn, Cygon 2E (23.4%) is used at 5 ml to 3.8 liters of water (1 tsp. per gal.) for foliage plants in general. As a spray for foliage plants, the recommended dosage is 7.5 ml per 3.8 liters of water (1½ tsp. per gal.). Treatments of 2.5 to 5 ml per 3.8 liters of water (½–1 tsp. per gal.) have been successful in tests on ferns. This product has restrictions and is unavailable in certain states.

Disulfoton (Di-syston) granules applied to the soil provide systemic protection against aphids and other insects. It is often included in rose-care products and is effective against scale insects, red spider-mite, and thrips.

Fluvalinate (Mavrik Aquaflow) is a synthetic pyrethrin-like chemical. The water-based formulation makes it safe for plants. Recommended dosage ranges from 1.3 to 3.3 ml per 3.8 liters of water (¼–⅔ tsp. per gal.) for foliage plants.

Imidacloprid (Marathon) is a broad-spectrum systemic insecticide. It comes in wettable powder or granular form. The active ingredient does not readily move in the soil, therefore drenches or granules must be applied to the root zone to be effective. It reportedly remains active in the soil for 8 to 12 weeks after one application. Some ferns reportedly do not respond to granular forms even if generously applied. It is not available to home growers.

Kinoprene (Enstar 5E) is safe for Boston fern (*Nephrolepis exaltata* 'Bostoniensis') and its cultivar 'Fluffy Ruffles' and for *Pteris cretica* 'Parkeri' when used at the manufacturer's recommended rate. It severely damages maidenhair fern (*Adiantum*), however, and its effect on other ferns is unknown.

Malathion is a broad-spectrum insecticide available as a wettable powder but more commonly as a dust or emulsion. The latter is most commonly used, and the manufacturer's recommended dosage for 50% malathion concentration on foliage plants in general is 10 ml per 3.8 liters of water (2 tsp. per gal.). This dosage severely burns or injures a variety of ferns, although commercial fern growers encountered little or no damage when the dosage was reduced to 2.5 ml per 3.8 liters of water (½ tsp. per 1 gal.), though this reduction violates the label laws.

Nicotine sulfate is no longer available in the United States, although a nicotine alkaloid aerosol is available to commercial growers. It is highly toxic.

Oxydemetron-methyl (Metasystox-R) is a systemic insecticide. The 25% emulsion is used at 7.5 to 10 ml per 3.8 liters of water (1½–2 tsp. per gal.) for foliage plants. It is reportedly safe for maidenhair and other ferns when applied to the soil.

Oxamyl (Vydate) controls aphids and a variety of insects, nematodes, and mites; however, it is available only to commercial growers.

Pyrethrin kills aphids and comes in many formulations. Synthetic pyrethrins (pyrethroids) are also available.

Resmethrin kills aphids and other pests and comes as a spray or aerosol. The aerosol form is favored by some commercial growers.

Soap sprays are discussed under "Alternatives to Chemical Controls."

EARWIGS

Earwigs are reddish brown insects about 13 mm (0.5 in.) in length, with prominent pinchers at the end of their tails. They ordinarily eat decaying vegetation, but they can damage ferns by nibbling at tender new growth. During the day earwigs hide under flower pots and plant debris. They forage at night.

PREVENTION AND CONTROL. Keep a clean culture. Trap earwigs during the night in a roll of damp newspaper, and destroy it in the morning.

Propoxur (Baygon) bait is the insecticide of choice. Baits or dusts of carbaryl (Sevin), chlorpyrifos (Dursban), and diazinon also control earwigs. Scatter the bait where earwigs congregate but not directly on the fern foliage.

FUNGUS GNATS

Fungus gnats resemble small mosquitoes less than 3 mm (0.1 in.) long. With a hand lens the feelers (antennae) are seen to be longer than the head, and the veins of the wing form a Y-shaped pattern. These features are absent on shore flies, a similar gnat. Fungus gnats frequent damp places and soils with high organic matter. When disturbed, the adults often run rapidly on the plant or soil before taking flight.

Both shore flies and fungus gnat adults can spread disease, but the fungus gnat causes the most damage when in its larval stage. In greenhouses and enclosed places they eat roots, root hairs, stems, and prothalli. Shore-fly larvae are maggot-like and eat detritus, whereas fungus gnats eat living plant tissue. Fungus-gnat larvae are small, whitish, translucent, legless worms with black heads. They can be found beneath the soil level or in the plant tissue being eaten. Affected plants grow slowly, lack vigor, may wilt, show yellow leaves, and have rotted roots. Prothalli appear wilted or have small but noticeable holes where the larvae have fed. The greatest damage is seen during plant growth stages in which there are few roots and the larvae have fed on them.

PREVENTION AND CONTROL. Keep a clean culture. Remove weeds and plant debris, and take steps to avoid excessive moisture in or on the soil and surrounding area. To control algae, which often flourish in unclean cultures and attract fungus gnats, use clean or new flats and pots (see "Algae, Mosses, and Liverworts"). On spore pots and flats covered with glass, seal any space between the glass cover and pot or flat, preferably with plastic foam strips instead of cotton. If feasible, reduce the organic content in the soil mix. Ammonium nitrate used as a drench at three-quarters the normal fertilizer concentration works for larval control, and acts as a fertilizer as well.

If drenches or sprays are used, remove surrounding debris before application. Avoid irrigation for one day after application. Drench, dust, or spray the plant, the soil, under benches, and any places where the gnat or its larvae might be. Yellow sticky cards are useful for trapping adult gnats and for monitoring the effectiveness of other control measures.

Biological controls include *Bacillus thuringiensis* and other organisms (see "Alternatives to Chemical Controls"). *Bacillus thuringiensis* H-14 (Gnatrol) kills larvae. The drench works within 24 hours after ingestion. Ferns are unharmed by the recommended dosages of 5 to 10 ml per 3.8 liters of water (1–2 tsp. per gal.) for light infestations, or 20 to 40 ml (4–8 tsp.) for heavy infestations. A nematode that kills the larval stages of the fungus gnat is sold as Exhibit.

Chemical treatments of choice include diazinon (also used in a capsule form called Knox-out), kinoprene (Enstar 5E), oxamyl (Vydate 10% granules for the larvae and Vydate 2L spray for the larvae and adults), and resmethrin (a synthetic pyrethrin). One percent resmethrin aerosol (PT1200 Resmethrin) did not damage Boston ferns, and growers reported no damage to the commonly grown species of *Pteris* and *Pellaea*. Resmethrin spray (SBP-1382-2EC) is recommended for foliage plants at 5 ml per 3.8 liters of water (1 tsp. per gal.); its toxicity to ferns is unknown. Less effective, but also registered as a control for fungus gnats, are dimethoate (Cygon 2E), carbaryl (Sevin), and malathion. See "Aphids" for details and precautions.

Although unregistered against fungus gnat larvae, fluvalinate (Mavrik Aquaflow) seems a promising control. Others products that are reportedly effective on fungus gnats include Fenoxycarb (an insect growth regulator), Citation, Orthene, and Dycarb.

MEALYBUGS

Several species of mealybugs attack fern fronds and (less frequently) roots. These small insects are characterized by a white mealy look (Figure 11.2). They weaken a plant by feeding on its sap. Ants are attracted to the mealybugs' honeydew secretion.

Figure 11.2. Mealybug (18×).

PREVENTION AND CONTROL. Adult mealybugs are more difficult to control than the immature stages (crawlers). Therefore you should inspect plants frequently for infestation and employ control measures promptly. Control the ants (as discussed earlier); also see "Alternatives to Chemical Controls." For root mealybugs, use the spray as a drench.

Acephate (Orthene), diazinon, and malathion are the insecticides of choice. Also used are dimethoate (Cygon 2E), imidacloprid (Marathon), kinoprene (Enstar 5E), oxydemetron-methyl (Metasystox-R), and oxamyl (Vydate). If you have a choice, use systemics. See "Aphids" for more details.

Millipedes

Millipedes generally feed on decaying plant debris but also eat healthy fern foliage. They appear worm-like but have many legs. The garden species is reddish brown, about an inch long, and emits a sweet, pungent odor when crushed (reminiscent of toasted almonds). Millipedes may be confused with predatory centipedes, which differ by having only one instead of two pairs of legs per body segment, and by generally moving faster. Millipedes are most active at night. During the day look for them under flowerpots and debris.

Prevention and Control. Keep a clean culture. Remove debris.

Propoxur (Baygon) bait is the pesticide of choice. Carbaryl (Sevin) dust or a spray from 50% wettable powder, at 30 ml per 3.8 liters (2 tbsp. per gal.), will also control millipedes. Spray into cracks, under containers, and in other hiding places, thoroughly wetting these surfaces. Avoid spraying on fern foliage.

Pesticides such as acephate (Orthene), chlorpyrifos (Dursban), diazinon, pyrethrin, and rotenone also kill millipedes. Be sure to follow the directions on the label, and avoid getting the insecticide on foliage.

Mites, Red Spider-Mites, Spider Mites, Two-Spotted Mites

Although many species of mites attack plants, red spider-mites are the most pernicious. They are about the size of a grain of salt and vary in color from red to green to cream. The adults have eight legs. When shaken onto white paper, the mites can be seen as tiny crawling specks. They leave a delicate webbing on the leaves. Plants damaged by mites decline in vigor and show a yellow, stippled pattern or larger yellowish areas that can eventually turn brown. By the time damage is noticed, the mites could have moved elsewhere. Since mites are attracted by dusty dry conditions, they seldom attack ferns.

Prevention and Control. Do not let the plants suffer from moisture stress and low humidity. Spray with water to wash off mites and accumulated dust and increase the humidity. Spraying is necessary only if the mites persist in large numbers. Spray thoroughly on the lower surface of the foliage. Soap sprays and biological controls are effective (see "Alternatives to Chemical Controls").

Chemical controls of choice include dicofol (Kelthane), which is relatively harmless to ferns. Dienochlor (Pentac, using the 50% wettable powder spray) is safe on Boston fern (*Nephrolepis exaltata* 'Bostoniensis') and its cultivar 'Fluffy Ruffles'. Other pesticides that may be used on mites include acephate (Orthene), diazinon, disulfoton (Di-syston), fluvalinate (Mavrik Aquaflow), oxydemetron-methyl (Metasystox-R), and oxamyl (Vydate). See "Aphids" for details and precautions. Carabyl (Sevin) and malathion seem to cause subsequent outbreaks of mite infestations; therefore, carabyl is often combined with dicofol in sprays. Sulfur dust is ineffective and might burn the plant.

Nemas or Nematodes

Leaf nematode blight is caused by minute worms (*Aphelenchoides fragariae*). The nematodes form reddish brown or black spots that are typically sharply marked on the leaf. They typically feed on the leaf tissue between the veins, seldom across the veins. Therefore the spots have an angular shape. On bird's-nest fern (*Asplenium nidus*) the discoloration is limited to tissue between the parallel veins. In other species and on young ferns, the affected area may be more irregular due to the pattern of the veins. Nematodes can be seen by placing a bit of infected tissue in a drop of water, then lightly mincing and examining it under about 20× magnification. With good light, you can see the characteristic thrashing movement of these nearly transparent, slender worms (about 0.5 mm long). Leaf nematodes thrive under cool moist conditions. They travel in a film of water or in drops from splashed water. Besides weakening and discoloring the plant, nematodes spread disease. Root-knot nematodes have not been reported to attack ferns.

It is unlikely that nematodes spread through fern spores, unless fragments of infected leaf tissue are sown with the spores. Rapid drying of the leaf tissue prevents nematodes from entering their rest stage. Otherwise, they can remain alive for a year or more.

Certain ferns are more susceptible to leaf nematode damage than others. These include *Asplenium* (*A. bulbiferum* and *A. nidus* in particular), *Blechnum, Pteris, Tectaria,* and *Woodwardia* (*W. fimbriata* and *W. radicans* in particular). Also susceptible are *Adiantum, Cyrtomium falcatum, Dicksonia antarctica, Diplazium dilatatum, Diplazium proliferum, Dryopteris filix-mas, Dryopteris hondoensis, Nephrolepis cordifolia, Polypodium, Polystichum munitum, Rumohra adiantiformis, Sphaeropteris cooperi,* and *Thelypteris.*

Prevention and Control. Prevention is easier than control. Start with disease-free stock and use only clean flats or pots. Beware of soil, materials, or tools that might harbor nematodes. Disinfect contaminated materials or tools, pasteurize suspected soil with steam at 82°C (180°F) for about 30 minutes, or treat with a soil fumigant. Because nematodes thrive in debris, discolored leaves should be discarded to where they will not reinfect other plants. Remove infected leaves and burn them. Avoid overhead watering and other conditions that wet the leaves. Remove weeds that might harbor nematodes. For the fern hobbyist with only a few infected plants, the best course is to dispose of them properly and enact preventative measures to protect against further spread. Bird's-nest fern (*Asplenium nidus*) has been successfully freed of nematodes by immersing the plant in hot water at 46°C (115°F) for 10 to 15 minutes.

If the infection is from the ground, the plants should be grown in pots on raised benches. Do not allow the infected soil to be splashed on benches, pots, or foliage. If planting the ferns in the ground, allow the soil to remain fallow and weed-free for a season or so. This will decrease but not eliminate the nematode population. Drying the soil also reduces the nematode population. Live mature marigolds (*Tagetes patula*) will release from their roots a chemical (ozone) that kills nematodes. This control practice is only effective if many marigolds are planted.

The chemicals used to control nematodes are generally unavailable to home growers because of their toxicity to humans and pets and their ability to remain in the soil or plants for a long time if improperly applied. Nematicides used on ferns include ethoprop (Mocap), oxamyl (Vydate), and phenamiphos (Nemacur). All of these have restrictions on their use. With the constant changes in labeling and laws, it is best to contact local agricultural agencies for current information. For more details, see Krusberg (1992) and anonymous (1986).

Psocids and Springtails

Psocids or book lice are small, pale insects that scurry around on damp soil or decaying vegetation. Springtails (Collembola) are similar in appearance but jump when disturbed. Both thrive in warm moist environments. Neither harms ferns directly, but they can spread fungi and bacteria.

Prevention and Control. If you encounter problems with a spreading disease, spray the soil with a soap spray or with the chemicals listed for controlling aphids.

Scale Insects

Adult scale insects live in a stationary, wax-like shell under which they suck plant juices. Extra juices are secreted as honeydew, which attracts ants and serves as the medium for the growth of a blackish mold.

Several species of scale insects feed on ferns. The most common is the brown soft-scale. It has black or brown spots on its back. Young scale insects (crawlers) continually emerge from the mother scale for about two months and grow to full size in two more months (Figure 11.3).

Prevention and Control. Adult scale insects are difficult to control, and therefore frequent inspection and enacting controls at an early stage are important. Although biological controls such as kino-

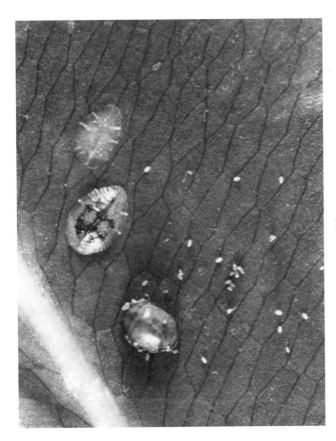

Figure 11.3. Scale insects (10×). Note the very young scale insects emerging from the older scale at the bottom.

prene (Enstar 5E) are available, natural predators can be encouraged by spraying the plants with water to keep off dust. Soaps may be effective against crawlers. Adults can be controlled by dabbing with alcohol- or oil-soaked swabs. Chemicals of choice to control the adults are diazinon, dimethoate (Cygon 2E), imidacloprid (Marathon), malathion, acephate (Orthene, more effective against the crawlers). Other pesticides that kill scale insects include oxydemetron-methyl (Metasystox-R), oxamyl (Vydate), and disulfoton (Disyston) granules. See "Aphids" for more details.

SNAILS AND SLUGS

The brown garden snail and various slugs can quickly devastate ferns. Other species that usually eat decaying vegetation can also damage certain ferns. Small snails, such as the rotund disc snail, do not leave a conspicuous slime trail and easily go unnoticed. Their damage causes small holes in the foliage and collapsed fiddleheads. Slugs do not have a shell like that of a snail, but they do leave a mucous trail. New growth and tender foliage are most vulnerable, as are certain fern genera (especially *Asplenium*). Slugs and snails come out of hiding and feed at night. During the day they hide in dark, moist, cool places.

PREVENTION AND CONTROL. Examine the plants and surrounding areas (especially if moist) in the late evening to handpick and destroy the snails and slugs. During the day, search under flower pots or in other hiding places. With snails, be certain that they are completely killed as they can easily repair cracked shells. Keep a clean culture by removing debris and other potential slug hideouts. Fill in cracks and crevices in walls, fences, and building foundations with mortar to reduce winter hiding places. Beer in cups or various traps attract snails, but not as well as methaldehyde baits. Coarse bark chips and various mulches discourage slug and snail movement. In particular, ashes inhibit the movement of slugs and snails but should not be applied in large amounts to the soil. Sharp sand, perlite, gritty materials, and ground peat moss are other mulches that snails dislike to traverse. Slugs do not seem to object to sand. Snails are stopped by vertical copper bands at least 4 cm (1.5 in.) wide, though slugs are less inhibited by this. Insecticidal soaps reportedly kill slugs and snails.

Decollate snails are predators of brown garden snails but will eat tender foliage, including that of some ferns. Slugs are rarely attacked by decollate snails. Toads, opossums, and other wildlife feed on snails and slugs.

For chemical controls, various baits, granules, and sprays can be applied on less exposed areas of flats, fences, and walls where snails and slugs travel and feed. The pests tend to return to the same hiding and feeding areas.

Methaldehyde attracts and stuns slugs and snails, and death is dependent on subsequent dehydration. Slugs and snails can recover and may live to develop resistant strains. Keep pets, particularly dogs, away from methaldehyde baits, which are poisonous. Baits in pellet form can become unsightly due to mold; other forms do not mold or the mold is less conspicuous. Methaldehyde is less effective at temperatures below 20°C (68°F) and loses potency in sunlight and high humidity. A special formulation (which can be obtained as Deadline, Corry's, and other brand names) resists sunlight and humidity damage and lasts longer. Sprays have the advantage of penetrating the soil where slugs may be hiding, but earthworms will also be harmed. Avoid spraying fern foliage.

Methiocarb (Mesurol) kills snails or slugs instead of stunning them. It also kills earthworms. The granular form should be applied when the foliage is dry. Increased humidity increases its toxicity; where humidity fluctuates widely, using methiocarb in combination with methaldehyde will give better control. For use in commercial greenhouses, methiocarb comes in aerosol form. It also kills aphids, scale insects, spider mites, moths, and whiteflies.

Mexacarbate (Zectran) is infrequently sold. Because direct sprays will burn maidenhair and possibly other ferns, it should be applied only to the soil and walkways. The dehydrating effect of aluminum sulfate applied as a drench of 56.7 grams per 3.8 liters of water (2 oz. per gal.) is reported to kill snails and slugs, but its effect on ferns is unknown. It might acidify the soil. For further details, see Parrella et al. (1985).

SOWBUGS AND PILLBUGS

Sowbugs and pillbugs are segmented, oval-shaped pests that eat decaying plants and the tender new growth of fronds, rhizomes, and roots. Pillbugs roll into a ball when disturbed; sowbugs do not. Both are also known as woodlice.

PREVENTION AND CONTROL. Keep a clean culture by removing debris and hiding places. Pour boiling water into hiding places, or attract the bugs to one spot with half a potato, apple, or turnip pulped on one side and placed cut side down. A small inverted flowerpot filled with damp moss can also be used.

The chemical controls are the same as for millipedes (which see). Diazinon is particularly effective, as are Sevin dust (carabyl) and pyrethroids.

THRIPS

Thrips are small, slender insects that cause noticeable white or bleached areas on ferns by sucking the plant juices. Bleached areas may become especially conspicuous during the summer months. Tiny, scattered black or brown dots (mold-infected honeydew) left by the thrips are visible with a hand lens on the underside of the damaged area of the frond (Figure 11.4). By the time the bleached areas appear, none or only a few lingering thrips will be seen. Greenhouse thrips, the species that attacks ferns, have dark brown to black adults, about 1 to 1.5 mm long. This species is common and found worldwide. It may attack ferns indoors or outdoors. The flower thrip does not form black dots on the foliage and has not been reported to attack ferns.

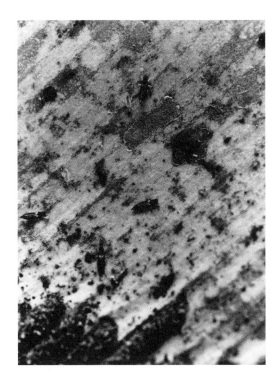

Figure 11.4. Thrips (6×). Note the dots of secretion and bleached leaf tissue.

PREVENTION AND CONTROL. Keep the surrounding grass mowed and remove weeds and badly damaged fronds. Ferns susceptible to thrips (such as *Polystichum* and some *Dryopteris*) should be placed in cooler, more humid sites of the garden. If in a greenhouse, use 0.178 mm (0.007 in.) brass mesh screen across openings. The chemical controls of choice are acephate (Orthene), disulfoton (Di-syston), malathion, and oxydemetron-methyl (Metasystox-R). Others include chlorpyrifos (Dursban), dimethoate (Cygon 2E), fluvalinate (Mavrik Aquaflow), oxamyl (Vydate), and imidacloprid (Marathon). See "Aphids" for more details; also see "Alternatives to Chemical Controls."

WHITEFLIES

Whiteflies are sucking insects about 3 mm (0.1 in.) long that fly upward when the foliage is disturbed. Examination of the leaf's underside will reveal many flattish, oval larvae and pupae adhering to the surface. Whiteflies are uncommon on ferns, although in some areas newly introduced species are attacking some ferns and are difficult to control.

PREVENTION AND CONTROL. See "Alternatives to Chemical Controls" for biological controls, soaps, and insect growth-regulators.

Chemical controls for greenhouse whiteflies are acephate (Orthene), diazinon, dimethoate (Cygon 2E), fluvalinate (Mavrik Aquaflow), malathion, oxydemetron-methyl (Metasystox-R), and resmethrin, among other registered controls. See "Aphids" for more details. Insecticides used for greenhouse whiteflies may not be effective against other whitefly species.

OTHER ANIMAL PESTS

Many insect pests feed on fern foliage or prothalli. They include cutworms, caterpillars, beetles (including weevils), crickets, grasshoppers, and cockroaches. Their presence is often indicated by damaged foliage, disturbed soil, or droppings. Earthworms and other soil dwellers do not directly damage ferns but may indirectly damage prothalli or young sporophytes by churning the soil around them. Mice may eat ferns.

Prevention and Control. The chemical control of choice is carbaryl (Sevin), but also used are acephate (Orthene), diazinon, and chlorpyrifos (Dursban). See "Aphids" for more details. Also see "Alternatives to Chemical Controls."

Fungi and Bacteria Attacking Ferns

Generally, cultivated ferns are not susceptible to fungal or bacterial diseases. These usually appear when the plants have been kept too wet at the roots or on the foliage. Prevention is better than attempting a cure. Ferns properly planted and cared for are less likely to succumb to disease. A number of symptoms common to virus infections on ferns have been noted but not well studied.

Prevention starts with healthy plants that show resistance to disease. Provide them with good drainage, and keep the crown of the plant above the soil. Foliage should not be allowed to stay wet for long periods. Avoid overwatering and splashing, and be sure to water in the early part of the day to allow time for the foliage to dry. Space the plants far enough apart so that there is adequate air circulation around and between them. Fronds should be gently shaken to remove the excess water, especially with finely divided foliage that becomes matted with water; better yet, avoid frequent overhead watering with such ferns. Keep a clean culture, because old leaves, plant debris, and weeds might harbor disease. Potted plants should be kept raised above the soil level to prevent possible contamination. Little is known about biological controls for fungal or bacterial diseases. Fungi (*Trichoderma* and *Gliocladium virens*) that control water molds are being studied.

Preventative measures involve sterilizing the soil, pots, and tools used in planting (see "Sterilizing Soils" in Chapter 5). Pots, tools, and benches can be disinfected with alcohol, 10% bleach solutions, quaternary ammonium compounds (Physan 20, Green Shield), or carbolic acid (Lysol). Formaldehyde is unsafe for people, pets, and the environment and has been withdrawn from the market for such use.

When disease symptoms appear, cut the diseased leaves back to healthy tissue and destroy the diseased parts (see "Leaf Spots" for more details). Fungal diseases tend to produce spots with a halo pattern that is lighter colored at the edge. Bacterial diseases generally cause discoloration that is shiny and water-soaked. Diseased parts should be discarded to where they will not infect other plants.

A last resort for home growers is to use chemicals (see Appendix IV). Most fungicides will only suppress the disease, not eradicate it. Some injure the plant, others are expensive, and most have not been tested on ferns. If they have been tested, it is usually only on the Boston fern and leather fern.

Fungicides should be sprayed to provide good coverage, especially on the lower leaf surfaces favored by fungi. Apply drenches to moist soil. Fungi that attack ferns fall into two categories: water molds and non-water molds. No spray exists to control both, but combinations of compatible fungicides are available to home growers, such as Banrot (contains etridiazole and thiophanate-methyl). If the specific fungus causing the disease is unknown, a broad-spectrum fungicide (usually compatible mixes) must be used. Compatible mixes sometimes work better than if the fungicides are used separately. Most broad-spectrum fungicides are effective against *Botrytis, Rhizoctonia,* and water molds that cause most of the blights and damping-off symptoms. Commercial growers routinely spray fungicides and apply drenches as preventative measures, but some fungicides accumulate in the soil to levels that are toxic to plants, and sometimes fungi will develop resistance. Rotating fungicides may be needed to avoid these problems.

Identifying pathogens to species requires time-consuming collaboration with a plant pathology laboratory, but commercial growers need quick identifications to begin treatment as soon as possible. To fill this need, kits (such as Alert) are available to identify certain diseases within minutes. Presently, these kits detect only three soil-borne diseases: *Rhizoctonia, Pythium,* and *Phytophtora* (the latter two are water molds).

Routine preventative fungicide treatments used by commercial growers include Chipco 26019 (or Cleary's 2226) and Subdue. They are registered for use in certain situations (such as outdoors, greenhouses, interiorscapes), for certain types of plants, and for certain users. As with pesticides, use of these chemicals other than as described on the label violates the law.

In the following section the common names of fungicides and some of their trade names are given. Trade names are used for convenience and do not imply endorsement. See Appendix IV for cross-references between trade names and the active ingredient.

Armillaria ROOT-ROT

Armillaria root-rot has been reported to kill *Dicksonia fibrosa* in southern California. It is widespread and attacks woody tissue, but some woody plants are more susceptible than others. The infected plants decline and eventually die. Prying into a dead stem will reveal the whitish growth of the mold. Eventually the characteristic honey-colored mushrooms may emerge, usually around the base of the stem.

PREVENTION AND CONTROL. Avoid planting *Dicksonia fibrosa* or woody plants in areas susceptible to *Armillaria* unless the species are resistant. The soil can be fumigated before planting, but recontamination is likely to occur.

BLIGHTS

Blights are caused by fungi or bacteria that attack young growing tissue. Affected young plants will wither and die, and the fronds of older plants will dry at the tips and margins (especially in Boston ferns). Blights can appear as water-soaked spots on bird's-nest ferns (*Asplenium nidus*). Also see the section "Tip Blight" later in the chapter.

PREVENTION AND CONTROL. Remove and destroy blighted parts and disinfect tools. Avoid getting the foliage wet, reduce humidity, and space the plants farther apart to facilitate drying and improve air circulation. If the specific disease organism is unknown, use a broad-spectrum spray (such as Banrot). Chemicals with the active ingredients propiconazole (Banner), chlorothalonil (Daconil 2787), iprodione (Chipco 26019), or mancozeb (Dithane M-45) might also be effective. Also see "*Rhizoctonia*" and "Water Molds."

DAMPING-OFF

Damping-off diseases attack young plants near the soil surface and cause them to fall over, wither, and die. Prothalli often reveal the symptoms of damping-off. Several different pathogens cause the disease.

PREVENTION AND CONTROL. Sterilize the soil if possible. Provide good ventilation, keep tops of young plants dry, and reduce the moisture level to a minimum. Broad-spectrum fungicides must be used unless the pathogen is known. Commercial growers favor Banrot or a combination drench of iprodione (Chipco 26019) and metalaxyl (Subdue). See also "Blights," "*Rhizoctonia*," and "Water Molds."

GRAY MOLD (*Botrytis*)

The fungus *Botrytis* forms delicate tufts of grayish white mold on dead, injured, or dying fronds. Infection typically starts from the upper part of the plant and proceeds toward the soil. Young ferns may survive for a short time but eventually produce deformed fronds or stop growing altogether. *Botrytis* spores are airborne and common. Cool moist conditions favor the fungus.

PREVENTION AND CONTROL. Remove dead and injured leaves. Maintain a warmer, drier environment. Promote free air circulation and use fans if necessary. The following fungicides are effective against gray mold: chlorothalonil (Daconil 2787), copper sulfate pentahydrate (Phyton 27), dimethyl 4,4′-*O*-phenylenebis (3-thioallophanate) (Cleary's 2226), iprodione (Chipco 26019), mancozeb (Dithane M-45), maneb (Dithane M-22), thiophanate-methyl (Zyban), and zineb (Dithane Z-78). All are registered for use on foliage plants, but often the only ferns that have been properly tested are the Boston fern and leather fern. Spray test before widely applying any fungicide to your ferns.

LEAF SPOTS

Spots and blotches on leaves are caused by factors such as poor air quality (see Chapter 4), physical damage, excessive moisture or shade, fungi, bacteria, and nematodes. Healthy ferns in well-ventilated places seldom become infected. Blemishes usually appear on older fronds, but new fronds can also become infected.

PREVENTION AND CONTROL. With minor infections, the disfigured fronds should be removed to prevent spreading. Cut the foliage back to healthy tissue, destroy the infected parts, and disinfect all tools. Reducing humidity, spacing the plants farther apart, increasing air circulation, and avoiding overhead watering or splashing will help prevent further infection. If the spots are few, smearing them with a cotton swab dipped in a strong solution of baking soda, a 10% bleach solution (avoid healthy tissue), or a quaternary ammonium compound (Physan 20 or Green Shield) may help stop the spots from enlarging. This treatment is particularly effective for the larger spots appearing on staghorn ferns. Experiments indicate that insecticidal soaps can increase or decrease leaf spots, depending on the disease and host. A 0.5% baking-powder solution has successfully been used to treat leaf spots but is not registered for such use. It is reportedly more effective when combined with a horticultural oil, such as Volck Oil Spray, a petroleum oil. Chemical sprays are a last resort. A broad-spectrum spray (see under "Blights") must be used unless the particular pathogen is known.

Some specific leaf-spot pathogens that have been identified on ferns include *Cercospora*, *Cladosporium*, *Colletotrichum*, *Cylindrocladium*, *Fusarium*, *Myrothecium*, *Peyronellaea*, *Phoma*, *Pseudomonas*, and *Xanthamomas campestris*. The latter two are bacteria that produce rot with a wet appearance (especially on base fronds of *Platycerium*). They can be controlled by Physan 20 applied with a cotton swab. Leaf blister (*Taphrina*), which forms a blister on both sides of the leaf, attacks mostly native ferns.

Rhizoctonia

Rhizoctonia is a fungus that usually attacks plants near the soil surface. The stems or stipes rot at the point of infection, and the weakened stalk cannot support the frond. The infection can also spread below the soil. Thicker roots turn yellow or brown and have cankers. Prothalli and young plants wither and damp off. Fronds may wilt, grow slowly, be deformed, or stop emerging altogether. This condition is called "hard crown" by some growers. *Rhizoctonia* often causes black-brown lesions on stems, leaf stalks, and roots. The base fronds (shields) of staghorn ferns may show wrinkly brown lesions.

The decaying parts of infected plants have brownish threads that can be seen with a hand lens. These threads are coarse enough to cling to soil particles (water molds have fine threads that do not cling to soil particles). Under the microscope, the characteristic T-shaped cells where the filaments branch are diagnostic.

Rhizoctonia also attacks tree ferns. The new fronds do not uncoil but seem to dry in place. Mature fronds will wilt, and the crown hardens and turns brown. Eventually the plant dies.

Overwatered plants or ones growing in poorly drained soils are most susceptible to infection. Infected plants continue to grow but usually languish and succumb to minor stresses. High humidity and temperatures of 21 to 27°C (70–80°F) favor the disease.

PREVENTION AND CONTROL. Discard infected plants. Make sure contaminated soil or equipment does not touch clean soil or equipment. Sterilize the soil before replanting contaminated areas. The disease is soil-borne and can easily spread by splashing or flowing water. Several chemicals can be applied as a drench, mainly as a preventative. They will inhibit the disease but not destroy it. The chemical of choice is pentachloronitrobenzene (PCNB, Terraclor), but it burns certain ferns. Also effective are chlorothalonil (Daconil 2787), Cleary's 2226, iprodione (Chipco 26019), captan, etridiazole (Truban), and the broad-spectrum Banrot. In all cases it is a good idea to test spray first.

Rots

Many species of fungi and bacteria can cause decay or rots. Rots caused by bacteria appear wetter and slimier than those caused by fungus.

Prevention and Control. Cut away rotting spots. Disinfect tools and treat as for blights (which see). Bacterial rots may respond to such bactericides as streptomycin (Agri-strep), copper sulfate pentahydrate (Phyton 27), and others. Some bactericides are expensive, and ferns may be sensitive to them. Small spots of rot can be dabbed with a cotton swab, as mentioned under "Leaf Spots." As a preventative measure, dust cut surfaces of the plant with fine sulfur or dip in a solution of general disinfectants (Physan 20 or Green Shield).

Rust

Rust diseases have long been known to affect wild ferns, but they are less frequently encountered on cultivated ones. The disease produces orange-brown pustules or white spots on the underside of the leaf. Discoloration can appear on the upper surface of the leaf opposite the pustules. Rust spores may be airborne. Moist, cool nights and warm days favor rust. The rust *Milesia* is common in England on hart's-tongue fern (*Phyllitis scolopendrium*).

Prevention and Control. Remove infected leaves to minimize airborne rust spores that can reinfect other leaves. Winter cleanup, particularly the removal of old fronds, will reduce infection in the spring. Propiconazole (Banner), folpet (Phaltan), chlorothalonil (Daconil 2787), mancozeb (Dithane M-45), maneb (Dithane M-22), and zineb (Diathane Z-78) are chemical sprays that kill rusts. Their effect on ferns is not known.

Sooty Molds

Sooty mold is a fungus (usually *Fumago*) that appears as black smutty patches on leaves. It also grows on the honeydew drops secreted by aphids and mealybugs. Although unsightly, sooty molds do not harm the plant. They do, however, intercept light to the fronds.

Prevention and Control. Control scale insects, aphids, mealybugs, and ants. Promote air circulation.

Tip Blight

The development of irregular, deformed fronds and a subsequent slowing or cessation of growth may appear among young and well-established species of tree ferns (such as *Dicksonia antarctica* and *Sphaeropteris cooperi*). Laboratory tests on diseased *Dicksonia* plants have tentatively identified the pathogen as the fungus *Phyllosticta*. This fungus is sometimes called tip blight because it causes the leaf tissue to appear sunburned along the margins, but the brown coloration can spread throughout the leaflet. Leaflets become distorted, undersized, appear moth-eaten, or are absent in places. Emerging fiddleheads can be irregularly twisted, and leaf-stalk cross sections sometimes reveal a central area of dead, darkened tissue. This disease has appeared in southern California, and similar symptoms have been reported in the Hawaiian Islands.

Prevention and Control. Generous applications of fertilizer may retard the disease symptoms for a time, but they eventually return. Broad-spectrum fungicides are reportedly effective against tip blight, including chlorothalonil (Daconil 2787) for home growers, and iprodione (Chipco 26019), mancozeb (Dithane M-45), and zineb (Dithane Z-78) for commercial growers. Overhead watering of tree ferns should be avoided.

Water Molds or Root-Rots

Plants overwatered or allowed to stand in water are usually killed by water molds of the genera *Pythium* and *Phytophthora*. These organisms thrive in cool temperatures. They first infect the roots, then the stem. Symptoms of water molds include stunted growth, yellow or wilted fronds, and reduced root growth. In addition, the stems, if not rotted away, become so soft that when washed the outermost tissue (cortex) readily separates from the tougher central strand. Both genera of water molds also attack prothalli and sporelings; these appear water-soaked when infected.

A few differences between the two types of water molds are evident, however. Generally, *Phytophthora* tends to attack woody plants, whereas *Pythium* favors herbaceous ones such as ferns. *Phytophthora* discolors the conducting tissue of the stem; *Pythium* discolors the softer tissue (the pith and cortex), often reducing it to a mush.

Water molds differ from *Rhizoctonia* by their tendency to infect the root tips and then progress upward, whereas *Rhizoctonia* infects the stem at the soil surface and progresses up and down. Also, the filaments of water molds, unlike those of *Rhizoctonia,* are so fine that they are invisible even with a hand lens, and they do not cling to soil particles.

Prevention and Control. Prevention is the best measure. Provide good drainage and do not overwater. Avoid splashing water, which will spread the disease from contaminated water and soil. As always, do not permit contaminated soil or other equipment to be mixed with clean soil or equipment. Infected plants should be discarded. Before replanting the contaminated areas, sterilize the soil. Peat moss may be a source of *Pythium*.

A biological control fungus, *Trichoderma,* kills water molds but is not widely available. A weak (light pink) solution of potassium permanganate used as a drench inhibits water molds. Metalaxyl (Subdue) is a systemic fungicide used as a drench. Commercial growers sometimes use it as a preventative measure at rates of 0.5 ml per 3.8 liters of water (about 5 drops per gallon). Granular forms are also available. Fenaminosulf (Dexon, Lesan) kills only water molds but degrades in light and must be used at once. Etridiazole (Terrazole, Truban), fosetyl-Al (Aliette), and captan are also used. All are registered for use on foliage plants, but sometimes only for Boston fern or leather fern, so test spraying should be done. Be careful with Aliette: it can burn ferns.

Algae, Mosses, and Liverworts

Algae, mosses, and liverworts can shade or crowd fern prothalli and sporelings. Some species of cyanobacteria (blue-green algae) produce toxins, and this may explain the decline in cultures so contaminated.

Algae

Of all the algae found in spore pans, the green algae and cyanobacteria (blue-green algae) cause the most trouble. *Oscillatoria* (a cyanobacteria) forms a blackish slime when growing under bright light, and a grayish mold-like mat under high humidity and dimmer light. It also emits a distinct odor. Studies indicate that some toxins produced by cyanobacteria reduce respiration in mammals and seed plants, which might account for the inhibition of sporeling growth when these algae are present. Nevertheless, some of the diminished growth probably results from the cyanobacteria robbing the plant of light, crowding it, and attracting fungus gnats. Ferns that are inherently slow growing or those growing in poor conditions in spore pans are most susceptible to algae. By providing optimum conditions for rapid fern growth, some of the algae problems may be averted.

PREVENTION AND CONTROL. Practice sanitation in planting and growing areas. Sterilize the soil before sowing spores. Use only distilled water because tap water might be contaminated with algae, and avoid any other possible contamination sources, such as unclean watering cans or pots. If algae appear, pick out the growth. In small plantings a light dab with a cotton swab will usually pick up the algae mat without disturbing the ferns. Dry soil additives such as pumice and sawdust placed on top of soilless mixes can reduce algae growth.

Algae can be controlled with quaternary ammonium compounds (Physan 20 or Green Shield). Sprays of these algaecides were harmless to small plants of *Cyrtomium falcatum*, *Dicksonia antarctica*, *Pteris cretica*, *Sphaeropteris cooperi*, and *Sphaeropteris medullaris* when used at a rate of 400 ppm (1.67 ml per 3.8 liters of water, or ⅓ tsp. per gal.). With either chemical, reapplications will probably be necessary.

A pale blue solution (0.1 ppm) of copper sulfate (bluestone) used as a drench will also inhibit algae growth. Do not allow any of the solution to get on the ferns. Various algaecides have been found to hurt young ferns, whereas others (such as Algamycin) do not. The synthetic antibiotic chloramphenicol (Parke-Davis or Rochelle) has been used to control cyanobacteria as a drench (at 20–40 ppm) but is not registered for this use. Chlorothalonil (Daconil 2787) and mancozeb (Dithane M-45) are other fungicides that have been reported as effective against some algae.

To prevent the spread of algae and to destroy the habitat of fungus gnats and other pests, the algae on benches, walkways, and walls should be controlled. Many commercial preparations are available for this purpose, but some are toxic to plants and must be used with care. Drenches or sprays of hydrated lime (at 681 g to 3.8 liters of water, or 1.5 lbs. per gal.) or copper sulfate (454 g to 3.8 liters, or 1 lb. per gal.) are effective.

MOSSES AND LIVERWORTS

Mosses and liverworts can become so abundant that they crowd and shade prothalli, especially in old cultures under bright light. Do not allow liverworts (particularly *Lunularia*) to establish among your ferns. They spread rapidly, carpeting the soil surface and preventing water, fertilizer, and air from getting into the soil.

PREVENTION AND CONTROL. Sterilize the soil before sowing spores, and water with distilled water. If mosses are a problem, do not put charcoal on the soil because many mosses flourish on it. Remove mosses and liverworts by hand if they grow over the ferns. When removing liverworts, try not to fragment them because the pieces will regenerate. Fern prothalli should be grown under lower light to weaken mosses. Most species of greenhouse mosses need more light to grow robustly than do ferns. Provide optimum conditions to hasten the growth of ferns, because slow-growing cultures tend to develop more mosses and liverworts. *Marchantia*, a liverwort, can be killed with a spray of quaternary ammonium compound (Physan 20) applied at 800 ppm (3.3 ml per 3.8 liters of water, or ⅔ tsp. per gal.). The effect of this spray on ferns is unknown; however, it is known that strong concentrations damage some plants.

12 How Ferns Get Their Names

There are about 12,000 species of ferns worldwide, but only about 30 are commonly cultivated. Most people know these cultivated species by easy-to-remember common names that are sometimes charmingly appropriate or even whimsical. Common names are useful when dealing with only a few species and when local usage is uniform, but they can cause confusion if many species and people from distant lands are involved. One reason for the confusion is that several different common names might apply to the same plant. *Phlebodium aureum,* for example, is known variably as the rabbit's-foot fern, the bear's-foot fern, the serpent fern, and golden polypody. Conversely, several different species might be referred to by the same common name; the name "lace fern" is used to describe plants in five different genera (*Cheilanthes gracillima, Microlepia strigosa, Nephrolepis exaltata* 'Smithii', *Odontosoria chinensis,* and *Paesia scaberula*). No rules are established for designating the correct common name for a species. Any number of names might exist, and new ones can be coined by anyone. Another problem with common names is that most plants don't have them.

Scientific names have the disadvantage of often being long, difficult to pronounce, and hard to remember. Because they are in Latin, their meaning is usually obscure to most people. But scientific names offer several advantages over common names. They are understood internationally. A trained botanist in Indonesia, Russia, or Mexico will know exactly what you mean when you utter "*Dryopteris.*" Using scientific names reduces confusion and increases accuracy in communication. The other great advantage is that they indicate a degree of evolutionary relationship. You can tell by the name, for example, that *Dryopteris intermedia* and *Dryopteris marginalis* are more closely related to each other than either is to *Polystichum acrostichoides.* If the common names of these three species were used—glandular wood fern, marginal shield fern, and Christmas fern—relationships are not apparent. If you deal with many species and want to be precise when communicating with other plant people, then it is worth the time to learn about scientific names.

Every species has only one correct scientific name. The situation is complicated, however, because many species have synonyms, or alternative scientific names, that arise as a result of new discoveries or hypotheses about relationships. For example, in the 1800s the Massachusetts fern was called *Dryopteris simulata,* but this name is now considered a synonym of *Thelypteris simulata* because the plant belongs with the thelypterioid ferns instead of the dryopteroids. The change resulted from greater knowledge based on new evidence about the relationships of the plant.

In the encyclopedic portion of this book, commonly encountered synonyms are given after the accepted scientific name, which is the one currently used in most floras, manuals, and monographs. The synonyms are given because they continue to be used by some gardeners and trade people. There is no mandate that new names be immediately adopted. Sometimes they are controversial, and even professional botanists disagree as to which name is correct. To avoid confusion, plant labels can give both names, placing the synonym in parentheses. The word "formerly" is sometimes added before the synonym. Adding this extra name to labels or catalog lists might be an inconvenience to the commercial growers, but gardeners are becoming more knowledgeable about species names and appreciate greater accuracy in labeling.

Naming Species

The scientific name of a species consists of two words. The first is like the surname of a person (Doe), the second is like the given name (Jane). The first word denotes the genus or larger group to which the plant belongs and indicates some degree of relationship. The second word denotes a particular kind of plant in the group. For instance, *Asplenium bulbiferum* is the scientific name for the mother fern. The first word, *Asplenium,* is the genus to which the mother fern belongs. The second word, *bulbiferum,* indicates the particular kind of *Asplenium.* There is a similar fern called *Asplenium daucifolium.* It is apparent from this name that the species is related to the mother fern because both are in *Asplenium.* It is also clear that the fern is not the same species as the mother fern because it has a different second word, or specific epithet. These two species differ not only in size and color but more significantly by the shape of the leaflets and the rhizome scales (Figure 12.1). Having the same specific epithet means nothing. *Botrychium virginianum* and *Polypodium virginianum* have the same specific epithet, but they belong to different genera and families. In this case the specific epithet indicates that the original specimens from which these species were described were collected in the State of Virginia.

How does a plant get a scientific name? A plant suspected as new to science is studied by a botanist who compares it to its relatives. If no match is found, and the plant is not a freak or variant of a known species, then the botanist names the plant according to the rules set forth in the *International Code of Botanical Nomenclature,* or the Code for short.

If the plant differs greatly from known plants, the botanist might decide to give it a genus name all its own. If, on the other hand, the botanist believes the plant belongs to an established genus, a specific epithet is added to the genus name to complete the species name of the plant. The botanist can name the plant after anything; it may be the name of the person who discovered it, the place where it was discovered, or a structural feature.

The botanist who names the plant is known as the author or authority. The author's name appears after the scientific name, although this is sometimes omitted in general use. The author's name may be given in full, or sometimes only the initials or a surname abbreviation are used. The author citations are important to botanists in determining the priority and application of names. The scientific name for the bird's-nest fern, for example, is *Asplenium nidus* Linnaeus (sometimes abbreviated "L." or "Linn.") for the famous Swedish botanist who began the consistent practice of giving species two names. This practice is called the binomial system, and it permits a systematic arrangement of species into a filing system.

Pronouncing Scientific Names

It matters little how one pronounces scientific names as long as they are understood by the listener. No one knows exactly how Latin was pronounced, and even in the heyday of the Roman Empire several dialects were probably spoken in different regions. So who's to say who's right? The best advice is to pronounce the names as the people around you do. When someone presumes to correct your pronunciation, a knowing smile is the appropriate response.

Figure 12.1. The fronds of the closely allied species *Asplenium bulbiferum* (left) and *A. daucifolium* (right).

Variation Within Species

Variation is a fundamental property of all living things. Just as species vary throughout their range, so do individuals within a given population. This variation might be in plant structure or function, such as producing fuller fronds or producing spores later in the season. The variation could be caused by growing conditions, such as the amount of shade or soil moisture, or by genetic differences, such as mutations or novel gene combinations. Variants with a hereditary basis can be named. Such a name appears after the species name. The common categories for these names are subspecies (subsp.), botanical varieties (var.), forms (forma or f.), and cultivated varieties (cultivar).

Cultivated Varieties

A cultivated variety, or cultivar, is a distinctive plant arising through selection from cultivated or wild stock or by hybridization in cultivation. Its distinctive attributes are uniform and stable and are retained when propagated. Whether or not the variant is distinct and worthy of being assigned a name is left to the individual naming the cultivar to decide. Not every fern variation is named, and many are unworthy of receiving a name. Some common variations seen in cultivated varieties of ferns include the following:

- Changes in the leaf margin, such as fringing, lobing, ruffling, cresting, or forking.
- Changes in size of the parts, such a depauperate, narrower, wider, smaller, or large pinnae or pinnules.
- Changes in position of the parts, such as overlapping or more distant pinnae.
- Changes in overall size of the plant, such as dwarfism or gigantism.
- Changes in color, such as variegation.
- Miscellaneous changes, such as formation of buds, failure to form spores, maintenance of juvenile foliage, and even physiological differences such as greater resistance to drought or cold.

Figure 12.2 shows the variations possible in cultivars of the lady fern.

The name of a plant cultivar is enclosed in single quotation marks and follows the species name. Older usage might have the abbreviation "cv." preceding the cultivar name. Valid cultivar names given after 1959 are in non-Latin form and in roman type, not italic. The main words of the name have the first letter capitalized, as in *Adiantum raddianum* 'Pacific Maid'. The species epithet can be omitted if there is no likelihood of confusion with another cultivar bearing the same name in the genus. Thus *Adiantum* 'Pacific Maid' is permissible.

Cultivar-groups are used to name an assemblage of two or more similar, named cultivars. (The word "named" was added to the definition of cultivar-group in the 1995 *International Code of Nomenclature for Cultivated Plants.* This precludes using the cultivar-group as a catchall category for variants belonging to the group but unworthy of recognition. This wording is currently being met with considerable controversy.) This category may also be used to recognize distinct groups within a species when the species itself is no longer recognized. For instance, plants known as *Davallia fejeensis* have been reduced by some botanists to *D. solida*. Plants known as *D. fejeensis* are prized by horticulturists and in this reduction to *D. solida* would be left without a name. However, it may continue to be recognized by using the cultivar-group category *D. solida* Fejeensis Group. If a particular cultivar in the Fejeensis Group needs to be identified, the group name is enclosed in parentheses, followed by the cultivar name in single quotation marks, as in *Davallia solida* (Fejeensis Group) 'Plumosa'.

Naming of cultivated plants is governed by rules set forth in the *International Code of Nomenclature for Cultivated Plants,* commonly referred to as the Cultivated Plant Code or *ICNCP* (Trehane 1995). The Cultivated Plant Code promotes uniformity, accuracy, and stability in naming horticultural plants. Growers, plant businesses, and producers of cultivated varieties should use these rules to minimize confusion. The assignment and use of cultivar names is a voluntary matter. It should not be confused with trademark names or patents, which are legal matters involving the government (discussed later in the chapter).

Unfortunately, despite these rules, the naming of fern cultivars in the trade and among hobbyist growers often makes it difficult to determine whether a given cultivar is new or a renamed older one. Most cultivars in circulation have not been named according to the rules in the *International Code of Nomenclature for Cultivated Plants,* and thus, technically speaking, have invalid names. Yet it is impossible to ignore these names because they are an important part of the commercial trade and of many gardens. Until a Fern Registration Authority is established, the problems with the valid naming and identification of many cultivars will be difficult to solve.

BOTANICAL VARIETIES AND FORMS

Species that show significant variation in different parts of their geographic range are said to have botanical varieties. These variations may be given botanical variety status (var.) and named. For example, the bracken fern (*Pteridium aquilinum*) has several botanical varieties (Figure 12.3). In the western United

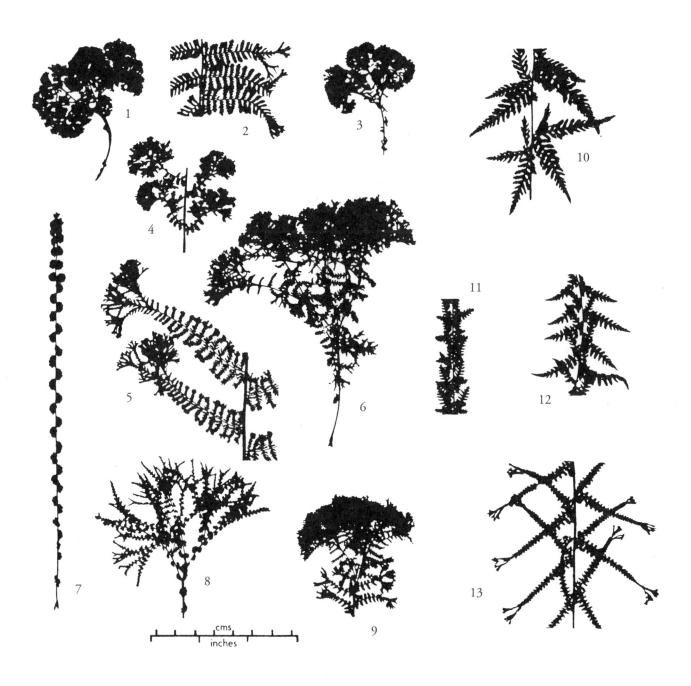

Figure 12.2. Variation in cultivars of the lady fern (*Athyrium filix-femina*): 1. 'Caput-Medusae'; 2. 'Foliosum Grandiceps'; 3. 'Grandiceps' (dwarf form); 4. 'Gemmatum Bolton' (original clone); 6. 'Acroladon' (original clone); 7. 'Frizelliae' (original clone); 8. 'Frizelliae Cristatum' (from spore); 9 'Corymbiferum'; 10. 'Pritchardii' (original clone); 11. 'Angustocruciatum Cristatum'; 12. 'Fieldii' (original clone); 13. 'Victoriae' (original clone); 14. 'Victoriae Foliosum'; 15. 'Flabellipinnulum'; 16. 'Minutissimum Congestum'; 17. 'Congestum Minus'; 18. 'Crispum Coronans'; 19. 'Veroniae' (original clone); 20. 'Plumosum Stansfield' (original clone); 21. 'Plumosum Druery' (original clone); 22. 'Plumosum Furcillans'; 23. 'Plumosum Penny' (original clone); 24. 'Plumosum Multifidum'; 25. 'Howardii' (original clone); 26. 'Clarissima Jones' (original clone); 27. 'Cristatum'; 28 'Clarissima Cristatum Garnett' (original clone). After Kaye (1965).

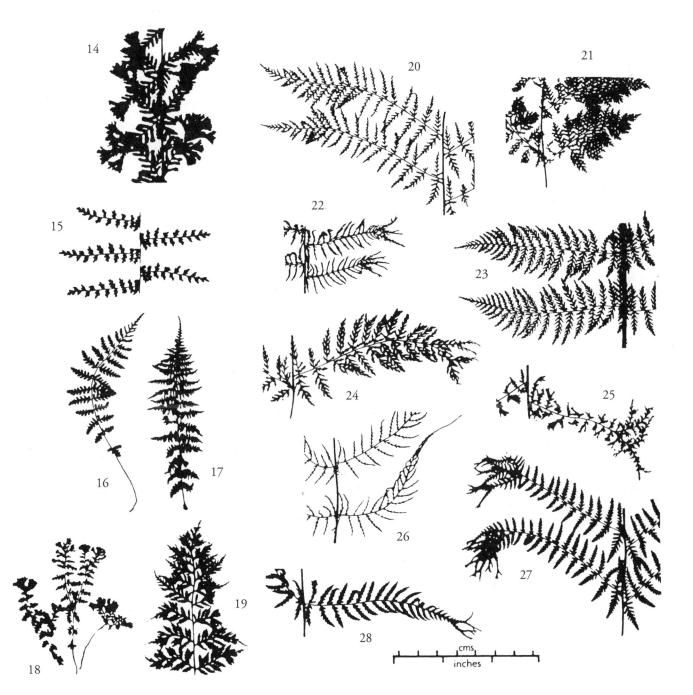

States there is *P. aquilinum* var. *pubescens,* the western bracken; common in the northeastern United States is *P. aquilinum* var. *latiusculum,* the eastern bracken. Besides geographical differences, the western bracken has pinnules nearly at right angles to the rachis and hairs on the indusia, while the eastern bracken has obliquely placed pinnules and hairless indusia. A third and more southeastern variety, *P. aquilinum* var. *pseudocaudatum,* the tailed bracken, has long, narrow terminal segments. A fourth variety occurs in southern Florida: *P. aquilinum* var. *caudatum,* the lacy bracken, with very stiff, wiry fronds. (Some botanists now believe var. *caudatum* to be a separate species and call it *P. caudatum.*) The abbreviations "subsp." or "ssp." stand for subspecies, a category used to imply an incipient species.

Figure 12.3. Comparison of the foliage of the botanical varieties of *Pteridium aquilinum* (left to right): var. *latiusculum,* var. *pubescens,* and var. *caudatum.*

A variation that appears sporadically among plants in nature is placed in a category known as a form (forma or f.). Additionally, the variation should be found sporadically throughout the range of the species. An example is *Blechnum spicant* f. *bipinnatum.* The typical form of the species (*B. spicant* f. *spicant*) has entire pinnae, but f. *bipinnatum* has deeply lobed pinnae. The lobed form, which is atypical, was found growing among typical plants in nature (Figure 12.4).

Sometimes botanical forms can be environmentally induced. Examples are the lobed types of sensitive fern (*Onoclea sensibilis*) and Christmas fern (*Polystichum acrostichoides*). In certain individuals of these species, abnormally deeply lobed pinnae are produced on plants that also produce typical pinnae. The deep lobes are caused by trauma from frost, mowing, fire, or transplanting (Beitel et al. 1981; Wagner 1942). These variants are often referred to as *Onoclea sensibilis* f. *obtusilobata* and *Polystichum acrostichoides* f. *incisum,* but they are unworthy of taxonomic recognition. If they were named, then two different form names would apply to the same plant—an illogical situation.

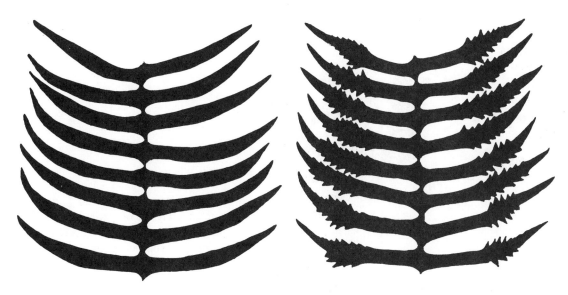

Figure 12.4. Comparison of the pinnae of the botanical forms of *Blechnum spicant:* forma *spicant* (left) and forma *bipinnatum* (right).

Early use of the category "varietas" did not distinguish between cultivated varieties, botanical varieties, and forms; hence, many plants listed as "var." are nowadays considered cultivars or forms. Actually, the distinction between cultivated varieties, botanical varieties, and forms is poorly defined and overlapping. A few plants might end up having both a botanical name and a cultivar name. The naming of subspecies, varieties, and forms is governed by rules set forth in the *International Code of Botanical Nomenclature*.

HYBRIDS

A hybrid is the offspring from a cross between two different species. Fern hybrids are often sterile because the chromosomes from the two parents cannot pair with each other during meiosis—the kind of cell division that gives rise to spores. The result is spore abortion, and under the microscope the spores appear irregular, misshapen, and often blackened. Ferns with aborted spores must be propagated by division of the rhizome or by buds.

When sterile, hybrids are designated by the hybrid sign "×" placed between the genus name and specific epithet. Examples are *Adiantum* ×*tracyi* (= *A. aleuticum* × *A. jordanii*), *Dryopteris* ×*triploidea* (= *D. carthusiana* × *D. intermedia*), and *Polystichum* ×*potteri* (= *P. acrostichoides* × *P. braunii*). A name such as "*Adiantum* ×*tracyi*" is the binomial; "*A. aleuticum* × *A. jordanii*" is the formula name.

Occasionally a sterile hybrid doubles its chromosome number, a process referred to as polyploidy. Polyploidy automatically confers fertility to the hybrid. The plant can now produce normal (not misshapen) spores that germinate upon sowing. Such fertile hybrids, also known as "nothospecies," take on an existence of their own, sometimes spreading far beyond the ranges of the parents. In this book, fertile species of hybrid origin are given binomials without using the hybrid sign "×." Examples of such plants are *Cystopteris tennesseensis,* which arose from a cross involving *C. bulbifera* and *C. protrusa,* and *Dryopteris clintoniana,* which arose from a cross involving *D. celsa* and *D. ludoviciana.*

Crosses between different genera may be placed in hybrid genera (Figure 12.6). To form the name of a hybrid genus, the generic names of the two parents are combined, and the hybrid sign "×" is placed before the name. For example, a hybrid between a species of *Aglaomorpha* and a species of *Drynaria* would be placed in the hybrid genus ×*Aglaonaria*.

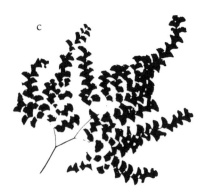

Figure 12.5. Hybrid of species in the same genus: a. parent *Adiantum jordanii;* b. parent *A. aleuticum;* c. hybrid offspring *A. ×tracyi.*

If naturally occurring hybrids are brought into cultivation, they must keep their hybrid name unless they were given an additional cultivar name at the time of publication (this rarely, if ever, happens). For example, *Adiantum ×tracyi* must be listed as such in horticultural use (Figure 12.5). But had this hybrid originated in cultivation (it did not), it would be permissible to list it as *Adiantum* 'Tracyi'.

Why Fern Names Change

Changing the accepted scientific name of a fern annoys growers and even professional botanists. But without name changes, new knowledge about ferns would be difficult to assimilate and organize. Maintaining existing names would be like keeping a static file. Newly discovered plants would have to be added to the existing categories in the file. Some categories would contain such large numbers of plants that they would be unwieldy to work with and difficult to understand. Unrelated plants would be inadvertently placed together, while related ones could be scattered in separate categories. It would be like trying to classify vehicles of today into categories made for the vehicles of 1900.

To accommodate our increasing knowledge of plants and to organize it into a meaningful relationship, files occasionally have to be changed. New categories might need to be added, and older ones combined or divided. As a result, there will be name changes. But of greater importance and broader interest is that the new knowledge of plants and their relationships is incorporated into the file, and the way the plants are organized in the file will reflect our updated knowledge. There are still many gaps in our knowledge of plant relationships, and until these plants are thoroughly studied and understood, name changes are sure to continue.

Figure 12.6. Hybrid of species of different genera: a. parent *Asplenium adiantum-nigrum;* b. parent *Phyllitis scolopendrium;* c. hybrid offspring ×*Asplenophyllitis jacksonii.* After Lovis and Vida (1969).

Trademarks and Plant Patents

A grower or originator of a cultivar may obtain a trademark or a trademark name for his or her plant. If approved by government authorities, the trademark does not prevent others from growing the particular plant, only from using the mark or name. Such trade names are not technically considered cultivar names, since the *International Code of Nomenclature for Cultivated Plants* stipulates that cultivar names must be available to all users. According to the Cultivated Plant Code, the trade names should be printed in capital letters to distinguish them from the true cultivar name and to indicate their special status. Trademarked names and plant patents are usually recognized by notations or symbols next to the names.

Patents are separate legal entities from trademarks and must be applied for separately. United States law grants a patent to anyone who has invented or discovered and asexually reproduced any distinct and new variety of plant. A plant patent excludes others from growing, using, or selling the plant for 17 years in the United States and its territories. Foreign countries may have reciprocal agreements with the United States, or they may have their own laws. Fees, illustrations, and descriptions of the plant and how it differs from others are some of the requirements of applying for a plant patent. Patented plants are primarily identified by a patent number and secondarily by a name. For added protection, patented plants may also have a trademark name, although growers often forego this additional expense. The issuing of trademarks and patents in the United States is governed by the Patent and Trademark Office of the U.S. Department of Commerce in Washington, D.C.

The Plant Variety Protection Act (Public Law 91-577), administered by the U.S. Department of Agriculture in Beltsville, Maryland, provides for a system of protection for cultivated varieties produced from seeds. Since ferns reproduce from spores, this law is not applicable to cultivated fern varieties.

Learning the Fern Genera

When looking at the diversity of cultivated ferns, we somehow know that a particular fern is a staghorn fern or a maidenhair fern. Some ferns are so distinct that we have little difficulty recognizing them. With these and other ferns, the overall appearance is enough to reveal to us its fern group. Other ferns require closer observation. For instance, if you look only at their foliage characteristics, the maidenhair spleenwort (*Asplenium trichomanes*) and the bird's-nest fern (*A. nidus*) appear very different—yet both are members of the

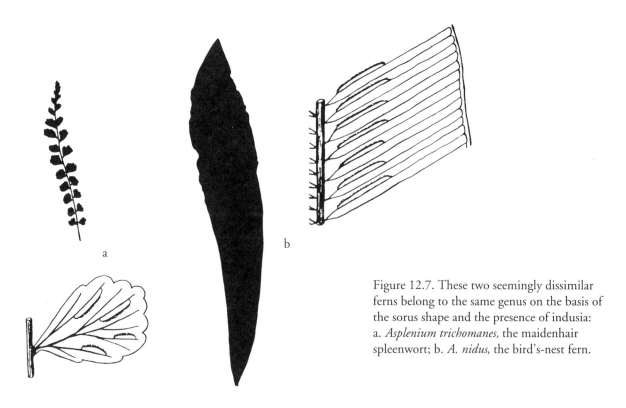

Figure 12.7. These two seemingly dissimilar ferns belong to the same genus on the basis of the sorus shape and the presence of indusia: a. *Asplenium trichomanes,* the maidenhair spleenwort; b. *A. nidus,* the bird's-nest fern.

genus *Asplenium* (Figure 12.7). What distinguishes this genus are the sori and indusia, not the shape of the frond. The sori and indusia of the two *Asplenium* species are long and narrow, and although longer in the bird's-nest fern, they are basically the same in both species. The indusium in both species is attached to the upper fork of a vein branch, and the rhizome scales are latticed or resemble a stained-glass window (clathrate) when observed through a hand lens. (They also all have two vascular bundles in the stipe.) Thus the relationships between ferns is not always obvious to the naked eye.

The fern student interested in learning how to recognize ferns in general should start by studying the genera. Start with a fern that you know, such as the maidenhair ferns of genus *Adiantum.* Select a fertile frond, and look up the scientific name of the plant in the index of this book. The discussion in Chapter 13 will describe a few of the more conspicuous features that distinguish this genus from others. Locate on your fern the features mentioned, then check your observations with the illustrations of the genus. A hand lens of 8 to 15× magnification will assist you greatly. Once you are satisfied that you can recognize the features mentioned, keep them in mind; the next time you see another kind of maidenhair fern, look for these features again. Soon you will associate maidenhairs with a certain set of features. You will also recognize features that do not belong with the maidenhairs. Select other fern genera that you know and repeat the process: (1) look up the scientific name; (2) locate the distinguishing features on your plant; (3) check your observations with the diagrams; and (4) examine other members of the genus for the same features to reinforce your observations. At this point you may be able to recognize some of the more technical differences between the species within the genus, but it is most important to concentrate on the features of the genus as a whole. The features used to distinguish a genus are generally less diversified and less confusing than those used to distinguish species. Besides, the species will be easier to recognize once you have become familiar with the genera. Most of the generic features are associated with the position, shape, and type of sorus and indusium. Also important is the rhizome, which may be erect or creeping, hairy or scaly. The venation and the shape of the frond may also be important. Chapters 2 and 13 and the glossary discuss or illustrate most of these distinguishing features.

13 Ferns and Fern Allies in Cultivation

This chapter describes the ferns and fern allies commonly cultivated in the United States. It omits those species found only in special collections and botanical gardens. Some species treated here may no longer be in cultivation; conversely, it was impractical to include all recent introductions. A few genera not cultivated in the United States are included because they were deemed worthy of culture, challenging to grow, or important in teaching botany. Most of the entries have been verified against botanical specimens and/or descriptions; however, specimens or sufficient data were not always available, and many species are poorly known. The correctness of the names must be considered in view of these problems.

Explanations of the Entries

GENUS ENTRIES

Common alternative names (synonyms), if any, are listed after each genus name. Synonyms are followed by common names, which are given only if widely used. The text that follows provides a general introduction to the genus, followed by a botanical description. Any special name problems encountered within a genus are also discussed.

If botanists agree on a particular genus name and there is little possibility of a new name change, the agreed-upon name is usually adopted. When a name has been changed, however, the traditional genus name will be cross-referenced.

Large genera such as *Athyrium, Cheilanthes, Davallia, Polypodium, Selaginella, Thelypteris,* and others have been subdivided formally or informally into smaller groups. The diagnostic characters and species are listed for each subgroup. This will assist the reader in identifying a fern to a particular subgroup without having to study each fern in the species entry.

SPECIES ENTRIES

Species within each genus are listed alphabetically by scientific name. Synonyms or misapplied names and common names, if any, follow. Cultural information is followed by a brief botanical description and information on the geographical area to which the fern is native.

Where species important in horticulture were reduced by botanists to another species (as is the case in the genus *Davallia*), the horticulturally important species name was retained with a note in the entry indicating the discrepancy. Keeping such names is the least disruptive stance to take at this time. If necessary, they may later be given cultivar status.

Only the most important synonyms are listed for a species; many synonyms not used in horticulture are omitted. You can get an idea of the other genera under which a species might be synonymized by looking at the generic synonyms after the genus name, or by referring to the Index of Plant Names. If the fern is widely known under an incorrect name, this name will be noted as being "misapplied to" or as a "trade name."

Subspecies, varieties, and cultivars. Within the species entries, plants below the rank of species, including subspecies, varieties, forms, and cultivars, are also discussed. Due to the tremendous number of cultivars—there are at least a thousand—including all cultivars is beyond the scope of this book and many are omitted. We have focused on those cultivars that are more common in the trade or among hobbyists and have a fairly distinct appearance. Cultivars with names that are believed to be in agreement with the *International Code of Nomenclature for Cultivated Plants* are also favored. As discussed in the previous chapter, the cultivar names circulating in the trade are not always reliable because they are often invalid or inconsistently or erroneously used. Where a name is known to be commonly misapplied to a particular plant, that is indicated in the text.

CULTURAL INFORMATION

For each species, information is provided on the temperature, light, soil, and water requirements of the plants. Ornamental attributes, including height and habit, and landscape uses are also discussed. The cultural information is meant only as a guide. Often little is known about a fern's requirements for growth, and what is known can vary greatly with different gardens, microclimates, and genetic races of the plants.

Height. As used in this chapter, fern size refers to the height of the whole plant, not the frond length. Because some ferns vary greatly, the given heights may have exceptions. The following general terms are used to describe fern height:

Very small: less than 15 cm (6 in.) tall
Small: less than 30 cm (1 ft.) tall
Medium: 30–100 cm (1–3 ft.) tall
Large: over 100 cm (3 ft.) tall

Temperature. It is difficult to give the minimum temperature tolerances of most introduced ferns. Little data exist on the subject, and what is reported is often insufficiently documented. Knowing the temperatures of the fern's native habitat helps, but ferns often grow well in colder or hotter places than might be expected from their natural distribution. The categories of hardiness used in this book are fairly broad and may overlap, but they offer workable categories for sorting out the hardiness of different ferns. The range of average annual minimum temperatures in the following section is based on the USDA Plant Hardiness Zone Map (United States Department of Agriculture, Agricultural Research Service, Miscellaneous Publication Number 1475; also see the map at the end of the color plates section). These ratings indicate the minimum temperature range at which a plant may be expected to survive. They do not necessarily represent the optimal winter temperature for the plant. Also keep in mind that the timing and duration of the minimum temperatures can profoundly affect a fern's survival, as can many other factors. Microclimates and genetic variations within a species often create exceptions to hardiness ratings. Two ferns might be listed as tolerating the same minimum temperatures, yet one might survive only with cool nights whereas the other only with warm nights.

Very hardy: Severe and extended winters, such as in alpine, tundra, taiga, and northern coniferous forest. The range of annual minimum temperature is −46°C and below to −29°C (−50°F and below to −20°F).

Hardy: Cold-temperate areas; tolerates long periods below freezing. The range of average annual minimum temperature is −29 to −15°C (−20 to 5°F).

Semi-hardy: Warmer temperate areas; tolerates short periods below freezing. The range of average annual minimum temperature is −15 to −10°C (5 to 15°F).

Semi-tender: Subtropical areas, with frost or subfreezing temperatures very rare; winter night temperatures often reaching 4 to 10°C (40 to 50°F). The range of average annual minimum temperature is −10 to −4°C (15 to 25°F).

Tender: Tropical areas, indoors, or greenhouses not below 16°C (60°F) at night, 18°C (65°F) or higher during the day. The range of average annual minimum temperature is −4 to 4°C and above (25 to 40°F and above).

Very tender: Temperatures should be maintained at about 21°C (70°F) or higher most of the time; some species will tolerate infrequent dips to 18°C (65°F). The range of average annual minimum temperature is 4°C and above (40°F and above).

With the dearth of data on introduced ferns, we have used broader categories of hardiness than the U.S. Department of Agriculture's hardiness zone map. Where USDA zones are known from reliable sources, they are cited. The rough equivalent between the USDA zones and those used in this book are given in Table 13.1.

Table 13.1. Geographical Areas and Their Hardiness Ratings

Geographical area	Range of average minimum temperature	USDA zones	Ratings in this text
Alpine, tundra	below −46°C to −40°C (below −50°F to −40°F); extremely cold, arctic climate	1, 2	very hardy
Coniferous forest, northern Midwest	−40°C to −29°C (−40°F to −20°F); very cold temperate	3, 4	very hardy
Northeast and central Midwest	−29°C to −18°C (−20°F to 0°F); cold temperate	5, 6	hardy
Far West inland areas, south to northern New Mexico	−29°C to −18°C (−20°F to 0°F); cold temperate	5, 6	hardy
Southeastern states, most of Texas to southern New Mexico	−18°C to −7°C (0°F to 20°F); temperate	7, 8	hardy to semi-hardy or semi-tender
Coastal Northwest	−12°C to −1°C (10°F to 30°F); warm temperate	8, 9	semi-hardy to semi-tender or tender
Pacific states slightly inland to southern Arizona	−12°C to −1°C (10°F to 30°F); warm temperate	8, 9	semi-hardy to semi-tender or tender
Coastal southern California	−1°C to 4°C and above (30°F to 40°F and above); subtropical and Mediterranean climate	10, 11	tender to very tender
Southern Florida, Hawaii	above 4°C (above 40°F); tropical climate	10, 11	tender to very tender

Light. Because light intensity interacts with humidity and temperature, these factors must be considered along with the light ratings given in this book. Light intensity is usually measured in units called foot-candles. Estimating foot-candles by eye is difficult. See Appendix I for information on calculating foot-candles with a camera light meter.

Low light: Dense shade, about 200 to 400 foot-candles.
Medium light: Partial shade and sun or medium shade, about 400 to 600 foot-candles.
High light: Bright shade, about 600 to 1000 foot-candles.
Direct sunlight: On a clear day, direct sunlight measures from 5,000 to 10,000 foot-candles. Plants tolerating direct sun usually can withstand higher temperatures as well.

Soil. The following terms are used in the plant entries to categorize soil types:

Garden soil: Garden soil, preferably a loam with a lot of humus.
Potting mix: Mostly soilless mixes; must be well-drained if containing soil.
Uncut moss: Coarse, uncut, or unground moss (green moss or sphagnum moss). Used in hanging baskets or tied to boards to give good drainage.
Drained: Provide with good drainage, which may be increased by planting on boards, hanging baskets, or mixing material such as bark pieces, coarse perlite, or coarse sand in the medium.
Acidic: Prefers acidic conditions (pH 4–7).
Basic: Prefers basic or limestone conditions (pH 7–8).

Water. Most ferns should be watered deeply but not too often; avoid light sprinkles. Expect the soil to be saturated after a thorough watering. Fortunately for most plants, this saturated condition does not last long as the extra water will drain away, the soil will start to dry, and much of the water will be replaced by air. The basic requirement is to keep the soil at the moisture level preferred by the plant for most of the time and not let it dry out. Water less during cool weather and more frequently during hot, dry weather.

Wet: The soil is saturated with water and the excess allowed to drain away (a condition known as field capacity). Plants that prefer such conditions have to be watered more frequently to maintain this level of wetness.
Moist-wet: The soil is not saturated with water but feels wet and tends to be sticky when handled. It is a condition between those described for wet and moist.
Moist: The soil feels moist but is not so wet as to be sticky when handled. Most ferns prefer this range of moisture.
Moist-dry: The soil feels damp but is not sticky to the hands. It is a condition between those described for moist and dry.
Dry: The soil feels dry and is light in weight due to the low water content.

EVERGREEN AND DECIDUOUS FERNS

As discussed in Chapter 9, the distinction between evergreen and deciduous is not always sharp. If the deciduous behavior of a species is known and is consistent in different climates, it is indicated as "deciduous" in the text. Otherwise, gardeners should evaluate each species for their particular climate. Most tropical and subtropical ferns grow slowly during cool months, and their fronds may become tattered and discolored, but once the temperature rises they resume active growth.

Evergreen. As used in this text, evergreen refers mainly to hardy ferns that remain green even in freezing temperatures. These ferns grow primarily in temperate climates. Tender ferns can be assumed to be evergreen (or nearly so) unless noted otherwise.

Deciduous. As used in this text, deciduousness indicates fronds that markedly wither and fall from the plant or wither in place (marcescent) even if temperatures remain constant. Some subtropical or tropical species (mainly native to seasonal climates) are deciduous at certain times of the year regardless of temperature changes.

DIAGNOSTIC FEATURES

Each species entry includes the main diagnostic characteristics, not a full botanical description. Because these descriptions are short, the accompanying illustration of the species should be examined. Refer to the preceding chapters and the glossary for explanations of unfamiliar terms.

Examining Ferns for Identification

When examining a fern, you should select recently matured fronds from adult plants. Fresh, clean plant material is especially important when looking at the indusia and scales. A good hand lens with 10× magnification is essential for observing smaller features. Hold the lens close to your eye to get the widest field of view and close-up of the subject. Keep the subject in full light, not in your shadow when examining it. Characteristics that require a microscope to be seen are omitted in this book.

Where vein patterns must be examined, use strong back lighting. If the blade is too thick, look for discolored portions where the veins might be more visible. Failing this, a small piece of the blade can be soaked in lye—a kitchen drain-opener such as Draino works well. Soak the tissue until it clears and the veins become visible; this will usually take one or two days unless the blade is very thick. Drain and rinse the tissue thoroughly because lye and drain-openers are extremely caustic. Veins may become more visible on fronds soaked in water for a week or two as the softer tissue disintegrates.

Sometimes you need to examine cross sections of the stipes to see the number and arrangement of the vascular bundles (conducting tissue). To do this, cut the stipe near the base and examine its cut surface. Use a sharp blade because a dull one will tear and distort the tissue.

Ferns can be identified by using floras, or books that treat the plants growing in a given geographical area. For fern genera from anywhere in the world, try Kramer and Green (1990); for the American tropics, try Tryon and Tryon (1982); for ferns in Canada and the United States, see Mickel (1979), Lellinger (1985), and Flora of North America Editorial Committee (1993). Lellinger (1994) includes a list of floras in print.

Sometimes botanists at universities, botanical gardens, and museums will agree to identify ferns or know of someone who will. Contact them first and ask for permission to send ferns for identification, and ask how the ferns should be prepared for shipment. The task of identification is greatly simplified if a portion of the rhizome with intact hairs or scales is included with the sterile and fertile fronds. Moreover, it is important to know the fern's country of origin and (especially in the tropics) its elevation. Small pieces of fronds are unsuitable for identification.

Acrostichum
Leather fern

FIGURES 13.1.1, 2

The genus *Acrostichum* includes bold-looking ferns with large, erect fronds up to 4 m (13 ft.) tall. Although the plants grow tall in the wild, they tend to be shorter in cultivation. In tropical climates or large indoor spaces with adequate light, they can be grown in ponds or in pots kept wet or set in water. *Acrostichum* is subject to damage by scale insects and slugs.

All three species of *Acrostichum* have fronds that are one-pinnate and leathery, with veins closely and uniformly netted. The fertile pinnae are slightly narrower than the sterile ones. The sporangia cover the entire lower surface of each pinna, and the sori lack indusia. *Acrostichum* is the name-sake of "acrostichoid sori," a term used to describe sori in which the sporangia are spread across the lower surface of the leaf, making the entire sorus resemble a mat of brown felt. Acrostichoid sori always lack indusia. This type of sorus characterizes *Acrostichum* and other, unrelated genera such as *Elaphoglossum* and *Platycerium*.

The genus occurs throughout the tropics, thriving primarily in mangroves and brackish marshes. Its name comes from the Greek *akros*, summit, and *stichos*, row, referring to the fertile pinnae borne toward the leaf apex in *Acrostichum aureum*.

Acrostichum aureum Linnaeus
Leather fern, coastal leather fern
Tender, thrives in Zone (9)10

FIGURE 13.1.3

A very large fern with erect rhizomes and fronds in clusters. Best grown under high light in garden soil or potting mix kept constantly wet. *Acrostichum aureum* can grow with its stems submerged but is typically found rooting in mud with the foliage held above water. It grows natively in brackish water but can be cultivated in fresh water.

Figure 13.1.1. *Acrostichum danaeifolium:* habit.

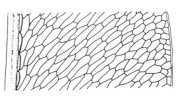

b

a

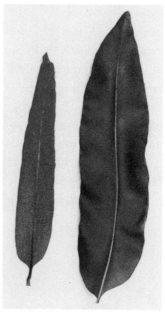

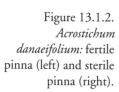

Figure 13.1.2. *Acrostichum danaeifolium:* fertile pinna (left) and sterile pinna (right).

Figure 13.1.3. *Acrostichum aureum:* a. habit, bar = 25 cm (10 in.); b. vein pattern, bar = 5 mm (0.2 in.). After Proctor (1985).

The blades of this species have up to 30 pairs of pinnae that are glabrous on their lower surfaces. The veins form areoles along the costae, and the areoles are about three times longer than wide. See *Acrostichum danaeifolium* for a comparison with that species. *Acrostichum aureum* occurs throughout the tropical regions of the world.

Acrostichum danaeifolium Langsdorff & Fischer

FIGURES 13.1.1, 2, 4

Giant fern, inland leather fern
Tender, Zone 9

A very large fern with erect rhizomes and fronds in clusters. Best grown under high light in garden soil or potting mix kept constantly wet.

The fronds of *Acrostichum danaeifolium* tend to be taller and more erect than those of *A. aureum.* The blades have 40–60 pairs of pinnae. The areoles formed by the veins along the costae are less than three times longer than broad. This species occurs only in the tropics of the New World.

Acrostichum danaeifolium resembles *A. aureum* but can be distinguished by hairs on the lower surface of the blade. The hairs are less than 0.5 mm long and are best seen with a hand lens. The pinnae of this species are also usually closer

together than those of *A. aureum.* If the plants are fertile, another distinction can be seen: the fertile pinnae of *A. danaeifolium* typically occur along the entire length of the leaf (on the basal, middle, and apical portions) whereas those of *A. aureum* occur only toward the apex (usually the apical one to seven pairs). In nature *A. danaeifolium* grows along coasts as well as farther inland—thus the common name inland leather fern—whereas *A. aureum* grows only near the coast.

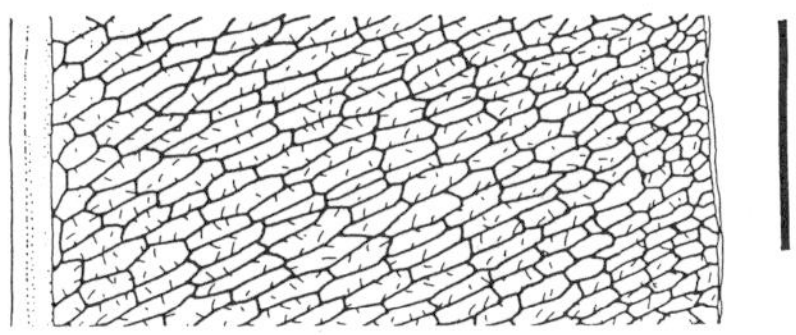

Actiniopteris

Grown as novelty plants for the attractive fan-shaped fronds, *Actiniopteris* is a genus of small, terrestrial ferns with short-creeping rhizomes and clustered fronds. Although attractive, the plants are difficult to grow. They seem to prefer moderately humid conditions, but excessive moisture around their roots should be avoided.

Actiniopteris is characterized by fan-shaped blades repeatedly forked into linear segments. Along the segment margins are the sori, which are protected by the enrolled edges of the segments. In the wild the species grow in dry habitats, and the blades, when dry, bend toward the leaf stalk.

The genus consists of five species and is native to Africa and the arid parts of tropical Asia. Its name comes from the Greek *aktis,* ray, and *pteris,* fern, alluding to the radiating segments of the blade. For additional information on this genus, see Pichi-Sermolli (1962) and the section on "Xerophytic Ferns" in Chapter 10 of this book.

Actiniopteris semiflabellata Pichi-Sermolli

FIGURES 13.2.1, 2

Tender to semi-tender

A small fern with short-creeping rhizomes and close-set stipes. Grows under high light in well-drained, sandy garden soil; avoid overwatering and excessive humidity. *Actiniopteris semiflabellata* is difficult to grow in cultivation.

Figure 13.1.4. *Acrostichum danaeifolium:* a. habit, bar = 25 cm (10 in.), after Proctor (1984); b. vein pattern, bar = 5 mm (0.2 in.), after Proctor (1985).

Figure 13.2.1. *Actiniopteris semiflabellata:* habit.

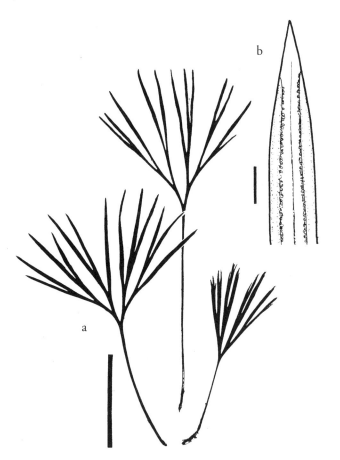

Figure 13.2.2. *Actiniopteris semiflabellata:* a. frond, bar = 5 cm (2 in.); b. sori and indusia, bar = 2 mm.

The base of the blade forms an angle of about 55 to 70 degrees, and the fertile blades consist of 10–24 closely placed, linear segments, with the apex of each segment ending in a tooth. The species occurs in eastern Africa, Arabia, Madagascar, Mauritius, and Nepal.

Actiniopteris semiflabellata is often misidentified in the trade as *A. radiata* (Swartz) Link, a species not cultivated in the United States. *Actiniopteris radiata* differs by its wide, fan-shaped blades that form a 150- to 180-degree angle at their base, and the apices of the broadest fertile segments have two to six teeth.

Adiantopsis

This genus consists of small- to medium-sized, terrestrial or rock-inhabiting ferns. Only one species is cultivated, grown primarily for the attractive radiating arrangement of its pinnae; other species have pedate or pinnate fronds. All species in the genus have erect or short-creeping and decumbent rhizomes. *Adiantopsis* is closely related to *Cheilanthes* but can be distinguished by the grooved upper surface of the rachis and the sharp wings on either side of the groove. The ultimate segments are asymmetrical and eventually fall off,

leaving a clean break. The segments have free veins ending in enlarged tips (hydathodes) on the upper surface. The sori are marginal, short, and covered by a round to crescent-shaped indusium that differs in texture and color from the blade.

Because of the dark stipes and rachises, the shape of the pinnules, and the marginal sori, *Adiantopsis* resembles certain species of *Adiantum*. The genus name, in fact, means "*Adiantum*-like," and comes from adding the Greek suffix *-opsis,* meaning like, to *Adiantum. Adiantopsis* consists of about 10 species and is indigenous to tropical America and Africa.

Adiantopsis radiata (Linnaeus) Fée   FIGURE 13.3.1
Tender to semi-tender

A small fern with short-creeping rhizomes. Best grown under medium to high light in garden soil with sand or potting mix kept moist but well drained. Avoid excessive watering and poor drainage. This species is moderately difficult to cultivate.

Figure 13.3.1. *Adiantopsis radiata:* fronds, bar = 5 cm (2 in.).

Adiantopsis radiata has blades that consist of four to nine one-pinnate pinnae radiating from the top of the stipe. The species occurs throughout most of the American tropics.

Adiantum   FIGURE 13.4.1
Maidenhair fern

Most maidenhairs are small- to medium-sized, terrestrial ferns prized for their fine, billowy foliage and shiny dark stalks. They generally require medium light, humidity, and moist soil but will not tolerate soggy soil. For this reason, keep the plants well drained, and do not overpot. *Adiantum* is mostly tender, but a few species are hardy or semi-hardy.

Figure 13.4.1. *Adiantum capillus-veneris:* habit.

Adiantum is characterized by shiny black or chestnut-brown stipes and sori borne at the margins of the segments. The indusium is formed by the enrolled margin of the segment, and sporangia are borne on its inner surface. This modified leaf margin is called a false indusium, in contrast to a true indusium which is formed by an outgrowth of the epidermis on the lower surface of the leaf. False indusia occur in such related genera as *Cheilanthes, Pellaea,* and *Pteris,* but only in *Adiantum* are the sporangia borne on the false indusium, not beneath it on the opposing leaf tissue. Another distinctive character of *Adiantum* is that the leaflets often lack midribs, and the veins are repeatedly and evenly forked. *Adiantopsis,* a similar genus, is distinguished by the grooving on the upper surfaces of the rachises and costae, with sharp wings on either side of the groove. In contrast, *Adiantum* species (except for *Adiantum flabellulatum*) have rounded and ungrooved rachises and costae.

Adiantum occurs worldwide and consists of about 200 species, most of which grow in the American tropics. The fronds of these species have the unusual property that, when wetted, water beads-up into silvery droplets that quickly roll off. The genus name comes from the Greek *adiantos,* meaning unwettable. For a further account of the cultivated species and their cultivars, see Goudey (1985),

Hoshizaki (1970a), and the section on "Maidenhair Ferns" in Chapter 10.

Adiantum aethiopicum Linnaeus   FIGURE 13.4.2
Semi-tender, Zone 8

A small to medium, clump-forming fern with fronds in loose-spreading clusters on medium- to short-creeping rhizomes. Best grown under medium light in moist garden soil or potting mix. This species is easy to grow.

Adiantum aethiopicum is characterized by finely divided blades up to three- or four-pinnate and by ultimate segments that are fan-shaped to broadly obovate, with up to three deep notches on the distal margin. Typically each segment has one to three sori. The plants are completely glabrous, and in fresh material the base of the segment stalks have an inconspicuous pale green swelling. The indusium is kidney-shaped with a deep, C-shaped sinus. The species is native to South Africa, Australia, New Zealand, and New Caledonia. The specific epithet *aethiopicum* sug-

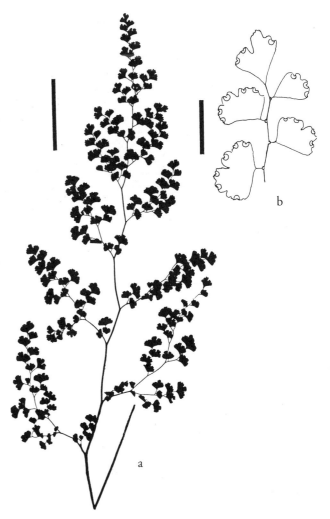

Figure 13.4.2. *Adiantum aethiopicum:* a. frond, bar = 5 cm (2 in.); b. fertile leaflets, bar = 1 cm (0.4 in.).

gests that the species occurs in northern Africa; however, in Africa it occurs only near the Cape.

Most of the plants sold as *Adiantum aethiopicum* in the United States are actually *A. raddianum* 'Triumph', which can be distinguished by its lack of a swelling at the base of the segment stalk and by veins that end in minute sinuses instead of teeth. *Adiantum capillus-veneris,* a similar species, differs by oblong indusia and the absence of swellings on the segment stalk base.

Adiantum aleuticum (Ruprecht) C. A. Paris

FIGURE 13.4.3

syn. *Adiantum pedatum* subsp. *aleuticum* Ruprecht
Western five-finger fern
Hardy, Zone 4(5)

A small to medium fern with fronds in clusters on a clump-forming rhizome. Grows in low to medium light in moist potting mix. *Adiantum aleuticum* can be difficult to grow in arid climates.

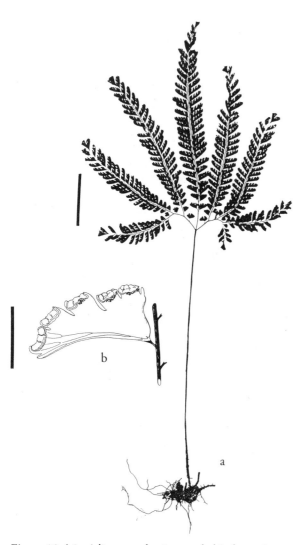

Figure 13.4.3. *Adiantum aleuticum:* a. habit, bar = 5 cm (2 in.); b. fertile leaflet, bar = 1 cm (0.4 in.).

The bluish green fronds are pedate with one-pinnate branches. The blade is fan-shaped or funnel-shaped in outline. The medial segments are more than three times longer than they are broad or somewhat long-triangular or reniform, their tips are sharply denticulate-lobed, and the lobes are separated by deep sinuses, 0.6–4.0 mm deep. *Adiantum aleuticum* is indigenous to the western United States and western Canada.

This species is very close to *Adiantum pedatum,* an eastern United States species that differs in having a rounder blade outline and shorter medial segments with rounded, crenulate or crenulate-toothed lobes. The lobes are separated by shallow sinuses (mostly 0.1–2.0 mm deep).

In the wild this species often grows on serpentine, a metamorphic rock that is often green and slippery to the touch. Serpentine has several traits inimical to plant growth. It is low in essential nutrients, such as nitrogen, calcium, potassium, and phosphorous, and high in toxic elements such as nickel and chromium. Its pH may be either highly acidic or basic. Soils derived from serpentine are often sterile and support unusual endemic plants.

subsp. *subpumilum* (W. H. Wagner) Lellinger (forma *imbricatum* Hoshizaki; 'Imbricatum'). Dwarf western five-finger fern. Smaller than the typical subspecies, with densely overlapping leaflets.

Adiantum anceps Maxon & C. V. Morton

FIGURE 13.4.4

Two-edged maidenhair
Tender

A medium-sized fern with fronds in loose clusters from a thick, short-creeping rhizome. Grows under low to medium light in moist potting mix.

Adiantum anceps has two- to three-pinnate blades with large, ovate to rhomboid segments that have a concavely long-acuminate apex. It resembles *A. peruvianum* but has larger, less rhomboid segments and concavely elongate tips. *Adiantum anceps* is native to the Andes of Colombia, Ecuador, and Peru.

Adiantum bellum T. Moore

FIGURE 13.4.5

Bermuda maidenhair
Semi-tender

A small to medium fern with fronds in loose clusters from a clump-forming rhizome. Grows in low to medium light in moist potting mix.

Adiantum bellum resembles *A. capillus-veneris* (and might be the same) but apparently differs in that the oblong indusia have irregularly jagged, rather than entire, margins. It is native to Bermuda and Guyana.

Some forms superficially resemble *Adiantum tenerum* 'Farleyense'. Some of the trade material circulating as *A. bellum* is actually *A. raddianum* 'Pacottii.'

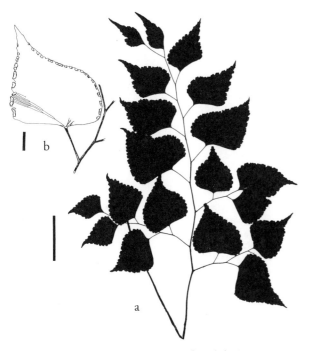

Figure 13.4.4. *Adiantum anceps:* a. frond, bar = 5 cm (2 in.); b. fertile leaflet, bar = 1 cm (0.4 in.).

Adiantum capillus-veneris Linnaeus

FIGURES 13.4.1, 6, 7

Southern maidenhair, Venus's hair
Semi-hardy, Zone 7

A small to medium fern with fronds in loose clusters from a much-branched, medium- to short-creeping rhizome. Grows best under low to medium light in moist, basic garden soil or potting mix. *Adiantum capillus-veneris* is easy to grow and is commonly cultivated. The plants die back with frost. They reportedly do not grow well in the Seattle area (Zone 8), perhaps due to soil that is too acidic.

Adiantum capillus-veneris is characterized by three- to four-pinnate blades and wedge-shaped segments with veins ending in marginal teeth. The color of the segment stalk gradually merges into the green of the veins, and the indusia are oblong and entire. *Adiantum capillus-veneris* is one of the most widely distributed ferns in the world, occurring primarily in warm-temperate to subtropical areas. It often grows on calcareous soil or rocks, especially around springs or caves. It is sometimes cultivated on limestone. This species is often confused with the commonly grown *A. raddianum* and *A. tenerum*.

'Fimbriatum'. Figure 13.4.7a. The distal margins of the segments are fimbriate.

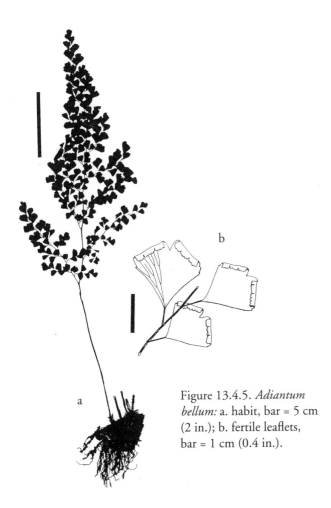

Figure 13.4.5. *Adiantum bellum:* a. habit, bar = 5 cm (2 in.); b. fertile leaflets, bar = 1 cm (0.4 in.).

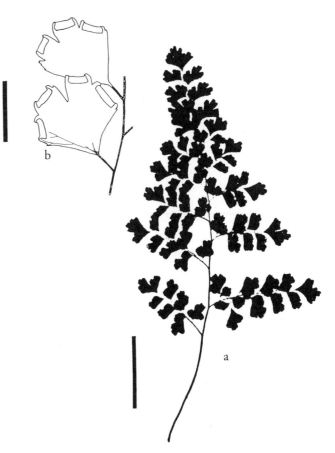

Figure 13.4.6. *Adiantum capillus-veneris:* a. frond, bar = 5 cm (2 in.); b. fertile leaflets, bar = 1 cm (0.4 in.).

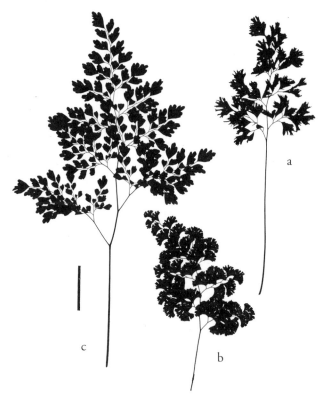

Figure 13.4.7. *Adiantum capillus-veneris* cultivars: a. 'Fimbriatum'; b. 'Imbricatum'; c. 'Mairisii'. Bar = 5 cm (2 in.).

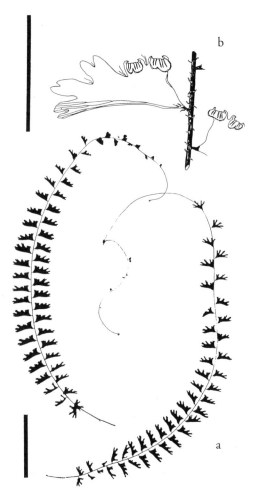

Figure 13.4.8. *Adiantum caudatum:* a. fronds, bar = 5 cm (2 in.); b. fertile leaflets, bar = 1 cm (0.4 in.).

'Imbricatum'. Green petticoats. Figure 13.4.7b. Fronds tend to be decumbent and have ruffled, densely overlapping segments. A beautiful plant, but more difficult to grow than the other cultivars. Avoid overhead watering. Semi-tender.

'Mairisii' ('Banksianum'). Figure 13.4.7c. Sparingly branched rhizomes up to 9 mm (0.4 in.) thick—thicker than those of the other cultivars. Stipes are erect and the blades broadly triangular to triangular, mostly three-pinnate, with segments asymmetrical, long-subrhomboid to triangular. Appears to be more cold hardy than the species. This selection apparently arose in the 1800s at the nursery of Mairis & Co., England, and was described as *Adiantum ×mairisii* T. Moore. Rush (1983) suggests that it was of hybrid origin, resulting from a cross between typical *A. capillus-veneris* and *A. aethiopicum*.

Adiantum caudatum Linnaeus   FIGURE 13.4.8
Trailing maidenhair
Tender

A small to medium fern with nearly erect rhizomes and fronds that arch downward. Grows in medium light in moist potting mix. The plants are best displayed in a hanging container.

Adiantum caudatum has extremely distinctive fronds: they are pendent, up to 50 cm (20 in.) long, narrow, one-pinnate, and bear a bud at the end of a whip-like tip. The pinnae are often coarsely lobed. This species is native to tropical Africa, India, and Asia.

Adiantum concinnum Humboldt & Bonpland ex
Willdenow   FIGURE 13.4.9
Brittle maidenhair
Tender

A small to medium fern with clump-forming rhizomes, glabrous stipes, and broadly triangular fronds. Grows in low to medium light in moist potting mix.

Adiantum concinnum can be distinguished by the innermost segments of the pinnae overlapping the rachis. It is native to tropical America, where it is common and sometimes weedy. The plants often grow on stone walls and steep banks.

'Edwinii'. Fronds and segments broader and larger than the typical species, with the inner upper pinnules hardly overlapping the rachis. The cultivar is easier to grow and is

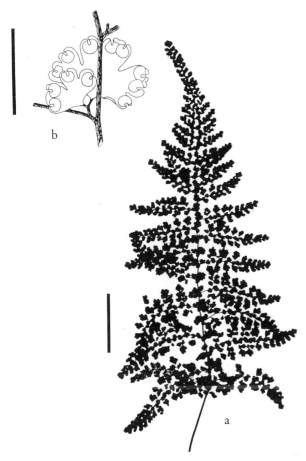

Figure 13.4.9. *Adiantum concinnum:* a. frond, bar = 5 cm (2 in.); b. leaflet pair at base of pinna, bar = 1 cm (0.4 in.).

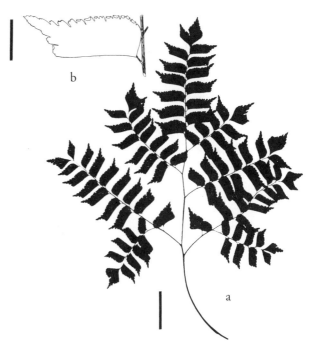

Figure 13.4.10. *Adiantum cultratum:* a. frond, bar = 5 cm (2 in.); b. fertile leaflet, bar = 1 cm (0.4 in.).

less tender than the species form. It might be a hybrid of *Adiantum concinnum* and *A. raddianum.*

Adiantum cultratum J. Smith ex Hooker

FIGURE 13.4.10

Tender

A medium-sized fern with fronds in a loose cluster from slender, creeping rhizomes. Grows under high-medium light in potting mix kept moist.

Adiantum cultratum resembles *A. trapeziforme* but differs by the slender, creeping rhizomes, narrower segments two to two-and-a-half times longer than broad, and shorter stalks (2–3 mm long). It is native to Mexico.

This species needs more study. It was originally described from the Lesser Antilles (St. Vincent) but has not been found there since. *Adiantum cultratum* is currently known from Mexico and has been confused with the plant traditionally called *A. trapeziforme.*

Adiantum diaphanum Blume

FIGURE 13.4.11

Filmy maidenhair

Semi-tender

A small fern with fronds in tufts on a short, semi-erect rhizome. Grows under low to medium light in moist potting mix with a lot of peat.

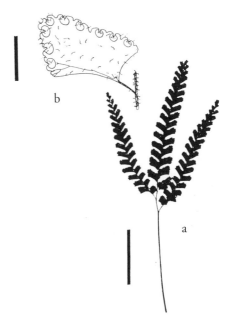

Figure 13.4.11. *Adiantum diaphanum:* a. frond, bar = 5 cm (2 in.); b. fertile leaflet, bar = 1 cm (0.4 in.).

Adiantum diaphanum is characterized by smooth stipes, and blades that are pinnate to some having one pair of pinnae at the base. The membranous segments bear black or reddish brown hairs on the lower surface. The indusium varies from round to nearly kidney-shaped and usually has dark hairs on the surface. An extremely unusual characteristic is the small barrel-shaped tubers borne by the roots. The species is native to Asia, Australia, New Zealand, and the Pacific Islands. It is a delicate fern that in nature usually thrives near water.

Adiantum excisum Kunze   FIGURE 13.4.12
Chilean maidenhair
Tender

A small fern with clustered fronds from clump-forming rhizomes. Grows in high to medium light in moist potting mix. The plants need humidity and can be difficult to grow.

Adiantum excisum resembles a delicate *A. raddianum* but differs by having dark green and airy foliage, often zigzag rachises, and broad segments with deep, spreading lobes. It is native to Chile.

Figure 13.4.12. *Adiantum excisum:* a. frond, bar = 5 cm (2 in.); b. fertile leaflets, bar = 1 mm (0.4 in.).

Adiantum flabellulatum Linnaeus   FIGURE 13.4.13
Tender or slightly hardier

A small to medium fern with fronds in a loose cluster from a clump-forming rhizome. Grows under medium light in potting mix kept moist. This species is easy to start from spores.

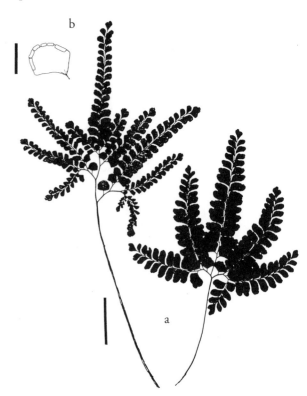

Figure 13.4.13. *Adiantum flabellulatum:* a. fronds, bar = 5 cm (2 in.); b. fertile leaflet, bar = 1 cm (0.4 in.).

Adiantum flabellulatum has pedate blade architecture, which only a few species of maidenhair have (such as *A. pedatum*), and its stipes are grooved on the upper surface, unlike those of all other species of *Adiantum*. This species can be further distinguished by the short, stiff, brownish hairs on the upper (but not lower) side of the stipe and rachis, and by the glabrous segments. The plants resemble a stiff *A. pedatum,* but the blades are not bluish green as in that species, and the segments are entire, not incised. The similar *A. hispidulum* differs by the presence of whitish hairs on the segment surfaces. *Adiantum flabellulatum* occurs from India west to China, Japan, and the Philippines.

Adiantum formosum R. Brown   FIGURE 13.4.14
Australian maidenhair
Semi-hardy to semi-tender

A medium to large fern with fronds spaced far apart on a long-creeping, branched rhizome. Grows under medium to low light in moist garden soil or potting mix. Because of

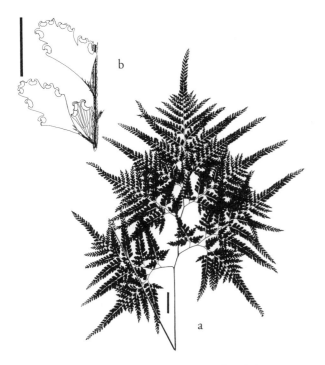

Figure 13.4.14. *Adiantum formosum:* a. frond, bar = 5 cm (2 in.); b. fertile leaflets, bar = 5 mm (0.2 in.).

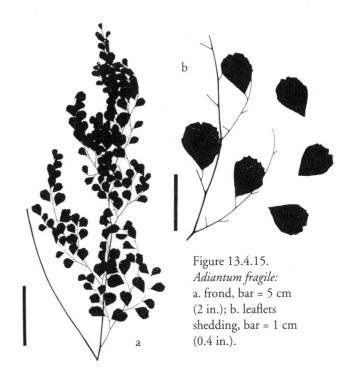

Figure 13.4.15. *Adiantum fragile:* a. frond, bar = 5 cm (2 in.); b. leaflets shedding, bar = 1 cm (0.4 in.).

its long-creeping rhizome, *Adiantum formosum* is best kept confined in a container. Withhold fertilizer to keep the fronds smaller. Divisions must be made with care because the deep-growing rhizomes and stipe bases break easily.

Adiantum formosum is characterized by large, broadly triangular fronds that are up to five-pinnate. The pinnae get smaller as they go from the base to the apex of the blade. The basal pinnae are by far the largest and are usually narrowly triangular. The species is native to Australia and New Zealand.

Adiantum fragile Swartz   FIGURE 13.4.15
Tender

A small to medium fern with fronds in a loose cluster from a clump-forming rhizome. Grows under medium light in moist, basic, well-drained garden soil or potting mix.

Adiantum fragile is characterized by bright yellowish brown rhizome scales; lance-ovate blades that are three- to four-pinnate at the base; delicately herbaceous, light green, segments that easily fall off; veins ending in marginal teeth; and subreniform to oblong indusia. It resembles *A. tenerum* but can be distinguished by the color of the rhizome scales. *Adiantum fragile* is native to the West Indies, where it often grows on limestone ledges, cliffs, and crevices of old stone walls.

Adiantum fructuosum Poeppig ex Sprengel
FIGURE 13.4.16

Tender

A medium-sized fern with fronds clustered on a short, knotted rhizome. Grows under low to medium light in moist garden soil or potting mix.

Adiantum fructuosum is characterized by bicolorous rhizome scales; stipes adjacent to each other; blades two-

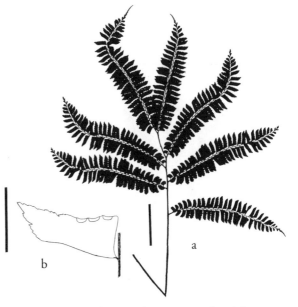

Figure 13.4.16. *Adiantum fructuosum:* a. frond, bar = 5 cm (2 in.); b. fertile leaflet, bar = 1 cm (0.4 in.).

pinnate with a terminal pinna resembling the lateral ones; fertile pinnules with tips mostly straight and obtuse, not falcate; and round apices. The blade features often overlap with *A. tetraphyllum*, which is distinguished by a long-creeping rhizome and more falcate segments. *Adiantum fructuosum* is native to the American tropics.

Adiantum hispidulum Swartz

FIGURE 13.4.17; PLATE 9

Rosy maidenhair, rough maidenhair
Semi-hardy or hardier, Zone 7

A small fern with clustered fronds from a clump-forming rhizome. Grows in low to high light in moist to moist-dry garden soil or potting mix. *Adiantum hispidulum* tolerates drier conditions than other maidenhairs. The plants are easy to cultivate and frequently seen in the United States trade. Young fronds are reddish.

Adiantum hispidulum is characterized by hairy stipes, pedate blades that are firm and have whitish hairs on the surface, and rounded indusia with slender, reddish brown hairs on the surface. The species is native to southern India, eastern Africa, and the Pacific Islands. It has escaped from cultivation in the United States (Connecticut and Georgia).

The name *Adiantum pubescens* Schkuhr applies to a variant with thinner and laxer hairs.

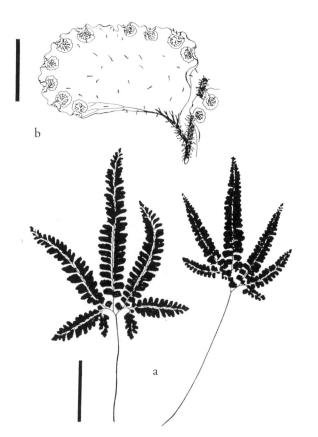

Figure 13.4.17. *Adiantum hispidulum:* a. fronds, bar = 5 cm (2 in.); b. fertile leaflet, bar = 5 mm (0.2 in.).

Some young plants of *Adiantum hispidulum* are circulating as *Adiantum* 'Birkenheadii', a name originally used in early English horticultural literature for a plant thought to have originated from *A. diaphanum*.

Adiantum jordanii K. Müller

FIGURE 13.4.18

California maidenhair
Semi-hardy to semi-tender

A small to medium fern with fronds in a cluster from a clump-forming rhizome. Best grown under high light in moist-dry garden soil or potting mix. The leaves usually wither in summer, and the soil should be kept drier at this time. This species is difficult to grow.

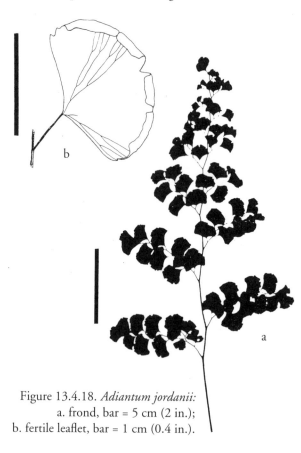

Figure 13.4.18. *Adiantum jordanii:*
a. frond, bar = 5 cm (2 in.);
b. fertile leaflet, bar = 1 cm (0.4 in.).

Adiantum jordanii resembles *A. capillus-veneris* but has broad, fan-shaped segments that are cleft or entire. *Adiantum jordanii* is native to the western United States (California and Oregon) and Mexico (Baja California). It hybridizes with *A. aleuticum* to form the sterile hybrid *A.* ×*tracyi*.

Adiantum latifolium Lamarck

FIGURE 13.4.19

Tender

A medium-sized fern with fronds widely spaced along a slender, creeping rhizome. Grows under low to medium light in moist garden soil or potting mix.

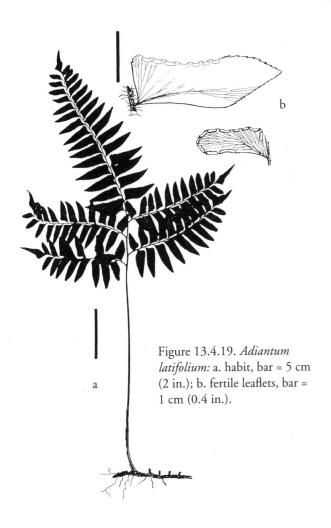

Figure 13.4.19. *Adiantum latifolium*: a. habit, bar = 5 cm (2 in.); b. fertile leaflets, bar = 1 cm (0.4 in.).

Figure 13.4.20. *Adiantum lucidum*: a. fronds, bar = 5 cm (2 in.); b. fertile leaflet, bar = 1 cm (0.4 in.).

Adiantum latifolium bears two-pinnate blades with up to four pairs of lateral pinnae and a terminal pinna that resembles the lateral ones. The segments are often glaucous beneath with a faint midrib basally, and the sterile segments are evenly serrate or denticulate. The oblong indusia are on the upper and sometimes lower margins of the segments. This species is native to tropical America and has escaped in Thailand and peninsular Malaya.

Adiantum lucidum (Cavanilles) Swartz

FIGURE 13.4.20

Tender

A small to medium fern with clustered fronds from a clump-forming rhizome. Grows under medium light in moist potting mix.

Only a few species of *Adiantum* have a single long sorus along both the upper and lower margins of the pinnae, and *Adiantum lucidum* is one such species. It can be distinguished by the combination of this soral characteristic and one-pinnate blades, scaly rachises, and free veins. Other characteristics include short-creeping rhizomes, asymmetrical pinna bases, and serrate pinna tips (where sterile). This species is native to lowland rain forests in tropical America.

Adiantum lunulatum N. L. Burman

FIGURE 13.4.21

syn. *Adiantum philippense* Linnaeus

Tender

A small to medium fern with erect or suberect rhizomes and arching fronds. Grows under medium light in well-drained garden soil or potting mix. The plants do best in humid conditions and are difficult to grow.

A delicate fern, *Adiantum lunulatum* sometimes roots at the leaf tips. It is characterized by one-pinnate blades, long-stalked pinnae with entire or bluntly toothed sterile margins, and oblong-linear indusia. It grows throughout the tropics of the world.

Adiantum macrophyllum Swartz

FIGURE 13.4.22

Large-leaved maidenhair

Tender

A medium-sized fern with clustered fronds from a short-creeping to semi-erect rhizome. Grows under low to medium light in moist potting mix. New fronds are often red or pink.

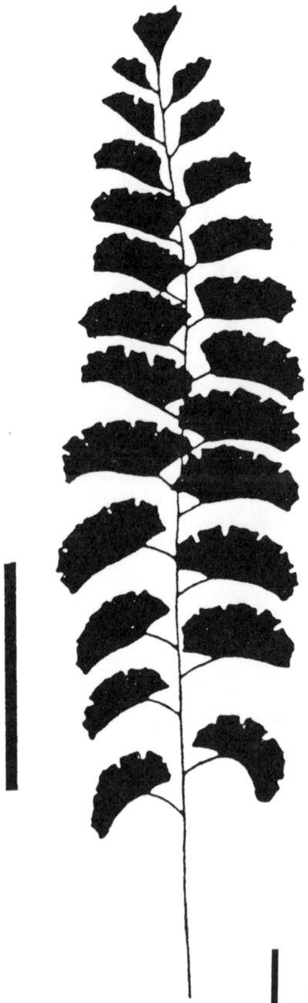

Figure 13.4.21. *Adiantum lunulatum:* frond, bar = 5 cm (2 in.).

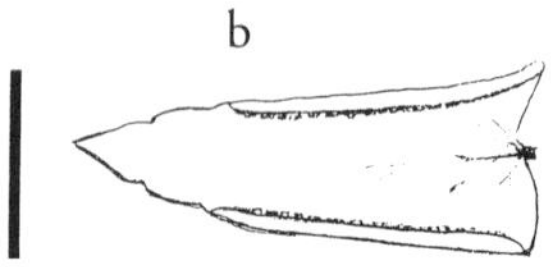

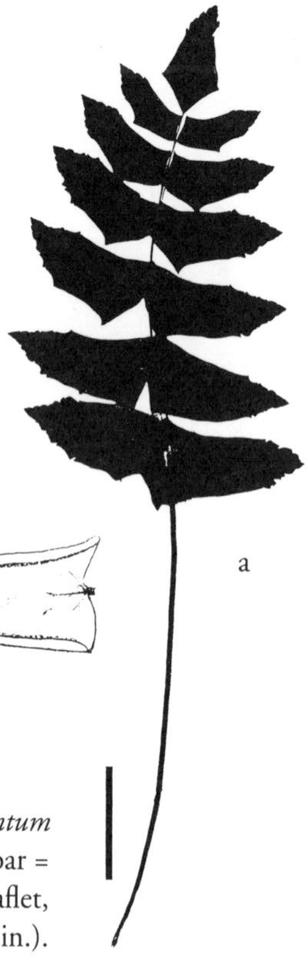

Figure 13.4.22. *Adiantum macrophyllum:* a. frond, bar = 5 cm (2 in.); b. fertile leaflet, bar = 1 cm (0.4 in.).

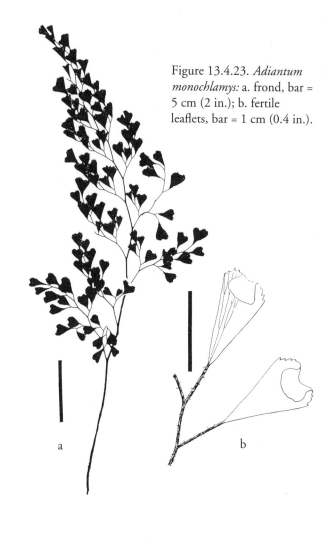

Figure 13.4.23. *Adiantum monochlamys:* a. frond, bar = 5 cm (2 in.); b. fertile leaflets, bar = 1 cm (0.4 in.).

Like *Adiantum lucidum, A. macrophyllum* has a single long sorus on both the upper and lower margins of the pinnae, but it can be distinguished from *A. lucidum* by its glabrous rachis. In addition, *A. macrophyllum* has one-pinnate blades and wide, sessile (or nearly so) pinnae that are glaucous beneath. It is native to the American tropics.

Adiantum monochlamys D. C. Eaton
FIGURE 13.4.23; PLATE 10

Hardy, Zone 6

A small fern with fronds clustered on short-creeping, clump-forming rhizomes. Grows under low to medium light in moist potting mix.

Adiantum monochlamys resembles *A. capillus-veneris* but has narrower wedge-shaped segments and usually only one sorus per segment. It is native to China, South Korea, and Japan.

Adiantum patens Willdenow
FIGURE 13.4.24

Tender

A small to medium fern with clustered fronds from a clump-forming rhizome. Grows under medium light in potting mix kept moist. This species is difficult to cultivate.

Adiantum patens resembles *A. pedatum* because of its pedate blades but differs by having crenate (not incised) segment margins, rachises beset with minute whitish hairs (not glabrous), and round-reniform (not oblong) indusia. The species occurs in the American tropics and Africa. The African plants are often distinguished as subspecies *oatesii* (Baker) Schelpe, but they hardly differ and should be considered the same.

Adiantum pedatum Linnaeus
FIGURE 13.4.25

American maidenhair, five-finger fern
Hardy to −37°C (−35°F), Zone 3

A small to medium fern, generally 30–60 cm (12–24 in.) tall, with fronds in clusters from the clump-forming rhizome. Grows under low to medium light in moist garden soil or potting mix. This species is difficult to grow in arid climates.

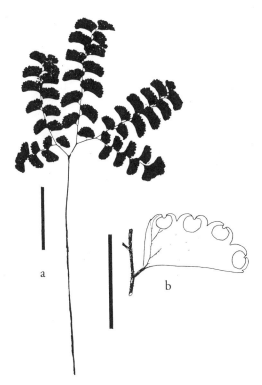

The most distinctive characteristics of *Adiantum pedatum* are its pedately divided blades, which are circular or nearly so in outline, and its incised segments. The leaf tissue is usually bluish green. The species resembles *A. patens* but differs by its glabrous stipes and rachises. It occurs in the central and eastern United States, Canada, and eastern Asia. Related plants of the western United States are now called *A. aleuticum*.

Adiantum pentadactylon Langsdorff & Fischer

FIGURE 13.4.26

Tender

A medium-sized fern with fronds clustered on a clump-forming rhizome. Grows under low to medium light in moist potting mix.

Adiantum pentadactylon resembles *A. trapeziforme* but differs in that the dark color of the segment stalk merges into the veins, rather than stopping abruptly, and its segments are more deeply lobed and have attenuate apices. It is native to Brazil.

Figure 13.4.24. *Adiantum patens:* a. frond, bar = 5 cm (2 in.); b. fertile leaflet, bar = 1 cm (0.4 in.).

Figure 13.4.25. *Adiantum pedatum:* frond, bar = 5 cm (2 in.).

Figure 13.4.26. *Adiantum pentadactylon:* a. frond, bar = 5 cm (2 in.); b. fertile leaflet, bar = 1 cm (0.4 in.).

Adiantum peruvianum Klotzsch   FIGURE 13.4.27
Silver-dollar fern, Peruvian maidenhair
Tender

A medium-sized fern with fronds clustered from a short-creeping to clump-forming rhizome. Grows under medium light in moist potting mix.

Adiantum peruvianum has large, rhombic, shiny segments borne on black slender stalks. The color of the stalk stops abruptly at the base of the segment; it does not enter the segment and gradually merge with the green of the veins as in some other species. *Adiantum peruvianum* is more common in collections than the similar *A. anceps,* from which it differs by having acute or rounded segment tips. It differs from *A. trapeziforme,* another similar species, by its inconspicuous serration on the pinnules. The species is native to Ecuador, Peru, and Bolivia.

Adiantum petiolatum Desvaux   FIGURE 13.4.28
Tender

A small to medium fern with fronds distributed along a creeping rhizome. Grows under medium light in moist potting mix.

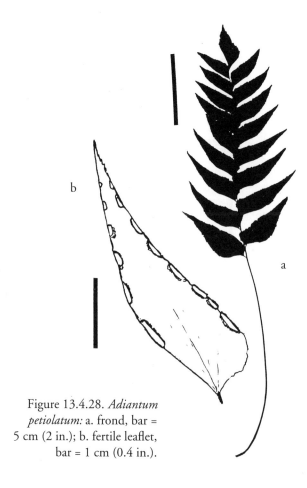

Figure 13.4.28. *Adiantum petiolatum:* a. frond, bar = 5 cm (2 in.); b. fertile leaflet, bar = 1 cm (0.4 in.).

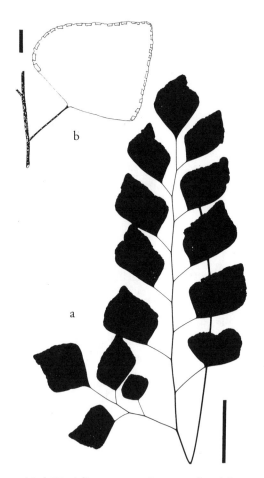

Figure 13.4.27. *Adiantum peruvianum:* a. frond, bar = 5 cm (2 in.); b. fertile leaflet, bar = 1 cm (0.4 in.).

The distinctive characteristics of *Adiantum petiolatum* are the long-creeping rhizomes, usually well-spaced fronds, one-pinnate blades, pinnae that are dull or glaucous beneath, and sterile segments with margins evenly serrate. The pinna bases tend to be broadly humped on the forward margin and often overlap the rachis. The species is widespread in tropical America.

Adiantum poiretti Wikström   FIGURE 13.4.29
Tender

A small to medium fern with fronds in loose clusters from a long-creeping rhizome. Grows under medium light in moist garden soil or potting mix.

Adiantum poiretti belongs to a group of species characterized by finely divided, billowy blades with stalked and small ultimate segments. This species can be distinguished from others in the group (such as *A. concinnum* and *A. tenerum*) by its long-creeping rhizomes and oblong-lunate sori. A yellow powder is frequently mixed among the sporangia, and if present the color is usually visible through the indusium. Other traits include golden-brown rhizome scales, blades up to three-pinnate, jointed segments that are wider than they are long, and sterile segments with poorly defined teeth. *Adiantum poiretti* is native to tropical America.

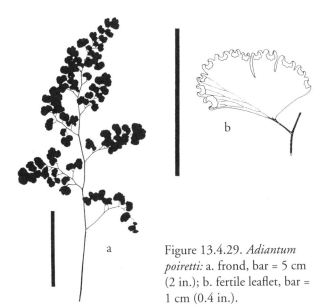

Figure 13.4.29. *Adiantum poiretti*: a. frond, bar = 5 cm (2 in.); b. fertile leaflet, bar = 1 cm (0.4 in.).

Adiantum polyphyllum Willdenow   FIGURE 13.4.30
Giant maidenhair
Tender

A large fern with clustered fronds from a clump-forming rhizome. Grows under medium light in moist potting soil.

Adiantum polyphyllum is a large, stiff fern with many jointed segments. The blades are broadly triangular and up to four-pinnate at the base. The lower pinnae have the pinnules on the basiscopic side with a pair of longer branches. Up to six indusia are found on the upper margin of the segment. The species occurs from Venezuela to Peru.

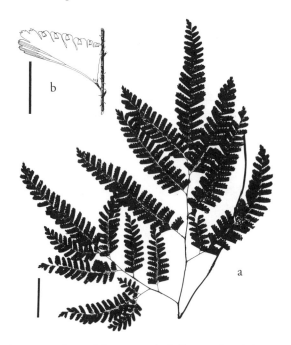

Figure 13.4.30. *Adiantum polyphyllum*: a. frond, bar = 5 cm (2 in.); b. fertile leaflet, bar = 1 cm (0.4 in.).

Adiantum pulverulentum Linnaeus   FIGURE 13.4.31
Tender

A medium to large fern with clustered fronds from a short-creeping rhizome. Grows in medium light in moist garden soil or potting mix.

Adiantum pulverulentum has two-pinnate blades with a terminal pinna resembling the lateral ones. This characteristic, plus the single sorus along the upper margin of the pinnules, makes *A. pulverulentum* one of the easiest maidenhairs to identify. (Other species with similar two-pinnate blades have more than one sorus along a pinnule margin.) The species is widespread in tropical America.

Figure 13.4.31. *Adiantum pulverulentum*: a. frond, bar = 5 cm (2 in.); b. fertile leaflet, bar = 5 mm (0.2 in.).

Adiantum pyramidale (Linnaeus) Willdenow
FIGURE 13.4.32

syn. *Adiantum cristatum* Linnaeus
Tender

A medium-sized fern with fronds clustered from a short-creeping, clump-forming rhizome. Grows under medium to high light in garden soil or moist potting mix.

Adiantum pyramidale can be identified by the small, hard bumps on the stipes; blades to three-pinnate at the base; the basal pinnae, which normally have a short to elongate branch on the basiscopic side; and oval to oblong, nearly straight indusia, mainly on the upper margin and sometimes around the apex. It is native to the West Indies.

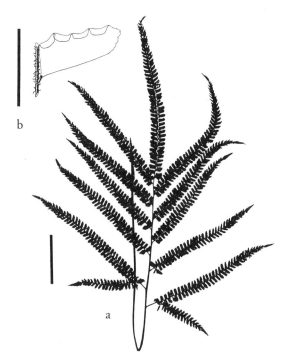

Figure 13.4.32. *Adiantum pyramidale:* a. frond, bar = 5 cm (2 in.); b. fertile leaflet, bar = 5 mm (0.2 in.).

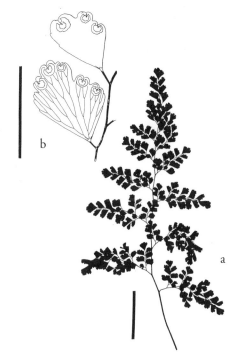

Figure 13.4.33. *Adiantum raddianum:* a. frond, bar = 5 cm (2 in.); b. fertile leaflets, bar = 1 cm (0.4 in.).

Adiantum raddianum C. Presl   FIGURES 13.4.33, 34
syn. *Adiantum cuneatum* Langsdorff & Fischer
Delta maidenhair
Semi-tender

A small to medium fern with clustered fronds from a clump-forming rhizome. Thrives in low to high light in moist garden soil or potting mix. The foliage dies back with light frosts.

Adiantum raddianum is characterized by mostly triangular, three- to four-pinnate blades, wedge-shaped segments without hairs, veins ending in a sinus between the teeth, and rounded indusia. It is native to the American tropics.

The delta maidenhair is the most commonly cultivated maidenhair in the United States. It has numerous, often poorly defined and confused cultivars. Some cultivars in the current trade not listed here include 'Fragrans', 'Fragrantissimum', 'Grandiceps', 'Lady Geneva', 'Micropinnulum', and 'Weigandii'.

'Croweanum'. Crowe maidenhair. Fronds more triangular, more foliaceous; fronds and segments larger than those of the species type. Easy to grow.

'Fritz Luth'. Figure 13.4.34a. Fronds triangular with even edges, flattened or with pinnae spreading over the next upper one, growth moderately compact, yet lacy and airy.

'Gracillimum'. Figure 13.4.34b. Blades up to five-pinnate, with very small segments, 2–4 mm (0.1–0.2 in.) long. Growth is loose but fine-textured.

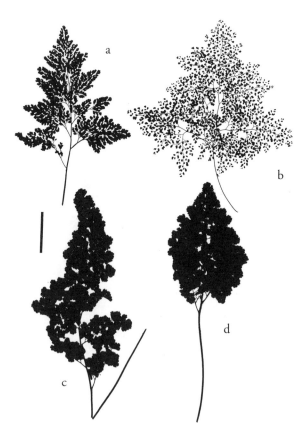

Figure 13.4.34. *Adiantum raddianum* cultivars: a. 'Fritz Luth'; b. 'Gracillimum'; c. 'Pacific Maid'; d. 'Pacottii'. Bar = 5 cm (2 in.).

'Ocean Spray'. Resembles 'Fritz Luth', but the blades are flatter and the pinnae are nearly all in the same plane. Slower, more compact growth, to 46 cm (18 in.) tall.

'Pacific Maid'. Pacific maid. Figure 13.4.34c. Fairly distinct by its crowded pinnae, pinnules, and segments. The segments are broadly fan-shaped. It grows rapidly and is looser and taller than 'Pacottii'.

'Pacottii'. (*Adiantum bellum* of trade, not of T. Moore). Double maidenhair. Figure 13.4.34d. Small, triangular, erect fronds; segments very densely placed; rarely more than 25 cm (10 in.) tall. Compared to other cultivars, it grows slowly from spores and transplants.

'Triumph'. Triumph maidenhair. Small-medium fronds, usually about 20 cm (8 in.) long, often with teardrop-shaped segments. An extremely variable plant. This cultivar is sometimes misnamed as *Adiantum aethiopicum.*

'Variegatum'. Variegated maidenhair. Segments sparingly variegated a cream-white. Grows slowly compared to other cultivars.

Adiantum reniforme Linnaeus   FIGURE 13.4.35
Tender to semi-tender

A small fern with fronds clustered from a short-creeping rhizome. Grows under low to medium light in moist potting soil. This species is usually difficult to grow.

Adiantum reniforme has small, kidney-shaped fronds with entire margins. It is native to Africa (Kenya), Madeira, the Canary Islands (Tenerife), and Comoros.

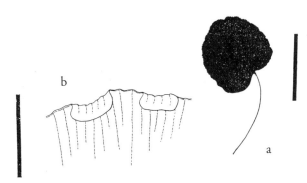

Figure 13.4.35. *Adiantum reniforme:* a. frond, bar = 5 cm (2 in.); b. indusia, bar = 5 mm (0.2 in.).

Adiantum seemannii Hooker   FIGURE 13.4.36
Seemann's maidenhair
Tender

A medium-sized fern with fronds clustered from a clump-forming rhizome. Grows in low to medium light in moist potting mix.

Adiantum seemannii is characterized by broadly triangular, one- or two-pinnate blades with a terminal pinna resembling the lateral ones. The pinnae are 5–8 cm (2–3 in.) long, usually ovate, and have serrate sterile margins. There

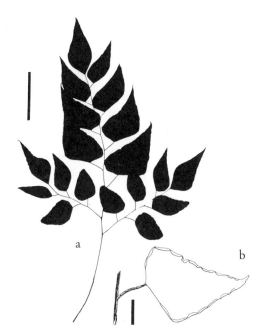

Figure 13.4.36. *Adiantum seemannii:* a. frond, bar = 5 cm (2 in.); b. fertile leaflet, bar = 1 cm (0.4 in.).

are usually several sori per pinna. This species resembles *A. anceps,* but its blade is whitish green (glaucous) beneath. *Adiantum seemannii* is native from Mexico to Panama and Colombia.

Adiantum tenerum Swartz   FIGURES 13.4.37, 38
Brittle maidenhair, fan maidenhair
Tender

A small to medium fern with fronds clustered on a short-creeping rhizome. Best grown under low to medium light in moist, basic potting mix.

Adiantum tenerum resembles *A. raddianum* but is larger, and it further differs by the dark color of its segment stalk ending abruptly at the segment where it is enlarged into a disk. The segments fall away freely (especially when dry), and the veins end in a tooth. This species is native to tropical America.

A number of cultivars exist, 'Farleyense' being the best known.

'Farleyense'. Farley maidenhair. Figure 13.4.38a. Fronds tend to be more arching than the typical species; the segment margins are ruffled and crowded. Avoid overhead watering. This cultivar originated in about 1865 on a Barbados sugar plantation named Farley Hill. The plant won instant acclaim in British horticultural circles and rapidly spread to gardens around the world. Rogers (1998) reviewed the history and classification of this cultivar.

'Fergusonii'. Figure 13.4.38b. Blades to three-pinnate but commonly two-pinnate, with pinnae long-stalked and pinnules crowded toward the pinna tips.

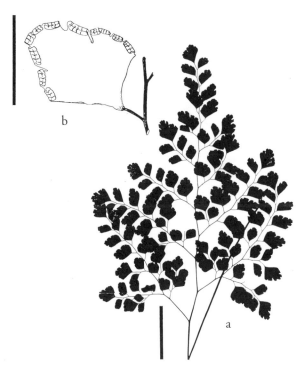

Figure 13.4.37. *Adiantum tenerum:* a. frond, bar = 5 cm (2 in.); b. fertile leaflet, bar = 1 cm (0.4 in.).

Adiantum tetraphyllum Humbold & Bonpland ex
Willdenow   FIGURE 13.4.39
Four-leaved maidenhair
Tender

A medium-sized fern with fronds spread along a short- to medium-creeping rhizome. Grows in moist garden soil or potting mix.

Adiantum tetraphyllum has two-pinnate blades with a terminal segment resembling the lateral pinnae. The rhizome scales are bicolorous, with dark centers and lighter margins. Fronds have two to six pairs of lateral pinnae, and these usually have slightly falcate apices. The pinnules are 1–4 cm (0.5–1.5 in.) long and have coarsely serrate margins when sterile. The indusia are oblong to oblong-lunate with short hairs on the upper surface, and they number three to six along the upper margin of the segment. This species is similar to *A. fructuosum*. It is widespread in the American tropics.

Figure 13.4.39. *Adiantum tetraphyllum:* a. frond, bar = 5 cm (2 in.); b. fertile leaflet, bar = 1 cm (0.4 in.).

Figure 13.4.38. *Adiantum tenerum* cultivars:
a. 'Farleyense'; b. 'Fergusonii'. Bar = 5 cm (2 in.).

Adiantum ×tracyi C. C. Hall ex W. H. Wagner

FIGURE 13.4.40

Semi-hardy

A small fern with loosely clustered fronds from a clump-forming rhizome. Grows under low to medium light in garden soil or potting mix kept moist.

Adiantum ×tracyi is characterized by broadly triangular blades that taper abruptly from a four- to five-pinnate base to a one-pinnate tip. It is native to the western United States (California and Oregon).

Adiantum ×tracyi is a naturally occurring sterile hybrid of *A. aleuticum* and *A. jordanii*. Its sterility is evinced by aborted spores that appear misshapen and irregular when seen under a microscope. These spores do not germinate, and the plant can be propagated only by divisions of the rhizome.

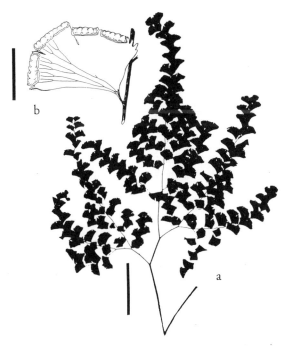

Figure 13.4.40. *Adiantum ×tracyi:* a. frond, bar = 5 cm (2 in.); b. fertile leaflet, bar = 5 mm (0.2 in.).

Adiantum trapeziforme Linnaeus

FIGURE 13.4.41

Diamond maidenhair

Tender

A medium-sized fern with clustered fronds from a short-creeping rhizome. Grows under low to medium light in moist potting mix.

Adiantum trapeziforme is characterized by triangular blades up to four-pinnate, with a terminal pinna similar to the lateral ones. The segments are trapeziform and stalked, with the stalks 4–7 mm (0.2–0.3 in.) long. The dark stalk color ends abruptly at the segment blade. This species is native to Central America and the West Indies.

Figure 13.4.41. *Adiantum trapeziforme:* a. frond, bar = 5 cm (2 in.); b. fertile leaflet, bar = 1 cm (0.4 in.).

Adiantum venustum G. Don

FIGURE 13.4.42

Himalayan maidenhair

Hardy

A small fern with fronds slightly distant along a medium- to short-creeping rhizome. Grows under low to medium light in moist potting mix. *Adiantum venustum* is slow to establish and is deciduous in colder climates. It forms dense, uniform colonies that make a good border planting.

Adiantum venustum is characterized by triangular blades up to three-pinnate, obovate segments, and sterile segment margins that are evenly and deeply dentate. The sori are

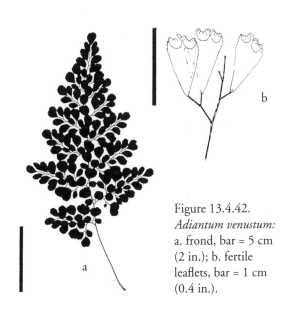

Figure 13.4.42. *Adiantum venustum:* a. frond, bar = 5 cm (2 in.); b. fertile leaflets, bar = 1 cm (0.4 in.).

reniform and generally occur two per segment. This species resembles some forms of *A. raddianum,* but the sterile segments are serrulate along the distal margin, not deeply lobed. It grows along the Afghanistan-Indian border.

Adiantum villosum Linnaeus   FIGURE 13.4.43
Tender

A medium-sized fern with fronds clustered along a short-creeping rhizome. Grows under medium light in moist garden soil or potting mix.

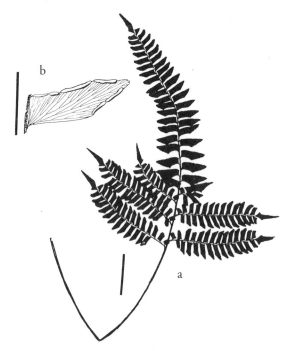

Figure 13.4.43. *Adiantum villosum:* a. frond, bar = 5 cm (2 in.); b. fertile leaflet, bar = 1 cm (0.4 in.).

Adiantum villosum has strongly nodose rhizomes and dark green, shiny blades that are up to two-pinnate and have terminal segments that are similar to but longer than the lateral pinnae. The pinnules are oblong to narrowly rhombic, with acuminate or acute tips and margins coarsely serrate when sterile. The indusia are oblong or linear and appear mostly on the upper margin. *Adiantum villosum* resembles *A. latifolium* but differs by its short-creeping rhizome. The species is native to the American tropics.

Aglaomorpha   FIGURES 13.5.1–3
syn. *Merinthosorus, Photinopteris, Pseudodrynaria, Thayeria*

Aglaomorpha is a genus of handsome and large epiphytic ferns that typically form a spreading cluster or nest of fronds. The blades are coarsely cut and form a bold pattern. The frond bases are often widened and turn brown and papery with age. They collect falling leaves and other

Figure 13.5.1. *Aglaomorpha coronans:* habit.

organic debris that eventually decay to provide a soil for the roots. The dry, papery texture of this humus-collecting leaf-base resists decay.

Aglaomorpha coronans and the hybrid ×*Aglaonaria robertsii* are the most frequently cultivated ferns in the genus. They are usually planted in hanging baskets but can also be grown in pots or even in the ground if given sufficient drainage by using a coarse medium. Though large, they are suitable as indoor plants because they tolerate low humidity and irregular watering. When the fronds become old, the pinnae fall off, but the rachises persist as long, brown spines. The shed pinnae litter the floor and can become untidy.

Figure 13.5.2. *Aglaomorpha coronans:* frond base.

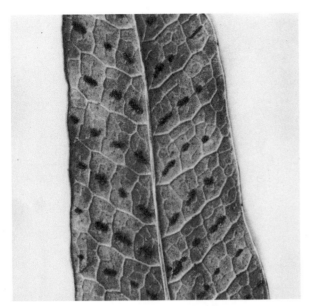

Figure 13.5.3. *Aglaomorpha coronans:* sori.

The genus is recognizable by the following characteristics: rhizomes short- to long-creeping, thick, fleshy, and scaly; fronds variable, some species with fronds entirely foliaceous, some with the basal part of the frond usually enlarged, dry, and papery (humus-collecting) and the upper part foliaceous; the foliaceous part one-pinnate or more often pinnatifid; pinnae jointed (articulate), with a true terminal pinna (segment) present; main veins raised and connected nearly at right angles by cross-veins; sporangia in discrete sori or spreading; no indusia.

Aglaomorpha was formerly defined as including only those plants bearing widened frond bases that turn brown and papery, deeply pinnate lobing at the upper part of the fronds, and discrete sori (not fused or acrostichoid). Nowadays, however, it is defined in a broader sense to include plants formerly placed in *Merinthosorus, Photinopteris,* and *Thayeria.* The characteristics of *Merinthosorus* are discussed under *Aglaomorpha drynarioides;* those of *Photinopteris,* under *A. speciosa;* and *Thayeria,* under *A. cornucopia.* Some botanists still recognize *Photinopteris* because of its fully one-pinnate fronds and the absence of humus-collecting frond bases. In this book we distinguish *Drynaria,* which is closely related to *Aglaomorpha,* by the separate humus-collecting and foliaceous fronds and the absence of a true terminal pinna or lobe on the foliaceous fronds. *Drynaria* can hybridize with *Aglaomorpha,* and one such hybrid, ×*Aglaonaria robertsii,* is commonly cultivated.

Aglaomorpha contains 14 species and occurs from the Asiatic tropics to New Guinea and nearby islands. See Chapter 10, the section "*Polypodium* and Relatives," for more information on culture; for a monographic treatment of the group, see Roos (1985). The genus name comes from the Greek *aglaios,* splendid, and *morphe,* shape. Aglaia was one of the Graces of Greek mythology.

Aglaomorpha cornucopia (Copeland) M. C. Roos
FIGURE 13.5.4

syn. *Thayeria cornucopia* Copeland
Very tender to tender

A medium-sized fern with branched, long-creeping rhizomes that tend to climb. Grows best under high light in potting mix or uncut moss kept moist-dry and well drained. It forms a nice display if allowed to climb.

The fronds of *Aglaomorpha cornucopia* are up to 60 cm (24 in.) long, sessile, and borne singly on special rhizome branches. The blade base wraps around the rhizome and is shaped like a cornucopia or oblong basket, becoming dry and papery. The blade above is green and pinnatifid. Fertile pinnae occur in the apical portion of the frond and resemble a string of beads, being constricted between the round sori. The species is native to the Philippines.

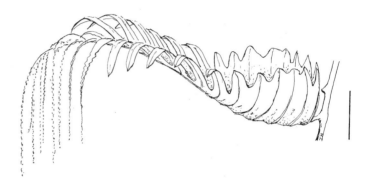

Figure 13.5.4. *Aglaomorpha cornucopia:* habit with fertile frond, bar = 10 cm (4 in.). Courtesy of T. Hoshizaki.

Aglaomorpha coronans (Wallich ex Mettenius)
Copeland   FIGURES 13.5.1–3, 5
Semi-tender or hardier

A medium to large fern with branched, short- to medium-creeping rhizomes. Best grown under high light in well-drained, moist-dry potting mix or uncut moss. The species is easy to grow and thrives in both humid and drier environments. It can be cultivated in the ground and in hanging baskets. *Aglaomorpha coronans* is the most commonly cultivated species in the genus, a testament to its durability and robust growth.

The fronds of *Aglaomorpha coronans* are stiff, pinnatifid, and sessile. They become brown and papery at the base but are shiny dark green above. The pinnae are connected to each other by wings, and the fertile pinnae are unmodified. The sori vary from oblong to linear, and several occur in a row between the lateral veins. This species is native to Bangladesh, India, China, Taiwan, southeastern Asia, Malaysia, and the Ryuku Islands of Japan.

'Angeli'. Fronds small, to about 30 cm (12 in.) tall, simple and entire or deeply and irregularly lobed.

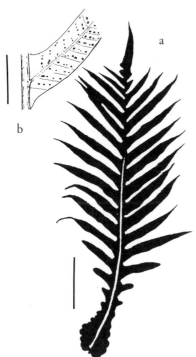

Figure 13.5.5. *Aglaomorpha coronans:* a. frond, bar = 10 cm (4 in.); b. part of fertile pinna, bar = 2.5 cm (1 in.).

Figure 13.5.6. *Aglaomorpha drynarioides:* fertile frond, bar = 10 cm (4 in.).

Aglaomorpha drynarioides (Hooker) M. C. Roos

FIGURE 13.5.6

syn. *Merinthosorus drynarioides* (Hooker) Copeland
Tender

Large to very large, with branched, short-creeping rhizomes. Grows under high light in well-drained, moist-dry potting mix or uncut moss.

Aglaomorpha drynarioides has soft rhizome scales, and its fronds grow to nearly 1.75 m (5.5 ft.) long. The fronds are sessile, pinnatifid, and brown-papery at the base but foliaceous above. The fertile pinnae toward the tip of the blade are long and linear, with sporangia covering the undersides or in linear patches on wider pinnae. The species is native to Malaysia, Indonesia, and New Guinea.

Aglaomorpha heraclea (Kunze) Copeland

FIGURE 13.5.7

Tender

Very large, with branched, short-creeping rhizomes. Grows best under high light in moist-dry potting mix or uncut moss kept well drained.

The fronds of *Aglaomorpha heraclea* are huge, up to 2 m (6.5 ft.) long. They are also pinnatifid, sessile, and brown-papery at the base but foliaceous distally. The fertile pinnae are about the same width as the sterile ones—not contracted, as is common in the genus. The sori are numerous, small, and scattered. This species is native from Sumatra to Malaysia, Java, Borneo, and New Guinea.

In the trade *Drynaria morbillosa* (C. Presl) J. Smith is often misapplied to *Aglaomorpha heraclea*.

Figure 13.5.7. *Aglaomorpha heraclea:* a. frond, bar = 10 cm (4 in.); b. part of fertile pinna, bar = 2.5 cm (1 in.).

Aglaomorpha meyeniana Schott
FIGURE 13.5.8

Tender

A medium-sized fern with branched, short-creeping rhizomes. Best grown under high light in well-drained, moist-dry potting mix or uncut moss.

Aglaomorpha meyeniana is characterized by orange rhizome scales and sessile fronds that are brown-papery at the base but foliaceous distally. The fertile pinnae are narrow and constricted between the sori, appearing like a string of beads. The sori are large and round. This species is native to Taiwan and the Philippines.

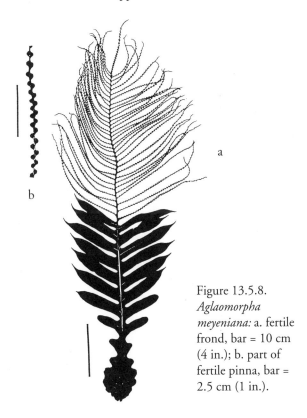

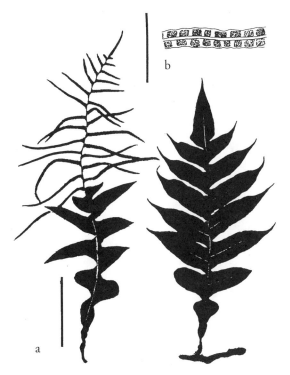

Figure 13.5.9. *Aglaomorpha pilosa:* a. fronds, fertile (left) and sterile (right), bar = 10 cm (4 in.); b. part of fertile pinna, bar = 2.5 cm (1 in.).

Figure 13.5.8. *Aglaomorpha meyeniana:* a. fertile frond, bar = 10 cm (4 in.); b. part of fertile pinna, bar = 2.5 cm (1 in.).

Aglaomorpha pilosa (J. Smith) Copeland
FIGURE 13.5.9

Tender

A medium-sized fern with branched, long-creeping rhizomes. Grows best under high light in a well-drained, moist-dry potting mix or uncut moss. Provide ample room to accommodate the creeping rhizomes.

The rhizome scales of *Aglaomorpha pilosa* are appressed, ovate-acuminate or triangular, pale-margined, and ciliate along the distal margins. The deeply pinnatifid blades lack any modifications for collecting humus. The pinnae are acuminate and hairy and are separated by mostly narrow sinuses; the lower pinnae gradually taper to a wing along the stipe. The fertile pinnae are narrow and occur only in the apical portion of the blade. The sori are oblong or occur in four-sided patches. Sporangial capsules bear four nee-

dle-like hairs. The soral patches resemble those of *A. splendens,* but the latter species differs by having larger fronds, shorter-creeping rhizomes, humus-collecting frond bases, and hairless sporangial capsules. *Aglaomorpha pilosa* is native to the Philippines.

Some plants circulating in gardens are misidentified as *Aglaomorpha brooksii* Copeland.

Aglaomorpha speciosa (Blume) M. C. Roos
FIGURE 13.5.10

syn. *Photinopteris speciosa* (Blume) C. Presl

Tender

A large fern with branched, short-creeping rhizomes. Grows best under medium to high light in well-drained, moist-dry potting mix or uncut moss.

Aglaomorpha speciosa bears one-pinnate fronds that lack humus-collecting bases. The ovate-oblong pinnae often have white dots on their upper surfaces and apices that are long-tapered and often drooping. A conspicuous nectary gland can be seen at the base of the pinna stalk. The fertile pinnae, which occur in the apical part of the frond, are extremely narrow, often drooping, and completely covered with sporangia on their undersides. This species is native to southeastern Asia, Malaysia, Indonesia, and the Philippines.

Aglaomorpha speciosa resembles certain species of *Polypodium* because of its fully one-pinnate fronds and the ab-

Figure 13.5.10. *Aglaomorpha speciosa:* fertile frond, bar = 10 cm (4 in.).

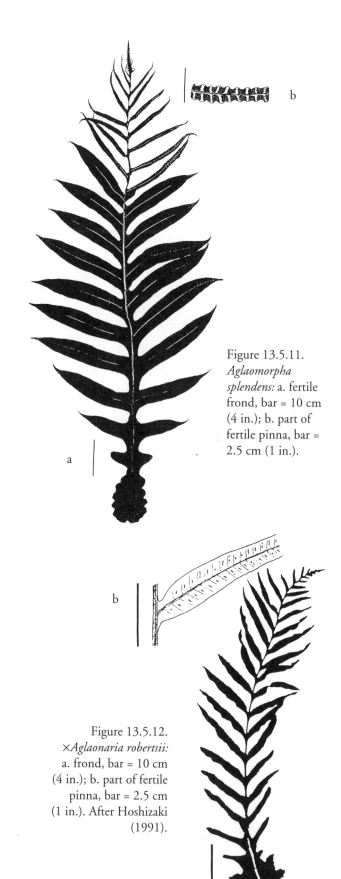

Figure 13.5.11. *Aglaomorpha splendens:* a. fertile frond, bar = 10 cm (4 in.); b. part of fertile pinna, bar = 2.5 cm (1 in.).

Figure 13.5.12. ×*Aglaonaria robertsii:* a. frond, bar = 10 cm (4 in.); b. part of fertile pinna, bar = 2.5 cm (1 in.). After Hoshizaki (1991).

sence of humus-collecting frond bases. Some authors still classify this species in *Photinopteris*.

Aglaomorpha splendens (J. Smith) Copeland

FIGURE 13.5.11

Tender

Large to very large, with branched, short-creeping rhizomes. Grows best under medium to high light in moist-dry, well-drained potting mix or uncut moss.

The fronds of *Aglaomorpha splendens* grow to 2 m (6.5 ft.) long and are sessile. They have brown, papery bases but are foliaceous above. They are deeply pinnatifid into triangular-lanceolate pinnae. The fertile pinnae occur toward the frond tips and are contracted about one-third to one-fifth the width of the sterile pinnae. The sori are quadrangular patches borne in rows on each side of the midrib. This species is native to the Philippines.

The plants are often confused with *Aglaomorpha brooksii* Copeland, a species from Borneo that differs mainly in having the quadrangular soral patches variously subdivided into smaller, sometimes irregular patches. *Aglaomorpha brooksii* has not been found in cultivation. *Aglaomorpha splendens* also often circulates in gardens as *A. pilosa*.

×*Aglaonaria robertsii* Hoshizaki

FIGURE 13.5.12

syn. *Aglaomorpha* 'Roberts'

Semi-tender or hardier

A medium to large fern with branched, short- to medium-creeping rhizomes. Grows best under high light in well-drained, moist-dry potting mix or uncut moss. The plants do well in humid or drier environments and are easy to cultivate.

×*Aglaonaria robertsii* is a hybrid of *Aglaomorpha coronans* and *Drynaria rigidula*. It resembles *A. coronans* but is softer textured and lighter green. The fronds become brown and papery at the base but remain green and foliaceous above. The blades are pinnatisect with apices pinnately lobed to a small terminal segment (or the terminal segment is absent). The pinnae are connected by a thin, cartilaginous margin, and each pinna is slightly narrowed above the broadly adnate base. The fertile pinnae resemble the sterile ones and are not narrowed as in most *Aglaomorpha* species. The sori vary from round to sublinear, with one or two sori united or separated and placed between the lateral veins.

This plant is a hybrid of horticultural origin and does not grow in the wild. Its parental species belong to the genera *Aglaomorpha* and *Drynaria;* thus the generic name of the hybrid is a compounding of those two names. In accordance with the *International Code of Nomenclature for Cultivated Plants,* the hybrid is also assigned the cultivar name 'Santa Rosa'. Santa Rosa Tropicals, California, was the nursery that first tissue cultured the plant.

'Starburst'. The pinna margins are sharply and narrowly incised; less robust than 'Santa Rosa'.

Alsophila
FIGURES 13.6.1–5

syn. *Nephelea*

The tree ferns of genus *Alsophila* are related to *Cnemidaria* (not cultivated), *Cyathea,* and *Sphaeropteris* in the family Cyatheaceae. *Alsophila* differs from these other genera by the black spines or sharp conical bumps on its stipes and the

Figure 13.6.2. *Alsophila tricolor:* frond.

Figure 13.6.3. *Alsophila tricolor:* sori, with an indusium visible on detached sorus, upper right.

Figure 13.6.1. *Alsophila tricolor:* habit.

Figure 13.6.4. *Alsophila tricolor:* tip of stipe scale, ending in a dark stiff bristle, bar = 0.1 mm.

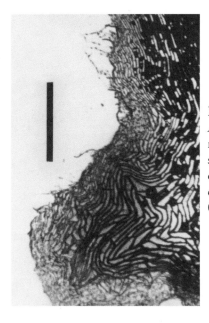

Figure 13.6.5. *Alsophila tricolor:* margin of stipe scale, marginal cells different from central cells, bar = 0.1 mm.

minute black bristles on its stipe scales (at least at the apex). The genus name comes from the Greek *alsos,* grove, and *philein,* to love, alluding to certain species that grow in shady groves. *Alsophila* contains about 235 species and is native to the Old and New World tropics. See *Cyathea* for a further comparison of the cyatheaceous genera and for general comments about tree ferns.

Alsophila australis R. Brown   FIGURE 13.6.6
syn. *Cyathea australis* (R. Brown) Domin
Rough tree fern, Australian tree fern
Semi-hardy to semi-tender

A large tree fern. Best grown under medium light in moist, acidic(?) garden soil or potting mix. The plants grow slowly and do best in cool, moist climates.

The stipe bases of *Alsophila australis* are beset with conical spines to 3 mm (0.1 in.) long and are covered by dark brown, glossy, slender, brittle scales. The tips of the scales are slightly contorted and bear a dark bristle. The scales

along the undersides of the pinnule and segment midrib are small, whitish, and puffy. The sori are partly covered with fringed scales and lack a true indusium. The species is native to Australia and Tasmania.

Almost all the plants listed as *Alsophila australis* in the United States trade (usually under the name *Cyathea australis*) are actually *Sphaeropteris cooperi.* True *A. australis* is rarely grown in the United States but is often cultivated in mild areas of England. The glossy, dark brown scales are distinctive of this species.

Alsophila tricolor (Colenso) R. M. Tryon
                    FIGURES 13.6.1–5, 7; PLATE 11
syn. *Cyathea dealbata* Colenso
Silver tree fern
Semi-hardy

A large tree fern, 3–9 m (10–30 ft.) tall, with blades white beneath. Grows best under medium light in moist garden soil or potting mix. The plants tend to grow slowly and should be placed in areas sheltered from the wind.

Alsophila tricolor is characterized by glaucous, slightly

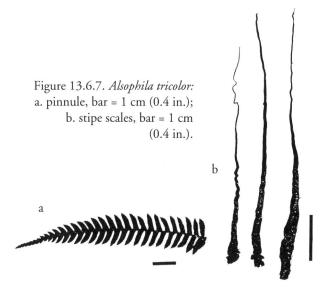

Figure 13.6.7. *Alsophila tricolor:* a. pinnule, bar = 1 cm (0.4 in.); b. stipe scales, bar = 1 cm (0.4 in.).

prickly stipes and shiny, slightly twisted, slender stipe scales to 7 cm (3 in.) long and tipped with a dark bristle. The globose indusia have an opening at the top. This species is native to New Zealand and is, in fact, the national fern of that country. It is depicted on New Zealand's coins, bills, passports, official seals, national airline planes, and most tourist posters.

Anemia   FIGURES 13.7.1, 2
Flowering fern

These small- to medium-sized terrestrial or epilithic ferns are particularly attractive for their erect, long-stalked, and branch-like fertile leaflets. The rhizome is erect or creeping

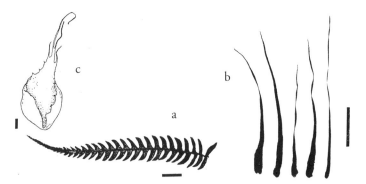

Figure 13.6.6. *Alsophila australis:* a. pinnule, bar = 1 cm (0.4 in.); b. stipe scales, bar = 1 cm (0.4 in.); c. bullate scale from the underside of the frond, bar = 0.1 mm.

and is covered by hairs, not scales. The blades can be up to three-pinnate but are mostly one- to two-pinnate-pinnatifid. Fertile fronds typically have the two lowermost pinnae fully contracted (skeletonized), erect, long stalked, and bearing sporangia. The sporangia are pear-shaped, with the annulus encircling the narrow end.

Anemia occurs in the tropics and subtropics of the world, though most of its 100 species grow in the Americas. The genus name comes from the Greek *aneimon,* naked, alluding to the exposed sporangia that lack an indusium.

Anemia adiantifolia (Linnaeus) Swartz

FIGURE 13.7.3

Pine fern
Semi-tender, Zone 9

A small to medium fern with an erect, seldom-branched rhizome. Grows best under medium to high light in basic, moist-dry garden soil or potting mix.

Anemia adiantifolia has fully three-pinnate fronds. It is native to tropical America and grows as far north as Florida.

Anemia phyllitidis (Linnaeus) Swartz

FIGURES 13.7.1, 2, 4

Semi-tender, Zone 9

A small fern with erect, seldom-branched rhizomes. Grows best under medium to high light in moist-dry garden soil or potting mix.

Figure 13.7.1. *Anemia phyllitidis:* habit.

Figure 13.7.2. *Anemia phyllitidis:* stalk-like fertile pinnae.

Figure 13.7.3. *Anemia adiantifolia:* frond, bar = 5 cm (2 in.).

Figure 13.7.4. *Anemia phyllitidis:* frond, bar = 5 cm (2 in.).

Anemia phyllitidis has one-pinnate fronds with a terminal pinna that resembles the lateral ones. The veins are netted. This species is native to tropical America.

Anemia rotundifolia Schrader   FIGURE 13.7.5
Semi-tender

A medium-sized fern with erect rhizomes and buds at the tips of the fronds. Grows best under medium light in moist garden soil or potting mix.

The fronds of *Anemia rotundifolia* are arching and one-pinnate with roundish pinnae, and the rachis is greatly extended, whip-like, and roots at the tip. This species is native to Brazil.

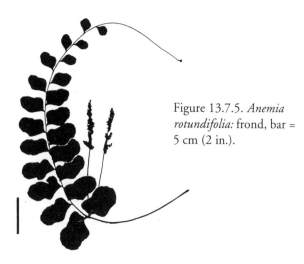

Figure 13.7.5. *Anemia rotundifolia:* frond, bar = 5 cm (2 in.).

Angiopteris   FIGURES 13.8.1–4
Mule's-foot fern

Members of *Angiopteris* are large, coarse, fleshy terrestrial ferns with massive stems. Their large size limits them to conservatories and outdoor gardens in the tropics. The plants need good drainage and must be protected from wind and frost. Do not let them dry, as wilted fronds recover only with difficulty.

Figure 13.8.1. *Angiopteris evecta:* habit.

These ferns bear fronds up to 7 m (23 ft.) long, although the fronds tend to be smaller in cultivation. The roots and stems are usually thick and fleshy, often massive; stems sometimes slender and creeping. The middle of the stipe often has a swelling or bump. The blades vary from one- to

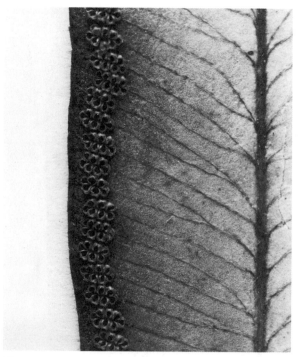

Figure 13.8.2. *Angiopteris evecta:* clusters of sporangia.

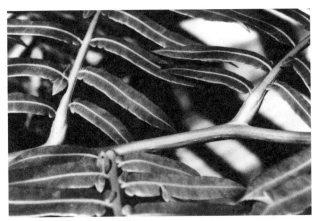

Figure 13.8.3. *Angiopteris evecta:* swollen pinna bases.

two-pinnate and often have a swelling at the juncture of the rachis and pinnae. The sori consist of a double row of free (unfused) sporangia, and an indusium is absent.

Angiopteris resembles the closely related *Marattia,* and sterile specimens are difficult to assign to either genus. Plants from both genera have fleshy flaps of tissue called stipules on either side of the stipe base. The stipules hug the swollen base of the fleshy stipe. The genera have similar cultural requirements.

New plants can be propagated from stipules cut from the stipe. The stipules should be planted in a moist, loose medium (gravel, perlite, sphagnum, or a loose, well-drained planting mix) at a slant or flat on the medium with either side up. Some growers notch the thin edges slightly to encourage plantlet formation at these points; otherwise, plants tend to form at the base of the stipule, usually one on each side. Apply bottom heat at 27°C (80°F) to hasten the appearance of buds, which may take several months or up to 2 years to appear; large stipules are slower to produce buds. The buds should be kept moist, but not so wet as to rot. After the buds produce roots and two or three leaves, they can be transplanted. *Angiopteris* can also be propagated by offshoots (more commonly produced on young plants) or spores. On all established plants, new roots that emerge from the stem base should be kept moist with a covering of mulch. For more information, see Hill (1984).

Angiopteris, which contains about 200 species, is native to the Old World tropics, where it grows in wet habitats. It has become naturalized in Jamaica and Hawaii. The genus name comes from the Greek *angeion,* case or capsule, and *pteris,* fern, referring to the sporangia that are larger than those of many other ferns.

Plants of the genus *Angiopteris* and the allied *Marattia* are so large that few adequate scientific specimens have been made, making study of the species particularly difficult. Although new *Angiopteris* continue to be introduced, their identities are uncertain, and many are named as varieties of *Angiopteris evecta.*

Angiopteris angustifolia C. Presl   FIGURE 13.8.5
Tender

Very large, with erect, stout, massive stems and whorled fronds. Best grown under medium light in well-drained garden soil or potting mix. *Angiopteris angustifolia* prefers a humid environment; do not permit the soil to dry.

The pinnules are 12–20 mm (0.5–0.75 in.) wide and have translucent false veins that run from the margin to nearly the midrib of the pinnule. This species occurs from Malaysia to the Philippines.

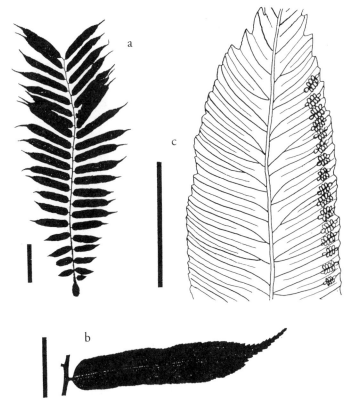

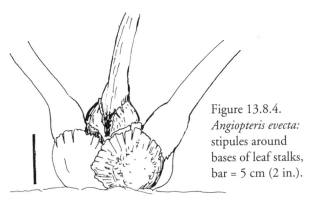

Figure 13.8.4. *Angiopteris evecta:* stipules around bases of leaf stalks, bar = 5 cm (2 in.).

Figure 13.8.5. *Angiopteris angustifolia:* a. pinna, bar = 5 cm (2 in.); b. pinnule, bar = 2 cm (0.8 in.); c. veins with long false vein (left) and sporangia (right), bar = 1 cm (0.4 in.).

Angiopteris evecta (G. Forster) Hoffmann

FIGURES 13.8.1–4, 6

Mule's-foot fern
Tender to marginally semi-tender

Very large, with erect, stout, massive stems and whorled fronds. Best grown under medium light in well-drained garden soil or potting mix. The plants prefer a humid environment; do not permit the soil to dry.

Angiopteris evecta is characterized by pinnules that are about 25 mm (1 in.) wide and translucent false veins that extend less than halfway from the margin to the midrib. The species occurs from Malaysia to Polynesia. One of the most spectacular plantings of *A. evecta* can be seen in the Foster Botanical Garden in Honolulu, Hawaii.

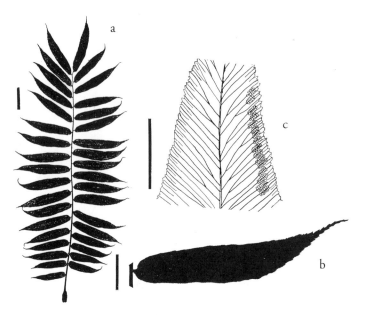

Figure 13.8.6. *Angiopteris evecta:* a. pinna, bar = 5 cm (2 in.); b. pinnule, bar = 2 cm (0.8 in.); c. veins with short false vein (left) and sporangia (right), bar = 1 cm (0.4 in.).

Anogramma

Anogramma has special appeal in terrariums because of its small size and delicate appearance. *Anogramma chaerophylla* should not be planted where volunteer ferns are not desired, such as in commercial greenhouses, because it readily spreads by spores.

The genus consists of terrestrial or epilithic ferns with erect rhizomes and mostly small, clustered fronds. The blades vary from one- to four-pinnate and are elongate-triangular, membranous, and glabrous (except for one species, *Anogramma leptophylla,* which is hairy). The veins are free, and the sporangia run along the veins. Indusia are absent.

Anogramma is closely related to *Pityrogramma,* differing mainly by its smaller size, thinner texture, and the lack of

powder on the lower surface of the blades. The life cycle of *Anogramma* is highly unusual because the gametophytes are perennial and the sporophytes are annual. In contrast, the gametophytes of all other ferns are ephemeral, dying after the sporophyte is formed. Thus, the leaves of *Anogramma* plants live less than a year and reappear the following growing season.

Anogramma grows in tropical and warmer temperate areas throughout the world and consists of five species. The genus name comes from the Greek *ano-,* upward, and *gramme,* line, referring to the elongate sori on the distal segments.

Anogramma chaerophylla (Desvaux) Link

FIGURES 13.9.1–3

Semi-tender

A small fern with erect rhizomes. Grows best under medium light in moist potting mix. Volunteer plants appear in spring, densely and luxuriantly, and usually wither within a few months. In terrariums it reproduces readily from spores.

Figure 13.9.1. *Anogramma chaerophylla:* habit.

Anogramma chaerophylla can be distinguished from closely related species by its glabrous stipes, broadly triangular and three- to four-pinnate blades, and white to tan spores. In nature the fronds can reach 40 cm (16 in.) long, but only about 15 cm (6 in.) in cultivation. The species is native to tropical America.

Anogramma leptophylla (Linnaeus) Link is cultivated in England and can be distinguished by its dark brown spores and 1 mm long hairs on the stipes. It is native to the Old World and Mexico.

Figure 13.9.2. *Anogramma chaerophylla:* sporangia along veins.

shaped indusium. Many species in the genus resemble broad-fronded polystichums, but their kidney-shaped indusia, anadromous frond plan, and (in most species) creeping rhizomes distinguish them. *Arachniodes* might be confused with certain species of *Dryopteris,* but that genus usually differs by having a catadromic frond plan and decumbent or erect rhizomes.

Arachniodes, which contains about 50 to 70 species and hybrids, grows in the tropics and subtropics throughout the world but is most diverse in Asia. The genus name comes from the Greek *arachnion,* spider's web, and *-odes,* meaning "having the form or nature of." No one knows why the fern received this name.

Arachniodes aristata (G. Forster) Tindale

FIGURES 13.10.1, 2

syn. *Polystichum aristatum* (G. Forster) C. Presl
East Indian holly fern
Hardy, Zone 6

A medium-sized fern with long-creeping rhizomes. Best grown under medium light in garden soil or potting mix. This species does well in moist to moist-dry soil. The plants are evergreen, easy to cultivate, and best displayed in wide pots or beds. They grow slowly from spores.

Arachniodes aristata is recognizable by its dark green, broad, five-sided sterile blades, which are up to four-pinnate. The fertile fronds are taller than the sterile ones and have slightly more contracted segments. This species is native to Africa, Australia, New Zealand, and the Pacific Islands.

Figure 13.9.3. *Anogramma chaerophylla:* habit, bar = 5 cm (2 in.).

Arachniodes

FIGURE 13.10.1

The arachniodes are medium-sized terrestrial ferns useful in pots or planting beds. One species in particular, the East Indian holly fern (*Arachniodes aristata*), is valued for its attractive shiny, dark green, divided foliage.

The rhizomes vary from short- to long-creeping; rarely are they erect. The blades are two-pinnate or more divided, broad, often triangular or pentagonal, anadromous, and dimorphic or not. The round sori are covered by a kidney-

Figure 13.10.1. *Arachniodes aristata:* habit.

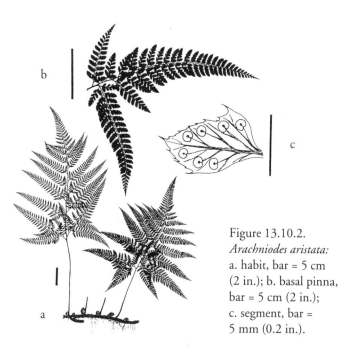

Figure 13.10.2.
Arachniodes aristata:
a. habit, bar = 5 cm
(2 in.); b. basal pinna,
bar = 5 cm (2 in.);
c. segment, bar =
5 mm (0.2 in.).

Arachniodes simplicior (Makino) Ohwi

FIGURE 13.10.3

Hardy, Zone (6)7

A medium-sized fern with long-creeping rhizomes. Best grown under medium light in moist-dry garden soil or potting mix. Some forms are especially attractive for their variegated foliage, bearing yellow-green lighter-colored tissue.

Arachniodes simplicior has evergreen fronds up to three-pinnate. The fronds are usually too few and far apart on the creeping rhizome to make a full, leafy pot plant. The

fertile fronds are taller and more contracted than the sterile. This species is native to Japan and China and has become naturalized in the southeastern United States.

A variegated form sometimes circulates under the misapplied name of *Arachniodes aristata* 'Variegatum'.

Arachniodes standishii (T. Moore) Ohwi

FIGURE 13.10.4

syn. *Polystichum standishii* (T. Moore) C. Christensen
Hardy, Zone 6

A medium-sized fern with slightly erect to short-creeping rhizomes. Grows best in humid environments under medium light in moist garden soil or potting mix. The plants are evergreen and slow-growing.

Arachniodes standishii is the largest and most finely dissected (up to four-pinnate) cultivated species of *Arachniodes*. The blades are elongate-triangular, monomorphic, dull, medium green, and softer textured than those of other species in cultivation. The sori, which are covered by broad reniform indusia, obscure most of the lower surface of the segments. The species is native to Japan, Korea, southern China, and Vietnam.

Argyrochosma

syn. *Notholaena* in part, *Cheilanthes* in part

Argyrochosma is a genus of small, wiry ferns that grow in dry rocky places. In the past the species have been classified with either the cloak ferns (*Notholaena*), lip ferns (*Cheilanthes*), or rock brakes (*Pellaea*). See *Cheilanthes* for a comparison of *Argyrochosma* to these and other genera. Windham (1987) showed that *Argyrochosma* is most closely

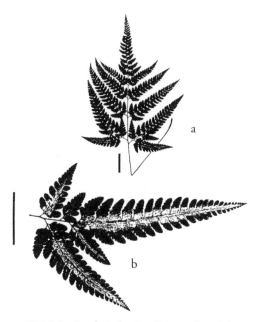

Figure 13.10.3. *Arachniodes simplicior:* a. frond, bar = 5 cm (2 in.); b. basal pinna, bar = 5 cm (2 in.).

Figure 13.10.4. *Arachniodes standishii:* a. habit, bar = 5 cm (2 in.); b. basal pinna, bar = 5 cm (2 in.); c. pinnule, bar = 1 cm (0.4 in.).

related to *Pellaea* but can usually be distinguished by the presence of a waxy powder (farina) on the lower surfaces of the blades (this is absent in *Argyrochosma jonesii* and *A. microphylla*) and other technical characteristics.

The blade surfaces of *Argyrochosma* lack hairs or scales. The segments are untoothed and distinctly stalked. The sporangia run along the veins, usually covering the outer one-third to two-thirds of the segments. The fertile margins are flat or slightly enrolled and have the same color and texture as the rest of the blade—that is, the fertile margins are not texturally modified like those of some other cheilanthoid ferns.

About 20 species occur in the genus, which is entirely native to the New World. Its name comes from the Greek *argyros,* silver, and *chosma,* powder, referring to the whitish powder found on the lower blade surfaces of most species.

Argyrochosma dealbata (Pursh) Windham

FIGURE 13.11.1

syn. *Cheilanthes dealbata* Pursh, *Notholaena dealbata*
(Pursh) Prantl
Powdery cloak fern
Hardy, Zone 5

A small fern with compact, erect to ascending, usually unbranched rhizomes and clustered fronds. Apparently prefers medium light with basic(?), moist-dry to dry, drained garden soil with sand.

Argyrochosma dealbata is distinguished from *A. jonesii* and *A. microphylla* by the white powder on the lower surface of the blades. It is further characterized by dark reddish brown, shiny stipes and triangular blades two- to three-pinnate and blue-green on the upper surface. The dark color of the stalk enters the segment bases and merges with the green of the blades. The ultimate segments are round to ovate-oblong, 3 mm (0.1 in.) or less long, and their margins enroll, covering the dark sporangia that are borne on the distal third of the secondary veins. The species is native to the south-central United States, where it grows on calcareous cliffs and ledges.

Argyrochosma jonesii (Maxon) Windham

FIGURE 13.11.2

syn. *Cheilanthes jonesii* (Maxon) Munz, *Notholaena jonesii* Maxon
Jones's cloak fern
Semi-hardy, Zone 8(9)

A small fern with compact, erect to ascending, usually unbranched rhizomes and clustered fronds. Best grown under high light in drained, basic(?) garden soil kept moist-dry to dry.

Figure 13.11.1. *Argyrochosma dealbata:* a. frond, bar = 2.5 cm (1 in.), after Tryon (1956); b. segments with sori and indusia, bar = 1 mm.

Figure 13.11.2. *Argyrochosma jonesii:* a. frond, bar = 2.5 cm (1 in.); b. fertile segment, bar = 1 mm. After Tryon (1956).

Argyrochosma jonesii has dark brown stipes and shiny, ovate-lanceolate, leathery blades that are two- to three-pinnate. The dark color of the segment stalks extends into the base of the segments and merges with the green of the blade; the stalks are not jointed to the segments, nor does the stalk color stop abruptly as in *A. microphylla*. The lower surface of the blade lacks white powder and has flat or slightly enrolled margins, with sporangia borne on outer third to half of the veins. The species is native to the southwestern United States and Mexico.

Argyrochosma microphylla (Mettenius ex Kuhn) Windham

FIGURE 13.11.3

syn. *Cheilanthes parvifolia* (R. M. Tryon) Mickel, *Notholaena parvifolia* R. M. Tryon

Small-leaved cloak fern
Semi-hardy, Zone 7

A small fern with compact, erect to ascending, usually unbranched rhizomes and clustered fronds. Grows under high light in basic(?), moist-dry, well-drained garden soil with sand.

Unlike the previous two species, *Argyrochosma microphylla* has its ultimate segments jointed to their stalks. This can be seen by the dark color of the stalk stopping abruptly at the segment base, not passing into the segment and merging with the green of the blade. The species is further characterized by brown stipes; triangular to ovate, three- to

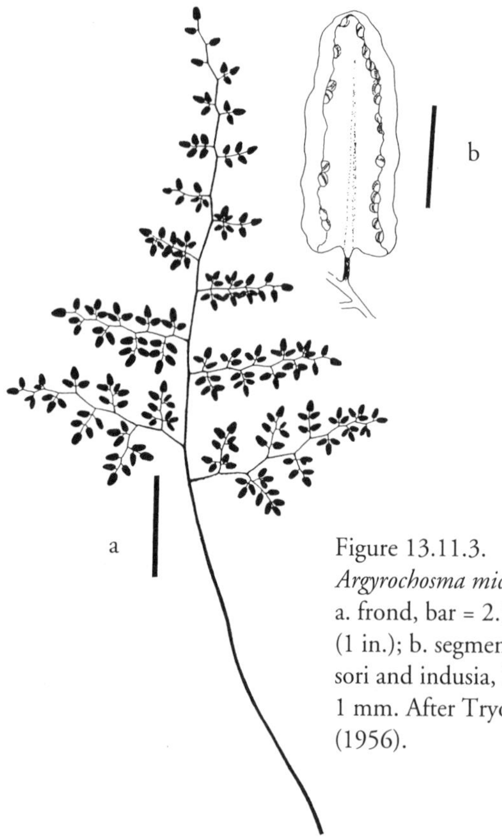

Figure 13.11.3. *Argyrochosma microphylla*: a. frond, bar = 2.5 cm (1 in.); b. segment with sori and indusia, bar = 1 mm. After Tryon (1956).

four-pinnate, glaucous (but not white-powdery) blades; and rachises grooved on the upper surface. The segment margins are enrolled, and the sporangia are borne on the outer third of the veins. The species is native to the southwestern United States and northern Mexico, where it inhabits rocky, limestone hillsides and cliffs.

Arthropteris

FIGURES 13.12.1, 2

Joint fern

Some species of *Arthropteris* look like a small *Thelypteris* with a long-creeping rhizome. Nevertheless, one species, *Arthropteris tenella,* is distinct for its small- to medium-sized, one-pinnate fronds. This small fern is handsomely displayed in baskets or by training it to grow up the trunks of trees. The latter growth habit can be started by planting the fern in the soil around the tree and training the rhizomes up the trunk, holding them in place with string or less visible plastic fishing line. A collar of uncut sphagnum moss placed around the base of the tree encourages rooting and more vigorous growth.

These terrestrial or epiphytic ferns have long-creeping, slender, scaly rhizomes, and the stipes are jointed. The joint is slightly raised and sometimes distant from the stipe base, often appearing as a faint dark line. Blades vary from one-pinnate to one-pinnate-pinnatifid and have sessile pinnae jointed to the rachis. The veins are either simple or forked, never netted. The round sori are covered by rounded, kidney-shaped indusia (this is absent in some species). The genus resembles certain species of *Thelypteris* but can be distinguished by the tiny, jointed, usually reddish (when dry) hairs on the upper surfaces of the rachises and costae; *Arthropteris* does not bear needle-shaped hairs, as is often the case in *Thelypteris*. Another distinction is that *Arthropteris* stipes have three or more vascular bundles, whereas *Thelypteris* stipes have only two.

Figure 13.12.1. *Arthropteris tenella*: habit.

Figure 13.12.2. *Arthropteris tenella:* sori.

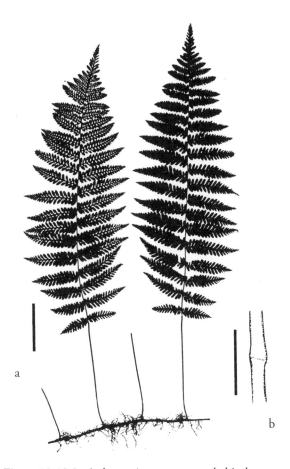

Figure 13.12.3. *Arthropteris monocarpa:* a. habit, bar = 5 cm (2 in.); b. joint near middle of stipe, bar = 1 cm (0.4 in.).

This genus is native to the Old World tropics, Japan, Polynesia, and temperate areas of Australia and New Zealand. One species occurs in South America (Juan Fernández Islands); the remaining 12 to 15 species are found in the Old World. The genus name comes from the Greek *arthron,* joint, and *pteris,* fern, alluding to the jointed stipes of some species.

Arthropteris monocarpa (Cordemoy) C. Christensen

FIGURE 13.12.3

Semi-tender to semi-hardy

A small to medium fern with medium- to long-creeping rhizomes. Best grown under medium light in moist-dry garden soil or potting mix. The plants can be used as a ground cover or confined in a wide container. They can also be used over logs or tree trunks if the substrate is sufficiently moist. The fronds are deciduous.

Arthropteris monocarpa is characterized by stipes jointed in the lower (basal) half, one-pinnate-pinnatifid blades, usually one sorus per lobe, and usually dark hydathodes on the vein tips of the upper surface of the blade. The indusium is kidney-shaped. This species is native to tropical Africa.

A similar species, *Arthropteris orientalis* (J. F. Gmelin) Posthumus, is not yet known in cultivation but has been confused with *A. monocarpa.* It differs by having stipes jointed in the upper (distal) half, one to eight sori per lobe, and the presence of whitish (not dark) hydathodes on the upper surface of the blade. The joint on the stipe appears as a faint dark line and is easily overlooked. This species is also native to tropical Africa. Introduced plants came from Zimbabwe.

Arthropteris tenella (G. Forster) J. Smith ex Hooker f.

FIGURES 13.12.1, 2, 4

syn. *Polypodium tenellum* G. Forster

Joint fern

Semi-hardy

A small to medium fern with medium- to long-creeping rhizomes. Best grown under low to medium light in moist to moist-dry garden soil or potting mix or uncut moss. The plants are versatile: they can form handsome displays if trained to grow up tree trunks, or they can be grown in baskets or as a ground cover. Any divisions should be made during periods of active growth.

Figure 13.12.4. *Arthropteris tenella:* a. habit, bar = 5 cm (2 in.); b. joint at stipe base, bar = 1 cm (0.4 in.).

Arthropteris tenella is characterized by one-pinnate blades with a terminal pinna resembling the lateral ones. The sori are non-indusiate, round, and close to the margin. It is native to New Zealand and Australia.

Aspidotis
Lace fern

These small ferns typically grow in dry, rocky areas. *Aspidotis* species are sometimes included in *Cheilanthes,* though they can be distinguished by their elongate, distally toothed segments with shiny, striated upper surfaces and broad, papery indusia. See *Cheilanthes* for a comparison with related genera. *Aspidotis* consists of four species, three of which occur primarily in western North America, and the remaining one in Mexico. The generic name comes from the Greek word *aspidotes,* shield-bearer, in allusion to the shield-like false indusia.

Aspidotis californica (Hooker) Nuttall ex Copeland
FIGURE 13.13.1
syn. *Cheilanthes californica* (Hooker) Mettenius
California lace fern
Semi-hardy, Zone 8

A small fern with compact, short-creeping to ascending rhizomes and clustered fronds. Grows under high light in well-drained, moist-dry to dry garden soil.

The blades of *Aspidotis californica* are pentagonal to triangular, four- to five-pinnate, with segments mostly lanceolate, 1.5–4 mm long, and pointed apices and margins coarse and sparsely toothed. The indusia are papery, light-colored, semi-circular, and entire or have two to six coarse

teeth. They occur one to three per segment. The species is native to the United States (California) and Mexico (northern Baja California).

Aspidotis carlotta-halliae (W. H. Wagner & E. F. Gilbert) Lellinger
FIGURE 13.13.2
syn. *Cheilanthes carlotta-halliae* W. H. Wagner & E. F. Gilbert
Semi-hardy, Zone 7

A small fern with compact, short-creeping to ascending rhizomes and clustered fronds. Grows under high light in well-drained, moist-dry to dry garden soil.

Aspidotis carlotta-halliae is a hybrid of *A. californica* and *A. densa.* It is best distinguished from its parents by the false indusia with 6–10 coarse irregular teeth or lobes. It is native to northern California, where it typically grows on serpentine rock.

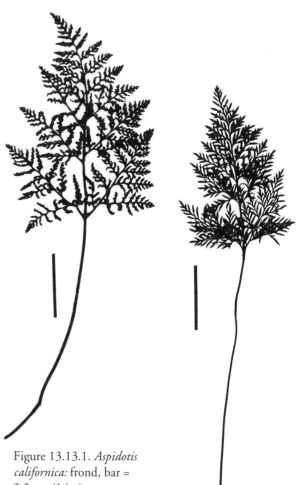

Figure 13.13.1. *Aspidotis californica:* frond, bar = 2.5 cm (1 in.).

Figure 13.13.2. *Aspidotis carlotta-halliae:* frond, bar = 2.5 cm (1 in.).

Aspidotis densa (Brackenridge in Wilkes) Lellinger

FIGURE 13.13.3

syn. *Cheilanthes siliquosa* Maxon, *Pellaea densa*
    (Brackenridge) Hooker
Indian's dream, cliff brake
Very hardy, Zone 4

A small fern with a more-or-less compact, short-creeping to
ascending, branching rhizome and clustered fronds. Grows
under high to medium light in well-drained, moist-dry to
dry garden soil with sand. Avoid getting water on the
fronds.

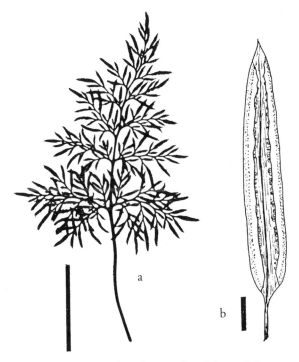

Figure 13.13.3. *Aspidotis densa:* a. frond, bar = 2.5 cm
(1 in.); b. fertile segment, bar = 1 mm.

An evergreen fern, *Aspidotis densa* is distinguished by
small triangular fronds with long segments. The blades vary
from pentagonal to triangular, three- to four-pinnate, and
have linear (not bead-like), entire segments. A glabrous
midrib is conspicuous on the lower surface. The fertile
fronds often have longer stipes and narrower segments than
the sterile ones. The indusium is linear, with 10–15 shallow, regular or irregular teeth. The species is native to the
northwestern United States and southwestern and eastern
Canada.

Asplenium   FIGURES 13.14.1–3
Spleenwort

Asplenium is a large, diverse genus of terrestrial or epiphytic
ferns. They range in size from the tiny European spleen-
worts, with fronds only a few centimeters long, to the giant

Figure 13.14.1. *Asplenium daucifolium:* habit.

bird's-nest ferns, with fronds more than one meter long.
The small species are favorites for rock gardens or terrariums. The larger subtropical and tropical species are well
adapted to growing indoors in pots. Several species of
bird's-nest ferns are in cultivation, mainly *Asplenium antiquum, A. australasicum,* and *A. nidus.* They are popular
indoor plants and are easy to grow if not overwatered. They
tend to get overwatered when planted in large pots, but fortunately they can thrive in relatively small pots. All species
of *Asplenium* must be protected from slugs and snails, especially emerging fronds and young plants.

A fern can usually be assigned to this genus if it has elongate sori (which vary from oblong to linear, depending on
the species) and clathrate rhizome scales. Another helpful,
but less easily seen, characteristic is the two vascular bundles
in the stipe. These bundles unite in the distal part of the
stipe to form an X-shape. The sori have a thin, flap-like indusium, although this trait is sometimes difficult to see because the indusium gets pushed aside and covered by the
sporangia as they mature. Unfortunately, frond form cannot be used to distinguish this genus because almost every
frond shape and degree of cutting, from simple to several
times pinnate, occur in *Asplenium.* The veins are free in
nearly all the species.

Most botanists now classify *Camptosorus, Ceterach, Phyllitis,* and *Schaffneria* in *Asplenium,* since these genera hybridize with *Asplenium* and are distinguished from it by

Figure 13.14.2. *Asplenium daucifolium:* frond.

only a few minor characteristics. In this book, however, these genera are kept separate, partly for convenience and partly because current studies indicate newer realignments of the genera.

Asplenium occurs worldwide and is one of the largest fern genera, containing about 650 species. The genus name comes from the Greek *splen,* spleen. The Greek physician and botanist Dioscorides thought that plants of this genus cured diseases of the spleen.

Asplenium adiantum-nigrum Linnaeus

FIGURE 13.14.4

Black spleenwort
Semi-hardy, Zone 8

A small fern with suberect rhizomes. Grows best under medium light in moist, basic garden soil with sand or potting mix.

Asplenium adiantum-nigrum is characterized by dark or black stipes and (typically) triangular, two-pinnate-pinnatifid blades. The basal pinnae are the largest and most divided. The species is cosmopolitan, growing mostly in temperate areas.

Asplenium aethiopicum (N. L. Burman) Becherer

FIGURE 13.14.5

Semi-hardy, perhaps more tender (?)

A medium-sized fern with short-creeping to suberect rhizomes. Grows under low to medium light in moist garden soil or potting mix.

Figure 13.14.3. *Asplenium daucifolium:* sori and indusia.

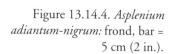

Figure 13.14.4. *Asplenium adiantum-nigrum:* frond, bar = 5 cm (2 in.).

Figure 13.14.5. *Asplenium aethiopicum:* frond, bar = 5 cm (2 in.).

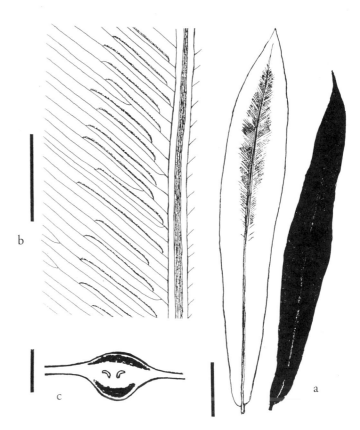

Figure 13.14.6. *Asplenium antiquum:* a. fronds, bar = 5 cm (2 in.); b. sori on upper vein fork, bar = 1 cm (0.4 in.); c. midrib cross section, bar = 5 mm (0.2 in.).

Asplenium aethiopicum can be distinguished by its dark stipes and rachises that bear numerous blackish, thread-like scales. The pinnules are distinctive by being wedge-shaped and deeply and irregularly incised, the incisions irregularly toothed. The blade is narrowly lanceolate to oblong and up to two-pinnate-pinnatifid. The species is native to tropical Africa, Madagascar, and Australia.

This species is closely related to *Asplenium praemorsum* Swartz, an American tropical species, and further research may show that they are the same. As presently recognized, *A. aethiopicum* is highly variable and includes five ploidy levels.

Asplenium antiquum Makino   FIGURE 13.14.6
Japanese bird's-nest fern
Semi-tender, perhaps hardier (?)

A medium-sized fern with erect, stout, unbranched rhizomes. Best grown under medium-high light in well-drained, moist to moist-dry potting mix or uncut moss. The plants do well in pots but are sensitive to overwatering.

Asplenium antiquum resembles the common bird's-nest fern (*A. nidus*) but has more compact growth and narrower fronds with more obvious short stipes. The midrib on the underside of the leaf is rounded, not keeled, and the veins in the middle of the blade are more than 1 mm apart. The vein tips are united into a connecting strand that runs parallel to the blade margin. The sori usually occur on the upper fork of forked veins. The indusium is more than 0.5 mm wide. This species is native to Taiwan and Japan.

Asplenium antiquum is sold widely. It was first introduced into the United States in 1969 from the spores of plants collected near Hakone, Japan. This species is a robust grower with a neater outline than *Asplenium nidus*. *Asplenium nidus* and *A. australasicum* differ from *A. antiquum* by having the veins closer, the sori on both forks of a vein, and the indusia less than 0.5 mm wide. *Asplenium australasicum* also has the lower side of the midrib keeled, not rounded. *Asplenium serratum,* a similar species from the American tropics, differs by having free, not connected, veins at the tips.

'Victoria'. Plate 12. Margins ruffled and fringed. A similar cultivar with narrower fronds is also in the trade.

Asplenium auritum Swartz   FIGURE 13.14.7
Eared spleenwort
Tender

A small fern with erect rhizomes. Best grown under medium light in moist potting mix.

Asplenium auritum has thick, lanceolate fronds, up to one-pinnate-pinnatifid at the base, with scattered clathrate

Figure 13.14.7.
Asplenium auritum:
frond, bar = 5 cm (2 in.).

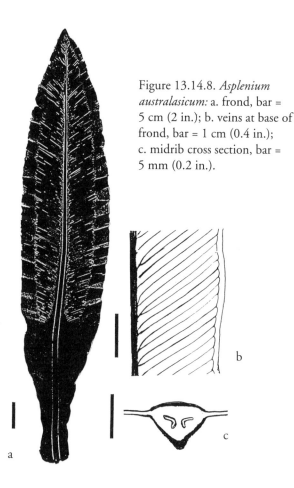

Figure 13.14.8. *Asplenium
australasicum:* a. frond, bar =
5 cm (2 in.); b. veins at base of
frond, bar = 1 cm (0.4 in.);
c. midrib cross section, bar =
5 mm (0.2 in.).

scales on the lower surfaces. The indusium is inconspicuous. The species is widespread in tropical America, where it typically grows as an epiphyte on tree trunks.

Asplenium australasicum (J. Smith) Hooker

FIGURE 13.14.8

syn. *Asplenium australis* Horticulture
Semi-tender

A medium to large fern with erect, stout, unbranched rhizomes. Grows well under medium light in well-drained, moist to moist-dry potting mix or uncut moss. The plants do particularly well in pots, but be careful not to overpot. Collectively, the fronds form a funnel or bowl. This species tends to be more cold hardy and less vulnerable to slugs than *Asplenium nidus,* which it resembles.

The fronds of *Asplenium australasicum* vary greatly in outline but are generally oblanceolate. They differ from those of *A. nidus* by having keeled undersides of the midribs, and the sori are usually spread along more than half the length of the vein. The species is native to Australia and the Pacific Islands.

Whether fronds are arranged in a narrow funnel or wide bowl is not consistent in Australian plants or those in cultivation. The most reliable feature for separating *Asplenium australasicum* from *A. antiquum* and *A. nidus* is the keeled rather than rounded midribs. Although infrequently grown, *A. serratum* also has simple leaves and a keeled midrib, but it can be distinguished because its veins are free at the tips, not connected.

Asplenium bulbiferum G. Forster

FIGURE 13.14.9

Mother fern
Semi-hardy to semi-tender

A medium-sized fern with short-creeping to suberect rhizomes and pale green, arching foliage. Grows under low to medium light in moist potting mix. This species is recommended for places with low light. It is easy to grow and can be easily propagated from the buds on the fronds; however, it has the disadvantage of being particularly susceptible to attack by slugs and snails. Narrowly segmented forms propagated from spores do not breed true.

Asplenium bulbiferum is characterized by highly divided blades (mostly two-pinnate-pinnatifid but sometimes up to nearly four-pinnate) that may bear numerous buds on the upper surfaces. The blades are oblong-ovate and thick. Each incurved lobe of the pinnules contain a single sorus. The species is native to India, Malaysia, Australia, New Zealand, and the Pacific Islands.

Asplenium ×crucibuli Horticulture

FIGURE 13.14.10

syn. *×Asplenosorus crucibuli* Horticulture
Hardy to semi-hardy, Zones 5

A small fern with erect rhizomes. Grows best under low to medium light in moist garden soil or potting mix. These evergreen plants are excellent for rock gardens.

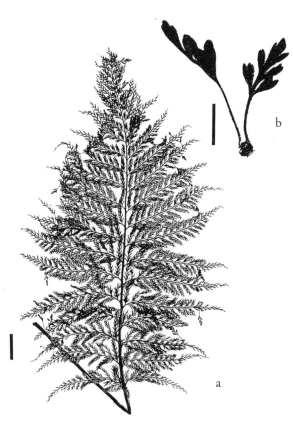

Figure 13.14.9. *Asplenium bulbiferum:* a. frond, bar = 5 cm (2 in.); b. leaf bud, bar = 1 cm (0.4 in.).

Figure 13.14.10. *Asplenium ×crucibuli:* fronds, bar = 5 cm (2 in.).

Asplenium ×crucibuli is a sterile hybrid characterized by linear fronds that are mostly pinnatifid but with a few pinnae at the base, and by elongate, tail-like blade tips. It was produced in horticulture from a cross between *A. platyneuron* and *Camptosorus sibericus.*

Asplenium cuspidatum Lamarck   FIGURE 13.14.11
Tender

A small fern with erect rhizomes and proliferous roots. Grows best under low-medium light in moist uncut moss. This species usually forms tufts of very small, delicate fronds in terrariums or bottle gardens. Like the filmy ferns, it prefers humidity and grows slowly during the winter.

Asplenium cuspidatum has triangular fronds up to three-pinnate, with ultimate segments narrowly obovate, sometimes forked at the tip. It is widespread in tropical America.

Figure 13.14.11. *Asplenium cuspidatum:* habits, bar = 5 cm (2 in.).

Asplenium daucifolium Lamarck
FIGURES 13.14.1–3, 12
syn. *Asplenium viviparum* C. Presl
Mauritius spleenwort, dwarf mother fern
Semi-tender

A small to medium fern with short-creeping to suberect rhizomes and bud-bearing fronds. Grows under low to medium light in moist potting mix. Though somewhat slow growing, this species is recommended for sites with low light. It is easy to start new plants from buds on the frond.

Asplenium daucifolium resembles *A. bulbiferum* but has smaller, stiffer, darker green fronds, and the underside of the rachis is beset with linear or thread-like scales. Similar scales also occur in *A. bulbiferum,* but they are ovate and cupped. The species is endemic to Madagascar and the Macarene Islands.

Figure 13.14.12. *Asplenium daucifolium:* frond, bar = 5 cm (2 in.).

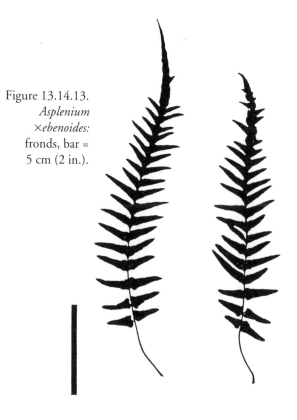

Figure 13.14.13. *Asplenium ×ebenoides:* fronds, bar = 5 cm (2 in.).

Asplenium ×ebenoides R. R. Scott   FIGURE 13.14.13
syn. *×Asplenosorus ebenoides* (R. R. Scott) Wherry
Scott's spleenwort, dragon-tail fern
Hardy, Zone (4)5

A small fern with erect rhizomes. Best grown under medium light in moist potting mix. Growth may be improved with ample humidity, as in terrariums.

Asplenium ×ebenoides is of hybrid origin, resulting from a cross between *A. platyneuron* and *Camptosorus rhizophyllus,* and the plants are variably intermediate between those species in frond shape and cutting. The intermediacy is best seen in the cutting of the blade, which is one-pinnate at the base, as in *A. platyneuron,* and entire or nearly so distally or long tapered, as in *C. rhizophyllus.* The central portion of the blade is lobed, often irregularly, expressing the intermediate condition. The venation is also intermediate: *A. platyneuron* has free veins, *C. rhizophyllus* has netted veins, and the hybrid has both.

This hybrid occurs naturally in the eastern United States where the two parents mingle. It produces aborted spores and is therefore sterile; however, at one site in Georgia, plants have doubled their chromosome number to become fertile, producing viable spores. Some commercial greenhouses have propagated these fertile plants from spores, and the fern is becoming more widely available in the trade.

Asplenium flabellifolium Cavanilles   FIGURE 13.14.14
Necklace fern
Semi-tender

A small fern with short-creeping to suberect rhizomes and fronds bearing buds at their tips. Grows best in humid environments in well-drained, moist potting mix. The plants prefer cool, moist, shaded areas.

The fronds of *Asplenium flabellifolium* are one-pinnate with round to fan-shaped pinnae, the larger pinnae three-

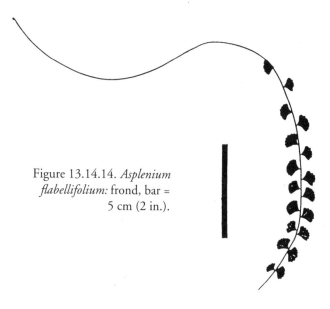

Figure 13.14.14. *Asplenium flabellifolium:* frond, bar = 5 cm (2 in.).

lobed or more. The rachis is long and trailing, often rooting at the tip. The species is native to Australia and New Zealand.

Asplenium fontanum (Linnaeus) Bernhardi   FIGURE 13.14.15

Smooth rock spleenwort
Hardy, Zone 5

Very small, to about 15 cm (6 in.) long, with clumped rhizomes. Grows under medium light in well-drained, moist, basic garden soil or sand and peat mix. The plants should be kept moist at all times.

Asplenium fontanum is characterized by lanceolate, two-pinnate-pinnatifid blades. It is native to Europe and the Himalayas.

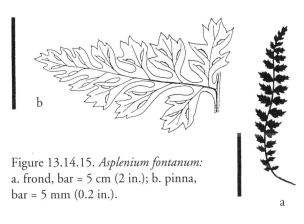

Figure 13.14.15. *Asplenium fontanum:* a. frond, bar = 5 cm (2 in.); b. pinna, bar = 5 mm (0.2 in.).

Asplenium longissimum Blume   FIGURE 13.14.16
syn. *Blechnum indicum* N. L. Burman
Tender

A medium to large fern with rhizomes erect or nearly so. Best grown under medium light in moist potting mix or uncut moss. The plants grow robustly and are best displayed in hanging baskets, but they must be watered frequently. The fronds can reach 1 m (3 ft.) long or more and often bear buds at the apex.

Asplenium longissimum is characterized by long, one-pinnate fronds narrowed at the base and by numerous narrowly triangular, sessile pinnae with coarse, doubly serrate margins. The pinna bases are mostly truncate or wedge-shaped on the lower pinnae, whereas the middle pinnae are unequal-sided, with the upper side slightly enlarged and eared and the lower side more oblique. The species occurs from Vietnam to Indonesia, Borneo, and the Philippines.

In the United States this species is often confused with *Asplenium pellucidum;* however, it differs from that species, and also from *A. polydon,* by the buds at the frond tips.

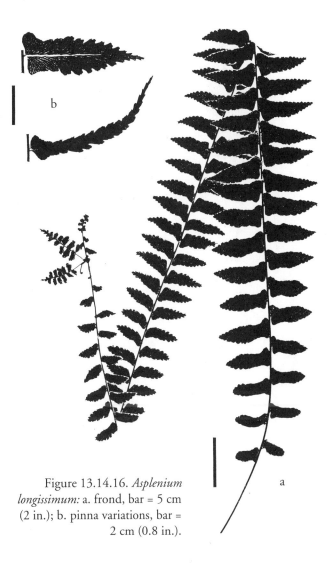

Figure 13.14.16. *Asplenium longissimum:* a. frond, bar = 5 cm (2 in.); b. pinna variations, bar = 2 cm (0.8 in.).

Asplenium marinum Linnaeus   FIGURE 13.14.17
Sea spleenwort
Semi-hardy

A small fern with clumped rhizomes. Best grown under medium light in moist potting mix. The plants are slow-growing and need humidity. In nature they grow along coasts on rocks subject to sea spray. This species is sensitive to frost.

Asplenium marinum is distinguished by lanceolate, one-pinnate fronds with fleshy, glossy blades. The pinnae vary from ovate-lanceolate to oblong and have crenate-serrate margins and blunt apices. This species is native to Europe and northern Africa.

Asplenium nidus Linnaeus   FIGURE 13.14.18
Bird's-nest fern
Tender

A medium to large fern with erect, stout, unbranched rhizomes. Best grown under medium to low light in moist-dry potting mix or uncut moss. The plants grow relatively slowly. Do not overpot, and keep well drained.

Figure 13.14.17. *Asplenium marinum:* frond, bar = 5 cm (2 in.).

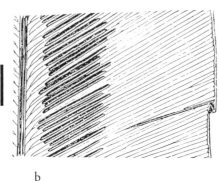

b

Figure 13.14.18. *Asplenium nidus:* a. frond, bar = 5 cm (2 in.); b. sori on both vein forks, bar = 1 cm (0.4 in.); c. midrib cross section, bar = 5 mm (0.2 in.).

a   c

The fronds of *Asplenium nidus* are up to 1.5 m (5 ft.) long, and most form a vase-shaped cluster. The stipe is short and inconspicuous, and the blades are simple, entire, and variable in shape but mostly oblanceolate. The midrib on the underside of the blade is rounded, not keeled as in related species. The vein tips unite in short arcs before the cartilaginous margin. The sori usually occupy less than half the vein length and are borne on both branches of the vein. The species is native to the tropics of the Old World and to Hawaii.

This variable species has several named varieties, which further research may prove to be valid species. Plants called *Asplenium nidus* in cultivation that have midribs keeled on the underside are mostly *A. australasicum.* Plants with midribs rounded on the underside and sori often only on the upper vein fork are *A. antiquum.*

A number of garden variants of *Asplenium nidus* exist, including plants with unusual characteristics such as lobed or fimbriate margins and narrow fronds. The most striking and well known is the lasagna fern.

var. *plicatum* van Alderwerelt van Rosenburgh ('Crispafolium', 'Crispum', and possibly 'Undulatum' of the trade). Lasagna fern. A smaller plant with pleated or wavy blades. The plants have thick, rigid fronds that twist slightly, resembling lasagna noodles. They grow slowly and need protection during winter in subtropical climates.

Asplenium oblongifolium Colenso   FIGURE 13.14.19
syn. *Asplenium lucidum* G. Forster
Glossy spleenwort
Semi-hardy

A medium-sized fern with short-creeping to suberect rhizomes. Grows best under medium light in moist garden soil or potting mix. The plants have attractive deep green, glossy fronds and are easy to cultivate.

Asplenium oblongifolium has one-pinnate blades with an apical pinna that resembles the lateral ones. The pinnae are short-stalked, entire, and tapered to the tip. The sori form a herringbone pattern and occupy most of the area between the midrib and margins. This species is endemic to New Zealand.

Asplenium oligophlebium Baker   FIGURE 13.14.20
Probably semi-tender

A small fern with erect rhizomes and fronds bearing buds at the apex. Seems to grow best under low light in moist potting mix. The plants are delicate, prefer humidity, and grow extremely well in terrariums. They root readily from the frond tips.

Asplenium oligophlebium is characterized by narrowly lanceolate, one-pinnate fronds with many linear-lanceolate to semi-triangular pinnae. The margins are irregularly lobed, especially the acroscopic margins, and the basal lobes of the pinnae are enlarged, often forked. The species is endemic to Japan.

Figure 13.14.19. *Asplenium oblongifolium:* frond, bar = 5 cm (2 in.).

Figure 13.14.20. *Asplenium oligophlebium:* frond, bar = 5 cm (2 in.).

Asplenium pellucidum Lamarck   FIGURE 13.14.21
Tender

A medium to large fern with suberect rhizomes and pendent fronds. Grows under medium light in moist potting mix or uncut moss.

The stipes of *Asplenium pellucidum* are short, and the pinnae are shorter toward the base of the blades. The pinna margins are serrate, and the middle pinnae are very unequal at the base. The rachis is beset by numerous dark scales that are rounded at the base and abruptly tapered to a bristle. *Asplenium pellucidum* is native to the Old World tropics except Africa. The plants cultivated in the United States are often misidentified as *A. longissimum.*

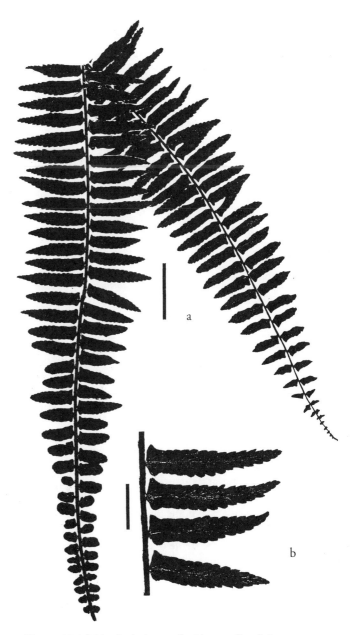

Figure 13.14.21. *Asplenium pellucidum:* a. frond, bar = 5 cm (2 in.); b. pinnae, bar = 2 cm (0.8 in.).

Asplenium pinnatifidum Nuttall   FIGURE 13.14.22
syn. ×*Asplenosorus pinnatifidus* (Nuttall) Mickel
Lobed spleenwort
Hardy

A small fern with erect rhizomes and clustered fronds. Best grown under medium light in moist gardening soil or potting mix. An excellent rock garden or, in arid climates, a good terrarium fern.

Asplenium pinnatifidum has narrowly lanceolate blades that are pinnatifid for most of their length except for one or two pinnae at the base. The blade apex is often long-attenuate. The species is native to eastern North America, where it usually grows in shaded sandstone crevices.

Asplenium pinnatifidum is a hybrid of *A. montanum* and *Camptosorus rhizophyllus,* and the lobing of the blade is variably intermediate between these two species. Although of hybrid origin, the plants are polyploid, having doubled their chromosome number, which means that they have normal, viable spores.

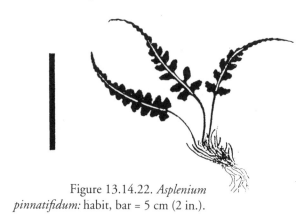

Figure 13.14.22. *Asplenium pinnatifidum:* habit, bar = 5 cm (2 in.).

Asplenium platyneuron (Linnaeus) Britton, Sterns & Poppenburg   FIGURE 13.14.23
Ebony spleenwort
Hardy, Zones 4 and 5

A small to medium fern with suberect rhizomes. Grows under low to high light in basic garden soil or potting mix kept moist-dry. The plants are easy to grow once established.

Asplenium platyneuron resembles *A. trichomanes* but differs by having larger and more erect fronds that are oblanceolate, and oblong pinnae eared near the base on the upper margin. The "ear" on the pinna often overlaps the rachis, which is ebony-colored. The fertile fronds are often tall and erect, whereas the sterile ones are smaller and spreading, sometimes forming a basal rosette. This species is common throughout the eastern United States; it also occurs in South Africa.

Asplenium platyneuron has been hybridized in cultivation with the Asian *Camptosorus sibericus* to form *A.* ×*crucibuli.* It is also one of the parents involved in the naturally occurring hybrids *A.* ×*ebenoides* and *A. pinnatifidum.*

Figure 13.14.23. *Asplenium platyneuron:* frond, bar = 5 cm (2 in.).

Asplenium polyodon G. Forster   FIGURE 13.14.24
syn. *Asplenium falcatum* Lamarck
Sickle spleenwort
Semi-tender or hardier

Short-creeping, stout rhizomes and often pendent fronds to 130 cm (52 in.) long. Grows under low to medium light in moist potting mix or uncut moss. The species is extremely variable in frond length. The long-fronded forms are best grown in baskets.

The stipe of *Asplenium polyodon* is dark brown, scaly, and about one-third to one-half the blade length. The larger stipe and rachis scales are long-triangular and smoky colored. The blades are narrowly oblong, one-pinnate, and widest at the base. The pinnae have unequal bases (excavate on the lower side), coarsely, doubly serrate margins, and gradually tapered tips. This species might be confused with *A. longissimum* or *A. pellucidum.* It is native from Madagascar to the Pacific Islands.

Asplenium prolongatum Hooker   FIGURE 13.14.25
Semi-hardy

A small fern with erect rhizomes and fronds bearing buds at the tips. Grows under low to medium light in moist soil or potting mix with good drainage. The plants grow well in terrariums or in rock crevices with adequate humidity.

Asplenium prolongatum is characterized by flattened stipes and oblong to narrowly triangular blades. The two-pinnate fronds have rachises extended into a whip-like tail bearing buds at the tip. It is native to India, China, and Japan.

Figure 13.14.24.
Asplenium polyodon:
a. frond, bar = 5 cm
(2 in.); b, c. pinna
variations, bar =
2 cm (0.8 in.).

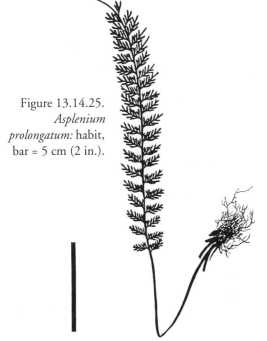

Figure 13.14.25.
*Asplenium
prolongatum:* habit,
bar = 5 cm (2 in.).

Asplenium kenzoi S. Kurata is presumably a hybrid of this species and *A. antiquum*. It resembles *A. prolongatum* but is less divided and more leathery.

Asplenium resiliens Kunze   FIGURE 13.14.26
Black-stem spleenwort
Hardy, Zone 6

A small fern with erect rhizomes. Grows best under medium light in moist, basic potting mix. The plants are moderately easy to grow.

Asplenium resiliens resembles *A. platyneuron* but has smaller, rounder pinnae, and the blades are often bluish green in color. It is apogamous, producing 32 diploid spores per sporangium. Native to the United States, Mexico, the West Indies, and South America, it grows on limestone rocks.

Asplenium ruta-muraria Linnaeus   FIGURE 13.14.27
Wall-rue
Very hardy, Zone 4

A small fern with clumped rhizomes. Grows under medium light in basic garden soil with sand or potting mix. This species tolerates moist to dry soil but needs good drainage and air circulation. It is difficult to establish.

Asplenium ruta-muraria is characterized by irregularly two-pinnate fronds, and the pinnules vary from rounded to fan-shaped. This species is native to North America, Europe, and Asia. It typically grows on limestone.

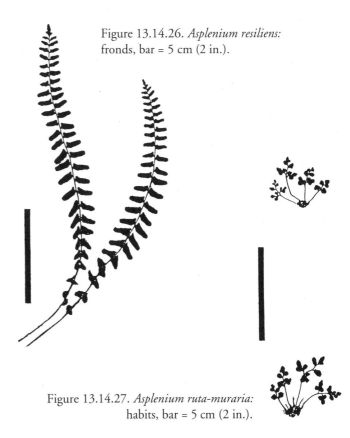

Figure 13.14.26. *Asplenium resiliens:*
fronds, bar = 5 cm (2 in.).

Figure 13.14.27. *Asplenium ruta-muraria:*
habits, bar = 5 cm (2 in.).

Asplenium septentrionale (Linnaeus) Hoffmann

FIGURE 13.14.28

Forked spleenwort
Very hardy, Zone 4

A small fern with clumped rhizomes. Grows under medium light in moist-dry potting mix. Water sparingly and give good drainage. The species is sensitive to root disturbances and is difficult to establish. It is infrequently offered by specialty nurseries as a novelty.

Asplenium septentrionale is characterized by linear blades and narrow, ascending segments. In general aspect, the plants resemble tufts of grass. They usually grow on limestone. This species is native to North America, Europe, and Asia.

Figure 13.14.29.
Asplenium serratum:
a. fronds, bar = 5 cm
(2 in.); b. sori,
indusia, and free
vein tips, bar = 2 cm
(0.8 in.).

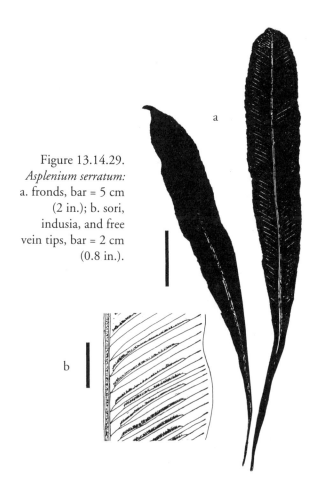

Figure 13.14.28. *Asplenium septentrionale:* fronds, bar = 5 cm (2 in.).

Asplenium serratum Linnaeus

FIGURE 13.14.29

Tender, Zone 10

A medium-sized fern with erect, stout, unbranched rhizomes. Grows under medium light in moist potting mix or uncut moss.

Asplenium serratum resembles the Old World bird's-nest ferns (such as *A. antiquum, A. australasicum,* and *A. nidus*) but differs by having veins that are free at the tips, not connected. It is not as robust as the Old World species and is infrequently grown. As presently circumscribed, *A. serratum* is extremely variable, apparently consisting of several closely related species that need to be distinguished through further research. It is native to tropical America.

Asplenium surrogatum P. S. Green

FIGURE 13.14.30

syn. *Asplenium mayii* Horticulture, *A. pteridoides* of
authors, not Baker
Semi-tender or hardier

A medium-sized fern with short-creeping to suberect rhizomes. Grows under medium light in moist garden soil or potting mix.

The fronds are oblong to ovate-oblong, one-pinnate-pinnatisect, leathery, and shiny. *Asplenium surrogatum* has linear-triangular and deeply pinnatisect pinnae, with the tips of the lobes irregularly cleft into sharp teeth. The species is endemic to Lord Howe Island in the southwest Pacific.

Figure 13.14.30. *Asplenium surrogatum:* frond, bar = 5 cm (2 in.).

The plant called *Asplenium mayii* in horticulture is the same as this species. In 1894 the original young plant of *A. mayii* was presumed to be a horticultural hybrid of *A. baptistii* and *A. pteroides,* a species sometimes confused with *A. surrogatum.*

Asplenium thunbergii Kunze   FIGURE 13.14.31
syn. *Asplenium belangeri* (Bory) Kunze
Tender

A medium-sized fern with suberect, branched, clumped rhizomes and bud-bearing fronds. Grows under medium light in moist, well-drained garden soil or potting mix. The plants are readily attacked by slugs and snails. Damage from these pests can be lessened by growing the plants in hanging pots. The species is easily propagated by leaf buds.

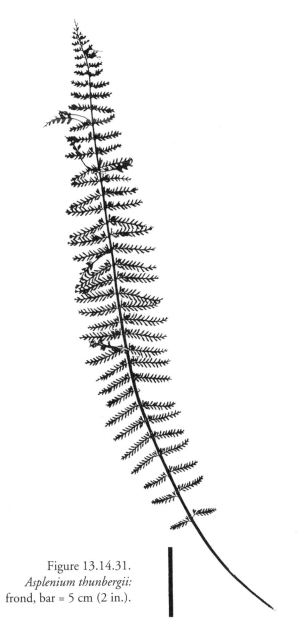

Figure 13.14.31. *Asplenium thunbergii:* frond, bar = 5 cm (2 in.).

The fronds of *Asplenium thunbergii* are narrowly oblong, up to two-pinnate near the base, with numerous pinnae divided into narrowly oblong, one-veined segments. There is one sorus per segment. The rachis is broadened by narrow wings on both sides, and buds form at the rachis-costa junctions. The species is native from southeastern Asia to Indonesia and Borneo.

Asplenium trichomanes Linnaeus
FIGURE 13.14.32; PLATE 13
Maidenhair spleenwort
Very hardy, Zone 2?

A small fern with erect rhizomes. Grows under low light in moist potting mix. Some plants adapt more easily to cultivation than others. Plants from China have adapted well to gardens in southern California. *Asplenium trichomanes* is an evergreen fern. The fronds often grow in a rosette pattern.

Asplenium trichomanes is characterized by dark rachises and one-pinnate blades with rounded to oblong pinnae. It resembles *A. resiliens,* but the pinnae are less elongate and the blade tissue is thinner and a brighter green (not dull blue-green). A cosmopolitan species, *A. trichomanes* occurs on every continent but mainly in temperate areas.

An infrequently seen but closely related species is *Asplenium tripteropus* Nakai, from eastern Asia, which differs by rooting at the frond tip.

In North America *Asplenium trichomanes* consists of two chromosomal races: one with two sets of chromosomes (diploid) and another with four (tetraploid). The two races differ in habitat, with the diploids tending to occur on acidic rocks such as sandstones, granites, and basalts, and the tetraploids occurring on basic rocks such as limestones and dolomites (Moran 1982).

'Cristatum'. A crested form.
'Incisum'. Pinna margins incised.

Figure 13.14.32. *Asplenium trichomanes:* fronds, bar = 5 cm (2 in.).

Figure 13.14.33. *Asplenium trichomanes-ramosum:* habit, bar = 5 cm (2 in.).

Asplenium trichomanes-ramosum Linnaeus

FIGURE 13.14.33

syn. *Asplenium viride* Hudson
Green spleenwort
Very hardy, Zone 2

A small fern with erect rhizomes. Grows under low light in basic, well-drained, moist potting soil. This species is infrequently cultivated and difficult to grow.

Asplenium trichomanes-ramosum resembles *A. trichomanes* but differs by having a green rachis. It usually grows on limestone and is native to North America, Europe, Asia, and Africa.

Astrolepis

Star-scale cloak fern

The genus *Astrolepis* consists of small to medium ferns that typically grow in dry, rocky places. They tolerate dryness and make excellent rock garden plants.

The blades of star-scale cloak ferns are linear to linear-oblong, one-pinnate to pinnate-pinnatifid, and somewhat leathery. The segments are shallowly lobed or entire and covered with star-shaped scales on the upper surface. The sporangia run along the veins and lack an indusium, the segment margins being more or less flat, not strongly enrolled, and of the same color and texture as the rest of the blade tissue (not differentiated as in other cheilanthoid ferns).

Until recently, the species of *Astrolepis* were classified with either *Notholaena* or *Cheilanthes;* however, they can be separated from these genera by the star-shaped scales on the upper surfaces of the blades and the two vascular bundles in the stipe (the other genera have only one). See *Cheilanthes* for a comparison to that genus and other cheilanthoid ferns.

Astrolepis is native to the Americas and contains about eight species. The common and generic names refer to the star-shaped scales on the upper surfaces of the blades: *astro* is Greek for "star" and *lepis* means "scale."

Astrolepis beitelii (Mickel) D. M. Benham & Windham

FIGURE 13.15.1

syn. *Cheilanthes beitelii* Mickel
Beitel's cloak fern
Semi-hardy

A medium-sized fern with compact to short-creeping rhizomes and clustered fronds. Grows under high light in well-drained, moist to moist-dry garden soil with sand. This species prefers heat.

Astrolepis beitelii resembles *A. sinuata* but usually differs by the larger pinnae, 13–35 mm (0.5–1.5 in.) long, with three to five pairs of lobes. The upper surface of the blade has star-shaped scales to 1 mm long, which are usually deciduous. The species grows from central Mexico to Guatemala, often on rocky slopes.

Astrolepis sinuata (Lagasca ex Swartz) D. M. Benham

FIGURE 13.15.2

syn. *Cheilanthes sinuata* (Lagasca ex Swartz) Domin,
    Notholaena sinuata (Lagasca ex Swartz) Kaulfuss
Semi-hardy, Zone 7(8)

A small to medium fern with compact to short-creeping rhizomes and clustered fronds. Grows under high light in

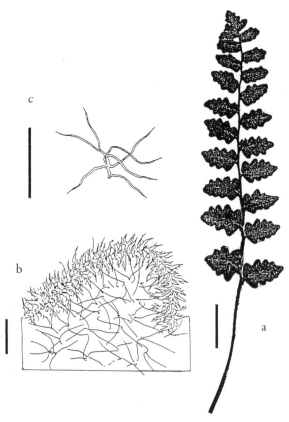

Figure 13.15.1. *Astrolepis beitelii:* a. frond, bar = 2.5 cm (1 in.); b. upper surface of lobe with scales, bar = 1 mm, by H. Fukuda; c. star-shaped scale, bar = 1 mm, by H. Fukuda. Courtesy of John T. Mickel.

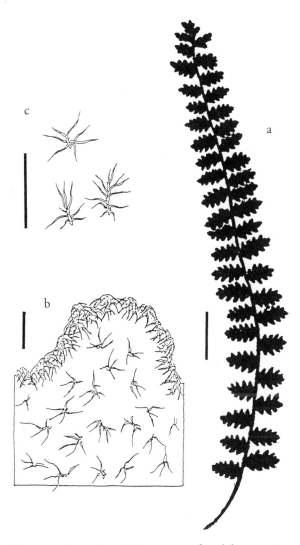

Athyrium

FIGURE 13.16.1

The lady fern (*Athyrium filix-femina*) and Japanese painted fern (*A. niponicum* 'Pictum') are well-known representatives of the genus *Athyrium*. The lady fern comes in a bewildering array of garden variations that are eye-catching in their unusual patterns. For example, the foliage can be regularly crisscrossed, finely divided, or bunched to form a dense, ball-like tuft. *Athyrium* is a favorite in temperate climates and is easy to grow, but the plants tend to have brittle fronds that break easily. In subtropical or warmer climates some species languish and die within a few seasons. Fertilizing and periodically replanting in fresh humusy soil can prolong the life of these plants. In arid climates it is necessary to keep the soil moist for best growth. Many species grow readily from spores.

The genus consists of terrestrial ferns, not epiphytes. They have long- to short-creeping, ascending, or erect rhizomes with nonclathrate scales. The blades are linear to broadly triangular, anadromic at least toward the base, one-pinnate or more divided, and usually herbaceous. The rachises have a V-shaped groove on the upper surface, and this groove is continuous with that of the costae. The grooves are often minutely hairy within. In many species a small green spine is found on the edge of the groove at the base of the costae or costules. The veins can be free or united. The sori are single, not in pairs (or rarely so), and they vary from linear to oblong to J-shaped or, less frequently, round. An indusium is present, rarely absent.

Figure 13.15.2. *Astrolepis sinuata*: a. frond, bar = 2.5 cm (1 in.); b. upper surface of lobe with scales, bar = 1 mm, by H. Fukuda; c. star-shaped scale, bar = 1 mm, by H. Fukuda. Courtesy of John T. Mickel.

drained, moist-dry to dry garden soil with sand. The plants seem to prefer heat and are relatively easy to grow.

The lower surface of the pinnae bear minute glandular hairs beneath the scales. *Astrolepis sinuata* resembles *Cheilanthes bonariensis* due to the linear, one-pinnate-pinnatifid blades, but it differs by having ciliate scales instead of long matted hairs on the lower surface of the pinnae. It also resembles *A. beitelii* but has smaller pinnae, only 12–20 mm (0.5–0.75 in.) long, with four to six pairs of lobes. It further differs by the star-shaped scales on the upper surface of the pinnae being shorter, to 0.5 mm long, and usually persistent. The species is native to the southwestern United States, Central America, the West Indies, and South America.

Figure 13.16.1. *Athyrium filix-femina:* habit.

A good characteristic to use for distinguishing *Athyrium* from similar genera such as *Arachniodes, Dryopteris,* and *Polystichum* is the presence of only two vascular bundles in the stipe. These bundles are concave, with the inner sides facing each other, and unite upward to form a U shape, not an X shape as in *Asplenium. Thelypteris* also has only two vascular bundles in the stipe, but it usually differs by having one-pinnate-pinnatifid blades and (usually) needle-shaped hairs.

Athyrium occurs worldwide, especially at higher elevations, and contains about 180 species. The genus name comes from the Greek *athyros,* doorless. What this refers to is uncertain.

Certain species in this genus are sometimes united with *Deparia* or *Diplazium,* which are recognized separately in this work. To assist in identification, the salient features of the genera are summarized here.

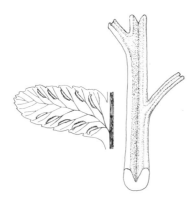

Athyrium: Sori single, not paired back-to-back on the same vein, usually linear to oblong, sometimes J-shaped; rachis grooves V-shaped and opening to admit the groove of the costae; conspicuous multicellular hairs absent on the blade. (*Athyrium alpestre, A. delavayi, A. distentifolium, A. filix-femina, A. niponicum, A. otophorum, A. vidalii*)

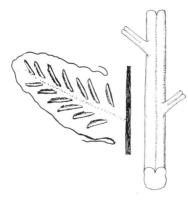

Deparia: Sori paired or not, variously shaped; rachis grooves variously shaped but not opening into the costae; conspicuous multicellular hairs present on the blade. (*Deparia acrostichoides, D. japonica, D. petersenii*)

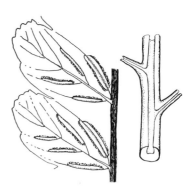

Diplazium: Some sori (usually the basal ones) paired back-to-back along the same vein, mostly linear; rachis grooves U-shaped or flat-bottomed and continuing into the costae; conspicuous multicellular hairs absent on the blade. (*Diplazium australe, D. dilatatum, D. esculentum, D. lonchophyllum, D. proliferum, D. pycnocarpon, D. subsinuatum, D. tomitaroanum*)

Athyrium alpestre (Hoppe) Clairville   FIGURE 13.16.2
syn. *Athyrium distentifolium* var. *americanum* (Butters) Cronquist
American alpine lady fern
Hardy, Zone (4)5

A medium-sized fern with short-creeping to suberect rhizomes and deciduous leaves. Grows under medium light in acidic, moist to wet garden soil or potting mix. This species is difficult to grow.

Athyrium alpestre resembles a small lady fern except that the sori are round and the indusia are reduced or absent. It is native to alpine and subalpine areas in North America, Europe, and Asia.

Athyrium delavayi H. Christ   FIGURE 13.16.3
Semi-hardy (?)

A medium-sized fern with erect, sparingly clump-forming rhizomes. Grows under medium light in moist garden soil or potting mix. The plants have a delicate aspect and attractive reddish costae.

Athyrium delavayi has ovate-oblong fronds with linear pinnae and small, nearly rhomboid pinnules. The basal pinnule is longer than the others and often pinnatifid and overlapping the rachis. The species is native to China.

Athyrium distentifolium Tausch ex Opiz
FIGURE 13.16.4
Alpine lady fern
Very hardy, Zones 1–4(?)

This species resembles *Athyrium alpestre* but is more coarsely cut, shorter, and obviously indusiate. It is easier to cultivate than *A. alpestre. Athyrium distentifolium* is native to Europe and Asia.

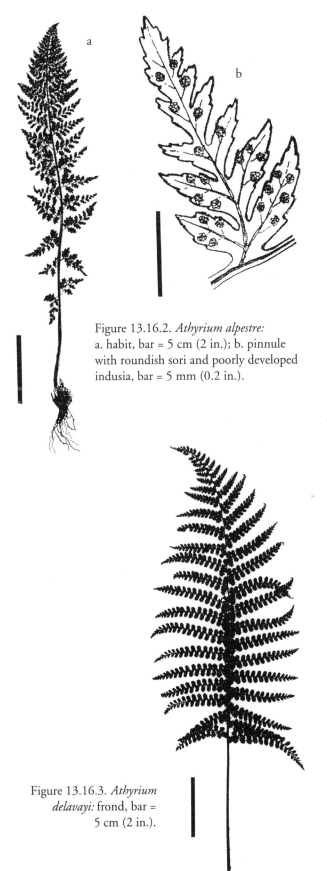

Figure 13.16.2. *Athyrium alpestre:*
a. habit, bar = 5 cm (2 in.); b. pinnule
with roundish sori and poorly developed
indusia, bar = 5 mm (0.2 in.).

Figure 13.16.4. *Athyrium
distentifolium:* frond, bar =
5 cm (2 in.).

Figure 13.16.3. *Athyrium
delavayi:* frond, bar =
5 cm (2 in.).

Athyrium filix-femina (Linnaeus) Roth

FIGURES 13.16.1, 5–9

Lady fern
Hardy, Zone 4

A medium-large fern with short-creeping to erect, clump-forming rhizomes and deciduous fronds. Grows best in low to high light in garden soil or potting mix kept amply moist-wet during the growing season. Most varieties are easily cultivated.

Athyrium filix-femina is extremely variable but generally is characterized by lanceolate to ovate, two-pinnate-pinnatifid blades and elongated or hooked indusia. It is widespread, occurring in North America, South America, Europe, and Asia.

The many cultivars of lady fern are derived from the European variety, var. *filix-femina,* and they differ in frond shape: highly branched, twisted, widened, narrowed, reduced, crested, crisscrossed, congested, rounded, or jagged (see Figure 12.2). Many cultivars must be propagated by divisions because they do not breed true from spores. Of the hundreds of cultivars, only a few are listed here. Some pteridologists raise the varieties listed here to the rank of species.

var. *angustum* (Willdenow) G. Lawson (*Athyrium angustum* (Willdenow) C. Presl). Northern lady fern. Figure 13.16.5. This variety is hardy to Zone 2. It is distinguished by stipes nearly as long as the blades, elliptic to lanceolate blades broadest near or just below the middle, and yellow spores. It is native to central to northeastern Canada and the United States.

Figure 13.16.5. *Athyrium filix-femina* var. *angustum:* frond, bar = 5 cm (2 in.).

Figure 13.16.7. *Athyrium filix-femina* var. *cyclosorum:* frond, bar = 5 cm (2 in.).

Figure 13.16.6. *Athyrium filix-femina* var. *asplenioides:* a. frond, bar = 5 cm (2 in.); b. pinnule with elongate sori and indusia, bar = 3 mm (0.1 in.), courtesy of Knobloch and Correll (1962); c. rhizome, bar = 2 cm (0.8 in.), courtesy of Knobloch and Correll (1962).

Figure 13.16.8. *Athyrium filix-femina* var. *filix-femina:* frond, bar = 5 cm (2 in.).

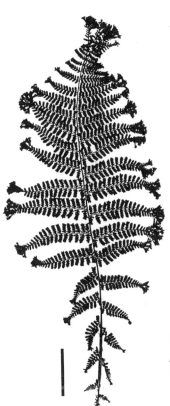

Figure 13.16.9. *Athyrium filix-femina* 'Cristatum': frond, bar = 5 cm (2 in.).

var. *asplenioides* (Michaux) Farwell (*Athyrium asplenioides* (Michaux) Hultén). Southern lady fern. Figure 13.16.6. This variety is hardy to Zone 5. It is distinguished by stipes shorter than the blades, ovate-lanceolate to lanceolate blades that are broadest just above the base, and dark brown spores. Native to the southeastern United States.

var. *californicum* Butters. California lady fern. This variety resembles var. *cyclosorum* but differs in having brown spores and narrower, more acute pinnules unequal at the base. It is slightly more difficult to grow than var. *cyclosorum* and is rarely cultivated.

var. *cyclosorum* Ruprecht. Northwestern lady fern. Figure 13.16.7. This variety is hardy to Zone 3(4). The stipe is half the length of the blade or less, blades are elliptic to oblanceolate, and spores yellow. It commonly volunteers in peat moss. Native from Alaska to the northwestern United States.

var. *filix-femina*. European lady fern. Figures 13.16.1, 8. This variety is hardy to Zone 3. It resembles var. *cyclosorum* except that the fronds are more lanceolate. It is easy to grow but the fronds break readily. Native to Europe. Numerous cultivars have been derived from this variety, some of which are shown in Figure 12.2. The more commonly cultivated ones are the following:

'Cristatum'. Crested lady fern. Figures 12.2.27, 13.16.9. Fronds medium-sized, the apices and pinnae heavily crested.

'Cruciato-cristatum'. Pinnae forked at their base, with the divisions crisscrossing over adjacent pinnae; tips crested.

'Frizelliae'. Figure 12.2.7. Fronds small-medium, linear, with the pinnae reduced to a congested cluster of fan-shaped, deeply toothed pinnules or segments.

'Minutissimum'. Dwarf lady fern. Resembles var. *filix-femina* but differs by having denser foliage with light green fronds up to 15 cm (6 in.) tall.

'Veroniae-cristatum'. Zone 4. Stipes crimson, blades broadly triangular, pinnae strongly ruffled, overlapping, and ending in a slender tassel.

'Victoriae'. Figure 12.2.13. Blades small and narrow with crested apices; the pinnae appearing crisscrossed, forming an X shape with the rachis at the center.

Athyrium niponicum (Mettenius) Hance
FIGURE 13.16.10; PLATE 14

Very hardy, Zone 3(4)

A medium-sized fern with short-creeping rhizomes and deciduous fronds. Grows best under high light in moist-wet garden soil or potting mix.

Athyrium niponicum is characterized by broad, two-pinnate-pinnatifid, soft herbaceous fronds, with the lower pinnae amply stalked. A herbaceous spine projects upward from the base of costae on the upper surface. The indusia are elongate and often hooked or J-shaped. This species is native to China and Japan.

Figure 13.16.10. *Athyrium niponicum* 'Pictum': frond, bar = 5 cm (2 in.).

Plants of *Athyrium niponicum* are often misidentified in the trade as *A. iseanum* Rosenstock or its synonym *A. goeringianum* (Kunze) T. Moore. *Athyrium iseanum* is not known in cultivation in the United States.

'Pictum'. Plate 14. Japanese painted fern. A variegated form with reddish and gray-silver colors. The colors develop best in high light. Crested, ruffled, and other forms have been reported. The ghost fern, a suspected hybrid between 'Pictum' and *Athyrium filix-femina,* is becoming available commercially and shows great horticultural promise. Its medium-sized leaves are a dull, "ghostly" grayish green.

Athyrium otophorum (Miquel) Koidzumi

FIGURE 13.16.11; PLATE 15

Hardy, Zone 4(5)

A medium-sized fern with short-creeping, clump-forming rhizomes and deciduous fronds. Grows under medium light in moist garden soil or potting mix.

Athyrium otophorum is characterized by broad, triangular, two-pinnate-pinnatifid, slightly leathery fronds with long, narrowly triangular pinnae. The stipe, rachis, and costa are reddish tinged. The species is native to Japan, Korea, and China.

Athyrium epirachis (H. Christ) Ching, a species from China and Japan with similar red-tinged rachises and costae, has been introduced into cultivation. It differs from *A. otophorum* by narrower, less foliaceous blades and erect rhizomes. It is a more vigorous grower and more evergreen than *A. otophorum.*

Athyrium vidalii (Franchet & Savatier) Nakai

FIGURE 13.16.12

Semi-hardy to hardier, Zone 6

A medium-large fern with ascending to suberect rhizomes and clustered, deciduous fronds. Grows well under medium light in moist garden soil or potting mix.

Athyrium vidalii is characterized by triangular, two-pinnate to two-pinnate-pinnatifid blades, sessile to short-stalked pinnae, spines present on the costule or base of the pinnule midribs (upper surface), and elliptic to oblong sori. The indusium is persistent, conspicuous, lunate, hooked or horseshoe-shaped, with margins irregularly toothed or entire. The species is native to China, Japan, Korea, and Taiwan.

Figure 13.16.11. *Athyrium otophorum:* a. frond, bar = 5 cm (2 in.); b. pinnule with elongate sori and indusia, bar = 5 mm (0.2 in.).

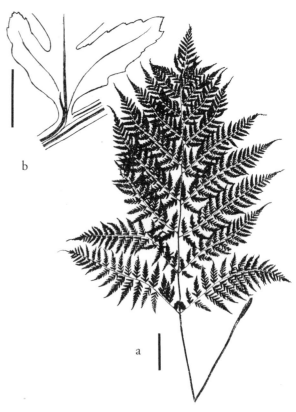

Figure 13.16.12. *Athyrium vidalii:* a. frond, bar = 5 cm (2 in.); b. spine at base of pinnule, bar = 5 mm (0.2 in.).

Azolla

FIGURES 13.17.1–3

Mosquito fern, fairy moss

Azolla consists of floating ferns that are grown as a novelty in aquariums, bowls, and ponds. These small, moss-like plants grow in warm, sluggish water or nearby muddy soils. They tend to die in cold weather after forming buds, which sink to the bottom of the pond and resume growth when warm weather returns. Mosquito ferns prefer full sunlight, warm temperatures, and silty water containing organic matter. High light encourages reddish growth. The common name is derived from the fern's supposed ability to discourage mosquito reproduction by densely carpeting the water's surface, thereby preventing the adults from laying eggs and preventing the larvae from getting air at the surface.

The plants have minute, plump, scale-like leaves. Filamentous roots extend down from the thread-like rhizome, which branches repeatedly and bears fronds in two rows. The fronds are bilobed, with the upper lobe fleshy and the lower lobe inconspicuous, thin, colorless, and submerged. The sori, which are rarely present, are round, whitish structures borne on the lower surface of the plant. There are two kinds of sori, one bearing female spores (megaspores) and the other male spores (microspores).

Identifying the species of *Azolla* is difficult because the distinguishing characteristics are microscopic. The number of cells composing the leaf hairs is helpful in distinguishing the species, but a magnification of at least 40× is needed to see this characteristic. A scanning electron microscope is needed to see surface details on the female spores, and even when these details can be seen, they can be difficult to interpret. Moreover, *Azolla* plants rarely bear spores, so these structures are often unavailable for identification.

Figure 13.17.2. *Azolla filiculoides:* habit, enlarged.

This genus occurs worldwide and has about seven species. Its name comes from the Greek *azo,* to dry, and *olluo,* to kill, presumably alluding to the fern's tendency to be killed by drying. *Azolla* is the world's most important economic fern because it is used as an organic fertilizer in rice paddies in China and Vietnam. The plants are a rich source of nitrogen, a nutrient often limiting to plant growth. The

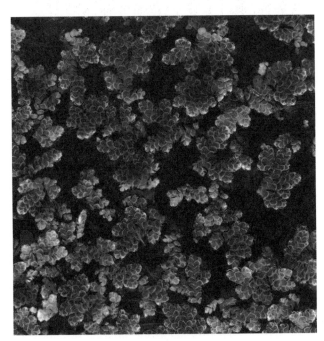

Figure 13.17.1. *Azolla filiculoides:* habit.

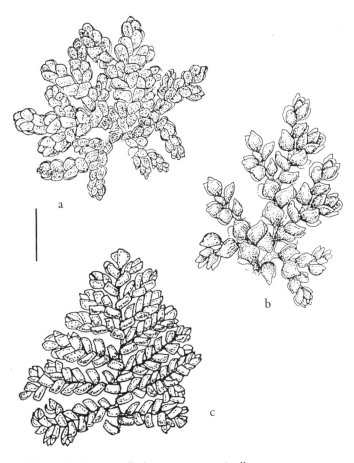

Figure 13.17.3. *Azolla,* bar = 2 mm: a. *Azolla caroliniana;* b. *Azolla filiculoides;* c. *Azolla pinnata.*

nitrogen enters the plant by the action of a cyanobacterium (blue-green algae), *Anabaena azollae,* that lives within the leaves of *Azolla.* The cyanobacterium combines, or "fixes," atmospheric nitrogen with hydrogen to make ammonia, a molecule that can be taken up by organisms and used to form nitrogen-containing compounds. Besides its use as fertilizer, *Azolla* is also fed to livestock and certain fish. For a popular account of the economic importance of *Azolla,* see Moran (1997); more technical accounts can be found in Moore (1969), Lumpkin and Plucknett (1982), van Hove (1989), and Wagner (1997).

Azolla caroliniana Willdenow   FIGURE 13.17.3a
Hardy, Zone (4)5; survives frost and ice

Small-sized. Prefers high light. This floating fern is the best species for growing on mud. The plants turn crimson in the fall, and several weeks later they die and sink to the bottom.

Azolla caroliniana plants are roughly circular to triangular and about the size of a dime. The largest hairs (papillae) on the upper surfaces of the leaves are two-celled. The megaspores lack angular bumps or pits and are densely covered with tangled filaments. Compared to *A. filiculoides,* the clumps of *A. caroliniana* tend to fragment more often and are more compact and rounder in outline. The species occurs in the Americas, Europe, and Asia.

Azolla mexicana C. Presl is less hardy but may be in cultivation. It differs by having megaspores sparingly covered with tangled filaments.

Azolla filiculoides Lamarck   FIGURES 13.17.1, 2, 3b
syn. *Azolla filiculoides* var. *rubra* (R. Brown) Strasburger, *A. rubra* R. Brown
Hardy, Zone (6)7

Small-sized. Grows best in high light. This floating species forms dense mats on the water's surface. Growth peaks in late spring and noticeably declines in winter. The plants can survive under thin ice. Most of the cultivated material in southern California is *Azolla filiculoides.*

Clumps of *Azolla filiculoides* are less likely to fragment than those of *A. caroliniana,* and they have a more open, branched aspect. The largest hairs on the upper leaf lobe are one-celled. The megaspores are warty with raised angular bumps. This species occurs in the Americas, Europe, northeastern Asia, southern Africa, and the Pacific Islands.

Azolla pinnata R. Brown   FIGURE 13.17.3c; PLATE 16
Ferny azolla
Tender

Small-sized. Best grown under high light. This floating fern has been used for centuries in China and Vietnam as a green manure for growing rice. The federal and some state governments list *Azolla pinnata* as an aquatic weed and prohibit its import, possession, and distribution.

Azolla pinnata is broadly triangular and regularly pinnately branched. The roots are branched and feathery, unlike the other species in the genus, all of which have unbranched, nonfeathery roots. It occurs in tropical Asia, Africa, Australia, New Zealand, and New Caledonia.

Belvisia

Members of this genus are small- to medium-sized, epiphytic ferns with undivided, narrow fronds bearing a fertile spike at the tip. They are infrequently cultivated but are generally grown in greenhouses or, in tropical areas, outdoors in pots or baskets. The gracefully arching fronds are closely spaced and best displayed in an elevated position.

The most distinctive characteristics of *Belvisia* are the simple leaves with narrowed, tail-like fertile tips. The rhizome is short- to long-creeping, unbranched, and covered by black or red-brown, clathrate scales. The veins are netted with irregular areoles containing forked veinlets. The sori lack indusia and are spread on the lower surface of the tail-like tip. Minute, scale-like paraphyses are mixed among the sporangia.

The genus, which consists of eight species, occurs in the Old World tropics, northeastern Australia, and Polynesia in tropical and warm-temperate climates. It is named for A. M. F. J. Palisot de Beauvois (1752–1820), a French traveler and agrostologist (grass specialist) whose Latinized name is *Belvisius.* For a technical treatment of *Belvisia,* see Hovenkamp and Franken (1993).

Belvisia mucronata (Fée) Copeland   FIGURE 13.18.1
syn. *Belvisia callifolia* (H. Christ) Copeland
Tender

A medium-sized fern with short-creeping rhizomes. Best grown under medium light in well-drained, moist potting mix or uncut moss.

The blades of *Belvisia mucronata* vary tremendously, especially in width, ranging mostly from 1 to 5 cm (0.5–2 in.) wide, and they are gradually narrowed below the fertile spike. The rhizome scales have dentate to ciliate margins, and the cells of the main body of the scales are all thick. The species is native to Sri Lanka, southeastern Asia, Malaysia, Australia, and the Pacific Islands.

Blechnum   FIGURES 13.19.1, 2
syn. *Lomaria*

Most *Blechnum* species are terrestrial plants with leaves that are reddish when young but turn green with age. Nearly all the species have pinnatifid or one-pinnate blades; never are they finely cut. The trunk-forming species, such as *Blechnum brasiliense* and *B. gibbum,* are particularly valued in pots for accent use. The species with creeping rhizomes are useful as ground covers or bedding plants. *Blechnum australe, B. penna-marina,* and *B. spicant* are favored in warm-temperate regions, whereas *B. appendiculatum* is used in

Figure 13.19.2. *Blechnum appendiculatum:* sori and indusia.

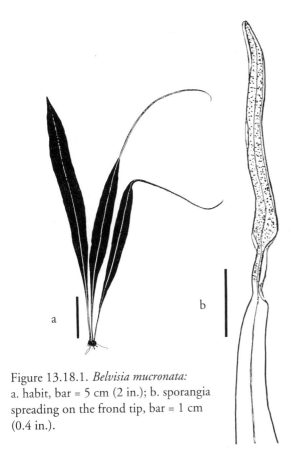

Figure 13.18.1. *Belvisia mucronata:*
a. habit, bar = 5 cm (2 in.); b. sporangia spreading on the frond tip, bar = 1 cm (0.4 in.).

Figure 13.19.1. *Blechnum appendiculatum:* habit.

subtropical climates. Many species apparently favor acidic soils, such as those suitable for azaleas and rhododendrons. Spores are often difficult to germinate.

The Australian and New Zealand species are widely cultivated in their native countries, and some of these are being tried in the United States. *Blechnum fraseri* (Cunningham) Luerssen is a small, attractive tree-like species from New Zealand but is, unfortunately, difficult to grow in the United States. A large, trunk-forming species from Costa Rica has also been tried but without success. *Blechnum tabulare* (Thunberg) Kuhn seems to be established in the South African trade. It resembles a cycad and would make an attractive addition to United States gardens.

The genus usually can be recognized by the pinnatifid or one-pinnate fronds, with long sori running parallel to and on both sides of the costae. Nearly all the species are terrestrial, although some are hemiepiphytes, bearing long-creeping rhizomes that climb tree trunks. The veins are free. If the sterile and fertile leaves are dimorphic, the fertile ones are often longer stalked and have narrower pinnae than the sterile ones.

The species with upright trunks seldom form offshoots, but others can be propagated by rhizome divisions or from stolons (if produced). *Blechnum* stolons are long and slender, and they are produced from a short, erect rhizome. When their tips emerge from the soil, they produce new plantlets that can, after they have rooted, be detached from the main plant and transplanted.

Blechnum consists of about 150 to 200 species worldwide, most of which grow in the Southern Hemisphere. The genus name comes from the Greek *blechnon,* which is an ancient name for ferns.

Blechnum amabile Makino   FIGURE 13.19.3
Hardy to semi-hardy, Zones 7 to 8

A medium-sized fern with creeping rhizomes and clustered fronds. Grows best under medium light in moist garden

Figure 13.19.3. *Blechnum amabile:* habit, showing dimorphic fertile frond (center) and sterile fronds, bar = 5 cm (2 in.).

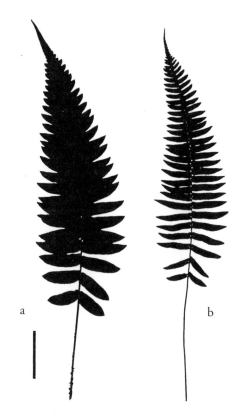

Figure 13.19.4. *Blechnum appendiculatum* variants: a. monomorphic sterile frond of the less red form with glandular hairs; b. monomorphic sterile frond of the redder form with needle-like hairs. Bar = 5 cm (2 in.).

soil or potting mix. Fronds gradually wither in place upon light frost. This species is a slow grower.

Blechnum amabile bears dimorphic, one-pinnate fronds. The sterile blades are lanceolate and narrow, 2–4 cm (0.75– 1.5 in.) wide, and the fertile fronds are barely longer. Sterile pinnae are numerous, linear, and decurrent on the rachis, with the lower pinnae shorter and triangular. The fertile pinnae are narrower and more contracted than the sterile ones. The species is native to China and Japan.

This plant is similar to *Blechnum niponicum,* which see.

Blechnum appendiculatum Willdenow
FIGURES 13.19.1, 2, 4; PLATE 1
syn. *Blechnum glandulosum* Link, *B. occidentale* var. *minor* Hooker
Semi-hardy, Zone 8

A small to medium fern with whorled fronds. Grows best under medium light in moist-dry garden soil or potting mix. This species spreads readily by stolons.

Blechnum appendiculatum greatly resembles *B. occidentale,* and cultivated plants have long been misidentified as that species. *Blechnum appendiculatum* differs, however, by being hairy on the rachis underside. It is native to the southern United States and American tropics.

Two kinds of *Blechnum appendiculatum,* apparently representing different species, are cultivated. The first (Figure 13.19.4b) has pointed hairs on the lower surface of the rachis, and the red of the young stipes and rachises is mostly retained as the frond matures. The second type (Figure 13.19.1, 2, 4a) has minute capitate-glandular hairs (the glands pale yellow) on the lower surface of the rachis and blade tissue. Although reddish when young, the stipe is less intensely red than that of the first type, and the color is lost as the fronds mature, so the stipes and rachises become greenish. In addition, the first type has darker green blades than the second.

Blechnum australe Linnaeus   FIGURE 13.19.5
Hardy to semi-hardy, Zone 7(8)

A small to medium fern with erect, stolon-forming rhizomes and fronds usually in an uneven whorl or cluster. Best grown under medium to high light in moist garden soil or potting mix. The plants spread easily from stolons and are easy to cultivate.

Blechnum australe has slightly dimorphic, one-pinnate fronds. The sterile fronds are narrowly elliptic with lanceolate pinnae, and the pinnae bear a mucronate lobe or "ear" on the upper side at the base. The fertile fronds are contracted, though the lower pinnae may be similar to the sterile pinnae. The typical variety, var. *australe,* is native to southern Africa, Madagascar, and the South Atlantic islands.

Blechnum australe var. *auriculatum* (Cavanilles) de la Sota occurs in Brazil, Uruguay, and Argentina.

Blechnum brasiliense Desvaux   FIGURE 13.19.6
Semi-tender to tender

A medium to large fern with a trunk-like stem (in older plants) and whorled fronds that collectively form a funnel or basket. Best grown under medium to high light in moist

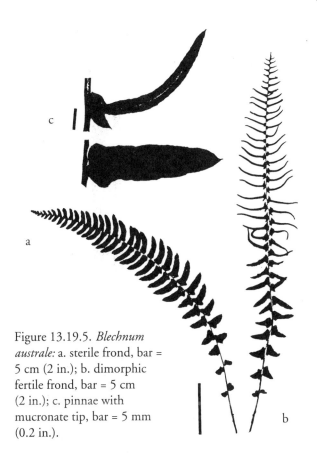

Figure 13.19.5. *Blechnum australe:* a. sterile frond, bar = 5 cm (2 in.); b. dimorphic fertile frond, bar = 5 cm (2 in.); c. pinnae with mucronate tip, bar = 5 mm (0.2 in.).

garden soil or potting mix. This species is sensitive to transplanting. Some variants have redder juvenile fronds than others.

Blechnum brasiliense is characterized by numerous sharp-pointed, ascending pinnae and oblanceolate fronds gradually tapered to the base. The stems form a short trunk and are covered by dark brown or blackish scales. The sterile and fertile fronds are monomorphic. The species is native to Guatemala, Ecuador, Peru, and Brazil.

'Crispum'. Pinna margins slightly ruffled.

Blechnum capense (Linnaeus) Schlechtendal

FIGURE 13.19.7

Semi-hardy

A large fern with short-creeping, branched rhizomes and clustered fronds. Grows under medium to high light in (acidic?) garden soil or potting mix kept moist or moist-wet. This species has proven difficult to grow in some gardens.

Blechnum capense has one-pinnate, dimorphic fronds. The sterile fronds are elliptic with 10–50 pairs of crowded, oblong to linear pinnae. The basal pinnae are highly reduced and rounded. The pinnae on the fertile fronds are linear but are rounded and sterile at the base of the blade. The species (as recognized here) is endemic to New Zealand.

The name *Blechnum capense* applies to several poorly known species. As used here, the name applies to the common New Zealand plant known in that country as kiokio.

Figure 13.19.6. *Blechnum brasiliense:* a. monomorphic fertile frond; b. sterile frond from young plant. Bar = 5 cm (2 in.).

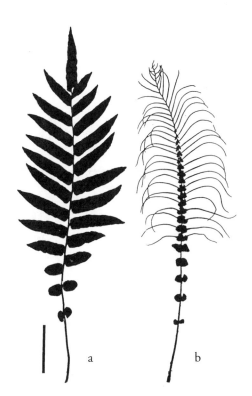

Figure 13.19.7. *Blechnum capense:* a. sterile frond; b. dimorphic fertile frond. Bar = 5 cm (2 in.). After Brownsey and Smith-Dodsworth (1989).

Plants circulating as *B. capense* in the United States may not be the New Zealand species.

Blechnum cordatum (Desvaux) Hieronymus

FIGURE 13.19.8

Semi–hardy to hardy, Zone 7

A medium-large fern with erect fronds that may be spaced along a creeping rhizome as well as clustered on an erect rhizome. Grows under medium light in moist-wet garden soil or potting mix. In the northwestern United States it may take full sun if well watered. Rhizomes and stolons below the ground usually survive freezing weather. The plants spread by stolons.

Blechnum cordatum has dimorphic fronds. The sterile fronds have oblong, dark green blades that are somewhat hard and leathery, with the terminal pinna resembling the lateral pinnae; the pinnae are oblanceolate and finely toothed. On the lower surface of the rachis opposite each pinna stalk is a small, elongated bump, a type of aerophore. Aerophores may be inconspicuous or absent on dried fronds but are easy to see on fresh fronds. They are usually whitish yellow and contrast strongly with the color of the surrounding tissue. The fertile pinnae are linear, with the mar-

gins strongly enrolled when old. The plant is native to South America.

In the United States and England, plants circulating as *Blechnum chilense* (Kaulfuss) Mettenius, *B. tabulare* (Thunberg) Kuhn, and *B. magellanicum* (Desvaux) Mettenius all seem to be *B. cordatum*. *Blechnum wattsii* Tindale of Australia is rarely cultivated in the United States. It can be distinguished from *B. cordatum* by the absence of aerophores, more oblong pinnae that are abruptly long acuminate at the tip, and fertile pinnae that are farther apart.

Blechnum falciforme (Liebmann) C. Christensen

FIGURE 13.19.9

Semi-tender

A large fern with ascending to erect rhizomes and whorled fronds. Grows under medium light in moist garden soil or potting mix.

The fronds of *Blechnum falciforme* are one-pinnate, dimorphic, and noticeably scaly. The stipe has a dense matting of twisted hair-like scales, and the sterile pinnae have cartilaginous, serrate margins. The basal pinnae are not reduced, and the undersurfaces of the costae are scaly. The species is native to Central and South America.

Blechnum gibbum (Labillardière) Mettenius

FIGURE 13.19.10; PLATE 17

Semi-tender to tender

A medium-sized fern with erect, trunk-like stems (in older plants) and fronds borne in a rosette-like whorl. Grows best in medium light in moist, well-drained garden soil or potting mix. This species is somewhat difficult to grow because

Figure 13.19.8. *Blechnum cordatum:* a. sterile frond from young plant; b. old dimorphic fertile frond. Bar = 5 cm (2 in.).

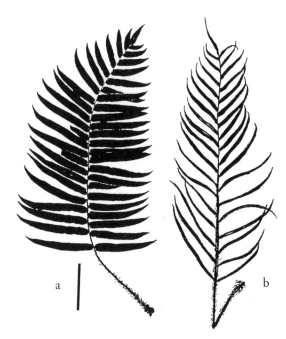

Figure 13.19.9. *Blechnum falciforme:* a. sterile frond; b. dimorphic fertile frond. Bar = 5 cm (2 in.).

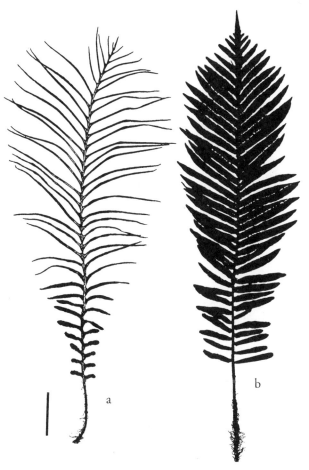

Figure 13.19.10. *Blechnum gibbum:* a. dimorphic fertile frond; b. sterile frond from young plant. Bar = 5 cm (2 in.).

Figure 13.19.11. *Blechnum gracile:* a. sterile frond; b. monomorphic fertile frond. Bar = 5 cm (2 in.).

of its sensitivity to transplanting, irregular watering, and wind.

Blechnum gibbum resembles *B. brasiliense* but has black rhizome and stipe scales, dimorphic fronds, and generally narrower sterile pinnae. It is native to New Caledonia and islands of the South Pacific.

An unnamed variant with wider and blunter pinnae is often misidentified as *Blechnum moorei* C. Christensen. True *B. moorei,* which is unknown in cultivation, differs by having spinulose-ciliate margins and pinna apices that are truncate, notched, or forked.

Blechnum gracile Kaulfuss   FIGURE 13.19.11
syn. *Blechnum fraxineum* of authors, not Willdenow
Semi-tender

Small-sized. Grows best under medium light in moist garden soil or potting mix. The plants spread readily by stolons.

Blechnum gracile is distinctive by its blade form: one-pinnate with only one to four pinna pairs and a terminal segment that is equal to or two times as long as the lateral pinnae. The sterile and fertile fronds have the same form (monomorphic), although the fertile ones tend to be more erect. The species is native to tropical America.

Blechnum niponicum (Kunze) Makino
FIGURE 13.19.12

Hardy

A medium-sized fern with erect rhizomes and fronds arranged in a rosette. Grows under medium light in moist garden soil or potting mix.

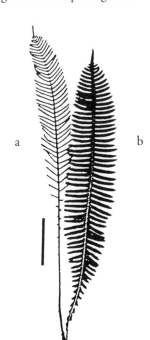

Figure 13.19.12. *Blechnum niponicum:* a. dimorphic fertile frond; b. sterile frond. Bar = 5 cm (2 in.).

Blechnum niponicum has dimorphic fronds, the fertile fronds taller than the sterile ones. The sterile fronds are one-pinnate and 5–10 cm (2–5 in.) wide. The scales on the base of the stipe are linear. This species is native to Japan.

Blechnum spicant resembles *B. niponicum* but differs by narrower, less oblanceolate sterile fronds and much taller fertile fronds. The similar *B. amabile* has a creeping rhizome, narrower sterile fronds, shorter fertile fronds, and ovate stipe scales.

Blechnum occidentale Linnaeus   FIGURE 13.19.13
Hammock fern
Probably tender

A small to medium fern with erect rhizomes and clustered fronds. Grows under medium light in moist garden soil or potting mix. The plants spread by stolons.

Blechnum occidentale is characterized by blades that are one-pinnate at the base but pinnatisect above and blade apices that are gradually tapered to the tip. The blades are usually narrowly triangular, with the lowest pinnae pointing downward and heart-shaped at the base. The rhizomes usually bear several stolons. The lower surface of the rachis is glabrous, not hairy as in the closely related *B. appendicu-*

Figure 13.19.13. *Blechnum occidentale:* a. monomorphic fertile frond; b. sterile frond. Bar = 5 cm (2 in.).

latum. The species is widespread in tropical America.

Most plants identified as *Blechnum occidentale* in gardens in the United States are actually *B. appendiculatum.*

Blechnum penna-marina (Poiret) Kuhn
                    FIGURE 13.19.14; PLATE 18
Hardy, Zone 5

A small fern with fronds spaced along a much-branched, creeping, stoloniferous rhizome. Grows under medium or high light in moist but well-drained, acidic garden soil or potting mix. The plants spread by stolons and make a useful ground cover in areas with mild winters.

Blechnum penna-marina bears one-pinnate, dimorphic fronds, the fertile ones much contracted and about twice as tall as the sterile. The species is native to South America, southeastern Australia, New Zealand, and the circum-antarctic islands.

An unnamed dwarf cultivar circulates in the trade, as well as the following:

'Cristata'. Tip of frond crested.

Blechnum polypodioides Raddi   FIGURE 13.19.15
syn. *Blechnum unilaterale* Swartz
Tender

A small to medium fern with erect, stoloniferous rhizomes and clustered fronds. Grows under medium light in moist garden soil or potting mix.

Blechnum polypodioides is characterized by pinnatisect to one-pinnate, lanceolate fronds tapered at both ends. The sterile and fertile fronds are monomorphic and minutely hairy on the lower surfaces. The pinnae tend to be numerous, oblong to linear, and essentially entire, and the lower ones are distant and much reduced. The species is widespread in tropical America.

Figure 13.19.14. *Blechnum penna-marina:* habit, showing sterile frond (shorter outer fronds) and dimorphic fertile fronds (taller inner fronds), bar = 5 cm (2 in.).

Figure 13.19.15. *Blechnum polypodioides:* monomorphic sterile frond, bar = 5 cm (2 in.).

Blechnum punctulatum Swartz   FIGURE 13.19.16
Hardy to semi-hardy

A medium-sized fern with branched, ascending rhizomes and clustered fronds. Grows under medium light in moist garden soil or potting mix. This species is slow growing.

Blechnum punctulatum has dimorphic, one-pinnate fronds. The sterile fronds vary from lanceolate to linear-elliptic and are reduced to short pinnae below. The fertile fronds are more oblanceolate compared to the sterile ones. Sori are absent from the lower, shorter pinnae of the fertile fronds. The blades resemble those of *B. australe* but have blunter pinna tips. *Blechnum punctulatum* is native to southern Africa.

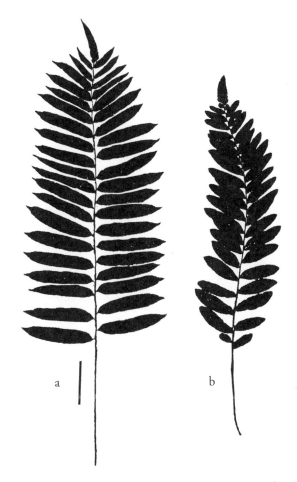

Figure 13.19.16. *Blechnum punctulatum:* a. dimorphic fertile frond; b. sterile frond. Bar = 5 cm (2 in.).

Figure 13.19.17. *Blechnum serrulatum:* a. monomorphic fertile frond; b. young sterile frond. Bar = 5 cm (2 in.).

Blechnum serrulatum L. C. Richard   FIGURE 13.19.17
syn. *Blechnum indicum* of authors, not N. L. Burman
Saw fern, swamp fern
Tender, Zone 9

A large fern with creeping rhizomes and clustered, shiny, thick fronds. Grows under medium to high light or direct sun. This species prefers moist garden soil or potting mix but tolerates wet soils. The fronds tend to grow upright in full sun. During the dry season, the pinnae are shed from the rachis by means of the abscission layer, leaving behind erect, naked rachises. The species often forms dense colonies in the wild.

Blechnum serrulatum is characterized by fronds one-pinnate throughout, with 20–40 pinna pairs and a single apical segment. The pinna margins are finely serrate, and careful inspection will reveal that the pinnae are jointed to the rachis, with the joint visible as a faint dark line or swelling. The stipes are often densely clustered. The sterile and fertile leaves are monomorphic. Sori are borne only on the distal pinnae and are covered by erose-lacerate indusia. This species is native to the United States (Florida), the West Indies, Central and South America, India, Malaysia, and Australia.

In the Old World this species has long been called *Blechnum indicum* N. L. Burman; however, that name is a synonym of *Asplenium longissimum* Blume (Morton 1967).

Blechnum spicant (Linnaeus) Smith   FIGURE 13.19.18
Deer fern
Hardy to semi-hardy, Zone 7

A medium-sized fern with erect, sometimes-branched rhizomes and fronds in a rosette or cluster. Best grown under low-medium light in moist, well-drained, acidic potting mix. Be sure to provide the plants with humidity and acidic soil, and avoid using hard water. This evergreen species has proven difficult to grow in the southwestern United States, possibly because of high summer heat and humidity. It grows readily from spores.

Blechnum spicant bears fronds that are one-pinnate and dimorphic. The sterile fronds vary from lanceolate to narrowly elliptic, and fertile fronds have taller and narrower pinnae. The species is native to western North America and Europe.

Several cultivars exist, including the following, which are common in the trade:

'Crispum'. Margins ruffled.
'Redwood Giant'. Plants large.
'Serratum'. Margins serrate.

Figure 13.20.1. *Bolbitis portoricensis:* habit. Photo courtesy of G. Hampfler.

Figure 13.19.18. *Blechnum spicant:* a. sterile frond; b. dimorphic fertile frond. Bar = 5 cm (2 in.).

Figure 13.20.2. *Bolbitis portoricensis:* sterile frond (left) and contracted fertile frond (right).

Bolbitis   FIGURES 13.20.1–3
syn. *Edanyoa*

This genus is infrequently cultivated. It consists mostly of medium-sized, coarse plants that typically grow along rocky streambanks in the tropics and less frequently in soil or on tree trunks.

Bolbitis is characterized by creeping rhizomes, dimorphic sterile and fertile fronds, and acrostichoid sori. The sterile fronds vary from simple to one-pinnate (or rarely two-pinnate). The veins can be either free or netted and, if netted, with or without veinlets. The fertile fronds have long stipes that elevate the blades above the sterile fronds.

Bolbitis heteroclita includes a tiny terrestrial (formerly *Edanyoa difformis*) that differs greatly from other *Bolbitis* species in general appearance. Its small size makes it popu-

Figure 13.20.3. *Bolbitis portoricensis:* sporangia spreading on under surface.

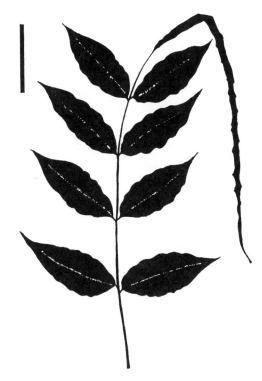

Figure 13.20.4. *Bolbitis heteroclita:* sterile frond, bar = 5 cm (2 in.).

lar for terrariums. *Bolbitis heudelotii* in the United States and *B. fluviatilis* in Europe are sometimes sold in aquarium supply stores as underwater plants. Some species are easy to grow but are rarely seen in cultivation, such as *B. aliena,* which needs warm temperatures year-round.

Bolbitis contains 85 species and occurs throughout the tropics of the world. The genus name comes from the Greek *bolbition,* diminutive of *bolbos,* bulb, alluding to the small bulblets borne on the leaves of some species. For a technical monograph of the genus, see Hennipman (1977).

Bolbitis heteroclita (C. Presl) Ching

FIGURES 13.20.4–8

syn. *Bolbitis simplicifolia* (Holttum) Ching, *Edanyoa difformis* Copeland

Tender

A medium-sized fern with medium- to long-creeping rhizomes and whip-like blade apices. Grows well under medium light in moist to moist-wet garden soil or potting mix.

The blades of typical *Bolbitis heteroclita* (Figure 13.20.4) are narrowly triangular, with entire to coarsely dentate-lobed lateral pinnae. The terminal pinna is often tailed or whip-like and bears a bud at the tip. The veins are netted in irregular areoles with few included veinlets. The species is native to Asia and Malaysia.

Bolbitis heteroclita is a variable and complex species, and several name changes have been required for the cultivated

plants. Many of the species reduced to *B. heteroclita* are recognized in horticulture and are here given cultivar status.

Difformis Group (*Edanyoa difformis* Copeland). Figure 13.20.5. A diminutive creeping fern often used in terrariums and easy to grow. Fronds are usually less than two-pinnate-pinnatifid and lack the terminal elongated pinna of the species. Native to the Philippines and long known as the species *Edanyoa difformis.* Hennipman believes this plant is a neotenous form (represents juvenile characteristics) of *Bolbitis heteroclita.* The *International Code of No-*

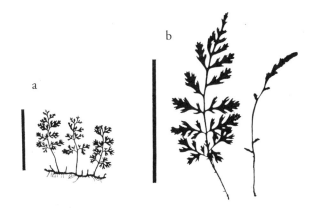

Figure 13.20.5. *Bolbitis heteroclita* Difformis Group: a. habit, bar = 5 cm (2 in.); b. sterile frond (left) and fertile frond (right), bar = 5 cm (2 in.).

Figure 13.20.6. *Bolbitis heteroclita* 'Malacca': habit, showing fertile frond third from left, bar = 5 cm (2 in.).

menclature for Cultivated Plants allows listing it as a cultivar in a group category.

'Malacca'. Figure 13.20.6. This variant is known among growers in the United States only as a small *Bolbitis heteroclita*. The small, triangular or oblong-triangular fronds and pinnatifid lower pinnae tend to be consistent features for recognition. 'Malacca' is easy to grow. It seems to be the same as the cultivated plants Hennipman (1977) lists as 'malaccensis', a smaller plant from the Philippines. Because the latter name is in Latin, it cannot be used as a cultivar name. Thus the plant is here listed as 'Malacca' to meet the requirement of the *International Code of Nomenclature for Cultivated Plants*.

Simplicifolia Group (*Bolbitis simplicifolia* (Holttum) Ching). Figure 13.20.7. Plants small-medium; rhizome creeping; fronds in compact clusters, erect, usually symmetrical; pinnae broad-elliptic; terminal pinnae resemble the lateral pinnae, though usually longer; seldom more than one pair of lateral pinnae; margins undulate to nearly entire. The plants in cultivation were reportedly introduced from Malaysia about 30 years ago. Long known as *B. simplicifolia,* this plant has been reduced to synonymy under *B. heteroclita.* The *International Code of Nomenclature for Cultivated Plants* of 1995 allows listing it as a cultivar in a group category.

Tenuissima Group. Figure 13.20.8. Produces highly variable fronds even on the same plant. The fronds are often asymmetrical with puckered surfaces. Hennipman

Figure 13.20.7. *Bolbitis heteroclita* Simplicifolia Group: habit with sterile fronds, bar = 5 cm (2 in.).

Figure 13.20.8. *Bolbitis heteroclita* Tenuissima Group: habits, showing variations in sterile fronds, bar = 5 cm (2 in.).

(1977) listed the plant as 'tenuissima', a Latin name meaning "more slender."

Bolbitis heudelotii (Bory ex Fée) Alston

FIGURE 13.20.9

Tender

A small fern with medium- to long-creeping rhizomes. Grows under medium light on rocks or in soil. This species can be used as an underwater plant for aquariums, or it can be potted in a peat-sand-soil mix and kept wet. It is rarely cultivated.

Bolbitis heudelotii has one-pinnate fronds, usually with ascending pinnae. If the plants are submerged, the sterile pinna margins are entire, but when held above water, they are irregularly and shallowly serrate. The fertile frond has narrower pinnae and emerges above the water during non-flood periods. This species is native to Africa, where it often grows along streambanks prone to flooding.

Bolbitis portoricensis (Sprengel) Hennipman

FIGURES 13.20.1–3, 10

syn. Bolbitis cladorrhizans (Sprengel) Ching
Tender

A medium to large fern with medium-long-creeping rhizomes and elongate blade apices bearing buds at their tips. Can grow submerged in an aquarium or out-of-water in pots with garden soil or a sand-peat mix in medium light. If grown in pots, the soil must be kept wet.

The fronds of Bolbitis portoricensis are triangular and one-pinnate, with the lower pinnae longer and lobed on the basiscopic side. The veins are netted. The apical portions of well-developed fronds often are elongate (sometimes whip-like or tailed) and bud-bearing at the tips. The species is native to tropical America.

Bommeria

Copper fern

Bommeria is a genus of attractive small ferns that produce triangular fronds covered with silky white hairs. They are rarely cultivated and are native to dry, rocky places.

The most distinctive characteristics of this genus are its small, triangular to pentagonal blades and sori that run

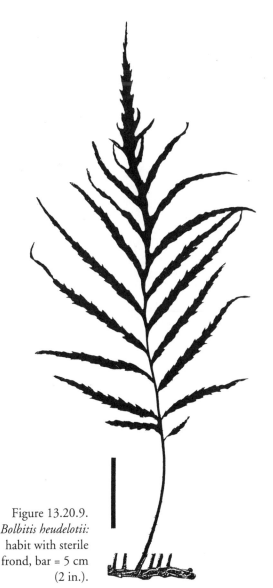

Figure 13.20.9. *Bolbitis heudelotii:* habit with sterile frond, bar = 5 cm (2 in.).

Figure 13.20.10. *Bolbitis portoricensis:* sterile frond and rhizome, bar = 5 cm (2 in.).

along the veins between the midribs and margins, often mostly near the margins. The blades are lobed, only two- to three-pinnatifid (never fully pinnate), whitish, hairy, and slightly scaly. The rhizomes vary from short- to long-creeping and are scaly, not hairy. The veins may be free or partly netted, and indusia are absent.

Bommeria contains only four species, and these are native to the southwestern United States, Mexico, and Central America. It is named for Joseph Edouard Bommer (1829–1895), a Belgian pteridologist.

Bommeria hispida (Mettenius ex Kuhn) Underwood

FIGURE 13.21.1

Semi-hardy, Zone 8

A small fern with medium-creeping rhizomes. Grows under medium light in moist-dry, well-drained potting mix with coarse sand. The plants are somewhat difficult to grow.

The fronds of *Bommeria hispida* range from 4 to 15 cm (1.5–6 in.) long and have pentagonal blades with surfaces covered with long, white hairs. The veins are free, not netted. It is native to the United States, Mexico, and Nicaragua.

Botrychium
Grape fern

FIGURES 13.22.1, 2

These very small- to medium-sized terrestrial ferns are named for the resemblance of their sporangia to clusters of grapes. In addition to the allusion in the common name, the genus name comes from the Greek *botrys,* meaning bunch or cluster, as in grapes. In the eastern United States

Figure 13.22.1. *Botrychium virginianum:* frond.

grape ferns are used mostly in natural plantings, although the medium-sized species are used as potted plants in other parts of the world. Grape ferns are hard to establish in gardens and are difficult if not impossible to grow from spores.

A well-drained loam mixed with compost is best for cultivating *Botrychium* species. Water about once a week, but avoid overwatering, which can promote root-rot. On the other hand, it is important to not let the roots dry out when the plants are in their deciduous period. Guard against slugs and snails, which readily attack the newly emerging fronds. Grape ferns also should be protected from wind. Transplant them with extra care, disturbing the roots as little as possible. Because each plant produces only one frond per year, the loss of a leaf is a potentially serious setback.

The most distinctive characteristic of the genus is its fronds, which are divided into two parts: a sterile part consisting of a green leafy blade, and a fertile part consisting of a long stalk bearing a branched cluster of globose sporangia at its apex. All members of *Botrychium* are terrestrial and have fleshy roots and short, erect, fleshy rhizomes. The genus, which consists of about 55 species, is cosmopolitan.

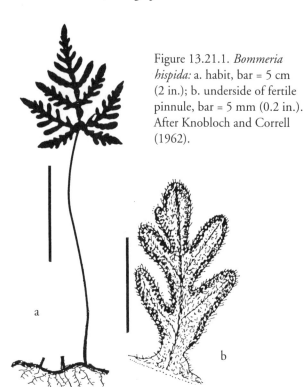

Figure 13.21.1. *Bommeria hispida:* a. habit, bar = 5 cm (2 in.); b. underside of fertile pinnule, bar = 5 mm (0.2 in.). After Knobloch and Correll (1962).

Figure 13.22.2. *Botrychium virginianum:* branches bearing sporangia.

Botrychium dissectum Sprengel   FIGURE 13.22.4
syn. *Botrychium obliquum* Muhlenberg
Dissected grape fern
Very hardy, Zone 4

A small fern with erect rhizomes. Grows under medium light in moist garden soil or potting mix. The blades typically turn bronze or coppery in late fall or winter, especially in exposed habitats.

Botrychium dissectum is characterized by having sterile blades with terminal segments divided all the way to the tip. The blades differ greatly in the amount of dissection, even in the same population. Two extreme forms are recognized: forma *dissectum,* with blades lacerate throughout and a highly dissected appearance, and forma *obliquum* (Willdenow) Fernald, with blades merely lobed or pinnatifid and a less cut appearance. Forma *dissectum* is not found in Florida and the Gulf States. The species is native to the eastern United States and southeastern Canada.

Botrychium virginianum (Linnaeus) Swartz
FIGURES 13.22.1, 2, 5

Rattlesnake fern
Very hardy, Zone 3

A small-medium fern with erect rhizomes. Grows under medium light in moist garden soil or potting mix. This species is difficult to establish.

Botrychium biternatum (Savigny) Underwood
FIGURE 13.22.3
syn. *Botrychium dissectum* var. *tenuifolium* (Underwood) Farwell
Sparse-lobed grape fern, southern grape fern, winter grape fern
Hardy, Zone 6

A small fern with erect rhizomes. Grows under medium light in moist garden soil or potting mix. The sterile blade stays green throughout the winter and often into spring, and a new frond develops in early summer. The fertile part of the frond, which is not always present, withers soon after the spores are shed.

The terminal segments of the sterile blade are elongate and nearly parallel-sided. The sterile blades of *Botrychium biternatum* remain green throughout the winter, in contrast to *B. dissectum,* which tends to turn bronze or coppery during the winter. The species is native to the southeastern United States.

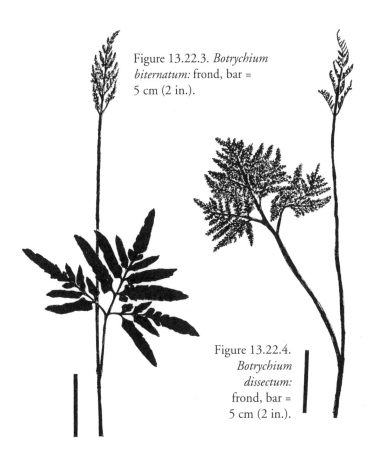

Figure 13.22.3. *Botrychium biternatum:* frond, bar = 5 cm (2 in.).

Figure 13.22.4. *Botrychium dissectum:* frond, bar = 5 cm (2 in.).

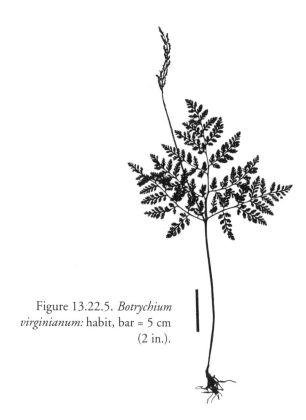

Figure 13.22.5. *Botrychium virginianum:* habit, bar = 5 cm (2 in.).

Botrychium virginianum is characterized by finely divided, green, triangular blades that are deciduous in late summer, not evergreen throughout the winter as in the previous two species. The fertile spike attaches just below the green blades, but it is not always fully developed and sometimes is represented only by an aborted stub. The spike withers in midsummer as soon as the spores are shed. The species is common in the forests of North America. It also occurs in Central America, South America, Europe, and Asia.

Camptosorus

syn. *Asplenium,* in part
Walking fern

The walking ferns are small, lime-loving terrestrials used in rock gardens or terrariums. The common name derives from the plant's ability to form plantlets at the tips of its long-tapered fronds, making the plant appear to "walk" over the rock surface. Although it can be grown in warmer climates outdoors or in terrariums, *Camptosorus* must have humidity and drainage. The plants grow best in temperate climates.

The genus is characterized by netted veins and fronds that taper to a long, whip-like apex, which roots at the tip. The rhizome is short and erect. The sori are elongate and scattered (not regularly arranged as in the closely related genus *Asplenium*) and covered by a flap-like indusium. This genus is often classified in *Asplenium* because it hybridizes with several species of that genus.

Camptosorus consists of only two species, one of which occurs in North America and the other in northeastern Asia. The genus name comes from the Greek *camptos,* curved, and *soros,* mound or heap, referring to the bent or crooked sori that distinguish it from *Asplenium.*

Camptosorus rhizophyllus (Linnaeus) Link
FIGURES 13.23.1

syn. *Asplenium rhizophyllum* Linnaeus
North American walking fern
Very hardy, Zone 3(4)

A small fern with erect rhizomes and leaves that bear buds at the apices. Grows under low to medium light in moist, basic potting mix. In arid climates, grow in a terrarium.

The fronds of *Camptosorus rhizophyllus* are about 10–20 cm (4–8 in.) long, long-tapered at the tip, and cordate or hastate at the base. This evergreen fern is native to eastern North America, where it reaches its greatest frequency and abundance on limestone. It grows less frequently on sandstone.

Camptosorus sibericus Ruprecht   FIGURE 13.23.2
syn. *Asplenium ruprechtii* Sa. Kurata
Asian walking fern
Very hardy, Zone 4

A small fern with erect rhizomes and long-tapered leaves bearing buds at the tips. Grows under low to medium light in moist, basic potting mix. In arid climates, grow in a terrarium.

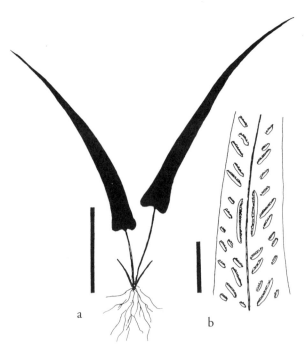

Figure 13.23.1. *Camptosorus rhizophyllus:* a. habit, bar = 5 cm (2 in.); b. sori and indusia, bar = 5 mm (0.2 in.), courtesy of T. Hoshizaki..

Figure 13.23.2. *Camptosorus sibericus:* a. habit, bar = 5 cm (2 in.); b. sori and indusia, bar = 5 mm (0.2 in.), courtesy of T. Hoshizaki.

Camptosorus sibericus has stouter and smaller evergreen fronds than *C. rhizophyllus*. They are usually up to about 5 cm (2 in.) long and often constricted above the tapered base. The species is native to Siberia, Japan, Korea, and northern China.

Asplenium ×*crucibuli* is a hybrid produced in horticulture from a cross between this species and *A. platyneuron.*

Campyloneurum
Strap fern

The more frequently cultivated strap ferns, such as *Campyloneurum angustifolium* and *C. phyllitidis,* are handsomely displayed in hanging containers, where their dense cluster of narrow fronds form a spreading or gracefully arching pattern. The frond width can vary greatly within a species.

Nearly all species of *Campyloneurum* have simple, entire, strap-shaped leaves. Their blades are glabrous except along the rachis, where there may be scattered scales. The veins are always netted, although this may be difficult to see in species with thick blades. In many species the main lateral veins are parallel and connected by curved crossveins to form areoles, and the areoles enclose veinlets that point toward the margin. The sori are round, lack indusia, and in most species are borne in one to four rows between the main veins. The rhizome varies from short- to long-creeping and may be clothed by clathrate or nonclathrate scales.

The genus name comes from the Greek *kampylos,* arched, and *neuron,* nerve, referring to the arched veinlets that form between the primary lateral veins. *Campyloneurum* contains about 50 species restricted to the American tropics. Most of the species are epiphytes. Lellinger (1988) gives a provisional key to the species. See *Polypodium* for a comparison of this genus to other polypodiaceous genera.

Campyloneurum angustifolium (Swartz) Fée
FIGURE 13.24.1

Narrow-leaved strap fern
Semi-tender, Zone 9

A medium-sized fern with short-creeping rhizomes and arched or pendent fronds borne in a cluster. Thrives under high-medium light in drained, moist to moist-dry potting mix.

Campyloneurum angustifolium is characterized by linear blades only 4–12 mm (0.2–0.5 in.) wide, with stipes short or absent. The veins are hard to see because of the thick-textured blade, but there are less than four areoles between midrib and margin, with the costal areoles more elongate than the marginal areoles. The sori are borne in one or two (rarely three) rows between midrib and margin. The species is widely distributed throughout tropical and subtropical America, often growing as an epiphyte on tree trunks.

Campyloneurum angustifolium varies greatly, and several unnamed variants are in cultivation. Some forms have consistently narrow fronds only 4 mm (0.2 in.) wide. Wild plants with twisted fronds and undulate margins have also been brought into cultivation from Costa Rica.

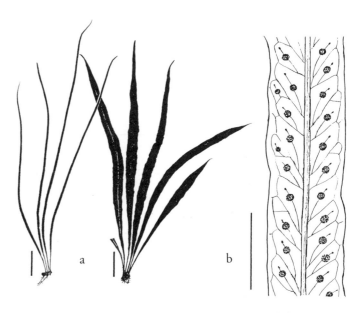

Figure 13.24.1. *Campyloneurum angustifolium:* a. habits of two plants, bar = 5 cm (2 in.); b. sori and vein pattern, bar = 1 cm (0.4 in.).

Campyloneurum brevifolium (Link) Link

FIGURE 13.24.2

syn. *Campyloneurum latum* T. Moore
Tender, Zone 10

A medium-large fern with short-creeping rhizomes and erect fronds borne in a cluster. Grows under medium light in moist, well-drained potting mix.

Campyloneurum brevifolium resembles *C. phyllitidis* but differs by often having three (versus two) veinlets within each areole. The stipes are 5–18 cm (2–7 in.) long, and the blades are mostly 5–13 cm (2–5 in.) wide, dark green, and abruptly contracted to the stipe. Sori are borne in two or more rows between the lateral veins, with up to 14 sori in a row between midrib and margin. The species is widespread in tropical America.

Campyloneurum costatum (Kunze) C. Presl

FIGURE 13.24.3

Tender, Zone 10

A medium-sized fern with short-creeping rhizomes and arched or pendent fronds borne in a cluster. Grows under medium light in well-drained, moist potting mix.

The stipes of *Campyloneurum costatum* are 4–14 cm (1.5–5.5 in.) long, and the blades are elliptic or oblong,

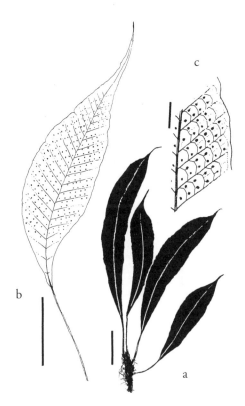

Figure 13.24.3. *Campyloneurum costatum:* a. habit, bar = 5 cm (2 in.); b. frond, bar = 5 cm (2 in.); c. sori and vein pattern, bar = 1 cm (0.4 in.).

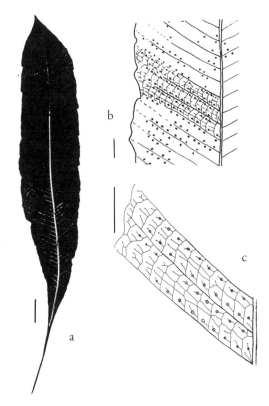

Figure 13.24.2. *Campyloneurum brevifolium:* a. frond, bar = 5 cm (2 in.); b. sori distribution, bar = 1 cm (0.4 in.), after Hoshizaki (1982); c. sori and vein pattern, bar = 1 cm (0.4 in.), after Hoshizaki (1982).

mostly 5 cm (2 in.) wide with acute apices. The main lateral veins are easily visible but the smaller, secondary ones are obscure. There are four to eight areoles between midrib and margin. The sori are in two rows between lateral veins, with four to eight sori in a row between midrib and margin. The species is widespread in tropical and subtropical America.

Campyloneurum phyllitidis (Linnaeus) C. Presl

FIGURE 13.24.4

Semi-tender, Zone 9

A medium-sized fern with short-creeping rhizomes and spreading to slightly arching fronds borne in a cluster. Grows under medium light in well-drained, moist to moist-dry potting mix. This species is the most common *Campyloneurum* in cultivation. It needs protection from slugs and snails.

The stipes of *Campyloneurum phyllitidis* are absent or up to 5 cm (2 in.) long. The yellowish green blades are 4–8 cm (1.5–3 in.) wide, gradually tapering toward the base or a short stipe, with acute to obtuse apices. The main lateral veins are clearly visible, but the smaller secondary ones that form areoles are hard to see. Two sori are usually borne between the main lateral veins, with 5 to 14 sori in series between the midrib and margin. This species is widespread in tropical and subtropical America.

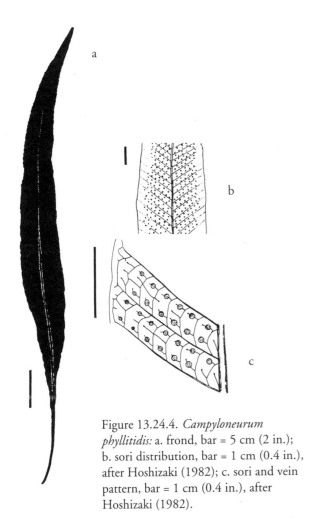

Figure 13.24.4. *Campyloneurum phyllitidis:* a. frond, bar = 5 cm (2 in.); b. sori distribution, bar = 1 cm (0.4 in.), after Hoshizaki (1982); c. sori and vein pattern, bar = 1 cm (0.4 in.), after Hoshizaki (1982).

The broader fronds of *Campyloneurum phyllitidis* are often mistaken for *C. brevifolium.* The short or absent stipe and the more regularly shaped areoles of *C. phyllitidis* help distinguish it from *C. brevifolium,* which has a well-defined stipe and irregularly shaped areoles with three included veinlets. Some plants, however, are difficult to distinguish. Crested and fimbriate forms of *C. phyllitidis* occur in cultivation.

Campyloneurum tenuipes Maxon   FIGURE 13.24.5
Tender to semi-tender

A medium-sized fern with short-creeping rhizomes and erect to spreading fronds borne in a cluster. Grows under medium light in moist potting mix with good drainage.

The fronds of *Campyloneurum tenuipes* reach 30–80 cm (12–32 in.) in length, with stipes about one-third the length of the frond. The blade is narrowly elliptic with a tapered base and abruptly narrowed to a tail-like apex. The main lateral veins are visible, but the finer veins are usually hard to see. The sori are borne in two rows between the main lateral veins, in series of 6–10 between the midrib and margin. The species occurs from southern Mexico to Honduras.

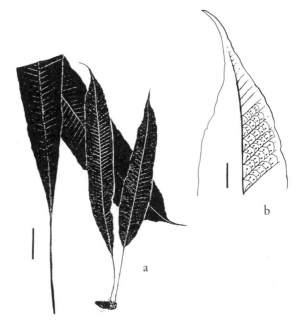

Figure 13.24.5. *Campyloneurum tenuipes:* a. habit and frond, bar = 5 cm (2 in.); b. frond apex with sori and vein pattern, bar = 1 cm (0.4 in.).

Campyloneurum xalapense Fée   FIGURE 13.24.6
Tender to semi-tender

A medium-sized fern with short-creeping rhizomes and fronds borne in a cluster. Grows under medium light in moist potting mix.

Campyloneurum xalapense is characterized by short or absent stipes, oblanceolate blades, acuminate to abruptly

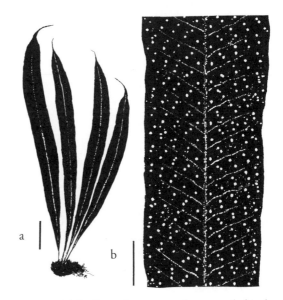

Figure 13.24.6. *Campyloneurum xalapense:* a. habit, bar = 5 cm (2 in.); b. white dots on upper blade surface, bar = 1 cm (0.4 in.).

caudate apices, and white dots on the upper blade surfaces. Veins are less obscure on the lower surfaces. The areoles are irregularly shaped, with generally five to eight between the costa and margin, and the sori are in two rows between the main lateral veins. The species occurs from southern Mexico to Costa Rica.

Ceratopteris   FIGURE 13.25.1
Water fern, water sprite

Ceratopteris is commonly used as an aquarium plant. These ferns either float on water, grow fully or partially submerged, or root in mud. The fertile leaves are erect and are produced above water. In Asia the foliage of *Ceratopteris thalictroides* is used in salads and is said to have a peppery taste.

Ceratopteris is characterized by short, erect, inconspicuous rhizomes bearing a few thin scales. The sterile and fertile fronds are dimorphic—the fertile ones are more finely cut with narrower segments—but both have triangular, glabrous blades. The veins are netted, not free. The large, marginal sporangia are protected by a continuous enrolled indusium.

This genus has the distinction of having the fastest life cycle of any fern. The plants can take as little as one month to go from spores to mature, spore-bearing plants, though three or four months is more typical. Because of this quick cycle, the plants are favorites of laboratory geneticists who study differences in heritable traits from one generation to the next.

The plants live about one year and are usually perpetuated by the numerous buds that form on the blade surface, typically in the margins of the sinuses. The buds detach and float away from the parent plant. Mature plants can be propagated by division of the rhizome, which may be allowed to float or, if grown submerged, held in place by coarse gravel. If plants are to be rooted in mud, garden soil with little organic matter will do. Some growers recommend a mixture of about half peat and half sand mixed with 10% top soil. Plants that are rooted in mud need their fronds kept moist. Temperatures must be maintained close to 27°C (80°F) for good growth. The plants and buds decline when temperatures are below 20°C (68°F), and if lost, new plants must be started from spores.

The genus, which consists of four species, is native to the tropics and subtropics worldwide. The name comes from the Greek *keras,* horn, and *pteris,* fern, alluding to the antler-like fertile leaves. The species are sometimes difficult to identify because the fronds vary considerably in form. Only *Ceratopteris thalictroides* and *C. pteridoides* are commonly cultivated. For more details on cultivation, see Curtwright (1995) and Lloyd (1974).

Ceratopteris pteridoides (Hooker) Hieronymus
FIGURES 13.25.2, 3
American water fern, triangular water fern
Tender, Zone 9

A small to medium fern with short, inconspicuous rhizomes. Grows under high light in wet garden soil or floating on water. In nature the plants float; rarely do they root in mud. This species reproduces readily from buds on the blades.

The best distinguishing characteristics of *Ceratopteris pteridoides* are the inflated stipe bases and the opposite pinnae or lobes of the sterile blade. The inflated stipe base is composed of aerenchyma, a type of tissue related to parenchyma that contains large intercellular air spaces that impart buoyancy to the plant. The buds generally develop into plantlets on the actively growing fronds, whereas in *C. thalictroides* the buds generally develop on older, senescing fronds. The species is native to the southern United States (Florida and Louisiana), tropical America, and southeastern Asia.

Ceratopteris cornuta Le Prieur, an Old World species, might be sold in aquarium stores. It differs from *C. pteridoides* by lacking an inflated stipe and by having mostly alternate basal pinnae and triangular, one- to two-pinnate blades with many buds.

Figure 13.25.1. *Ceratopteris* habit.

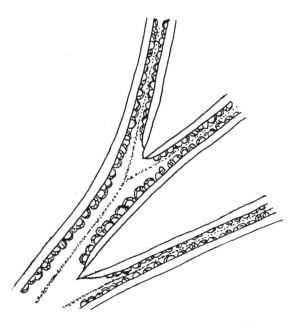

Figure 13.25.2. *Ceratopteris pteridoides:* sori and indusia.

Figure 13.25.4. *Ceratopteris thalictroides:* habit, with a more divided pinna in the upper right, bar = 5 cm (2 in.). After Beddome (1864).

Figure 13.25.3. *Ceratopteris pteridoides:* habit, bar = 5 cm (2 in.). After Tryon and Stolze (1989).

Ceratopteris thalictroides (Linnaeus) Brongniart

FIGURE 13.25.4; PLATE 19

Oriental water fern
Tender, Zone 9

A small to medium fern with short, inconspicuous rhizomes. Grows under high light in wet garden soil or floating on water. Typically, the plants root in mud.

Unlike the preceding species, *Ceratopteris thalictroides* has narrow (not inflated) stipe bases and mostly alternate basal pinnae or lobes. The sterile fronds are mostly lanceolate to lanceolate-ovate and two- to three-pinnate, with buds that tend to grow on dying fronds. The fertile fronds are usually two- to three-pinnate with narrow, linear segments. This species is found throughout the tropics of the world, except Africa.

Ceratopteris richardii Brongniart (syn. *C. deltoidea* Benedict), a species of the southern United States, tropical America, and Africa, is possibly in cultivation. Some authors consider it the same as *C. thalictroides,* from which it is sometimes difficult to distinguish. *Ceratopteris richardii* is said to have larger sterile fronds with more buds, and fertile fronds to three-pinnate. The only sure way to distinguish the species is by the number of spores per sporangium: *C. richardii* has 16 spores, whereas *C. thalictroides* has 32.

Ceterach   FIGURES 13.26.1, 2

Rusty-back fern

Ceterach is a genus of small, terrestrial ferns with numerous overlapping scales on the undersides of the fronds. It is used mostly in rock gardens in temperate climates (see "Xerophytic Ferns" in Chapter 10). During dry weather, the fronds enroll, exposing their scaly lower surfaces. During wet weather, they expand quickly. The scales on the lower surface of the blade absorb water to rehydrate the frond.

Ceterach is characterized by pinnatifid or one-pinnate blades that are densely scaly beneath, obtuse segment tips, and elongate sori with inconspicuous indusia. The scales are broad and clathrate. The veins join near the margin of the frond, and the sori are often obscured by the scales and therefore are difficult to see. The rhizomes of all species are short and erect. Many pteridologists classify *Ceterach* with

Figure 13.26.1. *Ceterach officinarum:* habit.

Figure 13.26.2. *Ceterach officinarum:* fertile pinnae.

Asplenium because it hybridizes with that genus. The two genera are distinguished in this book for convenience.

Only three species occur in *Ceterach,* and all are native to the Old World. The genus name comes from the Greek *sjetrak,* an old name applied to the plant by Persian physicians.

Ceterach aureum (Cavanilles) L. V. Busch

FIGURE 13.26.3

Rusty-back fern
Hardy

A small-medium fern with erect rhizomes and clustered fronds. Grows under medium light in moist-dry potting mix. This species is excellent for rock gardens.

Ceterach aureum resembles *C. officinarum* but has larger and broader fronds. The blades are generally two times longer than broad, and the scales beneath are toothed.

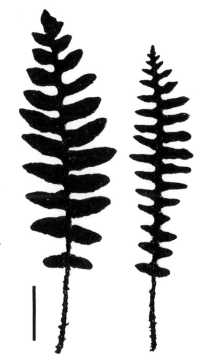

Figure 13.26.3. *Ceterach aureum:* fronds, bar = 5 cm (2 in.).

The species is native to the Madeira and Canary Islands. Some pteridologists considered this species a variety of *C. officinarum.*

Ceterach officinarum de Candolle

FIGURES 13.26.1, 2, 4; PLATE 20

syn. *Asplenium ceterach* Linnaeus
Scale fern
Hardy

A small-medium fern with erect rhizomes and clustered fronds. Grows under medium light in moist-dry, basic potting mix. This stout fern is excellent for rock gardens. In nature it grows on calcareous rocks and mortared walls.

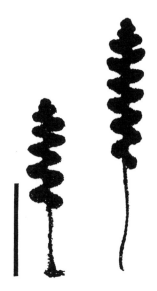

Figure 13.26.4. *Ceterach officinarum:* fronds, bar = 5 cm (2 in.).

The fronds of *Ceterach officinarum* are up to four times longer than broad, less than 30 cm (12 in.) long, and the blade scales are entire, not toothed. The species is native from the United Kingdom to the Pyrenees.

Cheilanthes   FIGURES 13.27.1–3
Lip fern

Cheilanthes is a genus of small, evergreen, terrestrial or rock-inhabiting ferns of dry climates. The plants often have woolly or scaly frond undersides. A number of species exist in special collections, and only a few are in general use in rock gardens and trough gardens. Although attractive for their small size and (often) fine texture, lip ferns can be difficult to grow. Care is needed to provide the proper amount of water, humidity, and drainage through the seasons. The plants prefer a medium with about 50% coarse sand or perlite. The soil should be kept moderately moist during periods of active growth but drier during inactivity. Avoid wetting the foliage but maintain moderate humidity. Wide, frequent fluctuations in moisture level seem harmful to lip ferns. Fluctuations can be reduced by locating plants next to large rocks or by planting them in clay pots that are in turn planted into larger pots (double potting) or directly in the ground. Excessive shade can cause the fronds to become weak and abnormally elongated; sites located to receive direct sun in the early morning and late afternoon can help prevent this. Some species grow well in full sun. For more details on the culture of *Cheilanthes* species, see the section on "Xerophytic Ferns" in Chapter 10.

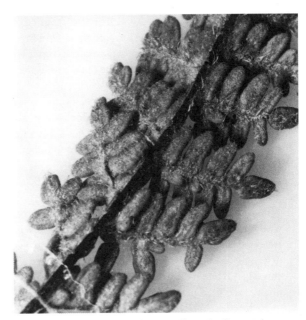

Figure 13.27.2. *Cheilanthes gracillima:* leaflets with indusia.

Cheilanthes is large, variable, and hard to characterize. All species have free veins, and the sori are typically found along the margins and protected by a false indusium. The rhizomes vary from compact and erect to decumbent or long-creeping. The fronds have one- to five-pinnate blades

Figure 13.27.1. *Cheilanthes gracillima:* habit.

Figure 13.27.3. *Cheilanthes lanosa:* sori with indusia pushed back.

that may be glabrous, glandular, hairy, scaly, or covered with a colored powder on the lower surface. Some species have numerous bead-like segments that are circular or nearly so and often cupped, with the open end of the cup facing downward.

Cheilanthes contains about 180 species and is widespread in the temperate and tropical regions of the world. The genus name comes from the Greek *cheilos,* lip, and *anthos,* flower, alluding to the position of the sporangia beneath the lip-like false indusium.

Some species of *Notholaena* and *Pellaea* are difficult to distinguish from *Cheilanthes.* In view of this problem, *Notholaena* has been redefined to include only those species with a dense white or yellow waxy powder on the lower surfaces of the blades and with sporangia at the tips of the veins in a more or less continuous marginal band covered by an enrolled but texturally unmodified frond margin. This definition, accepted here, places all the cultivated species formerly listed as *Notholaena* into *Cheilanthes.* Many *Cheilanthes* species go in and out of cultivation rather frequently, and therefore all could not be treated here. The reader is referred to floras, particularly of drier regions, for more information.

Pteridologists now distinguish several genera formerly included in *Cheilanthes.* To help with identification, these genera are described here.

Argyrochosma: Upper surface of the blade without stellate scales, not striate; lower surface of the blade usually has a yellowish or whitish powder; margin of the fertile segments enrolled to cover the sporangia or not; ultimate segments entire and stalked. (*Argyrochosma dealbata, A. jonesii, A. microphylla*)

Aspidotis: Upper surface of the blade without stellate scales, striate; lower surface of the blade not powdery; margin of the fertile segments enrolled to cover the sporangia, white-papery; ultimate segments entire and short-stalked. (*Aspidotis californica, A. carlotta-halliae, A. densa*)

Astrolepis: Upper surface of the blade with stellate scales, not striate; lower surface of the blade not powdery; margin of the fertile segments flat, not enrolled to cover the sporangia; pinnae stalked to subsessile. (*Astrolepis beitelii, A. sinuata*)

Cheilanthes: Upper surface of the blade without stellate scales, not striate; lower surface of the blade not powdery; margin of the fertile segments slightly enrolled to cover the sporangia; ultimate segments entire, stalked or sessile. (*Cheilanthes alabamensis, C. argentea, C. arizonica, C. bonariensis, C. buchtienii, C. covillei, C. eatonii, C. farinosa, C. feei, C. fendleri, C. gracillima, C. hirta, C. lanosa, C. lendigera, C. lindheimeri, C. newberryi, C. tomentosa, C. villosa, C. wrightii*)

Mildella: Upper surface of the blade without stellate scales, not striate; lower surface of the blade not powdery; margin of the fertile segments enrolled to cover the sporangia; ultimate segments entire, sessile, adnate; indusium linear, attached below the margin of the segment and thus leaving a narrow band of blade tissue between the edge and the indusium. (*Mildella intramarginalis*)

Notholaena: Upper surface of the blade without stellate scales, not striate; lower surface of the blade often with a yellowish or whitish powder; margin of the fertile segments enrolled to cover the sporangia; ultimate segments entire, sessile to subsessile. (*Notholaena standleyi*)

Cheilanthes alabamensis (Buckley) Kunze

FIGURE 13.27.4

Alabama lip fern
Hardy, Zone 7

A small to medium fern with short-creeping to compact rhizomes and clustered fronds. Grows best under medium-high light in moist-dry to dry, basic garden soil and sand.

Cheilanthes alabamensis has black stipes, rachises, and costae, with the color entering the pinnules. The hairs on the upper rachis surface are dense, short, and twisted; those beneath are long and sparse or absent. The blade is lanceolate to linear-oblong, two-pinnate to two-pinnate-pinnatifid, with segments elliptic to elongate-triangular, not bead-like. The blade surface varies from hairy to nearly glabrous. The species is native to the United States and Mexico, where it typically grows on limestone.

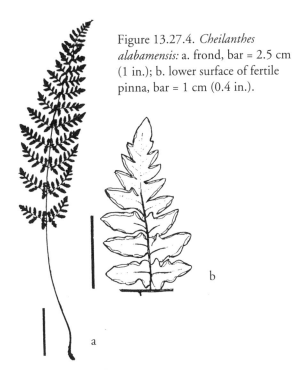

Figure 13.27.4. *Cheilanthes alabamensis*: a. frond, bar = 2.5 cm (1 in.); b. lower surface of fertile pinna, bar = 1 cm (0.4 in.).

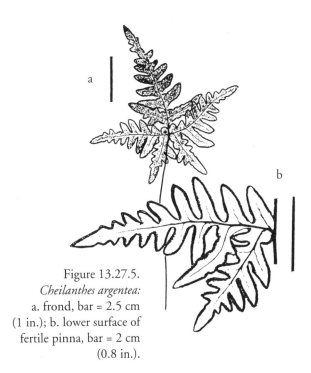

Figure 13.27.5. *Cheilanthes argentea:* a. frond, bar = 2.5 cm (1 in.); b. lower surface of fertile pinna, bar = 2 cm (0.8 in.).

Cheilanthes argentea (J. F. Gmelin) Kunze
FIGURE 13.27.5; PLATE 21

syn. *Aleuritopteris argentea* (J. F. Gmelin) Fée
Hardy, Zone 5

A small fern with compact rhizomes and clustered fronds. Grows under medium to high light in moist to moist-dry, well-drained garden soil with sand. The plants are easy to grow from spores. One variant in cultivation has white lower blade surfaces.

Cheilanthes argentea is distinctive by its pentagonal, one-pinnate-pinnatifid to two-pinnatifid blades covered by a yellow or white powder on the lower surfaces. The basal pinnae are asymmetrical, being larger on the basiscopic side, and the stipes are dark purplish and shiny. The sporangia are covered by a continuous, entire indusium. The species is native from northern Asia to Malaya and India.

Cheilanthes arizonica (Maxon) Mickel
FIGURE 13.27.6

syn. *Cheilanthes pyramidalis* subsp. *arizonica* Maxon
Arizona lip fern
Semi-hardy, Zone 8

A small fern with short-creeping rhizomes and clustered fronds. Grows under high light in well-drained, moist-dry to dry garden soil and sand.

Cheilanthes arizonica is distinguished by elongate-pentagonal blades up to four-pinnate, basal pinnae conspicuously larger than the above pair, and the ultimate segments elliptic to linear-oblong (not bead-like), the largest 4–10 mm (0.2–0.4 in.) long. The lower surface of the blade bears scattered reddish glands, but the upper surface is glabrous.

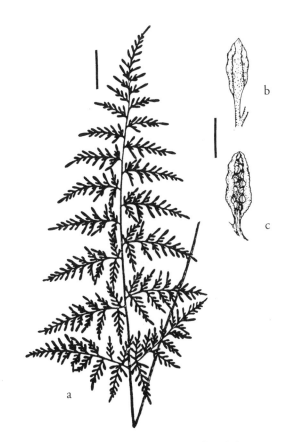

Figure 13.27.6. *Cheilanthes arizonica*: a. frond, bar = 2.5 cm (1 in.); b. underside of sterile segment, note glands, bar = 5 mm (0.2 in.); c. underside of fertile segment, bar = 5 mm (0.2 in.). After Knobloch and Correll (1962).

The species is native to southeastern Arizona, Mexico, Guatemala, and Honduras. In nature it occurs on quartzite or igneous rocks.

Cheilanthes bonariensis (Willdenow) Proctor

FIGURE 13.27.7

syn. *Notholaena aurea* (Poiret) Desvaux
Bonaire lip fern, slender cloak fern
Hardy to semi-hardy, Zone 7

A small-medium fern with short-creeping to compact rhizomes and clustered fronds. Grows under high light in moist-dry to dry, well-drained garden soil with sand.

Cheilanthes bonariensis has narrow, one-pinnate-pinnatifid blades with densely hairy lower surfaces. The pinnae are numerous (often about 40 pairs) and have four to seven pairs of lobes. They may be shed from the rachis (jointed). The hairs on the lower surface are dense, long, and matted, varying from white to creamy yellowish in color. The species is widespread in the American tropics and subtropics.

Cheilanthes buchtienii (Rosenstock) R. M. Tryon

FIGURE 13.27.8

syn. *Notholaena buchtienii* Rosenstock
Buchtien's lip fern
Semi-hardy, to Zone 9 or colder

A small fern with short-creeping rhizomes and clustered fronds. Seems to thrive in gardens under high light in moist-dry, well-drained garden soil with sand.

Figure 13.27.8. *Cheilanthes buchtienii:* a. frond, bar = 2.5 cm (1 in.); b. lower surface of fertile pinna, bar = 1 cm (0.4 in.).

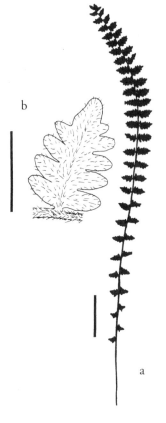

Figure 13.27.7. *Cheilanthes bonariensis:* a. frond, bar = 2.5 cm (1 in.); b. upper surface of pinna, bar = 5 mm (0.2 in.).

The stipe of *Cheilanthes buchtienii* is about half as long as the blade or shorter. The blade is narrowly linear and one-pinnate-pinnatifid or two-pinnate at the base. The pinnae vary from triangular to triangular-lanceolate and are densely hairy beneath with matted, pale brown hairs. The species is native to Bolivia and Argentina.

Cheilanthes covillei Maxon

FIGURE 13.27.9

Coville's lip fern
Semi-hardy, Zone 7

A small fern with compact, short-creeping rhizomes and clustered fronds. Grows under high light in well-drained garden soil kept moist-dry to dry.

Cheilanthes covillei has dark brown stipes, and the lanceolate to ovate-triangular blades are three- to four-pinnate with bead-like segments. Both surfaces of the blade are glabrous, or a few small scales may be near the base on the underside. The rachises, costae, and costules are densely scaly, the scales broadly ovate and ciliate toward the base, darker in the center, and nearly covering the segments on the undersides. This species resembles *C. fendleri,* but its rhizome scales are strongly appressed, instead of loosely overlapping, and the costal scales are entire to erose. It is na-

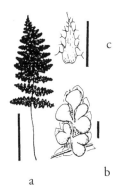

Figure 13.27.9. *Cheilanthes covillei*: a. frond, bar = 2.5 cm (1 in.); b. upper surface of segments, bar = 1 mm, after Hickman (1993); c. scale on lower side of segments, bar = 1 mm, after Hickman (1993).

tive to the southwestern United States and Mexico (Baja California), where it grows on rocky cliffs and ledges, usually on igneous rocks.

Cheilanthes eatonii Baker in Hooker & Baker

FIGURE 13.27.10

Eaton's lip fern
Hardy, Zone 6

A small fern with compact rhizomes and clustered fronds. Thrives under high light in moist-dry to dry, well-drained garden soil with sand. The plants are relatively easy to grow.

Cheilanthes eatonii has dark brown stipes. The blades are oblong-lanceolate, three- to four-pinnate, and hairy on both surfaces (more so beneath). The segments are oval to round and bead-like, and the rachis has scattered linear scales and is hairy. This species resembles *C. tomentosa*. It is native to the southern United States, Mexico, and Costa Rica, usually growing on rock slopes and ledges.

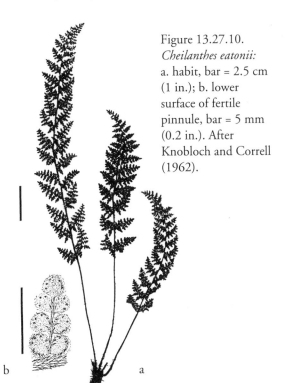

Figure 13.27.10. *Cheilanthes eatonii*: a. habit, bar = 2.5 cm (1 in.); b. lower surface of fertile pinnule, bar = 5 mm (0.2 in.). After Knobloch and Correll (1962).

Cheilanthes farinosa (Forsskål) Kaulfuss

FIGURE 13.27.11

syn. *Aleuritopteris farinosa* (Forsskål) Fée
Semi-tender (?)

A small to medium fern with compact rhizomes and clustered fronds. Grows under high light in drained, moist-dry garden soil or potting mix.

Cheilanthes farinosa is characterized by triangular to narrowly triangular blades that are two-pinnate and have a white or yellow powder on the lower surface. The stipe is dark and shiny. The basal pinnae are enlarged on their lower side, and the segments are not bead-like. This species is native to the tropics of the world.

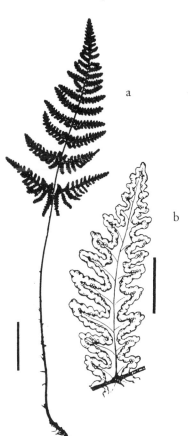

Figure 13.27.11. *Cheilanthes farinosa*: a. frond, bar = 2.5 cm (1 in.); b. lower surface of fertile pinna, bar = 5 mm (0.2 in.), after Knobloch and Correll (1962).

Cheilanthes feei T. Moore

FIGURE 13.27.12

Slender lip fern
Very hardy, Zone 4

A small fern with compact to short-creeping rhizomes and small, rosette-like clusters of blue-green fronds. Grows under high light in moist-dry to dry, basic, well-drained garden soil with sand.

The most distinctive characteristic of *Cheilanthes feei* is its small, blue-green, finely divided blades with numerous bead-like segments. The stipe bears multicellular (septate) hairs. The lower surface of the segment is dense with long,

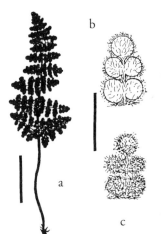

Figure 13.27.12. *Cheilanthes feei:* a. frond, bar = 2.5 cm (1 in.); b. upper surface of pinnule, bar = 5 mm (0.2 in.), after Knobloch and Correll (1962); c. lower surface of pinnule, bar = 5 mm (0.2 in.), after Knobloch and Correll (1962).

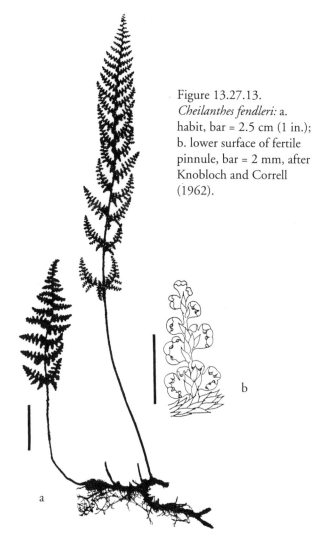

Figure 13.27.13. *Cheilanthes fendleri:* a. habit, bar = 2.5 cm (1 in.); b. lower surface of fertile pinnule, bar = 2 mm, after Knobloch and Correll (1962).

lax hairs; the upper surface is sparsely hairy to glabrous. This species is native to North America (mostly the central United States), where it grows on limestone cliffs.

Cheilanthes fendleri Hooker

FIGURE 13.27.13; PLATE 22

Fendler's lip fern
Hardy, Zone 5

A small fern with evergreen fronds scattered along a long-creeping rhizome. Grows under high light in well-drained, moist-dry garden soil. The plants are relatively easy to grow.

Cheilanthes fendleri is distinctive by the combination of long-creeping rhizomes, dark brown stipes, and bead-like segments. The blades are lanceolate to ovate-triangular, three- to four-pinnate, and glabrous on both sides or with a few scales near the base on the lower surface. The primary and secondary costae, however, are densely scaly, the scales nearly covering the segments. This species resembles *C. covillei,* which differs by having rhizome scales strongly appressed rather than loosely so, and costal scales ciliate near the base rather than entire to erose. *Cheilanthes fendleri* is native to the southwestern United States and Mexico.

This species is sometimes misnamed in the trade as *Cheilanthes lanosa* or *C. tomentosa.*

Cheilanthes gracillima D. C. Eaton

FIGURES 13.27.1, 2, 14

Lace fern
Hardy, Zone 5

A small fern with short-creeping rhizomes and clustered, dark green fronds. Grows under high light in drained, moist-dry garden soil with sand. This is a compact, evergreen fern.

Cheilanthes gracillima has dark brown stipes, and the blades are linear-oblong, two- to three-pinnate, 1–2.5 cm (0.5–1 in.) wide, and densely woolly beneath. The rachis bears scattered scales but no hairs. The scales along the costa of the pinnae are long-ciliate and do not conceal the seg-

ments, which are oblong, or rarely oval, and bead-like. The lower surfaces of the blades are densely covered with branched hairs and small ciliate scales. The margins are hardly or not modified into a false indusium. This species is native to the northwestern and central United States.

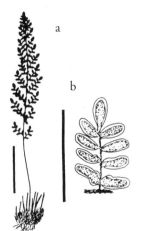

Figure 13.27.14. *Cheilanthes gracillima:* a. habit, bar = 2.5 cm (1 in.); b. lower surface of fertile pinnule, bar = 5 mm (0.2 in.).

Plate 1. In this subtropical garden in the American Southwest, *Blechnum appendiculatum* (foreground) grows with *Platycerium bifurcatum* (above, on tree) and the tree fern *Sphaeropteris medullaris* (background).

Plate 2. Cooper's tree ferns *(Sphaeropteris cooperi)* create an attractive grove in southern California.

Plate 3. A tree fern planting: *Sphaeropteris cooperi* (right, background), *Cibotium glaucum* (right), and *Dicksonia antarctica* (left).

Plate 4. A narrow space can accommodate a large number of ferns.

Plate 5. Several epiphytic ferns growing in baskets hung on a wall (clockwise from top left): *Davallia mariesii* var. *stenolepis*, *Nephrolepis exaltata*, *Davallia mariesii* var. *stenolepis*, *Microsorum scandens*, *Platycerium bifurcatum* (on tree), and *Phlebodium pseudoaureum*. (Photo by Arthur Takayama)

Plate 6. This fern garden in the Pacific Northwest effectively displays *Osmunda regalis* (left) and *Polystichum braunii* (right).

Plate 7. A temperate-climate rock garden.

Plate 8. Cinnamon fern *(Osmunda cinnamomea)* offers attractive foliage color in autumn, as shown here in Maine.

Plate 9. *Adiantum hispidulum,* rosy maidenhair

Plate 10. *Adiantum monochlamys*

Plate 11. *Alsophila tricolor,* silver tree fern

Plate 12. *Asplenium antiquum* 'Victoria'

Plate 14. *Athyrium niponicum* 'Pictum', Japanese painted fern

Plate 13. *Asplenium trichomanes,* maidenhair spleenwort

Plate 15. *Athyrium otophorum*

Plate 16. *Azolla pinnata*, ferny azolla

Plate 17. *Blechnum gibbum*

Plate 18. *Blechnum penna-marina*

Plate 19. *Ceratopteris thalictroides,* oriental water fern

Plate 20. *Ceterach officinarum,* scale fern

Plate 21. *Cheilanthes argentea*

Plate 22. *Cheilanthes fendleri,* Fendler's lip fern

Plate 23. *Cryptogramma crispa*, European parsley fern

Plate 24. *Cyrtomium falcatum*, house holly fern

Plate 25. *Drynaria rigidula* 'Whitei'

Plate 26. *Dryopteris erythrosora*, autumn fern

Plate 27. *Dryopteris wallichiana*, Wallich's wood fern

Plate 28. *Goniophlebium subauriculatum* 'Knightiae', Knight's polypody

Plate 29. *Gymnocarpium dryopteris,* common oak fern

Plate 30. *Hemionitis arifolia*

Plate 31. *Lygodium japonicum,* Japanese climbing fern

Plate 32. *Marsilea mutica*

Plate 33. *Matteuccia struthiopteris,* ostrich fern

Plate 34. *Microsorum punctatum* 'Ramosum', cobra plant

Plate 35. *Nephrolepis cordifolia*, erect sword fern

Plate 36. *Ophioglossum pendulum*

Plate 37. *Osmunda claytoniana*, interrupted fern

Plate 38. *Phlebodium pseudoaureum*

Plate 39. *Phyllitis scolopendrium,* hart's-tongue fern

Plate 40. *Pityrogramma austroamericana,* goldback fern

Plate 41. *Pityrogramma austroamericana,* close-up on the underside of a frond segment

Plate 42. *Platycerium bifurcatum*, common staghorn fern

Plate 43. *Platycerium superbum*, giant staghorn fern

Plate 44. *Polypodium formosanum*

Plate 45. *Polypodium pyrrholepis*

Plate 46. *Polystichum setiferum* 'Plumoso-divisilobum Group', divided soft shield fern

Plate 47. *Pteris argyraea,* silver brake

Plate 48. *Pyrrosia polydactyla*

Plate 49. *Selaginella uncinata,* blue spike moss

Plate 50. *Woodwardia radicans,* European chain fern

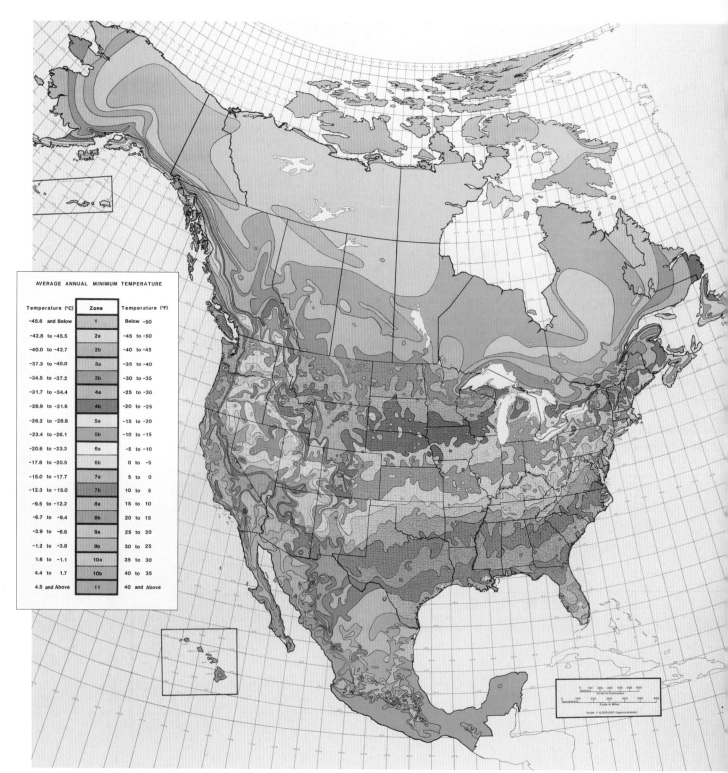

AVERAGE ANNUAL MINIMUM TEMPERATURE

Temperature (°C)	Zone	Temperature (°F)
-45.6 and Below	1	Below -50
-42.8 to -45.5	2a	-45 to -50
-40.0 to -42.7	2b	-40 to -45
-37.3 to -40.0	3a	-35 to -40
-34.5 to -37.2	3b	-30 to -35
-31.7 to -34.4	4a	-25 to -30
-28.9 to -31.6	4b	-20 to -25
-26.2 to -28.8	5a	-15 to -20
-23.4 to -26.1	5b	-10 to -15
-20.6 to -23.3	6a	-5 to -10
-17.8 to -20.5	6b	0 to -5
-15.0 to -17.7	7a	5 to 0
-12.3 to -15.0	7b	10 to 5
-9.5 to -12.2	8a	15 to 10
-6.7 to -9.4	8b	20 to 15
-3.9 to -6.6	9a	25 to 20
-1.2 to -3.8	9b	30 to 25
1.6 to -1.1	10a	35 to 30
4.4 to 1.7	10b	40 to 35
4.5 and Above	11	40 and Above

USDA Plant Hardiness Zone Map

Cheilanthes hirta Swartz   FIGURE 13.27.15

Parsley fern
Semi-hardy to hardier (?)

A small to medium fern with short-creeping rhizomes bearing fronds in a loose cluster. Best grown under medium-high light in well-drained, moist to moist-dry garden soil or potting mix. This species is relatively easy to grow.

The short, dark brown stipes of *Cheilanthes hirta* are covered with reddish brown, long, stiff, hair-like scales. The blades vary from linear-elliptic to narrowly oblanceolate and are two- to three-pinnate-pinnatifid. The segments have rounded lobes (not bead-like) and scattered, long, gland-tipped hairs on both surfaces. The costa is dark brown with reddish brown hairs. The marginal lobes are curved over discrete sori, and the false indusium is minute or absent. The species is native to southern Africa.

Cheilanthes lanosa (Michaux) D. C. Eaton in Emory
FIGURES 13.27.3, 16

syn. *Notholaena vestita* Desvaux
Hairy lip fern
Hardy, Zone 5

A small to medium fern with short-creeping rhizomes bearing clustered, grayish fronds. Grows under medium-high light in well-drained, acidic garden soil or potting mix kept

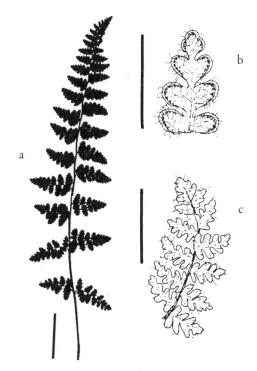

Figure 13.27.16. *Cheilanthes lanosa:* a. frond, bar = 2.5 cm (1 in.); b. lower surface of fertile pinnule, bar = 5 mm (0.2 in.); c. upper surface of pinna, bar = 1 cm (0.4 in.).

moist-dry to dry. *Cheilanthes lanosa* is easy to cultivate. Some of the plants sold by this name in the trade are *C. fendleri*. It usually grows on the ground in or among sandstone; it does not grow on vertical cliff faces.

Cheilanthes lanosa has narrow-triangular to lanceolate, two-pinnate-pinnatifid blades that are sparsely hairy on both surfaces. The stipe, rachis, and costae are purple-brown and have long hairs, but no scales, and the ultimate segments are oblong to lanceolate (not bead-like) and pinnately lobed. The species is native to the eastern United States.

Cheilanthes lendigera (Cavanilles) Swartz
FIGURE 13.27.17

Beaded lip fern
Semi-hardy or hardier, Zone 8

A small fern with fronds scattered or clustered along a long-creeping rhizome. Grows well under high light in drained, moist-dry to dry garden soil or potting mix. The plants are relatively easy to grow.

Cheilanthes lendigera has dark brown stipes with long, soft, whitish hairs. The blades are triangular-lanceolate, to three-pinnate, with the costae nearly scaleless beneath. The segments are small and bead-like, with the upper surfaces smooth and the lower surfaces covered with long, tawny hairs. The sporangia are covered by a prominent, broad,

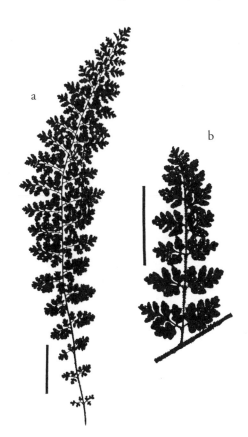

Figure 13.27.15. *Cheilanthes hirta:* a. frond, bar = 2.5 cm (1 in.); b. pinna, bar = 2 cm (0.8 in.).

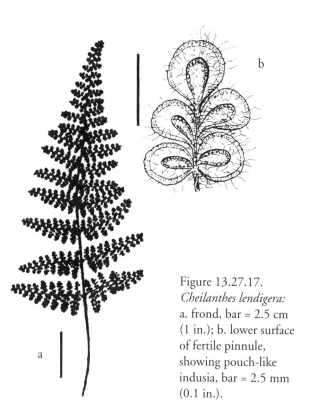

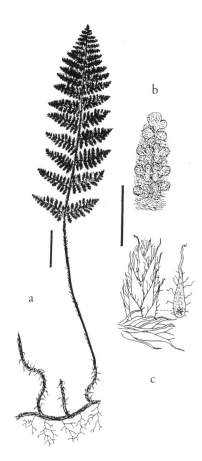

Figure 13.27.17. *Cheilanthes lendigera:* a. frond, bar = 2.5 cm (1 in.); b. lower surface of fertile pinnule, showing pouch-like indusia, bar = 2.5 mm (0.1 in.).

Figure 13.27.18. *Cheilanthes lindheimeri:* a. habit, bar = 2.5 cm (1 in.); b. upper surface of pinnule, bar = 2 mm, after Knobloch and Correll (1962); c. lower surface of pinnule and enlargement of scale, bar = 2 mm, after Knobloch and Correll (1962).

translucent false indusium that nearly covers the underside of the segment. The species occurs from the southwestern United States to South America and the West Indies.

Cheilanthes lindheimeri Hooker   FIGURE 13.27.18
Lindheimer's lip fern
Semi-hardy, Zone 7

A small fern with fronds scattered or clustered on a long-creeping rhizome. Grows well under high light in drained, moist-dry to dry garden soil. This species is relatively easy to grow.

The blades of *Cheilanthes lindheimeri* are oblong-lanceolate to ovate-triangular, to four-pinnate, and 2–5 cm (0.75–2 in.) wide. The rachis has some scales and hairs, and the costal scales are lanceolate with truncate or subcordate bases. The margins have fine, curly hairs that form a tangled mass partly concealing the segments. The minute, bead-like segments are nearly smooth on both surfaces but appear hairy due to the hairy costal scales. The species is native to the southwestern United States and Mexico.

Cheilanthes newberryi (D. C. Eaton) Domin
FIGURE 13.27.19
syn. *Notholaena newberryi* D. C. Eaton
Newberry's lip fern, cotton fern
Semi-hardy to hardy, Zone 7

A small fern with short-creeping to compact rhizomes and clustered fronds. Grows under high light in drained, moist to moist-dry garden soil with sand.

The fronds of *Cheilanthes newberryi* are a distinctive cottony, whitish gray. The stipes are wiry, and the blades are linear to ovate-lanceolate, two- to four-pinnate, and 1–5 cm (0.5–2 in.) wide. The rachis is hairy on both surfaces, and the segments are round and flat, only somewhat bead-like, up to 3–5 mm wide, with the lower surface conspicuously woolly with fine, cobwebby hairs (some of these also occur on the upper surface). The species is native to the

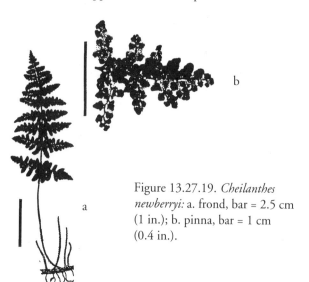

Figure 13.27.19. *Cheilanthes newberryi:* a. frond, bar = 2.5 cm (1 in.); b. pinna, bar = 1 cm (0.4 in.).

United States (southern California) and Mexico (Baja California) and usually grows on igneous rocks.

Cheilanthes tomentosa Link   FIGURE 13.27.20

Woolly lip fern
Hardy, Zone 6

A small-medium fern with compact rhizomes and clustered fronds. Grows well under high light in well-drained, moist-dry to dry garden soil with sand. The plants usually bear attractive gray-green fronds. This species is relatively easy to grow.

Cheilanthes tomentosa has dark stipes and oblong-lanceolate, four-pinnate blades, 1.5–8 cm (0.6–3 in.) wide. The rachis bears scattered inconspicuous linear scales and hairs, and the scales on the costae are narrow, not concealing the segments. The ultimate segments are oval, rarely oblong, bead-like, up to 1–2 mm wide, with the lower surface densely hairy with matted hairs and the upper surface with fine hairs. The species resembles C. eatonii, which differs by having more prominent, wider scales on the rachis and costae. Cheilanthes tomentosa is native to the southwestern United States and Mexico, where it grows on a variety of rock types.

Cheilanthes villosa Davenport ex Maxon

FIGURE 13.27.21

Villous lip fern
Semi-hardy

A small fern with erect to ascending, compact rhizomes and clustered fronds. Grows best under high light in drained, moist to moist-dry, basic garden soil with sand. This species is relatively easy to grow.

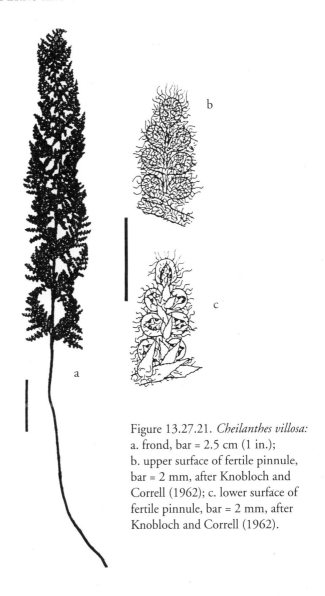

Figure 13.27.21. Cheilanthes villosa: a. frond, bar = 2.5 cm (1 in.); b. upper surface of fertile pinnule, bar = 2 mm, after Knobloch and Correll (1962); c. lower surface of fertile pinnule, bar = 2 mm, after Knobloch and Correll (1962).

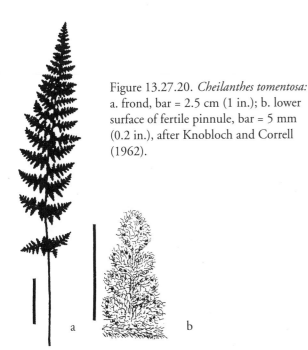

Figure 13.27.20. Cheilanthes tomentosa: a. frond, bar = 2.5 cm (1 in.); b. lower surface of fertile pinnule, bar = 5 mm (0.2 in.), after Knobloch and Correll (1962).

Because of its bead-like segments, Cheilanthes villosa resembles C. lendigera. It differs by its dense covering of broadly ovate scales on the costae and crinkled hairs on the upper surface of the segments. It is native to the southwestern United States and northern Mexico.

Cheilanthes wrightii Hooker   FIGURE 13.27.22

Wright's lip fern
Semi-hardy, Zone (7)8

A small fern with long-creeping rhizomes and clustered to scattered fronds. Grows under high light in drained, moist-dry to dry garden soil with sand.

Cheilanthes wrightii is characterized by two-pinnate-pinnatifid, lanceolate to ovate-triangular blades that are 1–4 cm (0.5–1.5 in.) wide. The segments vary from oblong to linear and are glabrous on both surfaces. The species is native to the southwestern United States and Mexico. It usually grows on igneous rocks.

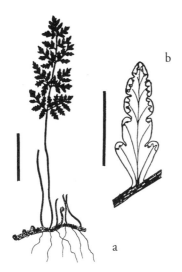

a

b

Figure 13.27.22.
Cheilanthes wrightii:
a. habit, bar =
2.5 cm (1 in.);
b. lower surface of
fertile pinnule, bar =
2.5 mm (0.1 in.).
After Knobloch and
Correll (1962).

Cibotium   FIGURES 13.28.1–3

Cibotiums are large to huge tree ferns, usually with tall trunks. The Mexican tree fern long known in cultivation, *Cibotium schiedei,* does not form an erect trunk but has a massive crown that produces lacy, gracefully arching fronds. Hairs taken from the trunks and stipes of the Hawaiian tree fern (*C. glaucum*), called hapu, were used to stuff pillows and mattresses, but they had the disadvantage of deteriorating with age. During the mid-1950s, plants of *C. glaucum* from the island of Hawaii were sold in the continental United States under the incorrect name "*C. chamissoi.*" In southern California they are grown outdoors, and in colder climates they are used as indoor pot plants. They are still popular and nowadays are propagated from spores instead of from trunks collected from wild populations. Shipments

Figure 13.28.2. *Cibotium glaucum:* stipes and trunk with hairs.

of the trunks would occasionally contain trunks of the man fern (*C. menziesii*), which can be distinguished by the blackish, stiff hairs on its stipes and trunk. Man fern has never been abundant in the trade and is harder to grow than *C. glaucum.*

The stems of *Cibotium* vary from prostrate to crown-like to tall trunks, depending on the species. They bear long, densely matted hairs, which also occur on the stipe bases. The blades are two-pinnate-pinnatifid or more divided, broadly triangular, and lightly to strongly whitish on the undersides. Some species have eared segments; that is, they have a slightly longer basal lobe that points forward. The secondary costa and its midribs are ridged on the upper surface. As in all tree ferns of the family Dicksoniaceae, the

Figure 13.28.1. *Cibotium glaucum:* habit.

Figure 13.28.3. *Cibotium chamissoi:* sori and indusia details, bar = 5 mm (0.2 in.). Courtesy of T. Hoshizaki.

sori are marginal and enclosed by a two-lobed indusium, the lower lobe fitting inside the upper one. This arrangement gives the sorus a clam-like appearance.

A member of the family Dicksoniaceae, *Cibotium* is readily separated from the cyatheaceous tree ferns by its marginal sori and the presence of hairs (not scales) on the stipe and trunk. *Dicksonia,* which also has hairs, differs by having fronds that are narrowed at the base and green (not whitish) on the undersides; the outer indusial lobe more like the leaf segment in color and texture; and the inner indusial lobe thin and brownish.

Cibotium contains 10 species and is native to Central America, Asia, and Hawaii. The genus name comes from the Greek *kibotos,* a small chest or casket, alluding to the shape of the indusium. For more on culture, see the section in Chapter 10 on "Tree Ferns." For a technical treatment of the species, see Maxon (1912) and Palmer (1994).

Cibotium barometz (Linnaeus) J. Smith

FIGURE 13.28.4

Scythian lamb, vegetable lamb
Tender

A large tree fern with prostrate stems, not upright trunks. Grows under medium light in moist potting mix. This species is rarely cultivated.

The rhizomes of *Cibotium barometz* are covered with golden-brown hairs, and similar hairs occur on the rachis and costae but are matted and woolly. The sori are limited to the lower half of segments. This species is native to southeastern Asia.

Because it is a tree fern, *Cibotium barometz* is banned from import in countries abiding by the CITES treaty, which bans trade in rare or endangered plants and animals (see Appendix III). In the pre-treaty days of the 1930s, *C. barometz* was listed in trade catalogs in the United States, but it is unknown whether the plants were actually this species.

The stems are occasionally sold in oriental markets for medicinal use. Concoctions from the rhizome are used to treat arthritis and joint pains, and the hairs are used to staunch bleeding. In some parts of China it is common for households to have a piece of *Cibotium* trunk with attached stipe bases from which the hairs can be pulled off and put on cuts and scrapes. The pieces of stem are fashioned into an article that resembles a small dog or lamb, with the stipe bases serving as the legs. Sometimes fiddleheads are attached to the rhizome to represent ears or the tail. In southern China, where *Cibotium barometz* is native, it is called the "golden-haired dog."

Cibotium barometz is associated with the legend of the vegetable lamb of Tartary, sometimes also called the Scythian lamb. During the Middle Ages it was believed that there existed a half-plant, half-lamb creature somewhere in the region north of the Black Sea (Tartary or Sythia) that

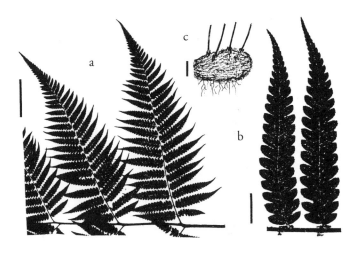

Figure 13.28.4. *Cibotium barometz:* a. pinnae from young plant, bar = 5 cm (2 in.); b. primary pinnules, bar = 1 cm (0.4 in.); c. prostrate rhizome from mature plant, bar = 5 cm (2 in.).

grew and remained attached to the soil by a "trunk" from its navel. It fed on the surrounding vegetation and died when this was exhausted. In the late 1700s botanists concluded that *C. barometz* was the source of this legendary plant, but the legend is actually based on the cotton plant. See Moran (1992a) and Lee (1887) for a fuller account of the legend.

Cibotium chamissoi Kaulfuss

FIGURES 13.28.3, 5

Tender

A large tree fern. Grows well under medium light in moist potting mix.

The stipes of *Cibotium chamissoi* are woolly only at the base, and the blades are dull green to slightly glaucous on the lower surfaces and noticeably covered with cobweb-like, tan hairs. The segments are not eared. Though endemic to the Hawaiian Islands, this species is rarely cultivated in Hawaii, and plants sold by this name in the continental United States are mostly *C. glaucum.*

Cibotium glaucum (Smith) Hooker & Arnott

FIGURES 13.28.1, 2, 6; PLATE 3

Hapu, Hawaiian tree fern
Semi-tender

A large tree fern, with trunks to 5 m (16 ft.). Grows well under medium to high light in moist garden soil or potting mix. This species is the most common *Cibotium* in cultivation. It may root from bare-root trunks, but most trade plants are grown from spores. It grows slowly and is not as cold hardy as *Sphaeropteris cooperi,* another very common tree fern.

The stipes of *Cibotium glaucum* are pale and woolly at the base or throughout. The segments are glaucous on the

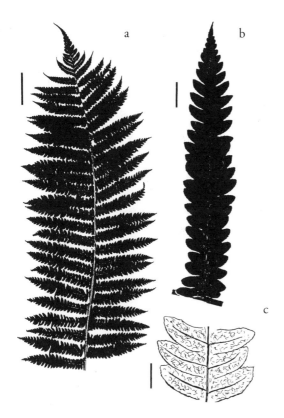

Figure 13.28.5. *Cibotium chamissoi:* a. pinna, bar = 5 cm (2 in.); b. primary pinnule, bar = 1 cm (0.4 in.); c. hairs on lower segment surface, bar = 5 mm (0.2 in.).

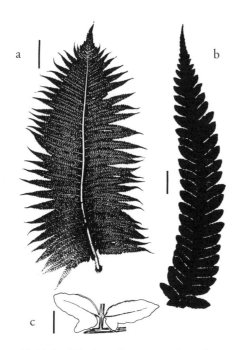

Figure 13.28.6. *Cibotium glaucum:* a. pinna, bar = 5 cm (2 in.); b. primary pinnule, bar = 1 cm (0.4 in.); c. eared segments at base of primary pinnule, bar = 5 mm (0.2 in.).

lower surface, glabrous or with cobweb-like white hairs, and one or both segments are eared at the base of at least some pinnules. The species is endemic to the Hawaiian Islands.

In the trade *Cibotium glaucum* is often misidentified as *C. chamissoi* Kaulfuss.

Cibotium menziesii Hooker   FIGURE 13.28.7
Man fern
Marginally semi-tender

A large tree fern, with trunks to 5 m (16 ft.). Grows well under medium light in moist potting mix. The plants require more heat and humidity than *Cibotium glaucum.*

Cibotium menziesii has stipes clothed with thick, waxy, stiff hairs. The segments are glossy and lack ears. Minute tufts of hairs are present on the lower surface. The species is endemic to the Hawaiian Islands.

Figure 13.28.7. *Cibotium menziesii:* a. pinna, bar = 5 cm (2 in.); b. primary pinnules, bar = 1 cm (0.4 in.); c. lower segment surface dotted with minute tufts of hair, bar = 5 mm (0.2 in.).

Cibotium schiedei Schlechtendal & Chamisso
FIGURE 13.28.8
Mexican tree fern
Semi-tender

A large tree fern with stout crowns and stems that form a trunk when very old. Grows well under medium light in moist, well-drained potting mix. This fast-growing species

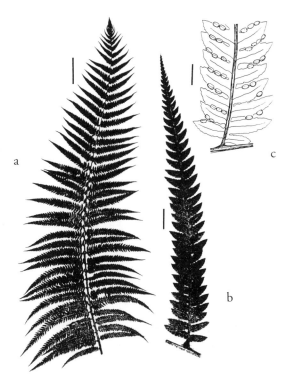

Figure 13.29.1. *Coniogramme japonica:* habit.

Figure 13.28.8. *Cibotium schiedei:* a. pinna, bar = 5 cm (2 in.); b. primary pinnule, bar = 1 cm (0.4 in.); c. sori protruding beyond segment margins, bar = 5 mm (0.2 in.).

has gracefully arching fronds, but older plants are often too big for most homes. Plantlets sometimes emerge as off-shoots at the base of the crown. These may be separated and rooted, but are usually hard to establish.

The stipe of *Cibotium schiedei* is clothed with yellow-brown silky hairs, and the blades are large, 2–3 m (6.5–10 ft.) long, and light green on the upper surface but glaucous on the lower. The segments lack ears, and the sori often protrude beyond the margin. The species is native to Mexico.

A similar species, *Lophosoria quadripinnata* (J. Gmelin) C. Christensen, is becoming more frequently cultivated. It might be identified as a *Cibotium* because it also has woolly hairs on the trunk and stipe base and large, finely divided leaves that are glaucous beneath. It can be distinguished from *Cibotium schiedei* by having sori borne on the lower surface of the leaf, rather than at the margin, and by the lack of indusia.

Coniogramme   FIGURES 13.29.1, 2

Coniogramme makes a good ground cover but needs protection from slugs and snails. These medium- to large-sized, creeping, terrestrial ferns have strap-shaped pinnae. The stipes contain one large vascular bundle, and the blades are mostly one-pinnate, except for the basal pair (or two) of pinnae, which tend to be more divided. The blade always

Figure 13.29.2. *Coniogramme japonica:* sporangia along veins.

terminates in an apical segment that resembles the lateral pinnae, and the veins tips are conspicuously enlarged on the upper surface of the leaf. The sori run along the veins between the midrib and margin of the segments. Indusia are absent. The cultivated species of *Coniogramme* mimic a large *Pteris cretica* but differ by having longer-creeping rhizomes, deciduous fronds, and sori that run between the midrib and margin of the segments, not along the margin as in *Pteris*.

The genus consists of about 20 species native to the Old World tropics, Japan, and in the Pacific to Hawaii. Its name comes from the Greek *konios,* dusty, and *gramme,* line, referring to the lines of sori along the veins.

Coniogramme intermedia Hieronymus

FIGURE 13.29.3

syn. *Coniogramme fraxinea* (G. Don) Diels
Hardy

A medium to large fern with deciduous fronds and medium- to long-creeping rhizomes. Grows well under low light in moist garden soil.

Coniogramme intermedia is characterized by free veins and strap-shaped ultimate segments. It is native to India, China, Korea, Japan, Malaysia, and Hawaii.

Figure 13.29.3. *Coniogramme intermedia:* frond, bar = 5 cm (2 in.).

Coniogramme japonica (Thunberg) Diels

FIGURES 13.29.1, 2, 4

Bamboo fern
Semi-hardy, Zone (7)8

A medium-large fern with deciduous fronds and medium- to long-creeping rhizomes. Grows well under low light in moist garden soil or potting mix.

Coniogramme japonica resembles the preceding one but has netted veins. It is native to China, Taiwan, Korea, and Japan.

'Variegata'. Segments with yellow along the midribs.

Figure 13.29.4. *Coniogramme japonica:* frond, bar = 5 cm (2 in.).

Cryptogramma

FIGURES 13.30.1–3

Rock brake, parsley fern

A coarse, parsley-like foliage characterizes *Cryptogramma,* which consists of small ferns used in rock gardens in cold-temperate climates. The plants are difficult to grow.

The fronds vary from two- to three-pinnate (rarely four-pinnate) and have toothed sterile segments and free veins. The segments of the fertile fronds appear pod-like due to the strongly enrolled margins (the false indusium) that cover the sporangia.

Cryptogramma contains about 10 species and occurs in North America, Europe, Asia, southern Chile, and Argentina. The genus name comes from the Greek *kryptos,* hidden, and *gramme,* line, alluding to the line of sori hidden by the enrolled leaf margin.

Figure 13.30.1.
Cryptogramma acrostichoides: sterile frond.

Figure 13.30.2.
Cryptogramma acrostichoides: fertile frond.

Figure 13.30.3. *Cryptogramma acrostichoides:* fertile segments.

Cryptogramma acrostichoides R. Brown
FIGURES 13.30.1–4

American parsley fern
Very hardy, Zone 2

A small fern with suberect to erect rhizomes and tufted evergreen fronds. Grows well under medium light in well-drained garden soil. The plants seem to grow best if the soil is kept moist in the spring but moist-dry other times of the year.

The rhizomes of *Cryptogramma acrostichoides* are hard, short, scaly, and much branched. The sterile fronds remain green during the winter and senesce the following spring. The stipes are dark brown toward the base, and the blades are up to three-pinnate and somewhat leathery. Minute, cylindrical hairs occur on the upper blade surface and in the grooves of the stipe, rachis, and costae. The sterile segments vary from oblong to ovate-lanceolate, with 6–12 teeth or shallow lobes. The species is native to North America and Asia.

The Cascade parsley fern, *Cryptogramma cascadensis* E. R. Alverson, resembles *C. acrostichoides* and might be cultivated in the northwestern United States. It differs from *C. acrostichoides* by having sterile fronds deciduous in autumn and by the lack of hairs on the upper surfaces of the blades and in the grooves of the stipes and rachises. It is native to the northwestern United States and adjacent Canada.

Figure 13.30.4. *Cryptogramma acrostichoides:* a. fertile frond (left) and sterile frond (right), bar = 5 cm (2 in.); b. fertile pinnule, bar = 5 mm (0.2 in.).

Some botanists consider *Cryptogramma acrostichoides* to be a variety of the European species, *C. crispa,* but they differ consistently in blade cutting and chromosome number ($2n = 60$ in *C. acrostichoides* and $2n = 120$ in *C. crispa*). They also differ in habitat. *Cryptogramma acrostichoides* grows on noncalcareous rocks, often in slightly drier habitats than is usual for other species in the genus. In contrast, *C. crispa* grows on calcareous rocks in more humid places.

Cryptogramma crispa (Linnaeus) R. Brown

FIGURE 13.30.5; PLATE 23

European parsley fern
Very hardy, Zone 2

A small fern with erect to suberect rhizomes. Grows best under medium light in well-drained garden soil. The plants seem to do best if the soil is kept moist in the spring but moist-dry other times of the year.

Cryptogramma crispa resembles *C. acrostichoides* but has thinner, deciduous leaves, and sterile blades up to four-pinnate. It is native to Europe.

Cryptogramma sitchensis (Ruprecht) T. Moore

FIGURE 13.30.6

Alaska parsley fern
Very hardy, Zone 2

A small fern with suberect to erect rhizomes and tufted evergreen fronds. Grows well under medium light in garden soil with good drainage. Probably does best if the soil is moist in spring and drier at other times.

Cryptogramma sitchensis greatly resembles *C. acrostichoides* and is believed to have arisen by hybridization between that species and possibly *C. raddeana* Formin of eastern Asia. It differs from *C. acrostichoides* by its obovate segments with two to six deep lobes and at least some three- to four-pinnate sterile fronds. It is native to northwestern Canada and Alaska, where it typically grows among rocks in acid soils.

Figure 13.30.5. *Cryptogramma crispa:* habit, with sterile fronds (left and right) and fertile frond (center), bar = 5 cm (2 in.). After Sowerby (1855).

Figure 13.30.6. *Cryptogramma sitchensis:* a. habit, with two sterile fronds (shorter) and two fertile fronds (taller), bar = 5 cm (2 in.); b. sterile pinnule, bar = 3 mm (0.1 in.). After Cody and Britton (1989).

Cryptogramma stelleri (S. G. Gmelin) Prantl

FIGURE 13.30.7

Slender rock brake, cliff brake, fragile rock brake
Very hardy, Zone 2

A small fern with deciduous fronds distributed along a slender (1–1.5 mm wide), creeping rhizome with few branches. Thrives under medium light in well-drained, moist, basic garden soil. The fronds die back by late summer and need less water at that time.

Cryptogramma stelleri bears stipes that are dark at the base but greenish above. The blades are up to two-pinnate, herbaceous to membranous, and thin. The segments of sterile leaves are ovate-lanceolate to fan-shaped and lobed halfway to the midrib. The species is native to northern North America, Europe, and Asia, where it typically grows on calcareous rocks, often forming dense colonies in crevices or ledges.

Figure 13.30.7. *Cryptogramma stelleri:* habit, sterile frond (left) and fertile frond (right), bar = 5 cm (2 in.). After Cody and Britton (1989).

Ctenitis

These medium- to large-sized, terrestrial ferns are infrequently cultivated, except in Florida. The Florida tree fern (*Ctenitis sloanei*) can form a trunk up to 1.3 m (4 ft.) tall.

Ctenitis can usually be distinguished by the following combination of characteristics: scaly rhizomes; three or more vascular bundles in the stipe; minute, jointed, often reddish hairs on the upper surfaces of the rachises and costae; free veins (not netted); and round sori. Usually the rachis is grooved on its upper surface and the costae are not. In those rare instances where both are grooved, the grooves are interrupted at the junctures, not continuous. This is in contrast to dryopteroid ferns such as *Cyrtomium, Dryopteris,* and *Polystichum,* in which the grooves are prominent on both the rachises and costae and run into one another.

Ctenitis contains 150 species and is native to tropical regions of the world. The genus name comes from the Greek *kteis,* comb, referring to the comb-like lobes of the pinnae in *Ctenitis submarginalis* (Langsdorff & Fischer) Ching, the type species of the genus.

Ctenitis sloanei (Poeppig ex Sprengel) C. V. Morton

FIGURES 13.31.1–4

syn. *Ctenitis ampla* auct. non (Humboldt & Bonpland ex Willdenow) Ching
American tree fern, Florida tree fern
Tender, Zone 10(11)

A large tree fern with erect stems that can form trunks up to 1.3 m (4 ft.) tall, although it infrequently does so in cultivation. Grows under medium light in moist, drained potting mix. This species is sensitive to transplanting and is difficult to establish.

The stipe scales of *Ctenitis sloanei* are dense, linear or thread-like, orange (rarely brown), and toothed. The veins reach all the way to the margin, and the indusium falls away early. The species is native to the United States (Florida) and American tropics.

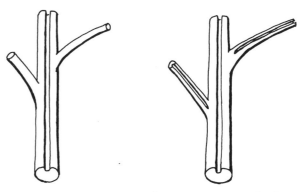

Figure 13.31.1. *Ctenitis sloanei:* habit.

Figure 13.31.2. *Ctenitis:* rachis, groove not opening into the costae, costae not grooved (left), costae grooved (right).

Figure 13.31.3. *Ctenitis sloanei:* sori and indusia.

Figure 13.31.4. *Ctenitis sloanei:* a. frond from mature plant, bar = 5 cm (2 in.); b. frond from immature plant, bar = 5 cm (2 in.); c. veins reaching the margin, bar = 5 mm (0.2 in.).

Cyathea

syn. *Hemitelia*

Tree fern

Cyathea is a genus of elegant tree ferns that typically bear a crown of large fronds on top of a tall, erect trunk. They can reach 15–20 m (50–65 ft.) tall in the wild, and some mountain slopes support dense stands of these stately trees. In temperate areas this genus is seen mainly in conservatories or large greenhouses. Tree ferns can be grown as houseplants, but most species seem to do best outdoors in subtropical or tropical gardens, where they can grow up to 5 m (16 ft.) in height. Most thrive under filtered light, but they will grow in full sun in coastal areas where heat and light are not too intense. Growth is best in rich, organic, moist soil. (See Chapter 10 for more information.)

Tree ferns have several uses. In some cultures they are used for food, fodder, or building material. The trunks are highly valued in backwoods construction because they are strong and resist decay. The thick layer of tough aerial roots (the root mantle) found around the trunk of some species is used as a growing medium for epiphytes, especially orchids. The scales on the trunk and stipes can shed readily, and care should be taken to avoid getting the scales into your eyes and on your skin. Although not toxic, the scales can cause severe irritation.

Most species of *Cyathea* have upright, scaly trunks and a layer of tough aerial roots, at least toward the base. The fronds are borne in a whorl at the top of the stem, forming a palm-like growth habit, and they usually have finely divided, two- to three-pinnate blades. The stipe scales lack dark bristles at the apex, in contrast to those of the similar genus *Alsophila,* and the marginal cells differ in orientation and often in color from the central cells (when viewed under 20× magnification). The round sori are borne on the undersides of the blades, and the indusia, when present, vary from scale-like to cup-like or globose.

To distinguish cyatheaceous ferns from other tree-fern groups, look at the indument or covering on the stem apex or stipe bases. *Cyathea* has a covering of scales, whereas dicksoniaceous tree ferns such as *Cibotium* and *Dicksonia* have hairs. *Sadleria* has scales on the trunk and stipe, but its fronds are narrow and the sori are covered by a conspicuous oblong indusium.

Cyathea is native to the Old and New World tropics, occurring mainly in cloud forests. It consists of about 115 species. The genus name comes from the Greek *kyathos,* a wine cup, referring to the cup-like shape of the indusium in certain species.

Cyathea is defined here in the narrow sense, excluding *Alsophila, Cnemidaria,* and *Sphaeropteris.* Although pteridologists agree that these genera represent natural groups, they disagree over whether the groups should be recognized as separate genera. Some pteridologists classify the species of all four groups into one large, inclusive genus, *Cyathea.*

For a reference to tree-fern taxonomy, see Kramer and Green (1990). The following guide to the cultivated genera of Cyatheaceae is provided to facilitate identification:

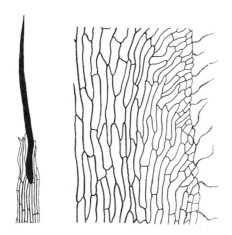

Alsophila: Stipe scales tipped with a dark bristle; marginal cells of scales are different from the central cells in orientation, size, and often color; stipes spiny, with spines black and shiny. (*Alsophila australis, A. tricolor*)

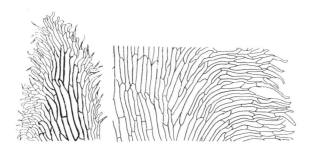

Cyathea: Stipe scales not tipped with a dark bristle; marginal cells of scales are different from the central cells in orientation, size, and often color; stipes spiny or not, but if spiny, the spines are not black and shiny. (*Cyathea arborea*)

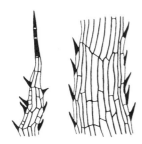

Sphaeropteris: Stipe scales tipped with a short, dark, spine-like hair, not a bristle; marginal cells of scales are similar to those in the center, except for occasional black teeth; stipes spiny or not, but if spiny, the spines are not black and shiny. (*Sphaeropteris aramaganensis, S. cooperi, S. excelsa, S. horrida, S. medullaris*)

Cyathea arborea (Linnaeus) Smith   FIGURES 13.32.1, 2
West Indian tree fern
Tender to very tender

A large tree fern. Grows best under medium light in moist potting mix. This species grows in southern Florida and seems to require warm nights.

The fronds of *Cyathea arborea* eventually fall away from the trunk. The stipe scales are mostly whitish, and the base of the segment midrib on the underside have one or two white, puffy scales. The saucer-shaped indusium forms a cup beneath the sporangia. The species is native to the West Indies, Venezuela, and Colombia.

Cyclopeltis

These medium-sized terrestrial ferns are grown in southern Florida and are sometimes used in public parks in the West Indies. The rhizome is thick, densely scaly, and ascending or erect. The blades are one-pinnate with many sessile pinnae and a terminal one resembling the laterals.

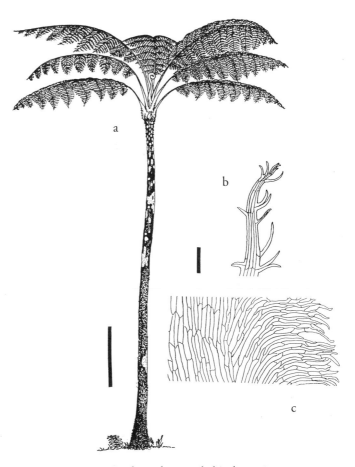

Figure 13.32.1. *Cyathea arborea:* a. habit, bar = 1 m (3 ft.), after Little and Wadsworth (1964); b. tip of stipe scale ending in several cells (not a bristle or hair), bar = 0.1 mm; c. margin of scale, with outer border of cells oriented at right angles to the central cells, bar = 0.1 mm.

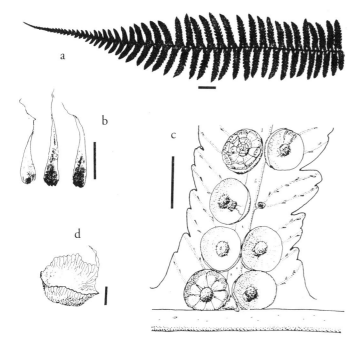

Figure 13.32.2. *Cyathea arborea:* a. pinnule, bar = 1 cm (0.4 in.); b. stipe scale, bar = 1 cm (0.4 in.); c. detail of segment with bullate scale at base, bar = 1 mm, illustration by P. J. Edwards, used with permission; d. enlargement of bullate scale, bar = 0.1 mm, illustration by P. J. Edwards, used with permission.

Figure 13.33.1. *Cyclopeltis semicordata:* a. habit, bar = 10 cm (4 in.); b. sori with peltate indusia, bar = 5 mm (0.2 in.).

The veins are free, and the sori are round and covered by peltate indusia.

The peltate indusium immediately separates *Cyclopeltis* from *Dryopteris* and *Thelypteris,* which it superficially resembles. It differs from *Polystichum* by having entire, not spiny, margins and pinnae that lack an inner, upward-pointing ear.

The genus, which consists of five species, is native to tropical America and southeastern Asia. The genus name comes from the Greek *kyklos,* circle, and *pelte,* shield.

Cyclopeltis semicordata (Swartz) J. Smith

FIGURE 13.33.1

Tender

A medium-sized fern with erect rhizomes. Best grown under medium light in moist garden soil. The plants are occasionally grown in Florida.

Cyclopeltis semicordata has one-pinnate fronds with sessile pinnae that have a semicircular basal lobe overlapping the rachis. The upper surfaces of the rachises and costae bear short hairs, as is typical for ferns related to *Ctenitis* and *Tectaria.* It is widespread in the American tropics where it typically grows on wet forest floors.

Cyrtomium

FIGURES 13.34.1, 2

syn. *Phanerophlebia*

This genus of terrestrial or rock-inhabiting ferns is well represented by the house holly fern (*Cyrtomium falcatum*), widely grown indoors in pots for its leathery, glossy green, durable foliage. The most common cultivar in nurseries is the Rockford fern (*C. falcatum* 'Rockfordianum'), which has irregularly fringed pinna margins. This plant is easy to grow, but its soil should be kept on the moist-dry side. It has become naturalized in parts of the United States with mild winters. In the wild *Cyrtomium* grows in the soil or on rocks, not as epiphytes.

Cyrtomium can usually be distinguished by erect, scaly rhizomes; one-pinnate, evergreen fronds; netted veins; and round sori covered by an umbrella-shaped indusium. The lateral pinnae tend to be nearly equal in size, and the terminal pinna usually resembles the lateral ones, except that the base can be lobed.

Some pteridologists classify the New World species of *Cyrtomium* (which are rarely cultivated) in *Phanerophlebia* because those species have casually to sparingly netted veins like *Phanerophlebia* and in contrast to the Old World species of *Cyrtomium.* At the other extreme, *Cyrtomium* and

Figure 13.34.1. *Cyrtomium falcatum:* habit.

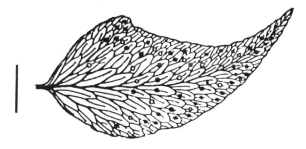

Figure 13.34.2. *Cyrtomium falcatum:* veins, sori, and indusia, bar = 1 cm (0.4 in.).

Figure 13.34.3. *Cyrtomium caryotideum:* a. frond, bar = 5 cm (2 in.); b. serrate-spinulose margin, bar = 5 mm (0.2 in.); c. indusium, bar = 1 mm.

Phanerophlebia are sometimes merged into *Polystichum*. For more information on the classification of these ferns, see Kurata (1963) and Yatskievych (1996).

Cyrtomium is native to the tropics and subtropics of the world and contains about 15 species. The genus name comes from the Greek *kyrtoma,* arch, referring to the veins that anastomose in arches in some species.

Cyrtomium caryotideum (Wallich ex Hooker & Greville) C. Presl   FIGURE 13.34.3
Dwarf holly fern
Hardy, Zone 6

A medium-sized fern with erect rhizomes. Grows well under medium light in moist-dry, basic(?) garden soil or potting mix. In some areas of the United States, such as the Southeast and southern California, the crown seems to succumb to a disease. For some reason the crowns often produce aborted fronds and eventually stop growing.

Cyrtomium caryotideum is characterized by three to six pairs of large pinnae. The pinnae are hastate or have a triangular acuminate ear or are earless. They are dull green and densely spiny-serrate along the margins. The sori are often sparse or absent near the margins, and the indusium margin is distinctly erose-dentate to fimbriate. The species is native to Japan, China, Taiwan, Vietnam, India, the Philippines, and Hawaii.

A putative hybrid with *Cyrtomium falcatum* occurs in the trade and needs further study. Its frond and pinnae resemble *C. falcatum,* but the pinnae are fewer and further apart and have sparingly spiny-serrate margins and erose-dentate to fimbriate indusia, as in *C. caryotideum.*

Cyrtomium falcatum (Linnaeus f.) C. Presl
FIGURES 13.34.1, 2, 4, 5; PLATE 24
House holly fern
Semi-hardy or hardier, reportedly to −12°C (10°F), Zone (6)7

A medium-sized fern with erect rhizomes. Grows well under medium to high light in moist-dry garden soil or potting mix. The plants are easy to cultivate and have attractive evergreen or semi-evergreen fronds. They tolerate drier air than most ferns.

The fronds of *Cyrtomium falcatum* are about 75 cm (30 in.) tall and bear 10 (rarely 8) or more pinna pairs. The pinnae are thick, leathery, and dark glossy green. In wild plants the margins are nearly entire, although a few obscure,

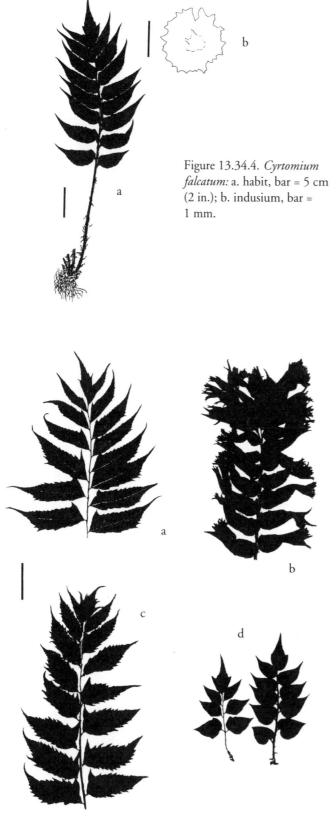

Figure 13.34.4. *Cyrtomium falcatum:* a. habit, bar = 5 cm (2 in.); b. indusium, bar = 1 mm.

minute teeth may be present. The indusia margins are erose. This species is native to India, China, and Japan.

The major cultivars are

'Butterfieldii'. Butterfield holly fern. Figure 13.34.5a. Margins coarsely serrate.

'Mayi'. May fern. Figure 13.34.5b. Fronds often forked or branched; pinna apices widened, somewhat ruffled, and irregularly lacerate-toothed.

'Rockfordianum'. Rockford holly fern. Figure 13.34.5c. Pinna margins regularly fringed, somewhat like a holly leaf. This cultivar is common in the trade.

An unnamed dwarf form (Figure 13.34.5d) is reported to be sexual whereas the other cultivars are apogamous. This dwarf form is a choice plant presently in limited circulation.

Cyrtomium fortunei J. Smith   FIGURE 13.34.6
Hardy, Zone 5(6)

A medium-sized fern with erect rhizomes. Grows well under medium light in moist-dry garden soil or potting mix. The plants are easy to grow from spores and have attractive evergreen fronds.

Cyrtomium fortunei resembles *C. falcatum* but has gray-green, less glossy, less leathery fronds. There are 10–25 pairs of pinnae and these have serrate margins, at least distally. The terminal pinna is smaller than the lower lateral ones, and the indusium margins are entire or subentire. The species is native to Japan, South Korea, southeastern China, and Indochina.

This species varies tremendously and its varieties sometimes intergrade.

Figure 13.34.5. *Cyrtomium falcatum,* frond variants: a. 'Butterfieldii'; b. 'Mayi'; c. 'Rockfordianum'; d. unnamed variant. Bar = 5 cm (2 in.).

Figure 13.34.6. *Cyrtomium fortunei:* a. frond, bar = 5 cm (2 in.); b. indusium, bar = 1 mm.

var. *clivicola* (Makino) Tagawa. Upper surfaces of the blades matte yellow-green; pinnae typically in about 10 (15) pairs, usually to 4 cm (1.5 in.) long, mostly eared at the base; indusium margins somewhat erose. Native to China and Japan.

var. *fortunei*. Upper surfaces of the blades deep green, shiny; pinnae in 15–25 pairs, less than 2–3 cm (0.75–1.2 in.) wide, generally truncate and nearly earless; indusium margins entire. The indusia are grayish white throughout (concolorous). Native to Japan, South Korea, southeastern China, Indochina, and Thailand.

var. *intermedium* Tagawa. Pinnae about 15 (8–19) pairs, bases widely wedge-shaped, weakly eared or not, gradually narrowed toward an attenuate apex. The indusia are blackish in the center. Native to Japan. Some of the trade material in the United States named as this variety probably represents var. *clivicola*.

Cyrtomium lonchitoides (H. Christ) H. Christ
FIGURE 13.34.7

Semi-hardy (?)

A medium-sized fern with erect rhizomes. Best grown under medium light in moist garden soil or potting mix.

Cyrtomium lonchitoides is characterized by stipes only 5–10 cm (2–4 in.) long and elongate, lanceolate, thin-tex-

tured blades about 30 cm (12 in.) long and 9 cm (3.5 in.) wide. The pinnae are distant from one another, nearly opposite or alternate, and crenate-serrate. The apex is unusual in being short and deeply pinnatifid. The indusium margins are erose. The species is native to China.

Cyrtomium macrophyllum (Makino) Tagawa
FIGURES 13.34.8, 9

Big-leaf holly fern
Semi-hardy, Zone 6(7)

A medium-sized fern with erect rhizomes. Grows under medium light in moist-dry garden soil or potting mix. The evergreen fronds are a lighter green than those of *Cyrtomium falcatum*.

Cyrtomium macrophyllum has 2–8 (12) pinna pairs, with the lateral pinnae more than 4 cm (1.5 in.) wide and entire or slightly toothed toward the tip. The pinna bases are rounded to broadly wedge-shaped, without ears, and the terminal pinna is larger than or nearly the same size as the lateral pinnae. The indusia are nearly entire. The species is native to Japan, China, and the Himalayas.

var. *tukusicola* (Tagawa) Tagawa (*Cyrtomium tukusicola* Tagawa). Figure 13.34.9. Separated from var. *macrophyllum* by wedge-shaped pinnae and indusia that are black-brown in the center but pale at the margins. Native to Japan (Honshu and Kyushu). Evergreen and hardy in Salt Lake City, Utah.

Figure 13.34.7. *Cyrtomium lonchitoides:* habit, bar = 5 cm (2 in.).

Figure 13.34.8. *Cyrtomium macrophyllum* var. *macrophyllum:* frond, bar = 5 cm (2 in.).

Figure 13.34.9. *Cyrtomium macrophyllum* var. *tukusicola:* frond, bar = 5 cm (2 in.).

Figure 13.35.1. *Cystopteris fragilis:* habit.

ing rhizomes and medium-sized, triangular fronds that are three-pinnate-pinnatifid. The plants are easy to grow from spores and may readily volunteer. This native of Japan and Taiwan prefers partial shade and moist garden soil. It is listed as hardy to Zone 8. In warmer zones, care must be taken not to overwater during the cool months and when the plant is in its deciduous period.

Cystopteris, which contains about 20 species, is native to the temperate zones and to montane areas in the tropics.

Cystopteris
Bladder fern

FIGURES 13.35.1, 2

The bladder-like indusia are the source of the common name of the genus *Cystopteris*. These mostly small ferns with delicate foliage are used in shaded rock gardens and on damp banks. They are hardy in cold-temperate areas, and a few species are adapted to boreal or alpine climates. *Cystopteris* is seldom cultivated in warmer climates because of its deciduous nature and need for a cold rest period. Many species thrive in basic soils.

The genus is characterized by two vascular bundles in the stipe; thin, herbaceous blades one- to three-pinnate-pinnatifid; free veins; and round sori covered by an arched-inflated indusium. The latter trait is often difficult to see because it gets pushed aside by the sporangia as they mature. On young leaves, the indusium appears scale-like or hood-shaped and is attached beneath the sorus on the side closest to the midrib.

The characteristics used to distinguish the species of *Cystopteris* overlap considerably, and therefore the species can be difficult to identify. The widespread *Cystopteris fragilis* is particularly variable and is considered by some botanists to comprise several species. *Cystopteris* might be confused with *Woodsia,* which differs by having the indusium surrounding the underside of the sorus rather than attached to one side.

Cystopteris also resembles *Acystopteris,* a genus represented in the trade by *Acystopteris japonica* (Luerssen) Nakai. It can be separated from *Cystopteris* by the multicellular hairs on its fronds and by the small or absent indusia. *Acystopteris japonica* is a deciduous species with long-creep-

Figure 13.35.2. *Cystopteris fragilis:* sori and indusia.

The genus name comes from the Greek *kystos,* bladder, and *pteris,* fern, and refers to the inflated indusium covering the sorus.

Cystopteris alpina (Lamarck) Desvaux   FIGURE 13.35.3
syn. *Cystopteris fragilis* subsp. *alpina* (Lamarck) Hartman,
   C. regia of authors, not (Linnaeus) Desvaux
Hardy

A small fern with short-creeping rhizomes and deciduous leaves. Grows under low-medium light in moist, basic garden soil or potting mix.

   Cystopteris alpina resembles *C. fragilis* in growth habit and leaf shape but differs by the pinnules being narrower and wedge-shaped, more finely divided, and the veins ending in a marginal notch. In nature it usually grows on limestone. It is native to the mountains of Europe, Asia Minor, and northeastern Africa.

Cystopteris bulbifera (Linnaeus) Bernhardi
FIGURE 13.35.4

Berry bladder fern, bulblet bladder fern
Very hardy, Zone 3

A small to medium fern with short-creeping rhizomes and deciduous fronds bearing buds along the rachises and (less frequently) the costae. Thrives under low-medium light in

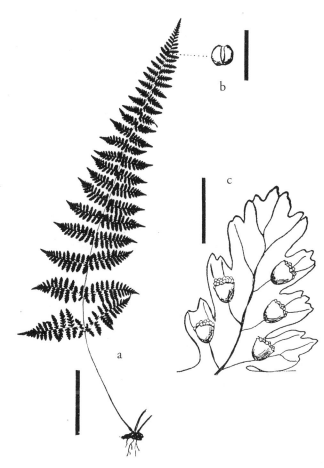

Figure 13.35.4. *Cystopteris bulbifera:* a. habit, bar = 5 cm (2 in.); b. leaf bud, bar = 1 cm (0.4 in.); c. pinnule with sori and indusia, bar = 3 mm.

Figure 13.35.3. *Cystopteris alpina:* habit, bar = 5 cm (2 in.).

moist-wet, basic garden soil or potting mix. The plants are easy to grow in temperate climates and are readily propagated from bulblets.

   Cystopteris bulbifera is the only species of this genus that bears large, green, fleshy bulblets along the rachises and costae, or has reddish stipes (although this color often fades with age). The blades are thin and one- to two-pinnate-pinnatifid, and the rachis and costa usually bear tiny gland-tipped hairs, especially while young (magnification needed). The veins end in teeth, not in sinuses. This species is native to (primarily) the eastern United States and adjacent Canada.

   'Crispa'. Margins ruffled.

Cystopteris dickieana Sim   FIGURE 13.35.5
syn. *Cystopteris fragilis* subsp. *dickieana* (Sim) Hylander
Dickie's bladder fern
Hardy

A small fern with deciduous leaves clumped along a short-creeping rhizome. Grows well under low-medium light in moist-wet, drained garden soil or potting mix.

Figure 13.35.5.
Cystopteris dickieana:
habit, bar = 5 cm (2 in.).

Figure 13.35.6.
Cystopteris fragilis:
a. habit, bar = 5 cm
(2 in.); b. sorus and
indusia, bar = 1 mm,
after Knobloch and
Correll (1962).

Cystopteris dickieana greatly resembles *C. fragilis,* and some pteridologists argue that it is not distinct. It is said to differ primarily by its wrinkled, warty (not spiny) spore surfaces. The blades and pinnules also tend to be narrower, and the pinnae are typically overlapping. The veins end mostly in marginal notches. The species is native to northern North America, Greenland, Iceland, Europe, Asia, and northern Africa.

Cystopteris fragilis (Linnaeus) Bernhardi

FIGURES 13.35.1, 2, 6

Brittle bladder fern, fragile bladder fern
Very hardy, Zone 1

A small fern with short-creeping rhizomes and deciduous leaves. Grows well under low-medium light in garden soil or potting mix kept moist-wet. This species is easy to grow.

The blades of *Cystopteris fragilis* are thin and herbaceous, with nonoverlapping pinnae and veins ending mostly in teeth, not shallow notches. The pinnules are roughly triangular and sessile or very short-stalked. Minute gland-tipped hairs, present in some other bladder ferns, are absent. The species is extremely variable and one of the most widespread ferns in the world, occurring on every continent.

An unnamed, crested form is reported in cultivation.

Cystopteris montana (Lamarck) Bernhardi ex Desvaux

FIGURE 13.35.7

Mountain bladder fern
Very hardy, Zone 1

A small fern with deciduous fronds and medium-creeping rhizomes. Grows well under low-medium light in basic, moist-wet, well-drained garden soil or potting mix.

Cystopteris montana is easily distinguished from other bladder ferns by its nearly black, medium-creeping rhizomes and wide, pentagonal blades. It is native to the mountains of North America, Europe, and Siberia.

The fronds of this species are cyanogenic; when crushed, they emit the pungent odor of prussic acid, which resembles the smell of burnt almonds. Presumably this deters herbivores.

Cystopteris protrusa (Weatherby) Blasdell

FIGURE 13.35.8

syn. *Cystopteris fragilis* var. *protrusa* Weatherby
Southern fragile fern, woodland bladder fern, lowland
    bladder fern
Hardy, Zone 5

A small fern with creeping rhizomes and clumped, deciduous fronds. Thrives under low-medium light in moist-wet garden soil or potting mix.

Cystopteris protrusa resembles *C. fragilis,* but its creeping rhizomes protrude 1–4 cm (0.5–1.5 in.) beyond the current year's cluster of fronds. Another difference is that the pinnules on large, fertile leaves tend to be distinctly stalked, whereas in *C. fragilis* they are sessile or nearly so. The rhizomes bear yellowish hairs not found in any other

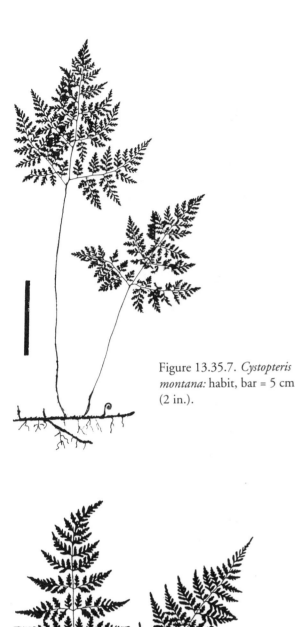

Figure 13.35.7. *Cystopteris montana:* habit, bar = 5 cm (2 in.).

Figure 13.35.8. *Cystopteris protrusa:* habit, bar = 5 cm (2 in.).

species of *Cystopteris.* This species is native to the eastern United States, where it grows on shaded forest floors.

Cystopteris reevesiana Lellinger   FIGURE 13.35.9
syn. *Cystopteris fragilis* subsp. *tenuifolia* Clute
Southwestern brittle fern
Hardy, Zone 5

A small fern with short-creeping rhizomes and clumped, deciduous leaves. Thrives under medium light in moist garden soil or potting mix.

Cystopteris reevesiana resembles *C. fragilis* but has longer creeping rhizomes, stipes that are mostly dark purple at base, and more finely divided blades, with the proximal pinnae one-pinnate-pinnatifid to two-pinnate. It is native to the southwestern United States.

Figure 13.35.9. *Cystopteris reevesiana:* frond, bar = 5 cm (2 in.).

Cystopteris tennesseensis Shaver   FIGURE 13.35.10
Tennessee bladder fern
Hardy, Zone 6

A small fern with short-creeping rhizomes and clumped, deciduous leaves. Thrives under low-medium light in moist-wet, basic garden soil or potting mix.

Cystopteris tennesseensis is a fertile hybrid resulting from a cross involving *C. bulbifera* and *C. protrusa.* It can be difficult to distinguish from its parents. Like *C. bulbifera, C. tennesseensis* bears bulblets on the lower surfaces of the

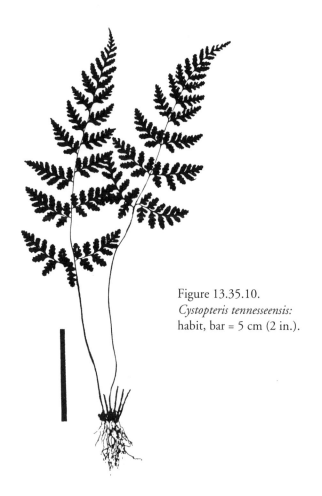

Figure 13.35.10.
Cystopteris tennesseensis:
habit, bar = 5 cm (2 in.).

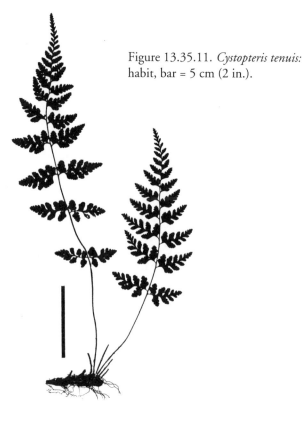

Figure 13.35.11. *Cystopteris tenuis:*
habit, bar = 5 cm (2 in.).

rachis and (sometimes) costae, but the bulblets are smaller, scalier, and less fleshy. Minute gland-tipped hairs occur on the rachises and costae (magnification needed), a trait imparted from *C. bulbifera.* The veins end in notches or teeth. A characteristic of the Tennessee bladder fern not shared by other bladder ferns is that nearly all the leaves, even the smallest, bear sori. This species is native to the central and eastern United States, where it grows on limestone. It is *the* common bladder fern in the Ozarks of Missouri and Arkansas.

Cystopteris tenuis (Michaux) Desvaux

FIGURE 13.35.11

syn. *Cystopteris fragilis* var. *mackayi* G. Lawson
Mackay's brittle fern
Very hardy, Zone 4

A small fern with short-creeping rhizomes. Grows best under medium light in moist soil or potting mix. The leaves are deciduous and absent during the winter months.

Cystopteris tenuis resembles *C. fragilis* and can be difficult to distinguish. It typically has pinnules that are wedge-shaped at the base, whereas those of *C. fragilis* are broadest at the base and triangular. The pinnae and pinnules also tend to be more ascending than those of *C. fragilis,* although

this takes practice to recognize. *Cystopteris tenuis* is a fertile hybrid originating from a cross between *C. fragilis* and *C. protrusa.* It is native to the United States and Canada.

Davallia

FIGURES 13.36.1–3

syn. *Araiostegia, Humata, Pachypleuria, Scyphularia, Trogostolon*

Davallias are among the most beautiful and treasured cultivated ferns. Their broad, lacy, often shiny fronds are usually displayed in hanging baskets in conservatories or greenhouses, where the entire basket may be hidden by the foliage. The most sought-after davallias are those with finely divided fronds, such as certain selections of the Fiji davallia (*Davallia fejeensis*) that bear numerous segments about the width of a pencil lead. The warm-temperate species are grown outdoors in mild climates of the United States, although most of the nursery stock is used indoors.

Besides hanging baskets, davallias are planted over rocks or as ground covers so that their creeping rhizomes can be seen—the rhizomes are often described as "furry feet." One species with such rhizomes is the bear's-foot fern (*Davallia tyermannii*). It is a choice fern of small to medium size with durable, triangular, moderately fine-divided fronds. Although slower growing than many other common species, *D. tyermannii* less frequently needs repotting. Resembling the bear's-foot fern, the squirrel's-foot fern, *D. mariesii* var. *stenolepis* (*D. trichomanoides* of trade) is the most common species in the trade. It has light brown, furry rhizomes and

Figure 13.36.1. *Davallia mariesii* var. *stenolepis:* habit.

Figure 13.36.3. *Davallia mariesii* var. *stenolepis:* sori and indusia.

Figure 13.36.2. *Davallia mariesii* var. *stenolepis:* frond.

is faster growing and softer in appearance than the bear's-foot fern, but it is just as robust and adaptable.

The small Japanese ball fern (*Davallia mariesii* var. *mariesii*) is now rarely seen in the United States. During the 1960s it was imported from Japan with the rhizomes tied and shaped into balls, monkeys, pergolas, and other figures. These were hung in gardens and patios, and when the fronds emerged, the plants would take on the outline of the ball or figure. In warm-temperate gardens the Japanese ball fern can be planted as a ground cover. Its small, triangular, deciduous fronds are attractive, and some forms appear densely leafy due to overlapping pinnae.

The diminutive *Davallia parvula* is another attractive species. It has finely dissected fronds and is often used in terrariums or bottle gardens where humidity is high and the tiny plant is safe from being stepped on.

Temperature tolerances of davallias are incompletely known, but *Davallia mariesii* var. *mariesii* can be grown outdoors where the average minimum January temperature is about −1°C (30°F). *Davallia tyermannii* probably tolerates a similar temperature minimum. Other warm-temperate species that are likely to tolerate short, infrequent freezes are *D. canariensis, D. griffithiana, D. pyxidata, D. mariesii* var. *stenolepis, D. tasmanii,* and (marginally) *D. trichomanoides.* Almost all the others are tender outdoors, except in areas of Florida and the Hawaiian Islands. For more information about cultivation, see Hoshizaki (1981) and the section in Chapter 10 titled "*Davallia* and Relatives."

The genus *Davallia* has several distinctive characteristics. Depending on the species, plants can be epiphytic, epilithic, or terrestrial. The rhizomes are always long-creeping and scaly, the scales being mostly ovate to lanceolate and peltate; if basally attached, the scales are reniform or cordate with overlapping bases. The stipes are jointed to the rhizomes and fall off cleanly, leaving a circular scar. The blades are anadromous and vary from simple to finely dissected (up to four-pinnate) and from lanceolate to triangular in shape. The rachis is raised and grooved on the upper surface, with the grooves running into those of the costae. The veins are free, not netted. Some species have false veins that run parallel to the main veins but are not connected to them. Unlike true veins, the false veins do not conduct water or mineral nutrients; presumably they lend mechanical support to the blade tissue. The sori are close to the margin and covered by an indusium that may be round, scale-like, shell-shaped, pouch-shaped, or more often cup- or tubular-shaped.

The two recent studies on the delineation of davalliod genera differ considerably. Kato (1985) recognized several genera whereas Nooteboom (1994) united most of them. In this work we have followed Nooteboom, but for those wishing to use the genera recognized by Kato, we list their differences below.

Davallia, in the traditional sense, has indusia that are attached all the way up the sides, forming a pocket with a single opening toward the leaf margin. The cultivated species that belong here are *Davallia canariensis, D. denticulata, D. divaricata, D. embolstegia, D. epiphylla, D. fejeensis, D. griffithiana* (though with the indusia attached only slightly up the sides), *D. lorrainii, D. mariesii, D. pyxidata, D. solida,* and *D. tasmanii.*

Humata was separated from *Davallia* by its leathery fronds and indusia attached only at the base, not along the sides. The cultivated species that belong here include *Davallia falcinella, D. heterophylla, D. parvula, D. repens,* and *D. tyermannii.*

Kato (1985) recognized several segregate genera from *Humata*, such as *Trogostolon* and *Pachypleuria*. Under this system, the genus *Trogostolon* includes *Davallia falcinella.* The characters of *Trogostolon* are dark brown, peltate, toothed rhizome scales with needle-like apices; fronds finely dissected with one vein in the ultimate segments; sori at a vein fork; and round indusia attached by the base and halfway up the sides. If Kato's findings are followed, *Pachypleuria* includes *D. parvula* and *D. repens.* The characters that define *Pachypleuria* are peltate, ciliate rhizome scales with wart-like outgrowths on the lower surface; fronds mostly small, leathery, linear to deltate, simple to bipinnatifid, rarely finely dissected; sori at a vein fork or bend; and firm indusia attached at the base or slightly up the sides.

Scyphularia was segregated from *Davallia* mainly by the needle-like and bristly scale tips of its rhizome. Cultivated species include *Davallia pentaphylla* and *D. triphylla,* although the latter's rhizome scales are not strongly needle-like and bristly.

Araiostegia was delineated primarily by its thin blades, finely divided fronds, scaly rachises and costae, and delicate, roundish or kidney-shaped indusia attached only at the base. The species in this group are rarely cultivated but include *Davallia hymenophylloides* and *D. pulchra.*

In his monograph on the genus *Davallia,* Nooteboom (1994) changed the names of several well-known cultivated species. These changes leave many plants with distinct and consistent characteristics (at least in horticulture) essentially without names. Because this will bring confusion to gardeners, many of the species synonymized by Nooteboom are still recognized in this book. Eventually, most of these reduced species should be given cultivar status under the cultivar-group category discussed in Chapter 12.

This genus is named for Edmond Davall (1763–1798), a Swiss plant collector. It contains about 35 species native to the Old World tropics, mainly in Asia and the eastern Pacific.

Davallia canariensis (Linnaeus) Smith   FIGURE 13.36.4
syn. *Davallia portugal* Horticulture
Canary Island davallia, hare's-foot fern
Semi-hardy to semi-tender

A medium-sized fern with medium- to long-creeping rhizomes. Grows well under medium light or full sun in drained, moist-dry garden soil, potting mix, or uncut moss. The plants are easily cultivated but are moderately slow growing. The new growth is seasonal.

Davallia canariensis is characterized by thick rhizomes up to 18 mm (0.75 in.) wide that are white-waxy beneath the scales. The blades are broadly triangular, about 40 cm (16 in.) long and wide, and have a fleshy lip present at the junction of the costa and rachis on the upper ridge. The indusia are cup-shaped. This species is native to Portugal, Spain, the Canary Islands, and Morocco.

Davallia denticulata (N. L. Burman) Mettenius ex
Kuhn   FIGURE 13.36.5
syn. *Davallia elegans* Hedwig
Toothed davallia
Tender

A medium-large fern with medium- to long-creeping rhizomes. Grows well under medium light in moist-dry potting mix or uncut moss with good drainage. The plants are easy to grow and tend to volunteer in suitable climates.

The rhizome scales of *Davallia denticulata* are toothed and narrowed abruptly from a broad base. The blade segments are oblong, often with a faint line (false vein) parallel to and between the true veins. The indusia are small and cup-shaped. This species is native to the Old World tropics.

A crested form with somewhat narrower fronds is presently cultivated.

Figure 13.36.4. *Davallia canariensis:* a. frond, bar = 5 cm (2 in.); b. rhizome scales, bar = 5 mm (0.2 in.); c. fertile segments, bar = 5 mm (0.2 in.); d. swollen lips at rachis-costa junctions, bar = 5 mm (0.2 in.).

Figure 13.36.5. *Davallia denticulata:* a. frond, bar = 5 cm (2 in.); b. rhizome scales, bar = 5 mm (0.2 in.); c. fertile segments, bar = 5 mm (0.2 in.); d. sterile segment with false veins, bar = 5 mm (0.2 in.).

Davallia divaricata Blume   FIGURE 13.36.6
Tender

A medium-large fern with medium- to long-creeping rhizomes. Grows well under low to high light in moist-dry potting mix or uncut moss with good drainage. The young fronds are red.

Davallia divaricata has rhizome scales that are thin, large, and uniformly reddish brown. The rachises and costae are reddish; the indusia, cup-shaped. This species is native to tropical Asia and Malaysia.

Davallia embolstegia Copeland   FIGURE 13.36.7
Tender

A medium-large fern with medium- to long-creeping rhizomes. Grows well under medium light in well-drained, moist-dry potting mix or uncut moss. This species needs heat and humidity to grow well. It is rarely cultivated.

The rhizome scales attach at a notch in the cordate base (not peltate), and the segments lack false veins. The stipe scales of *Davallia embolstegia* are mostly narrowly triangular to lanceolate and long-acuminate. Indusia are cup-shaped with an elongated free lip. This species resembles *D. epiphylla* but is larger and has ungrooved or only weakly grooved rachises and nonpeltate rhizome scales. *Davallia embolstegia* is native to Borneo and the Philippines.

Davallia epiphylla Sprengel   FIGURE 13.36.8
syn. *Davallia denticulata* var. *elata* (G. Forster)
    Mettenius ex Kuhn
Tender

A medium-sized fern with medium- to long-creeping rhizomes. Grows well under medium light in drained, moist-dry potting mix or uncut moss.

Davallia epiphylla has peltate rhizome scales, and the larger stipe scales are broadly heart-shaped at the base and abruptly narrowed above to a thread-like tip. The indusia are cup-shaped with an elongated free lip. This species is native to Malaysia, New Guinea, and the Pacific Islands.

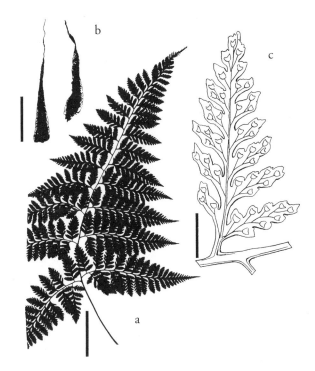

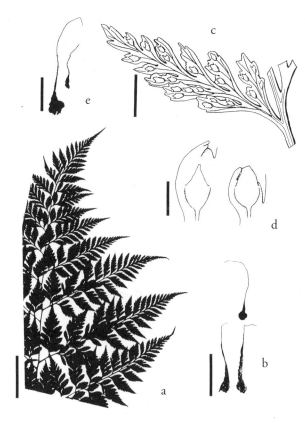

Figure 13.36.6. *Davallia divaricata:* a. frond, bar = 5 cm (2 in.); b. rhizome scales, bar = 5 mm (0.2 in.); c. fertile segments, bar = 5 mm (0.2 in.).

Figure 13.36.8. *Davallia epiphylla:* a. frond, bar = 5 cm (2 in.); b. rhizome scales, bar = 5 mm (0.2 in.); c. fertile segments, bar = 5 mm (0.2 in.); d. indusia, bar = 1 mm; e. stipe scales, bar = 2 mm.

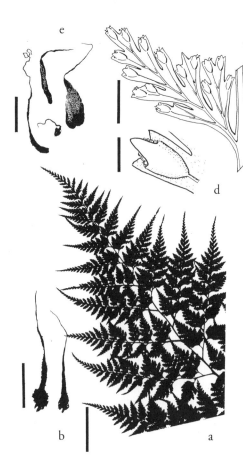

Figure 13.36.7. *Davallia embolstegia:* a. frond, bar = 5 cm (2 in.); b. rhizome scales, bar = 5 mm (0.2 in.); c. fertile segments, bar = 5 mm (0.2 in.); d. indusium, bar = 1 mm; e. stipe scales, bar = 2 mm.

This species is readily separated from all the others, except *Davallia embolstegia,* by the free lip on the indusium. The rarely grown *D. embolstegia* is much larger, more finely divided, and has nonpeltate rhizome scales.

Davallia falcinella C. Presl   FIGURE 13.36.9
syn. *Humata falcinella* (C. Presl) Copeland, *Trogostolon falcinellus* (C. Presl) Copeland
Very tender

A small fern with medium-creeping rhizomes and finely divided fronds. Grows best under medium light in well-drained, moist-dry uncut moss. The plants are sensitive to overwatering.

The rhizome scales of *Davallia falcinella* are peltate, but they narrow abruptly above the base into a firm, dark brown bristle. The blades are up to four-pinnate, and the indusia are round and attached halfway up the sides. The species is endemic to the Philippines.

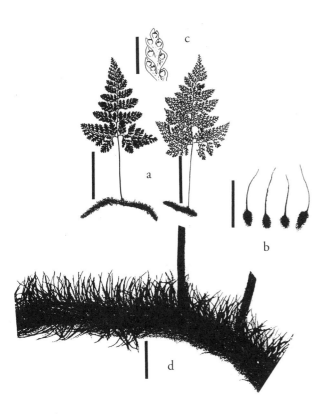

Figure 13.36.9. *Davallia falcinella*: a. habits, sterile frond (left) and fertile frond (right), bar = 5 cm (2 in.); b. rhizome scales, bar = 5 mm (0.2 in.); c. fertile segments, bar = 5 mm (0.2 in.); d. rhizome with bristly scales, bar = 5 mm (0.2 in.).

Figure 13.36.10. *Davallia fejeensis*: a. frond, bar = 5 cm (2 in.); b. rhizome scales, bar = 5 mm (0.2 in.); c. rhizome scale hairs, bar = 1 mm; d. fertile segments, bar = 5 mm (0.2 in.).

Davallia fejeensis Hooker   FIGURES 13.36.10, 11
syn. *Davallia solida* var. *fejeensis* (Hooker) Nooteboom
Fiji davallia
Tender

A small to medium fern with medium- to long-creeping rhizomes. Grows well under medium light in drained, moist-dry potting mix or uncut moss.

Davallia fejeensis produces fronds that are variable in size and degree of dissection. The blades can be up to five-pinnate, with linear segments supplied by a single vein. The rhizome scale margins bear long hairs. The indusia are tubular and occupy all or nearly all of the segment width. The plants resemble *D. solida* in other details. This species is native to Fiji and the Austral Islands.

This variable plant (see Figure 13.36.11) intergrades into *Davallia solida* (also highly variable) and is often classified as a variety of that species (Nooteboom 1994). The most distinctive cultivars include:

'Major'. Figure 13.36.11j. Fronds larger, to 60 cm (2 ft.) long, moderately finely divided; the segments oblanceolate, 1 mm at the narrowest part. The thick rhizomes grow straight and away from the substrate.

'Plumosa'. Figure 13.36.11i. Fronds medium-sized, pendulous, finely divided, the segments linear, to 0.5 mm wide.

Davallia griffithiana Hooker   FIGURE 13.36.12
syn. *Humata griffithiana* (Hooker) C. Christensen
Semi-tender

A small to medium fern with medium- to long-creeping rhizomes. Grows well under medium light in drained, moist-dry potting mix or uncut moss. This species is slow growing.

Davallia griffithiana resembles *D. tyermannii* but its rhizome scales are triangular rather than ovate-attenuate, and the blade is somewhat more foliaceous. In addition, the rounded indusia are attached a short ways up the sides, not at the base. Nooteboom (1994) considered *D. tyermannii* a synonym of *D. griffithiana*. This species is native to northern India, China, and Taiwan.

Figure 13.36.11. *Davallia fejeensis* variations: all lower pinnae (except h, a middle pinna), all unnamed cultivars, except d. 'Dwarf Ripple', e. 'False Plumosa', i. 'Plumosa', and j. 'Major'. Bar = 5 cm (2 in.).

Davallia heterophylla J. E. Smith   FIGURE 13.36.13
syn. *Humata heterophylla* (J. E. Smith) Desvaux
Tender to very tender

A small fern with medium-creeping rhizomes that often become hanging and vine-like. Grows well under humid conditions and medium light in drained, moist potting mix or uncut moss. The plants are frequently used for terrariums or hanging baskets.

Davallia heterophylla has dimorphic fronds. The sterile ones are simple, lanceolate-ovate, entire and often truncate at the base. In contrast, the fertile fronds are narrower and lobed. Semicircular indusia are attached by a broad base. The species is native to India, southeastern Asia, Malaysia, Indonesia, the Philippines, New Guinea, and the Pacific Islands.

Davallia hymenophylloides (Blume) Kuhn
FIGURE 13.36.14
syn. *Araiostegia hymenophylloides* (Blume) Copeland,
    Leucostegia hymenophylloides (Blume) Beddome
Tender to very tender

A medium-large fern with medium- to long-creeping rhizomes and deciduous, broad, thin, finely divided fronds. Grows best in drained, moist potting mix or uncut moss.

Davallia hymenophylloides has fleshy rhizomes covered by thin, nearly entire scales. The blades are up to four-pinnate-pinnatifid, sometimes elongate and narrowing toward the base, with ultimate segments narrowly oblong. The indusium is kidney-shaped, to 1 mm wide, and attached at the cordate base. This species is native to India, southeastern Asia, Malaysia, Indonesia, and the Philippines.

Figure 13.36.12. *Davallia griffithiana:* a. habit, with a variant frond on left, bar = 5 cm (2 in.); b. rhizome scales, bar = 5 mm (0.2 in.); c. fertile segments, bar = 5 mm (0.2 in.); d. indusium, bar = 1 mm.

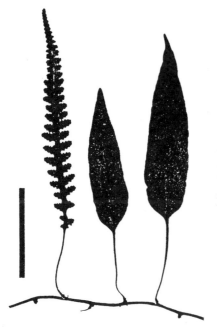

Figure 13.36.13. *Davallia heterophylla:* habit, fertile frond (left) and two sterile fronds (right), bar = 5 cm (2 in.).

Davallia lorrainii Hance   FIGURE 13.36.15

syn. *Davallia trichomanoides* var. *lorrainii* (Hance) Holttum

Tender

A small to medium fern with medium- to long-creeping rhizomes and deciduous fronds. Grows well under medium light in drained, moist-dry potting mix or uncut moss. Avoid overwatering during dormancy.

Davallia lorrainii has a strongly deciduous growth habit and rhizome scales that are dark brown to black with many even, pale hairs borne at nearly right angles to the margin. The round-ovate stipe scales have pale margins bearing hairs similar to those on the rhizome scales. *Davallia lorrainii* resembles *D. trichomanoides* Blume (not of trade), and Nooteboom (1994) considered it a variety of that species. It is native to Asia and the Malayan Archipelago.

Davallia mariesii T. Moore ex Baker

          FIGURES 13.36.1–3, 16, 17; PLATE 5

syn. *Davallia bullata* Hayata

Semi-hardy fern

A small to medium fern with medium- or longer creeping rhizomes and deciduous to semi-evergreen fronds. Best grown under medium light in drained, moist-dry garden soil, potting mix, or uncut moss.

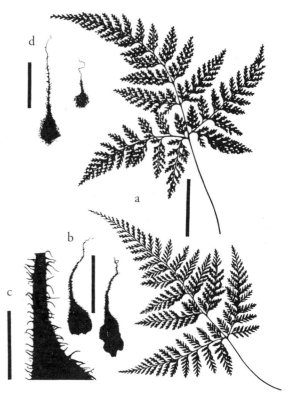

Figure 13.36.15. *Davallia lorrainii:* a. fronds, bar = 5 cm (2 in.); b. rhizome scales, bar = 5 mm (0.2 in.); c. rhizome scale cilia, bar = 1 mm; d. stipe scales, bar = 2 mm.

Figure 13.36.14. *Davallia hymenophylloides:* a. frond, bar = 5 cm (2 in.); b. fertile segments, bar = 2 mm.

Figure 13.36.16. *Davallia mariesii:* a. habit and larger frond (left), bar = 5 cm (2 in.); b. rhizome scales, bar = 5 mm (0.2 in.); c. rhizome scale cilia, bar = 1 mm; d. fertile segments, bar = 5 mm (0.2 in.); e. stipe scales, bar = 2 mm.

Figure 13.36.17. *Davallia mariesii* var. *stenolepis:* a. habit, bar = 5 cm (2 in.); b. rhizome scales, bar = 5 mm (0.2 in.); c. rhizome scale cilia, bar = 2 mm; d. fertile segments, bar = 5 mm (0.2 in.); e. stipe scales, bar = 2 mm.

Davallia mariesii has triangular fronds up to three-pinnate at the base, with stipe scales triangular to ovate or oblong, mostly narrowing abruptly to a long, twisted apex. The whitish tan to brown rhizome scales are lightly pressed to the rhizome, and the margins bear short cilia and teeth. The indusia are short and tubular. This species is native to Korea, Japan, Taiwan, and China.

Nooteboom (1994) considered *Davallia mariesii* to be the same as *D. trichomanoides* var. *trichomanoides.* The plants called *D. mariesii* in horticulture, however, are distinct and important enough in the trade to require maintaining the name.

var. *mariesii.* Japanese ball fern. Figure 13.36.16. Fronds to 15 cm (6 in.) long, triangular, deciduous, the pinnae closely placed, and the pinnules sometimes overlapping. This variety intergrades with var. *stenolepis.* Native to Korea and Japan. In Japan the live rhizomes are gathered when the plant is in its leafless period and tied into balls or other figures and subsequently hung out to grow as a basket fern.

var. *stenolepis* (Hayata) Hoshizaki (*Davallia stenolepis* Hayata, *D. trichomanoides* of trade, not Blume). Squirrel's-foot fern. Figures 13.36.1–3, 17. Fronds to about 20 cm (8 in.) long, nearly evergreen or with a short dormant period between shedding of the old fronds and emergence of the new ones. The pinnae and pinnules do not noticeably overlap. Variety *stenolepis* resembles var. *mariesii* but is only slightly deciduous, larger, and has less crowded, more attenuate pinnae. Native to the Ryuku Islands, South Korea, China, and Taiwan. The variety is easily cultivated but less cold hardy than var. *mariesii.* It is the most widely grown *Davallia* in the United States and is usually sold, incorrectly, as *D. trichomanoides.* Most Japanese botanists consider var. *stenolepis* merely a semi-evergreen, southern variant of *D. mariesii.*

Davallia parvula Wallich ex Hooker & Greville

FIGURE 13.36.18

syn. *Humata parvula* (Wallich) Mettenius, *Pachypleuria parvula* (Wallich) M. Kato

Tender

Very small, with medium-creeping rhizomes and finely divided, triangular blades. Grows well under low-medium light in drained, moist potting mix or uncut moss. The plants need humidity and are best used in terrariums. They are easily harmed by too much fertilizer.

The most distinctive characteristic of *Davallia parvula* is its small size: the fronds are only to 2.5 cm (1 in.) long and broad, with segments less than 1 mm wide. The indusia are rounded and attached at the base. This species is native from Malaysia and Indonesia to New Guinea.

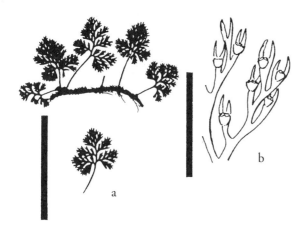

Figure 13.36.18. *Davallia parvula:* a. habit and frond, bar = 5 cm (2 in.); b. fertile segments, bar = 5 mm (0.2 in.).

Davallia pentaphylla Blume

FIGURE 13.36.19

syn. *Davallia pycnocarpa* Brackenridge, *Scyphularia pentaphylla* (Blume) Fée, *S. pycnocarpa* (Brackenridge) Copeland, *S. sinusora* Copeland

Tender

A small fern with medium- to long-creeping rhizomes. Grows best under medium light in well-drained, moist-dry potting mix or uncut moss. This species is easy to grow.

Davallia pentaphylla is distinctive for its one-pinnate blades, typically with five leaflets, and a terminal leaflet that resembles the lateral ones. The leaflets, particularly the basal pair, are sometimes lobed or forked. The rhizome scales are also distinctive by their widely spreading habit and black, needle-like tips, which imparts a bristly appearance. The indusia are tubular. This species is native to Malaysia, Indonesia, New Guinea, and the Pacific Islands.

Nooteboom (1994) did not recognize *Scyphularia pycnocarpa,* a variant that consistently produces lobed or forked lower leaflets (see Figure 13.36.19 lower left).

Figure 13.36.19. *Davallia pentaphylla:* a. habits, with the former *D. pycnocarpa* at lower left, bar = 5 cm (2 in.); b. rhizome and scales, bar = 5 mm (0.2 in.); c. sori and indusia, bar = 5 mm (0.2 in.).

Davallia pulchra D. Don

FIGURE 13.36.20

syn. *Araiostegia pulchra* (D. Don) Copeland

Tender

A small-medium fern with medium- to long-creeping rhizomes. Grows best under medium light in well-drained, moist-dry potting mix or uncut moss.

Davallia pulchra resembles *D. mariesii* var. *stenolepis* but has more-delicate blades and bean-shaped or rounded indusia attached only at the base. It is native from India to Tibet, southeastern Asia, and southern China.

Davallia pyxidata Cavanilles

FIGURE 13.36.21

syn. *Davallia solida* var. *pyxidata* (Cavanilles) Nooteboom

Australian davallia, Australian hare's-foot fern

Semi-hardy to semi-tender, Zones 8–9

A small-medium fern with medium- to long-creeping rhizomes. Best grown under medium-high light in well-drained, moist-dry potting mix or uncut moss. The plants are sometimes used as bedding plants. The stiff, upward-growing rhizomes do not make for a good basket plant.

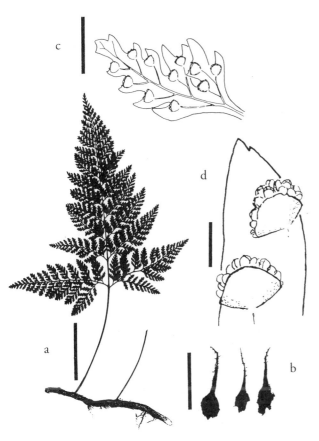

Figure 13.36.20. *Davallia pulchra:* a. habit, bar = 5 cm (2 in.); b. rhizome scales, bar = 5 mm (0.2 in.); c. fertile segment, bar = 5 mm (0.2 in.); d. sori and indusia, bar = 1 mm.

Figure 13.36.21. *Davallia pyxidata:* a. frond, bar = 5 cm (2 in.); b. rhizome scales, bar = 5 mm (0.2 in.); c. ascending rhizome, bar = 10 cm (4 in.); d. fertile segments, bar = 5 mm (0.2 in.); e. apex of sterile pinnule, bar = 5 mm (0.2 in.).

The rhizomes of *Davallia pyxidata* tend to grow stiffly upward and are covered by easily detached, nearly black scales with tapered apices and long-hairy margins. The stipes contain four (sometimes three or five) vascular bundles. The secondary pinnules are mostly pointed, with the apex ending in a dominant tooth. The indusia are short and tubular. This species is native to Australia.

Nooteboom (1994) classified *Davallia pyxidata* as a variety of *D. solida;* however, *D. solida* var. *solida* differs most conspicuously by having rhizomes that generally do not grow stiffly upward. Other differences are the lighter-colored rhizome scales, which are difficult to detach whole; stipes with six (three to nine) vascular bundles; more leathery and glossy blades; more obtuse secondary pinnules with apices not ending in a dominant tooth; more obscure veins; and longer indusia. Furthermore, *D. pyxidata* is hardier than the tender *D. solida.* Given these differences, *D. pyxidata* merits recognition as a distinct species.

Davallia repens (Linnaeus f.) Kuhn   FIGURE 13.36.22
syn. *Humata repens* (Linnaeus f.) Diels, *H. vestita*
  (Blume) T. Moore, *Pachypleuria repens* (Linnaeus f.)
  M. Kato
Semi-tender to tender

A small fern with medium-creeping rhizomes. Grows best under warm, humid conditions, preferring medium light and moist-dry, drained potting mix or uncut moss.

The rhizomes of *Davallia repens* are white-waxy beneath the scales. The blades are triangular and deeply pinnately lobed to two-pinnate at the base, with the lower lobes broader and lobed on the lower margin. The indusium is semi-circular and attached only at the base. This species is native from northern India to Japan, and the Mascarene Islands to Australia.

Nooteboom (1994) pointed out the tremendous variation in the group and reduced *Davallia vestita* and other species to *D. repens.*

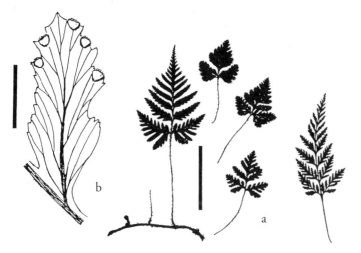

Figure 13.36.22. *Davallia repens:* a. habit and frond variations, with the former *D. vestita* at far right, bar = 5 cm (2 in.); b. fertile segment, bar = 5 mm (0.2 in.).

Figure 13.36.23. *Davallia solida:* a. frond, bar = 5 cm (2 in.); b. rhizome scales, bar = 5 mm (0.2 in.); c. fertile segments, bar = 5 mm (0.2 in.); d. stipe scales, bar = 2 mm.

Davallia solida (G. Forster) Swartz

FIGURES 13.36.23, 24

Polynesian davallia
Tender

A small to medium fern with medium- or longer creeping rhizomes. Grows well under medium light in potting mix or uncut moss kept moist-dry and given good drainage.

The blades of *Davallia solida* are coarsely cut and variable in size and shape. The rhizome scales are long-hairy on the margin and difficult to detach whole. The stipe scales vary greatly in shape, and their margins may have a sparse tangle of hairs. Sometimes the scales are so reduced that they appear as a fine scurf. The segment veins end short of the margin. The indusia are cup-shaped, longer than wide. This species is native to Asia, Malaysia, Australia, and Polynesia.

Many cultivated variants circulate under a variety of names, and often these are difficult to distinguish, except for the following:

'Ruffled Ornata'. Figure 13.36.24. Segments broad, margins ruffled, tips drooping.

Davallia tasmanii Field

FIGURE 13.36.25

Tasman's davallia
Semi-tender

A small fern with medium-creeping rhizomes. Grows well under medium light in drained, moist-dry potting mix or uncut moss. The plants are slow growing and are rarely cultivated.

The rhizome scales of *Davallia tasmanii* bear shaggy hairs, and the blades are often pentagonal and leathery. The veins are obscure, and the indusia are cup-shaped. This species is endemic to New Zealand.

Figure 13.36.24. *Davallia solida* 'Ruffled Ornata': frond, bar = 5 cm (2 in.).

Figure 13.36.25. *Davallia tasmanii:* a. fronds, bar = 5 cm (2 in.); b. rhizome scales, bar = 5 mm (0.2 in.); c. fertile segments, bar = 5 mm (0.2 in.).

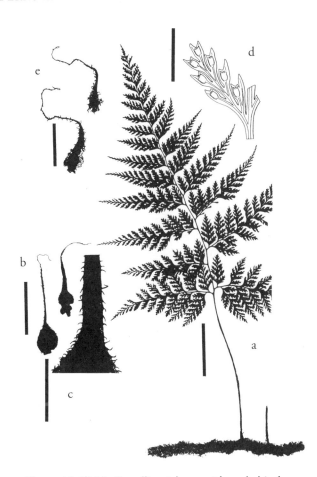

Figure 13.36.26. *Davallia trichomanoides:* a. habit, bar = 5 cm (2 in.); b. rhizome scales, bar = 5 mm (0.2 in.); c. rhizome scale cilia, bar = 1 mm; d. fertile segments, bar = 5 mm (0.2 in.); e. stipe scales, bar = 2 mm.

Davallia trichomanoides Blume   FIGURE 13.36.26
Squirrel's-foot fern
Semi-hardy to semi-tender

A small to medium fern with medium- or long-creeping rhizomes. Grows well under low to high light in drained, moist-dry potting mix or uncut moss. For trade material under the name *Davallia trichomanoides,* see *D. mariesii* var. *stenolepis.*

The reddish brown rhizome scales of *Davallia trichomanoides* spread widely or curl backward, imparting a ruffled appearance. The stipe scales are ovate-triangular, long-attenuate, and ciliate. The pinnae are long-attenuate, and the indusia are cup-shaped. This species is native to Malaysia, New Guinea, and Java. The plants of *D. trichomanoides* in cultivation came from New Guinea.

Nooteboom (1994) broadly construed *Davallia trichomanoides* to include *D. lorrainii, D. mariesii* var. *mariesii, D. mariesii* var. *stenolepis,* and others. *Davallia trichomanoides* resembles the common trade plant *D. mariesii* var. *stenolepis* but has larger, softer, more finely cut fronds and long-tapering pinna apices. The rhizome scales of *D. trichomanoides* also differ by being red-brown (not whitish brown) and widely spreading (not pointing forward).

Davallia triphylla Hooker   FIGURE 13.36.27
syn. *Scyphularia simplicifolia* Copeland, *S. triphylla* (Hooker) Fée
Tender

A small fern with medium- to long-creeping rhizomes. Best grown under low to high light in drained, moist-dry potting mix or uncut moss. The plants grow slowly. They infrequently produce fronds with three leaflets.

A distinctive characteristic of *Davallia triphylla* is the flattened rhizome covered by tightly appressed scales, the margins of which bear long, white hairs. The older scales tend to turn black. The fronds are simple and lanceolate, or trifoliate with entire leaflets. The indusia are longer than they are wide and stoutly tubular but slightly tapered. The species is native to Malaysia and Indonesia.

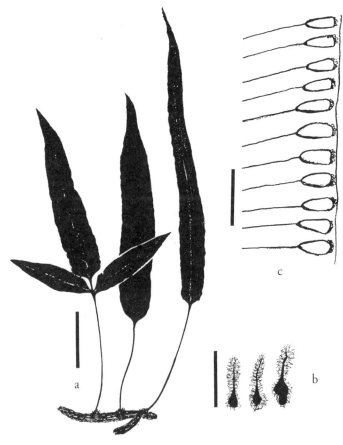

Figure 13.36.27. *Davallia triphylla*: a. habit, bar = 5 cm (2 in.); b. rhizome scales, bar = 5 mm (0.2 in.); c. sori and indusia, bar = 5 mm (0.2 in.).

Figure 13.36.28. *Davallia tyermannii*: a. habits, with dwarf form at upper left, bar = 5 cm (2 in.); b. rhizome scales, bar = 5 mm (0.2 in.); c. fertile segments, bar = 5 mm (0.2 in.); d. indusium, bar = 1 mm.

Davallia tyermannii (T. Moore) Hooker & Baker

FIGURE 13.36.28

syn. *Humata tyermannii* T. Moore
Bear's-foot fern, white rabbit's-foot fern
Semi-hardy

A small to medium fern with medium or longer creeping rhizomes. Best grown under medium to high light in well-drained, moist-dry garden soil or potting mix or uncut moss. The species is easy to grow (although somewhat slow growing) and extremely variable. It is a popular houseplant.

Davallia tyermannii is characterized by whitish rhizome scales and triangular blades up to three-pinnate-pinnatifid. The smallest segments are dilated. Roundish-oval indusia are attached only at the base. The species is native to China.

Nooteboom (1994) considered *Davallia tyermannii* a synonym of *D. griffithiana*. These two species are very close, separated mainly by the indusia being slightly attached on the sides in *D. griffithiana* and only at the base in *D. tyermannii*. The great variation, particularly in *D. tyermannii*, needs further study. Crested and dwarf forms of *D. tyermannii* are prized by gardeners.

Davallodes

Davallodes plants are medium-sized epiphytes with elliptic blades. They are mainly seen outdoors in Florida as basket ferns or in the greenhouses of fern collectors. Rarely they are offered in specialty catalogs.

Davallodes differs from the similar *Davallia* by having catadromous blades (at least on the larger pinnae) somewhat to strongly narrowed toward the base, not anadromous and widest at the base as in *Davallia*. Furthermore, the rachises, costae, and often the blade tissue are hairy, whereas *Davallia* is glabrous at maturity. *Davallodes* has creeping, fleshy rhizomes covered by needle-like, peltate scales. The roots are produced on the underside of the rhizome at the nodes, not along the internodes. The stipes are jointed to the rhizome. The blades vary from one-pinnate-pinnatifid to two-pinnate-pinnatifid, but they are always thin. Sori occur mostly at the vein fork and are covered by small, inconspicuous indusia that are either scale-like, reniform, or pouch-shaped. The attachment of the indusium varies from basal to half-way up the sides.

Davallodes consists of about 10 species (only 7 were recognized by Nooteboom 1994) that occur in wet forests from Sumatra to the Philippines and New Guinea. The genus name means "Davallia-like," adding the Greek suffix *-odes,* meaning like, to *Davallia.*

Davallodes hirsutum (J. Smith ex C. Presl) Copeland

FIGURE 13.37.1

Tender

A medium-sized fern with medium- to long-creeping rhizomes. Grows well under medium light in drained, moist potting mix or uncut moss. The plants are easy to grow if given sufficient warmth and humidity throughout the year.

A distinctive characteristic of *Davallodes hirsutum* is the spreading, needle-like tips of the blackened rhizome scales. The blades are hairy and lanceolate to narrowly elliptic. The indusia are small and inconspicuous, about 0.5 mm wide. The species is native to Malaysia, the Philippines, Sulawesi, and New Guinea.

Dennstaedtia

FIGURES 13.38.1–3

Cup fern

The cup ferns are medium- to large-sized terrestrial ferns with creeping rhizomes and finely divided foliage. They may be used in foundation plantings or as bedding ferns.

Figure 13.38.1. *Dennstaedtia davallioides:* habit.

The wide-creeping habit makes *Dennstaedtia* unsuitable as a pot plant. The rhizomes branch readily, and their growth can be controlled by cutting away unwanted parts of the rhizome and foliage.

The genus is characterized by creeping, hairy (not scaly) rhizomes, stipes containing a single U-shaped vascular bundle, and cup-shaped indusia borne at the margins of the blades. The fronds vary from medium-sized to huge, usually

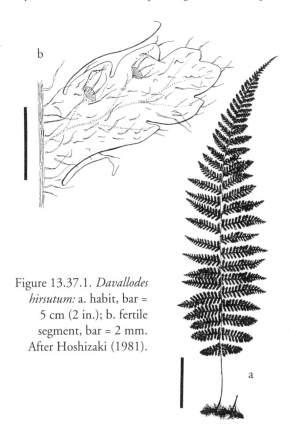

Figure 13.37.1. *Davallodes hirsutum:* a. habit, bar = 5 cm (2 in.); b. fertile segment, bar = 2 mm. After Hoshizaki (1981).

Figure 13.38.2. *Dennstaedtia davallioides:* segments bearing sori.

Figure 13.38.3. *Dennstaedtia bipinnata:* sori and cup-shaped indusia.

two- to three-pinnate and broadest at the base. The veins are free, not netted. The sori are usually turned slightly downward. Many species of *Dennstaedtia* bear branch-buds on the stipe base. These buds, called "epipetiolar buds," develop into creeping stems. They are not always present, but if so, they can be up to three or four per stipe.

The genus is native to the tropics and subtropics of the world and contains about 45 species. It is named for August Wilhelm Dennstaedt (1776–1826), a German botanist.

Dennstaedtia bipinnata (Cavanilles) Maxon

FIGURES 13.38.3, 4

Couplet fern
Tender, Zone 9

A medium-sized fern with long-creeping rhizomes. Prefers medium light in moist garden soil. This species does best in a climate with warm nights.

Dennstaedtia bipinnata can be distinguished from other cultivated species in the genus by the form of the upper sides of the rachises, costae, and costules. These axes are grooved, and the grooves of the costules run into those of the costae, which in turn run into that of the rachis. Furthermore, the grooves of the pinnules are bordered by an erect wing of green tissue. The leaf axes are ungrooved in other *Dennstaedtia* species or, if grooved, the grooves do not run into each other or have the green wings. Other characteristics of this species are triangular, glossy blades that are glabrous except for dark hairs present on the rachis opposite the larger pinnae. Epipetiolar buds are absent. It is native to the American tropics and southern Florida.

Dennstaedtia cicutaria (Swartz) T. Moore

FIGURE 13.38.5

Semi-tender

A medium-large fern with long-creeping rhizomes. Grows well under medium light in moist garden soil.

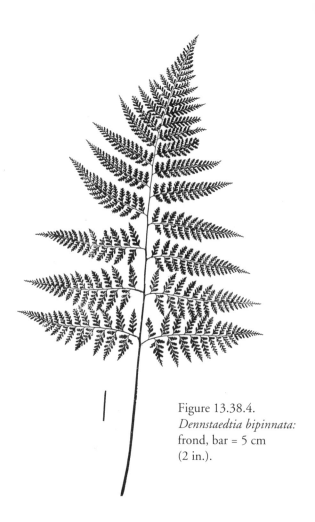

Figure 13.38.4. *Dennstaedtia bipinnata:* frond, bar = 5 cm (2 in.).

Figure 13.38.5. *Dennstaedtia cicutaria:* frond, bar = 5 cm (2 in.).

Dennstaedtia cicutaria can be distinguished from the other cultivated *Dennstaedtia* by the numerous needle-shaped hairs on the lower surfaces of the blades. The rhizomes are 12 mm (0.5 in.) thick or more, and branch-buds arise near the stipe bases. The triangular blades have dull green surfaces and are densely hairy within the rachis grooves. The species is native to the American tropics.

Dennstaedtia davallioides (R. Brown) T. Moore
FIGURES 13.38.1, 2, 6

Lacy ground fern
Semi-hardy to semi-tender

A medium-large fern with long-creeping rhizomes. Grows well under medium light in moist or moist-dry garden soil.

The rhizomes of *Dennstaedtia davallioides* grow to about 6 mm (0.2 in.) thick, and the blades are triangular, medium green, with hairs more or less evenly distributed over the rachis. The species is native to Australia.

Dennstaedtia punctilobula (Michaux) T. Moore
FIGURE 13.38.7

Hay-scented fern
Very hardy, Zone 3

A medium-sized fern with long-creeping rhizomes and deciduous fronds. Prefers low to high light in moist, acidic garden soil. This species spreads well in gardens, sometimes becoming a weed, but it is easy to control by pulling up the shallow rhizomes. New fronds are produced throughout the growing season. When crushed, the fronds emit an odor of freshly cut hay. The substance that produces the odor is contained within the enlarged, glandular cell of the hair covering the blades.

The blades of *Dennstaedtia punctilobula* are narrowly triangular to lanceolate and two-pinnate-pinnatifid, with gland-tipped hairs on the lower surface. Epipetiolar buds frequently occur at the stipe bases. The species is native to eastern North America.

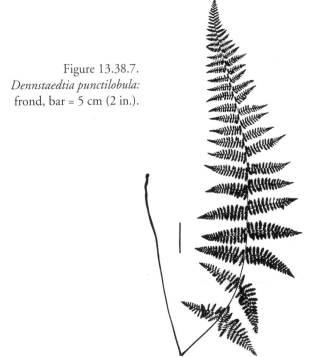

Figure 13.38.7.
Dennstaedtia punctilobula:
frond, bar = 5 cm (2 in.).

Figure 13.38.6. *Dennstaedtia davallioides:* habit, bar = 5 cm (2 in.).

Deparia
FIGURE 13.39.1

syn. *Athyrium* in part, *Diplazium* in part, *Dryoathyrium, Lunathyrium*

These terrestrial ferns are related to the lady ferns of genus *Athyrium*. They are easy to cultivate and can be used in beds or for background foliage in warm-temperate areas. The cultivated species of *Deparia* grow readily from spores.

Deparia consists of mostly medium-sized ferns with erect or short- to long-creeping rhizomes. The scales are not clathrate, in contrast to those of *Asplenium,* a genus

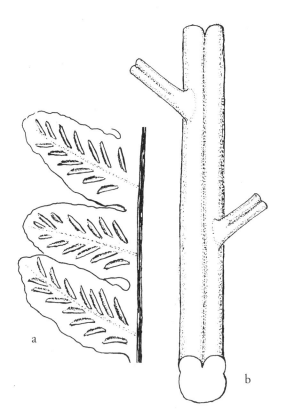

Figure 13.39.1. *Deparia:* a. segment with typical indusia; b. rachis and costae grooves not continuous.

with which *Deparia* could be confused. The stipes contain two vascular bundles at the base. The blades vary from one-pinnate to two-pinnate-pinnatifid. They are at least partly anadromous, and the costal grooves are interrupted at the juncture with the rachis—that is, they do not run into the groove of the rachis. The hairs of the rachises and costae are multicellular and jointed. The veins are free (not netted), and the sori vary from round to U- or J-shaped to linear. Sometimes the sori are paired, as in *Diplazium.*

Deparia species were formerly included in either *Athyrium* or *Diplazium.* The easiest way to distinguish this genus is by the multicellular hairs on the fronds (*Athyrium* and *Diplazium* lack such hairs). Furthermore, the costal grooves in *Deparia* do not run into the rachis groove, whereas in *Athyrium* and *Diplazium* the grooves are continuous. This characteristic is usually best developed in the middle of the blade. For further comparison, see *Athyrium;* for a technical treatment of many *Deparia* species, see Kato (1984).

Deparia contains about 40 species native mostly in the Old World east to Hawaii, North America, and are naturalized in Europe and tropical America. The genus name comes from the Greek *depas,* cup or beaker, alluding to the shape of the indusium in certain species.

Deparia acrostichoides (Swartz) M. Kato

FIGURE 13.39.2

syn. *Athyrium thelypteroides* (Michaux) Desvaux,
    Diplazium acrostichoides (Swartz) Butters
Silver glade fern, silvery spleenwort
Very hardy, Zone (3)4

A medium-large fern with short-creeping rhizomes and deciduous fronds. Grows well under medium light in moist garden soil or potting mix.

Deparia acrostichoides has swollen stipe bases, blades one-pinnate-pinnatifid, broadly lanceolate, noticeably narrowed below, and silvery on the lower surface. The indusia are linear or hooked. The species is native to the southeastern United States.

Deparia japonica (Thunberg) M. Kato

FIGURE 13.39.3

syn. *Athyrium japonicum* (Thunberg) Copeland
Hardy, Zone 6

A medium-sized fern with deciduous fronds from a short-creeping, branched rhizome. Grows well under medium light in moist-wet garden soil or potting mix. The plants tend to volunteer.

The sterile blades of most cultivated plants are triangular, one-pinnate-pinnatifid, and sometimes blackish green. The fertile fronds are taller, narrower, and more erect than the sterile ones. The indusia are linear with laciniate margins and are arranged in a herringbone pattern. This species is native from the Himalayas to China, Korea, and Japan, where it favors warm-temperate or temperate climates.

Figure 13.39.2. *Deparia acrostichoides:* frond, bar = 5 cm (2 in.).

Figure 13.39.3. *Deparia japonica*: frond, bar = 5 cm (2 in.).

Figure 13.39.4. *Deparia petersenii*: a. frond, bar = 5 cm (2 in.); b. pinna with elongate sori and indusia, bar = 1 cm (0.4 in.).

Deparia japonica is related to *D. petersenii* and is considered the same by some authors. It is said to differ from *D. petersenii* by its gradually acuminate, serrate blade and pinnae, oblique serrate-toothed segment, and incurved indusia. Some cultivated material is difficult to distinguish.

Deparia petersenii (Kunze) M. Kato   FIGURE 13.39.4
syn. *Athyrium petersenii* (Kunze) Copeland
Semi-hardy or hardier, Zone 8

A medium-sized fern with a short-creeping, branched rhizome. Grows well under medium light in moist garden soil or potting mix. This species is easy to grow, robust, and tends to volunteer. The fiddleheads are reportedly edible.

In cultivated material, the blades of *Deparia petersenii* vary from triangular to ovate-lanceolate and are up to two-pinnate, with the basiscopic pinnule next to the rachis reduced to a somewhat angular lobe. The indusia are linear with laciniate margins and arranged in a herringbone pattern. This species is extremely variable and is closely related to *D. japonica*. It favors subtropical and tropical climates in Asia and Australia and has been introduced in the Pacific Islands and the southeastern United States.

Dicksonia   FIGURES 13.40.1, 2
Tree fern

The genus *Dicksonia* consists of large tree ferns with narrow, leathery fronds. The Tasmanian dicksonia (*Dicksonia antarctica*) and Cooper's tree fern (*Sphaeropteris cooperi*) from Australia are the most commonly cultivated tree ferns in the United States. Both species are grown outdoors in Florida and in coastal California at least as far north as San Francisco. A handsome grove of Tasmanian tree ferns can be seen at Golden Gate Park in San Francisco. Tasmanian dicksonias also thrive in estate gardens in mild parts of

southwestern England. The tree-fern trunk fibers used in horticulture come from *D. sellowiana* of Latin America and should not be confused with the hapu fiber, which come from *Cibotium glaucum* of Hawaii.

All dicksonias have trunk-like stems that are clothed, along with the stipe bases, by bristly hairs. The old, dead fronds usually persist on the trunk and hang downward, forming a "skirt." The blades vary from two-pinnate-pinnatifid to four-pinnate and are oblong or lanceolate, narrowed at the base, and have a stiff, leathery texture. The sori are borne at the margins of the blades and appear clam-like because of the two-valved indusium. The outer lobe of the indusium is formed from the enrolled leaf margin and is greenish, resembling the leaf tissue in color and texture. The inner lobe, however, is brownish and thinner.

Dicksonia is readily separated from the cyatheoid tree ferns by having hairs rather than scales on the trunk and stipe and by sori borne on the blade margins, not the lower surfaces. The related genus *Cibotium* differs from *Dicksonia* by its broadly triangular blades with slightly glaucous lower surfaces, and by the inner and outer indusial lobes being of similar color and texture.

Figure 13.40.1. *Dicksonia antarctica:* habit.

Figure 13.40.2. *Dicksonia antarctica:* sori and indusia.

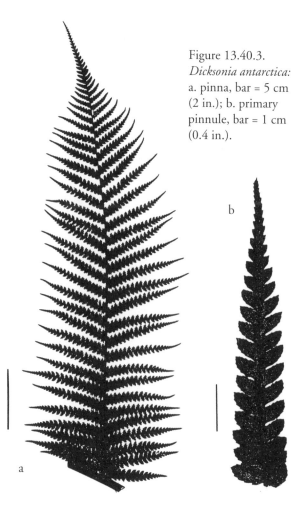

Figure 13.40.3. *Dicksonia antarctica:* a. pinna, bar = 5 cm (2 in.); b. primary pinnule, bar = 1 cm (0.4 in.).

The name *Dicksonia* comes from James Dickson (1738–1822), a Scottish physician and cryptogamic botanist. The genus contains about 20 species and occurs mostly in wet montane forests (especially cloud forests) of the tropics and warm-temperate regions of the world. For more information about these plants, see the section in Chapter 10 on "Tree Ferns."

Dicksonia antarctica Labillardière

FIGURES 13.40.1–3; PLATE 3

Tasmanian dicksonia
Semi-hardy to semi-tender

A large tree fern, with a trunk up to about 6 m (20 ft.) tall. Grows well under medium light or (if not too intense) full sun in moist garden soil or potting mix. This species is easy to grow and is by far the most common *Dicksonia* in the trade. The plants generally grow best in areas with cool, humid climates year-round, without dry, cold winds.

Dicksonia antarctica is characterized by dark brown trunks, stipes that soon loose their covering of hair, and tan or greenish rachises and costae. The blade is harsh and stiff, with central pinnae three to four times longer than broad and central pinnules long and acute to acuminate. It is native to Australia and Tasmania.

Cold weather easily damages or kills the fronds but not the trunks. Several nurseries in California reported that the frond tips were burnt when the temperature dropped to −7°C (19°F), and the fronds died completely when the temperature stayed this low for one week. The trunks, however, were not killed and soon recovered to produce new fronds. Dormant trunks in shipments have been known to survive −5°C (23°F) for two months. English gardeners report that the plants do not survive if the frost days number 20–40 per season.

Dicksonia fibrosa Colenso   FIGURE 13.40.4

Woolly tree fern, fibrous dicksonia
Semi-tender to semi-hardy; frost hardy

A large tree fern, to 6 m (20 ft.) or more tall. Grows under medium light or direct sun (if not too intense) in moist garden soil or potting mix. The plants prefer cool, humid climates, are rarely grown, and reportedly are susceptible to armillaria rot.

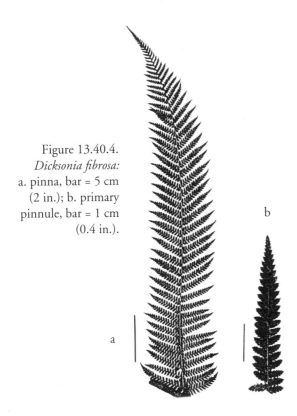

Figure 13.40.4.
Dicksonia fibrosa:
a. pinna, bar = 5 cm
(2 in.); b. primary
pinnule, bar = 1 cm
(0.4 in.).

Figure 13.40.5. *Dicksonia sellowiana:* a. pinna, bar =
5 cm (2 in.); b. primary pinnule, bar = 1 cm (0.4 in.);
c. sori and indusia, bar = 1 mm.

Dicksonia fibrosa has reddish brown trunks. The stipes retain some of their hairs, and the rachises and costae are tan or greenish. The blades are smaller, glossier, and more prickly than those of *D. antarctica*. The central pinnae are five to six times longer than broad, and the central pinnules short-acute. This species is endemic to New Zealand.

Dicksonia sellowiana Hooker   FIGURE 13.40.5
syn. *Dicksonia gigantea* H. Karsten
Semi-tender to slightly hardier

A large tree fern, with trunks to 6 m (20 ft.) tall in its native habitat. Grows best under medium light in moist garden soil or potting mix. This species is particularly attractive for its dark, glossy fronds, which are generally broader and glossier than those of *Dicksonia antarctica*. In the coastal areas of central and southern California this species can be grown year-round outdoors without difficulty.

The trunk of *Dicksonia sellowiana* tends to be thickest at the base because of the wide, dense layer of black rootlets. The fronds are widest above the middle and taper toward the base to a short stipe. The trunk apex and stipes are covered with long hairs. The blades are two- to three-pinnate-pinnatifid, up to 3 m (10 ft.) long, and slightly leathery. The pinnae are sessile, and the ultimate fertile pinnules are narrowly oblong, each bearing six or more sori. This species is widespread in the American tropics, where it generally grows at elevations above 2000 m (6500 ft.).

In Latin America (particularly Mexico and Central America) the trunks of *Dicksonia sellowiana* are harvested

and sculpted into animals such as ducks, swans, squirrels, and goats. These sculptures are used to adorn lawns and patios, much like cement statuary is used in the United States. The Mexicans call this type of sculpture *maquique*. Segments of the trunk are also carved into pots for growing plants or sawed into squares and used as a substrate for growing epiphytic orchids. In nature, many ferns and other epiphytes grow on the root mantles, some species being almost entirely restricted to it.

The similar *Dicksonia berteriana* (Colla) C. Christensen, an endemic to the Juan Fernández Islands, is cultivated in a few special collections. It differs from *D. sellowiana* by the fertile segments lacking a leafy apex or having only a small one.

Dicksonia squarrosa (Forster f.) Swartz

FIGURE 13.40.6

Slender tree fern, rough tree fern, New Zealand
    dicksonia
Semi-tender; tolerates light frost

A large tree fern, 5–6 m (16–20 ft.) tall. Grows best under
medium light in moist to moist-wet garden soil or potting
mix. This species prefers cool, humid climates. It tends to
form offshoots from stolons and can be propagated by removing the offshoots.

The trunk of *Dicksonia squarrosa* is slender and black,
and the stipes are rough with stiff hairs when young. The
rachises and costae vary from red-brown to blackish, and
the undersides of the blades are glaucous green. This species
is smaller than *D. antarctica*. It is endemic to New Zealand.

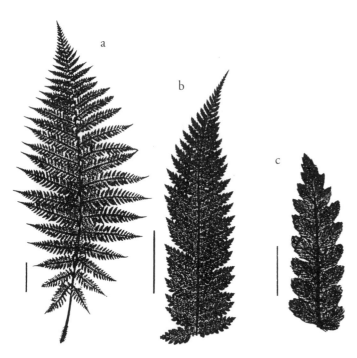

Figure 13.40.6. *Dicksonia squarrosa:* a. frond (from a
young plant), bar = 5 cm (2 in.); b. pinnae, bar = 5 cm
(2 in.); c. primary pinnule, bar = 1 cm (0.4 in.).

Dictymia

These small- to medium-sized ferns are suitable for use in
pots, baskets, or rock gardens. The rhizomes of *Dictymia*
plants are creeping and scaly, as is typical of polypodiaceous
ferns. The fronds vary from linear to lanceolate and are always dark green, glabrous, and leathery, with entire or wavy
margins. Netted veins are immersed in the blade tissue,
with many irregular areoles usually without included veinlets. The sori are large, round to elliptic or narrowly oblong, and lack indusia.

Dictymia can be confused with *Polypodium, Microsorum,*
or *Lepisorus* but differs from those genera by its venation

(many irregular areoles that mostly lack included free veinlets). *Lepisorus* further differs by the presence of peltate
paraphyses, at least on young sori. See *Polypodium* for a further discussion of related genera.

Only two species are found in *Dictymia,* occurring from
eastern Australia to Fiji. The genus name comes from the
Greek *diktyon,* net, alluding to the netted veins.

Dictymia brownii (Wikström) Copeland

FIGURE 13.41.1

Semi-tender (?)

A small-medium fern with creeping rhizomes. Grows under medium light in moist potting mix.

Dictymia brownii has stiff, leathery, and erect fronds.
The sori are large, round or oblong, and raised. The species
is native to eastern Australia.

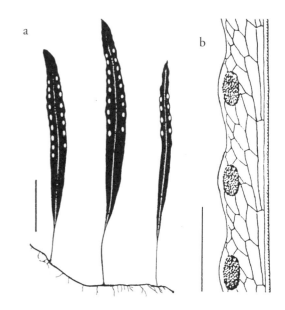

Figure 13.41.1. *Dictymia brownii:* a. habit, bar = 5 cm
(2 in.); b. sori and veins, bar = 1 cm (0.4 in.).

Didymochlaena

Mahogany fern

The mahogany ferns are medium- to large-sized plants with
erect rhizomes and fronds that form a basket-shaped whorl.
The new fronds are a striking reddish brown (hence the
common name), and the rectangular segments and horseshoe-shaped sori give the plants added interest. They are
sold as pot plants for indoor use but can be grown outdoors
in warmer climates.

The genus is characterized by two-pinnate fronds with a
terminal pinna resembling the lateral ones. The segments
are slightly leathery and rectangular. A minute spine occurs
at the bases of the segment stalks on the upper surfaces of
large, mature fronds. The sori are horseshoe-shaped.

Didymochlaena is generally thought to consist of one extremely variable species occurring throughout the tropics of the world. The genus name comes from the Greek *didymos*, double, and *chlaina*, cloak, apparently referring to the indusium that wraps around to cover both sides of the vein.

Didymochlaena truncatula (Swartz) J. Smith

FIGURES 13.42.1, 2

Semi-tender

A medium to large fern with erect rhizomes and clustered fronds. Grows well under medium light in moist garden soil or potting mix. *Didymochlaena truncatula* is easily grown and sometimes forms side crowns that can be separated for propagation. Older plants tend to topple unless replanted deeper or mulched at the base.

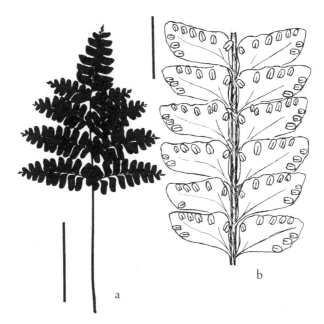

Figure 13.42.2. *Didymochlaena truncatula:* a. immature frond, bar = 5 cm (2 in.); b. pinnules with sori and indusia, bar = 1 cm. (0.4 in.).

Diplazium

FIGURES 13.43.1–3

syn. *Allantodia*

The small species of *Diplazium* are useful in borders, whereas the larger ones are grown in beds as background foliage or in pots. Generally the best growth is achieved under constant moist, cool, humid conditions; however, a few species are adapted to warm- or cold-temperate climates.

All species of *Diplazium* are terrestrial (never epiphytic), with rhizomes varying from long-creeping to erect. The rhizome scales are not clathrate as in *Asplenium*, a genus that has a similar soral shape and might be confused with *Diplazium*. The stipes contain two vascular bundles at the

Figure 13.42.1. *Didymochlaena truncatula:* mature frond.

Figure 13.43.1. *Diplazium tomitaroanum:* habit.

Figure 13.43.2. *Diplazium tomitaroanum:* indusia.

base. The blades vary from simple and entire to four-pin-nate-pinnatifid. The rachis groove is generally U-shaped, continuous with the grooves of the costae, and typically glabrous within. The veins can be either free or netted, depending on the species. The sori are indusiate, linear, and borne either singly or paired back-to-back along a vein; the paired sori are most frequent on the basal veins.

Diplazium species are sometimes included in *Athyrium* or *Deparia.* For a comparison of these three genera, see the discussion under *Athyrium.* The cultivated species of *Diplazium* tend to have more coarsely cut foliage than *Athyrium.*

The genus consists of about 400 species native to tropical regions throughout the world. Its name comes from the Greek *diplazios,* double, referring to the sori that sometimes occur on both sides of a vein.

Diplazium australe (R. Brown) N. A. Wake

FIGURE 13.43.4

Austral lady fern
Semi-hardy, Zone 8

A medium-large fern with short-creeping to suberect, clump-forming rhizomes and deciduous fronds. Grows

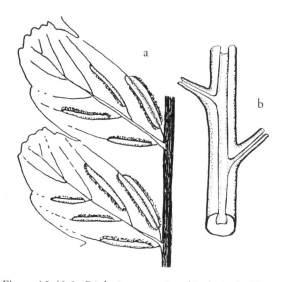

Figure 13.43.3. *Diplazium:* a. sori and indusia; b. U-shaped rachis groove continuous with costa groove.

Figure 13.43.4. *Diplazium australe:* frond, bar = 5 cm (2 in.).

well under low to medium light in moist garden soil or potting mix. This species is easy to grow.

Diplazium australe is characterized by broadly ovate or triangular, three-pinnate-pinnatifid blades. The sori are only 2–3 mm long, crescent-shaped, and only occasionally are they paired back-to-back along the veins. The species is native to Australia and New Zealand.

Diplazium dilatatum Blume   FIGURE 13.43.5
Semi-tender or somewhat hardier

A medium to large fern with short-creeping to suberect, branched rhizomes. Grows well under medium light in moist garden soil or potting soil. The plants are easily grown from spores.

Diplazium dilatatum has large, two-pinnate fronds with minute, stalked, transparent to reddish glands on the undersurface. The scales of the rhizomes and stipe bases have black margins and forked teeth (use hand lens). It is native to southern Asia, Malaysia, Australia, and New Guinea.

Diplazium maximum (D. Don) C. Christensen is closely related to this species, if not the same.

Figure 13.43.5. *Diplazium dilatatum:* frond, bar = 5 cm (2 in.).

Figure 13.43.6. *Diplazium esculentum:* frond, bar = 5 cm (2 in.).

Diplazium esculentum (Retzius) Swartz
FIGURE 13.43.6

syn. *Callipteris esculenta* (Retzius) J. Small
Vegetable fern
Semi-tender, Zone 9

A medium-sized fern, to 60 cm (2 ft.) tall, with erect rhizomes that can become trunk-like on older plants. Grows well under medium to high light in moist-wet garden soil or potting mix. Colonies of this species resemble a grove of short-stemmed, coarse-leaved tree ferns. The fiddleheads are edible. New plants frequently arise from root buds.

Diplazium esculentum is characterized by broad, two-pinnate fronds and veins that unite along the costae. The scales of the rhizomes and stipe bases have black margins and forked teeth (use hand lens). It is native to Africa, southeastern Asia, and Polynesia; it has been introduced in Florida and Louisiana.

Diplazium lonchophyllum Kunze   FIGURE 13.43.7
Semi-tender, Zone 9

A medium-sized fern with suberect rhizomes that often produce offshoots. Grows well in moist garden soil or potting mix; not adapted to climates with cool nights.

The blades of *Diplazium lonchophyllum* are triangular-lanceolate and two-pinnate at the base but one-pinnate-

pinnatifid above. The species is native to the southern United States (Louisiana) and Mexico to northern South America.

Diplazium proliferum (Lamarck) Thouars
FIGURE 13.43.8

syn. *Callipteris prolifera* (Lamarck) Bory
Tender

A large fern with erect rhizomes that form offshoots. Grows well under medium light in moist-wet garden soil or potting mix; it does best with warm nights. The plants are large and coarse but interesting for the large buds on the midrib. Stems of older plants may become trunk-like.

Diplazium proliferum has one-pinnate fronds with coarsely serrate-lobed pinnae and netted veins. The scales of the rhizomes and stipe bases have black margins and forked teeth (use hand lens). This species is native to Africa, Madagascar, and from Malaysia to Polynesia.

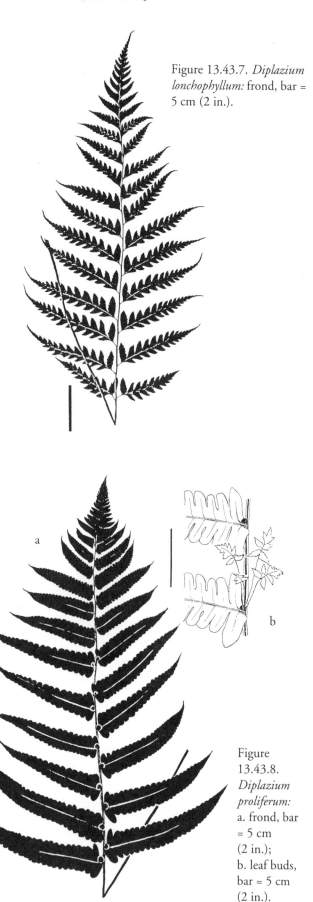

Figure 13.43.7. *Diplazium lonchophyllum:* frond, bar = 5 cm (2 in.).

Figure 13.43.8. *Diplazium proliferum:* a. frond, bar = 5 cm (2 in.); b. leaf buds, bar = 5 cm (2 in.).

Diplazium pycnocarpon (Sprengel) M. Broun
FIGURE 13.43.9

American glade fern, narrow glade fern
Very hardy, Zone 4

A medium-large fern with short-creeping, branched rhizomes and deciduous fronds. Grows well under medium light in moist, basic garden soil or potting mix. The leaves are often light green.

Diplazium pycnocarpon is characterized by one-pinnate fronds and nearly entire pinnae. It is native to eastern North America.

Figure 13.43.9. *Diplazium pycnocarpon:* fronds, bar = 5 cm (2 in.).

Diplazium subsinuatum (Hooker & Greville) Tagawa
FIGURE 13.43.10

syn. *Athyrium dubium* (D. Don) Ohwi, *Diplazium lanceum* (Thunberg) C. Presl
Semi-hardy, Zone 7(8)

A small fern with branched, medium- to long-creeping rhizomes. Grows well under medium light in moist garden soil or potting mix. The plants are useful for edging or as ground cover.

Figure 13.43.10.
Diplazium subsinuatum:
habit, bar = 5 cm (2 in.).

The fronds of *Diplazium subsinuatum* are simple, linear-lanceolate, thick, dark green, and glossy. The species is native to India, eastern Asia, the Philippines, and Borneo.

Diplazium tomitaroanum Masamune

FIGURES 13.43.1, 2, 11

Semi-hardy, Zone 7(8)

A small fern with branched, medium- to long-creeping rhizomes. Grows well under medium light in moist to moist-wet garden soil or potting mix. The plants can be used for edging, as ground covers, or as an attractive plant for small pots. It does grow slowly.

The blades are narrowly lanceolate, usually one-pinnate at the base and pinnatifid to lobed above, dark green, and glossy. *Diplazium tomitaroanum* is native to China, Japan, and Taiwan.

Doodia

FIGURE 13.44.1

Hacksaw fern, rasp fern

This genus of small- to medium-sized terrestrial ferns includes the commonly cultivated hacksaw fern, *Doodia media.* This species tolerates drier soil and less humidity than most ferns and is used in warm-temperate and subtropical gardens as an edging plant or indoors as a pot or terrarium plant. *Doodia* is easy to grow from spore, but the offspring vary, with some individuals more erect or having redder fronds. The species may spread by stolons.

Doodia is characterized by erect, narrow, pinnatifid or one-pinnate, harsh-leathery fronds and oblong indusia that run parallel and close to the costae. The rhizome varies from erect to ascending and bears dark scales. The numerous close-set pinnae are ovate or linear, sessile or broadly attached, and sharply toothed. The fertile fronds are often taller than the sterile ones and have narrower pinnae. The indusia open toward the costa, not the margin.

Doodia consists of 12 species. It occurs from Sri Lanka to Polynesia, Australia, and New Zealand. The genus is named for Samuel Doody (1656–1706), keeper of the Chelsea Physic Garden, London, and the first cryptogamic botanist in Britain.

Doodia aspera R. Brown

FIGURE 13.44.2

Prickly rasp fern
Semi-hardy

A small-medium fern with suberect rhizomes. Best grown under medium light in moist-dry garden soil or potting mix.

The pinnae of *Doodia aspera* are broadly attached (adnate) to the rachis, except the lowest pair is occasionally stalked. The blades are hairless. This species is native to Australia and New Zealand.

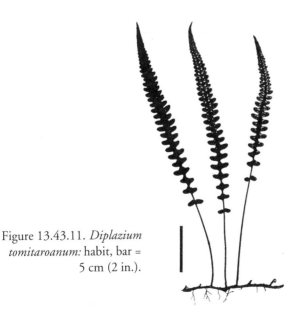

Figure 13.43.11. *Diplazium tomitaroanum:* habit, bar = 5 cm (2 in.).

Figure 13.44.1. *Doodia media:* habit, young plant.

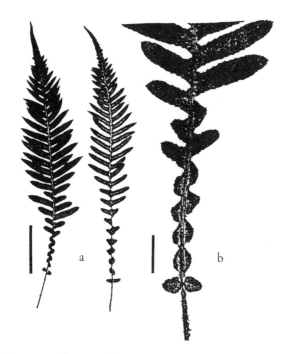

Figure 13.44.2. *Doodia aspera:* a. sterile frond (left) and fertile frond (right), bar = 5 cm (2 in.); b. frond base, bar = 1 cm (0.4 in.).

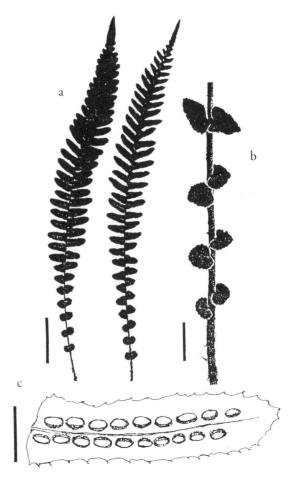

Figure 13.44.3. *Doodia media:* a. sterile frond (left) and fertile frond (right), bar = 5 cm (2 in.); b. frond base, bar = 1 cm (0.4 in.); c. sori and indusia, bar = 5 mm (0.2 in.).

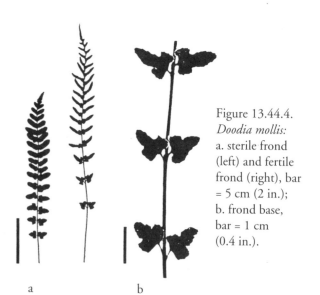

Figure 13.44.4. *Doodia mollis:* a. sterile frond (left) and fertile frond (right), bar = 5 cm (2 in.); b. frond base, bar = 1 cm (0.4 in.).

Doodia media R. Brown   FIGURES 13.44.1, 3
Hacksaw fern, rasp fern
Semi-hardy, Zone 8; tolerates light frost

A small-medium fern with suberect rhizomes. Grows best under high light in moist-dry garden soil. New growth tends to be redder if plants are placed in the sun. This species is easy to cultivate. When sown, the spores produce large prothalli.

Doodia media has fine, short hairs on the stipes and blades. The pinnae in the lower third of the blade are stalked or sessile but not adnate as in the preceding species. *Doodia media* is native to Australia and New Zealand. It is often confused with *D. aspera* in the United States trade.

Most of the trade material is subsp. *australis* Parris, which has pinnae gradually changing from decurrent to stalked over at least six pairs of pinnae, instead of abruptly changing as in subsp. *media.*

Doodia mollis Parris   FIGURE 13.44.4
Semi-hardy

A small fern with erect, clump-forming rhizomes. Grows well under medium light in moist garden soil or potting mix. This species is softer-textured than *Doodia media* and is rarely cultivated.

Doodia mollis has dimorphic sterile and fertile fronds, with the fertile ones taller and with narrower pinnae than the sterile. In the lower half of the fronds, the pinnae are stalked and have short "ears" at their base. Sometimes the lowermost pinnae appear trilobed because of the ears. This species is endemic to New Zealand.

Doryopteris   FIGURES 13.45.1–3

The eye-catching *Doryopteris* offers maple-like leaves borne on dark, shiny stalks. Most species are small- to medium-sized and usually grown in pots. In nature they grow in soil or on rocks. Some species produce buds at the base of the blade on either side of the stipe, and these buds can be used to propagate the plants. The cultivated species are tender and need warm temperatures year-round. Take care not to overwater the plants during the cool months, when their growth slows. These attractive ferns can be grown indoors if they are gradually hardened before being placed in a drier atmosphere.

The genus *Doryopteris* is characterized by dark, shiny stipes, broadly triangular blades that are basally lobed and then lobed again, and sori that run along the margin of the blade. The rhizome is scaly and varies from decumbent to suberect; rarely is it long-creeping. The sterile and fertile blades are usually the same size and shape, but in some species the fertile ones can be narrower and longer-petiolate. The sterile fronds can vary considerably, even on the same plant. The veins are free or netted, and the indusium is formed by the enrolled margin of the blade.

Figure 13.45.2. *Doryopteris concolor:* basal part of fertile frond.

Doryopteris contains about 30 species, most of which occur in tropical America. The genus also occurs in Africa, Madagascar, Australia, southern India, Malaysia, and the islands of the South Pacific. The genus name comes from the Greek, *dory,* lance, and *pteris,* fern, alluding to the shape of the blade in certain species.

Figure 13.45.1. *Doryopteris palmata:* habit.

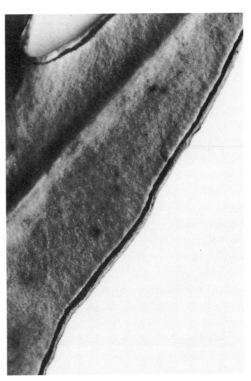

Figure 13.45.3. *Doryopteris palmata:* sori and indusia.

Doryopteris concolor (Langsdorff & Fischer) Kuhn in Decker   FIGURES 13.45.2, 4
syn. *Cheilanthes concolor* (Langsdorff & Fischer) R. M. Tryon & A. F. Tryon
Tender

A small fern with erect rhizomes. Grows well under medium light in moist potting soil.

Doryopteris concolor is characterized by free veins and glabrous stipes grooved on the upper surface, with sharp, raised ridges on either side of the groove. The sterile blades lack buds and are more deeply divided than those of *D. palmata,* a similar species. *Doryopteris concolor* is native to Central and South America, the West Indies, tropical Africa, Asia, Malaysia, Australia, and Polynesia.

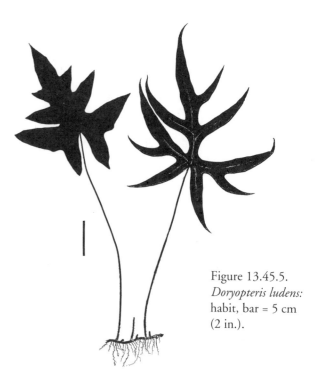

Figure 13.45.5. *Doryopteris ludens:* habit, bar = 5 cm (2 in.).

Figure 13.45.4. *Doryopteris concolor:* frond, bar = 5 cm (2 in.).

Doryopteris ludens (Wallich ex Hooker) J. Smith   FIGURE 13.45.5
Tender

A small-medium fern with slender, long-creeping rhizomes. Grows well under medium light in moist potting mix.

Doryopteris ludens resembles *D. nobilis* in blade shape and netted veins but differs by the long-creeping rhizomes and smaller sterile blades, only 4–45 cm (1.5–18 in.) long, that lack buds. It is native to northern India and southern China to Malaysia.

Doryopteris nobilis (T. Moore) C. Christensen   FIGURE 13.45.6
Tender

A small-medium fern with short- to medium-creeping rhizomes. Grows well under medium-high light in moist potting mix.

Doryopteris nobilis is the largest species in the genus, with sterile blades up to 65 cm (26 in.) long. The blades vary tremendously, ranging from lanceolate–arrowhead-shaped to palmately lobed to deeply pinnately lobed with lower pinnae again lobed (often only basiscopically). The blade bears buds at the base, and the veins are netted. The lobes of the fertile fronds often have serrate tips beyond the sori. This species is native to Colombia, Bolivia, Brazil, and northern Argentina.

Plants circulating among collectors as *Doryopteris sagittifolia* (Raddi) J. Smith are juvenile forms of *D. nobilis.* True *D. sagittifolia* has arrowhead-shaped blades, or if (rarely) five-lobed, the terminal lobe is the largest and the lateral lobes each bear a smaller basiscopic lobe.

Doryopteris palmata (Willdenow) J. Smith   FIGURES 13.45.1, 3, 7
syn. *Doryopteris pedata* var. *palmata* (Willdenow) Hicken
Spear-leaved fern, hand fern
Tender

A small fern with short-creeping to suberect rhizomes. Grows well under high light in moist potting mix.

Doryopteris palmata, which has netted veins, has previously been treated as a variety of *D. pedata;* however, it dif-

Figure 13.45.6. *Doryopteris nobilis:* fronds, bar = 5 cm (2 in.).

fers from that species by the presence of buds at the base of the blades, rounded and puberulent stipes (not grooved and glabrous), and wrinkled spores. It also has a different geographical distribution, occurring from Mexico to Venezuela and Bolivia, whereas *D. pedata* grows only in the West Indies. These differences warrant recognition at the species level.

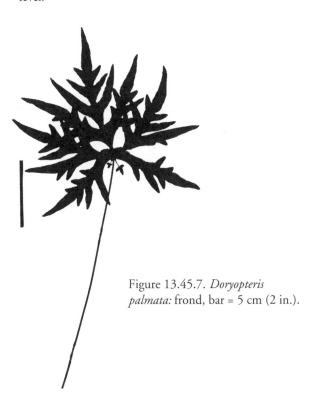

Figure 13.45.7. *Doryopteris palmata:* frond, bar = 5 cm (2 in.).

Drynaria
Oak-leaf fern

Drynaria is a genus of spectacular medium- to large-sized epiphytic ferns. The medium-sized species are suitable indoors with adequate light because the foliage usually tolerates the drier air indoors. During the dry season, or when fronds become old, the pinnae (or lobes) are shed from the midrib, but the midrib itself remains attached to the rhizome, sticking outward like a long spine. The green fronds may yellow when nighttime temperatures drop below 15°C (59°F) for more than a few weeks. If the temperature has not been too cold, growth resumes when warm weather returns. For more details on cultivation, see the section in Chapter 10 on "*Polypodium* and Relatives." For a technical monograph of the genus, see Roos (1985).

Drynaria has creeping, thick, fleshy, scaly rhizomes and netted veins. The genus bears two kinds of fronds (it is dimorphic). One type of frond is short and broad and turns brown and papery. These fronds sit close to the stem and collect falling debris that eventually decomposes to form humus from which the roots can absorb nutrients. They are always sterile and resemble oak leaves. The second kind of frond is longer, green, herbaceous, and fertile. Its function is to photosynthesize and produce spores, not collect humus. The fertile herbaceous fronds are pinnatifid or one-pinnate and lack a true terminal pinna or lobe, although the terminal position may be occupied by a slightly skewed lateral pinna or lobe. (The true apex aborts, and occasionally a partly aborted terminal pinna is produced.) The sori are round or nearly so and lack indusia.

This genus resembles *Aglaomorpha,* which differs by having a well-developed, true terminal pinna or lobe on the foliaceous frond. It also lacks the separate small, brown, papery, humus-collecting fronds characteristic of *Drynaria.* The close relationship of the two genera is evident in their ability to hybridize. One such hybrid, ×*Aglaonaria robertsii,* is important in horticulture.

Figure 13.46.1. *Drynaria sparsisora:* habit.

Figure 13.46.2. *Drynaria rigidula:* habit.

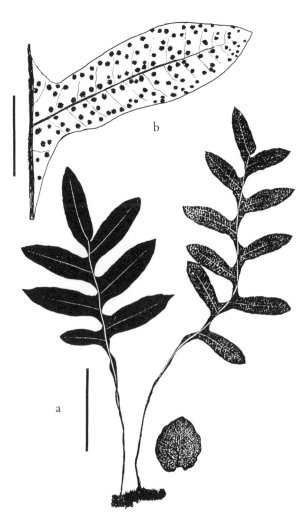

Figure 13.46.4. *Drynaria bonii:* a. habit, with a humus-collecting frond on the right, bar = 10 cm (4 in.); b. pinna and sori, bar = 2.5 cm (1 in.).

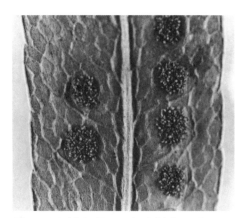

Figure 13.46.3. *Drynaria rigidula:* sori.

Drynaria contains 16 species and is native to the Old World tropics. The genus name comes from the Greek *dryinos,* of oaks, and refers to the plant's oak-like sterile fronds.

Drynaria bonii H. Christ   figure 13.46.4
Tender

A medium-sized fern with short-medium-creeping, branched rhizomes. Grows well under high light in moist-dry, drained potting mix or uncut moss.

Drynaria bonii is one of the smallest species in the genus. Its humus-collecting fronds are rounded and nearly entire, whereas the green, herbaceous fronds are pinnatisect with only a few pinnae, which are separated by broad sinuses. The pinnae are 2.5–4 cm (1–1.5 in.) wide, adnate to the rachis, and form wings on the rachis above and below their base. The sori are in two irregular rows between secondary veins. The species is native to India, southeastern Asia, and China.

Drynaria bonii is often confused with *D. descensa* Copeland, a Philippine species differing by crenate, humus-collecting fronds and smaller, less than 2.5 cm (1 in.) wide, and undulate lobes on the foliaceous fronds.

Drynaria propinqua (Wallich ex Mettenius) Beddome
figure 13.46.5

Probably tender

A medium-sized fern with branched, creeping rhizomes. Grows well under high light in drained, moist-dry potting mix or uncut moss. This species is reportedly difficult to grow.

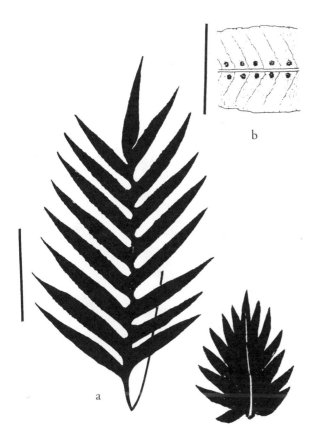

Figure 13.46.5. *Drynaria propinqua:* a. foliaceous frond (left) and humus-collecting frond (right), bar = 10 cm (4 in.); b. sori, bar = 2.5 cm (1 in.).

Figure 13.46.6. *Drynaria quercifolia:* a. foliaceous frond (left) and humus-collecting frond (right), bar = 10 cm (4 in.); b. rhizome scale, bar = 3 mm (0.1 in.); c. sori, bar = 2.5 cm (1 in.).

The humus-collecting fronds of *Drynaria propinqua* are deeply pinnatifid with narrowly acute lobes, and the foliaceous fertile fronds are deeply pinnatifid into lanceolate pinnae. The sori are borne in one row on both sides of, and close to, the costae. The species is native to India, southeastern Asia, and China.

Drynaria quercifolia (Linnaeus) J. Smith

FIGURE 13.46.6

Oak-leaf fern

Tender

A large fern with medium- to short-creeping, branched rhizomes and spreading fronds. Grows well under high light in drained, moist-dry potting mix, or uncut moss. The plants are easy to cultivate and are fast-growing.

The rhizome scales of *Drynaria quercifolia* are brownish, narrowly triangular, and spreading at about a 45-degree angle from the rhizome surface. The humus-collecting fronds vary from wavy to lobed. The foliaceous ones are deeply pinnatifid and up to about 90 cm (36 in.) long. The sori vary from round to oblong, but sometimes adjacent ones fuse into an elongate sorus. They are arranged in two fairly regular rows or scattered between the lateral veins.

This species is native from India to southeastern Asia, Malaysia, Indonesia, the Philippines, New Guinea, and Australia.

Drynaria rigidula (Swartz) Beddome

FIGURES 13.46.2, 3, 7

Semi-tender to slightly hardier

A large fern with medium- to short-creeping, branched rhizomes and usually gracefully arching fronds. Prefers high light and drained, moist-dry potting mix or uncut moss. The humus-collecting fronds develop poorly if the soil is kept too moist. The plants grow slowly.

Drynaria rigidula is the only species of *Drynaria* with one-pinnate fronds and sessile, wedge-shaped pinnae narrowly winged to the rachis. It grows in southeastern Asia,

Figure 13.46.7. *Drynaria rigidula:* a. foliaceous frond (center) and humus-collecting frond (right), foliaceous pinnae of 'Whitei' (lower left), bar = 10 cm (4 in.); b. pinna base and sori, bar = 2.5 cm (1 in.).

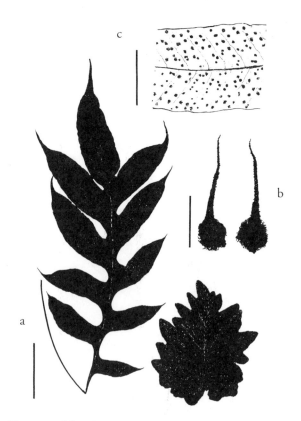

Figure 13.46.8. *Drynaria sparsisora:* a. foliaceous frond (left) and humus-collecting frond (right), bar = 10 cm (4 in.); b. rhizome scales, bar = 3 mm (0.1 in.); c. sori, bar = 2.5 cm (1 in.).

China, Malaysia, Indonesia, the Philippines, Australia, New Guinea, and southeastern Pacific Islands.

'Whitei'. Plate 25. Pinnae often broader, lacerate to irregularly lobed.

Drynaria sparsisora (Desvaux) T. Moore

FIGURES 13.46.1, 8

Tender

A large fern with medium- to short-creeping, branched rhizomes. Grows well under high light in drained, moist-dry potting mix or uncut moss.

Drynaria sparsisora resembles *D. quercifolia* but differs by blackish rhizomes scales that are bent above their base into a 90-degree angle to form a stiffly erect bristle. The foliaceous fronds are smaller, harder-textured, and more stiffly erect, and the sori are smaller and irregularly scattered between lateral veins. It is native to southeastern Asia, Malaysia, Indonesia, New Guinea, and Australia.

Dryopteris

FIGURES 13.47.1, 2

Shield fern, buckler fern, wood fern

These familiar ferns abound in the woods, fields, and wet areas of the eastern United States, Europe, Japan, and many other areas. *Dryopteris* is widely used in temperate gardens as accents, in borders, or for background foliage. The many species available in the trade range from small to large, coarsely to finely cut, and deciduous to evergreen. One garden favorite is the ornamental autumn fern (*Dryopteris erythrosora*) from Japan. It is widely available in the trade and

is sought after for its copper-red new foliage and bright red indusia. Generally, deciduous species from cold-temperate climates tend to have a shorter dormancy when grown in warmer climates. Deciduous fronds wither in place (marcescent) but may or may not lose their green color.

About 50 species of *Dryopteris* are cultivated in the United States, and new ones are constantly being introduced, replacing older ones that often disappear from the trade. Natural hybrids are common, and *Dryopteris complexa* (*D. affinis* × *D. filix-mas*), in particular, is widely sold, often under the trade name *D. filix-mas* 'Robusta'. Most of the cultivars originated from the European species, primarily *D. affinis* and *D. filix-mas*. As a group, the shield ferns pose no special problems in cultivation, although some of the species native to colder climates do not adapt well to gardens in warm climates, and some species thrive only in acidic soils. Most species are easy to propagate from spores or divisions. Offshoots come from the rhizome bases.

Dryopteris consists of terrestrial plants with thick, erect or suberect rhizomes that are surrounded by close, spirally arranged old leaf bases. Rarely, the rhizomes are short-creeping. The rhizome scales are nonclathrate. The stipes are grooved, scaly, and have 3 to 7 (9–10) vascular bundles

Figure 13.47.1. *Dryopteris uniformis* 'Cristata': habit.

Figure 13.47.2. *Dryopteris erythrosora:* indusia.

arranged in a C-shaped pattern. The blades are one- to four-pinnate, bearing scales but no hairs. The blades are usually catadromous but occasionally otherwise. The midrib is grooved, and the groove usually continues uninterrupted into the costae. Round sori are covered by kidney-shaped indusia, which are attached at a sinus (rarely the indusia are absent). The genus, which contains about 225 species, is cosmopolitan, but most of the species occur in temperate regions.

The species of *Dryopteris* are difficult to identify because there are so many of them, and they tend to form closely re-

lated groups of similar species. Furthermore, the fronds can vary even on a single plant. Identification requires examining large, mature leaves. Name changes also complicate the situation. Many such changes have occurred in certain European species (*Dryopteris affinis* complex) and North American ones (*D. spinulosa* complex). For a fuller treatment of the cultivated species, see Hoshizaki and Wilson (1999).

Due to the large number of cultivated species of *Dryopteris*, the following key is given to aid identification. After you limit the unknown species to a smaller group using the key, you can then compare it to the descriptions and illustrations of those species. The groups used in this key are the sections of *Dryopteris* recognized by Fraser-Jenkins (1986).

1. Scales on the lower surface of the blades strongly to slightly inflated or puffy (at least at the base).
 2. Basal pinnae with the downward-pointing basal pinnule longer than the adjacent pinnules: Section *Variae* (*Dryopteris bissetiana, D. formosana, D. sacrosancta,* and *D. varia*).
 2. Basal pinnae with the downward-pointing basal pinnule slightly shorter or about the same size as the others: Section *Erythrovariae* (*Dryopteris championii, D. cystolepidota, D. decipiens, D. erythrosora, D. fuscipes, D. hondoensis,* and *D. purpurella*).
1. Scales on the lower surface of the blades flat or nearly so.
 3. Blades one-pinnate to one-pinnate-pinnatifid.
  4. Pinnae entire: Section *Pycnopteris* (*Dryopteris sieboldii*).
  4. Pinnae pinnatifid.
   5. Pinnae cut less than halfway to the midrib: Section *Hirtipedes* (*Dryopteris cycadina* and *D. kuratae*).
   5. Pinnae cut nearly to the midrib: Section *Fibrillosae* (*Dryopteris affinis, D. complexa, D. crassirhizoma, D. lepidopoda, D. polylepis, D. pseudo-filix-mas,* and *D. wallichiana*).
 3. Blades two-pinnate to four-pinnate.
 6. Blades mostly narrowed toward the base (except slightly so in *Dryopteris clintoniana* and *D. goldiana*): Sections *Pandae* and *Dryopteris* (Section *Pandae: Dryopteris × australis, D. × bootii, D. celsa, D. clintoniana, D. cristata, D. ludoviciana,* and *D. tokyoensis;* Section *Dryopteris: D. caucasica, D. filix-mas, D. fragrans, D. goldiana, D. oreades,* and *D. sichotensis*).
 6. Blades mostly widest at the base (except narrowed in *Dryopteris lacera,* variable in *D. arguta*).
  7. Segment teeth not sharp or spine-tipped (variable in *Dryopteris stewartii*): Sections *Aemulae, Pallidae,* and *Remotae.* (Section *Aemulae: Dryopteris aemula;* Section *Pallidae: D. arguta, D. lacera, D. marginalis, D. mindshelkensis, D. stewartii, D. sublacera,* and *D. uniformis;* Section *Remotae: D. remota*).
  7. Segment teeth sharp-pointed or hair-tipped: Section *Lophodium* (*Dryopteris amurensis, D. campylop-*

tera, D. carthusiana, D. dilatata, D. expansa, and *D. intermedia*).

Dryopteris aemula (Aiton) O. Kuntze   FIGURE 13.47.3
Hay-scented wood fern
Hardy, Zone 6

A medium-sized fern. up to 80 cm (32 in.) long, with erect to suberect rhizomes and semi-evergreen fronds. Grows under medium light in moist, acidic garden soil or potting mix. This species grows slowly and prefers high humidity.

Dryopteris aemula resembles *D. dilatata* but has smaller, paler green, moderately ruffled blades, and the stipe scales are of one color, not darker in the center. The stipes are dark purple-brown at the base and as long as the blade, which is triangular-ovate, to three-pinnate-pinnatifid, with pinnules curving upward and appearing ruffled. When crushed, the blades emit an odor of drying hay. The species is native to western Europe.

Figure 13.47.3. *Dryopteris aemula:* a. frond, bar = 5 cm (2 in.); b. stipe scales, bar = 1 cm (0.4 in.). After Hoshizaki and Wilson (1999).

Dryopteris affinis (Lowe) Fraser-Jenkins
FIGURES 13.47.4, 5
syn. *Dryopteris abbreviata* (de Candolle) Newman, *D. pseudomas* (Wollaston) Holub & Pouzar
Yellow-golden-scaled male fern, common golden-scaled male fern, scaly male fern, hard male fern
Hardy, Zone 4(5)

A medium to large fern (some cultivars are dwarf), to 130 cm (52 in.) tall, with erect, stout rhizomes. Grows well under medium light in moist garden soil or potting mix. The fronds are deciduous in cold-temperate climates but nearly evergreen in warmer ones. The plants are easy to grow.

The stipe scales are golden, dense, and conspicuous, especially on new fiddleheads. *Dryopteris affinis* has glossy, lanceolate blades to two-pinnate. The undersides of the costae next to the rachis have a black blotch. The indusia are tucked under the sori when young. This species is native from Europe to the Caspian Sea and northwestern Africa.

The subspecies of *Dryopteris affinis* are difficult to distinguish. The many cultivars are confused as to their names and the subspecies from which they originated. In some

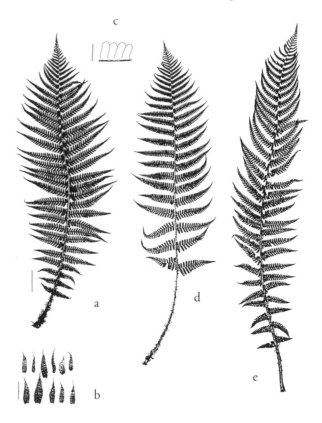

Figure 13.47.4. *Dryopteris affinis:* a. frond, bar = 5 cm (2 in.), after Hoshizaki and Wilson (1999); b. stipe scales, bar = 1 cm (0.4 in.), after Hoshizaki and Wilson (1999); c. pinnules from medial pinnae, bar = 1 cm (0.4 in.); d. subsp. *borreri,* bar = 5 cm (2 in.); e. subsp. *cambriensis,* bar = 5 cm (2 in.).

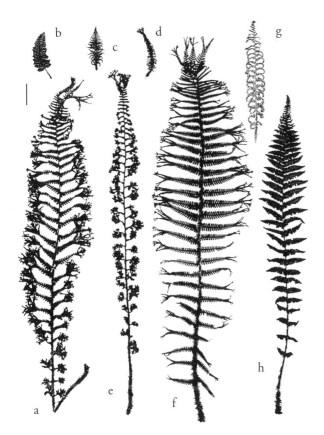

Figure 13.47.5. *Dryopteris affinis* cultivars: a. 'Cristata';
b. 'Congesta'; c. 'Crispa Gracilis'; d. 'Congesta Cristata';
e. 'Cristata Angustata'; f. 'Polydactyla'; g. 'Revolvens',
after Druery (1912); h. 'Stableri Crisped'. Bar = 5 cm
(2 in.).

case the names may correctly apply to *D. filix-mas*. In the
United States the hybrid between *D. affinis* and *D. filix-mas*, known as *D. complexa* (misnamed *D. filix-mas* 'Undulata-Robusta') was widely sold.

subsp. *borreri* (Newman) Fraser-Jenkins. Figure
13.47.4d. Fronds lanceolate to oblong, bases truncate, surfaces not glossy; deciduous in early winter in temperate climates.

subsp. *cambriensis* Fraser-Jenkins. Figure 13.47.4e.
Fronds oblanceolate to linear-elliptic, bases tapering, upper surfaces slightly glossy; deciduous in temperate climates.

'Congesta'. Figure 13.47.5b. Fronds dwarf, the pinnae
and pinnules congested but neatly overlapping.

'Congesta Cristata'. Figure 13.47.5d. Fronds dwarf,
congested, crested.

'Crispa'. Crisped male fern. In Victorian times this
name applied to plants with dwarf and broad fronds, to 20
cm (8 in.) long and 14 cm (5.5 in.) wide, with ruffled and
congested foliage. Plants in the current trade are normal-
sized with twisted segments. They are perhaps correctly
called 'Paleaceo Crispa'.

'Crispa Gracilis'. Figure 13.47.5c. Dwarf, congested,
upright leathery fern with pinna apices curved and hooked.

'Cristata'. ('Cristata the King', 'The King'). Figure
13.47.5a. Fronds arching, blade apex and pinnae ending
in a tassel or large crest. Zones 4–9.

'Cristata Angustata'. Figure 13.47.5e. Narrow frond, to
7.5 cm (3 in.) wide, apex and pinnae crested.

'Polydactyla'. Figure 13.47.5f. A group of crested forms
with long, finger-like, flat tassels on the pinna tips. Trade
plants usually listed as 'Polydactyla Dadd's'.

'Revolvens'. Figure 13.47.5g. Plants by this name vary.
The current trade plant has longer, wider fronds with the
margins curved downward; the original plant has shorter,
narrower fronds with the pinna tips curved downward.

'Stableri'. Fronds narrow, erect to slightly arching.

'Stableri Crisped'. Figure 13.47.5h. Like 'Stableri' but
with ruffled pinnae and pinnules.

Dryopteris amurensis H. Christ   FIGURE 13.47.6
Very hardy, Zone 4

A medium-sized fern, to 50 cm (20 in.), with short-creeping rhizomes and evergreen fronds. Grows under medium
light in moist garden soil or potting mix.

Dryopteris amurensis has stipes that are longer than the
blades. The blades are broadly triangular (wider than long),
three-pinnate pinnatifid at the base, membranous, and
bearing small scales along the veins on the lower surface.
The species is native to northeastern Asia.

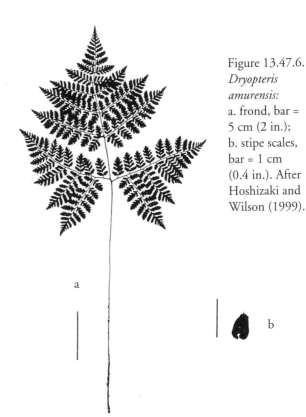

Figure 13.47.6.
*Dryopteris
amurensis:*
a. frond, bar =
5 cm (2 in.);
b. stipe scales,
bar = 1 cm
(0.4 in.). After
Hoshizaki and
Wilson (1999).

Dryopteris arguta (Kaulfuss) Maxon FIGURE 13.47.7
Coastal wood fern, California shield fern
Semi-tender, Zones 8–9

A medium-sized fern, to 65 cm (26 in.), with short-creeping to suberect rhizomes. Grows under low to medium light in moist-dry garden soil or potting mix with good drainage. This species is difficult to grow. The plants are usually semi-dormant in the dry season and sensitive to overwatering at that time.

The blades of *Dryopteris arguta* vary from triangular to ovate-lanceolate and are mostly pinnate-pinnatifid with serrate segments bearing spreading, spine-tipped teeth. The species is native to western North America.

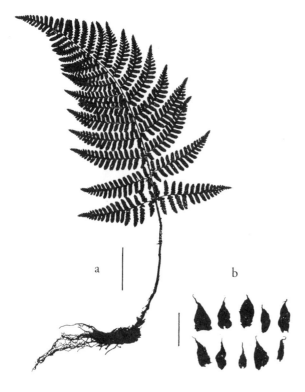

Figure 13.47.7. *Dryopteris arguta:* a. habit, bar = 5 cm (2 in.); b. stipe scales, bar = 1 cm (0.4 in.). After Hoshizaki and Wilson (1999).

Dryopteris ×australis (Wherry) Small FIGURE 13.47.8
Dixie wood fern
Hardy, Zone 5

A medium-large fern, to 115 cm (45 in.), with short-creeping rhizomes and deciduous fronds. Grows well under medium light in moist garden soil or potting mix. The plants are easy to grow. They cannot be propagated from spores because the spores are aborted. All plants sold in the trade are propagated by tissue culture.

Dryopteris ×australis is a sterile hybrid of *D. celsa* and *D. ludoviciana*. The plants are intermediate between the par-

Figure 13.47.8. *Dryopteris ×australis:* rhizome and frond, bar = 5 cm (2 in.). After Hoshizaki and Wilson (1999).

ents in appearance, but fertile parts tend to be contracted. The species is native to the southeastern United States.

Dryopteris bissetiana (Baker) C. Christensen
FIGURE 13.47.9

Beaded wood fern
Hardy, Zone 5

A medium-sized fern, to 45 cm (18 in.), with erect rhizomes and dark green, glossy, evergreen fronds with a bead-like aspect to the foliage. Grows well under medium light in moist garden soil or potting mix. Easy to grow.

Dryopteris bissetiana bears triangular, two-pinnate-pinnatifid, leathery blades, with the lowest basiscopic pinnule next to rachis elongate. The segment margins turn slightly downward and lack short spines or teeth. The scales on the costa undersides are weakly inflated. The species is native to eastern Asia.

Most of the current trade material called *Dryopteris bissetiana* is actually *D. erythrosora*.

Dryopteris ×boottii (Tuckerman) Underwood
FIGURE 13.47.10

Boott's wood fern
Very hardy, Zone 3

A medium-sized fern, to 70 cm (28 in.) tall, with short-creeping rhizomes that form offshoots. Grows well under medium light in moist garden soil or potting mix. The plants are deciduous. It cannot be propagated by spores because these are aborted.

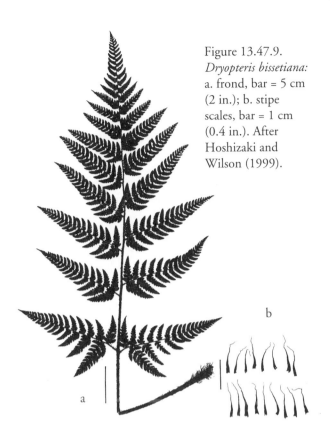

Figure 13.47.9. *Dryopteris bissetiana*: a. frond, bar = 5 cm (2 in.); b. stipe scales, bar = 1 cm (0.4 in.). After Hoshizaki and Wilson (1999).

Dryopteris×*boottii* is a sterile hybrid of *D. cristata* and *D. intermedia.* It mostly resembles *D. cristata,* but it bears the small, stalked glands typical of *D. intermedia.* The pinnae often twist horizontally to give a "venetian-blind" effect, as in *D. cristata. Dryopteris*×*boottii* is native to the northeastern United States and is commonly found where the two parents mingle.

Dryopteris campyloptera Clarkson   FIGURE 13.47.11
syn. *Dryopteris spinulosa* var. *americana* (Fischer) Fernald
Mountain wood fern, eastern spreading wood fern
Very hardy, Zone (3)4

A medium-sized fern, to 60 cm (2 ft.), with ascending to erect rhizomes and deciduous fronds. Grows under low to medium light in moist garden soil or potting mix. The plants need ample humidity and are unsuited for subtropical climates. Although this species is of hybrid origin, the plants are fertile and therefore can be propagated by spores.

Dryopteris campyloptera is a fertile hybrid of *D. expansa* and *D. intermedia.* It mostly resembles *D. expansa* but has a more erect habit and firmer texture. The basiscopic basal pinnule is two to four times longer than the opposite upward-pointing pinnule (the acroscopic pinnule). The species is native to northeastern North America.

Figure 13.47.10. *Dryopteris* ×*boottii*: frond, bar = 5 cm (2 in.). After Hoshizaki and Wilson (1999).

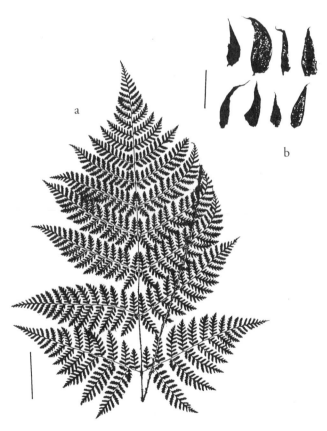

Figure 13.47.11. *Dryopteris campyloptera*: a. frond, bar = 5 cm (2 in.); b. stipe scales, bar = 1 cm (0.4 in.). After Hoshizaki and Wilson (1999).

Dryopteris carthusiana (Villars) H. P. Fuchs
FIGURE 13.47.12

syn. *Dryopteris spinulosa* (O. F. Müller) Watt
Spinulose wood fern, toothed wood fern, narrow buckler
fern
Very hardy, Zone 2

A medium-sized fern, to 40 cm (16 in.), with ascending to erect rhizomes. Grows well under medium light in moist, acidic garden soil or potting mix. The plants are deciduous and unsuited to subtropical climates.

The blades of *Dryopteris carthusiana* are two-pinnate-pinnatifid to three-pinnate and narrowly triangular-lanceolate. The lowermost, downward-pointing pinnule is less than two times as long as the basal upward-pointing pinnule above it. *Dryopteris carthusiana* is distinguished from the similar *D. dilatata* by its medium to light green fronds, flat margins, and stipe scales of one color. It also resembles *D. intermedia* but lacks the minute glandular hairs characteristic of that species. The species is native to North America, Europe, and Asia.

A foliose form of *Dryopteris carthusiana* is often sold in the trade and incorrectly identified as *D. stewartii*.

Figure 13.47.12. *Dryopteris carthusiana:* a. frond, bar = 5 cm (2 in.); b. stipe scales, bar = 1 cm (0.4 in.). After Hoshizaki and Wilson (1999).

Dryopteris caucasica (A. Braun) Fraser-Jenkins & Corely
FIGURE 13.47.13

Hardy, Zone 5

A medium-sized fern, to 80 cm (32 in.) tall, with deciduous fronds and erect rhizomes that form offshoots. Grows well under medium light in moist garden soil or potting mix.

Dryopteris caucasica resembles *D. filix-mas* (one of its parents) but differs by paler blades, pinnae widest at the middle (not the base), acute segments that are doubly toothed at the apex with acute teeth, and white, lacerate indusia. It is native to the Middle East.

Figure 13.47.13. *Dryopteris caucasica:* a. frond, bar = 5 cm (2 in.); b. stipe scales, bar = 1 cm (0.4 in.). After Hoshizaki and Wilson (1999).

Dryopteris celsa (W. Palmer) Knowlton, W. Palmer & Pollard
FIGURE 13.47.14

Log fern
Hardy, Zone (4)5

A medium-large fern, to 130 cm (52 in.), with medium- to short-creeping rhizomes and deciduous fronds. Grows well under medium light in moist-wet, acidic soil or potting mix. Though deciduous, it grows satisfactorily in southern California.

Dryopteris celsa is a fertile hybrid of *D. goldiana* and *D. ludoviciana*. It resembles *D. clintoniana* but differs by the dark brown stipe scales with a darker central stripe; in addition, on the basal pinnae, the basiscopic pinnule next to the rachis is equal to or shorter than the adjacent pinnules. It is native to the eastern United States.

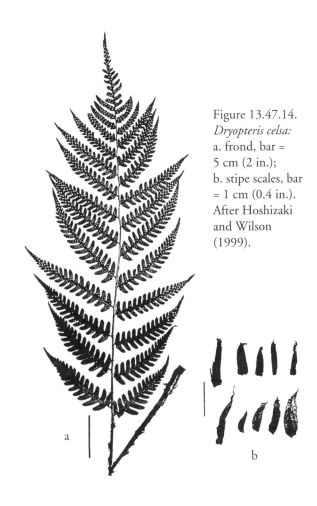

Figure 13.47.14. *Dryopteris celsa:* a. frond, bar = 5 cm (2 in.); b. stipe scales, bar = 1 cm (0.4 in.). After Hoshizaki and Wilson (1999).

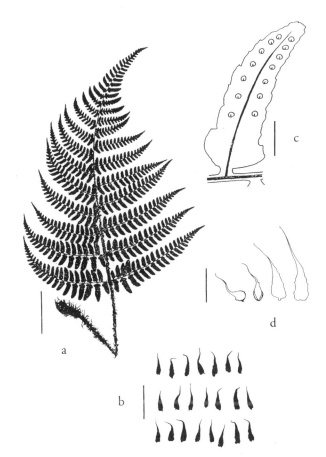

Figure 13.47.15. *Dryopteris championii:* a. frond, bar = 5 cm (2 in.); b. stipe scales, bar = 1 cm (0.4 in.); c. pinnule from medial pinna, bar = 5 mm (0.2 in.); d. bullate scales from costa, bar = 1 mm. After Hoshizaki and Wilson (1999).

Dryopteris championii (Bentham) C. Christensen ex Ching   FIGURE 13.47.15
Champion's wood fern
Hardy, Zone 5

A medium-sized fern, to 90 cm (36 in.), with erect rhizomes and evergreen fronds. Grows well under medium to high light in moist-dry garden soil or potting mix. In the northeastern United States the fertile leaves are not produced until the late fall. This species is particularly attractive in winter because its evergreen fronds remain upright, not reclining as in many species with evergreen fronds.

Dryopteris championii has narrowly triangular fronds and pinnules that are eared on both sides at the base. The stipe, rachis, and costae bear a dense covering of shiny red-brown scales, and those on the costae become strongly inflated. The species is native to eastern Asia.

Dryopteris clintoniana (D. C. Eaton) Dowell
    FIGURE 13.47.16

Clinton's wood fern
Very hardy, Zone 3

A medium-sized fern, to 95 cm (38 in.), with short-creeping rhizomes and deciduous fronds. Grows well under medium light in acidic, moist-wet garden soil or potting mix.

Dryopteris clintoniana is a hybrid of *D. cristata* and *D. goldiana.* It resembles *D. cristata,* but its basal pinnae are longer than they are wide and not twisted into a horizontal plane. The species is native to northeastern North America.

Dryopteris complexa Fraser-Jenkins   FIGURE 13.47.17
Robust male fern
Hardy, Zone 4(5)

A medium-large fern, to 130 cm (52 in.), with erect rhizomes that form offshoots and deciduous to semi-evergreen fronds (in warmer climates). Grows well under medium light in moist to moist-dry garden soil or potting mix. The plants are easy to cultivate and become rapid, vigorous growers with full foliage. The fronds are deciduous, but less so in warmer climates.

Dryopteris complexa is a fertile hybrid of *D. affinis* and *D. filix-mas.* The stipe scales are narrowly triangular and membranous. The middle and distal pinnae often overlap slightly, and the pinna midrib has a blackened spot on the

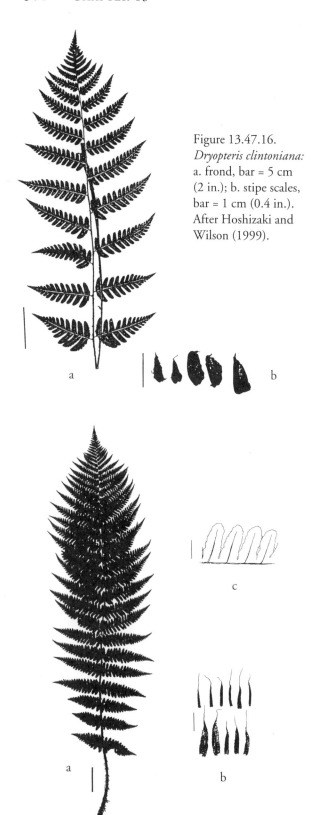

Figure 13.47.16.
Dryopteris clintoniana:
a. frond, bar = 5 cm
(2 in.); b. stipe scales,
bar = 1 cm (0.4 in.).
After Hoshizaki and
Wilson (1999).

underside next to the rachis. Unlike *D. affinis,* which also has the blackened spot, this species has segments that are toothed on the sides and has rounded apices. It is native to Europe.

The names *Dryopteris filix-mas* 'Undulata-Robusta' and *D. filix-mas* 'Robusta' are often misapplied in the United States trade to this species.

Dryopteris crassirhizoma Nakai   FIGURE 13.47.18
Thick-stemmed wood fern
Hardy, Zones 5–8

A medium-sized fern, to 1 m (3 ft.), with deciduous fronds and erect rhizomes that form offshoots. Grows well under medium light in moist-dry garden soil or potting mix. This species is easy to grow.

Dryopteris crassirhizoma forms an attractive vase-shaped cluster of fronds. Mickel (1994) reported that upon the onset of cold weather the fronds abruptly recline to the ground overnight (not gradually) and remain green throughout the winter. The erect, scaly crown of this fern is broad and massive, measuring 10–15 cm (4–6 in.) across. The fronds resemble those of *D. affinis* but differ by thick, glossy, brown stipe scales up to 2 cm (0.75 in.) long, one-pinnate-pin-

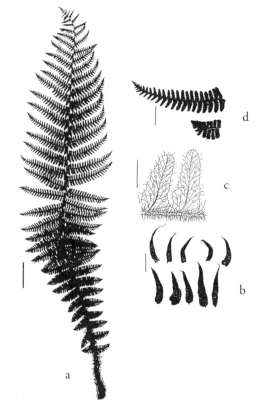

Figure 13.47.17. *Dryopteris complexa:* a. frond, bar = 5 cm (2 in.); b. stipe scales, bar = 1 cm (0.4 in.); c. pinnules from a medial pinna, bar = 5 cm (2 in.). After Hoshizaki and Wilson (1999).

Figure 13.47.18. *Dryopteris crassirhizoma:* a. frond, bar = 5 cm (2 in.); b. stipe scales, bar = 1 cm (0.4 in.); c. pinnules, bar = 1 cm (0.4 in.); d. medial pinna (above) and lower pinna (below), bar = 2 cm (0.8 in.). After Hoshizaki and Wilson (1999).

natifid blades, longer and narrower segments with margins entire or weakly crenate-serrate, and rounded and entire apices. The costae lack a black blotch at the base. The species is native to northeastern Asia.

Dryopteris cristata (Linnaeus) A. Gray

FIGURE 13.47.19

Crested wood fern
Very hardy, Zone 3

A medium-sized fern, to 50 cm (20 in.) tall, with deciduous fronds and short-creeping to erect rhizomes that form offshoots. Grows well under medium light in moist-wet garden soil or potting mix. The plants are easy to cultivate.

The fronds of *Dryopteris cristata* are one- to two-pinnate, narrowly lanceolate, and often have pinnae oriented more or less horizontally—the "venetian blind" effect. The basal pinnae are triangular, and fertile fronds are taller and more erect than sterile ones. The fertile pinnae occur mostly toward the apex of the blade and are slightly contracted. The species is native to the northern and southeastern United States. It commonly hybridizes in nature with *D. intermedia* to produce *D.* ×*boottii*.

Dryopteris cycadina (Franchet & Savatier) C. Christensen

FIGURE 13.47.20

Shaggy wood fern, black wood fern
Hardy, Zone 6

A medium-sized fern, to 1 m (3 ft.), with erect rhizomes and semi-evergreen fronds. Grows well under medium light in moist-dry garden soil or potting mix.

The common names of *Dryopteris cycadina* come from the dense, dark scales that cover the stipes and rachises. The blades are one-pinnate and leathery with about 30 pairs of pinnae, these mostly coarsely serrate to lobed one-third of the way to the costa. The basal pinnae point downward. The species is native to eastern Asia.

The cultivated plants of *Dryopteris cycadina* are often misidentified as *D. atrata* (Wallich) Ching or *D. hirtipes* Kuntze.

Dryopteris cystolepidota (Miquel) C. Christensen

FIGURE 13.47.21

syn. *Dryopteris nipponensis* Koidzumi
Hardy, Zone (5)6

A medium-sized fern, to 60 cm (2 ft.), with branched, short-creeping rhizomes and evergreen, glossy fronds. Grows well under medium light in moist garden soil or potting mix. The plants are easy to grow.

The blades of *Dryopteris cystolepidota* are broadly triangular, up to nearly three-pinnate at base, and thin-leathery. The segments have small spines turned up from the surface. The species is native to Japan and Korea.

Figure 13.47.19. *Dryopteris cristata:* a. frond, bar = 5 cm (2 in.); b. stipe scales, bar = 1 cm (0.4 in.). After Hoshizaki and Wilson (1999).

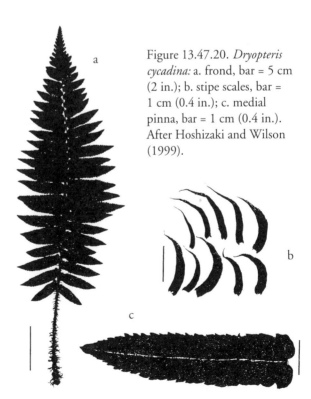

Figure 13.47.20. *Dryopteris cycadina:* a. frond, bar = 5 cm (2 in.); b. stipe scales, bar = 1 cm (0.4 in.); c. medial pinna, bar = 1 cm (0.4 in.). After Hoshizaki and Wilson (1999).

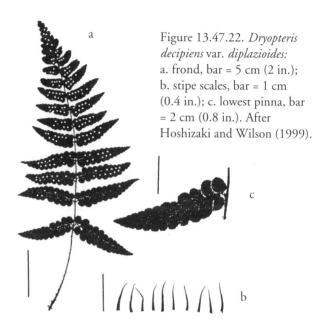

Figure 13.47.22. *Dryopteris decipiens* var. *diplazioides:* a. frond, bar = 5 cm (2 in.); b. stipe scales, bar = 1 cm (0.4 in.); c. lowest pinna, bar = 2 cm (0.8 in.). After Hoshizaki and Wilson (1999).

Figure 13.47.21. *Dryopteris cystolepidota:* a. frond, bar = 5 cm (2 in.); b. stipe scales, bar = 1 cm (0.4 in.); c. lowest pinna, bar = 2 cm (0.8 in.). After Hoshizaki and Wilson (1999).

Dryopteris dilatata (Hoffmann) A. Gray
FIGURES 13.47.23, 24

Broad wood fern, broad buckler fern
Hardy, Zone 4(5)

A medium to large fern, to 1 m (3 ft.) or more, with deciduous fronds and ascending to erect rhizomes that form offshoots. Grows well under low to medium light in acidic,

Dryopteris decipiens (Hooker) O. Kuntze
FIGURE 13.47.22

Hardy, Zone 5(7)

A small fern, to 30 cm (1 ft.), with ascending to erect rhizomes that form offshoots. Grows well under medium light in moist garden soil or potting mix. The fronds are deciduous in cold climates. They are coppery brown when young.

Dryopteris decipiens has one-pinnate-pinnatifid fronds with, generally, 15–18 pairs of shallowly lobed pinnae. The apices of the pinnae are curved slightly upward, toward the apex of the blade. The scales at the base of the stipes are purplish brown. The lower surfaces of the rachises and costae are beset with inflated scales. The species is native to Japan and China.

Plants in which the lower pinnae have a nearly free, round lobe next to the rachis are referred to as var. *diplazioides* (H. Christ) Ching (Figure 13.47.22).

Figure 13.47.23. *Dryopteris dilatata:* a. frond, bar = 5 cm (2 in.); b. stipe scales, bar = 1 cm (0.4 in.). After Hoshizaki and Wilson (1999).

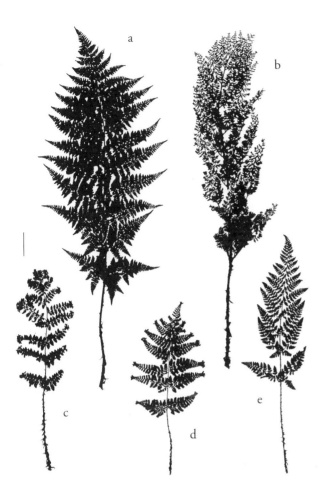

Figure 13.47.24. *Dryopteris dilatata* cultivars: a. 'Crispa Whiteside'; b. 'Lepidota Cristata'; c. 'Grandiceps'; d. 'Cristata'; e. 'Jimmy Dyce'. Bar = 5 cm (2 in.).

moist garden soil or potting mix. The plants are easy to grow. They are semi-evergreen and less vigorous in subtropical climates.

Dryopteris dilatata is a fertile hybrid of *D. expansa* and *D. intermedia*. It is often confused with *D. carthusiana*, which differs by darker green fronds with margins turned downward, larger stipe scales with a dark central stripe, and the downward-pointing pinnule next to the rachis two or more times as long as the opposite upward-pointing one. It is native to Europe.

Dryopteris dilatata is often mislabeled as *D. austriaca*.

'Crispa Whiteside'. Whiteside's crisped broad-buckler fern. Figure 13.47.24a. Ruffled foliage, lighter color than the species.

'Cristata'. Figure 13.47.24d. Frond and pinna tips crested when fully developed.

'Grandiceps'. Figure 13.47.24c. Frond apex crested into a dense tassel, pinnae crested.

'Jimmy Dyce'. Figure 13.47.24e. Fronds shorter, to 60 cm (24 in.), usually less stiff and erect, the pinnae close

together, slightly ruffled, blue-green in color. Hardy to Zone 6.

'Lepidota Cristata'. Figure 13.47.24b. Fronds finely dissected and crested, to 50 cm (20 in.), stipe and rachis with many brown, puffy scales. Hardy to Zone 4 and evergreen. Not as robust a grower as other cultivars.

'Recurved Form'. Segment margins strongly curved downward. Not as robust a grower as many of the other cultivars.

Dryopteris erythrosora (D. C. Eaton) O. Kuntze

FIGURES 13.47.2, 25; PLATE 26

Autumn fern
Hardy, Zone 5(6)

A medium-sized fern, to 1 m (3 ft.), with evergreen fronds and ascending to erect or prostrate, branching rhizomes. Grows well under low to medium-high light in moist to moist-dry garden soil or potting mix. The plants are easy to

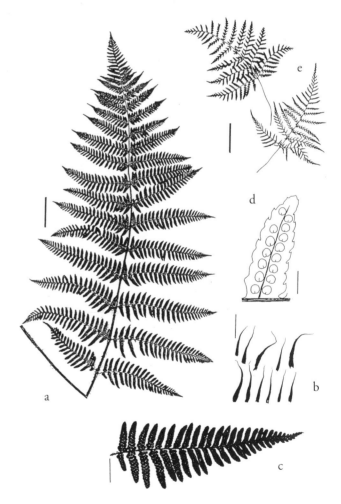

Figure 13.47.25. *Dryopteris erythrosora*: a. frond, bar = 5 cm (2 in.); b. stipe scales, bar = 1 cm (0.4 in.); c. lowest pinna, bar = 2 cm (0.8 in.); d. pinnule from medial pinna, bar = 5 mm (0.2 in.); e. forma *prolifica*, bar = 5 cm (2 in.). After Hoshizaki and Wilson (1999).

cultivate. New growth has an attractive reddish coppery color, turning dark, shiny green at maturity. New fronds are produced throughout the growing season, and in winter the fronds remain upright, not reclining as in many evergreen ferns.

Dryopteris erythrosora is highly variable but can be characterized as follows: the stipe scales are blackish and the blades are two-pinnate, mostly oblong-ovate, broad, and arching. The lowest basiscopic pinnules next to the rachis are short and have marginal teeth spinulose-tipped and incurved. The costal scales are strongly inflated and dark toward the tip. Set close to the midrib, the indusia are red or, rarely, greenish white (forma *viridosora* (Nakai ex H. Ito) H. Ito). The species is native to eastern Asia.

The variability of this species has caused considerable confusion in the trade. Most of the current plants circulating as *Dryopteris bissetiana* and *D. purpurella* are actually *D. erythrosora*.

forma *prolifica* (Maximowicz ex Franchet & Savatier) H. Ito. Blades shorter, 37 cm (15 in.), more triangular, usually with buds; pinnules narrow-linear, pointed.

Dryopteris expansa (C. Presl) Fraser-Jenkins & Jermy

FIGURE 13.47.26

syn. *Dryopteris austriaca* (Jacquin) Woynar
Arching wood fern, northern spreading wood fern
Very hardy, Zone 3(4)

A medium-sized fern, to 60 cm (2 ft.), with ascending or erect rhizomes and deciduous fronds. Grows well under low to medium light in acidic, moist garden soil or potting mix. The plants do not do well in subtropical climates.

Dryopteris expansa has tan stipe scales with a dark central stripe. The blades lack glands and are broadly triangular and three-pinnate-pinnatifid at the base, with the downward-pointing pinnule next to the rachis two to three times longer than the opposite upward-pointing pinnule. The pinnule margins are flat, not enrolled. The species is native to North America, Europe, and eastern Asia. It is a parent of *D. campyloptera* and is difficult to distinguish from the offspring.

Dryopteris filix-mas (Linnaeus) Schott

FIGURES 13.47.27, 28

Common male fern
Hardy, Zone 4(5)

A large fern, to 130 cm (52 in.), with deciduous fronds and short-creeping to erect rhizomes that form offshoots. Grows well under low to medium light in moist garden soil or potting mix. The usually deciduous fronds become semievergreen if the plants are grown in warmer climates. This species is easy to grow and has many garden variations.

Dryopteris filix-mas is of hybrid origin (but fertile) from a naturally occurring cross between *D. caucasica* and *D. oreades*. The fronds are one-pinnate-pinnatisect (nearly two-pinnate) with segments slightly tapered and toothed along

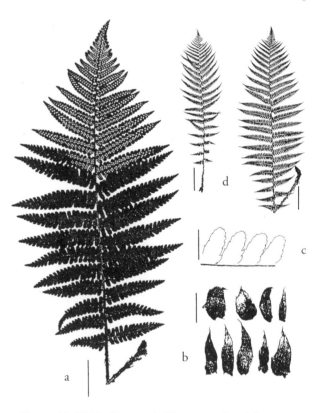

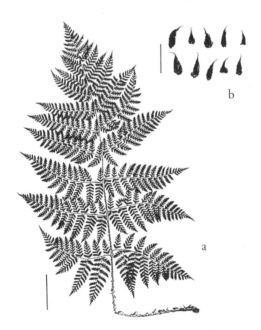

Figure 13.47.26. *Dryopteris expansa:* a. frond, bar = 5 cm (2 in.); b. stipe scales, bar = 1 cm (0.4 in.). After Hoshizaki and Wilson (1999).

Figure 13.47.27. *Dryopteris filix-mas:* a. frond, bar = 5 cm (2 in.); b. stipe scales, bar = 1 cm (0.4 in.); c. pinnules from medial pinna, bar = 1 cm (0.4 in.); d. other frond variations, bar = 10 cm (4 in.). After Hoshizaki and Wilson (1999).

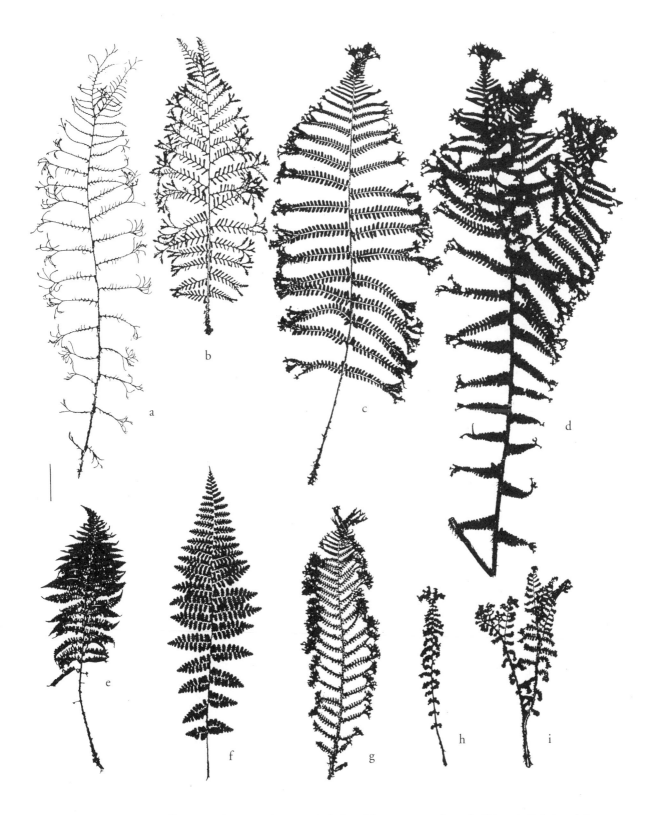

Figure 13.47.28. *Dryopteris filix-mas* cultivars: a. 'Linearis Polydactyla', an extreme form; b. 'Linearis Polydactyla'; c. 'Cristata'; d. 'Grandiceps'; e. 'Linearis Congesta'; f. 'Barnesii'; g. 'Crispa Cristata'; h. a dwarf, crisped, crested cultivar; i. 'Ramo Cristata'. Bar = 5 cm (2 in.).

the sides and apex. The teeth are acute and typically point toward the segment apex. The upper surface is puckered opposite the sori, and the young indusia have a flat, thin rim all around the edge. The species is native to North America and Europe.

'Barnesii'. Figure 13.47.28f. Barne's male fern. Fronds upright, narrow; pinnae short, to 5 cm (2 in.) long, wide, blunt; pinnules narrowed at base.

'Crispa Cristata'. Figure 13.47.28g. Frond apices and pinnae crested, pinnules ruffled.

'Cristata'. Figure 13.47.28c. Frond apices and pinnae crested; many different types.

'Grandiceps'. Figure 13.47.28d. Frond apices heavily tasseled, pinna tips less so.

'Linearis Congesta'. Figure 13.47.28e. Fronds to 37 cm (15 in.), pinnae crowded, pinnules narrow.

'Linearis Polydactyla'. Slender crested male fern. Figure 13.47.28a, b. Blades broad and elliptic, the blade and pinna apices crested, the segments finger-like, the segments of the pinnae skeletonized, mostly linear to nearly filiform. May grow better in acidic soil.

'Ramo Cristata'. Figure 13.47.28i. Fronds to 60 cm (24 in.), branched and crested.

'Undulata-Robusta'. See *Dryopteris complexa*.

Dryopteris formosana (H. Christ) C. Christensen
FIGURE 13.47.29

Hardy, Zone (6)7

A medium-sized fern, to 45 cm (18 in.), with short-creeping to erect rhizomes and evergreen fronds. Grows well under medium light in moist garden soil or potting mix.

Dryopteris formosana has broad, pentagonal fronds up to three-pinnate. The lowest basiscopic pinnule next to the rachis is quite long, and the segment teeth are short-aristate and tend to turn upward from the plane of the blade. The scales on the costa undersides are weakly inflated, appearing puffy (not flat). The species is native to Japan, Taiwan, and the Philippines.

Dryopteris fragrans (Linnaeus) Schott
FIGURE 13.47.30

Very hardy, Zone 2

A small fern, to 20 cm (8 in.), with erect rhizomes and marcescent fronds. Grows well under medium light in moist garden soil or potting mix. This species does best in cold-temperate areas. The plants grow in rock crevices and talus slopes in the wild.

Dryopteris fragrans has narrowly elliptic, one-pinnate-pinnatifid blades, the stipes only about one-third as long as the blades. The brown, withered fronds persist on the rhizome, sometimes accumulating as a thick mat. Yellowish, round glands dot the blade, especially on the lower surface, and they emit a distinctive fragrance when crushed. The indusia are circular, large, 1–2 mm wide, and overlap-

Figure 13.47.29. *Dryopteris formosana:* a. frond, bar = 5 cm (2 in.); b. stipe scales, bar = 1 cm (0.4 in.); c. pinnule from medial pinna, bar = 5 mm (0.2 in.). After Hoshizaki and Wilson (1999).

Figure 13.47.30. *Dryopteris fragrans:* a. habit, bar = 5 cm (2 in.); b. stipe scales, bar = 1 cm (0.4 in.). After Hoshizaki and Wilson (1999).

ping when young. The species is circumboreal, occurring in North America, Europe, and Asia.

Dryopteris fuscipes C. Christensen   FIGURE 13.47.31
Semi-hardy (?)

A medium-sized fern, to 50 cm (20 in.), with ascending to erect rhizomes and semi-evergreen fronds. Grows well under medium light in moist garden soil or potting mix.

Dryopteris fuscipes has triangular blades up to two-pinnate with narrow pinnae and stout, oblong segments. The scales on the lower surface of the costae are strongly inflated, appearing puffy (not flat). The species is native to eastern Asia.

Figure 13.47.32. *Dryopteris goldiana:* a. frond, bar = 5 cm (2 in.); b. stipe scales, bar = 1 cm (0.4 in.). After Hoshizaki and Wilson (1999).

Figure 13.47.31. *Dryopteris fuscipes:* a. frond, bar = 5 cm (2 in.); b. stipe scales, bar = 1 cm (0.4 in.). After Hoshizaki and Wilson (1999).

Dryopteris goldiana (Hooker ex Goldie) A. Gray
FIGURE 13.47.32
Giant wood fern, Goldie's fern
Very hardy, Zone 3(4)

A large fern, to 130 cm (52 in.), with ascending to erect rhizomes and deciduous fronds. Grows well under low to medium light in moist to moist-wet garden soil or potting mix. The blades are slightly bluish green.

The stipe scales of *Dryopteris goldiana* are narrowly triangular with thin, fragile, membranous margins and dark centers. The blades are mostly large, widely ovate, and one-pinnate-pinnatifid to two-pinnate, with wide truncate bases. The pinna apices are abruptly pointed, and the sori

lie close to the midrib. The species is native to eastern North America.

Dryopteris hondoensis Koidzumi   FIGURE 13.47.33
Very hardy, Zone 4

A medium-sized fern, to about 60 cm (2 ft.), with evergreen fronds and short-creeping, ascending, or erect rhizomes that form offshoots. Grows under low to medium light in moist to moist-dry garden soil or potting mix.

Dryopteris hondoensis is very similar to *D. erythrosora* except for its thinner leaf texture and short-stalked pinnae. In addition, the undersides of the costae have nonbullate or very weakly bullate scales. Plants with pinkish indusia are named forma *rubisora* Sa. Kurata. The species is native to Japan, Korea, and China.

Dryopteris intermedia (Muhlenberg ex Willdenow)
A. Gray   FIGURE 13.47.34
syn. *Dryopteris spinulosa* var. *intermedia* (Muhlenberg) Underwood
Evergreen wood fern, glandular wood fern, fancy fern
Very hardy, Zone 3

A medium-sized fern, to 70 cm (28 in.), with erect rhizomes and evergreen fronds. Grows well under low to medium light in moist garden soil or potting mix. The plants are easy to grow in temperate areas but are not suitable in subtropical ones.

Figure 13.47.33. *Dryopteris hondoensis:* a. frond, bar = 5 cm (2 in.); b. stipe scales, bar = 1 cm (0.4 in.); c. pinnule from medial pinna, bar = 5 mm (0.2 in.); d. lowest pinna, bar = 2 cm (0.8 in.).

Figure 13.47.34. *Dryopteris intermedia:* a. frond, bar = 5 cm (2 in.); b. stipe scales, bar = 1 cm (0.4 in.). After Hoshizaki and Wilson (1999).

Two characters will distinguish *Dryopteris intermedia* from similar ones (such as *D. carthusiana*) in the northeastern United States. First, the lower surfaces of the blades, especially the rachises and costae, are glandular pubescent, the glands appearing as minute hairs with swollen, head-like tips (a hand lens is needed to see this). Second, the innermost pinnule on the basal pinnae is shorter than the adjacent, outer ones (they are longer in similar species). The species is native to eastern North America.

Dryopteris kuratae Nakaike   FIGURE 13.47.35
Semi-hardy, Zone 6

A medium-sized fern, to about 1 m (3 ft.), with deciduous fronds. Grows well under medium light in moist garden soil or potting mix. Easy to grow.

Dryopteris kuratae bears one-pinnate-pinnatilobed blades, and the lobes have wide V- or U-shaped sinuses. The sori are scattered close to margin. The species is native to eastern Asia.

Figure 13.47.35. *Dryopteris kuratae:* a. frond, bar = 5 cm (2 in.); b. stipe scales, bar = 1 cm (0.4 in.); c. medial pinna, bar = 1 cm (0.4 in.). After Hoshizaki and Wilson (1999).

This plant is often confused with *Dryopteris pycnopteroides* (H. Christ) C. Christensen of Japan, a larger plant with sori scattered over the pinnae.

Dryopteris lacera (Thunberg) O. Kuntze
FIGURE 13.47.36

Hardy, Zone 5

A medium-sized fern, to about 60 cm (2 ft.), with ascending to erect rhizomes and deciduous fronds. Grows well under medium light in moist garden soil or potting mix. This species is easy to cultivate. The normally deciduous fronds tend to be slightly evergreen in warmer climates.

The broad lanceolate blades of *Dryopteris lacera* are one-pinnate-pinnatifid to two-pinnate and fertile only toward the tip. The segments or lobes are entire or nearly so, unlike many *Dryopteris* species that are lobed. At maturity the fronds are glabrous, without scales on the rachises or costae. The fertile pinnae are more contracted than the sterile and wither early. The species is native to eastern Asia.

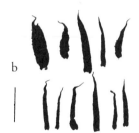

Figure 13.47.36. *Dryopteris lacera:* a. frond, bar = 5 cm (2 in.); b. stipe scales, bar = 1 cm (0.4 in.). After Hoshizaki and Wilson (1999).

Dryopteris lepidopoda Hayata
FIGURE 13.47.37

Hardy, Zone (5)6

A medium-sized fern, to 1 m (3 ft.), with erect rhizomes and evergreen fronds. Grows well under medium light in moist garden soil or potting mix. According to Mickel (1994), the young fronds are reddish gold.

Dryopteris lepidopoda has relatively long stipes with narrow, black, ciliate scales. The blades are oblong-triangular,

as wide at the base as in the middle, and the pinnae are pinnatisect with many oblong, shiny segments. Segments have rounded apices bearing sharp teeth. The species is native from eastern India to China and Taiwan.

Figure 13.47.37. *Dryopteris lepidopoda:* a. frond, bar = 5 cm (2 in.); b. stipe scales, bar = 1 cm (0.4 in.). After Hoshizaki and Wilson (1999).

Dryopteris ludoviciana (Kunze) Small
FIGURE 13.47.38

Southern wood fern
Hardy, Zone (5)6

A medium-large fern, to 130 cm (52 in.), with short-creeping to erect rhizomes that readily form offshoots. Grows well under medium light in moist-wet garden soil or potting mix. It is semi-evergreen. The plants are easy to grow in southern California.

The shiny dark green blades are one-pinnate-pinnatifid, with the fertile pinnae only in the apical part of the blade and markedly contracted. *Dryopteris ludoviciana* is native to the southeastern United States.

This species hybridizes with *Dryopteris celsa* to form the sterile hybrid *D. ×australis.*

Figure 13.47.38. *Dryopteris ludoviciana:* a. frond, bar = 5 cm (2 in.); b. stipe scales, bar = 1 cm (0.4 in.). After Hoshizaki and Wilson (1999).

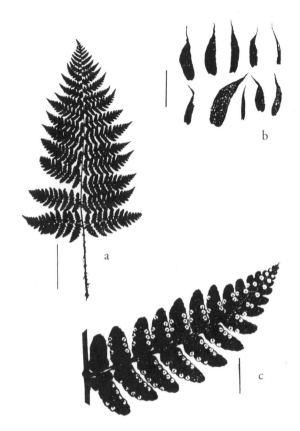

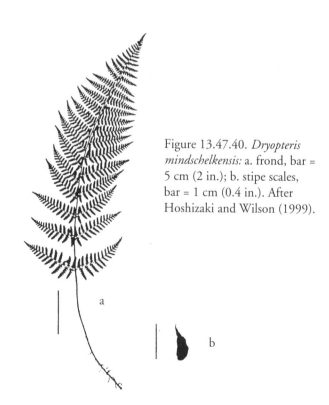

Figure 13.47.39. *Dryopteris marginalis:* a. frond, bar = 5 cm (2 in.); b. stipe scales, bar = 1 cm (0.4 in.); c. medial pinna, bar = 1 cm (0.4 in.). After Hoshizaki and Wilson (1999).

Dryopteris marginalis (Linnaeus) A. Gray

FIGURE 13.47.39

Eastern wood fern, marginal shield fern
Very hardy, Zone 2(3)

A medium-sized fern, to 60 cm (2 ft.), with erect rhizomes and evergreen fronds. Grows well under medium light in moist garden soil or potting mix. The plants are easy to grow and have bluish green blades. They do not do well in subtropical climates.

Dryopteris marginalis can be distinguished from many other *Dryopteris* by having sori that are close to the margin. The blades are one-pinnate-pinnatifid to two-pinnate and slightly leathery. The species is native to northeastern North America, where it grows on or among rocks.

Dryopteris mindshelkensis N. V. Pavlov

FIGURE 13.47.40

syn. *Dryopteris submontana* (Fraser-Jenkins) Fraser-Jenkins, *D. villarii* subsp. *submontana* Fraser-Jenkins & Jermy
Rigid buckler fern, limestone wood fern
Hardy, Zone (5)6

A medium-sized fern, to 60 cm (2 ft.), with ascending to erect rhizomes and deciduous fronds. Grows well in moist, basic garden soil or potting mix.

Figure 13.47.40. *Dryopteris mindschelkensis:* a. frond, bar = 5 cm (2 in.); b. stipe scales, bar = 1 cm (0.4 in.). After Hoshizaki and Wilson (1999).

Dryopteris mindshelkensis has narrowly triangular fronds densely covered on both surfaces with stalked, yellow glands that emit a fragrance when crushed. The species is native to Europe and northern Africa.

Dryopteris oreades Fomin
FIGURE 13.47.41

Mountain male fern
Hardy, Zone 4 (5–6)

A medium-sized fern, to 50 cm (20 in.), with deciduous fronds and erect rhizomes forming many offshoots. Grows well under medium to high light in acidic, moist garden soil or potting mix. The fronds arise in a strongly ascending fashion, forming shuttlecock-like clusters.

Dryopteris oreades resembles a small *D. filix-mas* but differs by gray-green, ruffled blade margins, segment apices with blunt teeth pointing away from the pinnule apex in a fan-shaped pattern, stipe scales dull, and young indusia thick and green. The species is native to the British Isles and western Europe.

Dryopteris polylepis (Franchet & Savatier) C. Christensen
FIGURE 13.47.42

Scaly wood fern
Hardy, Zone (5)6

A medium-sized fern, to about 60 cm (2 ft.), with deciduous fronds. Grows well under medium light in moist garden soil or potting mix.

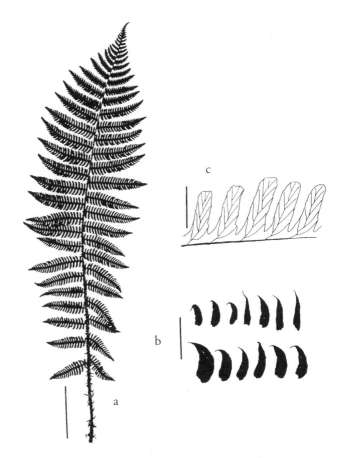

Figure 13.47.42. *Dryopteris polylepis:* a. frond, bar = 5 cm (2 in.); b. stipe scales, bar = 1 cm (0.4 in.); c. pinnules with unbranched veins, bar = 2 cm (0.8 in.). After Hoshizaki and Wilson (1999).

The pinnae are pinnatisect, and the veins are unforked, except for those in the basiscopic segments next to the rachis. *Dryopteris polylepis* is native to northeastern Asia.

Dryopteris pseudo-filix-mas (Fée) Rothmaler
FIGURE 13.47.43

Mexican male fern
Hardy, Zone 5(6)

A medium-sized fern, to 1 m (3 ft.), with semi-evergreen fronds and erect rhizomes forming offshoots. Grows well under medium light in moist garden soil or potting mix. The plants are easy to cultivate.

Dryopteris pseudo-filix-mas resembles *D. affinis* but differs by the basiscopic pinnule of the lowest pinnae usually elongate and pinnatifid on older plants (those of *D. affinis* are not elongated and are shallowly lobed). As in *D. affinis*, a black spot is present on the lower surface of the costa base. It is native to Mexico and Guatemala.

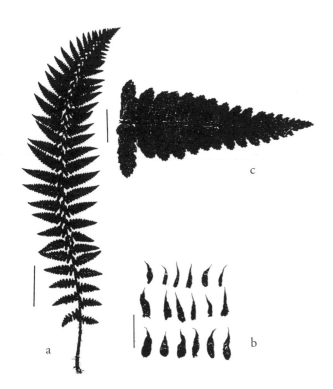

Figure 13.47.41. *Dryopteris oreades:* a. frond, bar = 5 cm (2 in.); b. stipe scales, bar = 1 cm (0.4 in.); c. pinna, bar = 1 cm (0.4 in.). After Hoshizaki and Wilson (1999).

Figure 13.47.43. *Dryopteris pseudo-filix-mas:* a. frond, bar = 5 cm (2 in.); b. stipe scales, bar = 1 cm (0.4 in.); c. lowest pinnae with variations in cut of the basiscopic pinnule, bar = 2 cm (0.8 in.). After Hoshizaki and Wilson (1999).

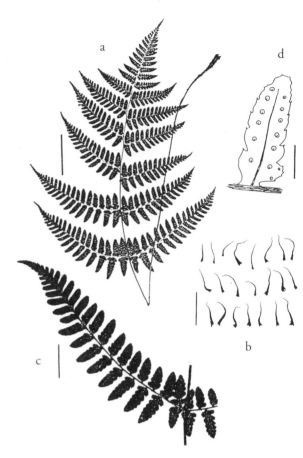

Figure 13.47.44. *Dryopteris purpurella:* a. frond, bar = 5 cm (2 in.); b. stipe scales, bar = 1 cm (0.4 in.); c. lowest pinnae, bar = 2 cm (0.8 in.); d. pinnule from medial pinna, bar = 5 mm (0.2 in.). After Hoshizaki and Wilson (1999).

Dryopteris purpurella Tagawa   FIGURE 13.47.44
Hardy, Zone 5

A medium-sized fern, to about 60 cm (2 ft.), with erect rhizomes and evergreen fronds. Grows well under low to medium light in moist garden soil or potting mix.

Dryopteris purpurella resembles *D. erythrosora,* but it differs by having purplish stipes and rachises; two-to three-pinnate-pinnatifid, smaller, coarser, and flatter blades; sessile, fewer (about six), and more distant pinnae; lower pinnae at nearly right angles to the rachis; and pinnules overlaying the rachis. The red color of the rachis and costae fades slowly. The underside of the costa bears strongly inflated scales, and the sori are submarginal. The species is native to Japan, Korea, and China.

Trade plants of *Dryopteris erythrosora* are often misidentified as *D. purpurella.*

Dryopteris remota (A. Braun) Druce   FIGURE 13.47.45
Scaly buckler fern
Very hardy, Zone 4

A medium-sized fern, to 1 m (3 ft.), with ascending to erect rhizomes and deciduous fronds. Grows well under medium light in moist garden soil or potting mix. In the northeastern United States this species volunteers when planted in gardens.

Dryopteris remota is of hybrid origin between *D. affinis* and *D. expansa.* Both normal and aborted spores are produced. The blades are narrowly triangular-lanceolate, two-pinnate, and nonglandular. The pinnules are acute. The species is native to Europe.

Dryopteris sacrosancta Koidzumi   FIGURE 13.47.46
Hardy, Zone (6)7

A medium-sized fern, to about 60 cm (2 ft.), with ascending to erect rhizomes. Grows well under low to medium light in moist garden soil or potting mix.

Figure 13.47.45. *Dryopteris remota:* a. frond, bar = 5 cm (2 in.); b. stipe scales, bar = 1 cm (0.4 in.). After Hoshizaki and Wilson (1999).

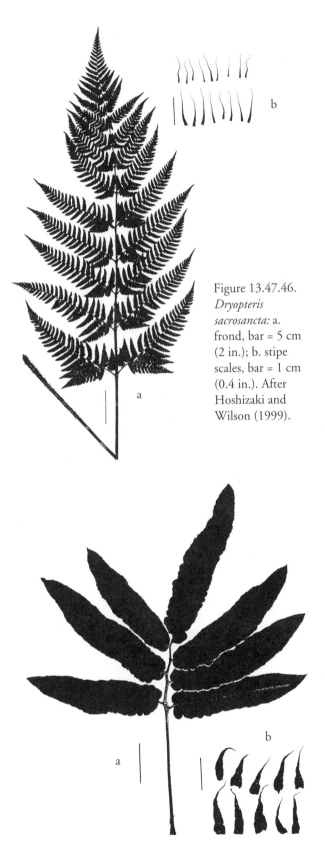

Figure 13.47.46. *Dryopteris sacrosancta:* a. frond, bar = 5 cm (2 in.); b. stipe scales, bar = 1 cm (0.4 in.). After Hoshizaki and Wilson (1999).

Dryopteris sacrosancta has large stipe scales with pale borders, and the scales on the undersides of the costae are weakly inflated (puffy) and dark tipped. The blades are triangular, three-pinnate, slightly glossy and leathery, and flat margined. The lowermost downward-pointing pinnule next to the rachis is elongate. The species is native to Japan, China, and Korea.

Dryopteris sieboldii (T. Moore) O. Kuntze

FIGURE 13.47.47

Japanese wood fern, Siebold's wood fern
Hardy, Zone 6

A medium-sized fern, to 50 cm (20 in.), with erect rhizomes and semi-evergreen fronds. Grows well under medium light in moist garden soil or potting mix. The plants are somewhat slow growing and tend to emerge rather late in the spring (late June in New York).

Dryopteris sieboldii is distinct from nearly all other wood ferns because it has a terminal segment that resembles the lateral pinnae (most wood ferns have a tapered pinnatifid apex). The blades are one-pinnate with two to seven large, leathery, oblong-lanceolate, entire pinnae. The species is native to Japan, Taiwan, and China.

Dryopteris sichotensis V. Komarov   FIGURE 13.47.48
syn. *Dryopteris coreano-montana* Nakai
Hardy, Zone 5(?) or hardier (?)

A medium-large fern, to 130 cm (52 in.), with erect rhizomes forming offshoots and upright, semi-evergreen

Figure 13.47.47. *Dryopteris sieboldii:* a. frond, bar = 5 cm (2 in.); b. stipe scales, bar = 1 cm (0.4 in.). After Hoshizaki and Wilson (1999).

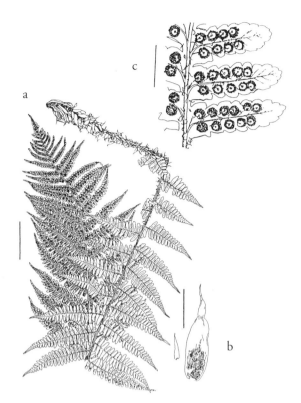

Figure 13.47.48. *Dryopteris sichotensis:* a. frond, bar = 5 cm (2 in.); b. stipe scales, bar = 1 cm (0.4 in.); c. pinnules, bar = 5 mm (0.2 in.). After Kurata and Nakaike (1979).

fronds. Grows under medium or stronger light in moist garden soil or potting mix.

Dryopteris sichotensis resembles *D. oreades,* but its pinnule teeth are slightly acute, not splayed out, the pinnule apices are more or less acute or rounded, the stipe scales more or less glossy, and the fronds yellow-green. The species is native to northeastern Asia.

Dryopteris stewartii Fraser-Jenkins   FIGURE 13.47.49
Hardy, Zone 6

A medium-large fern, to about 130 cm (52 in.), with deciduous fronds and ascending to erect rhizomes that form offshoots. Grows well under medium light in moist garden soil or potting mix. The plants are easy to grow. The normally deciduous fronds become semi-evergreen in warmer climates.

The blades of *Dryopteris stewartii* are triangular-lanceolate and two-pinnate-pinnatifid, and the segments are rounded and often bear spine-tipped teeth. The species is native to the Himalayas.

Plants circulating in the United States trade as *Dryopteris stewartii* are foliose forms of *D. carthusiana.* True *D. stewartii* is circulating in the trade incorrectly as *D. goeringiana* Koidzumi, a species not cultivated in the United States.

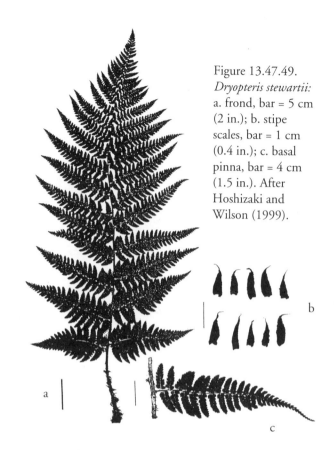

Figure 13.47.49. *Dryopteris stewartii:* a. frond, bar = 5 cm (2 in.); b. stipe scales, bar = 1 cm (0.4 in.); c. basal pinna, bar = 4 cm (1.5 in.). After Hoshizaki and Wilson (1999).

Dryopteris sublacera H. Christ   FIGURE 13.47.50
Hardy to semi-hardy, Zone 7

A medium-sized fern, to 30 cm (1 ft.), with evergreen fronds and erect rhizomes forming offshoots. Grows well under medium light in moist garden soil or potting mix. The plants are easy to cultivate.

Dryopteris sublacera bears abundant reddish to dark brown, minutely fringed scales on the stipes and rachises, and these scales leave a roughened surface when shed. The pinnules have rounded tips bearing short teeth. The species is native to India and eastern Asia.

Dryopteris tokyoensis (Matsumoto ex Makino)
C. Christensen   FIGURE 13.47.51
Tokyo wood fern
Hardy, Zone 5

A medium-sized fern, to 1 m (3 ft.), with deciduous fronds and ascending rhizomes that form offshoots. Grows well under medium light in moist, acidic garden soil or potting mix. This species is not suited for gardens in southern California.

Dryopteris tokyoensis is characterized by narrow, erect fronds that form a slender, vase-shaped cluster. The blades are widest above the middle and taper gradually toward the base, with 20–40 pairs of pinnae; the basal-most pinnae are nothing more than highly reduced, ear-like lobes. The cen-

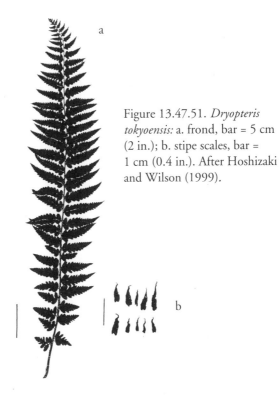

Figure 13.47.51. *Dryopteris tokyoensis:* a. frond, bar = 5 cm (2 in.); b. stipe scales, bar = 1 cm (0.4 in.). After Hoshizaki and Wilson (1999).

Figure 13.47.50. *Dryopteris sublacera:* a. frond, bar = 5 cm (2 in.); b. stipe scales, bar = 1 cm (0.4 in.); c. basal pinnae, bar = 2 cm (0.8 in.). After Hoshizaki and Wilson (1999).

tral pinnae are sessile or nearly so, with an auricle or "ear" on both sides of the base. The species is native to China, Japan, and Korea.

Dryopteris uniformis (Makino) Makino

FIGURES 13.47.1, 52

Hardy, Zone 5 (6)

A medium-sized fern, to 60 cm (2 ft.), with deciduous fronds and erect rhizomes that sometimes form offshoots. Grows in moist garden soil or potting mix. Although deciduous, this species is easy to grow, even in warmer climates.

Dryopteris uniformis is characterized by one-pinnate-pinnatifid to two-pinnate blades and densely scaly stipes and rachises. The scales are dark brown to black and have entire or fringed margins. The sori are borne on the upper pinnae. The species is native to Japan, Korea, and China.

'Cristata'. (*Dryopteris uniformis* forma *cristata* Ogata). Figures 13.47.1, 52d. Frond apices sometimes forked, pinnae crested. Said to volunteer readily from spores. Briefly deciduous in southern California.

Figure 13.47.52. *Dryopteris uniformis:* a. frond, bar = 5 cm (2 in.); b. stipe scales, bar = 1 cm (0.4 in.); c. medial pinna, bar = 2 cm (0.8 in.); d. 'Cristata', upper part of frond, bar = 5 cm (2 in.). After Hoshizaki and Wilson (1999), except d.

Dryopteris varia (Linnaeus) O. Kuntze

FIGURE 13.47.53

Hardy to semi-hardy, Zone 6(7)

A medium-sized fern, to 60 cm (2 ft.), with short-creeping to ascending rhizomes and semi-evergreen fronds. Grows well under medium light in moist garden soil or potting mix. The plants are easy to cultivate but grow slowly. The new fronds are bronze.

The blades of *Dryopteris varia* are triangular or pentagonal, abruptly narrowed in the distal third, stiff, thick, leathery, and dull gray-green. The lowest basiscopic pinnule next to the rachis is the longest. The costal scales are weakly inflated, flattened, or shallowly convex. The species is native to India and eastern Asia.

Dryopteris wallichiana (Sprengel) N. Hylander

FIGURE 13.47.54; PLATE 27

syn. *Dryopteris paleacea* (Swartz) Handel-Mazzetti, *D. parallelogramma* (Kunze) Alston

Wallich's wood fern

Hardy, Zone 5(6)

A medium-large fern, to 130 cm (52 in.), with semi-evergreen fronds and erect rhizomes that form occasional offshoots. Prefers medium light and moist garden soil or pot-

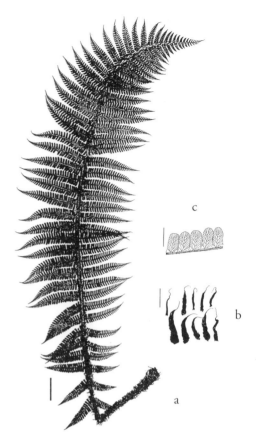

Figure 13.47.54. *Dryopteris wallichiana:* a. frond, bar = 5 cm (2 in.); b. stipe scales, bar = 1 cm (0.4 in.); c. pinnules from medial pinnae, bar = 1 cm (0.4 in.). After Hoshizaki and Wilson (1999).

ting mix. This species grows best in mildly cool, humid climates. The fronds are arranged in a handsome shuttlecock pattern.

Dryopteris wallichiana is characterized by one-pinnate-pinnatifid blades with 20–35 pairs of sessile pinnae. The segments of the pinnae are squared or oblong. The rachis is conspicuously covered by black, linear or thread-like scales. The species is native to subtropical and tropical mountains of the world.

Elaphoglossum

FIGURES 13.48.1, 2

syn. *Hymenodium, Peltapteris*

Paddle fern

The genus *Elaphoglossum* consists of mostly medium-sized ferns with simple, entire, often paddle-shaped blades. Fertile fronds are usually taller and narrower than the sterile ones and are produced infrequently. The sori are acrostichoid, appearing as if spread across the lower surface of the blade, not in discrete dots. Many species bear clustered fronds that are attractive in pots or baskets. Others are attractive for their metallic hues or unusual covering of hairs

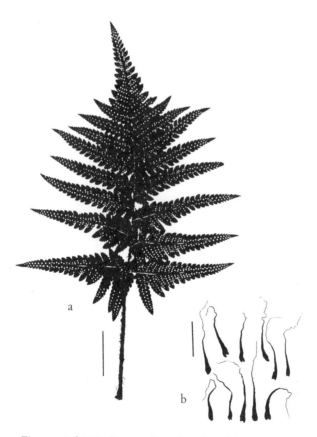

Figure 13.47.53. *Dryopteris varia:* a. frond, bar = 5 cm (2 in.); b. stipe scales, bar = 1 cm (0.4 in.). After Hoshizaki and Wilson (1999).

Figure 13.48.1. *Elaphoglossum crinitum:* habit.

or scales. Most of the species are epiphytes and need greenhouse or indoor protection during the cold months. The spores are often difficult to germinate.

Elaphoglossum species can usually be recognized by simple and entire fronds, free veins, and acrostichoid sori. The rhizomes are scaly and creeping or, rarely, erect. In many species the stipe base is jointed to a darker, stump-like extension (phyllopodium) of the rhizome. The blades vary in shape from broadly ovate to linear; rarely are they pinnatifid or deeply dichotomously cut, as is the case with *Elaphoglossum peltatum.* The blade tissue varies from glabrous to densely scaly and is mostly firm to leathery.

Peltapteris differs from *Elaphoglossum* by its deeply cut blades but is closely related to typical *Elaphoglossum* species and therefore is treated here in the latter genus. The name *Hymenodium* has been used for *Elaphoglossum crinatum,* which is distinct by having netted veins, but this characteristic alone is insufficient to distinguish another genus.

Elaphoglossum occurs in the tropics and subtropics of the world, though most of the species are American. It contains about 500 species, making it one of the world's most species-rich fern genera. Due to the large number, the species are difficult to identify, and many species have not received scientific names. Another obstacle with cultivated

material is the lack of information about the country of origin. The genus name comes from the Greek *elaphos,* stag, and *glossa,* tongue, alluding to the resemblance of the blades to a deer's tongue.

Elaphoglossum apodum (Kaulfuss) Schott ex J. Smith
FIGURE 13.48.3

Tender

A small-medium fern with erect, clustered fronds. Grows well under low to medium light in drained, moist potting soil or uncut moss.

The rhizome scales of *Elaphoglossum apodum* are dense, linear-attenuate, twisted, glossy, and pale orange-brown. The stipes are nearly absent, and the blades are widest above the middle, about 2.5–4 cm (1–1.5 in.) wide, and thin-herbaceous. Brownish orange, hair-like scales are found on both surfaces of the blade. The fertile fronds are short and narrow. This species is native to tropical America.

Elaphoglossum erinaceum (Fée) T. Moore, which is rarely cultivated, can be distinguished from *E. apodum* by longer stipes and more oval blades.

Figure 13.48.3. *Elaphoglossum apodum:* habit, bar = 5 cm (2 in.).

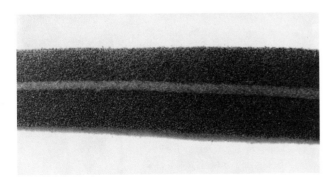

Figure 13.48.2. *Elaphoglossum:* sporangial area.

Elaphoglossum crinitum (Linnaeus) H. Christ

FIGURES 13.48.1, 4

syn. *Hymenodium crinitum* (Linnaeus) Fée
Elephant-ear fern
Tender

A small-medium fern with short-creeping rhizomes. Grows best with year-round heat under low to medium light in well-drained, moist-wet potting mix or uncut moss.

Elaphoglossum crinitum is a striking species, characterized by large, oblong blades with scattered, erect, black scales on both surfaces. Unlike most *Elaphoglossum* species, the veins are netted (without included veinlets). The species is native to the American tropics.

Elaphoglossum decoratum (Kunze) T. Moore

FIGURE 13.48.5

Tender

A small-medium fern with short-creeping rhizomes. Grows under low to medium light in well-drained, moist potting mix or uncut moss. This species is difficult to grow. Showy scales along the stipes and margins of the blades make for attractive foliage.

The scales on the stipes and blade margins are about 3.5 mm (about 0.1 in.) long, overlapping, yellowish brown, and heart-shaped. The blades of *Elaphoglossum decoratum* are linear-lanceolate to oblong, dark, thick, leathery, abruptly short-acuminate at the apex, and roundish to acute at the base. The surfaces of the blade are covered by minute, star-shaped scales; these are much less conspicuous than the marginal scales. The species is native to tropical America.

Elaphoglossum herminieri (Bory ex Fée) T. Moore

FIGURE 13.48.6

Tender

A medium to large fern with short-creeping rhizomes and often long, pendulous fronds. Grows under low to medium light in drained, moist potting mix or uncut moss. The fronds are attractive for their bluish green color and pendulous habit.

Elaphoglossum herminieri is characterized by pendent, nearly sessile fronds up to 1 m (3 ft.) or more long. Linear, metallic blue-green, leathery blades are dotted with minute, star-shaped, glandular scales on both surfaces. The fertile fronds, which are rarely produced, are rounded or kidney-

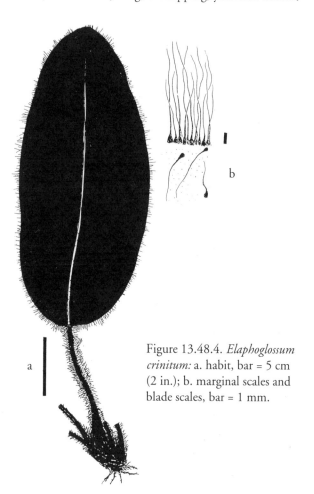

Figure 13.48.4. *Elaphoglossum crinitum:* a. habit, bar = 5 cm (2 in.); b. marginal scales and blade scales, bar = 1 mm.

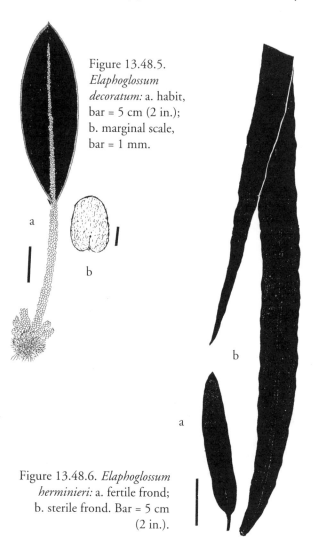

Figure 13.48.5. *Elaphoglossum decoratum:* a. habit, bar = 5 cm (2 in.); b. marginal scale, bar = 1 mm.

Figure 13.48.6. *Elaphoglossum herminieri:* a. fertile frond; b. sterile frond. Bar = 5 cm (2 in.).

shaped and much smaller than the sterile fronds. The species is native to tropical America.

Elaphoglossum luridum (Fée) H. Christ

FIGURE 13.48.7

syn. *Elaphoglossum schomburgkii* (Fée) T. Moore
Tender

A medium-sized fern with short-creeping to nearly erect rhizomes. Grows well under low to medium light in well-drained, moist potting mix or uncut moss.

    Elaphoglossum luridum is easy to recognize by its oblanceolate, medium-sized blades and dark, shaggy scales on the stipes and midribs. The lower surfaces of the blades have scattered small scales, and the rachises have dark star-shaped scales with twisted rays. The species is native to lowland forests of the American tropics.

Elaphoglossum maxonii Underwood ex Maxon

FIGURE 13.48.8

Semi-tender

A small to medium fern with medium-creeping rhizomes. Grows well under medium light in drained, moist garden soil or potting mix. This species is easy to cultivate.

The creeping rhizomes of *Elaphoglossum maxonii* are 8–15 mm (0.3–0.6 in.) wide, with phyllopodia hidden among the rhizome scales, the scales being narrowly triangular, golden or light brown, acuminate, and irregularly ciliate. The fronds are erect, leathery, and have ovate to narrowly elliptic blades, decurrent at the base. Minute and irregular star-shaped scales often with blackened centers are scattered on both blade surfaces. The fertile fronds are smaller than the sterile ones. The species is native to the Greater Antilles.

Figure 13.48.8. *Elaphoglossum maxonii:* habit, bar = 5 cm (2 in.).

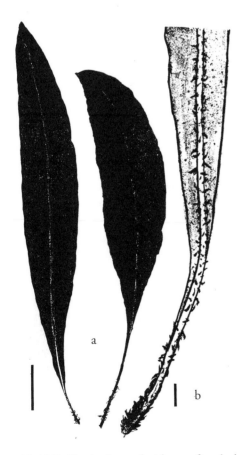

Figure 13.48.7. *Elaphoglossum luridum:* a. fronds, bar = 5 cm (2 in.); b. base of fronds, showing dark scales, bar = 5 cm (2 in.).

Elaphoglossum metallicum Mickel

FIGURE 13.48.9

Semi-tender

A medium-sized fern with short-creeping, branched rhizomes and fronds close together. Grows well under medium light in drained, moist potting mix or uncut moss. The fronds are attractive because of their iridescent, metallic blue blades.

    Elaphoglossum metallicum bears phyllopodia on its creeping rhizome. The stipes are densely covered with blackened and some lighter colored scales, and the blades are leathery and vary from lanceolate to broadly elliptic.

The scales on the undersurface are scattered, dark reddish brown, skeletonized, and about 1 mm long. There are fewer on the upper surface, and they tend to fall away. This species is known only from Peru.

Figure 13.48.9. *Elaphoglossum metallicum*: frond, bar = 5 cm (2 in.).

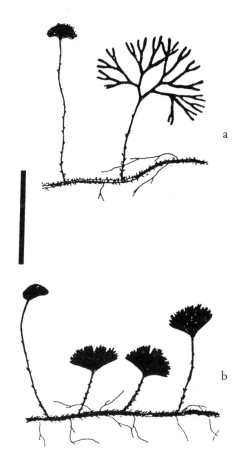

Figure 13.48.10. *Elaphoglossum peltatum*: a. habit, with fertile frond on left, sterile frond on right; b. forma *standleyi* habit, with fertile frond on left, sterile fronds on right. Bar = 5 cm (2 in.).

Elaphoglossum peltatum (Swartz) Urban

FIGURE 13.48.10

syn. *Peltapteris peltata* (Swartz) C. V. Morton,
    Rhipidopteris peltata (Swartz) Fée
Tender

A small fern with thin, long-creeping rhizomes and erect, peltately divided fronds. Grows well under low to medium light in drained, moist potting mix or uncut moss. The plants are suitable for use in bottle gardens.

Elaphoglossum peltatum is easily distinguished by the sterile blades typically deeply divided into narrow segments, although some forms are less divided. The rhizome and stipe scales are broadly ovate, thin, and tan or pale brown. Unlike the other cultivated species of *Elaphoglossum,* this species lacks phyllopodia. The fertile fronds are rounded and slightly taller than the sterile. This species is widespread in the American tropics.

Elaphoglossum sartorii (Liebmann) Mickel

FIGURE 13.48.11

Semi-tender or hardier

A small-medium fern with short- to medium-creeping rhizomes and erect, clustered to slightly distant fronds. Grows well under medium light in moist garden soil or potting mix. This species grows slowly and is often used as a ground cover or potted plant.

The rhizome of *Elaphoglossum sartorii* bears distinct phyllopodia and is covered by linear-lanceolate, entire scales. The fronds are about 30 cm (12 in.) long and 5 cm (2 in.) wide. The stipes are about one-quarter to one-third the frond length, glabrous or sparsely scaly with irregularly toothed scales. The blades are mostly elliptic, leathery, acuminate, the bases wedge-shaped, the surfaces glabrous or with minute, black, star-shaped scales on the lower surface. The fertile fronds are slightly narrower and taller than the sterile ones. The species is endemic to Mexico.

Elaphoglossum sartorii varies greatly and probably consists of several different species. The plant illustrated was

Figure 13.48.11. *Elaphoglossum sartorii:* a. habit; b. mature frond. Bar = 5 cm (2 in.).

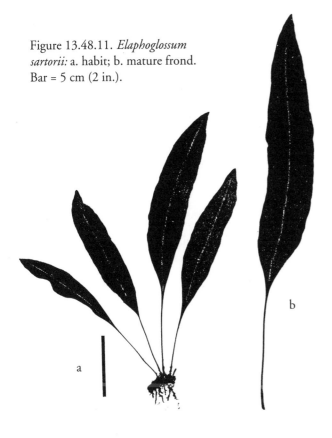

collected in Mexico. Plants from elsewhere should be referred to the *E. latifolium* complex, which also has not been fully studied. The rarely grown *E. maxonii,* also of the *E. latifolium* complex, differs from *E. sartorii* by its thicker rhizome and phyllopodia hidden by scales.

Elaphoglossum vestitum (Schlechtendal & Chamisso) Schott ex T. Moore   FIGURE 13.48.12
Semi-tender to tender

A small-medium fern with short-creeping rhizomes. Grows well under low to medium light in drained, moist potting mix or uncut moss.

Elaphoglossum vestitum has distinct phyllopodia and rhizome scales that are red-brown, shiny, linear-lanceolate, toothed, and 4–6 mm (0.2 in.) long. The stipes are slender and covered with narrowly triangular, red-brown, ciliate scales. The narrowly elliptic, gray-green blades are densely covered on the upper surface with whitish scales bearing filiform rays. Similarly shaped hairs on the undersurface are reddish brown. The species is native to southern Mexico.

This species has been misidentified in horticulture as *Elaphoglossum muelleri* (Fournier) C. Christensen, which lacks phyllopodia and is not cultivated.

Figure 13.48.12. *Elaphoglossum vestitum:* a. habit, with fertile frond on left, sterile fronds on right, bar = 5 cm (2 in.); b. blade scales, bar = 1 mm.

Equisetum   FIGURE 13.49.1
Horsetail, scouring rush

Equisetum is usually planted around ponds, bogs, and marshes, or it can be grown in pots, tubs, and small dish-gardens. Garden soil or potting mix are suitable if the plants are grown in pots and the soil is kept moist and drained. If the pots are set in standing water, a sand and peat-moss mix should be used to discourage the soil from "souring." Vigorously growing species such as *Equisetum hyemale* become weedy in gardens and are difficult to eradicate because of their deep rhizomes. *Equisetum* is often used in Japanese flower arrangements.

The plants can be propagated by dividing the rhizomes or by burying the stem segments shallowly in the soil. When buried in soil, new roots are eventually produced at

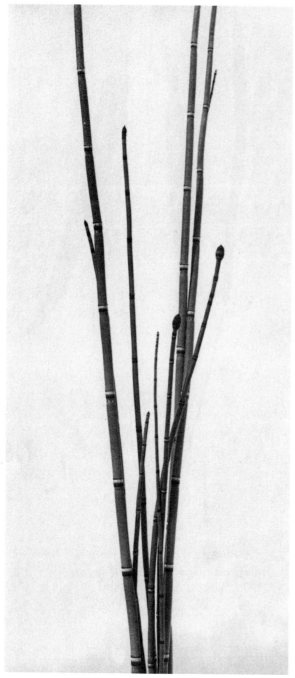

Figure 13.49.1. *Equisetum hyemale:* stems.

leaves united by their bases. The teeth on the sheath represent the tips of the leaves.

The common name of scouring rush was given to the reed-like (unbranched) species of *Equisetum* by American pioneers who used the silica-roughened stems to scrub pots and pans. The common name horsetail was given to those species with whorled branches, in allusion to their bushy, bristly appearance resembling a horse's tail. The genus name comes from the Greek *equis,* horse, and *seta,* bristle. *Equisetum* occurs worldwide, except New Zealand and Australia, and contains 23 species. The section on "Fern Allies" in Chapter 10 contains additional information on the genus.

Equisetum arvense Linnaeus   FIGURE 13.49.2
Common horsetail, field horsetail
Very hardy, Zone (1)2

A medium-sized plant with creeping rhizomes that send up irregularly spaced or clumped stems. Grows well under medium to high light in moist to wet garden soil. The aboveground stems are deciduous and have the general aspect of fine, feathery, bright-green foliage. This species is weedy in some parts of the United States and Europe.

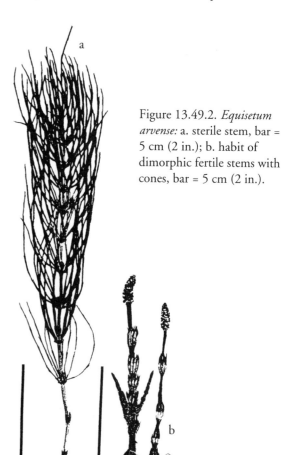

Figure 13.49.2. *Equisetum arvense:* a. sterile stem, bar = 5 cm (2 in.); b. habit of dimorphic fertile stems with cones, bar = 5 cm (2 in.).

the joints of the stem segments, and new stems soon follow. This method of producing new growth is how sterile hybrids of *Equisetum,* which cannot reproduce by spores because they abort, can become locally abundant or spread to distant sites where their parents do not grow.

The genus is easy to recognize by its green, usually hollow, jointed stems and spore-bearing cones at the stem tips; the cones, however, are not always present. The sheath around the stem joints represents a whorl of greatly reduced

The sterile stems of *Equisetum arvense* have dense whorls of branches from the joints, and sheaths of the main, erect stems tend to flare slightly outward and bear 8–12 teeth, some adhering in pairs. The fertile stems appear in the spring before the sterile ones. They are smaller, nongreen, and short-lived, withering soon after shedding their spores. This species is widely distributed in temperate North America, Europe, and Asia.

Equisetum diffusum D. Don   FIGURE 13.49.3
Semi-tender and perhaps hardier, Zone (8)9

A medium-sized plant with creeping, branching rhizomes. Grows in medium to high light in moist to wet garden soil. The plant's closely placed stems produce an attractive pot plant.

The aerial stems of *Equisetum diffusum* have branches in regular or irregular whorls. The stems have four ridges, with each ridge grooved and each side of the groove typically lined with a row of closely set, minute, blocky saw teeth (magnification needed). Ovoid-cylindrical cones may be produced at the tips of the stem late in the growing season (July–November). Tattered late-season stems are quickly replaced by new growth. This species is endemic to the Himalayas.

Equisetum ×ferrissii Clute   FIGURE 13.49.4
Ferriss's scouring rush
Very hardy, Zone 3

A medium-sized plant with creeping rhizomes that send up irregularly spaced or clumped stems. Grows under medium to high light in moist-wet to dry garden soil. When grown in pots, this hybrid produces fewer stems compared to its parents.

Equisetum ×ferrissii is of hybrid origin between *E. hyemale* and *E. laevigatum,* and its characteristics are intermediate between those two species. For example, *E. hyemale* has evergreen stems, and *E. laevigatum* has deciduous ones; the hybrid's stems are intermediate, being evergreen toward the base but deciduous in the upper part. The stem sheaths of the hybrid are also intermediate: those on the lower stem are ashy-white with black borders above and below (as in *E. hyemale*), but those on the upper part of the stem are green with a black border only at the top (as in *E. laevigatum*). The spores of the hybrid are whitish and aborted, not green and full as in the parental species. *Equisetum ×ferrissii* is native to and widespread in North America.

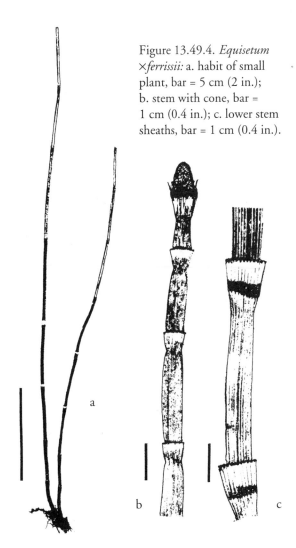

Figure 13.49.4. *Equisetum ×ferrissii:* a. habit of small plant, bar = 5 cm (2 in.); b. stem with cone, bar = 1 cm (0.4 in.); c. lower stem sheaths, bar = 1 cm (0.4 in.).

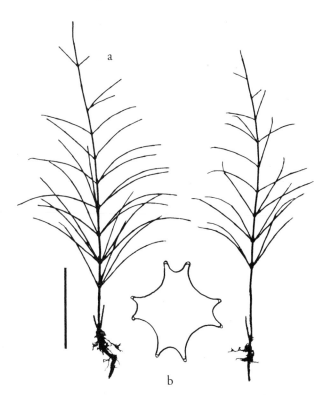

Figure 13.49.3. *Equisetum diffusum:* a. habit of stems from a young plant, bar = 5 cm (2 in.); b. outline of stem cross-section, enlarged to show stem with grooves in each of the four ridges.

Equisetum hyemale Linnaeus   FIGURES 13.49.1, 5
Scouring rush, rough horsetail, winter scouring rush
Very hardy, Zone 2

A medium to large plant with short- to long-creeping rhizomes. Grows well under medium to high light in moist to wet garden soil. It is easy to grow but becomes weedy in gardens and is difficult to eradicate because of its deep rhizomes. When grown in full sun the plants are more likely to produce cones.

Equisetum hyemale is characterized by rough, evergreen stems, and sheaths with a wide, ash-gray band bordered by a lower black band and an upper black rim. The stems are unbranched, but injury to the apex will result in lateral branches developing at some of the lower joints. The teeth are 14 or more at a joint, but most of them fall off at maturity. The cones have a minute point at the tip. This species is native to North America, Europe, and Asia. It typically forms large colonies along shaded riverbanks, streams, and in railroad ballast.

The thick-stemmed selection from the Washington area reverted to typical stem diameters when pot cultivated in southern California, whereas the slender-stemmed variants from Alaska maintained their distinctness.

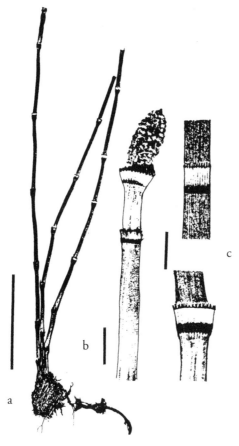

Figure 13.49.5. *Equisetum hyemale:* a. habit, bar = 5 cm (2 in.); b. stem with cone, bar = 1 cm (0.4 in.); c. sheaths, bar = 1 cm (0.4 in.).

Equisetum laevigatum A. Braun   FIGURE 13.49.6
Smooth horsetail
Very hardy, Zone 3

A medium-sized plant with creeping rhizomes that send up irregularly spaced or clumped stems. Grows well under medium to high light in moist-wet garden soil.

Equisetum laevigatum is characterized by smooth, usually unbranched (although sometimes sparsely and irregularly branched, especially if injured), deciduous stems and green (not ash-colored) sheaths with a black rim. The teeth at the rim typically fall off early and are therefore absent. The cones are blunt at the apex. The species is native to North America, often occurring in open, sunny habitats.

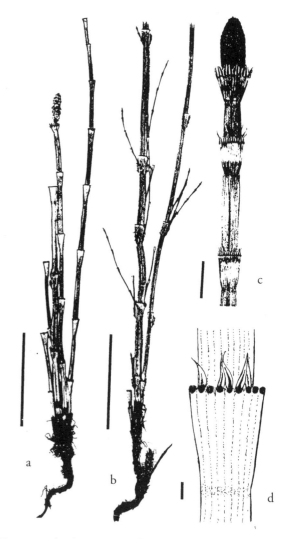

Figure 13.49.6. *Equisetum laevigatum:* a. habit of unbranched plant, bar = 5 cm (2 in.); b. habit of branched plant, bar = 5 cm (2 in.); c. stem with cone, bar = 1 cm (0.4 in.); d. sheath, bar = 1 mm.

Equisetum scirpoides Michaux   FIGURE 13.49.7

Dwarf scouring rush
Very hardy, Zone 2

A small plant that grows in loose clumps of evergreen, curly stems. Thrives under medium to high light in moist to wet garden soil. The plants are cultivated in dish gardens or as small novelty plants. Much of the trade material with this name is actually *Equisetum variegatum*.

Equisetum scirpoides is easy to recognize by its small size, clump-forming habit, and loosely twisted stems. Each stem-joint bears three teeth. Unlike other species in the genus, the stems are solid, not hollow. It is native to boreal North America, Europe, and Asia.

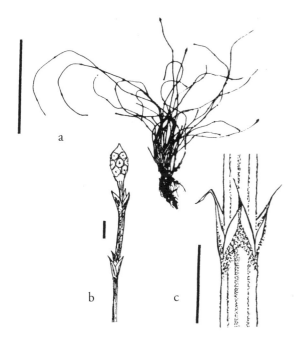

Figure 13.49.7. *Equisetum scirpoides:* a. habit, bar = 5 cm (2 in.); b. stem with cone, bar = 1 mm; c. sheath, bar = 1 mm.

Equisetum telmateia Ehrhart   FIGURE 13.49.8

Giant horsetail
Semi-hardy, Zone 8

A large plant with deciduous, branched, feathery stems that form extensive colonies. Thrives under medium to high light in moist-wet garden soil. The plants are generally too large and invasive for gardens.

Equisetum telmateia has deciduous stems with joints producing a whorl of slender branches. The teeth that occur at the rim of the sheath are pale or green at the base and dark at the tip. The fertile stems appear in early spring and are tan or brown. They wither soon after they shed their spores. The species is native to North America, Europe, northern Africa, and western Asia.

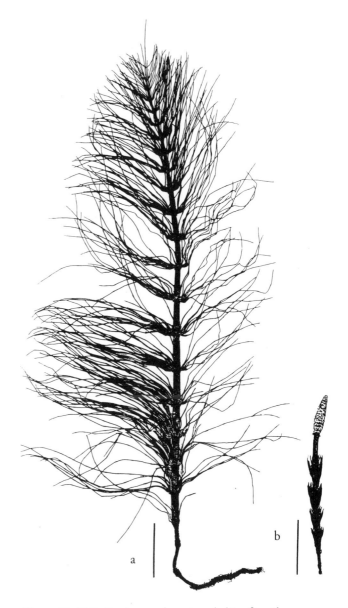

Figure 13.49.8. *Equiseum telmateia:* a. habit of sterile stem, bar = 5 cm (2 in.); b. dimorphic fertile stem with cone, bar = 5 cm (2 in.).

Equisetum variegatum Schleicher ex F. Weber & Mohr   FIGURE 13.49.9

Hardy, Zone 5

A small-medium plant with evergreen stems from short-creeping rhizomes. Thrives under medium or high light in moist-wet garden soil. Cultivated plants are smaller, up to 12.5 cm (5 in.) long, and more compact than those in the wild. This species is useful for small dish or water gardens.

The stems of *Equisetum variegatum* are unbranched and minutely grooved, and the sheaths have 3–12 teeth with conspicuous white margins. The species is native to the northern parts of North America, Europe, and Asia.

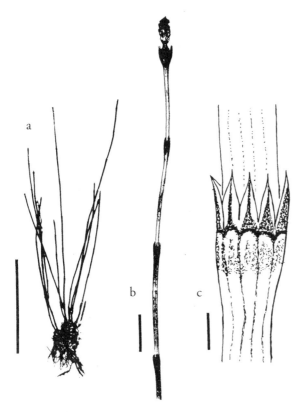

Figure 13.49.9. *Equisetum variegatum:* a. habit, bar = 5 cm (2 in.); b. stem with cone, bar = 1 cm (0.4 in.); c. sheath, bar = 1 mm.

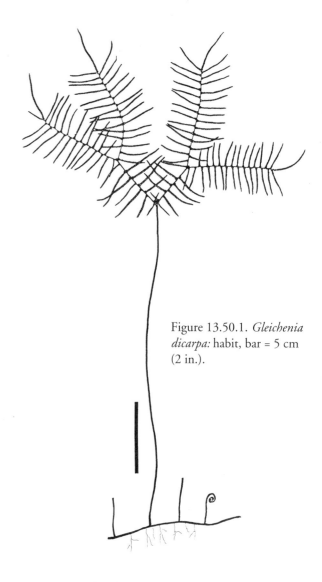

Figure 13.50.1. *Gleichenia dicarpa:* habit, bar = 5 cm (2 in.).

Gleicheniaceae
FIGURES 13.50.1, 2

Forking fern family

The family Gleicheniaceae includes five genera: *Dicranopteris, Diplopterygium, Gleichenella, Gleichenia,* and *Sticherus.* These genera are so distinctive in appearance and so widespread and abundant in the tropics that they are discussed here even though they are not cultivated in the United States. Gleicheniaceae consist of about 140 species in tropical and subtropical regions worldwide. Most of the species colonize poor soils and are too big and invasive for most greenhouses. But the family is eye-catching, and the smaller-sized species can be cultivated, as they are in New Zealand and Australia.

Members of this family, however, are difficult to cultivate. Victorian fern-growers apparently had some success, and one grower in Manchester, England, had an entire greenhouse devoted to 13 species. The grower said he placed the rhizomes in fibrous peat and silver sand, providing good drainage for the shallow roots.

More recently, growers in Australia successfully raised the following species from spores: pouched coral fern, *Gleichenia dicarpa* R. Brown (Figure 13.50.1); umbrella fern, *G. microphylla* R. Brown; and *G. rupestris* R. Brown. The growers reported that the pouched coral fern, which prefers poor, wet, acid soil, does not re-establish from mature plants. The umbrella fern, a more delicate and dainty plant, is more difficult to grow. It requires damp conditions and can be propagated by divisions thusly: a tip division with two fronds and attached roots is carefully lifted and re-planted in a peaty soil mix to about 2.5 cm (1 in.) deep. The transplant is kept damp until established (Best 1980).

Other growers have had further luck with the family. California hobbyists raised young plants of *Gleichenia microphylla* from spore in 1995, but the plants have grown slowly. The Royal Botanic Gardens at Kew, England, successfully grew a species in a loose, humusy woodland soil, and New Zealand growers have cultivated *Sticherus flabellatus* (R. Brown) H. St. John (Figure 13.50.2). One grower started young transplants in pure sand until established, then transferred them to a sand-soil-peat mix containing bone and blood meal.

Although plants may be grown from spores, growth is slow. Perhaps, like bracken fern (*Pteridium*), transplants of Gleicheniaceae do not establish readily but grow well once

Figure 13.50.2. *Sticherus flabellatus:* habit, bar = 5 cm (2 in.).

rooted. Because the United States Department of Agriculture requires that soil be removed from imported plants, any imported Gleicheniaceae stand little chance of success. It is generally thought that gleichenias need a mycorrhizal fungus in their roots to grow. The successes with spore-grown plants, however, raise questions about this need.

Members of this family can usually be recognized by their forked pinnae with a dormant bud in the fork's angle. In nature the plants are terrestrial, not epiphytic, although their leaves may rest on other plants for support. The rhizomes are always long-creeping, and the fronds are scrambling or trailing, one to many times forked, with the stipe containing a single, C-shaped vascular bundle. The pinnae are one to several times forked and have free veins. The sori are always round, located on the undersurface of the leaf, and lack an indusium.

In Alabama and Florida the native *Dicranopteris flexuosa* (Schrader) Underwood has not become well established, and colonies are known to have died out. The Hawaiian Islands have several native species of gleichenoids, some of which form extensive stands.

Plants of this family have only a few uses. A Japanese species of *Diplopterygium* has yearly growth that is well marked

on its fronds, and for this reason is widely used in Japan for New Year's Day decoration. In parts of southeastern Asia, baskets are woven from the tough, flexible rachises of several species. *Sticherus flabellatus* (R. Brown) H. St. John, *S. lobatus* N. A. Wakefield, and *Dicranopteris linearis* (N. L. Burman) Underwood are harvested in Australia and exported to Japan and elsewhere for cut-foliage use.

Goniophlebium

syn. *Polypodium,* in part; *Schellolepis*

Most gardeners know the genus *Goniophlebium* as *Polypodium*. It differs, however, by having jointed pinnae and goniophleboid venation—that is, several rows of regularly shaped, angular areoles with one free, included veinlet pointing toward the pinna margin. Some authors disregard the jointed pinnae and instead emphasize the presence of scattered, black, fibrous strands in the rhizome, clathrate rhizome scales, and (usually) hairy and scaly paraphyses in the sori. In this book, the species with nonjointed pinnae are left in *Polypodium* (*P. amoenum* and *P. formosanum*), except for the hybrid *Goniophlebium* ×*ekstrandii*. The plants with long fronds, such as the knight's polypody (*Goniophlebium subauriculatum* 'Knightiae'), are handsomely displayed in hanging baskets, where their fronds may reach 2.6 m (8.5 ft.) long.

The rhizome of *Goniophlebium* is creeping and often glaucous, and when viewed in cross section, many scattered, black fibers appear among the circle of vascular bundles. The rhizome scales are clathrate, and the blades vary from pinnatifid to one-pinnate. The pinnae are jointed, rarely scaly, with entire or toothed margins. The veins are netted, and the areoles have a regularly angular shape, those along the midribs large and containing a veinlet that points outward (toward the pinna margin). The sori are roundish, in one row on either side of the costa, and terminal on the veinlet contained within the areole. Usually hairs or scales are mixed among the sporangia. Like all polypodiaceous ferns, this genus lacks indusia.

Goniophlebium, which contains about 23 species, is native to Asia, Australia, and some Pacific Islands. The genus name comes from the Greek *gonia,* angled, and *phleps,* a vein, referring to the angular mesh of veins.

Goniophlebium ×*ekstrandii* Hoshizaki

FIGURE 13.51.1

Semi-tender

A medium-large fern with long-creeping rhizomes. Grows under medium light in moist, drained potting mix.

Goniophlebium ×*ekstrandii* has one-pinnate fronds with pinnae broadly attached to the rachis. The foliage is intermediate in shape between that of its parents, *Polypodium formosanum* and *Goniophlebium subauriculatum*. This sterile hybrid is known only in horticulture, and its cultivar name is 'Nola'.

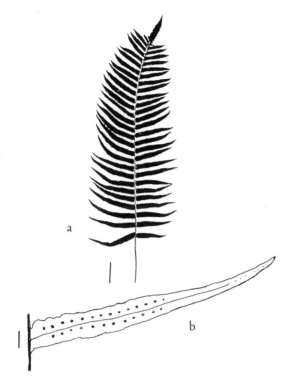

Figure 13.51.1. *Goniophlebium* ×*ekstrandii* 'Nola':
a. frond, bar = 5 cm (2 in.), after Hoshizaki (1991);
b. pinna, bar = 1 cm (0.4 in.).

Goniophlebium percussum (Cavanilles) W. H. Wagner & Grether   FIGURE 13.51.2

syn. *Goniophlebium verrucosum* (Hooker) J. Smith,
    Polypodium verrucosum (Hooker) Mettenius
Tender

A large fern with short- to medium-creeping rhizomes. Grows well under medium light in moist, drained potting mix. With marginal tropical conditions, the fronds tend to remain short.

Goniophlebium percussum bears fronds that are long, pendulous, and one-pinnate. The pinnae are jointed to the rachis, wedge-shaped at the base, and short-stalked. Fine white needle-like hairs are found on the pinna surface. The terminal pinna resembles the lateral ones or is longer. The sori are deeply sunken, circled with darkly toothed, stalked scales. The species is native from southeastern Asia to Malaysia, Indonesia, New Guinea, Australia, and the Philippines.

Goniophlebium persicifolium (Desvaux) Beddome   FIGURE 13.51.3

syn. *Polypodium persicifolium* Desvaux
Tender

A large fern with short- to medium-creeping rhizomes. Grows well under medium light in moist, drained potting mix.

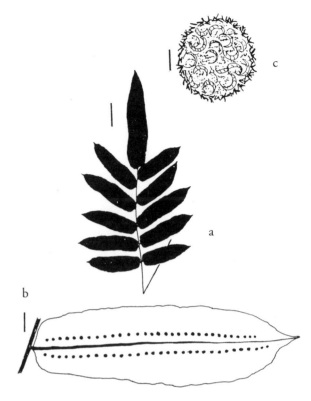

Figure 13.51.2. *Goniophlebium percussum:* a. frond, bar = 5 cm (2 in.); b. pinna, bar = 1 cm (0.4 in.), after Hoshizaki (1982); c. sorus circled with dark scales, bar = 1 mm, after Hoshizaki (1982).

Figure 13.51.3. *Goniophlebium persicifolium:* a. frond, bar = 5 cm (2 in.); b. pinna, bar = 1 cm (0.4 in.).

Goniophlebium persicifolium resembles *G. percussum* but differs by lacking needle-shaped hairs on the blades. In addition, the sori of this species are only slightly sunken, wider than 1.5 mm, and lack the ring of dark scales. *Goniophlebium persicifolium* is native from India to China, southeastern Asia to Malaysia, Indonesia, and the Pacific Islands.

Goniophlebium subauriculatum (Blume) C. Presl
FIGURE 13.51.4

syn. *Polypodium subauriculatum* Blume
Jointed polypody
Tender

A large fern with short- to medium-creeping rhizomes. Grows well under medium light in moist, drained potting mix. The fronds are long and pendulous, and the old fronds are shed in early to mid-spring as new ones emerge.

Figure 13.51.4. *Goniophlebium subauriculatum*: a. frond, bar = 5 cm (2 in.); b. pinna, bar = 1 cm (0.4 in.), after Hoshizaki (1982); c. 'Knightiae' frond, bar = 5 cm (2 in.).

The fronds of *Goniophlebium subauriculatum* are up to 2 m (6.5 ft.) long and one-pinnate with a pinnatifid apex. There are many pinna pairs and these are jointed, mostly cordate at the base, and sessile or nearly so. The species is native to China, southeastern Asia, Indonesia, Australia, and the Philippines.

'Knightiae'. (*Polypodium knightiae* Horticulture). Knight's polypody. Figure 13.51.4c; Plate 28. Pinnae irregularly and deeply incised. The plants tolerate more cold (semi-tender) and more irregular watering than the species.

Grammitidaceae
FIGURE 13.52.1
Grammitid family

Although not cultivated in the United States, the family Grammitidaceae is included here because of its large size and horticultural potential. Most plants in the family are small, tropical epiphytic ferns. Their attractive frond shapes and delicate aspect are reminiscent of tiny polypodiums; other species have fronds that resemble narrow strips trimmed by pinking shears. Among the genera in this family are *Acrosorus, Adenophorus, Calymmodon, Cochlidium, Ctenopteris, Grammitis, Lellingeria, Melpomene, Micropolypodium, Prosaptia, Scleroglossum, Terpsichore, Themelium,* and *Zygophlebia.* They are important in the tropics, especially in montane and cloud forests. Some species occur in subtropical or warm-temperate forests where humid conditions prevail. The Grammitidaceae contain about 450 species.

Although a few species were grown in Victorian times and some have been recommended for cultivation, no one seems to have cultivated the plants long-term. Usually they languish in terrariums and eventually die. Their cultural requirements are unknown. The proper combination of air movement, humidity, and light seem to be the main factors affecting their growth, but nutrients and mycorrhizal fungi might also be important.

The senior author has established *Cochlidium serrulatum* (Swartz) L. E. Bishop in a 3.8 liter (1 gal.) glass bottle (mayonnaise jar type) covered with a piece of glass. Medium indirect light is supplied through a large north-facing window. The fern grows in moist uncut sphagnum moss, which was lightly firmed into a 60-degree angle against one side of the bottle. Room temperature ranges from 16 to 24°C (60–75°F). Ordinary tap water is used but seldom required in the covered container. The plant appeared as a volunteer in a small clump of moss (collected in Costa Rica) that was planted at the top of the sphagnum moss slope. The plant is now over a year old, thriving and producing spores.

The plants resemble small polypodiums because of their pinnatifid or one-pinnate blades and round sori that lack indusia. They differ by having green, tetrahedral spores (not yellow, bean-shaped ones) and, usually, the rhizomes are erect or short-creeping, not long-creeping, as in many polypodiums.

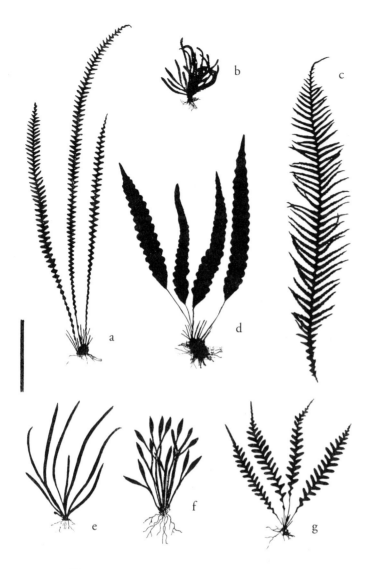

Figure 13.53.1. *Gymnocarpium disjunctum:* habit.

Figure 13.52.1. Grammitidaceae examples: a. *Grammitis palauensis,* from Palau; b. *Grammitis* from Costa Rica; c. *Ctenopteris blechnoides,* from Palau; d. *Enterosora trifurcata,* from Puerto Rico; e. *Grammitis adspersa,* from Malaya; f. *Cochlidium graminoides* (?), from Brazil; g. *Adenophorus pinnatifidus,* from Hawaii. Bar = 5 cm (2 in.).

Gymnocarpium   FIGURES 13.53.1, 2
Oak fern

These small- to medium-sized ferns are eye-catching because of their broadly triangular to pentagonal fronds, which are spaced far enough apart on the rhizomes to show off their pattern. The common oak fern (*Gymnocarpium dryopteris*) found on the floors of temperate forests is used as a ground cover or bed fern in the eastern United States and is considered invasive by some gardeners.

   Gymnocarpium can be distinguished by the combination of slender, long-creeping rhizomes, stipes with only

Figure 13.53.2. *Gymnocarpium disjunctum:* sori.

two vascular bundles, broadly triangular to pentagonal blades, and round (rarely elliptic), non-indusiate sori. The blades vary from pinnatifid to three-pinnate-pinnatifid and may have minute glands, but hairs are lacking. There is usually a slight swelling where the pinna joins the rachis. The veins are free, not netted.

The genus consists of five species and is native to North America, Europe, and Asia. Its name comes from the Greek *gymnos,* naked, and *karpos,* fruit, referring to the sori ("fruit") that lack an indusium.

Gymnocarpium disjunctum (Ruprecht) Ching
FIGURES 13.53.1–3

Western oak fern
Very hardy, Zone 4

A medium-sized fern with slender, long-creeping rhizomes and distant, deciduous fronds. Prefers low to medium light in moist garden soil or potting mix. This species is unsuitable for areas with warm winters.

The blades of *Gymnocarpium disjunctum* are broadly triangular-pentagonal, three-pinnate-pinnatifid, 8–24 cm (3–9 in.) long, and glabrous. The second pinna pair from the base is sessile, and its basiscopic basal pinnule is longer than the acroscopic one. The sori are round. The species is native to northeastern Asia and the northwestern coast of North America.

Gymnocarpium dryopteris (Linnaeus) Newman
FIGURE 13.53.4; PLATE 29

syn. *Polypodium dryopteris* Linnaeus
Common oak fern
Very hardy, Zone (3)4

A small fern, 15–25 cm (6–10 in.) tall, with slender, long-creeping rhizomes and deciduous fronds. Thrives under low to medium light in moist garden soil or potting mix. Be careful not to allow the soil to dry.

Gymnocarpium dryopteris has blades that are triangular-pentagonal, two-pinnate-pinnatifid, 3–14 cm (1.2–5.5 in.) long, and glabrous. The second pinna pair from the base is sessile, and the basal pinnules on both sides are essentially equal in length. The sori are round. The species is native to northern North America, north-central Europe, and northern Asia to China and Japan.

'Plumosum'. Pinnules thin, delicate, dense, the margins turned under.

Gymnocarpium oyamense (Baker) Ching
FIGURE 13.53.5

syn. *Currania oyamensis* (Baker) Copeland
Hardy

A small-medium fern with slender, long-creeping rhizomes and distant, deciduous fronds. Grows well under medium light in moist garden soil or potting mix.

Figure 13.53.3. *Gymnocarpium disjunctum:* a. frond, bar = 5 cm (2 in.); b. frond base, showing uneven basal pinnules in second pinna pair, bar = 2 cm (0.8 in.).

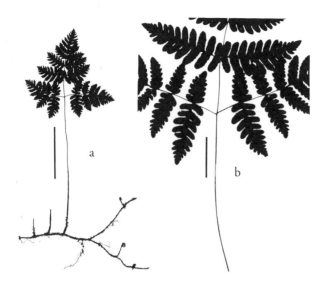

Figure 13.53.4. *Gymnocarpium dryopteris:* a. habit, bar = 5 cm (2 in.); b. frond base, showing even basal pinnules in second pinna pair, bar = 2 cm (0.8 in.).

Figure 13.53.5. *Gymnocarpium oyamense:* a. frond, bar = 5 cm (2 in.); b. sori, bar = 2 cm (0.8 in.).

Gymnocarpium oyamense has triangular-ovate, deeply pinnatifid or one-pinnate blades and round to elliptic sori. It is native to Nepal, China, Taiwan, Japan, the Philippines, Moluccas, and New Guinea.

Gymnocarpium robertianum (Hoffmann) Newman
FIGURE 13.53.6

Limestone oak fern
Very hardy, Zone 3

A small-medium fern with slender, long-creeping rhizomes and distant, deciduous fronds. Thrives under low light in basic, moist or moist-wet garden soil or potting mix.

The blades of *Gymnocarpium robertianum* are broadly triangular and two- to three-pinnate-pinnatifid. Both blade surfaces are minutely glandular (hand lens needed). The second pinna pair from the base is usually stalked. The sori are round. This species is native to eastern Canada and the north-central United States, Europe, and Asia (Caucus Mountains). It grows on calcareous rocks such as limestone and dolomite.

Hemionitis
FIGURES 13.54.1, 2

syn. *Gymnopteris, Parahemionitis*

Hemionitis is a genus of small, terrestrial or rock-inhabiting tropical ferns. The best-known species is the strawberry fern (*Hemionitis palmata*), named for a fancied resemblance of the leaves to those of a strawberry plant. It is occasionally

Figure 13.53.6. *Gymnocarpium robertianum:* a. frond, bar = 5 cm (2 in.); b. sori, bar = 1 cm (0.4 in.).

Figure 13.54.1. *Hemionitis palmata:* habit.

seen in fern collections, as is the closely allied *H. pinnatifida.* The two species are attractive for their broad, maple-like fronds. Both are grown in pots or terrariums or, in tropical climates, outdoors. They are easy to cultivate but are often attacked by scale insects, slugs, and mealybugs. The buds produced on the blade bases root readily when layered, or when large enough, they may be detached and transplanted.

The rhizomes are scaly and vary from erect to ascending. The stipes are often shiny and chestnut-brown to straw-colored. The fronds are herbaceous, often hairy and some-

times with a few scales, and they vary from simple and entire to deeply palmately or pinnately lobed to one-pinnate (noncultivated species can be up to three-pinnate). The veins are either free or netted, and if the latter, the areoles lack included veinlets. The sporangia run along the veins; an indusium is absent. Some species of *Hemionitis* might be confused with *Bommeria,* but the sori in that genus run along the margin, not between the margin and midrib as in *Hemionitis.*

The genus consists of seven species native to the American tropics. *Hemionitis arifolia,* which questionably belongs here, occurs in Asia. The genus name comes from the Greek *hemionos,* mule, and is of uncertain derivation.

Hemionitis arifolia (N. L. Burman) T. Moore
FIGURE 13.54.3; PLATE 30
syn. *Parahemionitis arifolia* (N. L. Burman) Panigrahi
Tender

A small fern with short-creeping to suberect rhizomes and fronds bearing buds at the base of the blade where it joins the stipe. Grows well under medium light in moist potting mix.

Hemionitis arifolia has dimorphic fronds: the sterile blades are heart-shaped; the fertile, triangular-hastate. Both fronds have hairs on the stipes and thinly on the blades, and the veins are netted with polygonal, elongate areoles. The species is native to the Old World tropics.

Some pteridologists classify this species in its own genus, *Parahemionitis* (Panigrahi 1993). Its evolutionary relationships with the New World species are questionable and require more study.

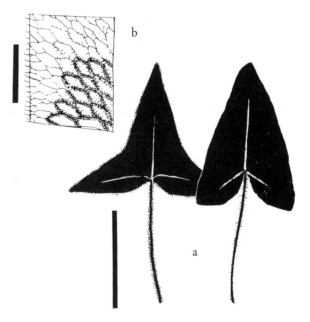

Figure 13.54.2. *Hemionitis palmata:* sporangia along veins.

Figure 13.54.3. *Hemionitis arifolia:* a. fronds, bar = 5 cm (2 in.); b. sporangia along veins, bar = 1 cm (0.4 in.). After Beddome (1864).

Hemionitis palmata Linnaeus   FIGURES 13.54.1, 2, 4
Strawberry fern
Tender

A small fern with short-creeping to suberect rhizomes and bud-bearing fronds. Grows well under medium light in moist potting mix.

In *Hemionitis palmata,* the sterile and fertile blades are palmately lobed and similar in size and shape. Usually one bud develops in a large marginal notch on the blade. The veins are netted. This species is native to Central and South America and the West Indies.

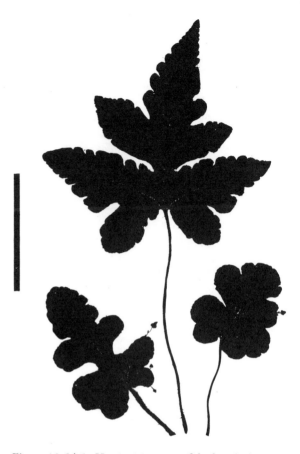

Figure 13.54.5. *Hemionitis pinnatifida:* fronds, bar = 5 cm (2 in.).

Figure 13.54.4. *Hemionitis palmata:* fronds, bar = 5 cm (2 in.).

Hemionitis pinnatifida Baker   FIGURE 13.54.5
Tender

A small fern with short-creeping to suberect rhizomes and bud-bearing fronds. Grows well under medium light in moist potting mix.

Hemionitis pinnatifida resembles *H. palmata* and is of hybrid origin between it and another unknown species in the genus. *Hemionitis pinnatifida* is distinguished by deeply pinnatifid terminal lobes and several buds that usually develop in smaller marginal notches. It is native to Central America.

Histiopteris
Bat fern, bat-winged fern

Histiopteris is a medium- to large-sized terrestrial fern infrequently cultivated. Because of its long-creeping rhizomes, it is best confined to large pots or tubs. The common name alludes to the wing-like appearance of the sessile pinnules. *Histiopteris incisa* is widely distributed in the tropics and subtropics and seems to vary in size, degree of blue-gray greenness, and adaptability to cold.

Histiopteris is easily recognized by long-creeping rhizomes; opposite, sessile (or nearly so) pinnae and sessile pinnules; and enrolled leaf margins that serve as indusia. The fronds are distant on the rhizome, and their tips grow continuously, never completely unfurling. The stipe contains one vascular bundle, and the blades are two-pinnate or more divided, often glaucous beneath. The basal pinnules of each pinna are opposite, often reduced and touching the rachis. The veins vary from free to netted. The sori run along the blade margin.

The genus is south-temperate to pantropical (mostly Malaysia) and contains five species. The genus name comes from the Greek *histion,* sail, and *pteris,* fern, alluding to shape of the basal pinnae.

Histiopteris incisa (Thunberg) J. Smith

FIGURE 13.55.1

Bat fern
Semi-tender to semi-hardy or hardier

A large fern with long-creeping rhizomes and fronds about 6 cm (2.5 in.) apart. Grows well under medium to high light in moist garden soil. This species often volunteers in spore cultures and is sometimes weedy in its native habitat. Plants from different geographical areas appear variable in blade cutting and tolerance to cold.

Histiopteris incisa has all the characteristics given above for the genus, except that the veins are netted. It is widely distributed in the tropics and southern subtropics of the world.

Hymenophyllum

FIGURES 13.56.1, 2

syn. *Mecodium, Sphaerocionium*
Filmy fern

The filmy ferns, or "filmies," are mostly small epiphytes native to humid habitats in the tropics. They are rarely cultivated but can be used to good effect in terrariums. The

Figure 13.56.1. *Hymenophyllum demissum:* habit.

most commonly grown species are those adapted to cool, humid climates. Some species adapt to cultivation readily but require vigilance in tending to their moisture and temperature needs. Where hot summer temperatures prevail, cultivation is difficult but may be improved by using a mist

Figure 13.55.1. *Histiopteris incisa:* a. frond, bar = 5 cm (2 in.); b. pinnule with sori and indusia, bar = 1 cm (0.4 in.).

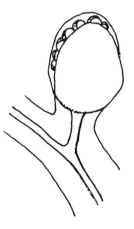

Figure 13.56.2. *Hymenophyllum:* sorus and indusium.

system. The delicate fronds of *Hymenophyllum* are only one cell-layer thick except around the veins.

The rhizomes are creeping, slender, and hairy (not scaly). The thin fronds are mostly small, with blades simple to four-pinnate. The sori are marginal and surrounded by a two-lipped or two-valved indusium. The receptacle is (usually) included within the indusium, not protruding. The spores are green and short-lived.

Only two genera of filmy ferns—*Hymenophyllum* and *Trichomanes*—are recognized in this book, following the practice of most pteridologists. A few pteridologists, however, divide these genera into many smaller ones (see the discussion under *Trichomanes*). *Hymenophyllum* can be distinguished from *Trichomanes* by the form of the indusium: two-valved or lipped in *Hymenophyllum*, and tubular or funnel-shaped in *Trichomanes*.

Hymenophyllum is native to the tropics and south-temperate areas of the world. It contains about 300 species. The genus name comes from the Greek *hymen,* membrane, and *phyllon,* leaf, referring to the membrane-like texture of the blades. For more information, see the section "Filmy Ferns" in Chapter 10.

Hymenophyllum demissum (G. Forster) Swartz
FIGURES 13.56.1, 3

syn. *Mecodium demissum* (G. Forster) Copeland
Semi-tender or hardier

A small fern with long-creeping rhizomes. Grows under low light in well-drained, moist to moist-wet potting mix or uncut moss. Keep the plants cool and humid during hot weather.

Hymenophyllum demissum has glabrous, three- or four-pinnate, mostly elliptic or ovate, 7–25 cm (3–10 in.) long blades and unwinged stipes. The sori are often in pairs. The species is endemic to New Zealand.

Hymenophyllum polyanthos (Swartz) Swartz
FIGURE 13.56.4

syn. *Mecodium polyanthos* (Swartz) Copeland
Tender

A small fern with medium-creeping rhizomes. Grows under low light in well-drained, moist to moist-wet potting mix or uncut moss under humid conditions.

Hymenophyllum polyanthos has unwinged stipes (or winged only toward the summit) and glabrous, three-pinnate blades. The sori are not in pairs. The species is native to the tropics and subtropics of the world.

Hypoderris

This genus has trilobed fronds reminiscent of *Tectaria,* to which it is related. *Hypoderris* differs from *Tectaria* only by the indusium, which encircles the base of the sorus and is strongly ciliate, as opposed to the indusia of *Tectaria,* which are absent or attached on one side of the sorus and arching

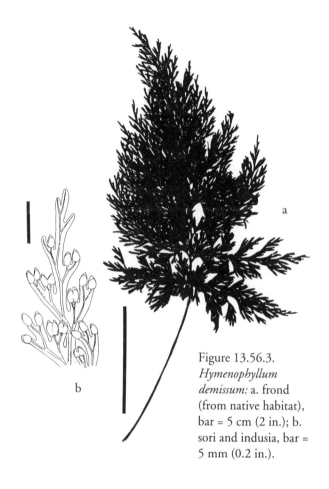

Figure 13.56.3. *Hymenophyllum demissum:* a. frond (from native habitat), bar = 5 cm (2 in.); b. sori and indusia, bar = 5 mm (0.2 in.).

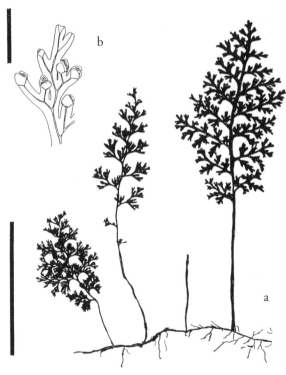

Figure 13.56.4. *Hymenophyllum polyanthos:* a. habit, bar = 5 cm (2 in.); b. sori and indusia, bar = 5 mm (0.2 in.).

above it. The indusium can be hard to see because it is often appressed to the leaf surface and covered by sporangia.

Hypoderris consists of a single species native to moist habitats of the West Indies and northern Venezuela. In the United States it is mainly cultivated outdoors in southern Florida, either in soil or pots. The genus name comes from the Greek *hypo,* below, and *derris,* covering, referring to the indusium below the sporangia.

Hypoderris brownii J. Smith
FIGURE 13.57.1
Tender

A small-medium fern with short- to medium-creeping rhizomes. Grows well under low to medium light in moist garden soil or potting mix. The plants respond well to nutrients but require greenhouse conditions in all but humid tropical climates.

Hypoderris brownii has scaly rhizomes that creep over soil or rocks. Its blades vary from simple to trilobed, with the central lobe the largest. The veins are netted with free, included veinlets in the areoles. Native to moist habitats of the West Indies and northern Venezuela.

Hypolepis
FIGURES 13.58.1, 2
Ground fern

Hypolepis has long-creeping rhizomes and finely divided, triangular fronds. These medium- to large-sized ferns are used as ground cover or, in warmer climates, as foundation plantings. They are sometimes seen growing in thick stands

Figure 13.58.1. *Hypolepis tenuifolia:* habit.

in parks of central and southern coastal California. Their spreading habit can be controlled by planting in large tubs. New plants are easily propagated by divisions or spores.

The best features for recognizing *Hypolepis* are the long-creeping, branched, hairy (not scaly) rhizomes, the finely divided, large, triangular fronds, and the roundish sori usually protected by tooth-like indusia formed by the blade margins (rarely the sori are below the margin and unprotected). In addition, the blades are two-pinnate-pinnatifid to four-pinnate-pinnatifid, thin, and often hairy.

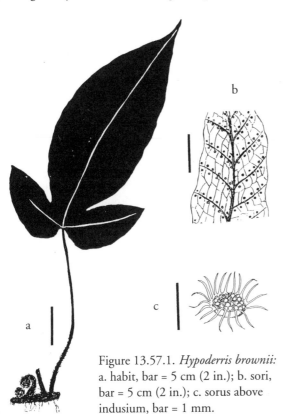

Figure 13.57.1. *Hypoderris brownii:* a. habit, bar = 5 cm (2 in.); b. sori, bar = 5 cm (2 in.); c. sorus above indusium, bar = 1 mm.

Figure 13.58.2. *Hypolepis tenuifolia:* sori and indusia.

The genus is native to the tropics and subtropics of the world and contains about 50 species. *Hypolepis millefolium* Hooker, a smaller species from New Zealand, is cultivated in the mild areas of England. *Hypolepis punctata* (Thunberg) Mettenius, an easily grown species introduced from Taiwan, is rarely seen in cultivation.

Hypolepis repens (Linnaeus) C. Presl   FIGURE 13.58.3
Bramble fern
Semi-tender

A medium-large fern with long-creeping rhizomes. Grows well under medium light in moist garden soil or potting mix. This species is easy to grow.

The stipes and rachises of *Hypolepis repens* are spiny and vary from glabrous to hairy. The indusia are thin and often inconspicuous. This species is native to Florida, Mexico to South America, and the West Indies.

Most of the horticultural material in Florida identified as *Hypolepis repens* is misidentified and actually represents *H. tenuifolia,* which differs by lacking prickles on the stipes and rachises.

Figure 13.58.4. *Hypolepis tenuifolia:* a. habit, bar = 5 cm (2 in.); b. pinna, bar = 5 cm (2 in.).

Figure 13.58.3. *Hypolepis repens:* a. pinna, bar = 5 cm (2 in.); b. rachis with small spines, bar = 1 cm (0.4 in.); c. sori and indusia, bar = 5 mm (0.2 in.).

Hypolepis tenuifolia (G. Forster) Bernhardi
FIGURES 13.58.1, 2, 4
Semi-tender or hardier

A large fern with long-creeping rhizomes. Grows well under medium or high light in moist garden soil or potting mix. This fern is easy to cultivate and is perhaps the most common species of *Hypolepis* cultivated in the United States.

Hypolepis tenuifolia has smooth stipes and rachises, without prickles. The rhizomes are more than 5 mm (0.2 in.) thick. The stipes and blades bear gland-tipped hairs, and the sori are protected by tooth-like false indusia. The species is native to Asia and Polynesia.

This species name is believed to apply to several different species yet to be fully sorted out.

Lastreopsis   FIGURES 13.59.1–3

The mostly medium-sized terrestrial ferns of genus *Lastreopsis* have broad, highly divided fronds. Some Australian and New Zealand species are suitable as a bedding plant in warm-temperate climates. They are easy to grow and have durable foliage. *Lastreopsis microsora* has been used for years as bedding plants in southern California, although some gardeners do not care for the dull, gray-green color of this species. The creeping rhizome is moderately slow-growing and easy to control. *Lastreopsis acuminata* is currently circulating among a few hobbyists and promises to be an excellent ornamental because of its fast growth and clustered, shiny leaves.

The rhizomes of *Lastreopsis* are creeping to nearly erect and scaly. The stipes contain three or more vascular bundles. The blades are usually pentagonal or triangular, several times pinnate, and the lowest pinna pair is enlarged on the lower side. The upper surface of the rachis and costae bear short hairs. The veins are free, not netted. The sori are round and, in most species, covered by a reniform indusium.

Lastreopsis can be distinguished from similar genera such as *Ctenitis, Dryopteris,* and *Tectaria* by the upper surface of the rachis, which has two thickened ridges and is densely

Figure 13.59.1. *Lastreopsis microsora* subsp. *pentangularis:* habit.

Figure 13.59.3. *Lastreopsis microsora* subsp. *pentangularis:* sori and indusia.

puberulent between the ridges. The ridges are continuous with the decurrent margins of the pinnules (also thickened). Unlike in dryopteroid ferns, the rachis and costae are rounded on their upper sides, not deeply grooved.

Lastreopsis is pantropical and contains 35 species. The genus name means "resembling *Lastrea,*" formed by adding the Greek suffix *-opsis,* like. For a taxonomic monograph of the genus, see Tindale (1965).

Figure 13.59.2. *Lastreopsis microsora* subsp. *pentangularis:* grooves of rachis and costae.

Lastreopsis acuminata (Houlston) C. V. Morton
FIGURE 13.59.4

syn. *Lastreopsis shepherdii* (Kunze ex Mettenius) Tindale
Shiny shield fern
Semi-hardy

A medium-sized fern with clump-forming and ascending rhizomes. Grows well under low to medium light in moist or moist-wet garden soil or potting mix. The plants are easy to grow from spores and establish readily.

Lastreopsis acuminata has tufted fronds often with pink-tinged stipes. The blades are narrowly triangular and two- to three-pinnate, coarser than those of most *Lastreopsis.* The lowest pinna pair are larger on the basiscopic side. This species is native to Australia and Tasmania.

Lastreopsis effusa (Swartz) Tindale   FIGURE 13.59.5
Semi-tender

A medium-large fern with clump-forming rhizomes. Grows well under low to medium light in moist garden soil or potting mix.

Lastreopsis effusa is characterized by highly dissected, pentagonal or broadly lanceolate blades that bear a scaly bud toward the tip of the rachis. Indusia are absent. It is native to tropical America.

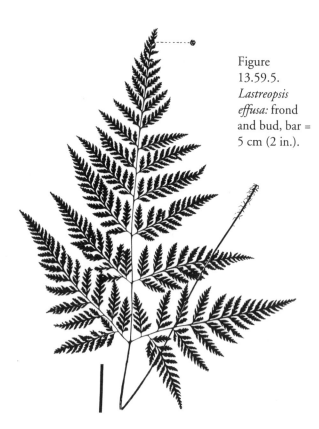

Figure 13.59.4.
Lastreopsis acuminata:
fronds, bar = 5 cm
(2 in.).

Figure
13.59.5.
Lastreopsis
effusa: frond
and bud, bar =
5 cm (2 in.).

Lastreopsis microsora (Endlicher) Tindale

FIGURES 13.59.1–3, 6, 7

Semi-hardy to semi-tender

A small to medium fern with moderately long-creeping rhizomes. Grows well under medium light in moist garden soil or potting mix. *Lastreopsis microsora* is easy to grow. Two subspecies are cultivated.

subsp. *microsora*. Figure 13.59.6. The rhizomes are short- to medium-creeping and branched. The blades are broadly pentagonal and bear a dense tuft of short pale hairs at the base of the costules and costa. The tips of ultimate segments are blunt, not acute, and the indusia are large and reniform. This subspecies is native to Australia. In the United States, plants of subsp. *microsora* have been confused with *Lastreopsis decomposita* (R. Brown) Tindale, which differs by having short-creeping rhizomes and inflated (bullate) scales at the base of the rachis. It is not known to be cultivated in the United States.

subsp. *pentangularis* (Colenso) Tindale (*Ctenitis pentangularis* (Colenso) Alston). Figures 13.59.1–3, 7. This subspecies resembles the previous one but is smaller, slightly less foliaceous, and more gray-green. It is native to New Zealand.

Figure 13.59.6. *Lastreopsis microsora:* frond, bar = 5 cm (2 in.).

Figure 13.59.7. *Lastreopsis microsora* subsp. *pentangularis:* frond, bar = 5 cm (2 in.).

Lecanopteris

syn. *Myrmecophila, Myrmecopteris*

Ant fern

The genus *Lecanopteris* has enlarged and hollow rhizomes that provide homes for ants. The ants, in turn, protect the plant by attacking anything that disturbs it. These small- to medium-sized epiphytes are grown as novelties where tropical conditions can be provided.

The rhizomes of *Lecanopteris* are bluish green when young and become blackish with age. The rhizome scales are absent or dense, round, peltate, and marginally membranous. The stipes are jointed to a small raised projection (phyllopodium), and the sterile blades vary from entire to lobed to deeply pinnatifid. The veins are netted, not free. The sori are round or oblong, usually sunken, and like all polypodiaceous ferns, lack indusia.

The species with scaly rhizomes, such as *Lecanopteris sinuosa*, have been placed in *Phymatosorus* (*Phymatodes*), but some pteridologists put them in *Myrmecopteris* (*Myrmecophila*). More study is needed to resolve these differences. For details, see Johns (1995). See *Polypodium* for a comparison of *Lecanopteris* to the other polypodiaceous genera.

Solanopteris, the only other genus of ferns to have ant-inhabited rhizomes, differs primarily by bearing globose tubers sporadically along a long-creeping rhizome; the entire rhizome is not enlarged and hollow, as in *Lecanopteris. Solanopteris* is entirely restricted to the American tropics, whereas *Lecanopteris* is native to southeastern Asia, mostly Malaysia.

Lecanopteris contains 13 species. The genus name comes from the Greek *lekane,* dish, and *lepis,* scale, referring to the dish-like flaps of the blade associated with the sori.

Lecanopteris carnosa (Reinwardt) Blume

FIGURE 13.60.1

Tender

A small-medium fern with medium-creeping rhizomes. Grows under high light in well-drained, moist-dry uncut moss. Culture is easier in constantly warm, humid, well-lighted greenhouses with good ventilation.

Lecanopteris carnosa is characterized by rhizomes lacking scales and pinnatifid, erect, leathery fronds. The rhizomes are sometimes described as a "mat of lumps." The sori are borne in cup-like depressions with each cup borne on a small projection from the frond margin. The species is native from Sumatra to the Philippines.

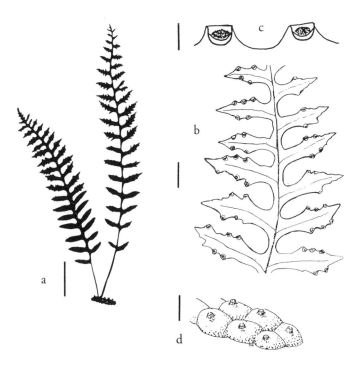

Figure 13.60.1. *Lecanopteris carnosa:* a. habit, bar = 5 cm (2 in.); b. fertile portion of frond, upper surface, bar = 1 cm (0.4 in.); c. sori on projection bent to upper frond surface, bar = 2 mm; d. swollen rhizome, bar = 1 cm (0.4 in.).

Lecanopteris crustacea Copeland   FIGURE 13.60.2

syn. *Myrmecopteris crustacea* (Copeland) Pichi-Sermolli,
Phymatodes crustaca (Copeland) Holttum
Tender

A small-medium fern with 3–5 cm (1.2–2 in.) wide, medium-creeping rhizomes. Grows well under high light in well-drained, moist-dry uncut moss. Culture is easier in constantly warm, humid, well-lighted greenhouses with good ventilation.

Lecanopteris crustacea is characterized by round, peltate rhizome scales, deeply pinnatifid fronds, and sunken sori. It is native to Sumatra, Malaysia, and Borneo.

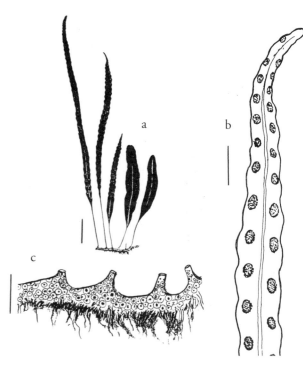

Figure 13.60.3. *Lecanopteris sinuosa:* a. habit, bar = 5 cm (2 in.); b. fertile portion of frond, bar = 1 cm (0.4 in.); c. rhizome, bar = 1 cm (0.4 in.).

Figure 13.60.2. *Lecanopteris crustacea:* a. habit, bar = 5 cm (2 in.); b. narrowed fertile segment, bar = 1 cm (0.4 in.); c. swollen rhizome, bar = 5 cm (2 in.); d. rhizome scale, bar = 1 mm, after Hoshizaki (1982).

Lecanopteris sinuosa (Wallich ex Hooker) Copeland   FIGURE 13.60.3

syn. *Myrmecopteris sinuosa* (Wallich ex Hooker) Pichi-Sermolli, *Phymatodes sinuosa* (Wallich ex Hooker) J. Smith
Tender

A small-medium fern with medium-creeping rhizomes 1–1.5 cm (0.5–0.6 in.) wide. Grows well under medium to high light in well-drained, moist-dry uncut moss. The cultural requirements are similar to those of *Lecanopteris carnosa,* but this species is easier to grow.

Lecanopteris sinuosa is characterized by round, peltate rhizome scales with whitish margins, and simple, oblong

to linear-lanceolate, entire to coarsely crenate fronds. The sori are round or oblong, large, and submarginal. It is native from Thailand to the Solomon Islands, and to Taiwan.

Lemmaphyllum   FIGURES 13.61.1, 2

The cultivated species of *Lemmaphyllum* are used as novelties in terrariums, pots, and small hanging containers. These small, creeping epiphytes have thick, oval, shiny, succulent leaves. The production of fertile fronds can be increased by growing the plants under higher light.

This genus has slender, creeping rhizomes covered by peltate, ovate-lanceolate, clathrate scales. The stipes are jointed to the rhizome, and the simple, entire blades vary from papery to succulent and rounded to elliptic, obovate, or lanceolate. Although often hard to see, the veins are netted, not free. The fertile fronds are narrower than the sterile ones. The sori are rounded or linear or running together, forming a row on each side of the midrib. As in all polypodiaceous ferns, the sori lack indusia, but in this genus they are protected by umbrella-shaped hairs mixed among the sporangia. *Lemmaphyllum* resembles *Microgramma,* though the commonly cultivated species differ by their thick, fleshy fronds and linear sori.

Lemmaphyllum is native to eastern Asia and contains six species. The genus name comes from the Greek *lemma,* scale, and *phyllon,* leaf, referring to the small, scale-like structures mixed among the sporangia.

Lemmaphyllum microphyllum C. Presl
FIGURES 13.61.1–3

Semi-hardy

A small fern with creeping rhizomes. Grows well under medium light in moist, drained potting mix. The plants are easy to grow once established but tend to grow slowly.

Lemmaphyllum microphyllum has dimorphic sterile and fertile fronds. The sterile fronds vary from circular to ob-lanceolate and are 1–4 cm (0.5–1.5 in.) long. In contrast, the fertile fronds are narrowly linear and up to 6 cm (2.5 in.) long. The sori are linear and in one row on either side of midrib. The species is native to Japan, South Korea, China, and Taiwan.

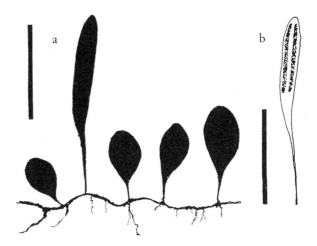

Figure 13.61.3. *Lemmaphyllum microphyllum:* a. habit, bar = 5 cm (2 in.); b. fertile frond, bar = 5 cm (2 in.).

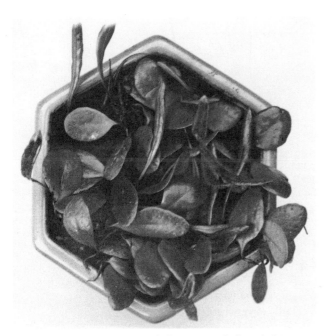

Figure 13.61.1. *Lemmaphyllum microphyllum:* habit.

Lemmaphyllum subrostratum (C. Christensen) Ching
FIGURE 13.61.4

Very tender

A small fern with medium-creeping rhizomes. Grows well under medium light in moist, drained potting mix. The plants grow slowly, possibly because of their heat requirement, and are rare in cultivation.

Lemmaphyllum subrostratum has only slightly dimorphic sterile and fertile fronds. The sterile fronds have green and

Figure 13.61.2. *Lemmaphyllum microphyllum:* sori on narrowed fertile fronds.

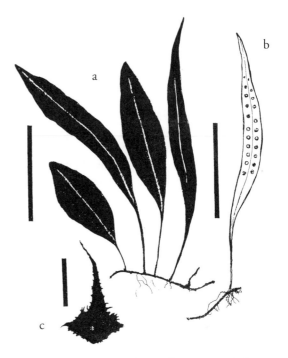

Figure 13.61.4. *Lemmaphyllum subrostatum:* a. habit, bar = 5 cm (2 in.); b. fertile frond, bar = 5 cm (2 in.); c. rhizome scale, bar = 1 mm.

well-defined stipes 1–3 cm (0.5–1.2 in.) long and blades that vary from elliptic to lanceolate, 5–10 cm (2–4 in.) long by 1–2 cm (0.5–0.8 in.) wide. In contrast, the fertile fronds have longer stipes and narrower blades. The sori are round. The rhizome scales are broadly rhomboid at base. The species is native to India and southeastern Asia.

Lemmaphyllum subrostratum was introduced commercially from India, and the plants were originally misidentified as *L. carnosum* (J. Smith ex Hooker) C. Presl, a species that differs by having ovate-lanceolate rhizome scales, sessile (or nearly so) sterile fronds, narrowly linear fertile fronds, and acrostichoid sori.

Lepisorus

syn. *Polypodium* in part, *Pleopeltis* in part

The species of *Lepisorus* grow in soil, on rocks, or on tree trunks and branches. These are small- to medium-sized, creeping polypodiaceous ferns. The widespread *Lepisorus thunbergianus* is often seen on trunks and branches in the Hawaiian Islands, and many cultivars of this species are commonly grown in pots or baskets in Japan. The cultivated species can be difficult to establish, but with patience the second or third attempt may succeed. Other species of *Lepisorus* are extremely difficult to grow.

The rhizomes vary from short- to long-creeping and contain scattered, blackish fiber strands (seen in cross section). Peltate, clathrate, entire or toothed scales cover the rhizomes, sometimes with one or two glandular projections on the margins. The stipes are short, and the blades are simple, entire, and lanceolate to linear, sometimes bearing clathrate scales. The fertile fronds are nearly the same size and shape as the sterile ones. The veins are netted with many irregular areoles, within which are free veins. The sori vary from round to elongate and are protected when young by partly or fully peltate, clathrate, entire scales. Like all polypodiaceous ferns, *Lepisorus* lacks indusia. The species of *Lepisorus* were first classified in *Polypodium* and later in *Pleopeltis*; see *Polypodium* for a comparison of this genus to other polypodiaceous genera.

Lepisorus is native mainly to the Old World tropics and subtropics. The number of species is unknown, but is probably less than 40. The genus name comes from the Greek *lepis,* scale, and *soros,* mound, referring to the scaly sorus.

Lepisorus longifolius (Blume) Holttum

FIGURE 13.62.1

syn. *Paragramma longifolia* (Blume) T. Moore
Probably tender

A medium-sized fern with short-creeping rhizomes. Grows well under medium light in moist, drained uncut moss or potting mix. This species is reportedly the easiest *Lepisorus* to grow in Florida.

Lepisorus longifolius has linear-lanceolate fronds. Oval to oblong, marginal sori are covered and surrounded by

Figure 13.62.1. *Lepisorus longifolius:* a. habit, bar = 5 cm (2 in.); b. fertile portion of frond, bar = 1 cm (0.4 in.); c. peltate scale of sori, bar = 0.1 mm.

peltate scales. This species is native from India to Malaysia and the Philippines.

Lepisorus thunbergianus (Kaulfuss) Ching

FIGURE 13.62.2

syn. *Polypodium lineare* Thunberg
Hardy to very hardy

A small fern with medium-creeping rhizomes. Grows under medium to high light in well-drained, moist-dry potting mix or uncut moss. This species is difficult to establish but is a popular pot plant in Japan, with many named cultivars.

The rhizome scales of *Lepisorus thunbergianus* are dark brown, ovate-cordate at base, and long-attenuate. The fronds are simple, leathery, tapered at both ends, linear-elliptic, 10–30 cm (4–12 in.) long, and 5–15 mm (0.2–0.6 in.) wide. Because of the leathery blades, the veins are hard to see. The sori are round or oval and disposed in one row on either side of midrib. The species is native to Japan, South Korea, China, Taiwan, Indochina, the Philippines, and the Hawaiian Islands.

The species is extremely variable, not only in blade size and shape, but also in habitat. The plants grow on rocks, steep banks, tree trunks, stone walls, and the roofs of houses.

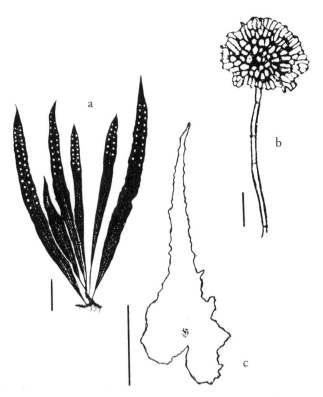

Figure 13.62.2. *Lepisorus thunbergianus:* a. habit, bar = 5 cm (2 in.); b. peltate scale of sori, bar = 0.1 mm; c. rhizome scale, bar = 1 mm.

Leptochilus Kaulfman
syn. *Colysis* C. Presl

These small- to medium-sized ferns have variously shaped leaves and are attractive in pots, baskets, or (in warmer climates) the ground. *Leptochilus,* better known to gardeners as *Colysis,* resembles *Microsorum* but differs by having elongate sori located in an even row between two veins. They are epiphytic or epilithic.

The genus has creeping rhizomes covered by peltate or false-peltate, clathrate or subclathrate scales. The fronds are simple or pinnatifid, with the fertile fronds contracted or not. The veins are visible, netted, and form areoles containing branched included veinlets pointing in various directions. The sori are mostly elongate or linear (rarely acrostichoid) and usually appear in one line or a fairly even row that is parallel to the secondary veins. The indusium is absent.

Leptochilus consists of about 10 species and is native to Asia, Malaysia, Australia, and the Solomon Islands. The genus name comes from the Greek *lepto,* meaning slender, and *-chilus,* meaning lipped, alluding to the blade tips of some species, which end in a slender, curled tip. For a technical comparison of *Leptochilus* to related genera, see Nooteboom (1997); also see *Polypodium* for a comparison of this genus to other polypodiaceous genera.

Leptochilus amplus (F. V. Müller ex Bentham)
Nooteboom FIGURE 13.63.1
syn. *Colysis ampla* (F. V. Müller ex Bentham) Copeland,
C. sayeri (F. V. Müller ex Bentham) Copeland
Tender

A medium-sized fern with long-creeping rhizomes. Grows well under low to medium light in moist, drained potting mix or uncut moss.

The stipe of *Leptochilus amplus* is winged to the base, and on mature plants the blade is deeply pinnatifid with about three pairs of oblong lobes, the terminal lobe resembling the lateral ones. The apices of the lobes are acuminate or long-attenuate, and the veins are conspicuous. The sori are slender, linear, and run obliquely between the midrib and margin. The species is native to Australia.

Leptochilus amplus circulates in horticulture as *Colysis sayeri,* a synonym. Australian botanists have traditionally recognized two species: (1) *L. sayeri,* with the stipe wing not reaching the base and with sori shorter and located midway between the midrib and margin of the lobes and, (2) *L. amplus,* with the stipe wing reaching the base and with longer sori, usually extending from near the lobe midrib to near the margin. According to Nooteboom (1997), however, these characteristics intergrade and the two species should be considered the same.

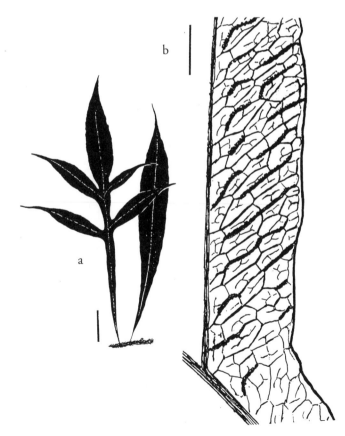

Figure 13.63.1. *Leptochilus amplus:* a. habit, bar = 5 cm. (2 in.); b. sori and vein pattern, bar = 1 cm (0.4 in.).

Leptochilus ellipticus (Thunberg) Nooteboom

FIGURE 13.63.2

syn. *Colysis ellipitica* (Thunberg) Ching, *C. pothifolia* (Buchanan-Hamilton) C. Presl
Semi-tender

A medium-sized fern with medium long-creeping rhizomes. Grows under medium to high-medium light in garden soil or potting mix kept moist to moist-dry. This species is subject to slug damage.

The fronds of mature *Leptochilus ellipticus* plants are broad and deeply pinnately lobed to a very narrow wing along the rachis or fully pinnate at the base. The lobes of sterile fronds are lanceolate and the veins are only slightly visible. Compared to the sterile fronds, the fertile ones are taller and have narrower lobes. The linear sori extend obliquely between the midrib and margin. The species is native to Japan, South Korea, China, Indochina, and Taiwan.

Leptochilus ellipticus was broadly construed by Nooteboom (1997) and consists of diverse-appearing plants that are considered species by other botanists.

Figure 13.63.2. *Leptochilus ellipticus:* a. habit, bar = 5 cm (2 in.); b. sori and vein pattern, bar = 1 cm (0.4 in.).

Leptochilus macrophyllus var. *wrightii* (Hooker) Nooteboom

FIGURE 13.63.3

syn. *Colysis wrightii* (Hooker) Ching
Semi-tender to slightly hardier

A medium-sized fern with medium- to long-creeping rhizomes and evergreen fronds. Grows well under medium light in moist to moist-dry garden soil or potting mix.

Widely known among gardeners as *Colysis wrightii, Leptochilus macrophyllus* var. *wrightii* is characterized by simple, narrow, oblanceolate blades that are long-tapered toward the base. It is native to Japan, southern China, Indochina, and Taiwan. In the wild it often grows on rocks.

'Monstrifera'. Blade tips widely fluted, tip and margins undulate.

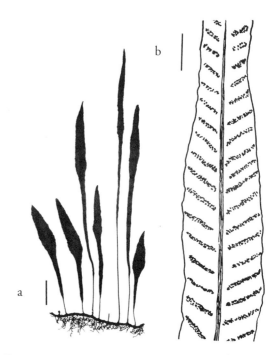

Figure 13.63.3. *Leptochilus macrophyllus* var. *wrightii:* a. habit, bar = 5 cm (2 in.); b. sori, bar = 1 cm (0.4 in.).

Leptopteris

The genus *Leptopteris* resembles large filmy ferns with striking delicate, plume-like fronds. The filmy texture and translucent appearance are due to the blades being only a few cell layers thick. These ferns are native to moist, humid habitats, where they can form woody trunks to 1 m (3 ft.) tall. *Leptopteris* should be grown in protected sites with above-freezing temperatures and ample humidity. If these conditions are unavailable, the plants should be grown indoors in large, shaded terrariums kept cool and humid year-round. They may be planted in high-quality uncut sphagnum moss.

Although rarely cultivated in the United States, *Leptopteris* is so striking that it merits further attempts. The genus is now on the endangered list in New Zealand, which prohibits the export of mature plants. They can be grown from spores, but the spores are green and presumably have short viability.

The rhizomes of *Leptopteris* are erect and trunk-forming. Medium- to large-sized fronds are arranged in a whorl and have finely hairy rachises and costae. The blades may be up to three-pinnate, are very thin, and have ultimate divisions that are often bilobed. The sporangia are scattered on the lower surfaces of the blades. Indusia are lacking.

Leptopteris, which contains six species, is native to Australia, New Zealand, and New Guinea to Samoa and New Caledonia. The genus name comes from the Greek *leptos,* thin, and *pteris,* fern, referring to the extremely thin fronds.

Leptopteris hymenophylloides (A. Richard) C. Presl

FIGURE 13.64.1

Semi-tender to semi-hardy

A medium-sized fern with erect rhizomes and fronds that collectively form a basket. Prefers low light and moist-wet, humusy potting mix or uncut sphagnum moss. The plants require high humidity and cool temperatures. This species is easier to grow than *Leptopteris superba* and tolerates slightly drier conditions.

Leptopteris hymenophylloides has ovate to triangular blades with flat segments (that is, in the same plane of the blade). The species is endemic to New Zealand.

Leptopteris superba (Colenso) C. Presl   FIGURE 13.64.2

Crape fern, Prince-of-Wales plume
Semi-tender to semi-hardy

A medium-sized fern with erect rhizomes and fronds that collectively form a basket. Grows under low light and in moist-wet, humusy potting mix or uncut sphagnum moss. This species grows slowly and is difficult to cultivate, requiring cool temperatures and constant high humidity. In nature it grows near waterfalls.

In contrast to the preceding species, *Leptopteris superba* has blades that taper gradually toward the base, ending in small pinnae. Another difference is that the segments turn up, out of the plane of the blade. The species is endemic to New Zealand.

Leucostegia

Although commonly used as a pot plant in Malaysia, *Leucostegia* is rarely cultivated in the United States. The genus is related to *Davallia,* which it resembles by its much-divided, broad fronds.

The plants are usually terrestrial and medium in size. Their rhizomes are thick, fleshy, more or less long-creeping,

Figure 13.64.1. *Leptopteris hymenophylloides:* frond, bar = 5 cm (2 in.).

Figure 13.64.2. *Leptopteris superba:* frond, bar = 5 cm (2 in.).

and root-bearing on all sides. They are covered by non-peltate scales, and hairs are often present as well. Grooves appear on the upper surfaces of the stipes. The blades are nearly three-pinnate to four-pinnate-pinnatifid, glabrous when mature, anadromous, and herbaceous or papery (chartaceous). The ultimate segments are rhombic-lanceolate. The sori are often impressed and borne at the vein tips. They are covered by delicate, kidney-shaped or rounded indusia—if the indusium is reniform, then it is attached at a point at the base; if rounded, then attached halfway up the sides.

Leucostegia, which consists of two species, occurs in southern China, the Himalayas, and southern India to Polynesia. The genus name comes from the Greek *leucos,* white, and *stege,* cover, referring to the whitish indusia.

Leucostegia pallida (Mettenius) Copeland

FIGURE 13.65.1

Tender

A medium-sized fern with creeping rhizomes and stipes 2–3 cm (0.75–1.2 in.) apart. Grows well under medium to high light in moist garden soil or potting mix. The plants can be grown in baskets or pots. The fronds tend to spread and should be given plenty of room.

Leucostegia pallida has triangular blades, up to four-pinnate, with obovate or rhombic ultimate segments. The sori appear as raised bumps on the upper surface of the blade. Roundish indusia are attached at the base and halfway up the sides. The species is native to the New Hebrides, Borneo, and Malaya.

This fern resembles *Leucostegia immersa* C. Presl, which is not cultivated in the United States but is reported to be cultivated in Australia. That species differs by indusia attached only by a narrow base.

Lindsaea

FIGURE 13.66.1

These attractive ferns are often seen in the tropics and sometimes in temperate areas, but they are difficult to grow and rarely cultivated in the United States. They are primarily seen in botanical gardens and special fern collections. In England, four species of *Lindsaea* are currently cultivated. Some species establish themselves if provided with a well-drained planting mix and anchored in place on uncut moss or a turf-like growing medium. The plants should be kept evenly moist in terrariums. The genus is mentioned here because of its horticultural potential and importance in the tropics.

Some of the species resemble maidenhair ferns (*Adiantum*), but there are several differences. *Lindsaea* almost always has light-colored (tan, green, or yellowish) stipes, rachises, and costae, and these are grooved on their upper surfaces, often with a sharp wing on either side of the groove. Furthermore, the indusium is formed on the lower

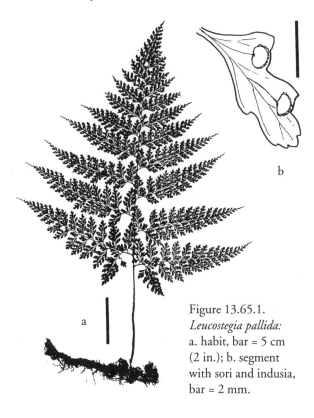

Figure 13.65.1. *Leucostegia pallida:* a. habit, bar = 5 cm (2 in.); b. segment with sori and indusia, bar = 2 mm.

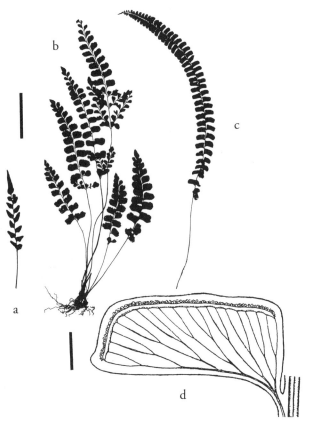

Figure 13.66.1. *Lindsaea:* a. frond (*Lindsaea ensifolia*); b. habit (*L. repanda*); c. frond (*L. stricta*), bar for a, b, and c = 5 cm (2 in.); d. sorus and indusium, bar = 2 mm.

surface of the blade and opens toward the margin. In contrast, *Adiantum* has brown or black rachises and costae that are ungrooved, and the indusium is formed by the enrolled margins of the leaf and therefore opens toward the center of the segments.

Lindsaea contains about 150 species and occurs worldwide. The genus is named for John Lindsay, a surgeon in Jamaica at the turn of the 19th century who studied the germination of fern spores.

Llavea

Llavea consists of one species, endemic to Mexico and Guatemala, that is rarely cultivated. *Llavea cordifolia* has an attractive airy appearance and bears many gray-green, oval segments. The plants are easy to grow from spores. They are sensitive to overwatering and susceptible to leaf-spot diseases when grown in extremely humid environments.

The genus has several distinctive characteristics, the most obvious being the strong differentiation in the shape and position of its sterile and fertile segments. The sterile segments are oval or nearly so and borne throughout the basal two-thirds of the blade, whereas the fertile ones are linear and borne only in the apical third. The sori are protected by the enrolled margin of the segments. The rhizome scales are mostly black but grade into bright yellow ones at the bases of the leaf stalks. The genus is named for Pablo de la Llave (1773–1833), a traveler in Mexico.

Llavea cordifolia Lagasca
FIGURES 13.67.1, 2
Tender to semi-tender

A medium-sized fern with short-creeping to suberect rhizomes. Grows under medium to high light in moist, drained potting mix. *Llavea cordifolia* is best used as a pot plant. Be careful not to overwater, and do not allow water to remain on the leaves. Provide adequate air circulation. See the genus entry for a botanical description.

Lonchitis
syn. *Anisosorus*

These terrestrial ferns are rarely cultivated. *Lonchitis* has rather coarsely cut fronds with a soft, hairy appearance. The rhizome is creeping, thick, and fleshy and bears hairs and scales. The stipe contains two vascular bundles. The fronds are slightly succulent, two- to three-pinnate-pinnatifid, broad, and hairy. The veins are free or occasionally netted. The sori are marginal, being borne at the sides of the segments or lobes. The indusium is formed by the enrolled leaf margin.

This genus is sometimes confused with *Blotiella* (not cultivated), which has hard, erect rhizomes and fully netted veins. *Lonchitis* is distinguished from the similar *Pteris* by hairy (not scaly) rhizomes.

The genus consists of two species that hardly differ. One, *Lonchitis hirsuta*, is native to tropical America, and

Figure 13.67.1. *Llavea cordifolia:* habit.

the other, *Lonchitis occidentalis* Baker, to Africa and Madagascar. The genus name comes from the Greek *lonche*, lance, and *-itis,* a suffix indicating a close connection. It comes from an ancient name that was used by the Greek physician and botanist Dioscorides.

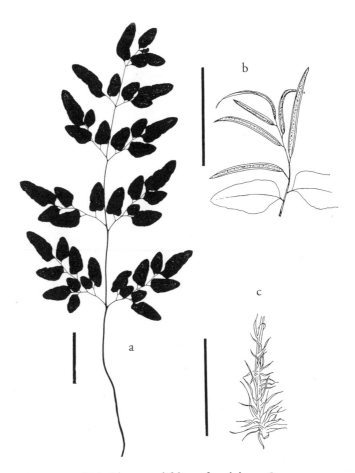

Figure 13.67.2. *Llavea cordifolia:* a. frond, bar = 5 cm (2 in.); b. distal portion of a fertile frond, bar = 5 cm (2 in.); c. stipe base, bar = 5 cm (2 in.).

Lonchitis hirsuta Linnaeus   FIGURES 13.68.1–3
Tender

A medium to large fern with short-creeping, succulent rhizomes and softly hairy fronds. Grows well under medium light in moist-wet potting mix.

All parts of *Lonchitis hirsuta* are hairy. The blade is soft and broadly cut, reminiscent of tomato foliage in shape. The veins are free. This species is native to the American tropics.

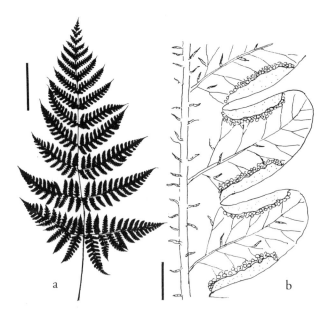

Figure 13.68.3. *Lonchitis hirsuta:* a. frond, bar = 5 cm (2 in.); b. hairs, sori, and indusia, bar = 5 mm (0.2 in.).

Figure 13.68.1. *Lonchitis hirsuta:* habit.

Figure 13.68.2. *Lonchitis hirsuta:* pinnae.

Lycopodium   FIGURES 13.69.1, 2
Club moss, ground pine, princess pine, tassel fern

In the north-temperate zone, *Lycopodium* is often seen on forest floors as small- to medium-sized, erect or trailing plants with scale-like leaves. Many tropical species are epiphytes; less often are they scandent or trailing on the ground. The epiphytic species with pendent stems are prized in horticulture. They can be handsomely displayed in hanging containers or on boards. The temperate species are difficult to grow and are seldom cultivated. They resent disturbance and often require the presence of special fungi (mycorrhizae) in the roots.

Lycopodiums have had several uses over the years. The evergreen species were used in wreaths and table decorations during the winter and Christmas season. The plants were so intensively gathered for this use that laws were enacted to protect them in forest preserves and parks. Another use involved the spores, which are full of volatile oils and highly flammable. These spores were a primary ingredient in fireworks and in flash powders used in photography. In the days when pills were hand-made by pharmacists, *Lycopodium* spores were used to coat the pills and prevent them from sticking. More recently, they have been used for the same purpose on rubber surgical gloves.

To cultivate the North American species that grow on forest floors, try transplanting them to woodland soils or rock gardens with loose, moist soil. Those species that grow in wetter areas need moist soil, but not so moist that the plants rot. A sandy soil mixed with peat moss and loam, carefully watered, might encourage rooting and new growth in transplants. Transplanting has been successful

Figure 13.69.1. *Lycopodium phlegmaria:* habit.

Figure 13.69.2. *Lycopodium squarrosum:* fertile leaves.

in oak-leaf mold, using aluminum sulfate to maintain acidity and preventing the plants from drying. A well-drained, slightly acidic soil or coarsely cut sphagnum moss (not too wet) has worked with *Lycopodium lucidulum.*

The epiphytic species are easy to grow, but most require warm temperatures, humidity, and adequate air circulation. The planting medium must be coarse and well drained. Care should be taken to guard against extremes: never let the plants dry out nor get too wet. Poor air circulation promotes leaf diseases and rot. Plants may need to have their roots covered by uncut sphagnum moss, which can be tied to a board or a tree-fern-fiber planter. Hanging pots or baskets can also be used, in which case a coarser planting mix (not soil) should be used. If lycopodiums are planted in pots with uncut sphagnum, the moss should be kept loose because packed moss holds too much water.

Lycopodium species can be propagated by divisions, tip cuttings, and layering. Propagators report that the new, lateral shoots tend to form between the sterile and fertile regions of the stem. Therefore when propagating by layering, this area should contact the growth medium. For further details on cultivation, see the section on "Fern Allies" in Chapter 10.

Lycopodium is easy to recognize by its small, usually scale-like leaves supplied by a single vein. Most plants are evergreen, but a few species are deciduous. Many species have cones, but some bear sporangia in the axils of leaves that resemble vegetative leaves, thus cones are absent. The sporangium can be seen as a bean-shaped or rounder structure, usually yellowish, on the upper surface of the scale (or leaf) near the base. The fertile leaves usually occur at the stem apex. The fertile leaves may be highly reduced and compact, thus forming a cone. The cones can also be sessile or borne on specialized stalks. Only one kind of spore is produced.

Some botanists divide *Lycopodium* into 3 to 12 genera, and it is only a matter of opinion how many of these, if any, should be recognized. *Selaginella* is sometimes confused with *Lycopodium,* but the cultivated species of *Selaginella* tend to have smaller leaves, softer foliage, and two kinds of sporangia: larger female ones at the base of the fertile zone and smaller male ones above.

Lycopodium occurs worldwide and contains about 450 species. The genus name comes from the Greek *lykos,* wolf, and *pous,* foot, alluding to a fancied resemblance between the branch tips and a wolf's paw.

Lycopodium carinatum Desvaux   FIGURE 13.69.3
syn. *Huperzia carinata* (Desvaux) Trevisan,
   Phlegmariurus carinatus (Desvaux) Ching
Keeled tassel fern
Tender

A medium-sized plant with slender, cord-like, pendulous, evergreen stems. Grows well under medium light in drained, moist potting mix or uncut moss attached to a board or in a hanging container.

   Lycopodium carinatum is a pendent epiphyte, several times branched, with a gradual transition from sterile to fertile leaves. The branches grow to about 80 cm (32 in.) long and 8–10 mm (0.3–0.4 in.) wide including the leaves. The sterile leaves are narrowly ovate, 10–13 mm (about 0.5 in.) long, 2 mm wide, thick, leathery, stiff, appressed, at about a 30-degree angle from the stem, closely overlapping, strongly keeled and folded along the midrib, entire, acute, and decurrent on the stem. The species occurs from India to Polynesia and Australia.

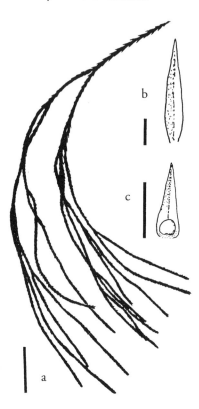

Figure 13.69.3. *Lycopodium carinatum:* a. branches with sterile and fertile leaves in spikes, bar = 5 cm (2 in.); b. sterile leaf, bar = 3 mm (0.1 in.); c; fertile leaf, bar = 3 mm (0.1 in.).

Lycopodium cernuum Linnaeus   FIGURE 13.69.4
syn. *Lycopodiella cernuua* (Linnaeus) Pichi-Sermolli,
   Palhinhaea cernua (Linnaeus) Vasconcellus & Franco
Nodding club moss
Tender to semi-tender, Zones 8–9

A medium to large plant with long, horizontal stems that branch and scramble. Grows under medium to high light in moist potting mix. The species resembles a miniature

Figure 13.69.4. *Lycopodium cernuum:* habit, bar = 5 cm (2 in.).

Christmas tree with nodding branch tips. In the southeastern United States the tips of the horizontal stems overwinter.

   The sterile leaves of *Lycopodium cernuum* are narrowly triangular, pale green, and entire. The cones are short, less than 1 cm (0.5 in.) long, and borne at the tips of the nodding branchlets. The fertile leaves are trowel-shaped and fringed along the margins. This is one of the most widespread club mosses in the tropical and subtropical regions of the world. It is often weedy in the wild, especially in disturbed habitats.

Lycopodium clavatum Linnaeus   FIGURE 13.69.5
Staghorn club moss, running pine
Very hardy, Zone (2)3

A medium-sized plant with long-creeping, horizontal stems that periodically send forth erect stems. Grows under medium light in moist-wet soil or potting mix. This species is difficult to grow.

   The hair-like tip of the sterile leaves will distinguish *Lycopodium clavatum* from all others in the genus. The plants are evergreen with antler-like branches and stalked cones.

Figure 13.69.5. *Lycopodium clavatum:* habit, bar = 5 cm (2 in.).

The species is one of the most widely distributed pteridophytes in the world, occurring on every continent. Japanese scientists report that spores can cause allergies.

Lycopodium complanatum Linnaeus   FIGURE 13.69.6
syn. *Diphasiastrum complanatum* (Linnaeus) Holub
Flat-branch club moss, ground cedar, running pine
Very hardy, Zone (1)2

A medium-sized plant with long-creeping horizontal stems that send up much-branched erect stems with flattened branchlets. Grows under medium light in moist soil or potting mix. The species is difficult to grow.

Lycopodium complanatum is an evergreen plant with flattened lateral branchlets that have constrictions marking annual growth. The sterile leaves of the branchlets are four-ranked (two laterals, one on top, and one on the bottom). The cones are elevated on slender, candelabra-like stalks. The species is native to North America, Europe, and Asia.

This species resembles *Lycopodium digitatum* A. Braun, which also grows in eastern North America. *Lycopodium digitatum* differs by the lack of growth constrictions on the branchlets and the fan-shaped arrangement of the horizontal branchlets.

Figure 13.69.6. *Lycopodium complanatum:* habit, bar = 5 cm (2 in.), after Beitel (1979).

Lycopodium dendroideum Michaux   FIGURE 13.69.7
syn. *Lycopodium obscurum* var. *dendroideum* (Michaux)
    D. C. Eaton
Prickly-tree club moss, princess pine
Very hardy, Zone 2

A medium-sized plant with long-creeping stems. Grows under medium light in moist soil or potting mix. The species is difficult to cultivate.

Lycopodium dendroideum is an evergreen species. The main stems are upright and branched into a miniature tree-like form. The lateral branches are round in cross section, and the sterile leaves are lanceolate and all of nearly equal size. Leaves of branchlets are arranged in two dorsal, two ventral, and two lateral rows, with those on the main stems beneath the first branch spreading at a 30- to 90-degree angle. The cones are sessile, and the fertile leaves are ovate-

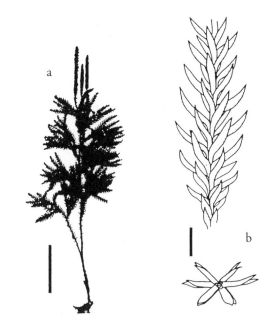

Figure 13.69.7. *Lycopodium dendroideum:* a. habit, bar = 5 cm (2 in.); b. dorsal view of branchlet (above) and cross section (below), bar = 3 mm (0.1 in.), after Hickey (1977).

triangular with an abruptly narrowing apex. The species is native to northern North America and Asia.

This species resembles *Lycopodium obscurum,* which see for comparison.

Lycopodium filiforme Swartz   FIGURE 13.69.8
syn. *Huperzia filiformis* (Swartz) Holub, *H. polytrichoides*
    (Kaulfuss) Trevisan, *Lycopodium filiforme* Kaulfuss
Tender

A medium-sized plant with pendulous, evergreen stems. Grows well under medium light in moist, drained potting mix or uncut moss attached to a board or in a hanging container.

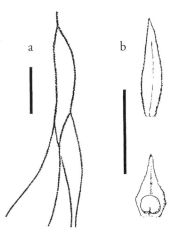

Figure 13.69.8. *Lycopodium filiforme:* a. branches with sterile and fertile leaves in spikes, bar = 5 cm (2 in.); b. sterile leaf above, fertile leaf below, bar = 3 mm (0.1 in.).

Like *Lycopodium carinatum*, *L. filiforme* has cord-like stems, but they are narrower, only 2–3 mm wide (including the leaves), to 60 cm (24 in.) long, and several times forked near the base. The sterile leaves are narrowly triangular to lanceolate, to about 3.5 mm long, about 1.5 mm wide at the base, keeled, with translucent and minutely irregularly toothed margins. The transition from the sterile to fertile zone is gradual. The species is endemic to Australia.

Lycopodium lucidulum Michaux   FIGURE 13.69.9

syn. *Huperzia lucidula* (Michaux) Trevisan, *Urostachys lucidulus* (Michaux) Nessel

Shining club moss

Very hardy, Zone 3

A small plant with erect stems that recline with age and take root. Grows under medium light in moist, acidic potting soil or coarsely cut moss. This species is difficult to grow. The plants are evergreen with shiny leaves and usually grow in open tufts. The upper tips of the branchlets form buds that are shed in the fall.

Lycopodium lucidulum has erect, dichotomously branched stems with constrictions marking annual growth. The sterile leaves are dark green, shiny, and oblanceolate, with the margins entire or papillate or with up to eight irregular teeth. Most of the leaves point downward and impart a shaggy appearance to the plant. The fertile leaves are similar to the sterile ones. The species resembles *L. selago*. It is native to eastern North America, where it grows on forest floors and rarely on rocks.

Figure 13.69.9. *Lycopodium lucidulum:* habit, bar = 5 cm (2 in.).

Lycopodium nummariifolium Blume

FIGURE 13.69.10

syn. *Huperzia nummulariifolium* (Blume) Chambers, Jermy & Crabbe, *Phlegmariurus nummulariifolius* (Blume) Ching

Tender

A medium-sized plant with long, pendent, stiff branches arising from a clump of rhizomes. Best grown in a hanging container with good drainage. The planting media should be kept moist, but the surroundings should have good air circulation and medium light.

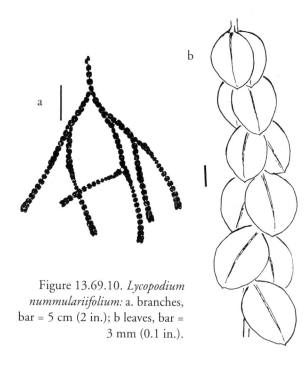

Figure 13.69.10. *Lycopodium nummulariifolium:* a. branches, bar = 5 cm (2 in.); b leaves, bar = 3 mm (0.1 in.).

Relatively large, circular leaves flattened against the stem readily distinguish *Lycopodium nummulariifolium* from other species in the genus. An epiphyte, it is native to Thailand, Malaysia, Polynesia, and New Guinea.

Lycopodium obscurum Linnaeus   FIGURE 13.69.11

Tree club moss, flat-branched tree club moss, ground pine, princess pine

Very hardy, Zone 3

A medium-sized plant with long-creeping stems. Grows under medium light in moist soil or potting mix. This species is difficult to grow.

Lycopodium obscurum resembles *L. dendroideum* and is sometimes difficult to distinguish. The easiest way to tell them apart is by looking at the leaves on the main, erect stem below the first branch: these leaves are appressed or slightly spreading-ascending in *L. obscurum* but widely spreading in *L. dendroideum*. Another difference (although you need to see the two species side by side to appreciate it) is that lateral branches are slightly flattened in *L. obscurum* but cylindrical in *L. dendroideum*. *Lycopodium obscurum* is native to the eastern United States and adjacent Canada.

Lycopodium phlegmaria Linnaeus

FIGURES 13.69.1, 12

syn. *Huperzia phlegmaria* (Linnaeus) Rothmaler, *Phlegmariurus phlegmaria* (Linnaeus) Sen & Sen

Common tassel fern

Tender

A medium-sized plant with short-creeping rhizomes and pendulous, evergreen stems. Grows well under medium

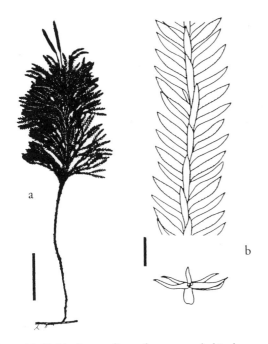

Figure 13.69.11. *Lycopodium obscurum:* a. habit, bar = 5 cm (2 in.); b. dorsal view of branchlet (above) and cross section (below), bar = 3 mm (0.1 in.), after Hickey (1977).

light in moist, drained potting mix or uncut moss attached to a board or in a hanging container.

The fertile parts of *Lycopodium phlegmaria* are slender and tassel-like, with fertile tips often continuing to grow and forming sterile leaves. (In other species, the fertile tips usually stop growing.) The sterile stems fork several times and are 1.5–3 cm (0.6–1.2 in.) wide (including the leaves). The leaves are spirally arranged, crowded, triangular to ovate-lanceolate, stiff, leathery, dark green, entire, prickly, short-stalked, and acute at the apex. The fertile branches are slender and much branched, and the fertile leaves are much shorter than sterile leaves, with the sporangia about as wide or wider than the fertile leaves. The species is native to Africa, Asia, and the Pacific Islands.

Lycopodium phlegmarioides Gaudichaud

FIGURE 13.69.13

syn. *Huperzia phlegmarioides* (Gaudichaud) Rothmaler
Layered tassel fern
Very tender, Zone 11

A medium-sized plant with pendulous stems, to 80 cm (32 in.) long, that are several-times branching. Grows best in medium light in coarse potting mix or uncut moss in hanging pots or on boards; keep moist but very well drained.

Lycopodium phlegmarioides is an epiphyte that resembles *L. phlegmaria* but has more yellowish green, stiffer, and fewer four-ranked leaves. The sterile leaves are broadly ovate, twisted at the base and adnate to the stem. The spo-

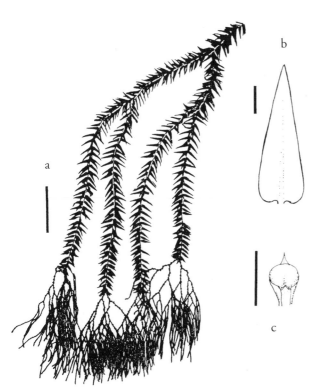

Figure 13.69.12. *Lycopodium phlegmaria:* a. branches with sterile and fertile leaves in spikes, bar = 5 cm (2 in.); b. sterile leaf bar = 3 mm (0.1 in.); c. fertile leaf, bar = 3 mm (0.1 in.).

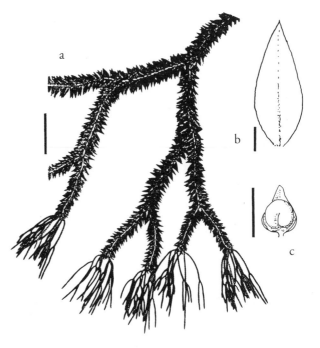

Figure 13.69.13. *Lycopodium phlegmarioides:* a. branches with sterile and fertile leaves in spikes, bar = 5 cm (2 in.); b. sterile leaf, bar = 3 mm (0.1 in.); c. fertile leaf, bar = 3 mm (0.1 in.).

rangia are shorter than the fertile leaves. This species is native from Australia and Malaysia to New Caledonia and the Pacific Islands.

Lycopodium selago Linnaeus   FIGURE 13.69.14

syn. *Huperzia selago* (Linnaeus) C. Martius & Shrank
Mountain club moss, fir club moss, alpine club moss
Very hardy, Zone 2

A small plant with evergreen, clump-forming stems. Grows under medium light in moist-wet sandy soil or drained potting mix. This species is difficult to grow.

The stems tend to be yellow-green (at least in cultivation), forked only once or twice, and produce buds near the tips. The sterile leaves are mostly narrowly triangular, pressed close to the stem, and have papillate or entire margins. The fertile leaves resemble the sterile. *Lycopodium selago* is similar to *L. lucidulum* but differs by having stomata on both surfaces of the leaves, whereas in *L. lucidulum* these are only on the lower surface. A hand lens is needed to see the stomata, which appear as tiny white dots. *Lycopodium selago* is native to northern North America (chiefly Canada).

Figure 13.69.14. *Lycopodium selago:* habit, bar = 5 cm (2 in.).

Lycopodium squarrosum G. Forster

FIGURES 13.69.2, 15

syn. *Huperzia squarrosa* (G. Forster) Trevisan,
   Phlegmariurus squarrosus (G. Forster) Löve & Löve
Water tassel fern, rock tassel fern
Very tender, Zone 11

A medium-sized plant with clump-forming, pendulous or erect, evergreen stems that are several-times branching. Grows best in medium light in coarse potting mix or uncut moss kept moist but very well drained. Plant in hanging containers or attach to boards.

The stems of *Lycopodium squarrosum* are up to 75 cm (30 in.) long, about 1.5–2.5 cm (0.5–1 in.) wide (including the leaves). The sterile leaves are narrowly ovate to linear-lanceolate, 1–2 cm (0.5–0.75 in.) long, entire, thin but somewhat stiff, crowded, and widely spreading except at the stem apex. The transition from the sterile to fertile regions is abrupt or gradual, but any cone-like structure is absent. The fertile leaves resemble the sterile ones, and their sporangia are inconspicuous, occupying less than one-fifth the length of the fertile leaf. The species is native to Africa, Australia, Asia, and Polynesia.

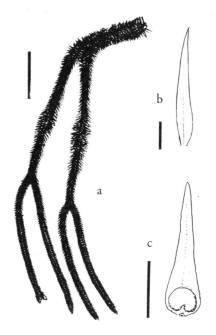

Figure 13.69.15. *Lycopodium squarrosum:* a. branches with fertile and sterile leaves in spikes, bar = 5 cm (2 in.); b. sterile leaf, bar = 3 mm (0.1 in.); c. fertile leaf, bar = 3 mm (0.1 in.).

Lygodium   FIGURES 13.70.1, 2

Climbing fern

Lygodium plants have twining, vine-like fronds and are grown in pots or in the ground. Emerging fronds can be trained on vertically strung wires or strings to produce a lacy green curtain. The fronds can grow up to 7 m (23 ft.) or more. The Japanese climbing fern (*Lygodium japonicum*) and the small-leaved climbing fern (*L. microphyllum*) have become naturalized in the southeastern United States. In temperate areas the foliage of these species dies to the ground in winter, and new fronds emerge in the spring. In milder climates the fronds linger more than a year and may produce new leaflets from dormant buds on the pinnae. Old fronds become untidy as their leaflets gradually turn brown and wither in place. Eventually the entire frond dies to the base and can only be removed, with difficulty, especially if it has become entangled with the new fronds. Propagation by rhizome divisions is unpredictable. Adult plants generally do not transplant well.

The rhizomes of lygodiums are short- to medium-creeping and hairy (not scaly). The fronds are vine-like, with the rachis twining and stem-like. The pinnae are one-pinnate or palmate. The fertile leaflets (as used here, the smallest stalked or free part of the blade) are narrower and have margins with spike-like extensions bearing two rows of scale-like indusia, each indusium covering one sporangium. Depending on the species, the veins can be either free or netted. The sporangia differ from those of other ferns because the annulus is located at the apex of the capsule, not encircling it.

Lygodium consists of 45 species and, except for one temperate species (*Lygodium palmatum*), is native to the tropics

Figure 13.70.1. *Lygodium japonicum:* habit.

Figure 13.70.2. *Lygodium japonicum:* indusia.

and subtropics worldwide. In southern Thailand, Malaya, Sumatra, the Philippines, and New Guinea, the twining leaf rachises are split and flattened for weaving into baskets, purses, and bracelets.

Lygodium circinnatum (N. L. Burman) Swartz
FIGURE 13.70.3

Very tender

A large fern with short-creeping rhizomes. Grows well under medium light in moist potting soil.

Lygodium circinnatum has sterile leaflets up to 20 cm (8 in.) long and about as wide. They are deeply palmately lobed into four or five linear-lanceolate lobes to 25 cm (10

Figure 13.70.3. *Lygodium circinnatum:* leaflets, sterile (above) and fertile (below), bar = 5 cm (2 in.).

in.) long. The species is native from India to southern China, southeastern Asia, Malaysia, and Melanesia.

Lygodium flexuosum (Linnaeus) Swartz

FIGURE 13.70.4

Tender

A large fern with short-creeping rhizomes. Grows well under medium light in moist potting soil. The new growth is often reddish.

Lygodium flexuosum resembles *L. japonicum,* but it has less-divided sterile leaflets, lateral leaflets mostly eared on one or both sides, and two- or three-lobed terminal leaflets 3–10 cm (1.2–4 in.) long. It is native to India, southern China, Japan, and Malaysia to Australia to Melanesia.

Figure 13.70.4. *Lygodium flexuosum:* leaflets, sterile (above) and fertile (below), bar = 5 cm (2 in.).

Lygodium japonicum (Thunberg) Swartz

FIGURES 13.70.1, 2, 5; PLATE 31

Japanese climbing fern
Semi-hardy to hardier, Zone (6)7

A large fern with short-creeping rhizomes. Grows well under high-medium light in moist garden soil or potting mix. This species is the most commonly cultivated of the climbing ferns. It is easy to grow from spores.

Lygodium japonicum is distinguished by its pinnately lobed sterile leaflets up to 3 cm (1.2 in.) long. The elon-

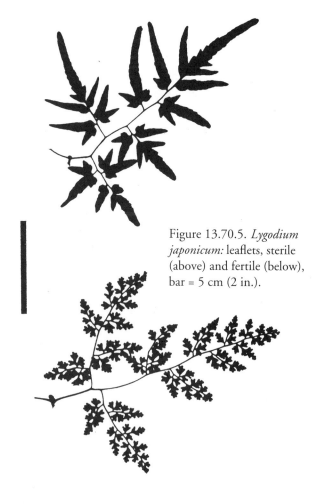

Figure 13.70.5. *Lygodium japonicum:* leaflets, sterile (above) and fertile (below), bar = 5 cm (2 in.).

gate triangular leaflets are five- to seven-lobed, with the terminal lobe the longest. The species is native to India, eastern Asia, Australia, and the Philippines. It has become naturalized in the southeastern United States. Its fronds are deciduous in the middle Atlantic states but evergreen farther south.

This species is often misidentified in the trade as *Lygodium scandens* (Linnaeus) Swartz, a synonym of *L. microphyllum.*

Lygodium microphyllum (Cavanilles) R. Brown

FIGURE 13.70.6

syn. *Lygodium scandens* (Linnaeus) Swartz
Small-leaved climbing fern
Semi-tender, Zone 9

A large fern with short-creeping rhizomes. Grows well under medium-high light in moist-wet garden soil or potting mix. This species is easy to grow from spores.

Lygodium microphyllum is characterized by slender, creeping rhizomes and ovate to oblong-ovate sterile leaflets to 2.5 cm (1 in.) long. The base is heart-shaped, and the segments ovate and heart-shaped. It is native to Africa, southeastern Asia, Australia, and Polynesia. It has become naturalized and weedy in Florida, especially in bald cypress

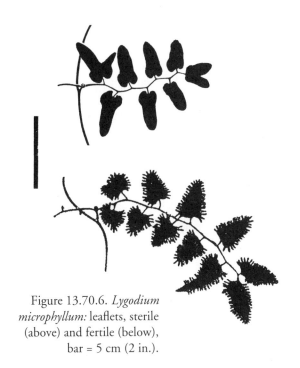

Figure 13.70.7.
*Lygodium
palmatum:* leaflets,
sterile (above) and
fertile (below), bar
= 5 cm (2 in.).

Figure 13.70.6. *Lygodium
microphyllum:* leaflets, sterile
(above) and fertile (below),
bar = 5 cm (2 in.).

swamps, where it smothers the native vegetation and can be a fire hazard by wicking fires up into the tops of trees.

Lygodium palmatum (Bernhardi) Swartz

FIGURE 13.70.7

Hartford fern
Very hardy, Zone 3

A large fern with short-creeping rhizomes. Grows under low light in sandy, acidic soil. This species is difficult to grow. Water the plants with rain water, especially in high-limestone areas. The plants can be propagated by spores, which mature in November or December, but they loose their viability quickly. Mickel (1994) reports that sporelings are easy to obtain but hard to get to grow to maturity.

The sterile leaflets of *Lygodium palmatum* are to 5 cm (2 in.) long, about as wide, and deeply palmately lobed with three to seven elongate lobes. The fronds remain green during the winter. This species is endemic to the eastern United States.

The evergreen fronds used to be collected during the winter and used for Christmas decorations. This destroyed so many populations that in 1869 the Connecticut legislature enacted a law to protect the plant—the first plant conservation law passed in the United States.

Macrothelypteris

syn. *Thelypteris* subgenus *Macrothelypteris*

Only a single species of *Macrothelypteris* is cultivated: *Macrothelypteris torresiana.* It was formerly classified in *Thelypteris,* but pteridologists now consider it sufficiently distinct because of its large, highly divided leaves and veins

that end before the leaf margin in a slightly swollen tip, among other technical characteristics.

This genus resembles dryopteroid or ctenitoid ferns such as *Dryopteris, Lastreopsis,* and *Megalastrum,* which contain species that have broadly triangular, two- to three-pinnate-pinnatifid blades like *Macrothelypteris.* It differs from these others, however, by having stipes with only two vascular bundles (not three or more), needle-like hairs on the blades, and ungrooved upper surfaces of the rachises, costae, and costules. The pinnae of *Macrothelypteris* are free from each other, not connected by a wing, thus differing from the related genus *Phegopteris.* The needle-like hairs on the lower surface of the costae are often more than 1 mm long and colorless. The sori are round and covered by inconspicuous indusia.

Macrothelypteris consists of 10 species and is native to the tropics and subtropics of the Old World. One species, *Macrothelypteris torresiana,* has become naturalized throughout the New World tropics and subtropics. The genus name comes from adding the Greek *macros,* large, to *Thelypteris.*

Macrothelypteris torresiana (Gaudichaud) Ching

FIGURE 13.71.1

syn. *Thelypteris torresiana* (Gaudichaud) Alston, *T. uliginosa* (Kunze) Ching

Torre's fern, Mariana maiden fern
Semi-hardy, Zone (7)8

A large fern with short-creeping to suberect rhizomes. Grows well under medium light in moist to moist-dry garden soil or potting mix. The plants are easy to cultivate and volunteer readily from spore and often appear as contaminants in spore pans.

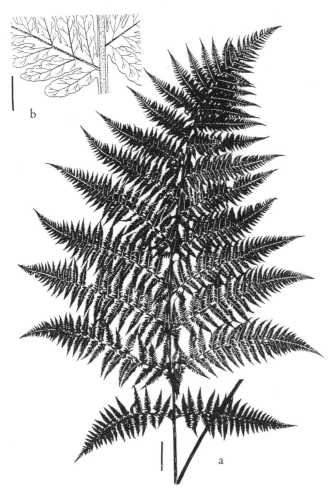

Figure 13.72.1. *Marattia:* habit.

Figure 13.71.1. *Macrothelypteris torresiana:* a. frond, bar = 5 cm (2 in.); b. winged costa and primary pinnule bases, bar = 1 cm (0.4 in.).

Besides the characteristics listed under the genus, *Macrothelypteris torresiana* has stipe bases with conspicuous white lines (aerophores) along their sides, and the blades are broadly triangular, light green, and two- to three-pinnate. The species is native to Asia and Africa, but is now widely naturalized in the American tropics, subtropics, and southeastern United States.

In the 1950s this species was commonly sold as *Dryopteris setigera* Kuntze and *Thelypteris setigera* (Blume) Ching (a species not cultivated).

Marattia   FIGURES 13.72.1–3

Marattia is a genus of huge ferns with mostly fleshy, globose stems and large, coarse, somewhat fleshy fronds. The succulent stems are full of starch that is sometimes eaten by people and wild pigs, the latter of which have decimated many populations. In the wild *Marattia* favors moist gullies and grows at somewhat higher elevations and in denser shade than *Angiopteris,* a related genus. Cultivated plants should be protected from frost, wind, and physical damage, as the fleshy fronds break easily. Do not permit the plants to wilt because the foliage recovers slowly.

The stems of *Marattia* are erect and bear fronds to 4 m (13 ft.) long. In appearance, growth habit, and method of propagation, *Marattia* resembles *Angiopteris* and is difficult to distinguish from it when sterile. When fertile fronds are present, the two genera are easy to distinguish: *Marattia* has fused sporangia, whereas those of *Angiopteris* are free. In *Marattia,* the middle of the stipe lacks the bump or swelling that is present in *Angiopteris,* and the distal portion of the rachis is usually winged. The sorus consists of a double row of fused sporangia (a synangium).

Figure 13.72.2. *Marattia fraxinea:* fused sporangia.

Figure 13.72.3. *Marattia fraxinea:* pinna.

Marattia contains 60 species native to the tropics throughout the world. The genus is named for Giovanni Francesco Maratti (1723–1777), a Benedictine abbot and later professor and head of the botanical garden in Rome.

Marattia fraxinea J. E. Smith ex J. F. Gmelin

FIGURES 13.72.2–4

Tender to semi-tender

A large fern with erect stems that tend to form trunks with age. Grows well under medium light in moist, drained garden soil or potting mix. Do not let the soil dry out, and be sure to protect plants from wind.

Marattia fraxinea has two-pinnate fronds with ultimate segments narrowly oblong-lanceolate to narrowly oblong

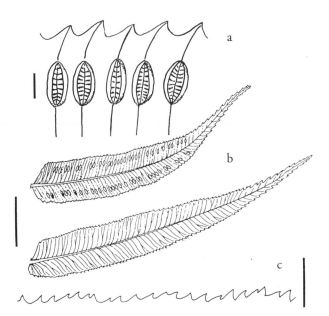

Figure 13.72.4. *Marattia fraxinea:* a. fused sporangia, bar = 1 mm; b. pinnules, fertile (above) and sterile (below), bar = 1 cm (0.4 in.); c. serrate margin, bar = 1 mm.

linear, with margins sharply serrate, rarely entire. The sporangial capsules are oval. This species is native to Africa and Madagascar.

Marattia salicina J. E. Smith

FIGURE 13.72.5

King fern, horseshoe fern

Tender to semi-tender; sensitive to frost

A large fern with erect stems. Grows well under medium light in drained, moist garden soil or potting mix. The plants need ample water. Do not permit the soil to dry because the fronds wilt readily and take a long time to recover. Set the plant in a place protected from winds.

The fronds of *Marattia salicina* are up to 2–3.5 m (6.5–11 ft.) long, and the segments are oblong to narrowly ovate with shallowly toothed to almost entire margins. The sporangial capsules are oblong to subglobose. This species is native to Australia, New Zealand, and Polynesia.

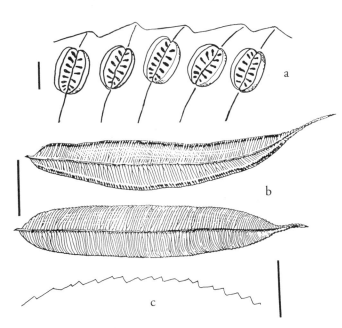

Figure 13.72.5. *Marattia salicina:* a. fused sporangia, bar = 1 mm; b. pinnules, fertile (above) and sterile (below), bar = 1 cm (0.4 in.); c. dentate margin, bar = 1 mm.

Marsilea

FIGURE 13.73.1

Water clover, pepperwort, nardoo

The four leaflets of *Marsilea* fronds resemble clover—thus the common name water clover. These ferns are grown as novelty plants in aquariums, ponds, and wide pots. If the pots are submerged a few inches in water, the plants may produce floating leaves. *Marsilea* usually grows vigorously and spreads by rhizomes. The plants do best in well-watered, sunny locations. They are typically planted in garden soil or a mixture of half sand and peat. Mixes with high

Figure 13.73.1. *Marsilea minuta:* habit.

amounts of organic matter are apt to sour in standing water.

Although the life cycle of *Marsilea* is the most complex of any fern, starting the plants from spores is easy and fun. The spores are of separate sexes (male and female) and contained in brown, hard, bean-like structures called *sporocarps.* These are extremely durable and remain viable for up to 100 years if kept dry. To germinate the spores, take a piece of sand paper or a rough nail file and abrade the sporocarp until the white inside is visible. Then put the sporocarp in shallow water under a bright light. Within minutes it will germinate and extrude a transparent, tail-like, gelatinous ring called the *sorophore,* to which the sori are attached. (If the sporocarp does not germinate, try abrading it some more, or it might be too young, in which case an older one should be used.) The sori resemble grains of white rice arranged in a row. Within a few more minutes the sori will release the small male and much larger female spores that will quickly germinate and fertilize in the water. After a week or so, the fertilized female spores, which will appear as conspicuous white dots, can be picked up with an eye dropper and released over wet sand or mud. Keep the planting wet and in bright light. Young plants should emerge and grow rapidly, maturing in 12 to 18 months.

The water clovers are subaquatic ferns that root in mud. New fronds are borne on long-creeping, branched rhizomes. The shorter side branches of the rhizome often ascend and bear many crowded fronds, each of which bears four leaflets and resembles a four-leaved clover. The sporocarps are usually borne at the base of the stipe.

The main characteristics used to distinguish the species of *Marsilea* are the sporocarps and roots. The sporocarps provide useful diagnostic features in their number and ar-

rangement on the stipe base, their shape, and whether they bear teeth. The position of the roots along the stem is also taxonomically important. In some species the roots are produced only at the nodes, whereas in others they are produced on the nodes *and* internodes. For a technical treatment of the American species, see Johnson (1986); for the African species, see Launert (1968).

Marsilea occurs worldwide and contains about 60 species. It is named for Count Luigi Ferdinando Marsigli (1656–1730), an Italian botanist from Bologna.

Marsilea angustifolia R. Brown   FIGURE 13.73.2
Dwarf water clover, narrow-leaved nardoo
Hardy, Zone 6 and possibly colder areas

One of the smallest *Marsilea* species in cultivation. Grows in full or filtered sun and responds well to ordinary soil or a mix of soil, sand, and peat. The plants can grow submerged and rooted in the mud with their leaves floating, or they can grow on damp ground and hold their leaves erect. With less soil water, the plants tend to produce tufts of foliage at the nodes and form dense mats. When provided with ample water and room, the rhizomes grow longer and the resulting mat of foliage is more open.

Marsilea angustifolia has 5–30 cm (2–12 in.) long fronds in clusters, with narrowly cuneate leaflets (broader in cultivated plants) that are glabrous or scaly. The sporocarps are in clusters, more or less globose, and hairy when young. Each is borne on a short, unbranched stalk. The sporocarps have a conspicuous blunt tooth on the upper edge and an inconspicuous tooth-like bump formed from the stalk (raphe) tip. *Marsilea angustifolia* is reported from all states of Australia except Tasmania.

The main distinguishing features of this species are the short sporocarp stalk, the blunt sporocarp tooth, and the inconspicuous tooth-like tip of the stalk. Cultivated plants are smaller than wild plants, have more obovate leaflets, and in live plants show a faint pale spot at the base of each leaflet. Also, the upper two leaflets are often smaller than the two lower leaflets. It is uncertain if this small cultivated plant, which appeared in a plant nursery, is a separate species.

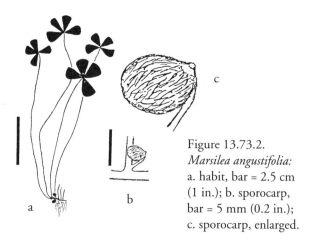

Figure 13.73.2.
Marsilea angustifolia:
a. habit, bar = 2.5 cm
(1 in.); b. sporocarp,
bar = 5 mm (0.2 in.);
c. sporocarp, enlarged.

Marsilea drummondii A. Braun   FIGURE 13.73.3
Nardoo
Probably semi-hardy (?)

A small fern with medium-creeping to erect rhizomes. Grows best under high light in aquatic conditions or in a moist to wet garden soil or sand-peat mix.

Marsilea drummondii is characterized by deciduous fronds with greenish gray leaflets and (in nonaquatic forms) conspicuous white, silky hairs. Roots are present on the nodes and internodes. The sporocarps have two teeth, and the sporocarp stalk usually bears one sporocarp. This species is native to Australia, where it is called "nardoo." It was eaten regularly by the Australian aborigines, and the early Europeans explorers consumed it as a last resort to avoid starvation. The sporocarps contain thiamase, an enzyme that destroys Vitamin B (thiamine), and eating sporocarps that were improperly prepared caused the death of several early Australian explorers (Moran 1995b).

Marsilea macrocarpa C. Presl   FIGURE 13.73.4
Probably semi-hardy (?)

A small fern with medium-creeping to erect rhizomes. Grows best under high light in aquatic conditions or in a moist to wet garden soil or sand-peat mix.

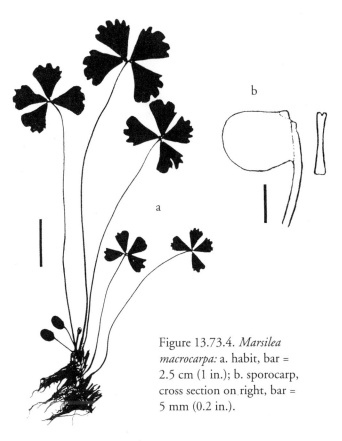

Figure 13.73.4. *Marsilea macrocarpa:* a. habit, bar = 2.5 cm (1 in.); b. sporocarp, cross section on right, bar = 5 mm (0.2 in.).

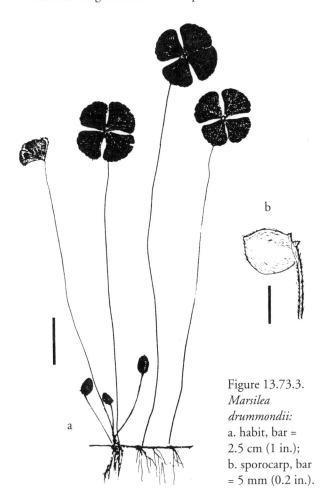

Figure 13.73.3. *Marsilea drummondii:* a. habit, bar = 2.5 cm (1 in.); b. sporocarp, bar = 5 mm (0.2 in.).

The distal margin of the leaflet is rounded and usually shallowly lobed. The sporocarp is borne singly at the base of the stipe and is oblong-rectangular, concave on both sides, with one short tooth on the upper edge. Some roots are present on internodes of the rhizome. *Marsilea macrocarpa* is native to Africa. The cultivated plants were introduced from Tanzania.

Marsilea macropoda Engelmann ex A. Braun
FIGURE 13.73.5

Semi-hardy

A small fern with medium-creeping to erect rhizomes. Prefers high light or full sun. The plants grow well in a wet sand-peat mix, but they can also be grown in drier soil if used as a ground cover. In central Texas this species has been used as a ground cover in full sun.

The stipes of *Marsilea macropoda* bear long, shaggy hairs. The leaflets are hairy on both sides with long, lax, whitish hairs (these sometimes lost on older leaves). The sporocarp stalk is branched near the base and bears several sporocarps, which are densely covered with long, soft, fine reddish hairs. The lower tooth on the sporocarp is obtuse and the upper one is inconspicuous or absent. The species is native to Texas and Mexico (introduced in Alabama and Louisiana), where it usually occurs on muddy clay soils or in shallow water.

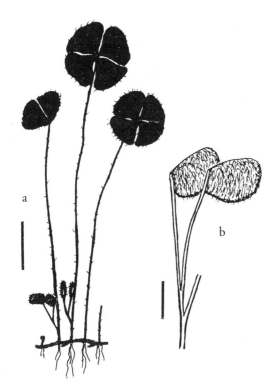

Figure 13.73.5. *Marsilea macropoda*: a. habit, bar = 2.5 cm (1 in.); b. sporocarps, bar = 5 mm (0.2 in.).

Marsilea minuta Linnaeus FIGURES 13.73.1, 6
Tender to semi-tender

A very small fern with medium-creeping to erect rhizomes. Grows well under high light in aquatic conditions or moist to wet sand-peat mix or garden soil.

Marsilea minuta is one of the smallest cultivated species, growing to 7 cm (3 in.) tall. Some roots are present on the internodes. The distal margin of the leaflet tends to be crenate. The sporocarp stalk branches near the base, bearing two or three (rarely four) sporocarps that are small, 2.6–4.1 mm long, with one conspicuous tooth. *Marsilea minuta* is a common, widespread, and often weedy species in Africa and India. It occurs in a few scattered locations in the New World tropics, but these populations probably represent escapes from cultivation.

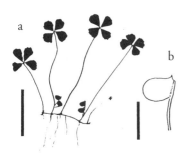

Figure 13.73.6. *Marsilea minuta*: a. habit, bar = 2.5 cm (1 in.); b. sporocarp, bar = 5 mm (0.2 in.).

Marsilea mutica Mettenius FIGURE 13.73.7; PLATE 32
Semi-hardy

A small to medium fern with medium-creeping to erect rhizomes. Grows well under high light in aquatic conditions or in moist to wet garden soil or sand-peat mix.

Marsilea mutica can be distinguished by its variegated leaflets that are pale green or yellowish green in the lower (proximal) part and a dark green in the upper (distal) part, often separated by a pale or brownish band. The sporocarp stalk arises from the stipe base or slightly higher, and the sporocarps are nearly globular and lack teeth. Roots are present on the nodes and internodes. The species is native to New Caledonia and Australia.

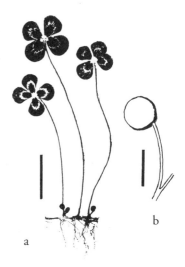

Figure 13.73.7. *Marsilea mutica*: a. habit, bar = 2.5 cm (1 in.); b. sporocarp, bar = 5 mm (0.2 in.).

Marsilea quadrifolia Linnaeus FIGURE 13.73.8
Hardy, Zone 5

A small fern with medium-creeping to erect rhizomes. Grows well under high light in aquatic conditions or moist-wet garden soil or sand-peat mix. The plants are used in China for treating infections.

Unlike many species of *Marsilea*, *Marsilea quadrifolia* has leaves glabrous or nearly so. Also, the stipes of the non-immersed fronds tend to recline on the soil instead of being stiffly erect as in many other species. The branched sporocarp stalks of *M. quadrifolia* are found elsewhere only in *M. macropoda*, a species that differs by its hairy leaves. Roots are present on nodes and internodes. The species is native to the northeastern United States, southeastern Europe, and Asia.

Marsilea schelpeana Launert FIGURE 13.73.9
Notched water fern
Semi-tender to (perhaps) hardier

A small fern with medium-creeping to erect rhizomes. Grows well under high light in aquatic conditions or moist-wet garden soil or sand-peat mix.

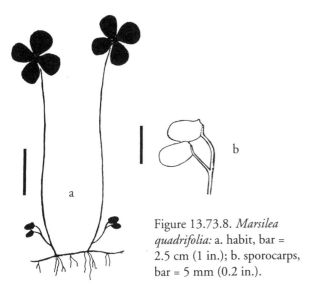

Figure 13.73.8. *Marsilea quadrifolia:* a. habit, bar = 2.5 cm (1 in.); b. sporocarps, bar = 5 mm (0.2 in.).

The leaflets of *Marsilea schelpeana* usually have two or three deep notches but are reported to be sometimes only slightly notched or, more rarely, not notched at all (entire). The sporocarp stalks are undivided, bearing only one sporocarp pointing upward at an oblique angle to the stalk. This sporocarp bears one tooth and a second, obsolete one. Roots are present on nodes and internodes. The species is endemic to South Africa.

This species is sometimes misnamed in the trade as *Marsilea crenata* C. Presl, a plant from eastern Asia with sporocarps in groups of two to seven and veins forming long areoles. It is unknown in cultivation in the United States.

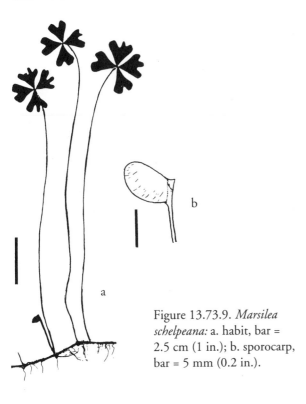

Figure 13.73.9. *Marsilea schelpeana:* a. habit, bar = 2.5 cm (1 in.); b. sporocarp, bar = 5 mm (0.2 in.).

Marsilea vestita Hooker & Greville   FIGURE 13.73.10
Very hardy, Zone 3

A small fern with medium-creeping to erect rhizomes. Grows well under high light in aquatic conditions or moist-wet garden soil or sand-peat mix.

Marsilea vestita has an erect, unbranched sporocarp stalk attached at the stipe base. The sporocarps are perpendicular or slightly nodding, thick, elliptic to nearly round, with a distal, acute tooth 0.4–1.2 mm long. Unlike most cultivated species, this one has roots that occur only at the nodes, not along the internodes. The species is native to the United States, Mexico, and Peru.

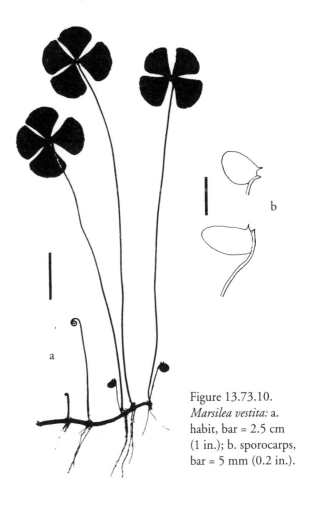

Figure 13.73.10. *Marsilea vestita:* a. habit, bar = 2.5 cm (1 in.); b. sporocarps, bar = 5 mm (0.2 in.).

Matteuccia   FIGURES 13.74.1, 2
syn. *Pteretis, Struthiopteris*
Ostrich fern

The ostrich fern native to the United States and Canada, *Matteuccia struthiopteris,* is a medium- to large-sized plant that produces an attractive vase-shaped cluster of fresh green fronds in spring. It forms dense stands in damp places as it sends out new plants from stolons. The common name refers to the feathery, plume-like fronds that resemble ostrich feathers.

Figure 13.74.1. *Matteuccia struthiopteris* var. *pensylvanica:* habit. Photo courtesy of R. Lloyd.

The genus *Matteuccia* is characterized by erect, stolon-producing rhizomes and dimorphic fronds. The sterile fronds are one-pinnate-pinnatifid. The veins are free, not netted. The fertile fronds are much shorter than the sterile ones, erect, brown, and woody. They persist over the winter. The pinnae of the fertile fronds are greatly contracted and strongly ascending. The sori are borne within the enrolled, leathery pinnae. Spores appear green under a microscope but black when viewed against a white background.

Matteuccia contains three species and is native to North America, Europe, and Asia. The genus name honors Carlo Matteucci (1800–1863), a physicist at the University of Florence in Italy.

Matteuccia orientalis (Hooker) Trevisan

FIGURE 13.74.3

Oriental ostrich fern
Hardy

A medium-large fern with erect, stoloniferous rhizomes and deciduous fronds. Thrives under medium to high light in moist-wet garden soil or potting mix.

The sterile fronds of *Matteuccia orientalis* have a stipe about half the length of the blade. Both the stipe and rachis are scaly, and the blades are broadly ovate with the basal

The fiddleheads of the ostrich fern are edible, and gathering them is a local industry in New England and Canada. The fiddleheads are boiled or steamed for 10 minutes and can be served many ways, but they are usually eaten with just salt and pepper or garlic and butter. They can sometimes be found in specialty food stores, either pickled or canned. The ostrich fern is the state vegetable of Vermont.

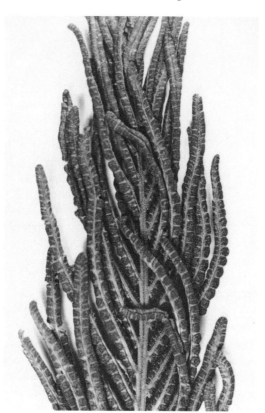

Figure 13.74.2. *Matteuccia struthiopteris* var. *pensylvanica:* fertile pinnae.

Figure 13.74.3. *Matteuccia orientalis:* fertile frond (left) and sterile frond (right), bar = 10 cm (4 in.).

pinnae slightly shorter or nearly the same as those above. The species is native to China and Japan.

Matteuccia struthiopteris (Linnaeus) Todaro

FIGURES 13.74.1, 2, 4, 5; PLATE 33

syn. *Matteuccia pensylvanica* (Willdenow) Raymond, *Pteretis nodulosa* (Willdenow) Fernald, *Struthiopteris pensylvanica* Willdenow

Ostrich fern

Very hardy, Zone 2

A large fern with fronds to 1.75 m (5.5 ft.) long and erect, stoloniferous rhizomes. Grows well under medium light in moist-wet garden soil or potting mix. This species is easy to grow and is one of the most frequently sold ferns in the eastern United States, where it is most often used as a foundation planting around houses. The sterile leaves are deciduous, but the fertile ones persist throughout the winter and shed their spores in early spring, sometimes over snow.

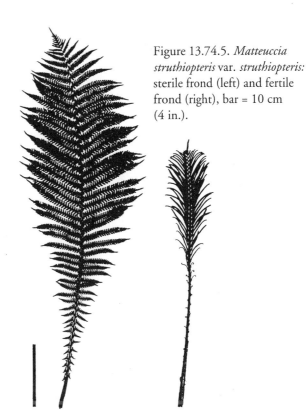

Figure 13.74.5. *Matteuccia struthiopteris* var. *struthiopteris*: sterile frond (left) and fertile frond (right), bar = 10 cm (4 in.).

Usually one or two new plants are produced each year from the stolons.

The sterile leaves of *Matteuccia struthiopteris* are green and oblanceolate, shaped like an ostrich feather, and gradually taper toward the base, ending in highly reduced pinnae. The fertile leaves are brown, smaller than the sterile ones, and have strongly ascending pinnae with enrolled margins that protect the sporangia within. The species is native to Europe, Asia, and North America.

var. *pensylvanica* (Willdenow) C. V. Morton. American ostrich fern. Figures 13.74.1, 2, 4. Stipe scales about the same color throughout (not darker in the center); pinna lobes rounded. This is the common and widely planted variety in North America.

var. *struthiopteris* (Figure 13.74.5). European ostrich fern. Stipe scales bicolorous, darker in the center; pinna lobes more truncate. This variety has been recently introduced into cultivation in the United States.

Megalastrum

syn. *Ctenitis* section *Subincisae* (C. Christensen) Tindale

These medium- to large-sized ferns have decumbent to erect rhizomes. The genus *Megalastrum* was previously classified in *Ctenitis,* but its basal basiscopic veins on the distal pinnules spring from the costa, not the costule, and the lobe supplied by this vein is widely adnate to the costa. Another difference, best seen on the upper surface of the blade, is that the veins end behind the margin in slightly enlarged, club-shaped tips—that is, they do not run all the way to

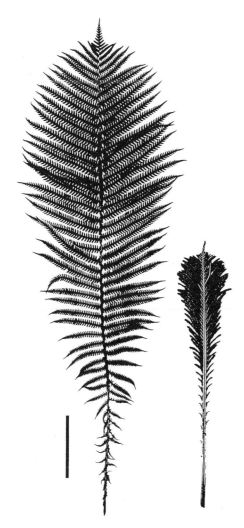

Figure 13.74.4. *Matteuccia struthiopteris* var. *pensylvanica*: sterile frond (left) and fertile frond (right), bar = 10 cm (4 in.).

margin, as is typical in *Ctenitis.* Finally, the hairs on the upper surfaces of the rachises, costae, and costules are coarse, whitish, and strigose, not fine, reddish, and erect as in *Ctenitis. Megalastrum* contains about 40 species and is native to the American tropics, Africa, and Madagascar. The origin of the genus name is unknown.

Megalastrum subincisum (Willldenow) A. R. Smith & R. C. Moran FIGURE 13.75.1
syn. *Ctenitis subincisa* (Willdenow) Ching
Tender

A large fern with an erect rhizome that sometimes forms a short trunk. Grows well under medium light in moist potting mix. This species is rarely grown and is not widely available.

Megalastrum subincisum has straw-colored to brown scales with curved marginal teeth. The blades are two- to three-pinnate-pinnatifid with sessile pinnules. The indusium tends to fall away early. The species is native to the American tropics.

Figure 13.75.1. *Megalastrum subincisum:* a. frond from mature plant, bar = 5 cm (2 in.); b. frond from immature plant, bar = 5 cm (2 in.); c. pinnule, showing thickened vein tips, bar = 5 mm (0.2 in.).

Micrograms

These appealing, small epiphytes are occasionally seen in fern collections. Their diminutive size makes them popular terrarium ferns, and they can also be grown on moss poles, bark, or in hanging baskets. Some species of *Microgramma* require more humidity than others, and these species do best in terrariums or greenhouses.

Micrograms can be identified by the following combination of characteristics: rhizomes long-creeping and densely scaly, the scales not clathrate; fronds simple, entire; veins netted; sori in one row between the midrib and margin; indusia absent. See *Polypodium* for a comparison of this genus to other polypodiaceous genera.

The genus contains about 20 species and is entirely native to the New World tropics, with the exception of two species that are native to Africa and Madagascar. The genus name comes from the Greek *mikros,* small, and *gramme,* line, referring to the slightly elongate sori in the species from which the genus was first described—although most species in the genus have round sori.

Micrograms heterophylla (Linnaeus) Wherry
FIGURE 13.76.1

Vine fern, climbing vine fern
Tender, Zone 10

A small fern with long-creeping rhizomes. Grows well under medium light in moist, drained potting mix or uncut moss. The plants are sometimes grown in terrariums.

The rhizomes of *Micrograms heterophylla* are slender, 0.5–1 mm wide, and the sterile blades reach 6 cm (2.5 in.) long and are usually about 1.5 cm (0.6 in.) wide. In cultivation the upper blade surface is wrinkled and glabrous. The species is native to southern Florida and the West Indies.

Figure 13.76.1. *Micrograms heterophylla:* a. habit, wild plant, bar = 5 cm (2 in.); b. habit, cultivated plant, bar = 5 cm (2 in.); c. fertile frond, bar = 5 cm (2 in.).

Microgramma lycopodioides (Linnaeus) Copeland
FIGURE 13.76.2

Tender

A small fern with long-creeping rhizomes. Grows well under medium light in moist, drained potting mix or uncut moss.

Microgramma lycopodioides is characterized by rust-colored rhizome scales and glabrous sterile blades that are linear to narrow-lanceolate, to 10 cm (4 in.) long, and acute at the apex. The species is native to tropical America.

Figure 13.76.2.
Microgramma lycopodioides: a. habit, bar = 5 cm (2 in.); b. fertile frond, bar = 5 cm (2 in.).

Microgramma megalophylla (Desvaux) de la Sota
FIGURE 13.76.3

syn. *Polypodium megalophyllum* Desvaux

Tender

A small-medium fern with long-creeping rhizomes. Grows well under medium light in moist, drained potting mix or uncut moss.

The most distinctive characteristic of *Microgramma megalophylla* is its strongly flattened rhizomes about 10–30 mm (0.5–1.2 in.) wide. This species also has the largest fronds in the genus: up to 24–50 cm (9–20 in.) long, 3–9 cm (1.2–3.5 in.) wide. The sori are round or slightly oblong and large, to 6 mm (0.2 in.) in diameter, and arranged in a medial, somewhat irregular row on both sides of the midrib. The species is native to South America, especially Amazonia. It is reportedly used as a remedy for coughs.

Microgramma nitida (J. Smith) A. R. Smith
FIGURE 13.76.4

syn. *Polypodium palmeri* Maxon

Tender

A small fern with long-creeping rhizomes. Grows well under medium light in moist-dry, drained potting mix or uncut moss. This species is easy to grow.

The rhizomes of *Microgramma nitida* are conspicuously flattened, as in the preceding species, but narrower, only 3–5 mm (0.1–0.2 in.) wide. The sterile blades are about 12 cm (5 in.) long, glabrous, slightly thick, and shiny. The sori are round and borne in a medial row on both sides of the midrib. This species is native to Mexico, Central America, Barbados, and Jamaica.

Figure 13.76.3.
Microgramma megalophylla: habit, bar = 5 cm (2 in.).

Exceptionally large plants of *Microgramma nitida* might be confused with *M. megalophylla*. The rhizome scales of the latter, however, are triangular-ovate, centrally dark from the base to the tip, and have a broad, thin, whitish border. The rhizome scales of *M. nitida* are linear-lanceolate, centrally dark at the base and infrequently so to the upper part of the scale, which is usually entirely whitish.

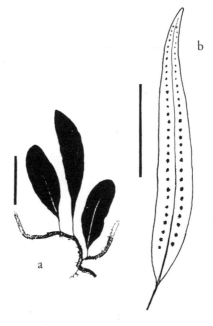

Figure 13.76.4.
Microgramma nitida: a. habit, bar = 5 cm (2 in.); b. fertile frond, bar = 5 cm (2 in.).

Microgramma percussa (Cavanilles) de la Sota

FIGURE 13.76.5

syn. *Pleopeltis percussa* (Cavanilles) Hooker & Greville,
   Polypodium percussum Cavanilles

Tender or slightly hardier

A small fern with long-creeping rhizomes. Grows well under high light in moist-dry, drained potting mix or uncut moss. This species is easy to grow, unlike *Pleopeltis,* from which it has been separated.

The thick-textured fronds of *Microgramma percussa* are narrowly linear-elliptic and have attenuate bases and apices. The young sori lack peltate scales but have a dense mass of persistent, branched, reddish filaments. The sporangia often appear as yellow dots among the reddish filaments. The species is widespread and common in tropical America.

Ferns circulating as *Pleopeltis macrocarpa* and *Polypodium lanceolatum* in the U.S. trade were found to be *Microgramma percussa.*

Microgramma piloselloides (Linnaeus) Copeland

FIGURE 13.76.6

Tender

A small fern with long-creeping rhizomes. Grows well under medium light in moist, drained potting mix or uncut moss.

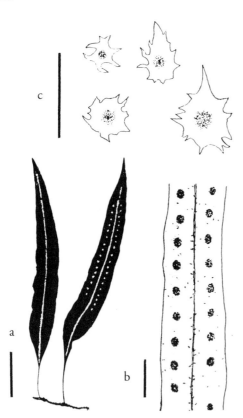

Figure 13.76.5. *Microgramma percussa:* a. habit, bar = 5 cm (2 in.); b. fertile portion of frond, bar = 1 cm (0.4 in.); c. blade scales, bar = 1 mm.

Microgramma piloselloides greatly resembles *M. reptans* but differs mainly by its slightly dimorphic sterile and fertile fronds (as opposed to strongly dimorphic ones in *M. reptans*). The fronds are typically oblong and densely whitish scaly on the lower surface. The sori do not project beyond the margin. It is native to the West Indies.

Figure 13.76.6. *Microgramma piloselloides:* a. habit, bar = 5 cm (2 in.); b. sterile frond (left) and fertile frond (right), bar = 5 cm (2 in.).

Microgramma reptans (Cavanilles) A. R. Smith

FIGURE 13.76.7

syn. *Microgramma ciliata* (Willdenow) Alston,
   Polypodium ciliatum Willdenow

Tender

A small fern with long-creeping rhizomes and dimorphic sterile and fertile fronds. Grows well under medium light in moist, drained potting mix or uncut moss.

The sterile fronds of *Microgramma reptans* are up to 5 cm (2 in.) long, vary from ovate to oblong, and are beset with many small, red-brown scales on the lower surface. The fertile fronds are linear and much narrower than the sterile ones, 2–4 mm wide, with sori projecting beyond the margin. The species is widespread throughout tropical America.

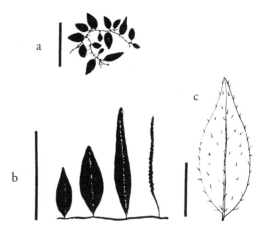

Figure 13.76.7. *Microgramma reptans:* a. habit of a small plant, bar = 5 cm (2 in.); b. sterile fronds (three on the left) and fertile frond (right), bar = 5 cm (2 in.), after Hoshizaki (1982); c. scales on frond, bar = 1 cm (0.4 in.), after Hoshizaki (1982).

Microgramma squamulosa (Kaulfuss) de la Sota

FIGURE 13.76.8

Tender or semi-tender

A small fern with long-creeping rhizomes. Grows well under medium light in moist-dry, drained potting mix or uncut moss. The plants have attractive dark green veins that contrast strongly with the lighter green of the blade tissue.

Microgramma squamulosa is characterized by whitish rhizome scales and scaly lower blade surfaces (especially the midrib) with highly dissected, scattered, whitish scales. The fronds grow to 16 cm (6.5 in.) long, are often reddish tinged, and have the veins conspicuously darker green. The species is native to tropical South America.

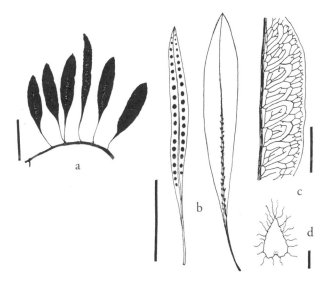

Figure 13.76.8. *Microgramma squamulosa:* a. habit, bar = 5 cm (2 in.); b. fertile frond (left) and sterile frond (right), bar = 5 cm (2 in.), after Hoshizaki (1982); c. vein pattern, bar = 1 cm (0.4 in.), after Hoshizaki (1982); d. rachis scale, bar = 1 mm, after Hoshizaki (1982).

Microgramma vacciniifolia (Langsdorff & Fischer) Copeland

FIGURE 13.76.9

Tender to semi-tender

A small fern with long-creeping rhizomes. Grows well under medium light in moist, drained potting mix or uncut moss.

Microgramma vacciniifolia has white rhizome scales and sessile or nearly sessile fronds. The sterile fronds are roundish-ovate or longer, only 4–6 cm (1.5–2.5 in.) long, with bases often obtuse-truncate. The fertile fronds tend to be narrower and longer than the sterile ones. The species is native to tropical America.

Microgramma vacciniifolia resembles *M. squamulosa,* a species that differs by having larger fronds and darkly out-

Figure 13.76.9. *Microgramma vacciniifolia:* a. habit, bar = 5 cm (2 in.); b. fertile frond, bar = 5 cm (2 in.). After Hoshizaki (1982).

lined veins. *Microgramma lycopodioides* differs by its rust-colored rhizome scale and larger size.

Microlepia

FIGURES 13.77.1, 2

Microlepia consists of medium- to large-sized terrestrial ferns found mostly in tropical or subtropical climates, with a few species extending into warm-temperate climates. The cultivated species have medium-creeping, clump-forming rhizomes that bear fronds close enough to give a full-foliage look to the plants. This appearance and their robust growth habit and tolerance to irregular watering makes them popular garden plants in warmer climates. They also make suitable houseplants.

Microlepia strigosa is widely used in beds and foundation plantings in southern California. This vigorous grower requires grooming to remove old fronds. It is the most common species in the trade but is often sold mixed with another species tentatively identified as *M. substrigosa.* A tall grower, *M. platyphylla* has large, bluish green segments and is useful in pots or as a screen in the landscape. Most species

Figure 13.77.1. *Microlepia strigosa:* habit.

Figure 13.77.2. *Microlepia platyphylla:* sori and indusia.

of *Microlepia* are grown easily from spore, and mature plants can be readily propagated by division of the rhizome.

The rhizomes of *Microlepia* are hairy, creeping, branched, and clump-forming. The fronds are two-pinnate to four-pinnate (rarely one-pinnate), anadromous, and usually have minute reddish hairs and a dense covering of short, transparent hairs on the rachis or costae. Longer hairs may also be present on various parts of the blade. The veins are free, not netted. The sori vary from marginal to submarginal and are covered by a shallow pouch or hood-shaped indusium attached by its base and sides.

Microlepia, which contains 45 species, is native to Asia and the Pacific basin, with one species, *Microlepia strigosa,* extending into Africa and the American tropics. The genus name comes from the Greek *mikros,* small, and *lepis,* scale, referring to the small, scale-like indusia.

Microlepia platyphylla (D. Don) J. Smith

FIGURES 13.77.2, 3

Semi-hardy to semi-tender

A large fern with medium-creeping, clump-forming rhizomes and blue-gray leaves. Grows well under medium to high light in moist-dry garden soil or potting mix. This species is easy to cultivate. It has erect, coarse foliage and can form large, dense clumps if not regularly divided.

Microlepia platyphylla is characterized by triangular blades up to two-pinnate-pinnatifid with narrowly triangular, pinnatifid to pinnately lobed, serrate pinnules. The midribs of the ultimate segments bear fine hairs, but otherwise the plants are glabrous. The species is native from India and southeastern Asia to the Philippines.

Figure 13.77.3. *Microlepia platyphylla:* frond, bar = 5 cm (2 in.).

Microlepia speluncae (Linnaeus) T. Moore

FIGURE 13.77.4

Semi-tender to tender

A mostly medium-large fern with medium-creeping, clump-forming rhizomes. Grows well under medium light in moist garden soil or potting mix. In the United States the crested form is more common in cultivation than the typical form. Because it is not as cold tolerant as *Microlepia strigosa,* which it resembles, *M. speluncae* is infrequently seen in the trade.

Microlepia speluncae resembles *M. strigosa* and *M. substrigosa* but differs by having more herbaceous blades that wilt quickly after picking, veins not raised on the lower blade surface, and smaller indusia attached mainly at the base and more submarginal (mostly about two lengths distant from the margin). This species is widely distributed in the tropics throughout the world.

'Corymbifera'. (*Microlepia pyramidata* Horticulture). Figure 13.77.4. Tips of blades and pinnae tasseled. Fronds light green, arching gracefully.

Figure 13.77.4. *Microlepia speluncae* 'Corymbifera': a. frond, bar = 5 cm (2 in.); b. lower pinna, bar = 2 cm (0.8 in.).

Microlepia strigosa (Thunberg) C. Presl

FIGURES 13.77.1, 5

Lace fern

Semi-hardy to semi-tender; reportedly can grow in Zone 6 if winter-protected

A medium-large fern with medium-creeping, clump-forming rhizomes. Grows well under medium or high light in moist-dry garden soil or potting mix. The plants are easy to cultivate and grow rapidly, although the species is known to tip-burn when exposed to temperatures of −7°C (19°F) or lower for several days. The fronds spread or arch gracefully.

Microlepia strigosa has yellowish brown or whitish rhizome hairs. The blades are two-pinnate-pinnatifid to three-pinnate (at the base of the larger pinnae), ovate, and herbaceous. The lower one or two pairs of pinnae are slightly reduced and narrowly linear-triangular. The veins are distinctly raised on the lower blade surface. The indusia are attached at the base and up the sides, and many appear at the base of a leaf-margin notch. Most have their upper edge

submarginal or reaching the leaf margin. The species is native to the Himalayas, Sri Lanka, and from southeastern Asia to Japan and Polynesia.

The native Hawaiian plant (also cultivated in Hawaii) and some trade plants imported from Holland are sometimes called *Microlepia strigosa* but are here referred to *M. substrigosa*.

Microlepia strigosa is a highly variable plant, but few of the cultivated variants are distinct except for forma *macfaddeniae* C. V. Morton (Figure 13.77.5d, e), which has narrowly linear fronds and pinnae greatly reduced and condensed, consisting of a cluster of fan-shaped pinnules.

Microlepia substrigosa Tagawa

FIGURES 13.77.6, 7

Semi-hardy to semi-tender

A large fern with medium-creeping, clump-forming rhizomes and fronds more than 1.5 m (5 ft.) tall. Grows well under medium to high light in moist-dry garden soil or potting mix. This species is easy to cultivate and is a rapid grower. *Microlepia substrigosa* is often misidentified as *M. strigosa* and *M. firma*.

Microlepia substrigosa resembles *M. strigosa*, but its blades are nearly triangular and up to three-pinnate-pinnatifid, with the lower pinnae triangular. Many indusia appear to be on a short lobe of the leaf margin, and the edges of most indusia do not reach the leaf margin. The species is native to Japan, Taiwan, China, and possibly the Hawaiian Islands (where it circulates as *M. strigosa*).

Two slightly different plants are encountered in cultivation, and they are tentatively identified here as *Microlepia substrigosa*. Both are mistakenly sold as *M. strigosa*, which has ovate, predominantly two-pinnate to two-pinnate-pinnatifid blades. One of these plants is widely distributed by a European grower and the other circulates in Hawaiian and southern California gardens (under the misapplied name of *M. firma*). The European plant has an erect habit and broadly triangular lower pinnae (Figure 13.77.6). The Hawaiian and southern California plant has a more spreading habit and narrower lower pinnae abruptly widened at the base (Figure 13.77.7). Although the identity of these plants is uncertain, they are not *M. strigosa* as generally known.

Microsorum Link

syn. *Diblemma, Phymatodes, Phymatosorus, Polypodium* in part

The polypodiaceous genus *Microsorum* is best known for the so-called cobra plant, a form of *Microsorum punctatum* that is heavily short-crested at the tips of its erect, strap-shaped fronds. The common name probably alludes to a fanciful resemblance to a cobra ready to strike. The cobra plant is widely used in Florida and the tropics as a ground cover or edging. In other parts of the United States it is used as a potted plant and does well indoors. Several forms

Figure 13.77.5. *Microlepia strigosa:* a. frond, bar = 5 cm (2 in.); b. lower pinna, bar = 2 cm (0.8 in.); c. lower pinnae, showing variations, bar = 2 cm (0.8 in.); d. forma *macfaddeniae* frond, bar = 5 cm (2 in.); e. forma *macfaddeniae* frond detail, bar = 1 cm (0.4 in.).

Figure 13.77.6. *Microlepia substrigosa* from European growers: a. frond, bar = 5 cm (2 in.); b. lower pinna, bar = 2 cm (0.8 in.).

Figure 13.77.7. *Microlepia substrigosa* from Hawaiian gardens: a. frond, bar = 5 cm (2 in.); b. lower pinna, bar = 2 cm (0.8 in.).

have long, arching fronds, and these are attractive as hanging plants.

Besides the cobra plant, the East Indian polypody (*Microsorum scolopendria*) is commonly cultivated. In tropical climates this species and its close relatives are used as ground covers, basket plants, or over rock walls. Although the branching rhizome is capable of growing to 6 m (20 ft.) in length, cultivated plants are seldom allowed to grow this long. As with many ferns, the fronds may differ in shape on the same plant, ranging from entire to pinnatifid.

The genus consists of medium- to large-sized epiphytes with long- or short-creeping rhizomes bearing peltate or false-peltate, clathrate or subclathrate scales. The blades are either entire, lobed, or pinnatifid, or (in *Microsorum lucidum*) pinnate. The veins are netted (this is hard to see in species with thick blades) and have within the areoles branched veinlets that may point in any direction. The sori are separate, small to larger, round or less often elongate, and irregularly scattered or in partly irregular rows, and they lack an indusium.

Most species of *Microsorum* have included veinlets pointing in all directions, not just toward the blade margin as in many other polypodiaceous ferns. The large sunken sori of *Phymatosorus* (*Phymatodes*) intergrades into *Microsorum,* and because other reliable distinguishing characters have not been found, Nooteboom (1997) reduced *Phymatosorus* to *Microsorum*. For more details, see Bosman (1991) and Nooteboom (1997). *Microsorum* species were formerly listed under *Polypodium* and may be more familiar to gardeners under that name. See Hoshizaki (1982) for details on cultivated species. The entry for *Polypodium* in this chapter includes a comparison of *Microsorum* with other polypodiaceous genera.

Microsorum consists of about 50 species native to tropical and subtropical regions of Africa, southeastern Asia, northern Australia, and the Pacific Islands. It has become naturalized in several areas in the New World. The genus name comes from the Greek *mikros,* small, and *soros,* mound, referring to the small, scattered sori, although some species have larger sori.

Microsorum commutatum (Blume) Copeland

FIGURE 13.78.1

syn. *Phymatosorus commutatus* (Blume) Pichi-Sermolli,
Polypodium vitiense Baker
Tender

A medium-sized fern with moderately-creeping rhizomes.
Grows well under medium light in moist, well-drained potting mix or uncut moss.

The *Microsorum commutatum* stipe is narrowly winged
toward the blade base; the blade is herbaceous, broad, and
deeply lobed. Both sides of the frond midrib have a few
small, dark, persistent, ovate-rounded scales. The sori are
small, in two irregular rows, and not sunken. The species is
native to Sumatra, Java, Borneo, Philippines, Sulawesi,
New Guinea, and certain Pacific Islands.

'Southern Cross'. Lobe margins irregularly and shallowly to deeply toothed, lobed, or fringed. Sori absent. This
is the cultivar grown in the United States. Sometimes circulates incorrectly as *Polypodium australe* 'Cambricum'.

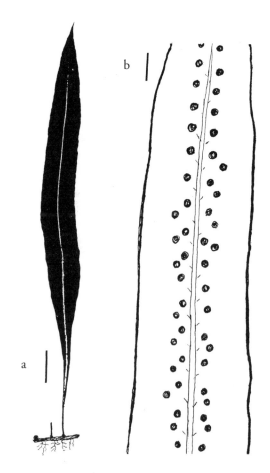

Figure 13.78.2. *Microsorum fortunei:* a. habit, bar = 5 cm
(2 in.); b. sori, bar = 1 cm (0.4 in.).

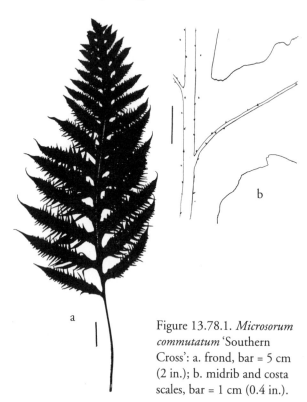

Figure 13.78.1. *Microsorum
commutatum* 'Southern
Cross': a. frond, bar = 5 cm
(2 in.); b. midrib and costa
scales, bar = 1 cm (0.4 in.).

Microsorum fortunei (T. Moore) Ching

FIGURE 13.78.2

syn. *Polypodium normale* D. Don
Semi-hardy

A medium-sized fern with short-creeping rhizomes. Grows
well under medium light in moist-dry potting mix. The
plants tend to become disfigured when grown under conditions of low humidity.

Microsorum fortunei has strap-shaped fronds to 60 cm (2
ft.) long and 3–5 cm (1.2–2 in.) wide. They are attenuate
on both ends. The sori are not sunken, round, up to 4 mm
(0.2 in.) wide, in one (rarely two) slightly irregular row on
either side of the midrib. The species is native to Indochina,
China, Taiwan, and Japan.

Microsorum grossum (Langsdorff & Fischer)

S. B. Andrews   FIGURE 13.78.3

syn. *Microsorum scolopendria* auct. non (N. L. Burman)
Copeland, *Phymatosorus grossus* (Langsdorff &
Fischer) Brownlie, *Polypodium grossum* Langsdorff &
Fischer
Tender

A medium-sized fern with long-creeping rhizomes. Grows
well under high light in drained, moist to moist-dry garden soil or potting mix. The plants are widely cultivated in
the tropics, where they are often used as a ground cover.
The foliage can be trimmed like a hedge. The rhizomes
tend to outgrow pots.

Microsorum grossum resembles *M. scolopendria* but differs by having up to 10 pairs of lobes (instead of 4) per

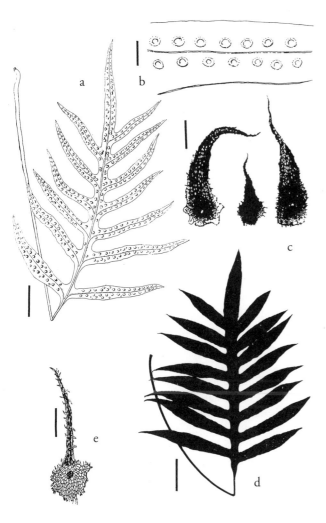

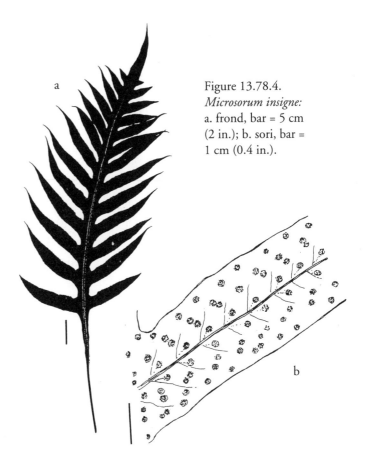

grower and less tender than *M. grossum* and *M. scolopendria*, it is favored in subtropical gardens. Otherwise all three plants have similar cultural requirements. Nooteboom (1997) considered *M. grossum* and *P. banjeriana* synonyms of *M. scolopendria*.

Microsorum insigne (Blume) Copeland
FIGURE 13.78.4

syn. *Colysis insignis* (Blume) J. Smith, *Microsorum dilatatum* (Beddome) Sledge, *M. hancockii* (Baker) Ching
Tender to semi-tender

A medium-sized fern with medium-creeping rhizomes. Grows best under medium to high light in moist-dry potting mix or uncut moss kept well drained. This species is a robust grower, thriving in humid or dry environments. Once established, it tolerates some irregular watering.

The fronds of mature *Microsorum insigne* are oblong to lanceolate and deeply pinnately lobed. The lobes are few to many and oblong-lanceolate with acuminate apices. The terminal lobe resembles the lateral ones. The sori are roundish, small, and scattered. The species is native to India, southeastern Asia, the Malayan Archipelago, China, and Japan.

This species varies in the size and number of lobes. Plants with many lobes are said to intergrade with the

Figure 13.78.3. *Microsorum grossum*: a. frond, bar = about 5 cm (2 in.), after Langsdorff and Fischer (1810); b. sori, upper frond surface, bar = 1 cm (0.4 in.), after Hoshizaki (1982); c. rhizome scales, bar = 1 mm, after Hoshizaki (1982); d. *Phymatodes* [= *Microsorum*] *banjeriana* frond, bar = 5 cm (2 in.); e. *Phymatodes* [= *Microsorum*] *banjeriana* rhizome scale, bar = 1 mm.

Figure 13.78.4. *Microsorum insigne*: a. frond, bar = 5 cm (2 in.); b. sori, bar = 1 cm (0.4 in.).

blade, and the plants tend to be larger and epiphytic rather than terrestrial. The species is native to Australia and central and eastern Polynesia.

Most plants cultivated in Hawaii and Florida are *Microsorum grossum*. A similar species that sometimes circulates under the incorrect name of *Polypodium alternifolium* is tentatively identified as *Phymatodes* [= *Microsorum*] *banjeriana* N. Pal & S. Pal (Figure 13.78.3d, e). This species is difficult to separate from *M. grossum;* the most reliable character is in the rhizome scale. Those of *Phymatodes banjeriana* are rounded at the base and abruptly narrowed into a long, slender, tapered apex, whereas the rhizome scales of *M. grossum* are triangular. Because *P. banjeriana* is a robust smaller, more triangular form previously known as *Microsorum hancockii* (Baker) Ching.

Microsorum linguiforme (Mettenius) Copeland

FIGURE 13.78.5

Tender or slightly hardier

A small to medium fern with medium- to long-creeping rhizomes. Grows well under medium light in moist potting mix or uncut moss. This species is a rapid and robust grower.

The long-creeping rhizome of *Microsorum linguiforme* is somewhat flattened and often has branches that are opposite or nearly so. The fronds are broadly ovate, entire, and often contracted above the base. The blade apex is roundish to acuminate, and the base varies from tapered to cordate. The veins are darkened. The sori are round and few. This species is native from India and the Malayan Archipelago to Fiji.

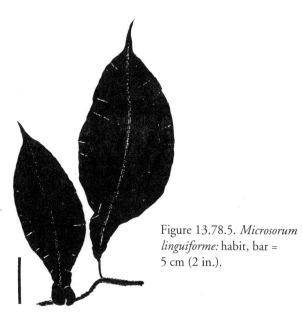

Figure 13.78.5. *Microsorum linguiforme:* habit, bar = 5 cm (2 in.).

Microsorum longissimum J. Smith ex Fée

FIGURE 13.78.6

syn. *Polypodium myriocarpum* C. Presl ex Mettenius; not *Polypodium longissimum* Blume

Tender

A medium-sized fern with short-creeping rhizomes and handsome shiny fronds bearing an attractive vein pattern. Grows well under medium light in drained, moist to moist-dry potting mix or uncut moss.

Microsorum longissimum has blackish rhizome scales. The shiny fronds are strap-shaped, to 35–95 cm (14–38 in.) by 1–9 cm (0.5–3.5 in.), with the primary veins conspicuous and forming one series of large areoles next to the midrib. The sori are round or elongate and 0.5–1.5 mm

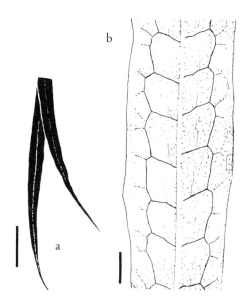

Figure 13.78.6. *Microsorum longissimum:* a. frond, bar = 5 cm (2 in.); b. vein pattern, bar = 1 cm (0.4 in.).

wide. *Microsorum samarense* also has strap-shaped fronds, but its veins are hard to see and the upper surfaces of the fronds are dull, not shiny. *Microsorum longissimum* is native to Borneo, Sarawak, and the Philippines.

Microsorum lucidum (Roxburgh) Copeland

FIGURE 13.78.7

syn. *Phymatosorus cuspidatus* J. Smith, *P. lucidus* (Roxburgh) Pichi-Sermolli

Semi-tender

A medium-large fern with medium- to long-creeping rhizomes. Grows well under medium light in drained, moist-dry garden soil or potting mix. This species is easy to cultivate once established, and it may overgrow surrounding plants.

The rhizome of *Microsorum lucidum* is green, fleshy, and 2.5 cm (1 in.) or more in diameter. The fronds are one-pinnate and dark green with obscure veins. The sori are arranged in one row, closer to the costa than the margin; they are not sunken. The species is native to India, southwestern China, and southeastern Asia.

Microsorum membranifolium (R. Brown) Ching

FIGURE 13.78.8

syn. *Microsorum alternifolium* of authors, *Phymatosorus nigrescens* (Blume) Pichi-Sermolli, *Polypodium nigrescens* Blume

Pimple fern

Tender

A large fern with medium-creeping rhizomes. Grows well under medium light in drained, moist potting mix or uncut moss. The plants often volunteer from spores. This species

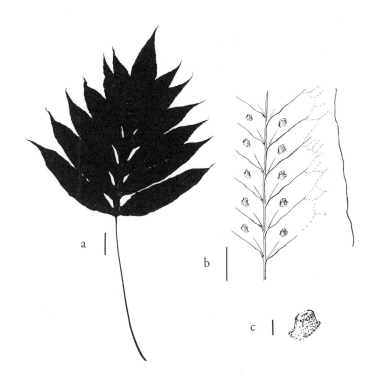

Figure 13.78.8. *Microsorum membranifolium:* a. frond, bar = 5 cm (2 in.); b. sori and vein pattern, upper surface, bar = 1 cm (0.4 in.); c. raised sorus, upper frond surface, bar = 2 mm.

Figure 13.78.7. *Microsorum lucidum:* a. frond, bar = 5 cm (2 in.); b. pinna, bar = 5 cm (2 in.), after Hoshizaki (1982).

has long been known as *Polypodium nigrescens* and is sometimes mislabeled in the trade as *P. diversifolium* Willdenow and as *P. alternifolium* Willdenow.

Microsorum membranifolium has large, deeply lobed fronds with distinct dark veins. The sori are deeply embossed on the upper surfaces of the blades, forming a stout cylindrical protuberance to 2 mm high. They are borne in one row between the costae and margins. The species is native from India to southeastern Asia and Australia.

Microsorum musifolium (Blume) Copeland

FIGURE 13.78.9

Tender

A large fern with short-creeping rhizomes and spreading fronds clustered into an irregular basket shape. Grows well under medium to high light in drained, moist potting mix or uncut moss. Keep the plants out of direct sun and avoid

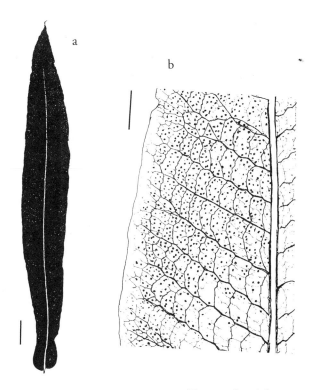

Figure 13.78.9. *Microsorum musifolium:* a. frond, bar = 5 cm (2 in.); b. sori and vein pattern, bar = 1 cm (0.4 in.).

overhead watering, which can cause leaf spots. The veins form a handsome pattern.

The fronds of *Microsorum musifolium* are oblanceolate, to 1 m (3 ft.) long, 10 cm (4 in.) wide, and sessile; the fronds are truncate to obtuse at the base and often narrowed above. The venation is regular and conspicuous, with 6–10 primary connective veins between the pairs of secondary veins. The species is native to southeastern Asia and the Malayan Archipelago.

We have not followed Nooteboom (1997), who concluded that this species was the same as *Microsorum punctatum*. *Microsorum musifolium* differs by its conspicuous veins and firm but thin translucent blades. In contrast, live plants of *M. punctatum* have inconspicuous veins and leathery blades.

Microsorum papuanum (Baker) Parris

FIGURE 13.78.10

Tender, Zone 9

A medium-sized fern with creeping rhizomes bearing fronds close or more distant from each other. Grows under high to medium light in well-drained, moist to moist-dry potting mix.

Microsorum papuanum differs from the closely related *Microsorum scolopendria* by its leathery and often crisped blade that is simple and entire or has one to three lobes, with the central lobe the longest. The sori are round to oval, often irregularly so, and deeply sunken into the frond (embossed on the upper surface). In cultivated plants, the sori reach 13 mm (0.5 in.) in length and to 8 mm (0.3 in.) in width. It is native to Malaysia, New Guinea, and the Pacific Islands.

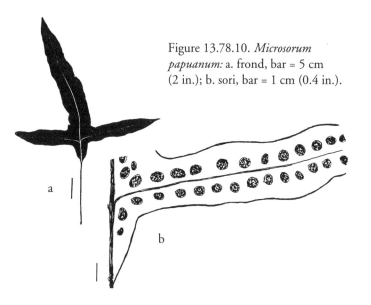

Figure 13.78.10. *Microsorum papuanum:* a. frond, bar = 5 cm (2 in.); b. sori, bar = 1 cm (0.4 in.).

Microsorum pteropus (Blume) Copeland

FIGURE 13.78.11

syn. *Colysis pteropus* (Blume) Bosman
Tender

A small fern with short-creeping rhizomes. Grows well under medium light in wet, coarse garden soil or potting mix with sand; can also be planted in drained pots or pots set in water. The plants can be grown submerged and are often used in aquariums. They can remain submerged for years without ill effects; however, sori are formed only on emergent fronds, not those under water. The fronds are vulnerable to leaf spots, which usually can be controlled by fungicide sprays.

The fronds of *Microsorum pteropus* are simple to trilobed, with the center lobe the largest. Submerged fronds are small and entire. The buds often form on the lower surface where sori would normally form. The species is native from India to southern China, the Malay Archipelago, New Guinea, and Japan. In nature it typically grows along stream banks prone to flooding, or in the spray of waterfalls.

Figure 13.78.11. *Microsorum pteropus:* habit, bar = 5 cm (2 in.), after Hoshizaki (1982).

Microsorum punctatum (Linnaeus) Copeland

FIGURES 13.78.12, 13

syn. *Microsorum irioides* (Poiret) Fée, *M. polycarpon* (Cavanilles) Tardieu, *Polypodium integrifolium* Lowe, *P. irioides* Poiret, *P. punctatum* (Linnaeus) Swartz
Tender to semi-tender

A medium-sized fern with very short-creeping rhizomes. Grows well under medium light in drained, moist-dry potting mix or uncut moss. It is easy to grow.

Microsorum punctatum has fronds that are strap-shaped or wider, to 1 m (3 ft.) long or more by 1.5–10 cm (0.6–4 in.) or more wide. They are mostly subcoriaceous, their apex round to acuminate, their base cordate to tapered. The leaves are often ruffled, fringed, or forked near or at the tips. The veins are hard to see because of the thick blades. The species is native to the Old World tropics and subtropics.

Wild plants are variable, and some may represent different species. *Microsorum whiteheadii* A. R. Smith & Hos-

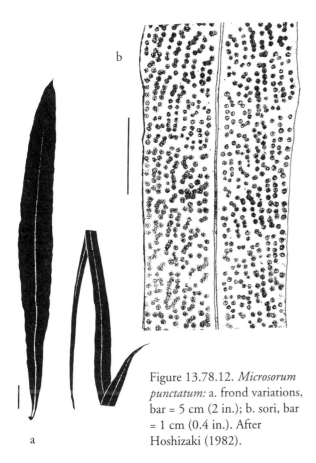

Figure 13.78.12. *Microsorum punctatum:* a. frond variations, bar = 5 cm (2 in.); b. sori, bar = 1 cm (0.4 in.). After Hoshizaki (1982).

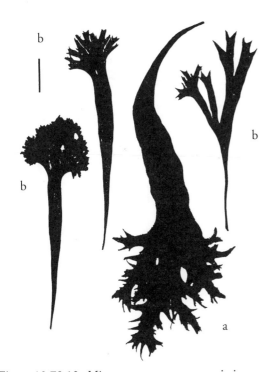

Figure 13.78.13. *Microsorum punctatum,* variations in cultivars: a. 'Grandiceps', fronds pendent; b. 'Ramosum', fronds erect, all from the same plant. Bar = 5 cm (2 in.). After Hoshizaki (1982).

kizaki is such a species and has recently been introduced into cultivation. It differs from *M. punctatum* by its thick, succulent, relatively broader oblanceolate blade.

Microsorum punctatum is the most common *Microsorum* in the trade and is available in many forms, such as wide or narrow, short or erect or nearly decumbent, crested, and variously emarginate. New selections are constantly being introduced, and the trade plants are loosely named. Some common cultivars are:

'Climbing-bird's-nest fern'. Fronds like the bird's-nest fern (*Asplenium nidus*) but softer and arching.

'Grandiceps'. Figure 13.78.13a. Similar to 'Climbing-bird's-nest fern' but loosely and thinly crested.

'Ramosum'. ('Cristatum') Figure 13.78.13b; Plate 34. Cobra plant. Fronds erect and densely crested.

Microsorum pustulatum (G. Forster) Copeland
FIGURE 13.78.14

syn. *Microsorum diversifolium* (Willdenow) Copeland, *Phymatosorus diversifolius* (Willdenow) Pichi-Sermolli, *Phymatosorus pustulatus* (G. Forster) M. F. Large, *Polypodium diversifolium* Willdenow, *Polypodium pustulatum* of authors, not G. Forster, *Polypodium scandens* of authors, not G. Forster

Kangaroo fern
Semi-hardy

A medium-sized fern with long-creeping rhizomes. Grows well under medium light in drained, moist potting mix or uncut moss. This species, long known as *Phymatosorus diversifolius,* grows slowly but tolerates cold better than others in the genus. It is grown outdoors in the warmer parts of England.

Microsorum pustulatum has ovate to narrowly ovate rhizome scales. The fronds are entire to broadly and deeply lobed, dark green, and leathery. The veins are clearly visible. The sori are in one row between the costa and margin. The species is native to Australia and New Zealand.

Microsorum scolopendria and its allies differ by ciliate or spiny rhizome scales, obscure veins, and the sori in one or two rows between the costa and margin.

Microsorum samarense (J. Smith ex Mettenius) Bosman
FIGURE 13.78.15

syn. *Diblemma tenuilore* (J. Smith ex Mettenius) Ching, *Polypodium tenuilore* J. Smith ex Mettenius

Tender

A small to medium fern with short-creeping rhizomes. Grows well under medium light in moist, drained potting mix or uncut moss.

Microsorum samarense is characterized by linear-lanceolate fronds, obscure veins, and (often) elongate sori. The leathery fronds are generally 25–45 cm (10–18 in.) long and 5–10 mm (0.2–0.4 in.) wide. The margins tend to roll inward when dry. The sori vary from round to (often) elon-

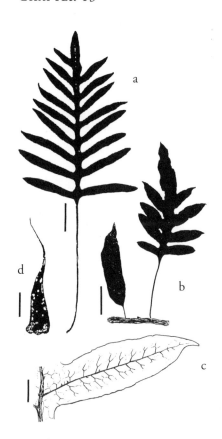

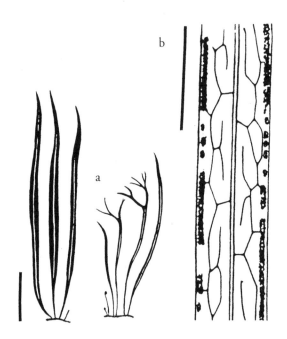

gate and are often concentrated on the marginal veins. The species is native to the Philippines, where it grows as an epiphyte and on limestone.

The plants vary tremendously in width. The narrowest form circulates in horticulture as *Diblemma tenuilore* and seems be shorter than usual, with many fronds having forked tips. The wider form is rarely grown.

Microsorum scandens (G. Forster) Tindale
FIGURE 13.78.16; PLATE 5

syn. *Phymatosorus scandens* (G. Forster) Pichi-Sermolli,
    Polypodium pustulatum of authors, not G. Forster,
    Polypodium scandens G. Forster

Fragrant fern
Semi-hardy

A small-medium fern with slender, long-creeping rhizomes. Grows well under medium light in moist garden soil, potting mix, or uncut moss. The plants are well suited to basket culture and will grow up tree trunks if initially provided

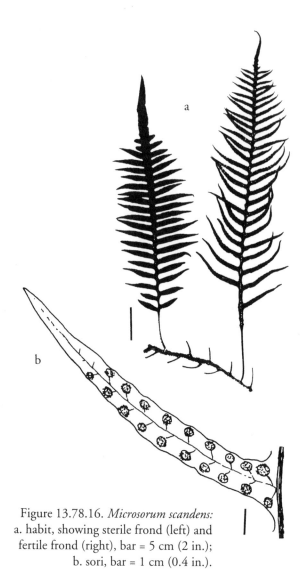

Figure 13.78.14. *Microsorum pustulatum:* a. frond, bar = 5 cm (2 in.); b. habit and frond variation, bar = 5 cm (2 in.); c. visible veins, bar = 1 cm (0.4 in.); d. rhizome scale, bar = 1 mm.

Figure 13.78.15. *Microsorum samarense:* a. habits, bar = 5 cm (2 in.); b. sori and vein patterns, bar = 1 cm (0.4 in.).

Figure 13.78.16. *Microsorum scandens:* a. habit, showing sterile frond (left) and fertile frond (right), bar = 5 cm (2 in.); b. sori, bar = 1 cm (0.4 in.).

with some moisture-retaining pockets in which to root. The fronds are evergreen and fragrant when crushed.

The fronds of *Microsorum scandens* are entire or pinnatifid, herbaceous, narrowly elliptic, to about 60 cm (24 in.) long, 16 cm (6.5 in.) wide. The frond base is long-decurrent on the stipe. The lobes of the blade are narrow, 4–10 mm (0.2–0.4 in.) wide, and separated by broad, U-shaped sinuses. The sori are round or elongate, borne in one row between costa and margin, and slightly raised on the upper surface of the frond. The species is native to Australia and New Zealand.

Microsorum scolopendria (N. L. Burman) Copeland
FIGURE 13.78.17

syn. *Phymatosorus scolopendria* (N. L. Burman) Pichi-Sermolli, *Polypodium scolopendria* N. L. Burman
East Indian polypody
Tender

A medium-large fern with long-creeping rhizomes. Grows well under high light in drained, moist to moist-dry garden soil, potting mix, or uncut moss.

The long-creeping rhizome bears triangular or ovate-triangular scales that are spiny or ciliate on the margins. The blade of *Microsorum scolopendria* is deeply lobed into four or fewer pairs of segments that are somewhat yellowish green, leathery, and flat. The veins are hard to see. The sori vary from round or oblong and are usually arranged in two irregular rows on each side of the midrib. The species is native to the tropics of the Old World.

As construed by Nooteboom (1997), *Microsorum scolopendria* consists of a single variable species; however, other botanists believe it consists of several. Plants of *M. scolopendria* with more than four pairs of lobes are recognized by some authors as *M. grossum,* whereas those with four or fewer are called *M. scolopendria* (and these plants are by no means uniform). Most plants cultivated in the United States are *M. grossum.*

Microsorum steerei (Harrington) Ching
FIGURE 13.78.18

Tender

A small-medium fern with short-creeping rhizomes and thick and leathery fronds up to 40 cm (16 in.) long, though usually shorter in cultivation. Prefers low to medium light and a well-drained, moist potting mix. Plants grow somewhat slowly and seem to do best at temperatures of 21°C (70°F) or more year-round. This species is striking because of its blue-green iridescent fronds.

The fronds of *Microsorum steerei* are like those of a small, fleshy *M. punctatum* but are more pointed and distinctly

Figure 13.78.17. *Microsorum scolopendria:* a. habit, bar = 5 cm (2 in.); b. sori, bar = 1 cm (0.4 in.); c. rhizome scale, bar = 1 mm.

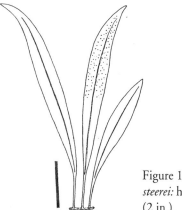

Figure 13.78.18. *Microsorum steerei:* habit, bar = 5 cm (2 in.).

iridescent. The plants in cultivation were introduced from Chumphon Province in southern Thailand by Chanin Thorut, who reported the plants growing on rocks in a deep, shady, humid forest. The fern has been reported to grow on limestone in China, Taiwan, and Vietnam.

Microsorum superficiale (Blume) Ching

FIGURE 13.78.19

syn. *Leptochilus buergerianum* (Miquel) Bosman,
    Microsorum buergerianum (Miquel) Ching,
    Neocheiropteris superficialis (Blume) Bosman
Semi-tender

A small fern with medium- to long-creeping rhizomes. Grows well under medium light in moist to moist-dry garden soil, potting mix, or uncut moss kept well drained.

Figure 13.78.19. *Microsorum superficiale:* a. habit, bar = 5 cm (2 in.); b. sori, bar = 1 cm (0.4 in.).

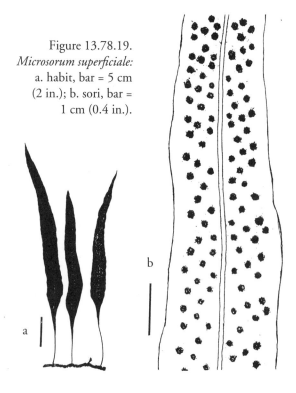

Once established, this species is a robust grower and may be trained to grow up tree trunks or branches.

Microsorum superficiale is characterized by simple, lanceolate, entire, herbaceous fronds that are borne apart on a slender rhizome. The sori are scattered on the lower surface. It is native to China, Japan, and Vietnam.

Microsorum viellardii (Mettenius) Copeland

FIGURE 13.78.20

syn. *Phymatodes viellardii* (Mettenius) Fournier
Semi-tender

A medium-large fern with long-creeping rhizomes. Grows well under medium to high light in drained, moist to moist-dry garden soil or potting mix. The plants are fairly robust growers in baskets or in the ground. This species cir-

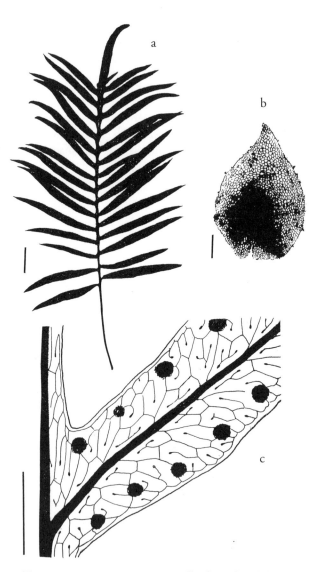

Figure 13.78.20. *Microsorum viellardii:* a. frond, bar = 5 cm (2 in.); b. sori and vein pattern, bar = 1 cm (0.4 in.), after Hoshizaki (1982); c. rhizome scale, bar = 1 mm, after Hoshizaki (1982).

culated among growers as "Mt. Elgan fern," a name of uncertain origin.

Microsorum viellardii has rounded rhizome scales up to 6 mm (0.2 in.) wide. The blade is deeply lobed, and the lobes are narrowed toward the base. The sori are submarginal and in one row between the midrib and margin. This species is endemic to New Caledonia.

Mildella

Mildella is barely distinct from *Cheilanthes* but is recognized here because it has been used in by most major floras. It differs from *Cheilanthes* by having a submarginal indusium with the green segment margin extending beyond it. The genus, which consists of about eight terrestrial species, occurs in Central America, the Galápagos Islands, Haiti, and from northern India to China. It is named in honor of Carl August Julius Milde (1824–1871), a German student of ferns and bryophytes. See *Cheilanthes* for a comparison of this genus to other cheilanthoid genera.

Mildella intramarginalis (Kaulfuss ex Link) Trevisan

FIGURE 13.79.1

syn. *Cheilanthes intramarginalis* (Kaulfuss ex Link) Hooker

Semi-tender (?)

A small to medium fern with clump-forming rhizomes and clustered fronds. Grows well under medium to high light in moist garden soil or potting mix.

Mildella intramarginalis resembles a small *Pteris*. It has short, triangular, sessile pinnae, the lowermost of which are prolonged on their basiscopic side. The narrowly ovate to long-pentagonal blades are one-pinnate-pinnatifid to two-pinnate, with linear, entire or serrate, adnate segments. The surfaces of the blades are smooth except for some fine hairs on the upper surface. The veins are prominent and free. The indusium is linear, distinctly submarginal, and up to 0.8 mm wide. The species occurs from Mexico to Central America and the Galápagos Islands.

Nephrolepis

FIGURES 13.80.1, 2

Sword fern, fish-bone fern

The genus *Nephrolepis* is best known for the Boston fern (*Nephrolepis exaltata* 'Bostoniensis') and the numerous cultivars derived from it. It is widely grown, and in temperate parts of the United States it is used mainly indoors but may be placed outdoors during warm weather. Some *Nephrolepis* plants can be grown outdoors year-round in subtropical areas, but they may show cold sensitivity. The tuber sword fern (*N. cordifolia*) is commonly grown as a ground cover in tropical and subtropical areas and tolerates cool weather much better than the Boston fern. Other species of *Nephrolepis* are rarely grown because they are tender and too large or coarse for ornamental purposes. All species grow better with strongly filtered light. The most common problem in caring for established plants is overwatering combined with poor drainage. These ferns generally tolerate short periods of dryness.

Nephrolepis reproduces vegetatively by runners or stolons. These parts are produced just behind the rhizome apex, and if their large numbers create an untidy appearance, they can be removed without harming the plant. Some stolons, however, should be encouraged to root so that fresh new growth can eventually replace older growth, which may last a few years or less.

The dividing and repotting of *Nephrolepis* is best done in the spring when new growth appears. In temperate or sub-

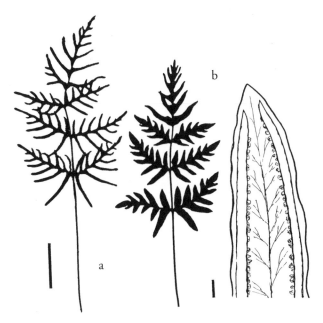

Figure 13.79.1. *Mildella intramarginalis:* a. fertile fronds (left) and sterile frond (right), bar = 2.5 cm (1 in.); b. tip of fertile segment, bar = 1 mm.

Figure 13.80.1. *Nephrolepis cordifolia:* habit.

Figure 13.80.2. *Nephrolepis* fronds: *N. exaltata* (left) and *N. cordifolia* (right).

Nephrolepis contains about 30 species and occurs throughout the tropics and subtropics worldwide. The genus name comes from the Greek *nephros,* kidney, and *lepis,* scale, referring to the kidney-bean-shaped indusia.

Nephrolepis acutifolia (Desvaux) H. Christ

FIGURE 13.80.3

Tender

A large fern with short, erect, stoloniferous rhizomes and fronds over 1 m (3 ft.) long. Grows well under high light in moist, well-drained potting mix.

Nephrolepis acutifolia can be distinguished by its leathery fronds, reddish scaly rachises, and linear, marginal indusia. It is native to tropical Africa and from southeastern Asia to Polynesia.

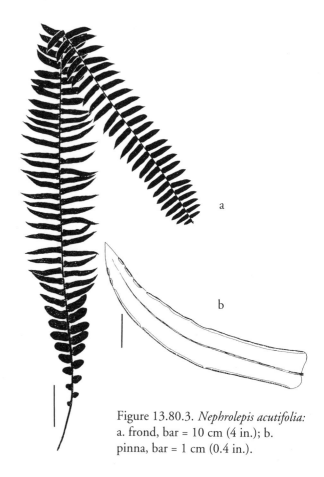

Figure 13.80.3. *Nephrolepis acutifolia:* a. frond, bar = 10 cm (4 in.); b. pinna, bar = 1 cm (0.4 in.).

tropical climates most new divisions made in cooler weather will not receive enough heat to allow them take hold; however, robust growers may take hold readily in cooler weather.

Nephrolepis can be identified by the combination of one-pinnate blades, numerous pinnae (generally 20–50 pairs) jointed to the rachis, and sori that are round, bean-shaped, or crescent-shaped (rarely linear) and covered by a similar-shaped indusium attached at its base. Another distinguishing trait is the many long, slender, scaly runners (stolons) formed at the base of the plant. An unusual characteristic is that the fronds are usually coiled at the apex, never completely unrolling. Most species are epiphytes, but some grow on rocks or, rarely, in soil. The main rhizomes are more or less short and erect, never long-creeping.

Some species of *Nephrolepis* are difficult to distinguish. The characteristics described in the species entries apply only to mature fronds. The scales and hairs on young fronds often differ from those of older plants and are unreliable for identification. Also, weathering can cause loss of hairs and scales, which are important identifying features.

Nephrolepis biserrata (Swartz) Schott   FIGURE 13.80.4
Giant sword fern
Tender, Zone 9

A medium to large fern with short, erect, stoloniferous rhizomes. Grows well under medium to high light in moist garden soil or potting mix. The pendent or arching fronds may reach 5 m (16 ft.) long, but the pinnae are too far apart for this plant to be an attractive ornamental. The fronds

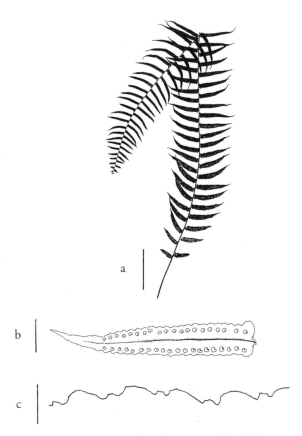

Figure 13.80.4. *Nephrolepis biserrata*: a. frond, bar = 10 cm (4 in.); b. pinna, bar = 1 cm (0.4 in.); c. pinna margin, bar = 3 mm (0.1 in.).

are lax and hairy in general aspect. Plants volunteer readily from spore, accounting for most of the plants in cultivation. Requires winter protection in southern California.

Nephrolepis biserrata can be separated from many others in *Nephrolepis* by the hairy lower surfaces of the pinnae, rachises, and costae. The stipe bases bear loose, spreading, narrow, light brown, concolorous scales, and the pinnae are typically 7 cm (3 in.) long or more with doubly crenate margins (large crenations alternating with small ones). The indusia are submarginal and round-reniform. The species is native to tropical America, Africa, and southeastern Asia.

Trade plants by this name are actually *Nephrolepis falcata*.

Nephrolepis cordifolia (Linnaeus) C. Presl
FIGURES 13.80.1, 2, 5, 6; PLATE 35
syn. *Nephrolepis auriculata* (Linnaeus) Trimen, *N. tuberosa* (Bory ex Willdenow) C. Presl
Tuber sword fern, erect sword fern
Semi-tender or slightly hardier, Zone 9

A medium-sized fern with erect, stoloniferous rhizomes. Grows well under medium to high light in moist to dry garden soil or potting mix. This species is easy to grow and

is widely used as a ground cover in tropical and subtropical climates, second only to the Boston fern (*Nephrolepis exaltata*) in United States use. Tuber sword fern is less sensitive to cool temperatures than Boston ferns—although the tips burn if temperatures last one week or more at −7°C (19°F)—and it maintains better color and active growth. This species is often mislabeled in the trade as *N. exaltata*.

Nephrolepis cordifolia has two particularly distinctive characteristics. First, whereas most species in the genus have pendulous or arching fronds, those of *N. cordifolia* are stiff and erect (except for a few cultivars), which is why it can be used as a low border hedge in the tropics. Second, on the runners are produced large, globose, scaly tubers, which are often underground. Other characteristics of the species include stipe bases with spreading whitish or tan scales; pinnae less than 4 cm (1.5 in.) long, usually overlapping, and mostly glabrous; and the upper surface of rachis scaly, the scales with a dark center. The indusia are bean-shaped to semi-circular, with a broad sinus or none, mostly opening toward the pinna apex. The species is native to tropical

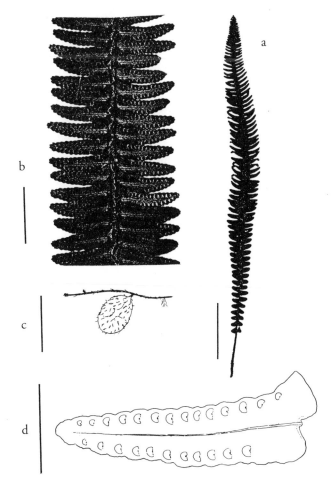

Figure 13.80.5. *Nephrolepis cordifolia*: a. frond, bar = 10 cm (4 in.); b. middle part of frond, bar = 2.5 cm (1 in.); c. tubers on stolons, bar = 2.5 cm (1 in.); d. pinna, bar = 1 cm (0.4 in.).

Figure 13.80.6. *Nephrolepis cordifolia,* fronds of cultivars: a. 'Duffii', pinnae bar = 1 cm (0.4 in.); b. 'Kimberly Queen'; c. 'Lemon Buttons', pinnae bar = 1 cm (0.4 in.); d. 'Plumosa'; e. 'Pom-pom'. All fronds, bar = 10 cm (4 in.).

America, Africa, Asia, Australia, Japan, and New Zealand (where it reportedly lacks tubers).

'Duffii'. Figure 13.80.6a. Fronds less than 30 cm (12 in.), erect, forked; pinnae small, to about 1 cm (0.5 in.) long, rounded or fan-shaped, often in pairs. This plant does not produced sori, and although considered a cultivar of *Nephrolepis cordifolia,* its parentage is doubtful, in part because it does not produce tubers and is more tender than *N. cordifolia.*

'Ecuadorian Fern'. Pinnae ruffled, undulate to irregularly lobed, finely toothed. A recent introduction from cultivation in Ecuador.

'Kimberly Queen'. Figure 13.80.6b. Fronds to 1 m (3 ft.) or more long and over 12.5 cm (5 in.) wide, sometimes slightly narrowly obovate; more arching and softer in appearance than the species. This cultivar grows vigorously. It is often misidentified in the trade as *Nephrolepis obliterata* (R. Brown) Carruthers, an Australian fern with narrow, distantly spaced pinnae, not known in cultivation.

'Lemon Buttons'. Figure 13.80.6c. Fronds to about 25 cm (10 in.) long, to 2.5 cm (1 in.) wide; pinnae reduced, oblong to roundish, not symmetrical at the base, not doubled as in 'Duffii'.

'Petticoats'. Fronds to about 70 cm (28 in.) long, ends forked several times in different planes; pinnae mostly oblong-rectangular, sometimes shallowly and bluntly forked at their tips. Forms with long fronds have been called 'Dennis Petticoats'; those with short fronds, 'Pom-pom' (Figure 13.80.6e); and a shorter, more erect form, 'Can-can'. The weight of the terminal tassel, especially on long fronds, causes the blades to bend and become pendent.

'Tesselata'. Fronds to about 75 cm (30 in.) long; pinnae one-pinnate in the distal half, except for lower pinnae; pinnules oblong-ovate. Variations in this cultivar include pinna and pinnule length, the degree to which the pinnae are bent backward, and the degree of emargination. Whether these variations are due to cultural conditions or are stable is not certain. Related (if not the same) plants are circulating as 'Plumosa' (Figure 13.80.6d) and 'Mildred Murray'.

Nephrolepis exaltata (Linnaeus) Schott

FIGURES 13.80.2, 7, 8; PLATE 5

Common sword fern, Boston fern
Tender to semi-tender

A medium-large fern with short, erect, stoloniferous rhizomes. Grows best under medium to high light in moist-dry potting mix. The wild form is stiff, upright, and has a rank appearance. Although the wild form is rarely cultivated, the cultivars derived from it are among the most loved and widely grown ferns. Natural hybrids between *Nephrolepis exaltata* and other species may be cultivated, especially a hybrid with *N. multiflora* in Hawaii. More information on cultivating Boston ferns is provided in Chapter 10.

The stipe bases of *Nephrolepis exaltata* have spreading, completely brown (concolorous) scales. The pinnae are usually less than 5 cm (2 in.) long, with the surfaces essentially glabrous or with a few hair-like scales on the upper surface. The rachises are sparsely to densely covered with hair-like scales on the upper surfaces, and the indusia are round to round–kidney-shaped with a U-shaped sinus, mostly opening toward the margin. This species is native to Florida, the West Indies, and the Pacific Islands.

Young plants of *Nephrolepis exaltata* are difficult to distinguish from those of *N. cordifolia* (which are often mistakenly sold as *N. exaltata*). In *N. exaltata* the scales on the upper surfaces of the rachises are uniform in color or, if darker in the center, then also with irregular darker spots on the rays of the scales. On young plants of *N. cordifolia,* these scales are usually whitish with a dark center sharply marked. The fronds are also narrower than those of *N. exaltata.* Sterile, adult plants of *N. cordifolia* are distinguished by their erect, stiff, narrower fronds, crowded pinnae, and tuber-producing runners. For commercial purposes *N. cordifolia* is grown mainly from spores, whereas the sterile Boston ferns are cloned mainly by tissue culture.

Nephrolepis exaltata has given rise to numerous cultivars, and these generally have the same cultural requirements as the wild form. So commonly grown are these ferns that commercial growers have established the precise cultural conditions for optimum growth: 2000 foot-candles of light, temperatures between 18 and 35°C (65–95°F), fertilizers with a 3-1-2 composition, micronutrients, and dolomite to adjust the pH to 5.5. Use a mix with good drainage, and water when the soil surface is slightly dry. To prevent breakage and decay of fronds, water should be applied at the soil level, not on the foliage. Poor foliage results when temperatures are below 18°C (65°F) for more than a month. Repotting just before the active growth in spring is recommended.

Those ferns with more finely cut or congested fronds might grow more slowly and need more care. You can expect cultivars with dense, compact foliage to show aborted pinnae where light does not penetrate into the center of the cluster. This does not harm the plant as long as the outer foliage is healthy. All declining fronds or pinnae, however, should be removed to promote air circulation and light penetration to underlying foliage, discouraging decay. The cultivars with long fronds are seldom found in the trade because these large ferns are not well accommodated to smaller homes, and nursery growers find it difficult to transport long fronds without damage.

English growers report that buds form on the foliage of their cultivars, but in the United States this has been documented only for 'Trevillian'. The buds are reported to produce plants that revert to the ordinary Boston fern, 'Bostoniensis'.

The names of Boston fern cultivars are greatly confused. Both old and new names have been loosely used and are poorly documented, except for the work of Sessions (1978). The delineation of cultivars is further complicated by their tendency to intergrade. Sometimes a given cultivar will produce fronds with different characteristics on the same plant. Cultivar variations include size and shape of divisions, number of times pinnate, margin patterns, and degree of

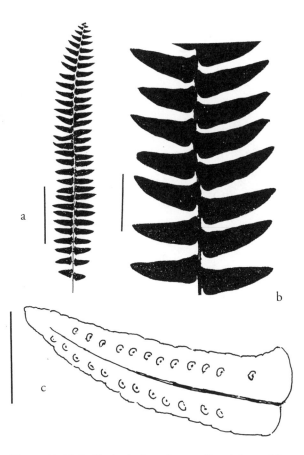

Figure 13.80.7. *Nephrolepis exaltata:* a. frond, bar = 10 cm (4 in.); b. middle part of frond, bar = 2.5 cm (1 in.); c. pinna, bar = 1 cm (0.4 in.).

Figure 13.80.8. *Nephrolepis exaltata* cultivars: a. 'Bostoniensis', middle part of frond; b. 'Dallas'; c. 'Elsevier' (frond enlarged at right); d. 'Fluffy Ruffles'; e. 'Gretnae', middle part of frond; f. 'Massii'; g. 'Mini-ruffles' (frond enlarged at right); h. 'Norwoodii', showing pinna; i. 'Rooseveltii', upper half of frond; j. 'Sassy'; k. 'Smithii'; l. 'Splendida'; m. 'Verona', showing pinna; n. 'Wanamaka'. Bar = 10 cm (4 in.).

ruffling, twisting, forking, or overlapping. Some of these variants tolerate cold better, tend to revert less, and retain their pinnae longer.

Only a small number of the hundreds of cultivars of *Nephrolepis exaltata* are mentioned here. They are selected to show the great diversity within the group.

'Bostoniensis' (var. *bostoniensis* Desvaux). Boston fern. Figure 13.80.8a. Fronds one-pinnate, up to about 120 cm (4 ft.) long, narrow, arching; pinnae slightly wavy; sori (if present) with aborted sporangia. 'Bostoniensis' is the parent of the many *Nephrolepis exaltata* cultivars. It is more compact and graceful than the wild plant, with the pinnae broader and not as flat as those of the wild form. It was first noticed in a Boston nursery in 1821, hence the name Boston fern.

'Dallas'. Dallas fern. Figure 13.80.8b. A compact plant with short fronds bearing oblong pinnae that are noticeably serrate with round apices.

'Elsevier'. Figure 13.80.8c. Fronds two-pinnate, miniature, less than 30 cm (12 in.) long. Resembles 'Mini-ruffles' but with narrowly elliptic, slightly twisted fronds.

'Fluffy Ruffles'. Figure 13.80.8d. Fronds two-pinnate, dwarf, less than 30 cm (12 in.) long, elliptic, stiff, upright; stipes thick; pinnae and pinnules overlapping, with entire to crenate margins. Tends to stay greener in winter.

'Gretnae'. Figure 13.80.8e. Like 'Bostoniensis' but with stouter pinnae forked at the apex into blunt lobes, the frond apex often several times forked.

'Golden Boston' ('Aurea'). Like 'Bostoniensis' but with yellow-green fronds.

'Gracillima' ('Irish Lace'). Resembles 'Smithii', but the fronds are three-pinnate and more ovate, and the pinnae arise uniformly, one behind the other.

'Massii'. Figure 13.80.8f. Short frond form with pinnae slightly twisted at apex.

'Mini-ruffles'. Figure 13.80.8g. Fronds miniature, to about 10 cm (4 in.) long, three-pinnate, broadly triangular, and erect, with overlapping pinnae.

'Norwoodii'. Figure 13.80.8h. Fronds three-pinnate, less than 40 cm (16 in.) long, ovate, spreading; pinnae and pinnules more or less in regular layers, overlapping and congested, pinnules divided into long narrow segments. The dense foliage on the blade has a fluffy but layered appearance with delicate details. The two-pinnate form also circulating as 'Norwoodii' is closer to 'Fluffy Ruffles'.

'Rooseveltii'. Figure 13.80.8i. Fronds to 1 m (3 ft.) long, pinnae wavy, usually eared on both sides of the base.

'Sassy'. Figure 13.80.8j. Fronds short; pinnae moderately twisted, ruffled, and irregularly finely dentate-serrate.

'Smithii'. Lace fern. Figure 13.80.8k. Fronds to four-pinnate, dwarf, about 30 cm (12 in.) long, widely ovate, arching to pendent, lacy; segments ovate, small, 2 mm or less long, spaced apart.

'Splendida'. Figure 13.80.8l. Fronds one- to two-pinnate, pendent, to 1 m (3 ft.) long, with the distal half many times forked and heavily crested. The pinna apex is acute or to three times forked. A large spectacular fern when well grown.

'Verona'. Figure 13.80.8m. Fronds three-pinnate, to about 40 cm (16 in.) long and half as wide, spreading to pendent, the segments ovate. All divisions are distant from each other, hence the blade appears open and imparts an airy appearance to the plant.

'Wanamaka'. Figure 13.80.8n. Fronds one-pinnate, dwarf, less than 30 cm (12 in.) long, narrow, stiff, upright, leathery, dark green; pinnae closely overlapping, curled and twisted, crenulate.

Nephrolepis falcata (Cavanilles) C. Christensen

FIGURE 13.80.9

Broad sword fern, macho fern
Tender

A large fern with erect, stoloniferous rhizomes and erect or pendulous, long fronds. Grows well under medium to high light in moist-dry potting mix or uncut moss.

The older stipe bases on *Nephrolepis falcata* have scales that are spreading to appressed, lanceolate or triangular, and nearly black with a pale margin. The pinnae are up to about 10 cm (4 in.) long and often curved toward the apex (falcate). The fertile pinnae are slightly narrowed compared to the sterile ones. A few scattered scales are found on both surfaces of the blades, but these tend to fall off with age. The upper surface of the pinna midrib is glabrous or with a few scales. The sori are near the margin, and the indusia are round with a narrow sinus. The species is native to Malaysia and extends northward into Burma and Indochina.

Nephrolepis falcata is often misidentified as *N. biserrata* and *N. ensifolia* C. Presl.

'Furcans'. Fishtail sword fern. Figure 13.80.9b. Fronds shorter and less pendent than typical for the species; pinna tips once- or twice-forked. In the tropics this plant is commonly grown in pots in full sun, although it produces better color in the shade.

'Ram's Horn'. Figure 13.80.9c. Pinnae twisted and curled backward.

Nephrolepis hirsutula (G. Forster) C. Presl

FIGURE 13.80.10

Rough sword fern, scurfy sword fern
Tender

A medium-large fern with short, erect, stoloniferous rhizomes. Grows well under medium to high light in garden soil or potting mix kept moist-dry.

The older stipe bases of *Nephrolepis hirsutula* bear appressed, convex scales with nearly black centers and pale margins. The pinnae are about 9 cm (3.5 in.) or more long, closely placed, and usually sharply eared. They bear filamentous scales on the lower surface. The upper surface of the pinna midrib has long hairy scales or is glabrous. The

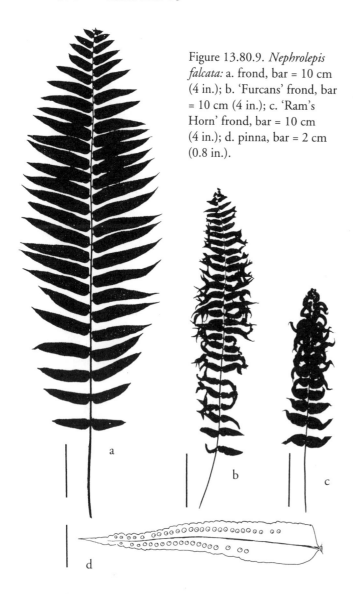

Figure 13.80.9. *Nephrolepis falcata*: a. frond, bar = 10 cm (4 in.); b. 'Furcans' frond, bar = 10 cm (4 in.); c. 'Ram's Horn' frond, bar = 10 cm (4 in.); d. pinna, bar = 2 cm (0.8 in.).

Figure 13.80.10. *Nephrolepis hirsutula*: a. frond, bar = 10 cm (4 in.); b. 'Superba' frond, bar = 10 cm (4 in.); c. pinna, bar = 2 cm (0.8 in.).

rachis appears scurfy-scaly. Round indusia have a narrow sinus and are arranged close to the margins. This species is native to Australia and tropical Asia to the islands of the Pacific; it has become naturalized in the American tropics.

The scurfy-scaly rachis is the source of the common name scurfy sword fern. The species greatly resembles *Nephrolepis multiflora,* a species that bears a stubble of short, erect hairs on the upper surface of the pinna midrib, whereas *N. hirsutula* has the hairs sparse or absent.

'Superba'. Figure 13.80.10b. Pinnae irregularly laciniate-lobed, ruffled. The plants are sterile. This cultivar is often confused with *Nephrolepis multiflora* 'Florist Fantasy'.

Nephrolepis lauterbachii H. Christ   FIGURE 13.80.11
Tender

A small-medium fern with short, erect, stoloniferous rhizomes. Grows well under medium to high light in moist-dry garden soil or potting mix.

Nephrolepis lauterbachii somewhat resembles *N. cordifolia* but has smaller, softer, thinner-textured fronds. The rhizomes do not produce tubers, and the stipes are about 1 mm thick and bear tan-brown scales. The pinnae are separate (not overlapping), less than 1.5 cm (0.6 in.) long, somewhat oblong-rectangular, and glabrous. The pinna bases are asymmetrical, being truncate or cordate on the acroscopic side and narrowly tapered on the basiscopic side. The rachis is glabrous or has a few concolorous scales. The indusia are round-reniform to lunate with an extremely broad sinus (or none), and they face the pinna apices. Up to five sori occur on the upper margin opposite or nearly opposite each major crenation. *Nephrolepis lauterbachii* is endemic to New Guinea.

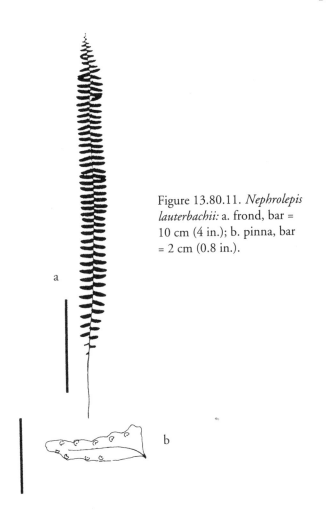

Figure 13.80.11. *Nephrolepis lauterbachii:* a. frond, bar = 10 cm (4 in.); b. pinna, bar = 2 cm (0.8 in.).

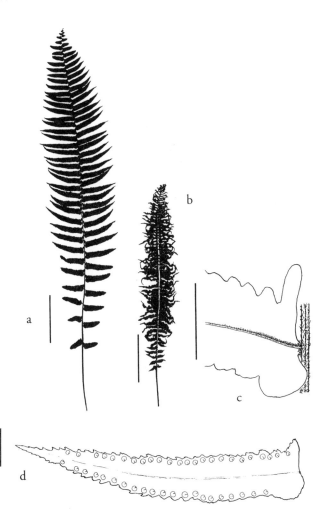

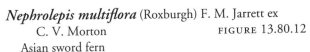

Figure 13.80.12. *Nephrolepis multiflora:* a. frond, bar = 10 cm (4 in.); b. 'Florist Fantasy' frond, bar = 10 cm (4 in.); c. hairs on upper surface of pinna base, bar = 1 cm (0.4 in.); d. pinna, bar = 1 cm (0.4 in.).

Nephrolepis multiflora (Roxburgh) F. M. Jarrett ex C. V. Morton   FIGURE 13.80.12

Asian sword fern

Tender

A medium to large fern with short, erect, stoloniferous rhizomes. Grows well under medium to high light in moist-dry garden soil or potting mix. The plants have a rank appearance and tend to be weedy. This species is widely cultivated outdoors in Florida and Hawaii.

Nephrolepis multiflora has pinnae about 10 cm (4 in.) long. The scales on the stipe bases are appressed, black in the center with pale tan borders, and minutely fibrillose along the margins (only *N. hirsutula* shares this characteristic). The pinnae may be eared or not, and their surfaces are covered by hair-like scales or ciliate-margined scales. The upper surface of the pinna midrib has a dense stubble of short, erect hairs 0.2–0.3 mm long. The sori are close to the margin, and the indusium is round with a narrow sinus. This species is native to the tropical regions of Africa and Asia and has become naturalized (and often weedy) in the American tropics.

'Florist Fantasy'. Figure 13.80.12b. Fronds shorter and more erect than the wild form; pinnae close together, some-

what twisted, ruffled, serrate, and attenuate. This cultivar has long been confused with *Nephrolepis hirsutula* 'Superba', which has laciniate-lobed, not ruffled, margins. An unnamed dull dark green cultivar resembling 'Florist Fantasy' but with stiffly erect fronds has recently been circulating in the trade.

Nephrolepis pendula (Raddi) J. Smith   FIGURE 13.80.13

Tender to semi-tender (?)

A large fern with short, erect, stoloniferous rhizomes. Grows well under medium light in moist potting mix. This species grows slowly and is less robust than *Nephrolepis cordifolia,* which it resembles. It is a choice fern for hanging baskets because of its long, narrow, pendent fronds.

Nephrolepis pendula differs from *N. cordifolia* by its flat, longer, pendent fronds and shorter pinnae. The pinnae are

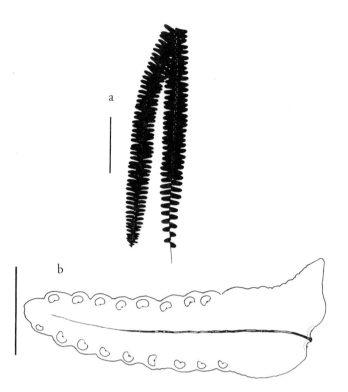

Figure 13.80.13. *Nephrolepis pendula:* a. frond, bar = 10 cm (4 in.); b. pinna, bar = 1 cm (0.4 in.).

about twice as long as broad and have rounded apices and mostly entire margins. The upper part of stipe and rachis (except at the point of pinna attachment) essentially lacks hairs or scales. The species is native to tropical America.

Niphidium

syn. *Pessopteris, Polypodium* in part

These epiphytic, epilithic, or terrestrial plants have medium- to large-sized, stiff, undivided, upright fronds. They are reminiscent of the bird's-nest fern (*Asplenium nidus*), but instead of the latter's neat rosette of light green fronds, *Niphidium* fronds are dark green and irregularly clustered. The two genera can be distinguished by the sori, which are linear and indusiate in *Asplenium* but round and non-indusiate in *Niphidium. Niphidium* also resembles the tropical American genus *Campyloneurum*, but that genus has two or more rows of sori between the main lateral veins, whereas *Niphidium* only has one.

The rhizomes of *Niphidium* vary from short- to long-creeping. The fronds are simple, entire, elliptic-lanceolate to oblong, and leathery, often with white dots on the upper surfaces. The main lateral veins are prominent and oblique to the rachis. In the cultivated species the sori are large, about 3 mm (0.1 in.) wide, usually round, and produced in a single row between the lateral veins. Each sorus is served by a small vein ring. As in all polypodiaceous ferns, indusia are lacking.

Niphidium contains 10 species and is native to the New World tropics. The genus name comes from the Greek *nipha,* snow, and *eidos,* like, referring to the whitish indument on the leaves of the type species. For a monographic treatment of the genus, see Lellinger (1972). Also see *Polypodium* for a comparison of *Niphidium* to other polypodiaceous genera.

Niphidium crassifolium (Linnaeus) Lellinger

FIGURE 13.81.1

Semi-hardy to hardier

A medium-large fern with short- to long-creeping rhizomes and clustered fronds. Does well under medium light in drained, moist-dry garden soil or potting mix. This species grows easily in the ground, pots, and hanging baskets. It can tolerate several consecutive days below freezing to −7°C (19°F).

The rhizome scales of *Niphidium crassifolium* are clathrate centrally but nonclathrate toward the margins. The fronds vary from narrowly oblanceolate to lanceolate, and from acute to rounded or sometimes mucronate at the tips. The upper surfaces of the blades, especially on older fronds, usually bear white dots that are accumulations of calcium carbonate secreted by the hydathodes beneath. This species is widely distributed in tropical America.

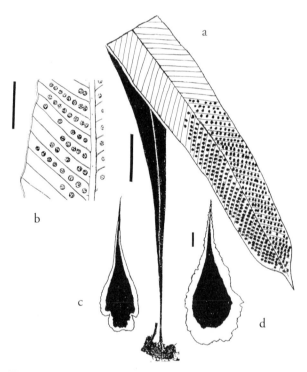

Figure 13.81.1. *Niphidium:* a. *N. crassifolium* frond, bar = 5 cm (2 in.); b. *N. crassifolium* sori, bar = 2.5 cm (1 in.), after Hoshizaki (1982); c. *N. crassifolium* rhizome scale, bar = 1 mm, after Lellinger (1972); d. *N. albopunctatissimum* rhizome scale, bar = 1 mm, after Lellinger (1972).

A few cultivated plants examined under the name *Niphidium crassifolium* turned out to be *N. albopunctatissimum* (Figure 13.81.1d), and these two species are difficult to distinguish. They have distinct rhizome scale characteristics—those of *N. albopunctatissimum* are irregular (erose) in the nonclathrate part of the margin toward the tip—but this trait is not always easy to use for identification, and when the scales are absent the species cannot be distinguished. In cultivated and wild plants, both species can have white dots on the upper surface of the frond (the name *albopunctatissimum* means "with many white dots"), so this is not a reliable characteristic to separate the two, either. The fronds of *N. albopunctatissimum* are slightly smaller and narrower than those of *N. crassifolium,* and in nature *N. albopunctatissimum* is mostly found on the ground or on rocks from Colombia to Bolivia, whereas *N. crassifolium* is occurs mostly throughout tropical America.

Notholaena
Cloak fern

A mostly rock-inhabiting fern of dry climates, *Notholaena* is difficult to grow and is found only in special collections. These small ferns have short-creeping, compact rhizomes. The genus resembles certain species of *Cheilanthes* and *Pellaea* but differs by the dense covering of white, cream, or yellow waxy powder (farina) on the undersides of the fronds and by the marginal, hardly enrolled, narrow indusia. The stipes are frequently longer than the blades, and the fronds may be linear-lanceolate to pentagonal and pinnate-pinnatifid to four-pinnate. Many species formerly classified in *Notholaena* have been transferred to *Cheilanthes* (which see for a comparison).

Notholaena consists of about 25 species native to North America, Central and South America, and the West Indies. The genus name comes from the Greek *nothos,* false, and *chlaena,* cloak, referring to the blade margins, which are not reflexed as in the similar genus *Cheilanthes.* For additional information on growing cloak ferns, see the section on "Xerophytic Ferns" in Chapter 10.

Notholaena standleyi Maxon   FIGURE 13.82.1
Hardy

A small fern with compact rhizomes and fronds in a cluster. Requires high light in moist-dry, well-drained garden soil preferably mixed with coarse sand or gravel.

Notholaena standleyi has pentagonal blades densely covered with a whitish powder on the lower surface, and the hardly enrolled indusium is narrow. It might be confused with the more frequently grown *Cheilanthes argentea,* which is less divided, less densely powdery, and has a more enrolled, broader indusium. *Notholaena standleyi* is native to the southwestern United States and Mexico.

Figure 13.82.1. *Notholaena standleyi:* fronds, the underside (left) with dense powder, and the upperside (right), bar = 2.5 cm (1 in.).

Odontosoria
syn. *Sphenomeris*

The cultivated species of *Odontosoria* are finely cut terrestrial plants of rocky areas. They are used in tropical gardens and are rarely seen elsewhere. Like many ferns that grow between rocks, these plants are difficult to remove without damaging the roots. Transplants with damaged roots often do not reroot readily, hence the genus is best propagated by spores.

The short-creeping to suberect rhizomes are covered with narrow or hair-like dark scales. The fronds are set close together and have two- to four-pinnate blades. The ultimate segments are linear or wedge-shaped and dichotomously lobed, with a single vein or the vein once or twice forked. Marginal sori are borne at the vein tips or, more rarely, are supplied by two or three veins. The rounded to oval indusium is attached by the base and more or less by the sides. It opens toward the margin of the segments.

The genus, which consists of 22 species, is native to the tropics and subtropics of America, Africa, and Japan. Its name comes from the Greek *odous,* tooth, and *soros,* mound, and refers to the sori borne at the extreme tips of small, marginal teeth.

Odontosoria chinensis (Linnaeus) J. Smith

FIGURE 13.83.1

syn. *Sphenomeris chinensis* (Linnaeus) Maxon, *S. chusana* (Linnaeus) Copeland
Lace fern
Tender

A medium-sized fern with short-creeping to suberect rhizomes. Grows well under medium to high light in well-drained, moist garden soil or potting mix. The species is commonly grown in Hawaii but only rarely in the continental United States.

The blades of *Odontosoria chinensis* vary from lanceolate to ovate and are up to four-pinnate. The pinna midrib is straight, not zigzag (as in many other species in the genus), and the ultimate segments are wedge-shaped or lobed. The sori are often two or more per segment. The species is native from Madagascar to Polynesia and Japan.

Figure 13.83.1. *Odontosoria chinensis:* a. habit, bar = 5 cm (2 in.); b. sori and indusia, bar = 5 mm (0.2 in.).

Oleandra

These primarily terrestrial ferns often require ample space for their wide-creeping or scrambling habit. *Oleandra pistillaris* grows erect and shrub-like but is unusual in appearance because its leaves are borne in whorls at intervals along the stems.

The genus is characterized by long-creeping rhizomes, jointed stipes, simple and entire blades, free veins, round sori scattered close to the midrib, and kidney-shaped to horseshoe-shaped indusia. The joint in the stipe can usually be seen as a faint dark line or a slight swelling. The fronds break off cleanly from these joints when they are shed.

Oleandra occurs throughout the tropical regions of the world and contains about 40 species. The genus name comes from oleander (*Nerium*), a flowering plant in the dogbane family (Apocynaceae), the leaves of which resemble those of several species in *Oleandra*.

Oleandra articulata (Swartz) C. Presl   FIGURE 13.84.1

syn. *Oleandra nodosa* (Willdenow) C. Presl
Tender

A medium to large fern with long-creeping, scrambling rhizomes. Grows well under high to medium light in moist garden soil or potting mix. This species requires ample room in the garden to spread; ideally, plant it in baskets to contain it.

Oleandra articulata is characterized by widely spreading rhizome scales, blades glabrous or nearly so on both sur-

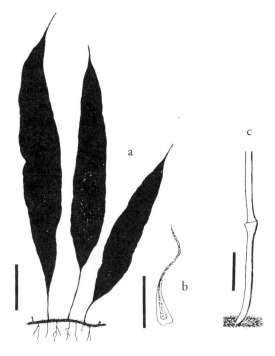

Figure 13.84.1. *Oleandra articulata:* a. habit, bar = 5 cm (2 in.); b. rhizome scale, bar = 2 mm; c. joint on stipe, bar = 1 cm (0.4 in.).

faces, and glabrous indusia. It is native to the American tropics.

Oleandra pilosa Hooker   FIGURE 13.84.2
Tender

A medium-sized fern with climbing, ascending to erect rhizomes. Grows well under high to medium light in moist garden soil or potting mix. This plant's growth habit is too upright for planting in baskets; it is probably best suited for growing against walls and other vertical surfaces.

Oleandra pilosa is characterized by tightly appressed, hairy-margined rhizome scales, blades hairy on both surfaces, and ciliate indusia. It is native to the American tropics.

Oleandra pilosa circulates among some gardeners as *O. neriiformis* Cavanilles, a species unknown in recent cultivation and native to Australia, tropical Asia, the Philippines, and Polynesia.

Oleandra pistillaris (Swartz) C. Christensen
FIGURE 13.84.3

Tender

A medium to large fern with long-creeping rhizomes and a shrubby or straggly appearance. Grows well under medium light in moist garden soil or potting mix. The species assumes a shrub-like appearance in tropical gardens. It can be suitably grown in large pots or tubs.

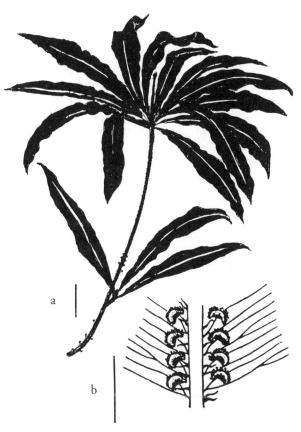

Figure 13.84.3. *Oleandra pistillaris:* a. habit, bar = 5 cm (2 in.); b. sori and indusia, bar = 5 mm (0.2 in.).

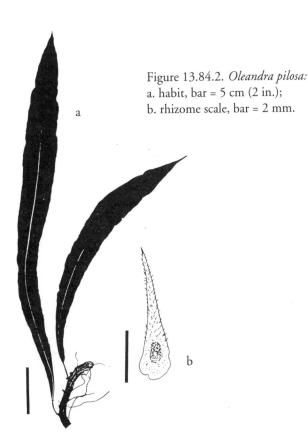

Figure 13.84.2. *Oleandra pilosa:* a. habit, bar = 5 cm (2 in.); b. rhizome scale, bar = 2 mm.

Oleandra pistillaris bears its fronds in distinct whorls along the stem, with the stem tip extending far beyond the last whorl. The sori are disposed in a row on both sides of the midrib. This species is native from Malaysia and Java to Polynesia(?).

This species might be confused with *Oleandra neriiformis,* which has creeping rhizomes that climb and produce aerial roots. The rhizomes of *O. pistillaris,* however, are erect, woody, and shrub-like.

Olfersia

Rarely cultivated, *Olfersia* grows in soil in the wild or scrambles over fallen logs or rocks. It occasionally climbs tree trunks, in which instances the rhizomes become long-creeping. Younger plants tend to maintain a short rhizome for some time and therefore can be confined to a wide pot.

Olfersia is medium-sized and can be distinguished from all other ferns by its creeping, densely scaly rhizomes and strongly dimorphic sterile and fertile fronds. The sterile fronds are one-pinnate with a terminal segment resembling the lateral pinnae. The veins are long-parallel and free for most of their length, joining just before the margin to form a submarginal connecting strand. The fertile fronds are bipinnate with linear pinnae and sori that merge. The indusium is absent.

This genus consists of one species widespread in the American tropics. Its name honors Ignaz Franz Werner von Olfers (1793–1871), a professor who collected in Brazil. See Moran (1986) for a technical treatment of the species.

Olfersia cervina (Linnaeus) Kunze   FIGURE 13.85.1
syn. *Polybotrya cervina* (Linnaeus) Kaulfuss
Tender

A medium-sized fern with medium- to long-creeping rhizomes. Grows well under medium light in moist garden soil. *Olfersia cervina* is easy to grow from spores. See the description of the genus for distribution and additional characteristics.

Figure 13.85.1. *Olfersia cervina:* sterile frond (left) and fertile frond (right), bar = 5 cm (2 in.).

Onoclea
Sensitive fern, bead fern

The bead-like appearance of the fertile fronds accounts for this genus's common name of bead fern. Some say that the name sensitive fern originates from the fronds' sensitivity to frost (they wither after the first subfreezing temperatures). These medium- to large-sized natives of temperate areas have coarsely cut but attractive foliage. The plants spread by creeping, branching rhizomes. *Onoclea* is useful in wet, temperate areas but will grow well in warmer climates even though it is deciduous. The fertile fronds are often used in dried flower arrangements.

Onoclea can be identified by its netted veins, triangular and deeply pinnatifid or (more often) one-pinnate-pinnatifid sterile blades, and strongly dimorphic sterile and fertile fronds. Other characteristics are medium-wide-creeping rhizomes and fertile pinnae that are strongly ascending and contracted into rounded, bead-like lobes enclosing the sori.

The genus, which consists of only one species, is native to North America and Asia. The genus name comes from the Greek *onos,* vessel, and *kleiein,* to close, referring to the pinnules of the fertile leaf, which roll up into bead-like segments to enclose the sori.

Onoclea sensibilis Linnaeus   FIGURES 13.86.1–3
Very hardy, Zone 2

A medium-sized fern with medium- to long-creeping rhizomes and deciduous fronds. Grows well under medium to high light in moist-wet garden soil. This species is easy to grow.

Onoclea sensibilis is characterized by pinnatisect fronds with lobed pinnae narrowed toward the base, and veins netted throughout. The margins of the blade are finely serrulate. The fertile fronds are brown, erect, and rigid with strongly ascending pinnae. The species is native to eastern North America and eastern Asia, often growing in wet habitats.

Onoclea sensibilis has been around for a long time. Fossils identical to modern plants have been found in Paleocene rocks in Canada—rocks that date back more than 54 million years (Rothwell and Stockey 1991).

Onychium
Claw fern

Onychium is a genus of terrestrial, clump-forming ferns that can be planted in the ground or in pots. Their finely divided fronds have a delicate, lacy appearance.

The rhizomes are short- to long-creeping and scaly. The fronds are dimorphic or monomorphic. The sterile blades

Figure 13.86.1. *Onoclea sensibilis:* habit.

Figure 13.86.2. *Onoclea sensibilis:* fertile pinnae.

vary from three- to five-pinnate and are anadromous and glabrous. The veins are free, not netted. Linear sori run along the margin. The indusium is formed by the enrolled leaf margin, and because the segments are extremely narrow, the indusium on one side of the segment meets the edge of the indusium on the opposite side.

Onychium contains about eight species native to the tropics and subtropics of Africa, the Near East, India, Asia, and New Guinea. The genus name comes from the Greek *onychion,* a small claw or nail, and refers to the shape of the ultimate segments of the blade.

Onychium japonicum (Thunberg) Kunze

FIGURES 13.87.1–3

Japanese claw fern, carrot fern
Semi-hardy, Zone 8

A small-medium fern with short-creeping, branched rhizomes. Grows well under high light in moist garden soil or potting mix. The plants are easy to cultivate and have attractive carrot-like foliage.

Figure 13.87.1. *Onychium japonicum:* habit.

Figure 13.86.3. *Onoclea sensibilis:* sterile frond (left) and fertile frond (right), bar = 5 cm (2 in.).

Figure 13.87.2. *Onychium japonicum:* sori and indusia.

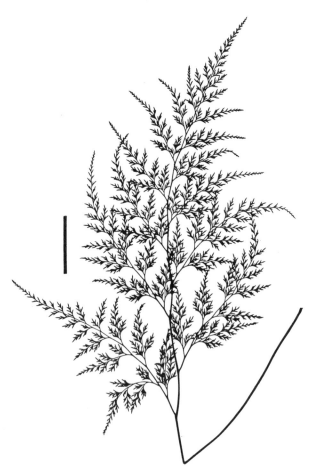

Figure 13.87.3. *Onychium japonicum:* frond, bar = 5 cm (2 in.).

Figure 13.88.1. *Ophioglossum petiolatum:* habit.

The stipes of *Onychium japonicum* are straw-colored toward the base, and the blades are three- to four-pinnate with segments narrowly lanceolate and acute. The sori are about 5 mm (0.2 in.) long. This species is native to India, the Himalayas, eastern Asia, the Philippines, and Java.

Ophioglossum

syn. *Cheiroglossa*

FIGURES 13.88.1, 2

Adder's-tongue fern, serpent's-tongue fern

Ophioglossum is a genus of mostly small ferns that are grown in natural gardens or in pots as novelties. They are hard to find in the wild, and some species are rare. The temperate ones are often overlooked because they grow in open grassy areas and resemble other plants, especially plantains (*Plantago*). One sure way to distinguish *Ophioglossum* from other plants is by the lack of a midrib on its blades—all other plants have a midrib or at least prominent parallel veins.

One of the most eye-catching tropical species is *Ophioglossum palmatum* (sometimes called *Cheiroglossa palmata* (Linnaeus) C. Presl), commonly known as the hand fern. It is an endangered species in Florida and should not be collected from the wild. This species is difficult to grow and rarely survives transplanting. The hand fern can be recognized by its fan-shaped sterile blade, which grows to 45 cm (18 in.) long and is deeply palmately lobed. The species is epiphytic and often grows in the old humus-filled leaf axils of palms.

Nearly all the species of *Ophioglossum* are terrestrial; only a few are epiphytic. Most have short, erect, fleshy rhizomes and whitish or tan, fleshy roots. The fronds are divided in two parts: a green, photosynthetic sterile blade and an erect, elongate stalk (the fertile spike). The fleshy blades lack a midrib, and they vary from simple and entire to strap-shaped and branched to fan-shaped and palmately lobed. The veins are netted, and the areoles may or may not contain veinlets. At the base of the sterile blade arises a long-stalked spike or (in the segregate-genus *Cheiroglossa*) several short spikes or a stalk branched into spikes at the top. Sporangia are borne at the apices of the fertile spikes. The sporangia are sunken on both sides of the spike and open by a horizontal slit.

Figure 13.88.2. *Ophioglossum petiolatum:* fertile spike. Photo courtesy of G. Hampfler.

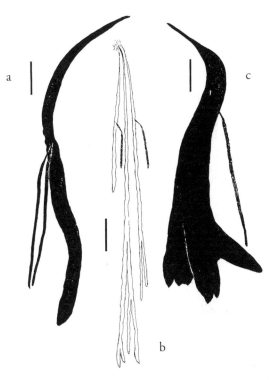

Figure 13.88.3. *Ophioglossum pendulum:* a. frond with two spikes, bar = 5 cm (2 in.); b. habit of mature plant, bar = 15 cm (6 in.), courtesy of T. Hoshizaki; c. frond with flared apex, bar = 5 cm (2 in.).

Ophioglossum occurs worldwide and consists of about 30 species. The common names are derived from the fancied resemblance of the erect fertile stalk to a snake's tongue. The genus name also alludes to this resemblance, being derived from the Greek *ophis,* snake, and *glossa,* tongue.

Ophioglossum pendulum Linnaeus

FIGURE 13.88.3; PLATE 36

Tender, Zone 10

A medium to large fern with short-creeping or suberect rhizomes and pendulous fronds. Grows under low to medium light in moist uncut sphagnum moss. The plants are typically grown on a suspended board or basket so that the fronds can hang downward as they do in nature (the plants are epiphytic). When grown in pots, however, the fronds tend to be more upright. A variant with two fertile spikes per blade is in cultivation.

Ophioglossum pendulum has long, pendent, strap-shaped sterile blades, up to 2 m (6.5 ft.) long, and occasionally several times branched. The veins form large areoles that lack included veinlets (the other species have included veinlets). The species is native to the Old World tropics.

Ophioglossum petiolatum Hooker

FIGURES 13.88.1, 2, 4

Semi-hardy, Zone 7

A small fern with erect rhizomes. Grows well under high light in moist garden soil. Fronds emerge during wet periods. The plants reproduce vegetatively from buds on the roots and may become weedy or volunteer in pots of other plants. The succulent leaves are readily attacked by millipedes, slugs, and snails.

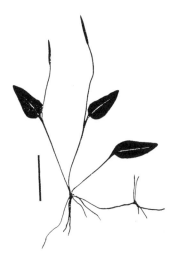

Figure 13.88.4. *Ophioglossum petiolatum:* habit, bar = 5 cm (2 in.).

Ophioglossum petiolatum produces two or three fronds per stem, instead of one as in other species. The fronds appear in one or more flushes of growth per year. The sterile blades have acute apices and the veins are netted, forming large areoles that contain free veins. The species is native to the southeastern United States, tropical America, Asia, and the Pacific Islands. In the Gulf States (Florida to Louisiana), the species is often abundant in sandy roadsides.

Ophioglossum vulgatum Linnaeus   FIGURE 13.88.5
Hardy to semi-hardy, Zone 6

A small fern with erect rhizomes. Grows under high light in moist garden soil. The plants reproduce by root buds and go dormant in hot weather.

The veins of *Ophioglossum vulgatum* resemble those of *O. petiolatum,* but the sterile blades have a rounded apex and the fronds are usually one per stem and appear once a year, not in several flushes. The species is native to the southeastern United States, Mexico, and temperate Eurasia.

Figure 13.89.1. *Osmunda regalis* var. *brasiliensis:* habit.

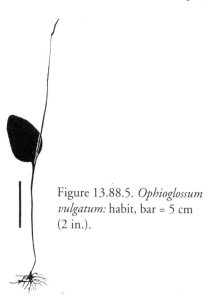

Figure 13.88.5. *Ophioglossum vulgatum:* habit, bar = 5 cm (2 in.).

Osmunda   FIGURES 13.89.1–3

Osmundas are familiar United States natives that produce fresh green growth in the spring and early summer. The fronds of these stately ferns form medium- to large-sized clusters or whorls. In gardens they are used as background foliage or accent plants. Although most osmundas grow in wet, acidic soil, the more common species can be cultivated in moist, neutral or very slightly acidic soil, although they do not become as massive as the wild plants. The royal fern (*Osmunda regalis*) attracts attention when contracted fertile areas develop at the frond tips and contrast with the foliaceous part of the frond. Because the thick, compact root mantle of the cinnamon fern (*O. cinnamomea*) does not decay rapidly, that species has been used as a substrate to grow orchids and other epiphytes.

Figure 13.89.2. *Osmunda regalis* var. *brasiliensis:* fertile pinnae.

Figure 13.89.3. *Osmunda regalis* var. *brasiliensis*: sporangia.

The tropical species *Osmunda vachellii* Hooker, which resembles a cycad, has recently been introduced to cultivation in southern California from the area around Hong Kong. Although not treated here, it seems promising as an ornamental. It has evergreen, one-pinnate fronds borne on an erect stem and entire, narrowly lanceolate pinnae. The fertile pinnae appear at or near the middle of the blade.

All species of *Osmunda* have erect rhizomes that can become massive and occasionally branch. They bear fronds in a spiral tuft. The lower part of the stipe bears wing-like outgrowths called stipules, although these are not equivalent to the stipules in marattiaceous ferns (*Angiopteris, Marattia*) or in angiosperms. The sterile blades vary from one- to two-pinnate, and mature blades are usually smooth except for a tuft of wool on the rachises and costae, usually at the pinna base. The blades are always catadromous. The pinnae are often jointed to the rachis, but the joints are non-functional. The veins are free, not netted. All or some of the fertile fronds are strongly contracted, lack green leafy tissue, and usually wither after the spores are shed. The sporangia are large and globose and not protected by an indusium. The spores are green and short-lived.

The genus consists of about 10 species and occurs worldwide. *Osmunda* is named for Osmunder, the Saxon equivalent of the god Thor.

Osmunda cinnamomea Linnaeus
FIGURE 13.89.4; PLATE 8

Cinnamon fern
Very hardy, Zone (2)3

A medium to large fern with erect rhizomes that form occasional offshoots. Grows well under low to high light in moist-wet to wet, acidic garden soil. The plants are robust growers with deciduous leaves. The fiddleheads are covered with a dense mat of tawny or cinnamon-colored hair.

Osmunda cinnamomea is characterized by completely dimorphic sterile and fertile fronds. The sterile blades are one-pinnate-pinnatifid, oblong-lanceolate, and bear a dense tuft of hair at the base of each pinna. The fertile fronds are two-pinnate with strongly ascending pinnae bearing globose sporangia. They wilt soon after the spores are shed. The species is cosmopolitan.

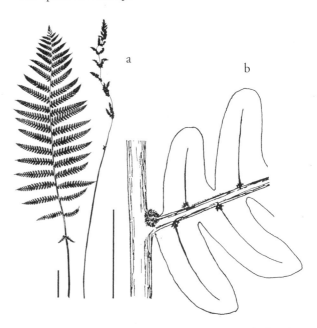

Figure 13.89.4. *Osmunda cinnamomea*: a. sterile frond (left) and fertile frond (right), bar = 5 cm (2 in.); b. pinnae base with tuft of hair, bar = 1 cm (0.4 in.).

Osmunda claytoniana Linnaeus
FIGURE 13.89.5; PLATE 37

Interrupted fern
Very hardy, Zone (2)3

A medium to large fern with erect rhizomes that form occasional offshoots. Grows well under low to medium light in moist-wet to wet, acidic garden soil. The plants have deciduous fronds and do poorly in the Gulf States and subtropical climates.

Osmunda claytoniana has one-pinnate-pinnatifid fronds with brown fertile pinnae borne in the middle of the blade —they appear to interrupt the green, sterile pinnae. The

Figure 13.89.5.
Osmunda claytoniana:
frond, middle pinnae
fertile, bar = 5 cm
(2 in.).

Figure 13.89.6. *Osmunda japonica:* sterile frond (left)
and fertile frond (right), bar = 5 cm (2 in.).

species is native to northeastern North America and Asia.

Osmunda×*ruggii* R. M. Tryon is a naturally occurring hybrid between this species and *O. regalis.* Although the two parental species frequently grow together, the hybrid is extremely rare, known from only two localities, one in Connecticut and the other in West Virginia. The hybrid is unavailable in the trade but would make an interesting addition to horticulture because it demonstrates hybrid intermediacy. It must be propagated vegetatively by division of the rhizome because the spores are aborted.

Osmunda japonica Thunberg   FIGURE 13.89.6
Japanese osmunda
Hardy

A medium-sized fern with suberect rhizomes and deciduous fronds. Grows well under medium light in moist garden soil. The fiddleheads of this species are edible and are available in markets in Japan. The cut rhizomes have been used as a substrate to grow epiphytes, much like tree-fern trunks, in horticulture.

Osmunda japonica resembles *O. regalis* but has completely dimorphic sterile and fertile fronds with finely serrate margins on the sterile pinnae. The fertile fronds are erect and emanate from the center of the plant, whereas the sterile ones tend to spread, forming a wide, loose basket. The species is native to eastern Asia.

Osmunda regalis Linnaeus
FIGURES 13.89.1–3, 7, 8; PLATE 6
Royal fern, flowering fern
Very hardy, Zone 2(3)

A medium to large fern with erect rhizomes that form occasional offshoots. Grows well under medium light in acidic, moist-wet to wet garden soil. The fronds are deciduous or semi-deciduous, and the new growth is sometimes reddish or purplish. When young, the sporangia appear green from the color of the spores within. After the spores are shed, the sporangia are rusty brown. Young leaves appear either purplish or green in spring—all the leaves on a given plant will be of the same color. Leaves that are purplish when young usually turn green with age.

Osmunda regalis is characterized by two-pinnate fronds that, when fertile, bear sporangia only in the apical third or so of the blade. The pinnules are oblong-lanceolate. This species occurs worldwide and varies geographically. The following geographic varieties are cultivated:

var. *brasiliensis* (Hooker & Greville) Pichi-Sermolli. Figures 13.89.1–3, 8. Fronds are slowly deciduous in temperate areas and nearly evergreen in subtropical ones. In greenhouses, this variety produces new fronds throughout the year. The rachis is glabrous. The fertile parts are conspicuously stalked and distant from the sterile pinnules below. Unlike var. *regalis,* the fertile pinnae are strongly ascending prior to withering and appear bunched together. The plants seem adapted to neutral or only slightly acidic soil. The cultivated material of this fern was collected in Brazil. Some botanists do not consider this variety distinct from var. *spectabilis*.

Figure 13.89.7. *Osmunda regalis:* fertile frond, bar = 5 cm (2 in.).

Figure 13.89.8. *Osmunda regalis* var. *brasiliensis:* fertile frond, bar = 5 cm (2 in.).

var. *regalis*. Figure 13.89.7. Fronds are completely deciduous. The fronds are more leathery than those of the other varieties and have thicker stipes and rachises. The pinnae and pinnules are sessile (or nearly so) and closer together than in var. *spectabilis*. The hairs on the rachis are ample and darker than those of var. *spectabilis*. The fertile pinnae spread at nearly right angles to the rachis and are borne in the same plane as the sterile pinnae. This robust grower is native to Europe and Asia. The following cultivars are derived from it: 'Cristata', pinnules or segments crested at the tips; 'Purpurescens', with purplish stipes, rachises, and costae.

var. *spectabilis* (Willdenow) A. Gray. Fronds are completely deciduous. The pinnae and pinnules are stalked and farther apart than in var. *regalis*. Also, the hairs on the rachises are fewer and lighter colored than in var. *regalis*. The fertile pinnae are slightly falcate and ascending, spreading in the same plane as the sterile pinnae. This variety is native to North America and might not be distinct from var. *brasiliensis*.

Paesia

Plants of the genus *Paesia* typically have finely divided fronds and zigzag rachises that allow them to scramble over other plants. *Paesia scaberula,* however, the only cultivated species, has only a slightly a zigzag rachis and less elongate fronds.

Paesia has slender, 3–5 mm (0.1–0.2 in.) long, creeping, hairy rhizomes. Other characteristics of the genus are two- to four-pinnate blades, free veins, and rachises and costae that are strongly ridged and grooved on the upper surfaces. The sori of *Paesia* have two indusia, an outer one formed from the modified, enrolled margin of the blade, and an inner one that is thin, colorless, and hidden by the outer one and, typically, by the sporangia. The sori are borne on an outer, marginal vein supplied by two or more lateral veins. In contrast, *Hypolepis* and *Odontosoria* (also in the family Dennstaedtiaceae) have only one indusium, and the sori are supplied by a single vein. *Paesia* is closely related to *Pteridium* but differs by having only one vascular bundle in the stipe, whereas *Pteridium* has several arranged in a horseshoe pattern.

Paesia consists of 12 species distributed in the American tropics, eastern Asia, and the western Pacific. It is named for Duke Fernando Diaz Paes Leme, who visited Brazil in 1660 on government service from Portugal.

Paesia scaberula (A. Richard) Kuhn   FIGURE 13.90.1
Hard fern, scented fern, lace fern
Semi-hardy, frost tolerant

A small to medium fern with hairy, long-creeping rhizomes and stiff fronds. Grows best in high to medium light in moist to moist-dry soil. Although difficult to transplant, this species grows vigorously once established. In its native

Figure 13.90.1. *Paesia scaberula:* habit, bar = 5 cm (2 in.).

New Zealand, it is weedy and volunteers readily in disturbed open areas, even in heavy soil. It will also volunteer in greenhouses and spore pans. When rubbed or crushed, the fronds emit a sweet odor, which is contained within the many glandular hairs on the surface of the blades.

The stipes and rachises of *Paesia scaberula* are straight or only slightly zigzag and bear red-brown, short, bristly hairs. The ovate or elliptic blades are three- to four-pinnate, finely cut into segments about 1 mm wide. They are yellow green, and the lower surfaces bear many short, yellowish, sticky, glandular hairs. The species is endemic to New Zealand.

Pecluma

Comb fern

The numerous narrow, comb-like segments give *Pecluma* its distinctive appearance. The genus, which is only occasionally grown and mainly in the collections of fern hobbyists, consists of handsome ferns of warm, humid climates. In nature the plants typically grow on tree trunks or branches, out of contact with the soil and its moisture. During the dry season the plants curl up and go dormant; however, they revive within minutes after the first rains of the next season. Most comb ferns are slow to establish in cultivation, requiring more humidity than most ferns. They respond well to frequent applications of nutrients. Although they grow in Zone 9 in Florida, the plants do not grow out-

doors in Zone 9 in southern California, where they need the heat and humidity of a greenhouse to thrive. The foliage is particularly susceptible to attack from slugs, snails, and scale insects.

The numerous (25 or more) narrow segments borne perpendicular, or nearly so, to the rachis are a distinctive aspect of *Pecluma.* Most species are medium-sized epiphytes. The plants of this genus are among the few ferns capable of spreading from root proliferations. The rhizomes are short-creeping and unbranched, never glaucous (as is sometimes the case in the related genus *Polypodium*), and the scales are nonclathrate and attached across the width of the base. The black to reddish brown stipes are round in cross section (not grooved) and jointed to the rhizome. Unlike in many species of *Polypodium,* the narrowly elliptic blades of *Pecluma* are never scaly, although a few scales may be present on the rachis. The veins are free or netted, simple or forked, but in some species are difficult to see because of thick blades. The sori are round and appear in one row between the costae and margins, and like all polypodiaceous ferns, they lack indusia.

The genus was formerly classified under *Polypodium* and informally called the "*Polypodium pectinatum-plumula* complex." *Pecluma* can be distinguished from *Polypodium* by its short, unbranched rhizomes, nonclathrate and basally attached rhizome scales, and the distinctive comb-like cutting of the blades.

Pecluma consists of about 25 species native to the American tropics and subtropics. The genus name was formed by compounding the specific epithets of two common, widespread species: *Pecluma pectinata* and *P. plumula.* For a monographic treatment of this genus, see Evans (1969); also see *Polypodium* for a comparison of *Pecluma* with related genera.

Pecluma dispersa (A. M. Evans) M. G. Price

FIGURE 13.91.1

Tender, Zone 9; does poorly outdoors in Zone 9 of southern California

A medium-sized fern with short-creeping rhizomes. Prefers medium light and moist but well-drained potting mix. This species can survive in Zone 9 but will not do well outdoors in Zone 9 of southern California.

Pecluma dispersa is characterized by the combination of black rachises bearing conspicuous scales, blades essentially glabrous on the lower surfaces, and twice-forked veins. It is widespread in the American tropics.

Pecluma pectinata (Linnaeus) M. G. Price

FIGURE 13.91.2

Tender

A medium-sized fern with short- to medium-creeping rhizomes. Grows well under medium light in moist, drained potting mix. This species responds well to fertilization.

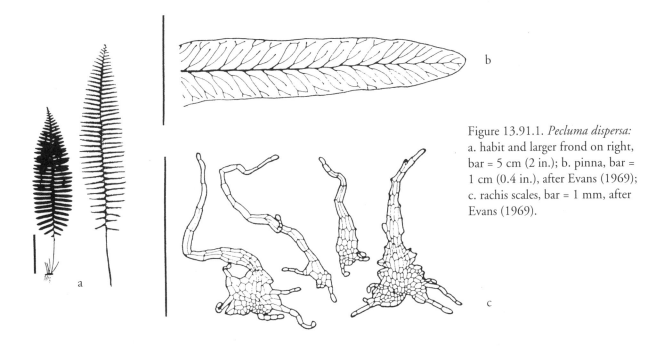

Figure 13.91.1. *Pecluma dispersa:* a. habit and larger frond on right, bar = 5 cm (2 in.); b. pinna, bar = 1 cm (0.4 in.), after Evans (1969); c. rachis scales, bar = 1 mm, after Evans (1969).

Pecluma pectinata is characterized by reddish brown, minutely hairy (but nonscaly) rachises, blades hairy on the lower surfaces with short-erect hairs, and twice-forked veins. The pinnae are greatly reduced toward the base of the blade but are not eared or pointing downward as in some species. *Pecluma pectinata* is widespread in the American tropics.

Pecluma plumula (Humboldt & Bonpland ex Willdenow) M. G. Price   FIGURE 13.91.3

Tender, Zone 9; does poorly outdoors in Zone 9 of southern California

A medium-sized fern with short- to medium-creeping rhizomes. Grows under medium light in moist, drained potting mix.

Pecluma plumula has black rachises beset with minute hairs and scales. The blades are glabrous on the lower sur-

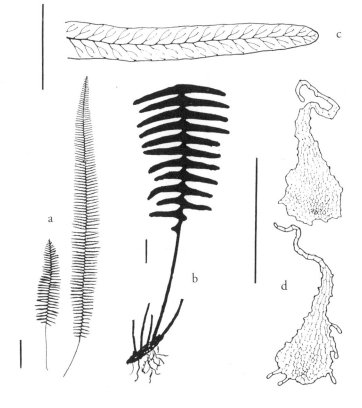

Figure 13.91.3. *Pecluma plumula:* a. fronds, bar = 5 cm (2 in.); b. rhizome and frond base, bar = 1 cm (0.4 in.); c. pinna, bar = 1 cm (0.4 in.), after Evans (1969); d. rachis scales, bar = 1 mm, after Evans (1969).

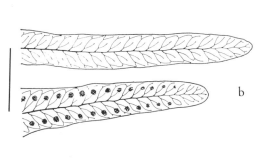

Figure 13.91.2. *Pecluma pectinata:* a. habit, bar = 5 cm (2 in.); b. pinnae, sterile (above) and fertile (below), bar = 1 cm (0.4 in.), after Evans (1969).

faces, and the pinnae at the base of the blades are reduced abruptly to small, downward-pointing lobes. The veins are once-forked. The species is widespread in the American tropics.

Pellaea

FIGURES 13.92.1, 2

syn. *Platyloma*
Cliff brake

The cliff brakes are small- to medium-sized ferns with mostly dark, polished stalks and gray-green, typically small but broad leaflets. *Pellaea* usually grows on rock crevices, ledges, and dry places, often in full sun. Semi-hardy species, such as the button fern (*Pellaea rotundifolia*) and the Australian cliff brake (*P. falcata*), are often sold as houseplants because they are adapted to the low humidity usually found indoors. Both species have narrow fronds and dark green foliage, and they are easy to grow outdoors in subtropical or warm-temperate climates. The taller, more divided green cliff brake (*P. viridis*) is also easy to grow but uncommon in the trade. All *Pellaea* species tolerate dryness and, to some extent, irregular watering. They are best grown in well-drained pockets of soil among rocks. Most of the native American species are propagated by spores because they do not transplant readily.

The genus *Pellaea* is characterized by short- to long-creeping rhizomes that bear bicolorous scales. The stipes are hard, often dark or blackish (some tan), and usually shiny. The blades vary from one- to three-pinnate, their apices bear a terminal leaflet (imparipinnate). The pinnules or segments are broad, stalked or sessile, naked or with only a few scattered hairs. Several to many sori are borne on the margins. They may be oblong or linearly joined. The sporangia are covered by false indusia (rarely absent) formed from the enrolled margins of the segments.

Pellaea can usually be identified by the combination of dark shiny stipes, pinnately divided blades ending in a terminal leaflet, and the false indusium. The genus, however,

Figure 13.92.2. *Pellaea viridis:* fertile pinnule.

is difficult to define because many of its characteristics are found in related genera. Pteridologists believe some species of *Pellaea* are not closely related and have accordingly transferred them to other genera. It is likely that the familiar trade species *Pellaea falcata* and *P. rotundifolia* will eventually be transferred to *Platyloma,* a genus characterized by slender, long-creeping rhizomes, jointed segments, false indusia differentiated from the margin, and spiny spores.

Pellaea is nearly cosmopolitan, but most of its 40 species occur in the southwestern United States and Mexico, with a secondary center of species richness in southern Africa. The genus name comes from the Greek *pellos,* dusky, and refers to the dull, bluish gray leaves of some species. See the section on "Xerophytic Ferns" in Chapter 10 for more information on cultivating cliff brakes.

Pellaea andromedifolia (Kaulfuss) Fée

FIGURE 13.92.3

Coffee fern
Semi-hardy, Zone (7)8; reportedly can endure
temperatures as low as −13°C (9°F)

A small to medium fern with slender, creeping rhizomes and loosely clustered fronds. Grows under high light in well-drained, moist-dry garden soil with coarse sand. The common name alludes to the mature leaflets, which bear a resemblance to coffee beans.

Figure 13.92.1. *Pellaea falcata:* habit.

Pellaea andromedifolia is characterized by bicolorous rhizome scales, tan stipes, up to three-pinnate blades, and oval, noncordate segments. The fiddleheads are densely scaly. This species is native to the United States (California and Oregon) and Mexico (Baja California).

Pellaea atropurpurea (Linnaeus) Link   FIGURE 13.92.4
Purple cliff brake
Very hardy, Zone 4

A small to medium fern with stout, ascending rhizomes and evergreen, clustered fronds. Prefers medium to high light and moist-dry, basic garden soil with coarse sand. This species can tolerate annual minimum temperatures of −28 to −35°C (−23 to −31°F).

Pellaea atropurpurea has rusty-tan and matted rhizome scales. The stipe and rachis vary from purplish to black and have a scruf consisting of minute, twisted hairs. The blade is bluish gray and two-pinnate, with the sterile segments oval to ovate-lanceolate. The fertile segments are longer and narrower than the sterile ones. This species occurs from Canada to Guatemala.

In the wild this species grows on calcareous rocks such as dolomite and limestone. It resembles *Pellaea glabella,* with which it often grows, but can be easily distinguished by the hairy stipe and stalked pinnae and pinnules.

Pellaea brachyptera (T. Moore) Baker   FIGURE 13.92.5
Sierra cliff brake
Hardy, Zone 7

A small fern with stout, ascending rhizomes and clustered evergreen fronds. Grows under medium light in drained, moist-dry garden soil with coarse sand. The plants are difficult to cultivate, but they have been recorded to endure temperatures as low as −14°C (7°F).

Pellaea brachyptera has bicolorous rhizome scales, and the stipes are dark brown and shiny. The blades are linear-oblong, two- to three-pinnate, and bluish green. The basal pinnae are one-pinnate, with the largest ones divided into 3–11 segments. The linear, tufted segments are crowded on a short costa. The segment margins are greenish and strongly enrolled, concealing nearly the entire lower surface of the pinnule. This species is native to the western United States (California, Washington, and Oregon).

Pellaea bridgesii Hooker   FIGURE 13.92.6
Bridges' cliff brake
Hardy, Zone (5)6

A small fern with stout, ascending rhizomes and clustered, deciduous fronds. Grows under high light in moist-dry, drained garden soil with coarse sand. This species is difficult to grow.

Figure 13.92.3. *Pellaea andromedifolia:* frond, bar = 5 cm (2 in.).

Figure 13.92.4. *Pellaea atropurpurea:* habit, bar = 5 cm (2 in.). After A. F. Tryon (1957).

Figure 13.92.5. *Pellaea brachyptera:* habit, bar = 5 cm (2 in.). After A. F. Tryon (1957).

Figure 13.92.6. *Pellaea bridgesii:* frond, bar = 5 cm (2 in.).

Some of the rhizome scales of *Pellaea bridgesii* are weakly bicolorous. The stipes and rachises are dark brown and shiny. The linear blades are one-pinnate throughout, with the pinnae round to ovate, entire, and leathery. The fertile pinnae are often folded lengthwise along the midvein. Sporangia are borne in a marginal band, but the margins remain flat, not enrolled as in many other species; *P. bridgesii* therefore lacks a false indusium. The species is native to the western United States.

Pellaea cordifolia (Sessé & Mociño) A. R. Smith

FIGURE 13.92.7

syn. *Pellaea cordata* (Cavanilles) J. Smith, *P. sagittata* var. *cordata* (Cavanilles) A. F. Tryon

Semi-hardy, Zone 8

A medium-sized fern with short-creeping rhizomes and lax, scrambling, bluish gray-green fronds. Grows well under high light in drained, moist-dry garden soil with coarse sand. The longer fronds tend to become tangled and will need support if grown upright.

Pellaea cordifolia is one of the few species in the genus that has tan stipes and rachises. The blades are ovate-triangular and up to three-pinnate, with rachises and costae straight, not zigzag. The segments vary from round-cordate to triangular-cordate, and the segment stalks are glabrous. Hairs occasionally occur on the enrolled margin of indusium. This species is native to the southern United States (Texas) and Mexico.

Pellaea falcata (R. Brown) Fée   FIGURES 13.92.1, 8

syn. *Platyloma falcata* (R. Brown) J. Smith

Australian cliff brake

Semi-hardy, Zone (7)8

A small-medium fern with dark green fronds in loose clusters from short- to medium-creeping rhizomes. Grows well under medium to high light in drained, moist-dry garden or potting mix. This species can withstand temperatures down to −7°C (19°F) for one week.

The stipes and rachises of *Pellaea falcata* bear spreading scales, and the blades are one-pinnate. The pinnae, which

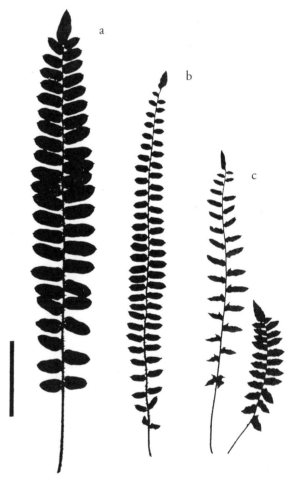

Figure 13.92.7. *Pellaea cordifolia:* a. frond, older, bar = 5 cm (2 in.); b. frond, younger; bar = 5 cm (2 in.). After A. F. Tryon (1957).

Figure 13.92.8. *Pellaea falcata* fronds: a. typical form; b. var. *nana;* c. 'Star Glow', older (left) and younger (right). Bar = 5 cm (2 in.).

are jointed to the rachis, are oblong and leathery, tapering to an obtuse or acute apex that is sometimes mucronate. The indusia are thin and narrow. This species is native to India, Australia, New Zealand, Norfolk Island, and New Caledonia.

Some plants in cultivation are intermediate with *Pellaea rotundifolia;* these have also been reported from New Zealand.

var. *nana* Hooker. Figure 13.92.8b. This variety resembles the type but is smaller and more compact, with pinnae close or overlapping. The pinnae are also smaller, about 5–20 mm long and 2–6 mm wide. It is endemic to Australia. Some botanists treat this variety as a species, *Pellaea nana* (Hooker) Bostock.

'Star Glow'. Figure 13.92.8c. Fronds dark green, shiny; pinnae margins subdentate, slightly enrolled, the larger pinnae sharply eared at the base on the upper margin. It differs from var. *nana,* from which it was apparently derived, by having emarginate pinnae. This cultivar is often misidentified as *Pellaea paradoxa* (R. Brown) Hooker, a species not in cultivation.

Pellaea glabella Mettenius ex Kuhn   FIGURE 13.92.9
Smooth cliff brake
Very hardy, Zone 3

A small fern with stout, ascending rhizomes and clustered evergreen fronds. Grows under medium light in well-drained, basic, moist-dry garden soil with coarse sand.

Pellaea glabella has rusty-brown rhizome scales that are spreading, not matted. The stipes are brown, shiny, smooth, and brittle. The bluish green blades vary from linear to ovate-lanceolate and one- to two-pinnate. The basal pinnae are deeply divided into three to seven oblong to linear-ovate lobes or pinnules. The species is native to eastern North America, where it typically grows on limestone.

Pellaea mucronata (D. C. Eaton) D. C. Eaton
FIGURE 13.92.10
Bird's-foot fern
Hardy, Zone 7

A small fern with stout, ascending rhizomes and evergreen, clustered fronds. Grows well under high light or full sun in coastal areas in well-drained garden soil with coarse sand. This species is difficult to grow. The common name bird's-foot fern alludes to the segment clusters, which resemble a bird's foot.

Pellaea mucronata has bicolorous rhizome scales, and the stipes are dark brown and shiny. The ovate-triangular to lanceolate blades are up to three-pinnate toward the base, with costae much longer than the ultimate segments. The larger pinnae have more than 10 segments. The indusia margins are uneven or erose. This species is native to the western United States and Mexico.

Figure 13.92.9. *Pellaea glabella:* habit, bar = 5 cm (2 in.). After A. F. Tryon (1957).

Figure 13.92.10. *Pellaea mucronata:* habit, bar = 5 cm (2 in.). After A. F. Tryon. (1957).

Pellaea ovata (Desvaux) Weatherby   FIGURE 13.92.11
Flexuous cliff brake
Semi-hardy, Zone 8

A medium-sized fern with short-creeping rhizomes and lax fronds. Grows well under medium-high light in moist-dry, drained garden soil with coarse sand. The longer fronds tend to become tangled and need support.

Pellaea ovata can be distinguished from all others in the genus by its tan, zigzag stipes and rachises. Other characteristics are bicolorous rhizome scales and elongate-triangular blades to 84 cm (34 in.) long and 30 cm (12 in.) broad, mostly three-pinnate and gray-green. The segments vary from elliptic to ovate and are sagittate to cordate at the base. The segment stalks bear short, reddish hairs. The enrolled indusium margin is glabrous. This species is native to the United States (Texas), Central and South America, and the West Indies.

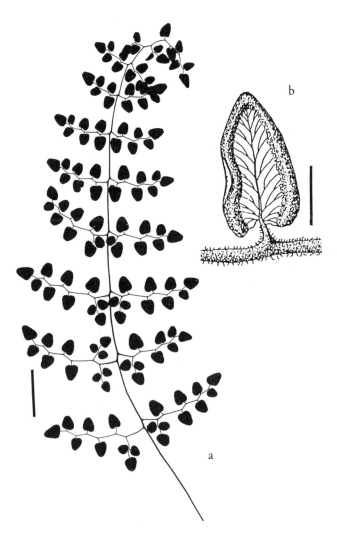

Figure 13.92.11. *Pellaea ovata:* a. frond, bar = 5 cm (2 in.); b. fertile pinnule, bar = 1 cm (0.4 in.), after Vareschi (1968).

Pellaea rotundifolia (G. Forster) Hooker

FIGURE 13.92.12

syn. *Platyloma rotundifolia* (G. Forster) J. Smith
Button fern, New Zealand cliff brake
Semi-hardy, Zone 8; can tolerate temperatures as low as
−7°C (19°F) for one week

A small-medium fern with short-medium-creeping rhizomes and fronds in a loose cluster. Grows well under medium to high light in moist-dry, well-drained garden soil with coarse sand. The plants are easy to grow and thrive indoors. Do not water until the soil is nearly dry.

Pellaea rotundifolia resembles *P. falcata* (which see) but has smaller and narrower fronds. The round to oval pinnae are up to 2 cm (0.75 in.) long and 1.3 cm (0.5 in.) wide, with margins minutely but shallowly toothed and apices rounded but abruptly narrowed to a sharp point. The species is endemic to New Zealand.

Pellaea ternifolia (Cavanilles) Link   FIGURE 13.92.13
Semi-hardy, Zone 8

A small to medium fern with ascending, stout rhizomes and clustered fronds. Grows under high light in well-drained, moist-dry garden soil or potting mix.

Pellaea ternifolia has particularly distinctive pinnae, which are three-parted and sessile or nearly so. These characteristics easily separate this species from others in the genus. Additional traits include bicolorous rhizome scales; black or dark purple, shiny stipes and rachises; and linear, one-pinnate-pinnatifid blades. The pinnae are entire or deeply three-lobed with mucronate apices. The species is native to the United States (Texas), Central and South America, and the Hawaiian Islands.

Pellaea viridis (Forsskål) Prantl   FIGURES 13.92.2, 14
syn. *Cheilanthes viridis* (Forsskål) Swartz, *Pellaea hastata*
    (Thunberg) Prantl
Green cliff brake
Semi-hardy

A medium-sized fern with short-creeping rhizomes and clustered fronds. Grows well under high light in well-drained, moist-dry garden soil or potting mix.

Pellaea viridis has bicolorous rhizome scales and shiny

Figure 13.92.12. *Pellaea rotundifolia:* frond, bar = 5 cm (2 in.).

Figure 13.92.13. *Pellaea ternifolia:* habit, bar = 5 cm (2 in.). After A. F. Tryon (1957).

Figure 13.92.14. *Pellaea viridis:* frond, bar = 5 cm (2 in.).

Figure 13.92.15. *Pellaea wrightiana:* habit, bar = 5 cm (2 in.).

dark brown to black stipes and rachises grooved on upper surface. The blades are lanceolate to triangular, commonly two- to three-pinnate, and have basal pinnae that are more developed on the lower side. The segments vary from cordate to hastate to wedge-shaped but are most commonly lanceolate to ovate. The veins are free (not netted) and easily visible. The false indusium is thin and subentire. This species is native from Africa to India.

Pellaea viridis is extremely variable in blade cutting. Most cultivated plants are typical *P. viridis,* but a few are intermediate with var. *macrophylla* (Kunze) Sim (*P. adiantoides* J. Smith), which is one-pinnate, or sometimes two-pinnate at the base, with large pinnae. Some botanists consider this species best placed in *Cheilanthes.*

Pellaea wrightiana Hooker   FIGURE 13.92.15
syn. *Pellaea ternifolia* var. *wrightiana* (Hooker) A. F. Tryon
Hardy, Zone 6

A small to medium fern with ascending, stout rhizomes and clustered grayish fronds. Grows well under high light in well-drained, moist-dry garden soil or potting mix.

Pellaea wrightiana resembles *P. ternifolia,* but it has more narrowly triangular blades, longer and more divided pinnae lobed or divided into 3–11 pinnules, and fully two-pinnate basal pinnae. It differs from *P. brachyptera* by having longer costae and whitish bordered segments. *Pellaea*

wrightiana is native to the southwestern United States and Mexico.

Pentagramma
Goldback fern, silverback fern

The genus *Pentagramma* consists of small ferns of dry habitats. They are distinguished by powdery yellow or white undersides and pentagonal fronds. Mature plants grow best in pots or rock gardens but are sensitive to overwatering and must be transplanted with care. If landscape effect is of prime importance, a similar growth form can be obtained by planting *Cheilanthes argentea,* which is much easier to grow. All species of *Pentagramma* germinate easily from spore.

The ascending rhizomes of *Pentagramma* are covered with sharply bicolorous scales. The stipes are dark brown to black and round or nearly so in cross section; they contain only one vascular bundle. The blades are triangular-pentagonal and one- to two-pinnate-pinnatifid, and the pinnae are sessile or adnate, usually with white or yellow powdery undersides. Sporangia are borne along the free, dichotomously branched veins. An indusium is absent. The two species of *Pentagramma* were formerly included in the genus *Pityrogramma* because of their powdery lower blade surfaces and sori that run along the veins. Pteridologists currently consider these genera distantly related within the Pteridaceae and best placed in different subgroups of the family.

Pentagramma contains two species and is native to the southwestern United States and northwestern Mexico. The genus name comes from the Greek *penta*, five, and *gramme*, line, alluding to the pentagonal outline of the blade.

Pentagramma triangularis (Kaulfuss) Yatskievych, Windham & E. Wollenweber   FIGURE 13.93.1
Semi-hardy, Zone 7

A small fern with short-creeping rhizomes. Grows under medium-high light in dry, well-drained garden soil. This species is difficult to cultivate, and the plants are sensitive to overwatering.

The stipes of *Pentagramma triangularis* are shiny and generally not powdery. The blades are white- or yellow-powdery below, appearing bright green or sometimes yellowish green when fresh. The species is extremely variable and four subspecies have been described to accommodate the variation. It is native to western North America and northwestern Mexico. In nature the plants occurs in rock crevices, at the base of overhanging boulders, and on roadbanks.

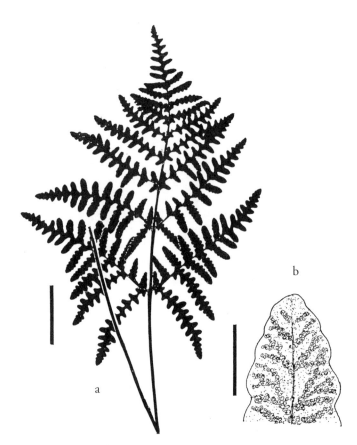

Figure 13.93.1. *Pentagramma triangularis*: a. frond, bar = 2.5 cm (1 in.); b. sporangia along veins, bar = 3 mm (0.1 in.).

Pentagramma pallida (Weatherby) Yatskievych, Windham & E. Wollenweber differs by having dull and powdery stipes and blades that are white-powdery on both surfaces, appearing grayish when fresh. It is endemic to the foothills of the Sierra Nevada in California and may be cultivated by local hobbyists. Its cultural requirements are the same as for *P. triangularis*.

Phegopteris
syn. *Thelypteris* subgenus *Phegopteris*
Beech fern

These medium-sized, terrestrial ferns have creeping rhizomes. *Phegopteris* was previously considered a subgenus of *Thelypteris* but can be distinguished from that genus by pinnae that are broadly adnate in the distal half of the blade and connected by wings along the rachis. Like all thelypteriod ferns, *Phegopteris* has only two vascular bundles in the stipe (most other similar fern groups have four or more) and needle-shaped hairs. Indusia are absent. The species with broadly triangular blades might be confused with *Gymnocarpium*, but that genus lacks the needle-like hairs.

Phegopteris contains three species, all of which are cultivated, native to the temperate regions of North America, Europe, and Asia. The genus name comes from the Greek *phegos*, beech, and *pteris*, fern, since *Phegopteris* commonly grows under beech trees.

Phegopteris connectilis (Michaux) Watt
FIGURE 13.94.1
syn. *Thelypteris phegopteris* (Linnaeus) Slosson
Narrow beech fern, long beech fern
Very hardy, Zone 2

A medium-sized fern with medium-creeping rhizomes and deciduous fronds. Grows well under low light or full shade in moist, acidic garden soil or potting mix.

Phegopteris connectilis has slender, creeping rhizomes and triangular blades. The basal pair of pinnae are sessile or adnate to the rachis but not connected to those above by a wing. The rachises and costae bear conspicuous brown scales, and the veins in the segments of middle pinnae are mostly simple. This species is native to the northern regions of North America, Europe, and Asia.

Phegopteris decursive-pinnata (H. C. van Hall) Fée
FIGURE 13.94.2
syn. *Thelypteris decursive-pinnata* (H. C. van Hall) Ching
Winged beech fern
Very hardy, Zone 4

A medium-sized fern with suberect rhizomes and erect, deciduous fronds. Grows well under medium light in moist-wet garden soil or potting mix. This species is easy to grow from spores and generally does well in gardens in the eastern United States. Several new plantlets are produced each

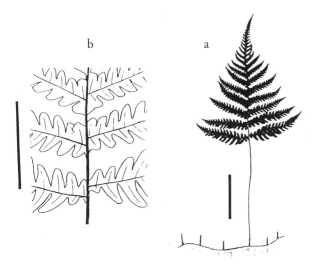

Figure 13.94.1. *Phegopteris connectilis:* a. habit, bar = 5 cm (2 in.); b. incompletely winged rachis, bar = 2.5 cm (1 in.).

year from short runners. The green of the fronds lasts until the first hard frost.

The rhizomes of *Phegopteris decursive-pinnata* are erect or suberect, and the blades are narrowly elliptic and tapered toward both ends, rather than broadly triangular as in the other two species. The pinnae are hairy on both surfaces, and their bases are connected to the rachis by a broadly lobed wing, but the lower pinnae are often free. The rachis is also hairy and bears ciliate scales. The species is native to eastern Asia.

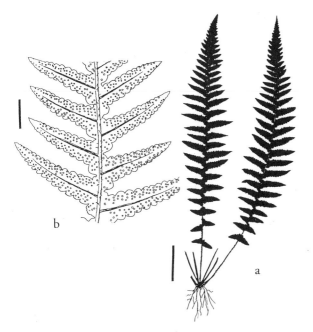

Figure 13.94.2. *Phegopteris decursive-pinnata:* a. habit, bar = 5 cm (2 in.); b. winged rachis, bar = 1 cm (0.4 in.).

Phegopteris hexagonoptera (Michaux) Fée

FIGURE 13.94.3

syn. *Thelypteris hexagonoptera* (Michaux) Nieuwland
Southern beech fern, broad beech fern
Very hardy, Zone 3

A medium-sized fern with medium-creeping rhizomes and deciduous fronds. Grows well under low light or full shade in moist, slightly acidic garden soil or potting mix. It grows readily from spores.

Phegopteris hexagonoptera has slender, creeping rhizomes and broadly triangular blades. The rachises and costae are hairy and bear a few inconspicuous, narrow scales. A wing along the rachis connects the basal pinnae to those above. The veins are always forked or pinnate. This species is native to eastern North America.

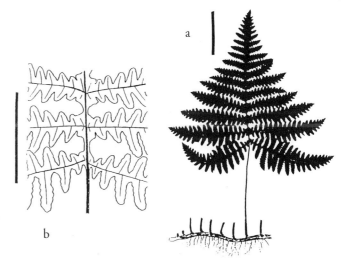

Figure 13.94.3. *Phegopteris hexagonoptera:* a. habit, bar = 5 cm (2 in.); b. winged rachis, bar = 2.5 cm (1 in.).

Phlebodium

syn. *Polypodium* in part
Rabbit's-foot fern, golden polypody

Phlebodium aureum is well known in the trade as a pot or basket plant, though it can also be grown in soil with good drainage. Its fronds and those of *P. pseudoaureum* vary considerably, from gray-green to blue-green shades, from stiff and erect to arching or pendant, from medium to large in size, from entire to fringed lobes, from sparsely to heavily crested tips, and so on. These characteristics are affected by the amount of nutrients and exposure to light. *Phlebodium aureum* is less cold hardy and needs more protection than *P. pseudoaureum,* which is also a robust grower. For more details on *Phlebodium* cultivars, see Hoshizaki (1982).

Phlebodium is closely related to *Polypodium,* and some pteridologists prefer to classify it in that genus. Like *Polypodium,* it has creeping rhizomes with two ranks of fronds on the upper surface, round, non-indusiate sori, and yellow bean-shaped spores. But *Phlebodium* differs by its venation: the areoles contain two veinlets that supply the sorus, and the areoles next to the costae are long, narrow, and lack included veinlets. The frond shape also differs from that of many polypodiums, being large and broadly cut with wide, adnate segments and a terminal segment that resembles the lateral ones. See *Polypodium* for a comparison with other polypodiaceous genera.

Phlebodium contains four species native to tropical America. The genus name comes from the Greek *phlebodes*, full of veins, in reference to the highly branched veins.

Phlebodium aureum (Linnaeus) J. Smith

FIGURE 13.95.1

syn. *Polypodium aureum* var. *aureum*
Hare's-foot fern, rabbit's-foot fern, bear's-paw fern, serpent fern, golden polypody
Tender to semi-tender, Zone 9(10)

A medium to large fern with moderately long-creeping rhizomes. Grows well under medium light in moist to moist-dry garden soil or potting mix kept well drained. This species is easy to cultivate and has more gracefully arching fronds than *Phlebodium pseudoaureum*, which it resembles, although it is less cold hardy.

Phlebodium aureum resembles *P. pseudoaureum* but differs by having the sori arranged in two rows between the costa and margin. The fronds are deeply lobed into narrow segments. *Phlebodium aureum* is believed to be a fertile hybrid of a cross involving *P. decumanum* and *P. pseudoaureum*. It is native to tropical America.

Some cultivated plants may be hybrids between *Phlebodium aureum* and *P. pseudoaureum*, as evidenced by their irregular venation and irregular rows of sori (inconsistently ranging from 1 to 2 rows). See Figure 13.95.1c.

'Cristatum'. Frond tips several times branched, tips of pinnae less so.

'Ekstrand'. Pinnae irregularly lobed, the lobes crowded, twisted, and irregularly and coarsely cut into teeth; blades strongly ruffled.

'Mandaianum'. Figure 13.95.1. Pinnae coarsely and irregularly incised to laciniate, weakly ruffled.

'Mayi'. Blades ruffled and fringed.

'Undulatum'. Blades wavy.

Phlebodium decumanum (Willdenow) J. Smith

FIGURE 13.95.2

syn. *Polypodium decumanum* Willdenow
Tender, Zone 10

A large fern with moderately long-creeping rhizomes. Grows well under medium light in moist, well-drained potting mix. This species is easy to cultivate and volunteers readily from spores. The orange rhizome scales are highly attractive.

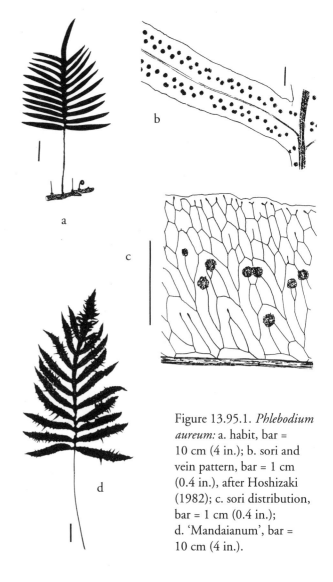

Figure 13.95.1. *Phlebodium aureum:* a. habit, bar = 10 cm (4 in.); b. sori and vein pattern, bar = 1 cm (0.4 in.), after Hoshizaki (1982); c. sori distribution, bar = 1 cm (0.4 in.); d. 'Mandaianum', bar = 10 cm (4 in.).

Phlebodium decumanum can be distinguished from the other cultivated species by its sori, which are arranged in three to seven rows (not one or two) between the segment midrib and margins. The fronds are generally larger, often over 1 m (3 ft.) long. The species is widespread in tropical America.

Phlebodium pseudoaureum (Cavanilles) Lellinger

FIGURE 13.95.3; PLATES 5, 38

syn. *Phlebodium areolatum* (Humboldt & Bonpland ex Willdenow) J. Smith, *Polypodium areolatum* Humboldt & Bonpland ex Willdenow
Tender to semi-tender, Zone (8)9

A medium to large fern with moderately long-creeping rhizomes. Grows well under low to high light in well-drained, moist to moist-dry garden soil or potting mix. The plants are easy to cultivate and robust growers. The fronds are typically firmer and stiffer than those of *Phlebodium aureum*.

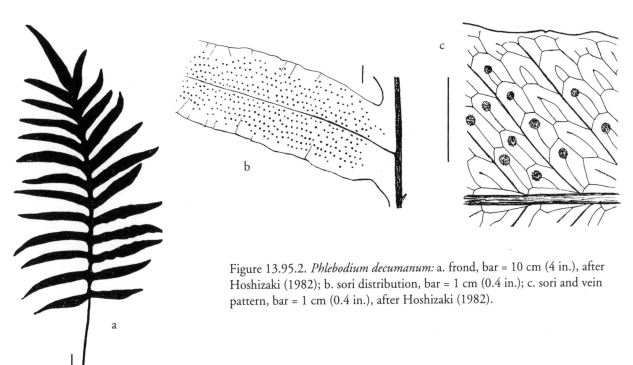

Figure 13.95.2. *Phlebodium decumanum:* a. frond, bar = 10 cm (4 in.), after Hoshizaki (1982); b. sori distribution, bar = 1 cm (0.4 in.); c. sori and vein pattern, bar = 1 cm (0.4 in.), after Hoshizaki (1982).

The sori of *Phlebodium pseudoaureum* are arranged in one row between the costa and margins, but a few may be scattered in a second row. The species is widespread in tropical America.

Within *Phlebodium pseudoaureum,* the blue-green (glaucous) plants vary considerably and circulate in the trade under a variety of loosely applied cultivar names under *P. glaucum* and *P. glaucopruniatum.* Some of the blue-green cultivars include the following:

'Mexican Tasseled'. Segment apices densely tasseled.

'Leatherman'. Pinnae falcate, attenuate; fronds lax.

Phlebodium ×schneideri Horticulture

FIGURE 13.95.4

Schneider's rabbit-foot fern
Semi-tender (?)

A medium to large fern with moderately long-creeping rhizomes. Grows under medium light in well-drained, moist to moist-dry potting soil or uncut moss. The plants are notable for their cascading fronds. Avoid watering the ruffled foliage because the extra weight might snap the stipe.

Phlebodium ×schneideri is reported to be a sterile hybrid of horticultural origin resulting from a cross between *Phlebodium aureum* (?) and *Polypodium vulgare* 'Elegantissimum', but it resembles other cultivars of *Phlebodium aureum* and *P. pseudoaureum,* only with more divided blades. The pinnae are deeply lobed (almost fully divided), and the lobes are in turn shallowly lobed and strongly ruffled.

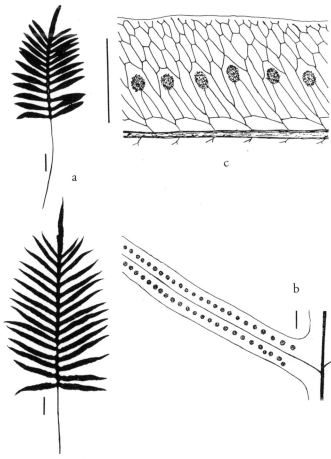

Figure 13.95.3. *Phlebodium pseudoaureum:* a. frond variations, bar = 10 cm (4 in.); b. sori distribution, bar = 1 cm (0.4 in.); c. sori and vein pattern, bar = 1 cm (0.4 in.), after Hoshizaki (1982).

Figure 13.95.4. *Phlebodium ×schneideri:* frond, bar = 10 cm (4 in.).

Figure 13.96.1. *Phyllitis scolopendrium:* habit.

Phyllitis

Hart's-tongue fern

The hart's-tongue ferns are small, terrestrial, evergreen plants with tongue-shaped fronds. The fiddleheads of *Phyllitis* were used as the model for the scrolls at the ends of violins. There is wide variation in spore-grown plants, and many garden forms are seen in cultivation. *Phyllitis* may also be propagated from basal pieces of the stipe, a process described in Chapter 8. The genus is susceptible to root-rot, so avoid overwatering and provide good drainage. For details about cultivars, see Druery (1912), Kaye (1968), and Dyce (1972).

The distinguishing characteristics of the genus are its simple, entire blades and paired sori in which each sorus in the pair opens toward its partner. Additional traits include the heart-shaped blade bases, leathery texture, once- or twice-forked veins, and linear indusiate sori. *Phyllitis* is closely related to *Asplenium* and hybridizes with it. Some pteridologists prefer to classify *Phyllitis* under *Asplenium;* it is only a matter of opinion whether to do so. *Phyllitis* is used here because of its long use by horticulturists.

The genus contains five species and is native to North America, Europe, and Asia. The name comes from the Greek *phyllos,* meaning leaf, which was an ancient Greek name for the fern.

Phyllitis scolopendrium (Linnaeus) Newman
FIGURES 13.96.1–4; PLATE 39

syn. *Asplenium scolopendrium* Linnaeus
Hart's-tongue fern
Hardy, Zone 4(5)

A small-medium fern with suberect rhizomes and evergreen fronds. Grows well under low light in well-drained, basic, moist-dry potting mix. The plants are sensitive to poor drainage and root-rot.

Figure 13.96.2. *Phyllitis scolopendrium:* fronds.

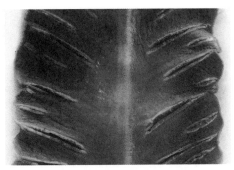

Figure 13.96.3. *Phyllitis scolopendrium:* sori and indusia.

Phyllitis scolopendrium has tongue-shaped fronds with cordate bases. The stipes are short and scaly. The species is native to North America and Europe.

Only the European variety (var. *scolopendrium*) is cultivated. The smaller, American variety (var. *americana* Fernald) is rare and difficult to grow. It tends to bear sori in the distal half of the frond but is otherwise similar to the European variety.

The hart's-tongue fern is extremely variable. In the late 1800s, one British fern grower listed 445 varieties (Lowe 1890). For representative examples of the numerous cultivars, see Figure 13.96.4 and those listed here:

'Crispum'. Blade margins frilly.
'Cristatum'. Frond apices crested.
'Laceratum'. Blade margins deeply and irregularly cut.
'Muricatum'. Blade surfaces roughened by ridges.
'Ramosum'. Fronds branched.
'Undulatum'. Blade margins wavy.

Pilularia
Pillwort

The pillworts are small, inconspicuous, sedge-like or grass-like plants. They can be distinguished from grasses and sedges by the coiled tips of their young leaves. *Pilularia* is related to the water clover (*Marsilea*) but lacks the distinctive clover-like leaves. Of little ornamental value, this genus is best used as part of a small, aquatic dish-garden or in bog or marsh plantings.

The rhizome is slender and creeping, bearing a filamentous stipe at each node. The fertile part, which is not always present, is a stalked, bean-like structure (sporocarp) borne at the base of the stipe. The sporocarp encloses the sporangia, which contain either male or female spores.

Pilularia is cosmopolitan and consists of five species. The genus name comes from the Greek *pilula*, little ball, and refers to the globose sporocarps.

Pilularia americana A. Braun   FIGURE 13.97.1
Hardy, Zone 5

A small fern with medium-creeping rhizomes. Grows well under high light in sandy or silty garden soil kept wet. The plants can also grow submerged or partly submerged. Do not let them dry completely.

Pilularia americana resembles *P. globulifera* by its small, grass-like leaves but differs by having sporocarps borne

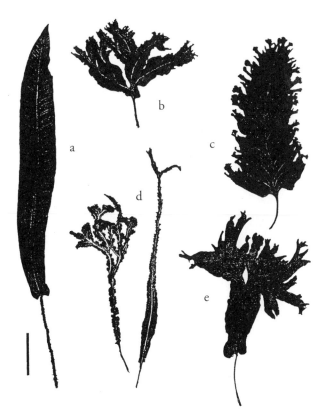

Figure 13.96.4. *Phyllitis scolopendrium* fronds: a. wild form; b. 'Ramo-cristatum'; c. 'Kaye's Lacerate'; d. 'Marginato-multifidum'; e. 'Capitatum'. Bar = 5 cm (2 in.).

Figure 13.97.1. *Pilularia americana:* habit, bar = 1 cm (0.4 in.).

below, rather than above, the soil. It is native to the United States and Mexico.

Pilularia globulifera Linnaeus   FIGURE 13.97.2
Hardy, Zone 5

A small fern with medium-creeping rhizomes. Grows well under high light in sandy or silty garden soil kept wet. The plants can also grow submerged or partly submerged. Do not let them dry completely. This species is a rapid and robust grower in moist to wet soil.

Pilularia globulifera resembles the preceding species, but its sporocarps are borne above the soil. Submerged plants do not form sporocarps. Native to Europe.

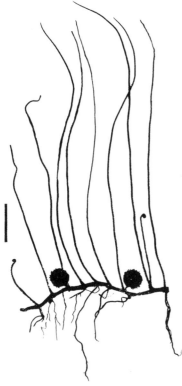

Figure 13.97.2. *Pilularia globulifera:* habit, bar = 1 cm (0.4 in.).

Pityrogramma   FIGURES 13.98.1, 2
syn. *Trismeria*
Goldback fern, silverback fern

The genus *Pityrogramma* is noted for its powdery yellow or white lower blade surfaces. These small- to medium-sized terrestrial ferns grow quickly; some species are short-lived. On older plants, the roots often fail to support the ascending rhizome and fronds. Support can be provided by adding mulch and rocks around the base of the plant and removing some of the older fronds. The roots are sensitive to disturbance, and so these ferns should be transplanted with care. Many species of *Pityrogramma* are easy to grow from spores and may become weedy in the greenhouse or spore pans. Avoid overwatering and check that the soil is well drained.

Figure 13.98.1. *Pityrogramma argentea:* habit.

Pityrogramma has short-creeping to erect rhizomes covered with scales of one color or with a poorly defined darker central portion. The stipes are dark and shiny, often stiff, grooved on the upper surface, and have two or more vascular bundles. The blades vary from linear-lanceolate to triangular, and their lower surfaces usually have a white, yellow, or orangish powder (farina). The lower pinnae are stalked, and the veins are free, not netted. The sori run along the veins, forming dark lines that sometimes become confluent as the sporangia mature. An indusium is absent.

The genus presents several taxonomic and nomenclatural problems that might confuse gardeners. The species

Figure 13.98.2. *Pityrogramma argentea:* underside of pinnule, showing powder and sporangia (dark spots) along vein.

vary morphologically and hybridize readily, which complicates identification. Many previously accepted species have been reduced to varietal rank, and most pteridologists now merge *Trismeria* with *Pityrogramma*. *Pityrogramma triangularis*, often called the goldback fern (as are other species of *Pityrogramma*), has long been placed in this genus but is now classified in *Pentagramma* (which see). For taxonomic details on the species of *Pityrogramma*, see Tryon (1962).

Pityrogramma, which contains 16 species, is native to tropical and subtropical America, Africa, and Madagascar. One species, *Pityrogramma calomelanos*, has become naturalized in many parts of the Old World tropics. The genus name comes from the Greek *pityron*, scurf, and *gramme*, line, referring to the powdery lower blade surface, which has sporangia in lines along the veins.

Pityrogramma argentea (Willdenow) Domin

FIGURES 13.98.1–3

Semi-tender

A small to medium fern with suberect rhizomes. Grows under high light in moist-dry, drained garden soil or potting mix.

Pityrogramma argentea is characterized by silver or gold lower blade surfaces and somewhat wedge-shaped ultimate segments that lack a well-defined midrib. The basal pinnae are the largest. It is native to Africa and Madagascar.

Pityrogramma austroamericana Domin

FIGURE 13.98.4; PLATES 40, 41

syn. *Pityrogramma calomelanos* var. *aureoflava* of authors, not (Hooker) Weatherby ex L. H. Bailey, *P. calomelanos* var. *austroamericana* (Domin) Farwell

Semi-tender, Zone 9

A medium-sized fern with suberect rhizomes. Grows well under high-medium to high light in moist-dry garden soil or potting mix kept well drained. The plants volunteer readily from spores.

Pityrogramma austroamericana differs from *P. calomelanos* by its bright yellow blade undersides and firmer texture in live plants. It is native to the New World tropics and naturalized in the Hawaiian Islands.

For many years this fern was misidentified as *Pityrogramma hybrida* Domin, a hybrid that is not cultivated.

Pityrogramma calomelanos (Linnaeus) Link

FIGURE 13.98.5

Silver fern

Tender, Zone 10

A medium-sized fern with suberect rhizomes. Grows well under high light in drained, moist-dry garden soil or potting mix. It prefers some air circulation.

Pityrogramma calomelanos has scales on the rhizome and stipe tipped with a long conical cell. The stipe is often as long as the blade, which is two-pinnate-pinnatifid to three-

Figure 13.98.3. *Pityrogramma argentea*: frond, bar = 5 cm (2 in.).

Figure 13.98.4. *Pityrogramma austroamericana*: frond, bar = 5 cm (2 in.).

pinnate, white on the underside, and has ascending distal pinnae and segments. This species resembles *P. ebenea*. It is common and widespread in the American tropics and has become naturalized in many parts of the Old World tropics.

Pityrogramma ebenea (Linnaeus) Proctor

FIGURE 13.98.6

syn. *Pityrogramma tartarea* (Cavanilles) Maxon

Tender

A medium-sized fern with suberect rhizomes. Grows well under high light in moist-dry, well-drained garden soil or potting mix.

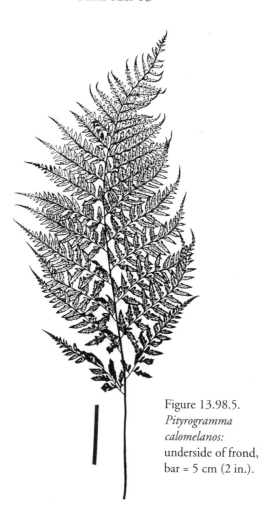

Figure 13.98.5. *Pityrogramma calomelanos:* underside of frond, bar = 5 cm (2 in.).

Figure 13.98.6. *Pityrogramma ebenea:* a. frond, bar = 5 cm (2 in.); b. underside of pinnule, bar = 2.5 cm (1 in.).

The scales of the rhizomes and stipes are tipped with several single cells ending in a short, round cell. The pinnules of *Pityrogramma ebenea* are white to cream or colorless on the lower surface and broadest at the base. They are inserted at right angles to the pinna rachis. This species is common and widespread in the American tropics.

Pityrogramma ebenea resembles *P. calomelanos* but differs by having wider basal pinnae on the lower side and the distal pinnae perpendicular to the rachis. In contrast, the basal pinnae of *P. calomelanos* are equally wide on both sides, and the distal pinnae are ascending. An elevational difference between the two species occurs in the wild: *P. ebenea* grows above 1000 m (3300 ft.), whereas *P. calomelanos* generally grows below that elevation.

Pityrogramma trifoliata (Linnaeus) R. M. Tryon

FIGURE 13.98.7

syn. *Trismeria trifoliata* (Linnaeus) Diels

Tender; survives Zone (9)10 with warm nights

A large fern with suberect rhizomes. Grows well under high light in moist-wet garden soil or potting mix.

Pityrogramma trifoliata has bicolorous rhizome scales, and the fronds are large, erect, coarse, linear or narrowly

Figure 13.98.7. *Pityrogramma trifoliata:* frond, bar = 5 cm (2 in.).

lanceolate, and usually white on the lower surfaces. The pinnae are usually two- to three-parted (rarely up to seven-parted) and spread in three dimensions around the rachis, thus the blade is not flat. This species is native to southern Florida and tropical and subtropical America.

This species differs from all others in the genus by having pinnae deeply parted into two or three (or more) segments. (The pinnae are not always three-parted as the specific epithet suggests.) Because of this difference, *Pityrogramma trifoliata* is sometimes classified in the genus *Trismeria*. Nowadays, however, pteridologists classify it with *Pityrogramma*, partly because it readily hybridizes with several species in the genus. The hybrids are usually common where the species grow together, such as along roadsides.

Platycerium   FIGURES 13.99.1–3
Staghorn fern, elkhorn fern

Staghorn ferns are bizarre-looking, medium- to large-sized epiphytes grown primarily on walls, tree trunks, baskets, and pots. The base of the plant is composed of highly modified, thick, spongy fronds that provide anchorage and rooting media for the fertile foliage fronds. Australian species, such as *Platycerium bifurcatum* and its relatives, are easy to grow outdoors in subtropical climates. In many parts of the United States they can be grown outdoors until the first frost. Indoors, they should be kept in a well-lighted, airy place but out of direct sun. The thick foliage fronds of *Platycerium* tolerate the lower humidity indoors. Some species form new plants (pups) from root buds, which can be separated from the parent plant when they produce base fronds about 13 cm (5 in.) wide. For more information, see "Staghorn Ferns" in Chapter 10.

Platycerium can be identified by the star-shaped hairs on its blades and the striking frond dimorphism, with the layers of sessile brown fronds appressed to the substrate and larger, green leafy fronds that are upright, arching, or pendulous. The latter type of frond bears sori; the former does not. Other characteristics of the genus are scaly, very short-creeping, stout rhizomes that are concealed by the base fronds, except at the tip. The thick and spongy base fronds are green at first but soon turn brown and persist on the plant. The edges are thinner, and in some species the upper margin is extended and foliaceous, lobed or not. The foliage fronds vary from simple and entire to dichotomously lobed or forked into strap-shaped segments. The sporangia are formed in large patches on the lower surface and are covered with star-shaped hairs. Indusia are absent.

The genus contains 15 to 18 species and occurs entirely in the Old World tropics, except for a single South American species, *Platycerium andinum*. The genus name comes from the Greek *platys,* flat, and *keras,* horn, referring to the flattened, antler-like leaves.

A large number of loosely named platyceriums have appeared in the trade in recent years. If you come across a

Figure 13.99.1. *Platycerium willinckii:* habit.

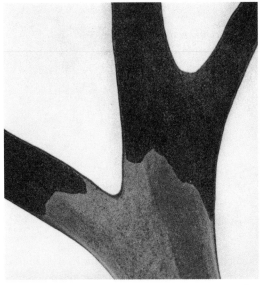

Figure 13.99.2. *Platycerium willinckii:* sporangial area.

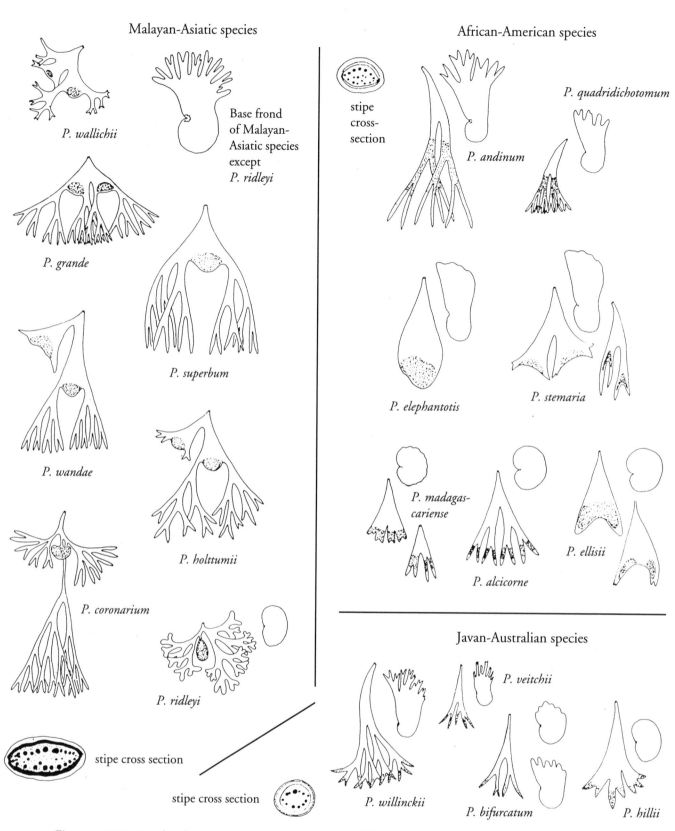

Malayan-Asiatic species

P. wallichii

Base frond
of Malayan-
Asiatic species
except
P. ridleyi

P. grande

P. superbum

P. wandae

P. holttumii

P. coronarium

P. ridleyi

stipe cross section

African-American species

stipe
cross-
section

P. andinum

P. quadridichotomum

P. elephantotis

P. stemaria

*P. madagas-
cariense*

P. alcicorne

P. ellisii

stipe cross section

Javan-Australian species

P. veitchii

P. willinckii

P. bifurcatum

P. hillii

Figure 13.99.3. Frond and stipe (in cross section) characters of *Platycerium* species: Malayan-Asiatic species, with a dark ring of tissue in the stipe, vascular bundles present or absent in the center; African-American species, with a pale ring of tissue in the stipe, vascular bundles scattered in the center; Javan-Australian species, with a pale ring of tissue, the vascular bundles in a circle, not scattered. After Hoshizaki (1972).

plant not named here, it probably represents a variant of the *Platycerium bifurcatum* complex (*P. bifurcatum, P. hillii, P. veitchii,* and *P. willinckii*), the members of which are widely grown and noted for their variability. For a discussion of this complex, see *P. bifurcatum*. For more horticultural information on the species and cultivars, see Joe (1964), Franks (1969), and Vail (1984); for scientific treatments, see Hoshizaki (1972), Hennipman and Roos (1982), and Hoshizaki and Price (1990).

To identify the species, use the outline of the three groups given here and in Figure 13.99.3. Once an unidentified species is limited to one of the groups, it can be compared to the illustrations and descriptions of the individual species in that group.

Malayan-Asiatic species. Some species may extend to Indonesia, New Guinea, and Australia. Stipe cross section has a dark ring of tissue, and vascular bundles are arranged in a circle with some bundles scattered within the circle or not; base fronds spreading, upper margin deeply lobed (except for *Platycerium ridleyi,* which has reniform base fronds); roots do not produce buds; mostly large plants. (*Platycerium coronarium, P. grande, P. holttumii, P. ridleyi, P. superbum, P. wallichii, P. wandae*)

African-American species. Stipe cross section does not have a dark ring of tissue, and vascular bundles are arranged in a circle with some scattered within the circle; base fronds variable, and if spreading, seldom as wide as the Malayan-Asiatic species; roots produce buds; mostly medium-sized or smaller plants compared to the Malayan-Asiatic species. (*Platycerium alcicorne, P. andinum, P. elephantotis, P. ellisii, P. madagascariense, P. quadridichotomum, P. stemaria*)

Javan-Australian species. Stipe cross section does not show a dark ring of tissue, and vascular bundles are arranged in a circle with no bundles within the center of the circle; base fronds variable, and if spreading, seldom as wide as the Malayan-Asiatic species; roots produce buds; mostly medium-sized or smaller plants compared to the Malayan-Asiatic species. (*Platycerium bifurcatum, P. hillii, P. veitchii, P. willinckii*)

Platycerium alcicorne Desvaux   FIGURE 13.99.4
syn. *Platycerium vassei* Poisson
Tender to slightly hardier

A medium-sized fern with a short rhizome and bud-forming roots. Grows well under high light in drained, moist-dry, coarse potting mix or uncut moss. The plants are easy to cultivate.

Platycerium alcicorne has round–kidney-shaped base fronds with entire margins. The center of the stipe in cross section shows scattered vascular bundles. The foliage fronds are erect and evenly forked several times into narrow segments, with the soral patch on the ultimate fork. This species is native to eastern Africa and Madagascar.

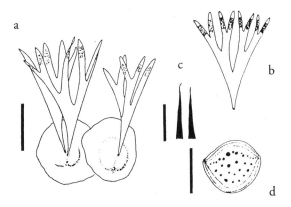

Figure 13.99.4. *Platycerium alcicorne:* a. habit, bar = 10 cm (4 in.); b. sporangial area placement; c. rhizome scales, bar = 5 mm (0.2 in.); d. stipe cross section, bar = 1 cm (0.4 in.).

Platycerium alcicorne resembles *P. bifurcatum,* which differs by the circular (not scattered) arrangement of the vascular bundles in the stipe and often lobed (not entire) upper margins of the base fronds. Some pteridologists consider *P. vassei* the same as *P. alcicorne,* but in horticulture the former name has been applied to a plant that has lighter green blades and very convex, smooth base fronds. The main radiating veins on the base fronds of older plants of *P. alcicorne* from Madagascar are often raised, but the main cross-veins are not. In the related species *P. madagascariense* the main cross-veins are also raised, forming a waffle-like pattern.

Platycerium andinum Baker   FIGURE 13.99.5
American staghorn
Semi-tender to tender

A large fern with a short rhizome and bud-forming roots. Grows well under high light in drained, moist-dry, coarse potting mix or uncut moss.

In *Platycerium andinum* the distal part of the base fronds are extended, arching forward, forked, and lobed. The decumbent foliage fronds are more than 1 m (3 ft.) long, hairy, and gray-green. The sporangial patch is borne on the strap-shaped segments, typically near the middle of the frond but may be more distal. The species is native to Bolivia and Peru.

Platycerium bifurcatum (Cavanilles) C. Christensen
FIGURE 13.99.6; PLATES 1, 5, 42
Common staghorn
Semi-tender

A medium to medium-large fern with a short rhizome and bud-forming roots. Grows well under medium to high light in well-drained, moist-dry to dry, coarse potting mix or uncut moss. It is easy to cultivate and is a common but variable species.

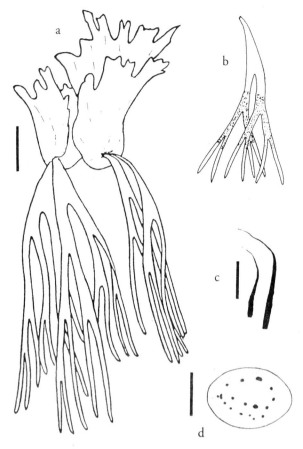

Figure 13.99.5. *Platycerium andinum:* a. habit, bar = 10 cm (4 in.); b. sporangial area placement; c. rhizome scales, bar = 5 mm (0.2 in.); d. stipe cross section, bar = 1 cm (0.4 in.).

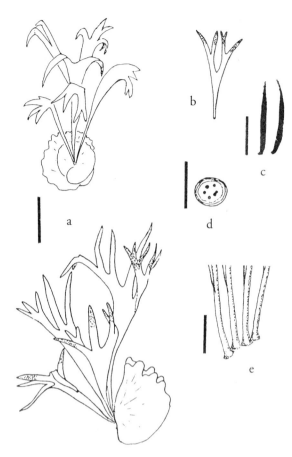

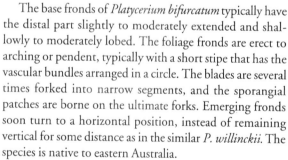

Figure 13.99.6. *Platycerium bifurcatum:* a. habits, bar = 10 cm (4 in.); b. sporangial area placement; c. rhizome scales, bar = 5 mm (0.2 in.); d. stipe cross section, bar = 1 cm (0.4 in.); e. stipe bases, bar = 2 cm (0.8 in.).

The base fronds of *Platycerium bifurcatum* typically have the distal part slightly to moderately extended and shallowly to moderately lobed. The foliage fronds are erect to arching or pendent, typically with a short stipe that has the vascular bundles arranged in a circle. The blades are several times forked into narrow segments, and the sporangial patches are borne on the ultimate forks. Emerging fronds soon turn to a horizontal position, instead of remaining vertical for some distance as in the similar *P. willinckii.* The species is native to eastern Australia.

The preceding description excludes *Platycerium hillii, P. veitchii,* and *P. willinckii,* which are sometimes considered varieties or subspecies of *P. bifurcatum* but are here treated as separate species. Collectively, these species and *P. bifurcatum* are referred to as the "*P. bifurcatum* complex." They all have a circular arrangement of vascular bundles in the stipes and lack dark tissue encircling the bundles. (This trait can be seen by making a clean cut across the stipe with a razor blade or sharp knife.) Most of the numerous, loosely given *Platycerium* names in the trade represent vari-

ations of the members of this complex. Some of these trade plants may be recognized as belonging to one of the four species in the complex, whereas others are more difficult to identify because of intergrading or inconstant characters. The particular frond form of a plant may not be the same in later growth or under different cultural conditions. Fronds can vary by season and age.

Platycerium willinckii var. *venosum* Hughes is closer to *P. bifurcatum* than to *P. willinckii* because of its strongly stalked (not sessile) foliage fronds. It differs from typical *P. bifurcatum* by having widely spreading base fronds, usually longer foliage fronds, and strongly raised major veins on the upper surface (but depressed on the lower) especially near the blade base. It was collected in northeastern Australia. Native var. *venosum* reportedly intergrades into typical *P. bifurcatum* plants (Roy Vail, personal communication).

'Netherlands'. Fronds arching, grayish, the base fronds swept upward, lobed on the upper margins. Common in the trade.

Platycerium coronarium (König ex Müller) Desvaux

FIGURE 13.99.7

syn. *Platycerium biforme* (Swartz) Blume
Disk staghorn
Tender

A large fern with a short rhizome that may branch and become longer; new plants form when the tip of the branch reaches the surface. Grows well under high light in drained, moist-dry, coarse potting mix or uncut moss.

The base fronds of *Platycerium coronarium* have the distal part extended, deeply lobed, and forward-arching. The foliage fronds are long, pendent, and several times forked. The sporangial patch is typically a kidney-shaped lobe. This species is native to southeastern Asia, Malaysia, Indonesia, and the Philippines.

Platycerium ×*elemaria* Hoshizaki & M. G. Price

FIGURE 13.99.8

Tender

A medium-large fern with a short rhizome and bud-forming roots. Grows well under medium to high-medium light in drained, moist to moist-dry, coarse potting mix or uncut moss.

Platycerium ×*elemaria* is a sterile hybrid of *P. elephantotis* and *P. stemaria*. Its base fronds resemble those of the parents, and the foliage fronds resemble those of *P. elephantotis* but have the apical margins shallowly and irregularly forked or lobed. Hydathodes are absent. This plant originated as a hybrid in horticulture and does not occur in the wild. The cultivar name of this hybrid is 'Sanchez'.

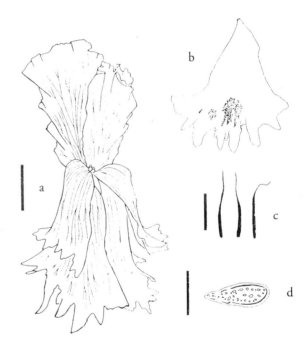

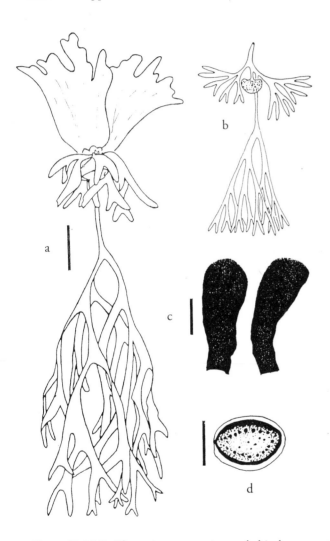

Figure 13.99.7. *Platycerium coronarium:* a. habit, bar = 10 cm (4 in.); b. sporangial area placement; c. rhizome scales, bar = 5 mm (0.2 in.); d. stipe cross section, bar = 1 cm (0.4 in.).

Figure 13.99.8. *Platycerium* ×*elemaria:* a. habit, bar = 10 cm (4 in.); b. sporangial area placement; c. rhizome scales, bar = 5 mm (0.2 in.); d. stipe cross section, bar = 1 cm (0.4 in.).

Platycerium elephantotis Schweinfurth

FIGURE 13.99.9

syn. *Platycerium angolense* Wellwitsch ex Baker
Angola staghorn
Tender

A medium-large fern with short rhizomes and bud-forming roots. Grows well under medium to high-medium light in drained, moist to moist-dry, coarse potting mix or uncut moss. The plants quickly show water stress and are prone to attack by scale insects.

The base fronds of *Platycerium elephantotis* are much extended, unlobed, and spreading slightly forward distally.

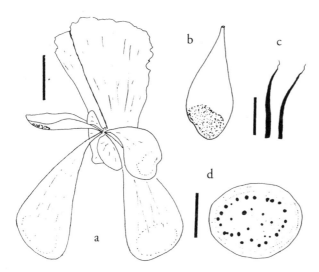

Figure 13.99.9. *Platycerium elephantotis:* a. habit, bar = 10 cm (4 in.); b. sporangial area placement; c. rhizome scales, bar = 5 mm (0.2 in.); d. stipe cross section, bar = 1 cm (0.4 in.).

The foliage fronds are spreading to pendent, asymmetrically obovate, and entire; they have hydathodes. The sporangial patch is apical. The species is native to Africa.

Platycerium ellisii Baker   FIGURE 13.99.10
syn. *Platycerium diversifolium* Bonaparte
Tender

A medium-sized fern with short rhizomes and bud-forming roots. Grows under high light in drained, moist to moist-dry, coarse potting mix or uncut moss. The plants are somewhat difficult to grow.

Platycerium ellisii resembles *P. alcicorne* but has typical foliage fronds usually shallowly once-forked at the tip. It is endemic to Madagascar.

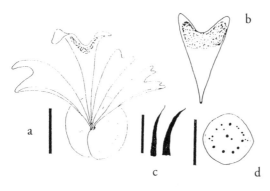

Figure 13.99.10. *Platycerium ellisii:* a. habit, bar = 10 cm (4 in.); b. sporangial area placement; c. rhizome scales, bar = 5 mm (0.2 in.); d. stipe cross section, bar = 1 cm (0.4 in.).

Platycerium grande (Fée) Kunze   FIGURE 13.99.11
Tender

A large fern with short rhizomes. Grows under high light in drained, moist-dry, coarse potting mix or uncut moss.

The base fronds of *Platycerium grande* have much-extended, deeply lobed, and usually forward-arching distal parts. The foliage fronds have two sporangial patches per frond, each typically borne on a semicircular extension jutting out into the sinus of the second fork. The species is endemic to the Philippines.

Platycerium superbum is often misidentified in the trade as *P. grande,* but it differs in having only one sporangial patch per frond. The similar but smaller *P. wallichii* has outer branches that are shorter than the inner ones and green instead of brown spores.

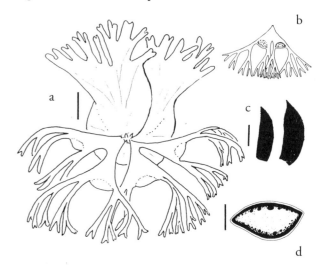

Figure 13.99.11. *Platycerium grande:* a. habit, bar = 10 cm (4 in.); b. sporangial area placement; c. rhizome scales, bar = 5 mm (0.2 in.); d. stipe cross section, bar = 1 cm (0.4 in.).

Platycerium hillii T. Moore   FIGURE 13.99.12
syn. *Platycerium bifurcatum* var. *hillii* (T. Moore) Domin
Green staghorn
Semi-tender

A medium-sized fern with short rhizomes and bud-forming roots. Grows well under medium to high light in drained, moist-dry, coarse potting mix or uncut sphagnum moss. This species is easy to grow.

Platycerium hillii has entire, round to kidney-shaped base fronds. The wedge-shaped or fan-shaped foliage fronds are erect with short stipes. They are several times forked, usually in the distal third of the frond. The forks are short and stout. The species is native to eastern Australia.

This species is distinguished by the entire base fronds and the short-stalked, erect foliaceous fronds that are two or more times shallowly forked distally. All other members of

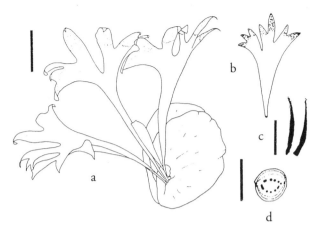

Figure 13.99.12. *Platycerium hillii:* a. habit, bar = 10 cm (4 in.); b. sporangial area placement; c. rhizome scales, bar = 5 mm (0.2 in.); d. stipe cross section, bar = 1 cm (0.4 in.).

the *Platycerium bifurcatum* complex have extended base fronds and are shallowly to deeply lobed. See also the discussion under *P. bifurcatum.* Some of the choice cultivars of *P. hillii* include 'Mona Loa', 'Panama', and 'Talnadge'.

Platycerium holttumii de Joncheere & Hennipman

FIGURE 13.99.13

Tender

A large fern with short rhizomes. Grows under medium light in drained, moist-dry, coarse potting mix or uncut moss.

Platycerium holttumii resembles *P. grande,* but its foliage frond has the outer primary branch and its divisions shortened. It is also resembles *P. wandae,* which differs by having the outer primary branch wedge-shaped without any further branching and by the presence of fringes on the base frond above or around the bud. *Platycerium holttumii* is native to southeastern Asia and the Malay Peninsula.

Platycerium madagascariense Baker

FIGURE 13.99.14

Tender

A medium-sized fern with short rhizomes and bud-forming roots. Grows under medium light in drained, moist-dry to moist, coarse potting mix or uncut moss. This species is difficult to grow and has a dormant period. The base fronds are not thick and spongy and are loosely layered. Therefore, water drains readily from the plant and extra care must be taken to provide sufficient water. Control the many pests that like to live between the loose layers of base fronds.

Platycerium madagascariense is distinctive for its waffle-like depressions on the base fronds. By contrast, the main veins of *P. alcicorne* are raised, but not the cross-veins. The base fronds of *P. madagascariense* are thick and papery when dry (not spongy as in *P. alcicorne*) and sometimes

Figure 13.99.13. *Platycerium holttumii:* a. habit, bar = 10 cm (4 in.); b. sporangial area placement; c. rhizome scales, bar = 5 mm (0.2 in.); d. stipe cross section, bar = 1 cm (0.4 in.).

have denticulate margins and short stipes. The foliage fronds are wedge-shaped with the apical margins mostly shallowly forked one to three times, and the sporangial patches occur in the apical part of frond. This species is endemic to Madagascar.

The trade plant circulating as 'Horne's Surprise' is a presumed hybrid of *Platycerium madagascariense* and *P. alcicorne.*

Platycerium ×mentelosii Hoshizaki   FIGURE 13.99.15
Tender

A medium-large fern with short rhizomes. Grows well under medium light in drained, moist-dry, coarse potting mix or uncut moss. Although a hybrid, this fern reportedly produces some viable spores from which the plant can be propagated.

Platycerium ×mentelosii has characteristics intermediate between those of its parents, *P. stemaria* and *P. superbum.* The stipe cross section has the dark band of the *P. superbum* parent and the scattered vascular bundles of *P. stemaria.*

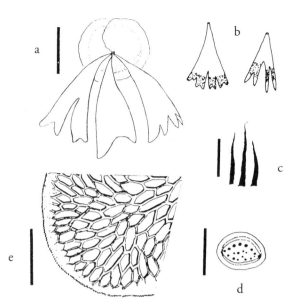

Figure 13.99.14. *Platycerium madagascariense:* a. habit, bar = 10 cm (4 in.); b. sporangial area placement; c. rhizome scales, bar = 5 mm (0.2 in.); d. stipe cross section, bar = 1 cm (0.4 in.); e. depressions between veins of base frond and minutely dentate margin, bar = 5 cm (2 in.).

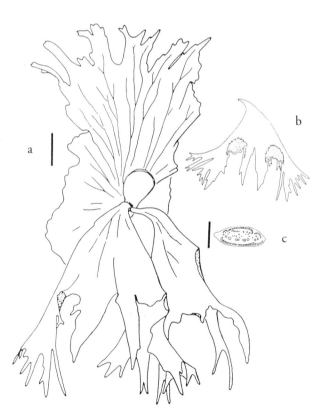

Figure 13.99.15. *Platycerium ×mentelosii:* a. habit, bar = 10 cm (4 in.); b. sporangial area placement; c. stipe cross section, bar = 1 cm (0.4 in.).

This sterile hybrid originated in horticulture; it does not occur in the wild. The cultivar name for this hybrid is 'Fantastic Gardens'.

Platycerium quadridichotomum (Bonaparte) Tardieu
FIGURE 13.99.16

Tender

A medium-sized fern with a short rhizome and bud-forming roots. Grows under high-medium light in drained, moist-dry to dry, coarse potting mix or uncut moss. This species is difficult to grow and prone to fungal attacks. The plants have a distinct dormant period.

Platycerium quadridichotomum is extended, irregularly lobed, and foliaceous in the distal part of the base fronds. The foliage fronds are spreading to pendent, several times forked, and up to 20–50 cm (8–20 in.) long. The sporangia are borne on strap-shaped branches and typically occupy a medial position on the frond. *Platycerium quadridichotomum* is endemic to Madagascar.

Platycerium andinum has the same general structure but is a much larger plant with long, thick, densely hairy foliage fronds.

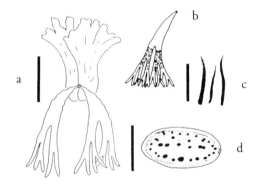

Figure 13.99.16. *Platycerium quadridichotomum:* a. habit, bar = 10 cm (4 in.); b. sporangial area placement; c. rhizome scales, bar = 5 mm (0.2 in.); d. stipe cross section, bar = 1 cm (0.4 in.).

Platycerium ridleyi H. Christ
FIGURE 13.99.17

Tender

A medium-sized fern with short rhizomes. Grows under high light in drained, moist-dry to dry, coarse potting mix or uncut moss. This species is difficult to grow and is attacked by a variety of insect pests.

Platycerium ridleyi has round to kidney-shaped base fronds with unlobed or coarsely dentate margins. The foliage fronds are erect, and the sporangial patch is borne on an obovate lobe. This species is native to western Malaya and Indonesia.

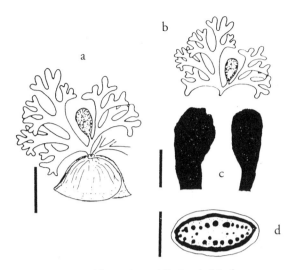

Figure 13.99.17. *Platycerium ridleyi:* a. habit, bar = 10 cm (4 in.); b. sporangial area placement; c. rhizome scales, bar = 5 mm (0.2 in.); d. stipe cross section, bar = 1 cm (0.4 in.).

Platycerium stemaria (Beauvaux) Desvaux
FIGURE 13.99.18

Triangular staghorn
Tender

A medium-large fern with a short rhizome and bud-forming roots. Grows well under medium to high-medium light in drained, moist to moist-dry, coarse potting mix or uncut moss. The plants quickly show water stress.

The base fronds of *Platycerium stemaria* have the upper margin much extended, unlobed, and spreading slightly forward. The spreading to pendent foliage fronds are twice-forked, with the sporangial patches typically below the sinus of the second fork. The typical variety, var. *stemaria,* is native to central and western Africa.

var. *laurentii* de Wilde. Differs from the typical variety by having irregularly dentate or laciniate apical margins on the broad primary fork. It is native to Africa.

Platycerium superbum de Joncheere & Hennipman
FIGURE 13.99.19; PLATE 43

syn. *Platycerium grande* var. *tambourinense* Domin
Giant staghorn
Semi-tender

A large fern with short rhizomes. Grows well under medium or high light in drained, moist-dry to dry, coarse potting mix or uncut moss. This species is a choice but extremely large fern that may be grown outdoors in subtropical climates.

In *Platycerium superbum* the distal part of the base fronds are much extended, deeply lobed, and usually forward-arching. The foliage fronds are several times forked. One sporangial patch is produced per frond, typically on a semicircular extension jutting out into the sinus of the first fork. The species is native to Australia.

Platycerium veitchii (Underwood) C. Christensen
FIGURE 13.99.20

syn. *Platycerium bifurcatum* subsp. *veitchii* (Underwood) Hennipman & Roos
Semi-tender

A medium-sized fern with short, ascending rhizomes and bud-forming roots. Grows well under medium to high light

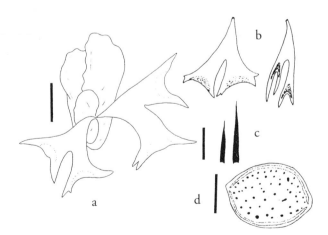

Figure 13.99.18. *Platycerium stemaria:* a. habit, bar = 10 cm (4 in.); b. sporangial area placement and frond variations; c. rhizome scales, bar = 5 mm (0.2 in.); d. stipe cross section, bar = 1 cm (0.4 in.).

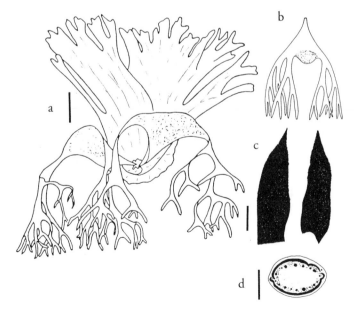

Figure 13.99.19. *Platycerium superbum:* a. habit, bar = 10 cm (4 in.); b. sporangial area placement; c. rhizome scales, bar = 5 mm (0.2 in.); d. stipe cross section, bar = 1 cm (0.4)in.

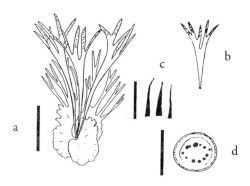

Figure 13.99.20. *Platycerium veitchii:* a. habit, bar = 10 cm (4 in.); b. sporangial area placement; c. rhizome scales, bar = 5 mm (0.2 in.); d. stipe cross section, bar = 1 cm (0.4 in.).

in drained, moist-dry to dry, coarse potting mix or uncut moss. The plants tolerate considerable heat. The whitish gray foliage and lobes on the base fronds develop best in high light.

Platycerium veitchii resembles *P. bifurcatum* but differs by the base frond typically extended on the upper margin into an erect, narrow, deep lobe that browns readily, and the foliage fronds are more erect, densely hairy, and gray-green. When the narrow lobes of the base frond do not develop, the plant may be difficult to distinguish from *P. bifurcatum*. It is endemic to Australia.

Platycerium wallichii Hooker   FIGURE 13.99.21
Indian staghorn
Tender

A medium-large fern with short rhizomes. Grows under high-medium to high light in moist to moist-dry, coarse potting mix or uncut moss. This species is difficult to cultivate, and new growth is seasonal. A mature specimen ex-

hibited at the 1997 International Fern Society show in Los Angeles produced an offshoot—something that rarely happens with this species in cultivation. It is uncertain whether the buds came from a root or from a rhizome branch.

Platycerium wallichii has base fronds that are extended and deeply lobed distally. The foliage fronds are several times forked, with the outer primary fork shorter, and typically two, sometimes three, sporangial patches are usually below the sinuses of the second fork. This species is native to eastern India, Burma, Thailand, and China.

Platycerium wandae Raciborski   FIGURE 13.99.22
syn. *Platycerium willhelminae-reginae* van Alderwerelt
    van Rosenburgh
Queen staghorn
Tender

A large fern with short rhizomes. Grows well under high-medium light in moist-dry, coarse potting mix or uncut moss. This is the largest *Platycerium* species, and plants may spread to 2 m (6.5 ft.) across.

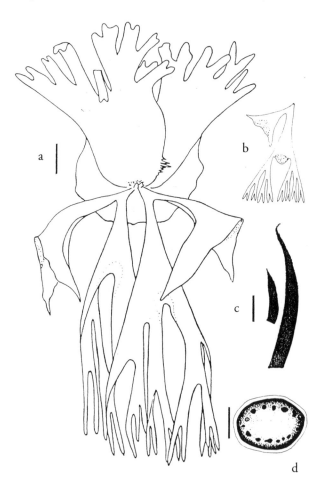

Figure 13.99.22. *Platycerium wandae:* a. habit, bar = 10 cm (4 in.); b. sporangial area placement; c. rhizome scales, bar = 5 mm (0.2 in.); d. stipe cross section, bar = 1 cm (0.4 in.).

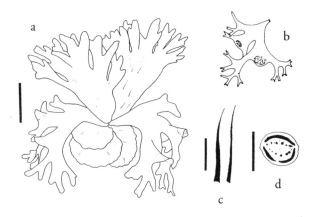

Figure 13.99.21. *Platycerium wallichii:* a. habit, bar = 10 cm (4 in.); b. sporangial area placement; c. rhizome scales, bar = 5 mm (0.2 in.); d. stipe cross section, bar = 1 cm (0.4 in.).

Platycerium wandae resembles *P. holttumii,* but the margins of the base fronds around the growing point or above it have small fringes. The outer branch of the foliage fronds is reduced to a wedge. There are two sporangial patches, one on the wedge and the other on the inner primary branch (around the sinus of the next fork). This species is endemic to New Guinea.

Platycerium willinckii T. Moore

FIGURES 13.99.1, 2, 23

syn. *Platycerium bifurcatum* subsp. *willinckii* (T. Moore) Hennipman & Roos, *P. sumbawense* H. Christ

Java staghorn

Tender to semi-tender

A medium-large fern with short rhizomes and bud-forming roots. Grows well under high-medium light in moist-dry, coarse potting mix or uncut moss. This species is easy to grow if protected from cold. The leaves are thick and gray-green.

The distal part of the base fronds of *Platycerium willinckii* are extended and swept upward, deeply lobed, and arched forward. The foliage fronds are long and pendent, typically sessile, and several times forked, usually with the most forking in the distal part of the frond. *Platycerium willinckii* is native to Java and the Lesser Sunda Islands.

Platycerium bifurcatum differs in having shorter, less-pendent foliage fronds, short stipes, and emerging fronds that are more horizontal, rather than remaining in a vertical position for some time and distance.

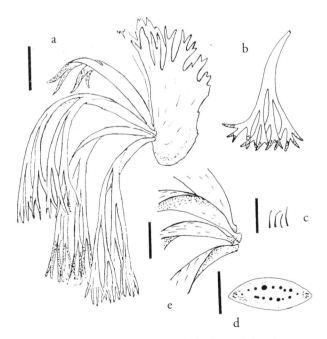

Figure 13.99.23. *Platycerium willinckii:* a. habit, bar = 10 cm (4 in.); b. sporangial area placement; c. rhizome scales, bar = 5 mm (0.2 in.); d. stipe cross section, bar = 1 cm (0.4 in.); e. stipe bases, bar = 2 cm (0.8 in.).

Polybotrya

The rhizomes of these rarely cultivated tropical ferns become long and scandent and may climb tree trunks up to over 8 m (26 ft.) high. Because they are tender plants with long-creeping rhizomes, their use in the landscape is limited to tropical climates or large greenhouses, where they are usually trained on tree trunks. *Polybotrya* is difficult to maintain in baskets because of the long-creeping, scandent habit.

Polybotrya is characterized by long-creeping, densely scaly rhizomes and strongly dimorphic sterile and fertile fronds. The apex of the blade is gradually tapered, not with a terminal pinna resembling the lateral ones. The fertile fronds resemble a highly dissected, skeletonized version of the sterile ones, and the sori always lack indusia.

The genus is native to the New World tropics and contains 35 species. Its name comes from the Greek *poly,* many, and *botrys,* bunch or cluster, alluding to the sporangia clustered on the fertile leaves. For a technical account of the species, see Moran (1987).

Polybotrya osmundacea Humboldt & Bonpland ex

Willdenow   FIGURE 13.100.1

Tender

A medium-large fern with long-creeping rhizomes that can climb to about 8 m (26 ft.). Grows well under high-medium light in moist garden soil or potting mix.

Polybotrya osmundacea has roughly triangular, two- to three-pinnate-pinnatifid sterile fronds with free veins. The fertile fronds are contracted and have hardly any green tissue. The sporangia form linear or oblong sori. The fertile fronds are only produced on the climbing portion of the rhizome. The species is widespread in the New World tropics.

Polypodium   FIGURES 13.101.1, 2

Polypody

The common polypodies of genus *Polypodium* are probably the most widely known ferns. They occur throughout the world and are frequently depicted in designs and mentioned in folklore of Western cultures. In gardens they can be used among rocks, on walls, or in pots or baskets. The larger species are usually grown in hanging baskets or pots. Most polypodies are tender. Some can be grown in the ground in warm climates if given good drainage. Certain species make suitable indoor plants. The spores may be slow to germinate but give many sporelings.

The genus *Polypodium* can be identified by its long-creeping rhizomes with two ranks of fronds on the dorsal surface. The fronds are jointed to the rhizome and fall away cleanly to leave a low, elevated base (the phyllopodium). The blades are typically pinnatisect to one-pinnate (rarely more finely divided) with pinnae continuous with, not jointed to, the rachis. The large, round sori lack indusia.

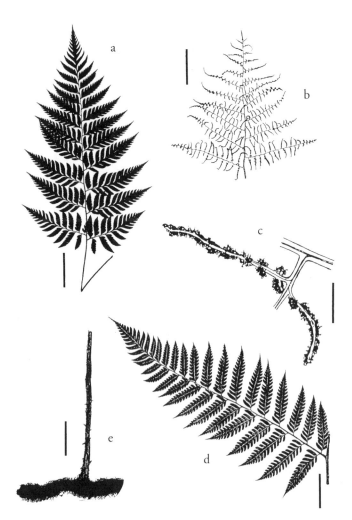

Figure 13.101.1. *Polypodium cambricum:* habit.

Figure 13.100.1. *Polybotrya osmundacea:* a. sterile frond from immature plant, bar = 5 cm (2 in.); b. apical portion of fertile frond, bar = 5 cm (2 in.); c. two fertile pinnules (tertiary), bar = 5 mm (0.2 in.); d. sterile pinna from mature plant, bar = 5 cm (2 in.); e. rhizome and stipe from mature plant, bar = 5 cm (2 in.).

The spores are yellow, at least when fresh. No other fern genus has this combination of characteristics.

Polypodium consists of about 125 species worldwide, with most of the species in the American tropics. The genus name comes from the Greek *poly,* many, and *podion,* foot, alluding to the resemblance of the rhizome's numerous branches to feet. For more information on this and related genera, see "*Polypodium* and Relatives" in Chapter 10.

Early pteridologists placed any fern with round, non-indusiate sori in *Polypodium.* Defined as such, *Polypodium* included species in unrelated genera such as *Ctenitis, Dryopteris,* and *Thelypteris.* Nowadays *Polypodium* is subdivided into many smaller genera, and these are compared here. The comparisons are only for the cultivated species and do not cover all the species within the genus.

Figure 13.101.2. *Polypodium cambricum:* frond apex and sori.

Campyloneurum: Rhizomes short-creeping; rhizome scales clathrate; fronds medium-sized, simple, entire, strap-shaped or linear-lanceolate, monomorphic; veins netted, lateral veins parallel and connected by curved cross-veins to form the areoles, the included veinlet unbranched and pointing toward the margin; sori round, borne below the free veinlet tip. Native to tropical and subtropical America. (*Campyloneurum angustifolium, C. brevifolium, C. costatum, C. phyllitidis, C. tenuipes, C. xalapense*)

Dictymia: Rhizomes short-creeping; rhizome scales peltate, broadly ovate, clathrate, usually with glandular marginal projections; fronds medium-sized, simple, entire, linear to lanceolate, subleathery, smooth; veins netted, included veinlets absent or rare; sori round to narrowly oblong, slightly to strongly embossed on the blade. Native to Australia and the islands of the southwestern Pacific. (*Dictymia brownii*)

Goniophlebium: Rhizomes medium- to long-creeping; rhizome scales peltate, clathrate, toothed, often with one- or two-celled, glandular marginal appendages; fronds medium- to large-sized; blades pinnatifid to pinnate with a terminal pinna resembling the lateral ones; pinnae jointed; veins netted, areoles angular and in several rows, costal areoles large, with one included veinlet pointing outward. Native to Asia. (*Goniophlebium ×ekstrandii, G. percussum, G. persicifolium, G. subauriculatum*)

Lecanopteris: Rhizomes short-creeping and swollen, with internal chambers inhabited by ants; rhizome scales peltate, clathrate centrally but not at the margin; fronds small-sized; blades entire to deeply pinnatifid; veins netted, the areoles with included free veinlets. Native to Malaysia. (*Lecanopteris carnosa, L. crustacea, L. sinuosa*)

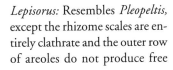
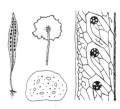

Lepisorus: Resembles *Pleopeltis,* except the rhizome scales are entirely clathrate and the outer row of areoles do not produce free

veins pointing toward the margins. Native to Africa and Asia. (*Lepisorus longifolius, L. thunbergianus*)

Leptochilus (*Colysis*): Rhizomes short- to long-creeping; rhizome scales peltate, clathrate; fronds medium-sized; stipes often winged; blades simple to one-pinnate, monomorphic or dimorphic; veins netted, included veinlet pointing in various directions; similar to *Microsorum* except sori are mostly elongate to linear and oblique to the axis. Native to Asia. (*Leptochilus amplus, L. ellipticus, L. macrophyllus* var. *wrightii*)

Micrugramma: Rhizomes long-creeping, often slightly flattened; rhizome scales elongate, not clathrate, attached well above their base; fronds less than 39 cm (15 in.) long; blades simple, entire, lanceolate to oblong, slightly dimorphic; veins netted with unbranched included veinlets pointing outward toward the margin; sori round. Native to the American tropics and subtropics. (*Microgramma heterophylla, M. lycopodioides, M. megalophylla, M. nitida, M. percussa, M. piloselloides, M. reptans, M. squamulosa, M. vacciniifolia*)

Microsorum (*Phymatosorus*): Rhizomes short- to long-creeping; fronds medium- to large-sized, simple, margins entire, lobed, or pinnatifid; veins netted, included veinlets simple or branched, variously directed, always ending in a hydathode; sori scattered dots or larger, round to oval, immersed in the blade tissue or not. Native to Africa, Asia, Australia, and islands of the southwestern Pacific. (*Microsorum commutatum, M. fortunei, M. grossum, M. insigne, M. linguiforme, M. longissimum, M. lucidum, M. membranifolium, M. musifolium, M. pteropus, M. punctatum, M. pustulatum, M. samarense, M. scandens, M. scolopendria, M. steerei, M. superficiale, M. viellardii*)

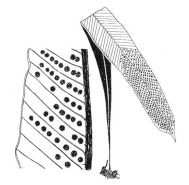

Niphidium: Rhizomes creeping to ascending; fronds clustered, medium- to large-sized, simple, entire, upper surfaces often have many white dots; sori round, large

(3–5 mm in diameter), in a single row between the main lateral veins, not sunken; sporangial capsules with minute hairs. Native to the American tropics and subtropics. (*Niphidium crassifolium*)

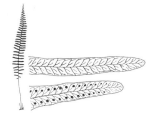

Pecluma: Rhizomes very short-creeping; rhizome scales attached along their base; fronds small- to medium-sized; blades deeply pinnatisect, comb-shaped, the many divisions narrow and close together, with small one-celled hairs on lower surfaces; sori round. Native to the American tropics and subtropics. (*Pecluma dispersa, P. pectinata, P. plumula*)

Phlebodium: Rhizomes medium- to long-creeping; rhizome scales usually orangish when freshly mature, not clathrate; fronds medium- to large-sized, pinnatilobed or pinnatifid; 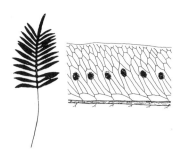 areoles next to the midrib mostly narrow and without included veinlets; other areoles with included veinlets or not, if present the veinlets are united or, if free, usually pointing outward toward the margin; sori supplied by two veinlets. Native to the American tropics and subtropics. (*Phlebodium aureum, P. decumanum, P. pseudoaureum, P. ×schneideri*)

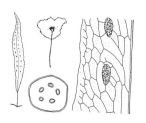

Pleopeltis: Rhizomes long-creeping; rhizome scales clathrate centrally but not at the margins; fronds small- to medium-sized, simple, entire (rarely dichotomously forked), surfaces with peltate scales; veins netted with included branched(?) veinlets pointing in various directions, the marginal row of areoles with free veins pointing toward the margins; sori usually round, covered with peltate paraphyses when young. Native to the American tropics and subtropics, and Africa. (No cultivated species; plants brought into cultivation have not survived.)

Polypodium: Rhizomes short- to long-creeping; fronds small to large; blade pinnatifid or pinnate; pinnae not jointed; veins free or netted, with or without a free included veinlet; sori round or oblong, at tip or junction of vein,

paraphyses (if present) not peltate. Cosmopolitan. (*Polypodium amoenum, P. appalachianum, P. attenuatum, P. bombycinum, P. brasiliense, P. calirhiza, P. cambricum, P. dissimile, P. formosanum, P. glycyrrhiza, P. guttatum, P. hesperium, P. hirsutissimum, P. interjectum, P. ×leucosporum, P. levigatum, P. loriceum, P. maritimum, P. menisciifolium, P. pellucidum, P. plebeium, P. polypodioides, P. ptilorhizon, P. pyrrholepis, P. rhodopleuron, P. sanctae-rosae, P. scouleri, P. thyssanolepis, P. triseriale, P. virginianum, P. vulgare*)

Selliguea (*Crypsinus*): Rhizomes long-creeping, conspicuous black fiber strands within; rhizome scales peltate; fronds medium-sized, simple, entire, lanceolate to oblong-lanceolate, some species (formerly in *Crypsinus*) hastate, pinnatifid to pinnate with cartilaginous and often notched margins; fertile fronds taller, more contracted; veins netted, lateral veins conspicuous; sori brown, round but usually elongate or linear, borne between adjacent lateral veins in one or two rows. Native to southern Africa, Asia, Australia, and the islands of the Pacific. (*Selliguea feei*)

Solanopteris: Rhizomes long-creeping, with ant-inhabited tubers, without black fiber stands within; rhizome scales peltate, round; fronds small-sized, simple to pinnatifid; fertile fronds usually narrower and longer than the sterile; veins netted with included veinlets; sori round or linear. Native to the American tropics. (*Solanopteris bifrons, S. brunei*)

Even with the removal of these segregate genera, *Polypodium* contains many species. To facilitate identification of these species, *Polypodium* is divided into three groups.

The Vulgare Group (*Polypodium vulgare* complex). This group is characterized by free veins (rarely with a few netted ones) and pinnatifid (or pinnatilobed) blades with scaleless surfaces. The sori are always in one row between the midrib and margin of the blade. The vulgare group contains about 25 species, most of which are native to the boreal and temperate regions of North America, Europe, and Asia. A few occur in Mexico, and one species (*Polypodium pellucidum*) is native to Hawaii.

The most commonly cultivated species in the group are of European origin. Other species may be cultivated but are usually difficult to establish. Pteridologists have named and described many species and hybrids that may be difficult for nonspecialists to identify, especially if the plant's original habitat is unknown. Even if this is known, fertile fronds and a microscope are usually needed for accurate identification.

The cultivated species of the vulgare group treated here include *Polypodium appalachianum*, *P. calirhiza*, *P. cambricum*, *P. glycyrrhiza*, *P. hesperium*, *P. interjectum*, *P. pellucidum*, *P. scouleri*, *P. virginianum*, and *P. vulgare*. They are illustrated together in Figure 13.101.34.

The Loriceum Group *(Polygoniophlebium).* This group is characterized by pinnatifid to pinnate, rarely simple blades that have scaleless surfaces (a few scales might be present on the rachis or costae). The veins form at least one row of regular areoles along the pinna midrib. Each areole contains a veinlet that points toward the blade margin. The pinnae are continuous with the rachis, not jointed to it by an abscission layer. The sori appear in one to several rows between the costae and margins. The group contains about 40 species, most of which are native to the New World.

Two widely grown species in the loriceum group are *Polypodium triseriale* and *P. menisciifolium*. The former is grown as a basket plant in gardens in Florida. *Polypodium menisciifolium*, which is cultivated in baskets in southern California, grows vigorously and tolerates irregular watering. Another species in the group, *P. formosanum*, is often found in the trade and is prized for its attractive pale grayish green fronds and rhizomes. A cultivar with repeatedly forked and congested rhizomes, 'Cristatum', adds further interest to this species.

The cultivated species treated here are *Polypodium amoenum*, *P. attenuatum*, *P. brasiliense*, *P. dissimile*, *P. formosanum*, *P. levigatum*, *P. loriceum*, *P. maritimum*, *P. menisciifolium*, *P. ptilorhizon*, *P. rhodopleuron*, and *P. triseriale*.

The Scaly-Polypody Group. This group is characterized by pinnatifid (or pinnatilobed) blades that are scaly, especially on the lower surface. Often the scales are dense and conspicuous. The veins vary from free to netted, but they are usually hard to see because of the thick blade tissue or because they are hidden by the scales. The sori are in one row between the costa and margin. All the species in the scaly-polypody group, of which there are about 40, are native to tropical America.

This group is closely related to *Pleopeltis*, and probably all the species should be transferred to that genus, as has already been done with some species. The cultivated species treated here are *Polypodium bombycinum*, *P. guttatum*, *P. hirsutissimum*, *P. ×leucosporum*, *P. plebeium*, *P. polypodioides*, *P. pyrrholepis*, *P. sanctae-rosae*, and *P. thyssanolepis*.

Polypodium amoenum Wallich ex Mettenius
FIGURE 13.101.3
syn. *Goniophlebium amoenum* (Wallich ex Mettenius) J. Smith ex Hooker & Greville
Semi-tender to hardier

A small to medium fern with long-creeping rhizomes. Grows well under low to high light in moist-dry, well-drained garden soil or potting mix. The plants are subject to slug and snail attack and require a lot of humidity.

The rhizomes of *Polypodium amoenum* contain scattered dark fibers, and the fronds are generally 14–50 cm (5.5–20 in.) long and 8–27 cm (3–11 in.) wide, with pinnatifid, dull green blades. The segments typically have pentagonal areoles next to the rachis. The sori are in one row between the pinna midrib and margin. The species is native to the Himalayas, southeastern Asia, China, and Taiwan.

Some pteridologists classify this species in *Goniophlebium*, but it lacks jointed pinnae (a defining characteristic of that genus) and is therefore retained in *Polypodium* until further study.

Polypodium appalachianum Haufler & Windham
FIGURES 13.101.4, 34d
Appalachian polypody
Very hardy, Zone 3

A small fern with short- to medium-creeping rhizomes. Grows under medium light in drained, moist potting mix. This species adapts poorly to gardens in southern California.

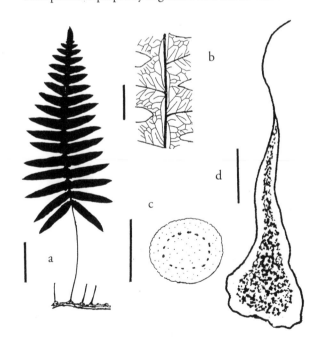

Figure 13.101.3. *Polypodium amoenum:* a. habit, bar = 5 cm (2 in.); b. vein details along the rachis, bar = 1 cm (0.4 in.), after Hoshizaki (1982); c. rhizome cross section, showing vascular bundles and scattered fibers, bar = 1 cm (0.4 in.); d. rhizome scale, bar = 1 mm.

Figure 13.101.4.
*Polypodium
appalachianum:*
a. habit, bar = 5 cm
(2 in.); b. paraphysis,
top view, bar =
0.1 mm.

Polypodium appalachianum was recently separated from
P. virginianum and is distinguished from it by the elongate-
triangular blades and golden-brown rhizome scales nearly
of all one color. The species is native to eastern North
America.

Polypodium attenuatum Humboldt & Bonpland ex

Willdenow   FIGURE 13.101.5
syn. *Polypodium kuhnii* Fournier
Tender

A medium-sized fern with a short-creeping rhizome surrounded by a dense root mass. Grows well under medium
light in moist, drained potting mix.

Polypodium attenuatum resembles *P. triseriale* but differs by deeply pinnatisect blades, falcate pinnae, a single
row of sori between the pinna midrib and margin, and a
dense mass of hairy, brown roots around the rhizome. The
species is native to lowland forests in tropical America.

Polypodium bombycinum Maxon   FIGURE 13.101.6
Tender

A medium-sized fern with short-creeping rhizomes. Grows
well under medium light in moist-dry, well-drained potting mix or uncut moss.

Polypodium bombycinum has short-creeping, branched
rhizomes that are 3–5 mm (0.1–0.2 in.) thick and covered
by rigid, dark brown scales. The stipes are short and close
together. The blades are stiff, erect, and linear to narrowly
elliptic or oblanceolate, tapering in the lower half with basal
pinnae reduced to small lobes. Appressed scales are so
abundant that they hide the lower blade surface. A small,
slightly swollen gland is found on the inside upper edge of
the segments, although this trait is often hard to see. The
species grows as an epiphyte in the tropical forests of Central and South America.

Polypodium brasiliense Poiret   FIGURE 13.101.7
Tender

A large fern with short- to medium-creeping rhizomes.
Grows well under medium light in moist, drained potting
mix.

Polypodium brasiliense resembles *P. triseriale* but differs
by its larger size, pinnae with five to six series of areoles be-

Figure 13.101.5. *Polypodium attenuatum:* a. frond, bar =
5 cm (2 in.); b. segment with sori, bar = 5 cm (2 in.);
c. rhizome scales, bar = 1 mm.

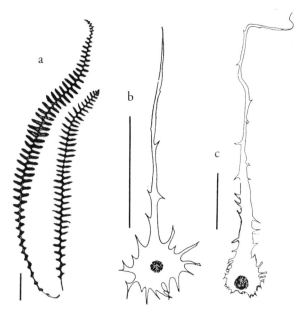

Figure 13.101.6. *Polypodium bombycinum:* a. fronds, bar
= 5 cm (2 in.); b. scale from lower surface of blade, bar =
1 mm, after Sota (1966); c. rhizome scale, bar = 1 mm,
after Sota (1966).

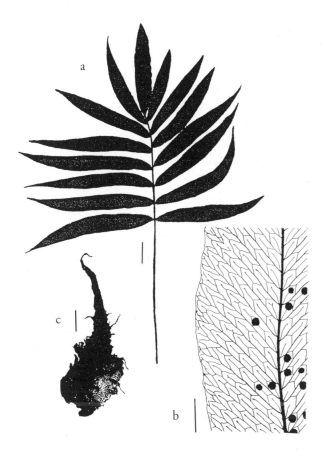

Figure 13.101.7. *Polypodium brasiliense:* a. frond, bar = 5 cm (2 in.); b. venation and sori, bar = 1 cm (0.4 in.); c. rhizome scale, bar = 1 mm. After Hoshizaki (1982).

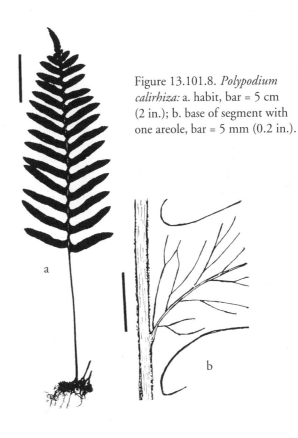

Figure 13.101.8. *Polypodium calirhiza:* a. habit, bar = 5 cm (2 in.); b. base of segment with one areole, bar = 5 mm (0.2 in.).

tween the pinna midribs and margins, slightly scaly pinna midribs, and long-attenuate, sparsely and irregularly fimbriate rhizome scales. It is native to tropical America.

'Cristata'. See *Polypodium triseriale* 'Cristatum'.

Polypodium calirhiza S. A. Whitmore & A. R. Smith

FIGURES 13.101.8, 34i

Semi-hardy, Zone 8

A small fern with short- to medium-creeping rhizomes. Grows well under medium light in drained, moist to moist-dry garden soil or potting mix. The rhizome has an acrid or slightly sweet flavor.

Polypodium calirhiza has pinnatifid blades that are widest above the base, with one or no areoles on each segment. The upper surface of the rachis has minute hairs, the lower surface with lanceolate to ovate scales. This plant is a fertile hybrid of *Polypodium glycyrrhiza* and *P. californicum* Kaulfuss (Figure 13.101.34g). It is native to California and Mexico and is grown in gardens on the West Coast of the United States.

Polypodium cambricum Linnaeus

FIGURES 13.101.1, 2, 9, 34a

syn. *Polypodium australe* Fée
Southern polypody
Semi-hardy to hardy

A small fern with short- to medium-creeping rhizomes. Grows well under medium light in moist, drained, basic garden soil or potting mix. The plants produce new fronds in late summer.

Polypodium cambricum is characterized by broadly ovate, pinnatifid blades, with the longest pair of pinnae often second from the base. Oval sori have paraphyses consisting of branched hairs. It is native to Europe.

Polypodium cambricum, a member of the *P. vulgare* complex, has long been considered a fringed (two-pinnatifid) variant of *P. australe.* Because *P. cambricum* is an earlier name, however, it must be used instead of the name *P. australe.* The unfringed form is typically found in nature (Figure 13.101.9a).

Most of the English *Polypodium* cultivars belong to *P. cambricum,* but they are uncommon in the United States trade and tend to grow slowly. The following are some cultivars that may be encountered in the United States:

'Cambricum' (var. *cambricum*). Figure 13.101.9b. Fronds two-pinnatifid, sterile, never producing sori. Some plants circulating in the trade as 'Cambricum' are large, tender plants belonging either to *Microsorum commutatum* 'Southern Cross' or *Polypodium triseriale* 'Cambrioides'.

Figure 13.101.10. *Polypodium dissimile:* habit, bar = 5 cm (2 in.).

Figure 13.101.9. *Polypodium cambricum:* a. habit of species, bar = 5 cm (2 in.); b. frond of 'Cambricum'; c. paraphysis (left) and sporangium (right), bar = 0.5 mm, after Shivas (1962).

'Cornubiense'. Fronds nearly three-pinnatifid, segments linear.

'Pulcherrimum'. Resembles 'Cambricum', but with blades to three-pinnatifid and fully fertile.

Polypodium dissimile Linnaeus   FIGURE 13.101.10
syn. *Polypodium chnoodes* Sprengel
Tender

A medium-sized fern with medium-creeping rhizomes. Grows well under medium light in moist, drained potting mix. The fronds are arching, herbaceous, and gray-green.

Polypodium dissimile is easily recognized by its distinctly clathrate rhizome scales, hairy blades (both surfaces), and two to four rows of areoles between the pinna midrib and blade margin. The lower pinnae are bent downward and clasp the rachis. This species is native to tropical America.

Polypodium formosanum Baker
    FIGURE 13.101.11; PLATE 44
syn. *Goniophlebium formosanum* (Baker) Rödl-Linder
Semi-tender to hardier

A small to medium fern with medium- to long-creeping rhizomes. Grows well under medium light in drained, moist-dry garden soil or potting mix. The new fronds emerge at the end of the summer, and old fronds are shed in late spring.

The rhizomes of *Polypodium formosanum* are 7–8 mm (0.3 in.) thick, conspicuously glaucous, and contain scattered dark fiber strands (seen in cross section). The pinnatifid, light gray-green blades are hairy on the margins and both surfaces of the rachis. This species is native to southern China, Japan, and Taiwan.

Some pteridologists classify this species in *Goniophlebium,* but it lacks the jointed pinnae characteristic of that genus. For this reason it is left in *Polypodium* pending further study.

'Cristatum'. Rhizomes forked many times and congested.

Polypodium glycyrrhiza D. C. Eaton
    FIGURES 13.101.12, 34h
syn. *Polypodium vulgare* var. *occidentale* Hooker
Licorice fern
Hardy, Zone 5(6)

A small fern with short- to medium-creeping rhizomes. Grows well under medium light in moist, drained potting mix or uncut moss. This species is easy to cultivate and often volunteers in the bales of green moss used to line hanging baskets.

The rhizomes of *Polypodium glycyrrhiza* have a distinct, sweet, licorice taste. The upper surface of the rachis has minute hairs and the lower surface has linear or hair-like scales. The pinnae shape varies (a rock form has rounder

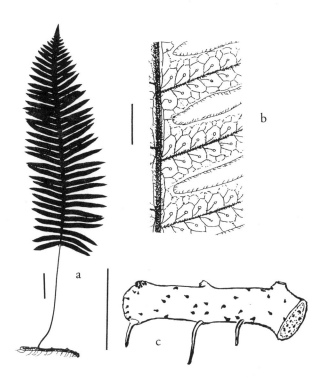

Figure 13.101.11. *Polypodium formosanum:* a. habit, bar = 5 cm (2 in.); b. vein details and hairs along the rachis, bar = 1 cm (0.4 in.); c. rhizome with rhizome scales, bar = 1 cm (0.4 in.).

Figure 13.101.12. *Polypodium glycyrrhiza:* frond variations, bar = 5 cm (2 in.), after Hoshizaki (1982).

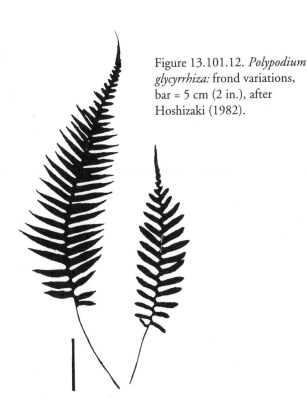

tips), and the sori vary from round to oval and lack paraphyses. The species is native to Asia and the western coast of North America.

Polypodium guttatum Maxon   FIGURE 13.101.13
Semi-tender, Zone 9

A small fern with short- to medium-creeping rhizomes. Grows well under medium light in moist-dry, drained potting mix.

Polypodium guttatum lacks scales on the upper surface of its blade, but scales are sparsely scattered on the lower surface, imparting a speckled appearance. This species is native to Mexico.

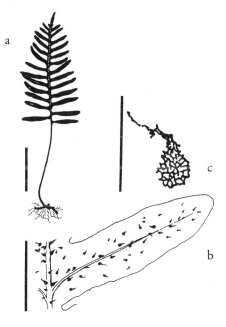

Figure 13.101.13. *Polypodium guttatum:* a. habit, bar = 5 cm (2 in.); b. segment underside with scales, bar = 1 cm (0.4 in.); c. scale from lower blade surface, bar = 1 mm. Courtesy of Knobloch and Correll (1962).

Polypodium hesperium Maxon
FIGURES 13.101.14, 34k

Western polypody
Very hardy, Zone (3)4

A small fern with short- to medium-creeping rhizomes. Grows under medium light in moist-dry, drained potting mix. This species bears evergreen fronds. It is difficult to grow and doubtfully in cultivation.

Polypodium hesperium has pinnatilobed blades, and the rachises are smooth above but bear linear-lanceolate scales below. The oval sori lack paraphyses. It is a fertile hybrid of *Polypodium amorphum* Suksdorf (Figure 13.101.34j) and *P. glycyrrhiza* and is native to western North America from Canada to Mexico.

Figure 13.101.14. *Polypodium hesperium:* habit, bar = 5 cm (2 in.).

Polypodium hirsutissimum Raddi   FIGURE 13.101.15

Semi-hardy (?)

A medium-sized fern with short- to medium-creeping rhizomes. Grows well under medium light in moist-dry, drained potting mix or uncut moss.

Polypodium hirsutissimum has densely scaly, narrowly oblong, pinnatisect blades. On the inside upper edge of the segments is a small, slightly swollen gland. This species is native to South America, where it grows epiphytically in wet forests.

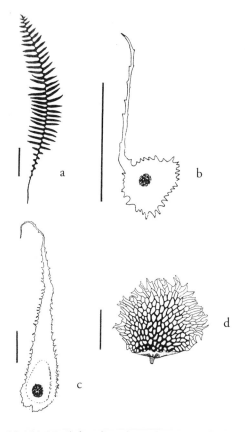

Figure 13.101.15. *Polypodium hirsutissimum:* a. frond, bar = 5 cm (2 in.); b. scale from lower surface of blade, bar = 1 mm, after Sota (1966); c. rhizome scale, bar = 1 mm, after Sota (1966); d. scale from around the sorus, bar = 0.25 mm, after Sota (1966).

Polypodium interjectum Shivas

FIGURES 13.101.16, 34c

Intermediate polypody
Hardy, Zone 5

A small fern with short- to medium-creeping rhizomes. Grows well under medium light in drained, moist to moist-dry garden soil, potting mix, or uncut moss. This species is easy to grow and produces new fronds in the late summer and autumn.

Polypodium interjectum has firm, ovate, pinnatifid fronds, often with longest pinnae in the fourth to sixth pair from the base. The young sori are oval and lack paraphyses. The species is native to Europe.

This member of the *Polypodium vulgare* complex is a fertile hybrid of *P. cambricum* and *P. vulgare.*

Figure 13.101.16. *Polypodium interjectum:* a. frond variations, bar = 5 cm (2 in.); b. sporangium, bar = 0.5 mm, after Shivas (1962).

Polypodium ×*leucosporum* Klotzsch

FIGURE 13.101.17

syn. *Pleopeltis* ×*leucospora* (Klotzsch) E. G. Andrews,
     ×*Pleopodium leucosporum* (Klotzsch) Mickel & Beitel
Semi-tender or hardier

A small-medium fern with medium-creeping rhizomes. Grows well under medium light in drained, moist-dry potting mix.

The ovate-elliptic fronds of *Polypodium* ×*leucosporum* are deeply and coarsely lobed nearly to the midrib, with the lower lobes sometimes much reduced. The sori are produced in a medial row. This fern is native to the American tropics.

Polypodium ×*leucosporum* is a sterile hybrid of *Pleopeltis macrocarpa* (Bory ex Willdenow) Kaulfuss and *Polypodium thyssanolepis* A. Braun ex Klotzsch. It was studied in detail by Wagner and Wagner (1975). The spores are misshapen, irregular, and aborted. Sterile hybrids such as this one are one reason pteridologists believe that the scaly-polypody group is more closely related to *Pleopeltis* than to other groups of *Polypodium*.

Polypodium levigatum Cavanilles FIGURE 13.101.18
syn. *Polypodium glaucophyllum* Kunze ex Klotzsch
Tender

A small fern with creeping, gray-green rhizomes bearing a few minute, scattered scales. Grows in medium light in moist to moist-dry, well-drained potting soil or uncut moss.

The simple and entire fronds of *Polypodium levigatum* are unusual. They are gray-green, elliptic-lanceolate, and smooth except for a few ovate-acuminate scales on the lower surface of the rachis. The veins are netted. It is native from Central America to South America.

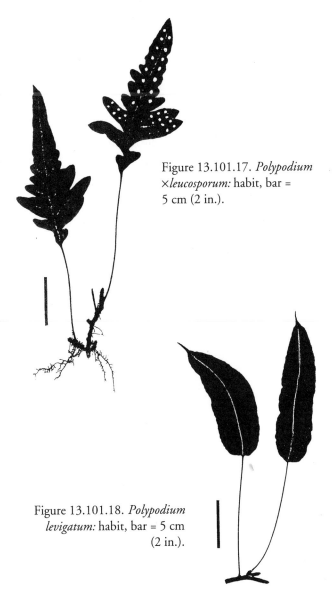

Figure 13.101.17. *Polypodium ×leucosporum:* habit, bar = 5 cm (2 in.).

Figure 13.101.18. *Polypodium levigatum:* habit, bar = 5 cm (2 in.).

Polypodium loriceum Linnaeus FIGURE 13.101.19
Tender

A small-medium fern with medium-creeping rhizomes. Grows well under medium light in drained, moist potting mix.

Polypodium loriceum resembles *P. maritimum,* but its rhizome scales are less distinctly clathrate, its blades are glabrous, and only one row of sori is found between the pinna midrib and margin. This species is widespread in the American tropics.

As presently defined, *Polypodium loriceum* is extremely variable and includes several geographic entities that probably represent different species. This matter, however, needs further research.

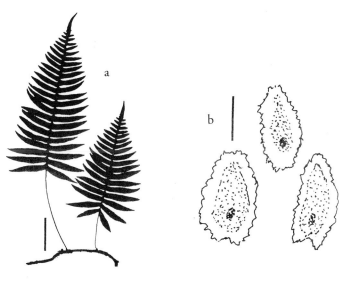

Figure 13.101.19. *Polypodium loriceum:* a. habit, bar = 5 cm (2 in.); b. rhizome scales, bar = 1 mm.

Polypodium maritimum Hieronymus
FIGURE 13.101.20

Tender

A small-medium fern with medium-creeping rhizomes. Grows well under medium light in drained, moist potting mix.

Polypodium maritimum is distinguished by pinnatisect, long-tapered blades and by two or three rows of areoles between the pinna midrib and margin. The rhizomes are densely covered with roundish scales. The species is native to Central America and northern South America.

Polypodium menisciifolium Langsdorff & Fischer
FIGURE 13.101.21

Semi-tender to hardier

A medium-sized fern with a medium- to long-creeping rhizome. Grows well under medium light in drained, moist to

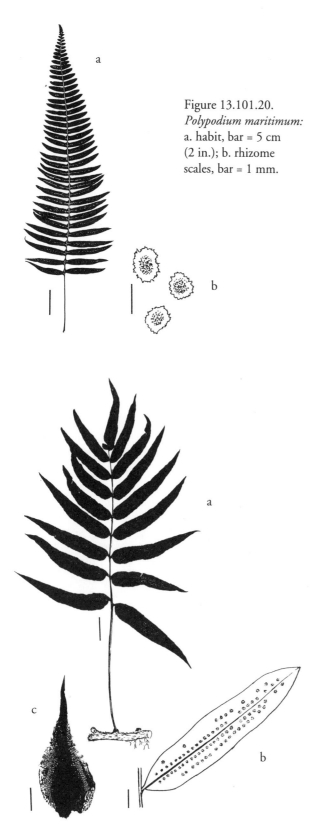

Figure 13.101.20.
Polypodium maritimum:
a. habit, bar = 5 cm
(2 in.); b. rhizome
scales, bar = 1 mm.

Figure 13.101.21. *Polypodium menisciifolium:* a. habit,
bar = 5 cm (2 in.); b. pinna with sori, bar = 1 cm
(0.4 in.), after Hoshizaki (1982); c. rhizome scale, bar =
1 mm, after Hoshizaki (1982).

moist-dry potting mix or uncut moss. The plants are robust growers and easy to cultivate.

Polypodium menisciifolium has one-pinnate fronds, and the pinna bases are rounded or obtuse. The rachises are glabrous on their upper surfaces. This species is native to southern Brazil.

This species is sometimes misidentified as *Polypodium fraxinifolium* Jacquin, a species not in recent cultivation.

Polypodium pellucidum Kaulfuss

FIGURES 13.101.22, 34m

Pellucid polypody
Tender to semi-tender

A small-medium fern with short- to medium-creeping rhizomes. Grows well under medium light in drained, moist to moist-dry potting mix or uncut moss. When grown in high light, the fronds become short and compact.

The fronds of *Polypodium pellucidum* are shiny, bright green, and evergreen. The veins are free (not netted), and a false vein ends at each marginal notch. The sori vary from round to oval and lack paraphyses. This species is endemic to the Hawaiian Islands.

Polypodium plebeium Schlechtendal & Chamisso

FIGURE 13.101.23

Semi-tender or hardier

A small fern with short- to medium-creeping rhizomes. Grows well under medium light in drained, moist-dry potting mix. This species can be grown in soil or as an epiphyte.

The rhizome scales of *Polypodium plebeium* have a dark central strip and lighter margins. The dark green fronds

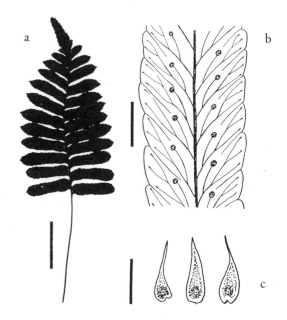

Figure 13.101.22. *Polypodium pellucidum:* a. frond, bar
= 5 cm (2 in.); b. segment with veins, bar = 3 mm
(0.1 in.); c. rhizome scales, bar = 3 mm (0.1 in.).

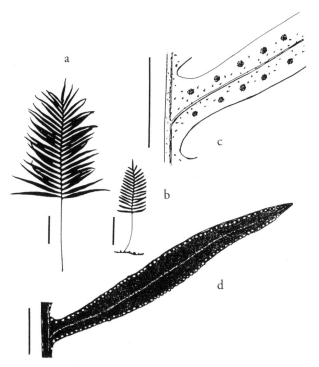

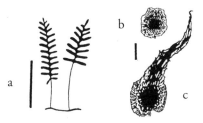

Figure 13.101.24. *Polypodium polypodioides:* a. habit, bar = 5 cm (2 in.); b. blade scale, bar = 1 mm; c. rhizome scale, bar = 1 mm. After Hoshizaki (1982).

Figure 13.101.23. *Polypodium plebeium:* a. frond grown under garden conditions, bar = 5 cm (2 in.); b. frond from the wild, bar = 5 cm (2 in.); c. base of segment with sori and scales, bar = 1 cm (0.4 in.); d. hydathodes along segment margin, upper surface, bar = 1 cm (0.4 in.).

have many pinnae (up to about 18 pairs) that are narrow and close together. Scales are on the lower surface of the blade only, 0.5–1.0 mm long, few, and inconspicuous. The veins are hard to see because the blades are thick. This species is native to Central America.

Polypodium polypodioides (Linnaeus) Watt
FIGURE 13.101.24

syn. *Pleopeltis polypodioides* (Linnaeus) E. G. Andrews
Resurrection fern
Hardy, Zone 6(7)

A small fern with short- to (mostly) long-creeping rhizomes. Grows under medium light in drained, acidic, moist-dry potting mix or uncut moss. The plants are slow-growing and difficult to establish. Avoid disturbing the roots during transplanting.

Polypodium polypodioides has small fronds, to 20 cm (8 in.) long and 4 cm (1.5 in.) wide. They are sparsely scaly above and more densely scaly beneath. The sori are slightly sunken and partially hidden by the covering of scales; they may appear slightly embossed on the upper surface of the blade. This species is native to the New World. Weatherby (1939) subdivided it into six varieties on the basis of frond size and scale characteristics of the blades and rhizomes:

var. *aciculare* Weatherby, of Central America; var. *burchellii* (Baker) Weatherby, of South America; var. *ecklonii* (Kunze) Weatherby, of southwestern Africa; var. *michauxianum* Weatherby, of the southeastern United States, Central America, the West Indies, and northern South America; var. *minus* (Fée) Weatherby, of southern Brazil, Uruguay, Paraguay, and Argentina; and var. *polypodioides,* of Central America, the West Indies, and northern South America.

In the southeastern United States the resurrection fern variety *michauxianum* (sometimes called *Pleopeltis polypodioides* var. *michauxianum* (Weatherby) E. G. Andrews & Windham) commonly grows on tree trunks or (more rarely) rocks and is occasionally cultivated. In the Gulf States it is a nearly constant associate of the live oak (*Quercus virginiana*). During dry weather the fronds curl into rough C- and J-shapes and can lose up to 97% of their normal moisture content. They can survive for months in this condition without any ill effects. The fronds rehydrate with rain and expand within hours. Physiological studies have shown that the scales on the lower surface of the blade funnel water into the middle layer of the leaf, thus helping to rehydrate the frond. For a nontechnical account of this, see Moran (1998).

Polypodium ptilorhizon H. Christ   FIGURE 13.101.25
Tender

A small fern with medium-creeping rhizomes. Grows well under medium light in moist, drained potting mix.

Polypodium ptilorhizon resembles a small *P. loriceum* but differs by having minute, scattered rhizome scales and fewer (generally 10–22) pairs of pinnae. The blades are glabrous, and there is only one row of areoles and sori between the pinna midrib and margin. The species is native to tropical America.

Polypodium pyrrholepis (Fée) Maxon
FIGURE 13.101.26; PLATE 45

Semi-hardy

A medium-sized fern with short- to medium-creeping rhizomes. Grows well under medium light in moist-dry gar-

Figure 13.101.25. *Polypodium ptilorhizon:* frond, bar = 5 cm (2 in.), after Hoshizaki (1982).

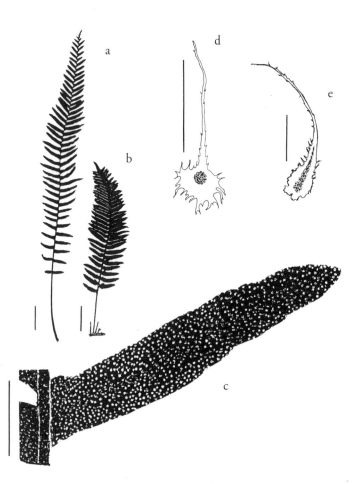

Figure 13.101.26. *Polypodium pyrrholepis:* a. frond grown in shade, bar = 5 cm (2 in.); b. habit, bar = 5 cm (2 in.); c. segment with scales, upper surface, bar = 1 cm (0.4 in.); d. scale from lower surface of blade, bar = 1 mm, after Sota (1966); e. rhizome scale, bar = 1 mm, after Sota (1966).

den soil or potting mix kept well drained. The plants are easy to cultivate in hanging baskets or in the ground.

Polypodium pyrrholepis has tufted, bright rusty-red rhizome scales. The fronds are set close together, with blades narrowly linear-oblong, pinnatisect, and densely scaly on both surfaces. A small, slightly swollen gland is on the inside, upper edge of the segments. This species is native to southern Mexico.

Polypodium rhodopleuron Kunze   FIGURE 13.101.27
Semi-tender

A small fern with creeping rhizomes. Grows under medium light in moist, drained potting mix. This species can be difficult to cultivate but is attractive because of the reddish rachises and (sometimes) other leaf parts. The color is best developed on young fronds.

Polypodium rhodopleuron has whitish rhizome scales, and the fronds are glabrous, pinnatisect, to about 30 cm (12 in.) long, and have red-tinged rachises. The veinlets next to costae have enlarged whitish tips. The species is native to Central America and Mexico.

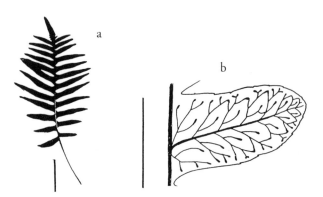

Figure 13.101.27. *Polypodium rhodopleuron:* a. frond, bar = 5 cm (2 in.); b. segment with veins, bar = 1 cm (0.4 in.). After Hoshizaki (1982).

Polypodium sanctae-rosae (Maxon) C. Christensen
FIGURE 13.101.28
Semi-tender

A small-medium fern with short- to medium-creeping rhizomes. Grows well under medium light in moist, drained potting mix. The plants tend to wilt easily if the light becomes too intense. Older fronds are silvery white, gray-green.

The rhizome scales of *Polypodium sanctae-rosae* are ovate to ovate-deltoid, small, appressed, and overlapping. The stipes and rachises of young fronds are speckled with dark scales. On the upper surface of the blades the scales are pale tan to white, whereas those on the lower surface are shiny, pale rust colored. The sori are tightly enclosed by a rosette of scales. The species is native to Mexico and Central America.

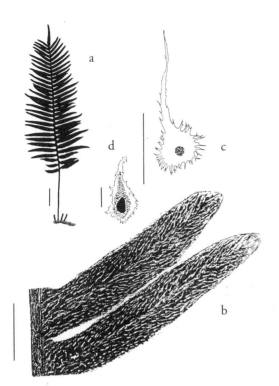

Figure 13.101.28. *Polypodium sanctae-rosae:* a. habit, bar = 5 cm (2 in.); b. segment, upper surface, bar = 1 cm (0.4 in.); c. scale from lower surface of blade, bar = 1 mm, after Sota (1966); d. rhizome scale, bar = 1 mm, after Sota (1966).

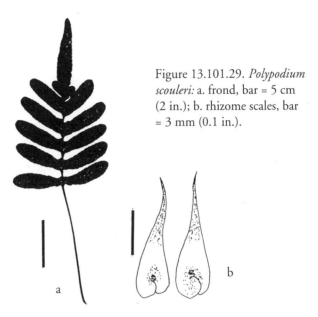

Figure 13.101.29. *Polypodium scouleri:* a. frond, bar = 5 cm (2 in.); b. rhizome scales, bar = 3 mm (0.1 in.).

The stipes of *Polypodium thyssanolepis* are longer than the blades, which are deeply pinnatifid, about 10 cm (4 in.) long, 7 cm (3 in.) wide, and broadest at the base. The pinnae are few (three to seven pairs) and glabrous or sparsely scaly on the upper surface but densely scaly on the lower. The sori are not sunken. The species occurs from the southwestern United States to South America and Jamaica. It grows terrestrially or on or among rocks.

Polypodium scouleri Hooker & Greville
FIGURES 13.101.29, 34l
Leathery polypody, coast polypody
Semi-hardy, Zones 8–9

A small to medium fern with medium-creeping rhizomes. Grows well under medium light in drained, moist-dry garden soil or potting mix or in uncut moss. The plants are evergreen, slow growing, and adapted to salt spray.

Polypodium scouleri has glaucous, stout rhizomes that produce stiff, leathery fronds with pinnae more than 12 mm (0.5 in.) wide. The veins are netted and form one row of areoles. The sori are more than 3 mm (0.1 in.) wide. This species is native to the West Coast of North America, from Canada to Mexico.

Polypodium thyssanolepis A. Braun ex Klotzsch
FIGURE 13.101.30
syn. *Pleopeltis thyssanolepis* (A. Braun ex Klotzsch) E. G. Andrews
Scaly polypody
Semi-hardy, Zone 8

A small fern with medium-creeping rhizomes. Grows well under medium light in drained, moist-dry garden soil or potting mix.

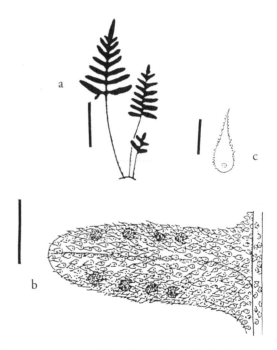

Figure 13.101.30. *Polypodium thyssanolepis:* a. habit, bar = 5 cm (2 in.); b. segment with sori and scales, bar = 5 mm (0.2 in.), after Knobloch and Correll (1962); c. blade scale, bar = 1 mm, after Knobloch and Correll (1962).

Polypodium triseriale Swartz

FIGURE 13.101.31

Tender to slightly hardier

A medium-sized fern with medium-creeping rhizomes. Grows well under medium light in drained, moist garden soil or potting mix. The species is extremely variable throughout its range.

Polypodium triseriale has ovate rhizome scales with pale margins. The fronds are one-pinnate at least at the base, with linear-lanceolate pinnae; the lower pinnae are narrowed toward the base and nearly free on the basiscopic side, narrowly adnate on the acroscopic side. The rachises are glabrous on the upper surface, and the veins form up to five series of areoles. The sori are in one to three rows. This species is common and widespread throughout tropical America.

'Cambrioides'. Pinnae sterile, irregularly lacerate, and ruffled. This cultivar grows slowly. Its fronds tend to be too heavy for the stipes, which often break. Since the plant is sterile, its placement with *Polypodium triseriale* is tentative. For a similar plant, see *Microsorum commutatum* 'Southern Cross'.

'Cristatum'. Pinnae several times forked to form a crest. Reportedly found in Brazil by Barbara Varga of Varga Nursery, Pennsylvania. Circulating in the United States trade as *Polypodium brasiliense* 'Cristata'.

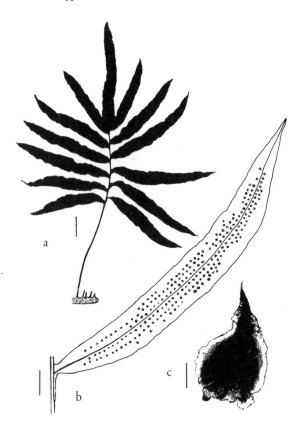

Figure 13.101.31. *Polypodium triseriale:* a. habit, bar = 5 cm (2 in.); b. pinna with sori, bar = 1 cm (0.4 in.); c. rhizome scale, bar = 1 mm. After Hoshizaki (1982).

Polypodium virginianum Linnaeus

FIGURES 13.101.32, 34f

Virginia polypody, rock polypody, American wall fern
Very hardy, Zone 2

A small fern with short- to medium-creeping rhizomes. Grows under low-medium light in drained, moist potting mix. The plants establish slowly and are susceptible to attack from snails and slugs. The fronds are evergreen.

The rhizome scales of *Polypodium virginianum* are dark brown and often weakly marked with a darker central stripe. The pinnatisect, thin-leathery fronds bear round sori. The paraphyses are modified sporangia with glands. This species is native to the eastern half of North America.

Polypodium virginianum is a fertile plant of hybrid origin from an ancient cross involving *P. appalachianum* Haufler & Windham and *P. sibericum* Siplivinsky. It differs from *P. appalachianum* by its more-linear fronds and light brown or bicolorous rhizome scales. The plants from boreal Canada and Alaska previously called *P. virginianum* have been transferred to *P. sibericum,* the Siberian polypody, which lacks glands on the paraphyses and has smaller spores.

Polypodium vulgare Linnaeus

FIGURES 13.101.33, 34b

Common polypody
Hardy, Zone (4)5

A small fern with short- to medium-creeping rhizomes. Grows well under medium light in drained, moist potting mix or uncut moss. The plants grow slowly, with new growth appearing in early summer.

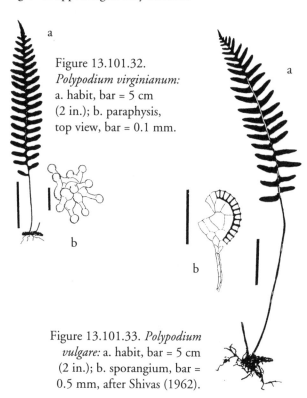

Figure 13.101.32. *Polypodium virginianum:* a. habit, bar = 5 cm (2 in.); b. paraphysis, top view, bar = 0.1 mm.

Figure 13.101.33. *Polypodium vulgare:* a. habit, bar = 5 cm (2 in.); b. sporangium, bar = 0.5 mm, after Shivas (1962).

Figure 13.101.34. Frond silhouettes of species in the *Polypodium vulgare* complex. European species: a. *P. cambricum;* b. *P. vulgare;* c. *P. interjectum.* Eastern North American species: d. *P. appalachianum;* e. *P. sibericum;* f. *P. virginianum.* Western North American species: g. *P. californicum;* h. *P. glycyrrhiza;* i. *P. calirhiza;* j. *P. amorphum;* k. *P. hesperium;* l. *P. scouleri.* Hawaiian species: m. *P. pellucidum.* Bars = 5 cm (2 in.). Plants c, f, i, and k of hybrid origin; see text entries for details.

The blades of *Polypodium vulgare* are flat, pinnatisect, and lanceolate, and almost all the pinnae are equal in length. The sori are round, without paraphyses. This species is native to Europe.

Polypodium cambricum and *P. interjectum* differ from this species by their broader fronds, their forward-projecting lower pinnae, and in sori details. For more information, see Rickard (1981).

'Ramosum Hillman'. Fronds branched near the base of the blade; tips of the branches forked to form a crest.

Polystichum
Shield fern

FIGURES 13.102.1–3

The shield ferns of the genus *Polystichum* are small- to medium-sized terrestrial ferns commonly grown in temperate gardens. Many of the species are particularly attractive for their dark green, glossy, evergreen foliage. The plants are used in rock gardens, borders, or pots, and larger species can be used as foundation plants or for background foliage. They are often slow to grow from spores.

Eastern and western North America harbor distinctive species of *Polystichum*. In the eastern region the Christmas fern (*Polystichum acrostichoides*) is one of the most common native species and is widely cultivated. It is easily recognized by its one-pinnate fronds with narrowed fertile pinnae toward the tip. The western sword fern (*P. munitum*) is abundant in the coastal forests of western North America, and it is commonly grown in gardens. Its narrow, one-pinnate fronds may grow to 1.6 m (5 ft.) tall but are usually 30–100 cm (1–3 ft.) in cultivation.

Besides the North American species, several European and Asian ones are commonly planted in certain regions of the United States. The bristle fern, *Polystichum polyblepharum* (widely sold as *P. setosum*), is cultivated in the Southwest and elsewhere. Its fronds are two-pinnate, dark, and

Figure 13.102.2. *Polystichum* pinnae: *P. proliferum* (left), *P. munitum* (center), *P. polyblepharum* (right).

glossy green. The soft shield fern (*P. setiferum*), a native of Europe, and its bewildering array of more than 300 garden varieties are grown throughout the United States. The wild form of the species resembles the bristle fern but has dull, lighter green blades.

Western North American *Polystichum* species do not grow as well on the East Coast, and vice versa, but the European and Asiatic species are adaptable in both areas, ex-

Figure 13.102.1. *Polystichum polyblepharum*: habit.

Figure 13.102.3. *Polystichum proliferum*: sori and indusia.

cept in very hot, humid places. The northwestern species can be grown in the southwest if provided with high humidity and acid soils. Because only a few species produce multiple crowns that can be divided, most polystichums are propagated from spores. Many species also form buds along their rachises or at the tips of the fronds. These buds are easily rooted by pegging the leaf to the soil. Thrip damage is often conspicuous on fronds of *Polystichum,* appearing as a grayish silvering on the blade.

Polystichum has erect, ascending (rarely short-creeping) rhizomes. The fronds are mostly one- to two-pinnate, less often three-pinnate, pinnatifid. They are elongate, often narrowed at the base, with the apex gradually reduced. The pinnae often have an upward-pointing "ear" at their base—a characteristic helpful in distinguishing the genus from *Dryopteris,* which often lacks the ear. Some one-pinnate species have terminal pinnae that resemble the lateral ones. The marginal teeth generally bear a short bristle or spine. The veins are anadromic and free, not netted. Round sori are formed in one row (or infrequently two) between the midrib and margin. Indusia may be present or absent; when present, they are peltate.

Some authors believe that *Cyrtomium* (including *Phanerophlebia*) is so closely related to *Polystichum* that it should be combined with it. *Cyrtomium,* however, differs by having netted veins and sori in two or more series.

The genus *Polystichum* contains 180 species and is cosmopolitan. For details on the many varieties, see Dyce (1963), Kaye (1968), and Mickel (1994). The genus name comes from the Greek *poly,* many, and *stichos,* row, referring to the sori of the type species (*Polystichum aculeatum*), which are arranged in many regular rows on the pinnae.

Because *Polystichum* contains so many species, the following subgroups are given to aid identification. Once an unknown species is limited to one of these subgroups, it can be compared to the descriptions and illustrations of other species in the group. The groups are based on typical fronds (not cultivars) from mature plants.

Fronds one-pinnate, the pinnae entire, serrate, or crenate, not pinnatifid: *Polystichum acrostichoides, P. craspedosorum, P. imbricans, P. lepidocaulon, P. lonchitis, P. munitum, P. nepalense, P. stenophyllum, P. stimulans*

Fronds one-pinnate-pinnatifid, lower pinnae may have a free pinnule at their base: *Polystichum andersonii, P. californicum, P. kruckebergii, P. lentum, P. scopulinum, P. setigerum, P. xiphophyllum*

Fronds two-pinnate or nearly so in the proximal part: *Polystichum aculeatum, P. xiphophyllum*

Fronds fully two-pinnate in most parts of the frond, not more divided: *Polystichum braunii, P. dudleyi, P. lemmonii, P. makinoi, P. neolobatum, P. polyblepharum, P. proliferum, P. rigens, P. setiferum, P. tripteron, P. tsus-simense*

Fronds two-pinnate-pinnatifid or up to three-pinnate, at least at the base of the lower pinnae: *Polystichum proliferum, P. richardii, P. silvaticum, P. tagawanum, P. tsus-simense, P. vestitum*

Polystichum acrostichoides (Michaux) Schott
FIGURE 13.102.4

Christmas fern
Very hardy, Zone 3

A medium-sized fern with ascending, clump-forming rhizomes and evergreen leaves. Grows well under low to medium light in moist garden soil or potting mix. Although easily cultivated in the eastern United States, the plants are difficult to grow on the West Coast. In winter, the fronds recline to the ground, forming a rosette around the rhizome apex.

Polystichum acrostichoides is characterized by one-pinnate blades with the distal, fertile pinnules narrower than the sterile ones. The pinnae have an upward-pointing "ear" at the base, and the margins are spinulose. When the sori mature they tend to become confluent, resembling acrostichoid sori. The species is native to eastern North America.

A sterile hybrid, *Polystichum* ×*potteri* Barrington (= *P. acrostichoides* × *P. braunii*), is sometimes cultivated. The hybrid is native to Pennsylvania, New England, Nova Scotia, New Brunswick, and Quebec.

Various cultivar names are listed in the trade, such as 'Crispum', 'Cristatum', and 'Incisum'.

Figure 13.102.4. *Polystichum acrostichoides:* frond, bar = 5 cm (2 in.).

Polystichum aculeatum (Linnaeus) Roth

FIGURE 13.102.5

syn. *Polystichum lobatum* (Hudson) C. Presl
Hard shield fern
Very hardy, Zone 4

A medium-sized fern with ascending to erect rhizomes and stiff, glossy, evergreen leaves. Grows well under medium light in moist, basic garden soil or potting mix. This species is easy to grow.

The stipes of *Polystichum aculeatum* are often short, and the fronds are lanceolate and nearly two-pinnate, with the basal pinnae half the length of the middle ones. The pinnules are sessile or nearly so, and the spores are dark brown. This species is native to Europe.

Polystichum aculeatum is often difficult to distinguish from *P. setiferum,* which is softer, fully two-pinnate, often not or only slightly narrowed at the blade base, has pinnules clearly stalked, and yellow spores. A sterile hybrid, *Polystichum×illyricum* (Burbas) Hahne (= *P. aculeatum× P. lonchitis*), is reported to be cultivated and appears intermediate between its parents.

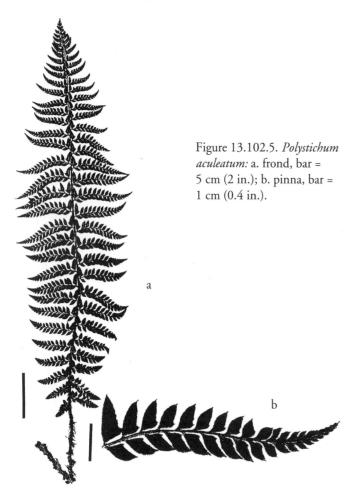

Figure 13.102.5. *Polystichum aculeatum:* a. frond, bar = 5 cm (2 in.); b. pinna, bar = 1 cm (0.4 in.).

Polystichum andersonii M. Hopkins

FIGURE 13.102.6

Anderson's sword fern, Anderson's holly fern
Hardy, Zone 5(6)

A medium-sized fern with ascending to erect rhizomes and evergreen, bud-bearing leaves. Grows well under medium light in moist garden soil or potting mix. The plants prefer moist, cool climates. This species adapts poorly on the East Coast and in southern California.

Polystichum andersonii has short stipes and elliptic-lanceolate, one-pinnate-pinnatifid blades that are narrowed toward the base. The pinnules are adnate to the costae, the adnation 2 mm wide or more. The bud(s) form on the distal third of the rachis. The indusium is dentate. This species is native to western North America.

The buds of this species do not drop from the leaf as in some ferns. Instead, they take root after the leaf has reclined in late fall and is prostrate on the soil. In the wild the plants form colonies by this method of reproduction.

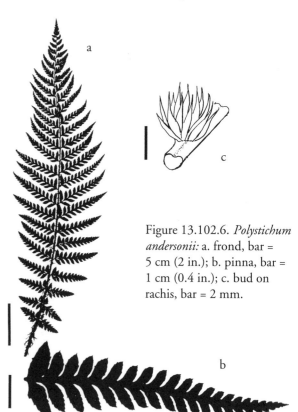

Figure 13.102.6. *Polystichum andersonii:* a. frond, bar = 5 cm (2 in.); b. pinna, bar = 1 cm (0.4 in.); c. bud on rachis, bar = 2 mm.

Polystichum braunii (Spenner) Fée

FIGURE 13.102.7; PLATE 6

Braun's holly fern, prickly shield fern
Very hardy, Zone 3(4)

A small to medium fern with clump-forming rhizomes and dark green, shiny, evergreen fronds. Grows well under medium light in moist potting mix. The plants do best if

Figure 13.102.7. *Polystichum braunii:* frond, bar = 5 cm (2 in.).

placed in a cool site. The fiddleheads are particularly attractive because they are densely covered by silvery scales, which turn light brown with age.

Polystichum braunii has short stipes, usually about one-quarter the length of the frond. The stipes are densely scaly, and the blades are two-pinnate and elliptic-lanceolate, gradually narrowed toward the base. The pinnules are short-stalked and bristly. This species is native to North America, Europe, and Asia.

Polystichum californicum (D. C. Eaton) Diels
FIGURE 13.102.8

California sword fern, California holly fern
Semi-hardy, Zone 8

A medium-sized fern with ascending to erect rhizomes and evergreen fronds. Grows under low to medium light in moist, drained potting mix. The plants are slow to establish. The new growth has silvery scales.

The blades of *Polystichum californicum* vary from one-pinnate-pinnatifid to almost two-pinnate and have adnate pinnules, the adnation 2 mm or more wide. The species is native to western North America.

This species is of hybrid origin, resulting from an ancient cross involving *Polystichum dudleyi* and either *P. munitum* or *P. imbricans*. According to Mickel (1994), some forms are sterile, others fertile.

Figure 13.102.8. *Polystichum californicum:* a. frond variations, bar = 5 cm (2 in.); b. pinna variations, bar = 2 cm (0.8 in.), after D. Wagner (1979).

Polystichum craspedosorum (Maximowicz) Diels
FIGURE 13.102.9

Hardy, Zone 5

A small fern with ascending to erect rhizomes and evergreen fronds. Grows well under medium light in moist potting soil.

Polystichum craspedosorum has linear-lanceolate, one-pinnate blades, with the rachises prolonged and rooting at tip. It is native to eastern Siberia, China, Japan, and Korea.

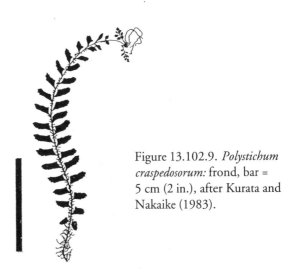

Figure 13.102.9. *Polystichum craspedosorum:* frond, bar = 5 cm (2 in.), after Kurata and Nakaike (1983).

Polystichum dudleyi Maxon   FIGURE 13.102.10

Woodrustic fern, Dudley's sword fern, Dudley's holly
    fern

Marginally semi-hardy, Zone 8

A medium-sized fern with ascending to erect rhizomes and
evergreen fronds. Grows well under medium light in moist,
drained potting mix. The plants do best in a cool, moist
climate, but they establish slowly. The fronds are slightly
brittle.

Polystichum dudleyi has scaly stipes and rachises, and the
blades are lanceolate, two-pinnate, and hardly tapered toward base. The pinnules are stalked and bear a tangle of
long, narrow, tan scales on their lower surfaces. The species
is native to California.

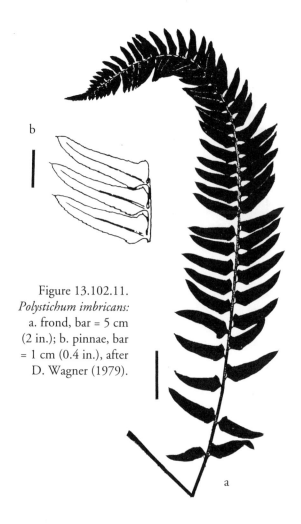

b

Figure 13.102.11.
Polystichum imbricans:
a. frond, bar = 5 cm
(2 in.); b. pinnae, bar
= 1 cm (0.4 in.), after
D. Wagner (1979).

a

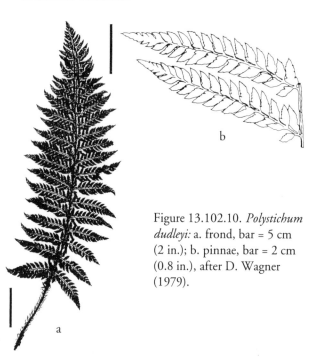

b

Figure 13.102.10. *Polystichum
dudleyi:* a. frond, bar = 5 cm
(2 in.); b. pinnae, bar = 2 cm
(0.8 in.), after D. Wagner
(1979).

a

Polystichum imbricans (D. C. Eaton) D. H. Wagner
    FIGURE 13.102.11

syn. *Polystichum munitum* var. *imbricans* (D. C. Eaton)
    Maxon

Imbricate sword fern

Hardy, Zone 6

A small to medium fern with ascending to erect rhizomes.
Grows well under medium to high light in moist garden
soil or potting mix with good drainage.

The scales on the stipes and rachises of *Polystichum imbricans* are shed early; the largest of these scales are less than
1 mm wide. The blades are linear-lanceolate and one-pinnate with oblong to lanceolate pinnae that are tipped by a
sharp, rigid, short point. The indusia are toothed or entire,
not ciliate. This species is native to the West Coast of Canada and the United States. See also *P. munitum.*

subsp. *curtum* (Ewan) D. H. Wagner. Pinnae slender,
lanceolate, falcate, plane, larger than those of subsp. *imbricans;* fronds up to 18 cm (7 in.) long. Native to California.

subsp. *imbricans.* Dwarf western sword fern. Pinnae
short, oblong, folded inward, oriented horizontally, overlapping; fronds dark green, stiff, erect, up to 50 cm (20 in.)
long. Native to southwestern Canada and the northwestern
United States.

Polystichum kruckebergii W. H. Wagner
    FIGURE 13.102.12

Kruckeberg's holly fern

Hardy, Zone 6

A small to medium fern with ascending to erect rhizomes
and dark green, glossy, evergreen fronds. Grows under medium to high light in moist garden soil or potting mix with
good drainage. This species is difficult to grow.

Polystichum kruckebergii has narrow and one-pinnate-
pinnatifid blades with ovate-triangular pinnae that tend to
overlap. The species is native to western North America.

This species is the fertile hybrid of *Polystichum lemmonii*
and *P. lonchitis.* Because it is fertile, it can be propagated by
spores.

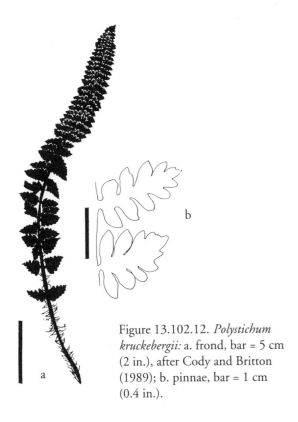

Figure 13.102.12. *Polystichum kruckebergii:* a. frond, bar = 5 cm (2 in.), after Cody and Britton (1989); b. pinnae, bar = 1 cm (0.4 in.).

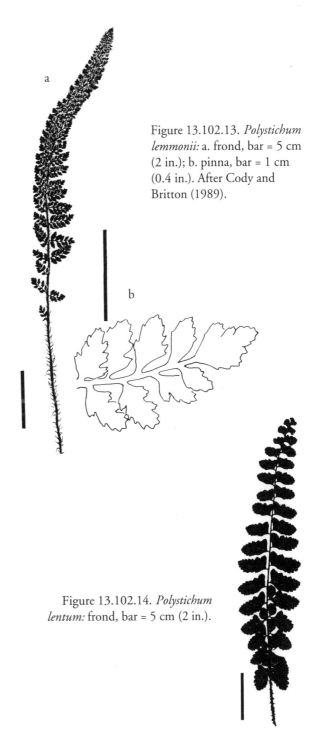

Figure 13.102.13. *Polystichum lemmonii:* a. frond, bar = 5 cm (2 in.); b. pinna, bar = 1 cm (0.4 in.). After Cody and Britton (1989).

Figure 13.102.14. *Polystichum lentum:* frond, bar = 5 cm (2 in.).

Polystichum lemmonii Underwood   FIGURE 13.102.13
syn. *Polystichum mohrioides* var. *lemmonii* (Underwood) Fernald

Shasta holly fern
Hardy, Zone 6

A small fern with ascending to erect rhizomes and semi-evergreen(?) fronds. Grows under medium to high light in moist potting mix with good drainage. The plants are difficult to grow.

Polystichum lemmonii has narrowly lanceolate, two-pinnate-pinnatifid blades with stalked pinnules that lack a spine at their tips. The species is native to western North America.

Polystichum lentum (D. Don) T. Moore
FIGURE 13.102.14

Himalayan holly fern
Semi-hardy, Zone 7

A small-medium fern with ascending to erect rhizomes and semi-evergreen(?) fronds. Grows well under medium light in moist garden soil or potting mix.

The blades of *Polystichum lentum* are narrowly elliptic and one-pinnate-pinnatifid to two-pinnate at the base. The pinnae are only deeply toothed, although some of the lower pinnae have a distinct basal pinnule. Buds are borne near the end of rachis. The species is native to Tibet, China, and Burma.

Polystichum lepidocaulon (Hooker) J. Smith
FIGURE 13.102.15

Semi-hardy, Zone 7

A small-medium fern with ascending to erect rhizomes and dark green, leathery, evergreen fronds. Grows well under medium light in moist garden soil or potting mix.

Polystichum lepidocaulon has scaly stipes and one-pinnate blades with long falcate, dark green, leathery pinnae.

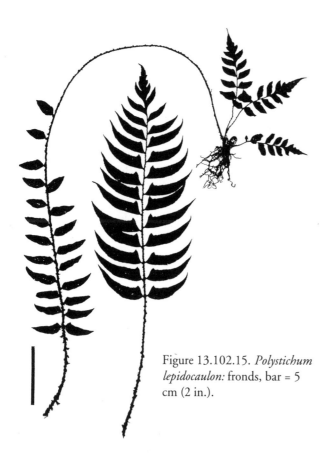

Figure 13.102.15. *Polystichum lepidocaulon:* fronds, bar = 5 cm (2 in.).

Figure 13.102.16. *Polystichum lonchitis:* a. frond, bar = 5 cm (2 in.); b. lowermost pinna, bar = 1 cm (0.4 in.).

The densely scaly rachis extends well beyond the blade and roots at the tip upon touching the ground. The species is native to Japan, Korea, eastern China, and Taiwan.

Mickel (1994) noted that this species was tried outdoors at the New York Botanical Garden without success but that it should be hardy in milder climates to the south.

Polystichum lonchitis (Linnaeus) Roth

FIGURE 13.102.16

Northern holly fern
Very hardy, Zone 3

A medium-sized fern with ascending to erect rhizomes and dark green, evergreen fronds. Grows under medium light in moist, basic garden soil or potting mix. The plants are difficult to grow even in cool climates.

The stipes are short, and the blades are linear-lanceolate, one-pinnate, and narrowed toward the base. The triangular basal pinnae are spinulose-margined, with the spines close and spreading. *Polystichum lonchitis* is native to northern North America and Greenland.

Two hybrids involving this species are also cultivated: *Polystichum ×illyricum* (Burbas) Hahne (= *P. aculeatum × P. lonchitis*) and *P. ×lonchitiforme* (Halacsy) Becherer (= *P. lonchitis × P. setiferum*).

Polystichum makinoi (Tagawa) Tagawa

FIGURE 13.102.17

Makino's holly fern
Hardy, Zone 5

A medium-sized fern with ascending to erect rhizomes and dark, glossy, evergreen fronds. Grows well under medium light in moist garden soil or potting mix.

The stipes and rachises of *Polystichum makinoi* bear numerous brown scales with paler margins. The blades are two-pinnate, the lower pinnae not or slightly reduced in size. The segments are rhombic and have soft, narrow, aristate teeth. The species is native to eastern India, southern China, Japan, and the Philippines.

Polystichum munitum (Kaulfuss) C. Presl

FIGURES 13.102.2, 18

Western sword fern, common sword fern
Hardy, Zone 7

A medium-large fern with ascending to erect rhizomes and evergreen fronds. Grows well under low to medium light in moist garden soil or potting mix with a lot of humus. This species does best in moist, cool climates and does not grow well in the eastern of southeastern United States. The fronds are frequently used in floral decorations.

The stipes and rachises of *Polystichum munitum* bear persistent ovate-lanceolate scales, to 1 mm wide or more in the distal part of the rachis. The blades are linear-lanceolate, one-pinnate, and plane, and the pinna apex is acuminate and short-spinulose (not with a sharp, short, rigid point).

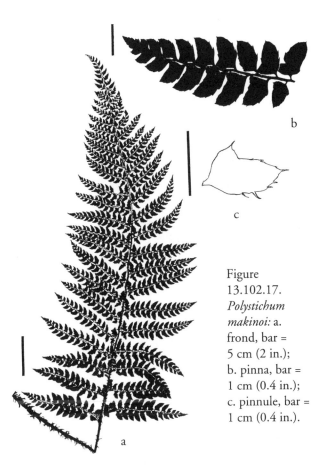

Figure 13.102.17. *Polystichum makinoi:* a. frond, bar = 5 cm (2 in.); b. pinna, bar = 1 cm (0.4 in.); c. pinnule, bar = 1 cm (0.4 in.).

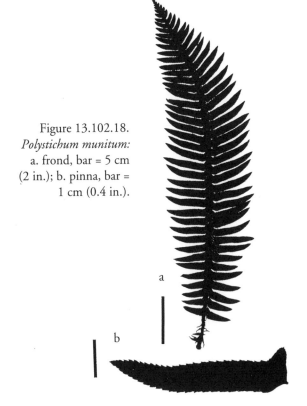

Figure 13.102.18. *Polystichum munitum:* a. frond, bar = 5 cm (2 in.); b. pinna, bar = 1 cm (0.4 in.).

The indusia are ciliate. Also see *P. imbricans.* The species is native to the western United States, Canada, Alaska (Yukon), and Mexico (Guadalupe Island); it is naturalized in Europe.

Polystichum neolobatum Nakai　　FIGURE 13.102.19
Long-eared holly fern
Hardy, Zone 5

A medium-sized fern with ascending to erect rhizomes and glossy, hard-textured, evergreen fronds that have a neatly trimmed appearance. Grows well under low to medium to high light in moist garden soil or potting mix. The plants are easy to cultivate.

Polystichum neolobatum bears shaggy scales on its stipes and rachises, and the blades are lanceolate, two-pinnate, and sparsely scaly on the undersides. The pinnule teeth are stiff and spiny. The acroscopic pinnule next to the rachis is large and ear-like. This species is native to Nepal, the Himalayas, Tibet, Burma, China, Taiwan, and Japan.

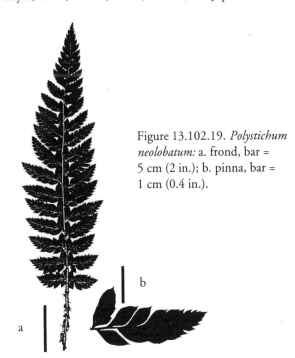

Figure 13.102.19. *Polystichum neolobatum:* a. frond, bar = 5 cm (2 in.); b. pinna, bar = 1 cm (0.4 in.).

Polystichum nepalense (Sprengel) C. Christensen
FIGURE 13.102.20

Nepal holly fern
Hardy, Zone 5

A medium-sized fern with ascending to erect rhizomes and evergreen fronds. Grows well under medium light in moist potting soil with good drainage.

Polystichum nepalense has narrowly lanceolate, one-pinnate blades with pinnae that are lanceolate, curved, eared, and finely toothed. The species is native to the Himalayas, China, Taiwan, and the Philippines.

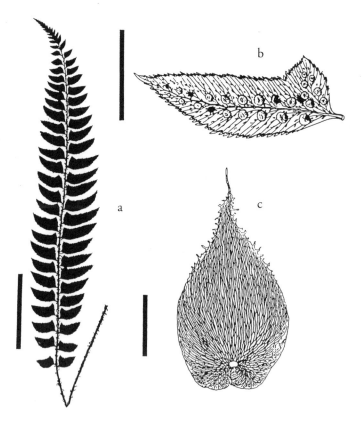

Figure 13.102.20. *Polystichum nepalense:* a. frond, bar = 5 cm (2 in.); b. pinna, bar = 1 cm (0.4 in.); c. stipe scale, bar = 1 mm. After Hu and Ching (1930).

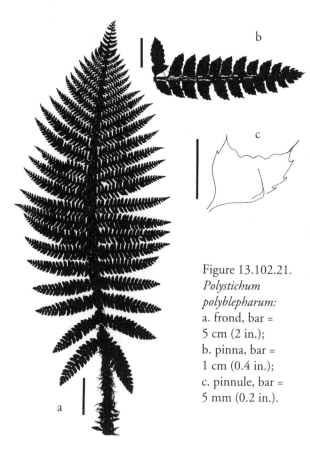

Figure 13.102.21. *Polystichum polyblepharum:* a. frond, bar = 5 cm (2 in.); b. pinna, bar = 1 cm (0.4 in.); c. pinnule, bar = 5 mm (0.2 in.).

Polystichum polyblepharum (J. Roemer ex Kunze) C. Presl　　　　FIGURES 13.102.1, 2, 21
Bristle fern, Japanese sword fern
Hardy, Zone 5(6)

A medium-sized fern with erect rhizomes and dark green, glossy, evergreen fronds. Prefers high-medium light and moist or moist-dry garden soil or potting mix. This species is easy to grow.

Polystichum polyblepharum has densely scaly stipes and rachises. The blades are elongate-elliptic to oblong and two-pinnate. The pinnules are eared, with the acroscopic ear prominent and spine-tipped and the basiscopic ear inconspicuous with its spine often bent over the upper pinnule surface. This species is native to Japan, southern Korea, and eastern China.

The plants in the trade are widely misidentified as *Polystichum setosum* Horticulture.

Polystichum retrosopaleaceum (Kodama) Tagawa somewhat resembles *P. polyblepharum* but differs by lower stipe scales broadly ovate with a long point (versus lanceolate-triangular), the pinnae apices more acuminate-pinnatifid (versus acute and subconform), and the foliage clear green (versus dark green). It is rarely cultivated in the United States but might be a handsome addition to gardens. It is hardy to Zone 5. This species is native to Japan and Korea.

Polystichum proliferum (R. Brown) C. Presl
FIGURES 13.102.2, 3, 22
Mother shield fern
Hardy, Zone 5

A medium-sized fern with erect rhizomes and dark green fronds that are evergreen in warmer climates. Grows well under medium light in moist garden soil or potting mix. This species is easy to grow and can be propagated from the bulbils on the fronds.

The blades of *Polystichum proliferum* are lanceolate to broader at the base and two- to three-pinnate, with a bud forming on the apical part. The pinnules are toothed. The species is native to Australia and New Zealand.

This species resembles *Polystichum vestitum* but is identifiable by the bulbils produced near the frond apices and by the glossy stipe scales with dark centers and pale borders. The name *Polystichum proliferum* might be confused with *P. setiferum* cultivars that bear buds on their rachis and have circulated incorrectly under the same name.

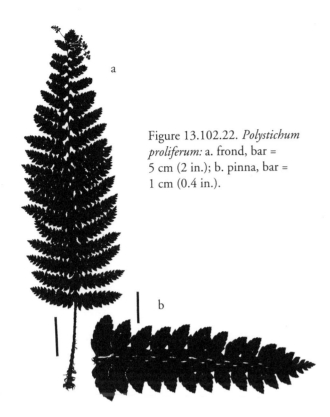

Figure 13.102.22. *Polystichum proliferum:* a. frond, bar = 5 cm (2 in.); b. pinna, bar = 1 cm (0.4 in.).

Figure 13.102.23. *Polystichum richardii:* frond, bar = 5 cm (2 in.), after Brownsey and Smith-Dodsworth (1989).

Polystichum richardii (Hooker) J. Smith

FIGURE 13.102.23

Richard's holly fern
Semi-hardy, Zone 7

A small to medium fern with erect rhizomes and evergreen fronds that vary from dark bluish green to olive green. Grows under medium light in moist garden soil or potting mix.

The stipes and rachises of *Polystichum richardii* are dark and densely covered with blackish brown scales with pale fringes at their base. The blades are narrowly oblong-elliptic to narrowly triangular and two- to three-pinnate. The indusia have a dark center and pale margins. The species is native to New Zealand.

Polystichum rigens Tagawa

FIGURE 13.102.24

Hardy, Zone 5

A medium-sized fern with erect rhizomes and evergreen, trim, rigid, glossy green fronds. Grows well under medium light in moist garden soil or potting mix.

The stipe scales have an apical cluster of cilia, and the blades are triangular and two-pinnate. *Polystichum rigens* has lanceolate to narrow-triangular pinnae, the apices of which have a spine-like tip. This species somewhat resembles *P. tsus-simense*, which has lanceolate stipe scales and is a smaller plant. *Polystichum rigens* is native to Japan and China.

Figure 13.102.24. *Polystichum rigens:* a. frond, bar = 5 cm (2 in.); b. pinnule, bar = 1 cm (0.4 in.); c. lower stipe scales, bar = 1 cm (0.4 in.). After Kurata and Nakaike (1979).

Polystichum scopulinum (D. C. Eaton) Maxon

FIGURE 13.102.25

Rock sword fern, western holly fern
Very hardy, Zone 4

A small to medium fern with ascending to erect rhizomes and leathery, semi-evergreen fronds. Grows under medium to high light in moist garden soil or potting mix with good drainage. This species is difficult to grow.

Polystichum scopulinum has narrow, one-pinnate-pinnatifid blades. The pinnae are deeply toothed distally and have on the acroscopic side a large, free "ear" that is adnate, the adnation 2 mm or more wide. The species is native to western North America.

This species is a hybrid of *Polystichum imbricans* and *P. lemmonii*.

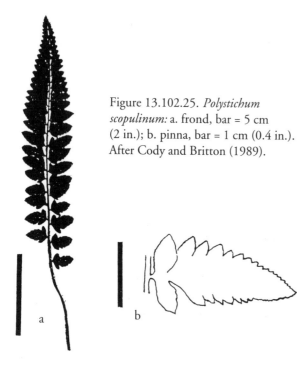

Figure 13.102.25. *Polystichum scopulinum:* a. frond, bar = 5 cm (2 in.); b. pinna, bar = 1 cm (0.4 in.). After Cody and Britton (1989).

Polystichum setiferum (Forsskål) T. Moore ex Woynar

FIGURES 13.102.26, 27

syn. *Polystichum angulare* (Willdenow) C. Presl
Soft shield fern
Hardy, Zone 6

A medium to large fern with erect rhizomes and fronds that are evergreen in warmer climates. Grows well under medium light in moist to moist-dry garden soil or potting mix. Many variants of this species form buds along the rachis. The plants do not like very high humidity.

The stipes of *Polystichum setiferum* are more than one-sixth the length of frond, and the blades are lanceolate and two-pinnate, with the lowest pinnae equal in length to the middle pinnae or sometimes shorter. The pinnules have a distinct stalk. This species is native to Europe.

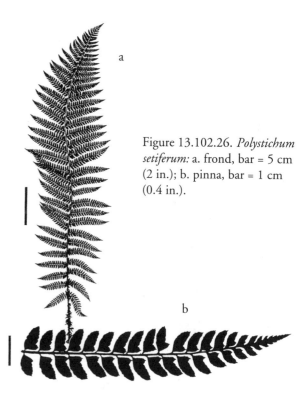

Figure 13.102.26. *Polystichum setiferum:* a. frond, bar = 5 cm (2 in.); b. pinna, bar = 1 cm (0.4 in.).

Because it varies tremendously (mostly in garden plants), this species is difficult to characterize. It is also confused with the infrequently cultivated *Polystichum aculeatum*.

Many cultivars can be found in the trade and special collections, and only a few are listed here. Sporelings frequently vary, and many of these intergrade and are not particularly distinct or deserving of cultivar names. The cultivar names are greatly confused in the trade and among collectors, creating controversy among growers. The cultivars have been reorganized according to a different set of characteristics than those previously used. For more information, see Dyce (1963, 1987) and Kaye (1968).

'Congestum'. Figure 13.102.27a. Dwarf soft shield fern. Fronds 15–30 cm (6–12 in.) long, darkish gray-green; pinnae and pinnules close and overlapping. This cultivar differs from typical plants by the smaller, upright, compact blades that are thicker textured due to the congestion of pinnae and pinnules. It is suited for use in borders because of its small size.

Divisilobum Group. Figure 13.102.27b. Blades narrow; pinnae less foliaceous than those of the species; pinnules narrowly ovate, apices acute, base oblique and eared. This selection includes the common trade cultivar that has narrow fronds and buds along the rachis. It is widely known in the United States trade under the incorrect names *Polystichum angulare* 'Proliferum' and *P. angulare* 'Alaska' and should not to be confused with the Australian and New Zealand species *P. proliferum*.

Imbricatum Group. Figure 13.102.27c. Parts less congested than 'Congestum', and fronds larger.

Figure 13.102.27. *Polystichum setiferum* cultivars: a. 'Congestum'; b. Divisilobum Group; c. Imbricatum Group; d. Multilobum Group; e. Plumoso-Divisilobum Group; f. 'Trilobum'. Bar = 5 cm (2 in.).

Multilobum Group. Figure 13.102.27d. Resembles Divisilobum Group but with pinnules stouter, nearly rectangular, and not overlapping; some variants are bud-bearing.

Plumoso-Divisilobum Group ('Plumoso-Multilobum'). Divided soft shield fern. Figure 13.102.27e; Plate 46. Fronds 60–100 cm (2–3 ft.) long, horizontally spreading, to three-pinnate; pinnae overlapping; basiscopic pinnules linear-lanceolate, longer than the acroscopic pinnules. This beautiful fern has a feathery, neatly three-dimensional aspect due to the spreading angle of the overlapping pinnae.

'Trilobum' ('Divisilobum Grandiceps'). Figure 13.102.27f. Pinnules have the same shape as those of Divisilobum Group, but the distal half of the blade is a mass of branches. Blades to about 30 cm (12 in.) long, rachises branched, branches often irregular and branched one or more times making the far (distal) part of the blade broad and congested; fronds bud-bearing. A very distinct, compact plant. Sometimes circulates as 'Divisilobum Grandiceps' or 'Divisilobum Cristatum' in the United States trade.

Polystichum setigerum (C. Presl) C. Presl

FIGURE 13.102.28

syn. *Polystichum braunii* subsp. *alaskense* (Maxon) Calder & R. L. Taylor
Alaskan holly fern
Hardy, Zone

A medium-sized fern with ascending to erect rhizomes and evergreen fronds. Grows under medium light in moist potting mix. The plants do best in cool, moist climates.

The stipes of *Polystichum setigerum* are about half the length of the fronds, and the blades are lanceolate and one-

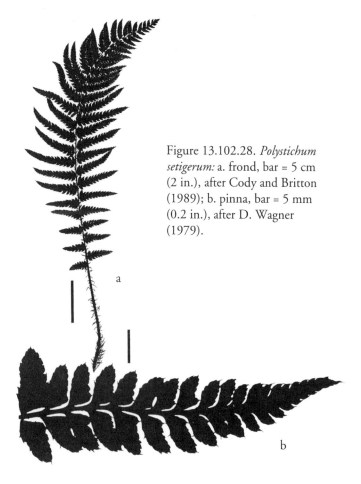

Figure 13.102.28. *Polystichum setigerum:* a. frond, bar = 5 cm (2 in.), after Cody and Britton (1989); b. pinna, bar = 5 mm (0.2 in.), after D. Wagner (1979).

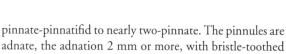

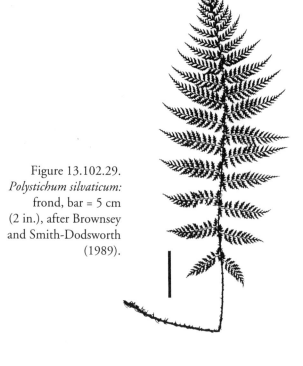

Figure 13.102.29. *Polystichum silvaticum:* frond, bar = 5 cm (2 in.), after Brownsey and Smith-Dodsworth (1989).

pinnate-pinnatifid to nearly two-pinnate. The pinnules are adnate, the adnation 2 mm or more, with bristle-toothed margins. This species is native to Alaska and Canada.

This species is of hybrid origin, resulting from a cross between *Polystichum munitum* and *P. braunii.* The trade material sold as *Polystichum* 'Alaska' is a cultivar of *P. setiferum.*

Polystichum silvaticum (Colenso) Diels

FIGURE 13.102.29

Semi-hardy, Zone 8(9)

A small to medium fern with erect rhizomes and shiny, soft, evergreen fronds. Grows well under low to medium light in moist garden soil or potting mix. The plants grow best in damp, shady sites.

The scales on the stipes and rachises are broad, glossy, and dark in the center. *Polystichum silvaticum* has lanceolate, two-pinnate-pinnatifid blades. The blade and pinna tips are long and slender. Indusia are absent. The species is native to New Zealand.

This species is closely related to *Polystichum vestitum* but has more-finely dissected blades, narrowly winged costae, and no indusium. In New Zealand the two species hybridize freely whenever they grow together.

Polystichum stenophyllum H. Christ

FIGURE 13.102.30

Hardy, Zone 6

A small fern with ascending to erect rhizomes and evergreen leaves. Grows under medium light in moist potting mix.

Polystichum stenophyllum has short stipes clothed in broadly ovate, ciliate scales with tailed apices. The linear-lanceolate, one-pinnate blades are up to 2.5 cm (1 in.) wide, and they bear buds below the apex. The many pinnae are ovate, serrate, and eared, with the lower ones smaller and pointing downward. The species is native to India, Tibet, China, and Taiwan.

Polystichum stimulans C. Presl   FIGURE 13.102.31
syn. *Polystichum illicifolium* T. Moore
Hardy, Zone 6

A small fern with ascending to erect rhizomes and evergreen fronds. Grows under medium light in moist potting mix.

Polystichum stimulans has linear-lanceolate, one-pinnate fronds up to 2.5 cm (1 in.) wide. The pinnae are very short and deeply bristle-toothed, reminiscent of holly leaves. This species is native to the Himalayas, China, and Taiwan.

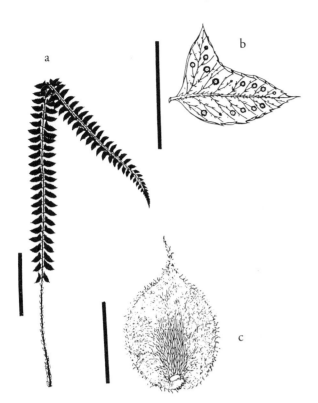

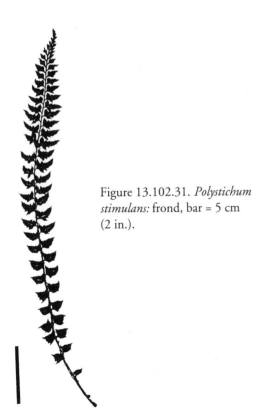

Figure 13.102.30. *Polystichum stenophyllum:* a. frond, bar = 5 cm (2 in.); b. pinnule, bar = 1 cm (0.4 in.); c. stipe base scale, bar = 3 mm (0.1 in.). After Hu and Ching (1930).

Figure 13.102.31. *Polystichum stimulans:* frond, bar = 5 cm (2 in.).

Polystichum tagawanum Sa. Kurata

FIGURE 13.102.32

Tagawa's holly fern
Very hardy, Zone 4

A medium-sized fern with ascending to erect rhizomes and shiny, evergreen fronds. Grows well under medium light in moist potting mix. The plants are easy to grow.

The stipe and rachis scales of *Polystichum tagawanum* are reddish brown, ovate to lanceolate, and toothed. The blades are ovate-lanceolate and two-pinnate to two-pinnate-pinnatifid. The pinnae are shorter at the base of the blade and point downward. The pinnules are eared and irregularly spinulose-lobed. This species is native to Japan.

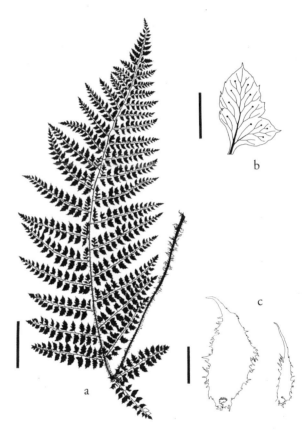

Figure 13.102.32. *Polystichum tagawanum:* a. frond, bar = 5 cm (2 in.); b. pinnule, bar = 5 mm (0.2 in.); c. stipe scales, bar = 2 mm. After Kurata and Nakaike (1983).

Polystichum tripteron (Kunze) C. Presl

FIGURE 13.102.33

Trifid holly fern
Hardy, Zone 5

A medium-sized fern with short-creeping to clump-forming rhizomes and (in temperate climates) deciduous fronds. Grows under medium light in moist potting mix. The plants are moderately difficult to grow.

Figure 13.102.34. *Polystichum tsus-simense* var. *tsus-simense:* a. frond, bar = 5 cm (2 in.); b. pinna, bar = 1 cm (0.4 in.).

Figure 13.102.33. *Polystichum tripteron:* frond, bar = 5 cm (2 in.).

Figure 13.102.35. *Polystichum tsus-simense* var. *mayebarae:* a. frond, bar = 5 cm (2 in.); b. pinna, bar = 1 cm (0.4 in.).

Polystichum tripteron is distinctive by its greatly elongated basal pinnae, which impart an inverted T-shape to the blades. The blades are two-pinnate. The long apex is one-pinnate above the lateral pinnae. The pinnules are dull green (not shiny) and coarsely toothed, without bristly teeth. This species is native to eastern Siberia, eastern China, Korea, and Japan.

Polystichum tsus-simense (Hooker) J. Smith

FIGURES 13.102.34, 35

Tsus-sima holly fern
Hardy, Zones (5)6

A small-medium fern with clump-forming rhizomes and dark green, shiny fronds that are evergreen in warm climates. Grows well under medium light in moist-dry potting mix or garden soil. In the 1950s and 1960s this species was widely grown in dish gardens. The plants, however, were not as robust as the current trade material, some of which has been identified as var. *mayebarae* (Tagawa) Sa. Kurata and sold as the "Korean rock fern."

var. *mayebarae* (Tagawa) Sa. Kurata. Korean rock fern. Figure 13.102.35. The trade plant is more foliaceous and larger than var. *tsus-simense*. The larger fronds are two-pinnate-pinnatifid to three-pinnate on the acroscopic pinnule of the lower pinnae. The larger stipe scales are dark brown and lanceolate to ovate. Native to China and Japan.

var. *tsus-simense.* Figure 13.102.34. This variety has oblong-triangular, two-pinnate blades. The basal acroscopic pinnule is conspicuously separate and larger than the others. It is also eared; occasionally the ear is free. The larger stipe scales are mostly blackish brown and narrow-lanceolate. This variety is native to the Himalayas, Thailand, Indochina, China, Taiwan, Korea, and Japan.

Polystichum vestitum (G. Forster) C. Presl

FIGURE 13.102.36

Prickly shield fern
Hardy, Zone 6

A medium-sized fern with erect rhizomes and harsh, prickly, semi-deciduous fronds that are dark green above, lighter below. Grows under medium light in moist potting mix or garden soil. This species grows in cool, moist climates.

The stipes and rachises of *Polystichum vestitum* are conspicuously and densely scaly with stiff, broad, shiny scales that are black-brown with pale margins. The blades are two-pinnate and narrowly oblong or elliptic. The pinnules have a basal acroscopic lobe ending in a sharp point. This species is related to *P. proliferum*. It is native to New Zealand.

Polystichum xiphophyllum (Baker) Diels

FIGURE 13.102.37

Hardy, Zone 6

A medium-sized fern with erect rhizomes and evergreen fronds. Grows well under medium light in moist garden soil or potting mix. This species is easy to grow.

Polystichum xiphophyllum is characterized by stipes and rachises with dark, narrowly lanceolate to linear scales. The blades are narrowly triangular, and the pinnae are pinnate in the basal half. The pinnae are lanceolate, triangular, short stalked, serrate, and lobed-crenate to one-pinnate. The acroscopic pinnule at the pinna base is free or adnate, large, and ovate. The species is native to India and China.

Polystichum yaemonense Horticulture

Semi-hardy, Zone 8

A medium-sized fern with erect rhizomes. Grows best under medium light in moist garden soil or potting mix.

Polystichum yaemonense has medium-sized fronds, the blades of which are narrowly triangular and two-pinnate. The pinnules are ovate-rectangular, and the sori submar-

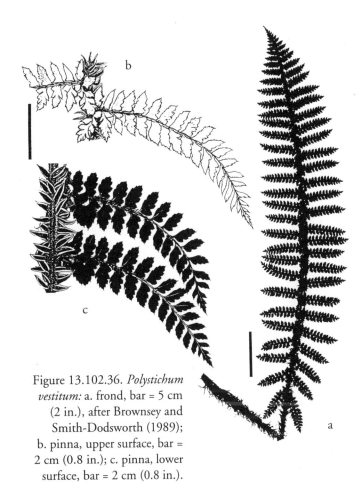

Figure 13.102.36. *Polystichum vestitum:* a. frond, bar = 5 cm (2 in.), after Brownsey and Smith-Dodsworth (1989); b. pinna, upper surface, bar = 2 cm (0.8 in.); c. pinna, lower surface, bar = 2 cm (0.8 in.).

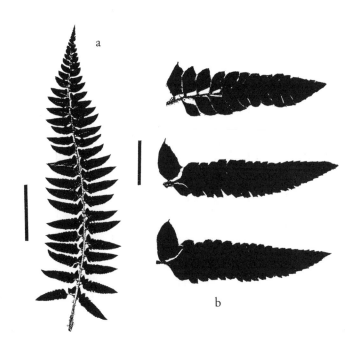

Figure 13.102.37. *Polystichum xiphophyllum:* a. frond, bar = 5 cm (2 in.); b. pinna, variations, bar = 1 cm (0.4 in.).

ginal. The name is of uncertain origin, but it applies to a fern cultivated in the Pacific Northwest. It is possibly a misspelling of *P. yokohamense* T. Oka & Ohtani, a hybrid whose parents are presumed to be *P. fibrilloso-paleaceum* (Kodama) Sa. Kurata and *P. tagawanum* Sa. Kurata. It is not *P. yaeyamense* (Makino) Makino, a one-pinnate species not known in cultivation in the United States.

Psilotum   FIGURES 13.103.1, 2
Whisk fern

The whisk ferns are small- to medium-sized plants with repeatedly branched stems bearing inconspicuous scale-like leaves. *Psilotum* is a primitive plant with no roots or vascularized leaves, making for interesting study in botany classes. It is cultivated mostly as a novelty plant. When grown in greenhouses, the whisk fern tends to volunteer in pots of other plants, either by spores or by underground gemmae that spread as the potting soil is reused. The plants respond well to applications of bonemeal. In the tropics *Psilotum* is often found growing in the old leaf bases of palms, where humus has accumulated.

Psilotum is easily recognized by its repeatedly forked green stems that lack broad, flat green leaves. It grows as an epiphyte or terrestrial plant. Roots are lacking, but the stems bear fine hairs (rhizoids) that absorb water and mineral nutrients. The leaves are small, distant, and scale-like, without veins. Large, three-lobed sporangia are borne on upper branches, and they turn yellow when mature.

The genus, which contains two species, occurs in the tropics and subtropics of the world. For more information on growing these plants, see the section on "Fern Allies" in Chapter 10. The genus name comes from the Greek *psilos,*

Figure 13.103.2. *Psilotum nudum:* sporangia.

naked or smooth, referring to the smooth, nearly naked branches.

Psilotum nudum (Linnaeus) Palisot de Beauvois
                                 FIGURE 13.103.1–3
Semi-hardy, Zone 8

A small-medium plant with aerial stems in a cluster arising from a clump of root-like stems. Grows well under medium to high light in moist-dry garden soil, potting mix, or uncut moss with good drainage. Hundreds of cultivars of *Psilotum nudum* have been grown in Japan for several centuries. Plants are propagated mainly by divisions, as spores may take as long as 3 months to germinate, if at all.

Psilotum nudum has evergreen, erect to semi-pendent stems, to 50 cm (20 in.) long and triangular in cross section. The species is widespread in the tropics and subtropics as an epiphytic or terrestrial plant.

The second species in the genus, *Psilotum complanatum* Swartz, can be distinguished by its wider, flattened branches. It is reportedly difficult to grow and is not found in the trade, although a hybrid between the two species from Hawaii, *P. ×intermedium* W. H. Wagner, shows horticultural promise.

Pteridium
Bracken

This well-known native of open fields and slopes is a medium- to large-sized terrestrial fern that spreads from a slender, wide-creeping, underground rhizome. Its triangular fronds are spaced far apart and are several times divided. *Pteridium* is rarely used as an ornamental because it spreads invasively in the garden. It is a terrible weed in many parts of the world.

The fiddleheads of bracken are harvested in Japan for food, and in the United States the packages are sold in some

Figure 13.103.1. *Psilotum nudum:* habit.

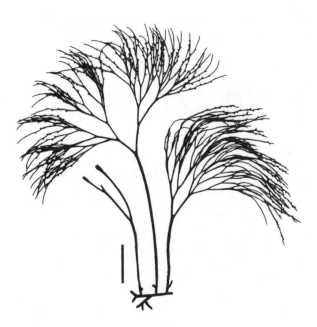

Figure 13.103.3. *Psilotum nudum:* habit, more arching form, bar = 5 cm (2 in.).

Asian food markets. Nevertheless, eating the fiddleheads is dangerous. They contain a carcinogen that causes stomach cancer, and the disease has a higher incidence in areas where bracken is consumed. Also, the fiddleheads contain thiaminase, an enzyme that destroys vitamin B (thiamine). Bracken has several chemical defenses against insects. It produces ecdysones, a hormone that promotes molting (ecdysis) in insects, thus causing the insects to molt prematurely and die. It is also cyanogenic, producing hydrogen cyanide locally where an insect is eating the plant. For a popular account of the chemical defenses of bracken, see Moran (1993).

Pteridium can usually be identified by its large (0.5–4.5 m [1.5–15 ft.] long), broadly triangular, two- to four-pinnate blades and its long-creeping, hairy rhizomes. It is also characterized by sori that run along the segment margins and are covered by a linear enrolled indusium. An unusual trait is that the sterile segment margins are enrolled to form a false indusium even when there are no sporangia—*Pteridium* is the only fern genus that does this. Other characteristics include fronds set far apart on the rhizome and sori continuous around the tips and bases of the lobes and smaller leaflets.

Pteridium traditionally has been construed as containing a single species with 2 subspecies and 12 varieties worldwide. Recently, however, pteridologists have recognized some varieties as species because they do not intergrade with the other varieties and maintain their distinctness when growing in mixed populations. The genus name comes from the Greek *pteridion,* meaning "a small fern."

Pteridium aquilinum (Linnaeus) Kuhn

FIGURES 13.104.1–3

Hardy to semi-tender, depending on the variety

A large fern with long-creeping rhizomes and large, triangular, deciduous fronds. Prefers medium to high light or full sun and moist-dry garden soil. *Pteridium aquilinum,* defined in the broad sense, occurs worldwide.

var. *caudatum* (Linnaeus) Sadebeck. Lacy bracken. Figure 13.104.3b. Fertile ultimate segments narrow, mostly only 1–2 mm wide. Semi-tender, Zone 9. Native to Florida and tropical America.

var. *latiusculum* (Desvaux) Underwood ex A. Heller. Eastern bracken. Figure 13.104.3c. Pinnule margins with shaggy hairs. Very hardy, Zone 3. Native to the United States, Mexico, Europe, and Asia.

var. *pseudocaudatum* (Clute) A. Heller. Tailed bracken. Figure 13.104.3e. Terminal segment of pinnule long and narrow, often 6–15 times longer than wide, mostly 2–5 mm wide. Grows in acid, sandy soil. Semi-hardy, Zone 7. Native to the eastern United States.

var. *pubescens* Underwood. Western bracken. Figures 13.104.1, 2, 3a, 3d. Blades densely hairy on the lower surface. Very hardy, Zone 3. Native to North America.

Figure 13.104.1. *Pteridium aquilinum* var. *pubescens:* habit.

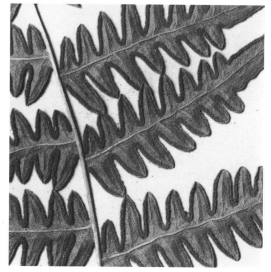

Figure 13.104.2. *Pteridium aquilinum* var. *pubescens:* sori and indusia.

Figure 13.104.3. *Pteridium aquilinum* varieties: a. var. *pubescens* habit; b. var. *caudatum* frond tip; c. var. *latiusculum* frond tip; d. var. *pubescens* frond tip; e. var. *pseudocaudatum* frond. Bar = 5 cm (2 in.).

Pteris   FIGURES 13.105.1, 2
Brake fern

Pteris is a genus of small- to large-sized ferns that are popular and readily available in the trade. The plants grow in soil or on rocks and are commonly used in terrariums, planter beds, and indoor pots. They can also be grown outdoors in mild climates. The fronds are variously divided, but generally not finely so, and they grow in clusters to give a full-foliage effect.

The most common species in the trade are the Cretan brake (*Pteris cretica*), spider brake (*P. multifida*), Victorian brake (*P. ensiformis* 'Victoriae'), Australian brake (*P. tremula*), and rusty brake (*P. vittata*). Most species are fairly rapid, vigorous growers adapted to a range of soils. Brake ferns generally do not like to be kept moist or wet, and many prefer moist-dry conditions. The Cretan brake and its cultivars tolerate low humidity indoors. Some of the medium-sized or larger species with sparingly branched rhizomes (mainly those in the *P. quadriaurita* complex) tend to lose vigor with age. They also tend to topple, as the rhizome and roots cannot support the foliage. Such plants can be staked for support, and soil built up around the rhizome encourages root development. Alternatively, the entire plant can be replanted deeper in the soil. Young plants respond better to this replanting. Species with much-branched rhizomes are easily propagated by divisions.

The rhizomes of *Pteris* are scaly (not hairy) and vary from short-creeping to ascending and sparingly to amply branched. The stipes are clustered, and the blades are usually one to several times pinnately divided with narrow, often sessile or adnate segments. The veins are usually forked and free; less frequently they have a few areoles or are completely netted. The sori run along the margins of the

Figure 13.105.1. *Pteris cretica:* habit.

Figure 13.105.2.
Pteris vittata:
sorus and
indusium.

Figure 13.105.3. *Pteris altissima:* frond, bar = 5 cm
(2 in.).

segments and are covered by an enrolled leaf margin (false indusium). Several fern genera have marginal indusia that resemble those of *Pteris,* namely *Histiopteris, Mildella, Pellaea,* and *Pteridium.* It is easy to misidentify these genera as *Pteris.*

Pteris contains about 250 species widespread in the tropics and subtropics of the world. See Joe (1958) and Walker (1970) for further details on the cultivated species. An ancient Greek term for ferns in general, the genus name comes from the Greek *pteron,* wing or feather, derived from a fancied resemblance of fern leaves to wings or feathers.

Pteris altissima Poiret   FIGURE 13.105.3
Forest brake
Tender

A large fern with clustered fronds. Grows well under medium light in moist garden soil or potting mix.

The fronds of *Pteris altissima* are up to 2.5 m (8 ft.) long and two- to three-pinnate-pinnatifid, with the basal pinnae larger on their lower side. The veins are netted. This species is native to the American tropics.

Pteris argyraea T. Moore   FIGURE 13.105.4; PLATE 47
syn. *Pteris quadriaurita* var. *argentea* Beddome, *P.*
    quadriaurita var. *argyraea* Horticulture
Silver brake, striped brake
Semi-tender

A medium-sized fern with clustered fronds. Grows well under medium light in moist-dry garden soil or potting mix.

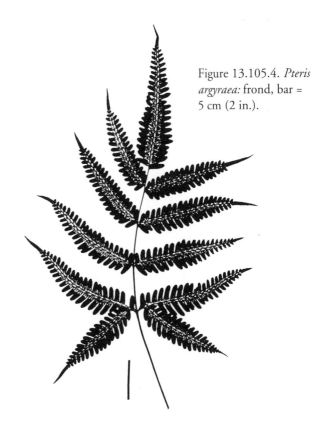

Figure 13.105.4. *Pteris argyraea:* frond, bar = 5 cm (2 in.).

The blades of *Pteris argyraea* resemble those of *P. quadri-aurita* but differ by a whitish band down the center of the pinnae. It also resembles *P. biaurita,* but that species's lowest veins are fused to form an areole on either side of the midrib. *Pteris argyraea* is native to Sri Lanka and Java. The cultivated plants are said to be robust like the plants from Java and unlike those from Sri Lanka.

Pteris aspericaulis Wallich ex J. Agardh

FIGURE 13.105.5

Semi-tender (?)

Medium-large fern with clustered fronds. Grows well under medium light in moist-dry garden soil or potting mix.

The blades of *Pteris aspericaulis* resemble those of *P. quadriaurita* but differ by having deep red stipes, rachises, and costae and by the small, nearly erect red spines along the costae and costules on the upper surface. This species is native to India and the Himalayan region.

var. *tricolor* (Linden) T. Moore ex Lowe (*Pteris tricolor* Linden). The stipes, rachises, and costae are red, but the pinnules are white in their basal half and green distally. Native to India. The plants under this name in the recent trade are typical var. *aspericaulis.* The true var. *tricolor* has not been seen in United States cultivation for at least 25 years.

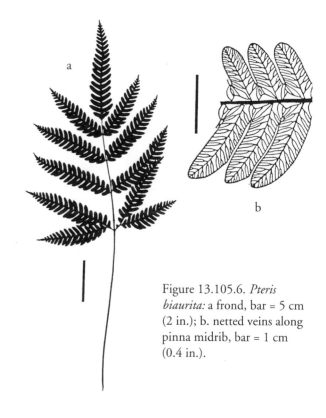

Figure 13.105.6. *Pteris biaurita:* a frond, bar = 5 cm (2 in.); b. netted veins along pinna midrib, bar = 1 cm (0.4 in.).

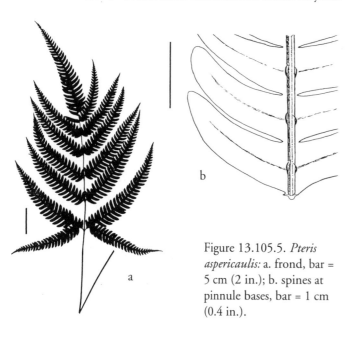

Figure 13.105.5. *Pteris aspericaulis:* a. frond, bar = 5 cm (2 in.); b. spines at pinnule bases, bar = 1 cm (0.4 in.).

Pteris biaurita Linnaeus

FIGURE 13.105.6

Tender

Medium-large fern with clustered fronds. Grows well under medium light in moist garden soil or potting mix.

The blades of *Pteris biaurita* differ from those of *P. quadriaurita* by having netted (not free) veins on either side of the pinna midrib. This species is native to the tropics throughout the world.

Pteris catoptera Kunze

FIGURE 13.105.7

Semi-hardy to semi-tender

A large fern. Grows well under medium light in moist-wet to moist garden soil or potting mix.

The blades of *Pteris catoptera* resemble those of *P. quadriaurita* but differ by pinna apices acute to long-caudate and the ultimate segments narrow and parallel sided. The veins are free, not netted. This species is native to Africa.

Pteris cretica Linnaeus

FIGURES 13.105.1, 8, 9

Cretan brake

Semi-hardy, Zone 7; may die back in cooler temperatures

A small to medium fern with clump-forming rhizomes and densely clustered fronds. Grows best under high-medium light in moist-dry garden soil or potting mix. This species is easy to grow.

Pteris cretica has dimorphic sterile and fertile fronds. The sterile blades are one-pinnate, except for the basal pinnae that are forked once or twice. The rachis is winged between the upper first or second pinna pairs. The pinnae are serrate, and the veins are free. The fertile blades have narrower pinnae than the sterile ones and tend to be more erect and longer petiolate. This species is native to tropics worldwide.

This highly variable species has numerous cultivars that essentially breed true from spore. Some cultivars are confused with *Pteris multifida* and other species. Only a few of the many cultivars are listed here.

'Albo-lineata' (var. *albolineata*). See *Pteris nipponica.*

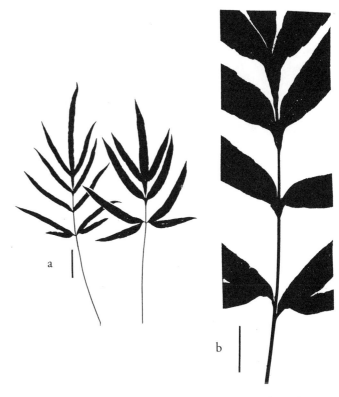

Figure 13.105.7. *Pteris catoptera:* a. frond, bar = 5 cm (2 in.); b. larger pinna with caudate tip, bar = 5 cm (2 in.); c. veins and spines along midrib of pinna and pinnules, bar = 1 cm (0.4 in.).

Figure 13.105.8. *Pteris cretica:* a. fertile frond (left) and sterile frond (right), bar = 5 cm (2 in.); b. rachis wing limited to upper pinnae pair, bar = 1 cm (0.4 in.).

'Childsii'. Figure 13.105.9a. Pinnae irregularly fringed, their tips often crested. The plants are sterile, but a similar, fertile form has recently appeared in the trade.

'Distinction'. Blades more open, margins more fringed but with fewer crests than 'Wimsettii'.

'Mayii' ('Cristata Mayii'). Figure 13.105.9b. Blades weakly variegated, pinnae crested.

'Ouvrardii'. Figure 13.105.9c. Resembles typical *Pteris cretica* except larger and with more pinnae. It is a robust grower.

'Parkeri'. Figure 13.105.9d. Fronds larger than typical *Pteris cretica,* the blades dark green, firm, leathery.

'Rivertoniana'. Figure 13.105.9e. Margins with irregular broad, acute to acuminate fringes or segments.

'Roweri'. Figure 13.105.9f. Plants compact, fronds crested. This cultivar is questionably distinct from early crested forms.

'Wilsonii'. Figure 13.105.9g. Plants compact, pinnae crested.

'Wimsettii'. Figure 13.105.9h. Pinnae irregularly fringed, the fringes long to very long and narrow; the tips of the pinnae and some of the larger fringes are split or crested.

Pteris dentata Forsskål   FIGURE 13.105.10
syn. *Pteris flabellata* Thunberg
Toothed brake
Semi-hardy to semi-tender

A medium-large fern with clustered fronds and sparingly branched rhizomes. Grows well under medium light in moist-dry garden soil or potting mix.

Pteris dentata has ovate, two-pinnate-pinnatifid to nearly three-pinnate blades. The ultimate segments and pinnules tend to fold inward along the midrib and have margins somewhat coarsely and irregularly serrate-toothed. This species is native to Africa.

Pteris ensiformis N. L. Burman   FIGURE 13.105.11
Semi-tender

A small fern with short- or longer-creeping rhizomes that may sparingly branch and form separate clusters of fronds. Grows well under medium light in moist-dry garden soil or potting mix. The typical form of the species is infrequently grown, although the cultivar 'Victoriae' is common.

Pteris ensiformis has dimorphic sterile and fertile leaves. The sterile blades are triangular to ovate and two-pinnate-pinnatifid, with the ultimate divisions oval-elliptic to more elongate. The fertile blades are long-stalked with the ulti-

Figure 13.105.9. *Pteris cretica* cultivars: a. 'Childsii'; b. 'Mayii'; c. 'Ouvrardii'; d. 'Parkeri'; e. 'Rivertoniana'; f. 'Roweri'; g. 'Wilsonii'; h. 'Wimsettii'. Bar = 5 cm (2 in.).

mate divisions narrowly linear. This species is native to India, China, Malaysia to Australia, and Polynesia.

'Evergemiensis'. Variegation more cream-white than in 'Victoriae', and the white extends between the lateral veins.

'Victoriae'. Victorian brake. Figure 13.105.11b. Cream-white band down the center of pinnae and pinnules, with only some white extending along the lateral veins.

Pteris grandifolia Linnaeus　　FIGURE 13.105.12
Tender

A large fern with short-creeping rhizomes and clustered fronds. Grows well under high-medium light in moist garden soil or potting mix. Too large for most gardens, this huge plant is grown only in south Florida.

Pteris grandifolia has one-pinnate blades throughout, and the pinnae are simple and entire. The veins are free near the midrib but netted toward the margin. This species is native to the American tropics.

Pteris longifolia Linnaeus　　FIGURE 13.105.13
Ladder brake
Tender

A medium fern with short-creeping rhizomes and clustered fronds. Grows well under medium to high light in moist garden soil or potting mix.

Pteris longifolia has oblanceolate, one-pinnate blades. The stipes and rachises of unweathered plants are amply covered with scales and hairs. The pinnae are numerous, simple, and jointed to the rachis. The veins are free. The indusium is erose-fimbriate. This species is native to the United States (Florida), Mexico, Guatemala, and the West Indies.

Figure 13.105.10. *Pteris dentata:* a. frond, bar = 5 cm (2 in.); b. pinna tip, bar = 1 cm (0.4 in.).

Figure 13.105.12. *Pteris grandifolia:* a. frond, bar = 5 cm (2 in.); b. pinnae, bar = 5 cm (2 in.).

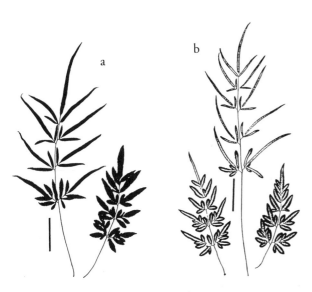

Figure 13.105.11. *Pteris ensiformis:* a. fertile frond (left) and sterile frond (right), bar = 5 cm (2 in.); b. 'Victoriae' fertile frond (center) and sterile fronds (left and right); bar = 5 cm (2 in.).

Figure 13.105.13. *Pteris longifolia:* frond, bar = 5 cm (2 in.).

Most of the plants sold in the United States under this name are actually *Pteris vittata*. The two species are often difficult to distinguish. The best characteristic to separate them is the jointed pinna bases of *P. longifolia*. These bases have a dark abscission layer where the pinna attaches to the rachis, and the juncture is usually thickened. (*Pteris vittata* never has thickened rachises at the juncture with the pinnae.) These characteristics are often hidden by scales, which must be scraped away to identify the plant.

Pteris multifida Poiret   FIGURE 13.105.14
syn. *Pteris serrulata* Linnaeus f.
Spider brake
Hardy, Zone 6

A small fern with clump-forming rhizomes and fronds in dense, irregular clusters. Grows well under medium light in moist to moist-dry garden soil or potting mix. The plants tend to be weedy.

Pteris multifida resembles *P. cretica* but differs by narrower pinnae and the rachis fully winged between each of the three upper pinna pairs. (*Pteris cretica* is unwinged or winged only between two upper pinna pairs or less.) This species is native to China and Japan.

A few crested and compact-growing cultivars are sometimes seen.

Pteris nipponica W. C. Shieh   FIGURE 13.105.15
syn. *Pteris cretica* var. *albolineata* Hooker
Semi-hardy, Zone 8

A small to medium fern with short- to medium-creeping rhizomes and fronds forming somewhat open clumps. Grows well under medium light in moist to moist-dry garden soil or potting mix. This species is more commonly known by its synonym: *Pteris cretica* var. *albolineata* (or 'Albo-lineata').

Pteris nipponica is distinguished by a pale band of tissue on both sides of the pinna midrib. It differs from *P. cretica* by having a more open-spreading habit, by the absence of a distinct wing on the distal part of the rachis, and by other microscopic spore details. This species is native to Japan, South Korea, and Taiwan.

Pteris quadriaurita Retzius   FIGURE 13.105.16
Semi-tender

A medium-large fern with clustered fronds and infrequently branched, short-creeping rhizomes. Grows best under medium light in moist-dry garden soil or potting mix.

The blades of *Pteris quadriaurita* are herbaceous and one-pinnate-pinnatifid except for the basal pinnae that are forked at the base. The costa (but not the costules) bears

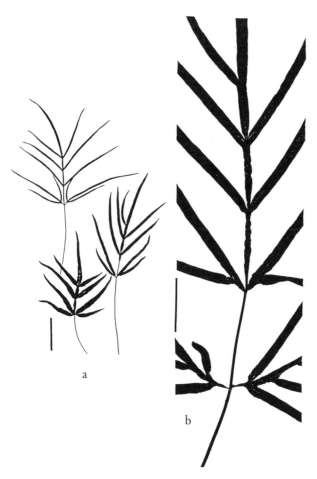

Figure 13.105.14. *Pteris multifida:* a. fertile frond (upper left), others sterile, bar = 5 cm (2 in.); b. rachis winged to or just above the base, bar = 1 cm (0.4 in.).

Figure 13.105.15. *Pteris nipponica:* a. habit, with sterile frond (left) and fertile frond (right), bar = 5 cm (2 in.); b. rachis not winged below terminal pinna, bar = 1 cm (0.4 in.).

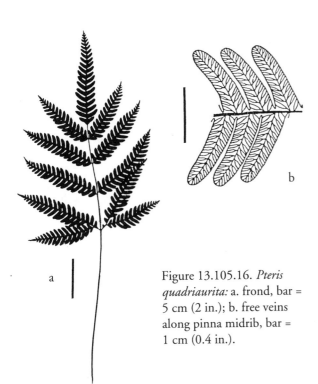

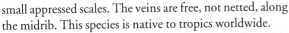

Figure 13.105.16. *Pteris quadriaurita:* a. frond, bar = 5 cm (2 in.); b. free veins along pinna midrib, bar = 1 cm (0.4 in.).

Figure 13.105.17. *Pteris semipinnata:* frond, bar = 5 cm (2 in.).

small appressed scales. The veins are free, not netted, along the midrib. This species is native to tropics worldwide.

Pteris quadriaurita comprises a complex of variable plants not fully studied. Plants examined in the trade labeled as *P. fauriei* Hieronymus are actually *P. quadriaurita.* True *P. fauriei*, native to eastern Asia, has leathery fronds and pinnae that are widest in the middle with caudate apices.

Pteris semipinnata Linnaeus   FIGURE 13.105.17
Semi-hardy to semi-tender

A medium-sized fern with clustered fronds. Grows well under medium light in moist garden soil or potting mix.

Pteris semipinnata has distinctive pinnae: the larger ones are straight and entire on the upper side, but the lower side is lobed. The blades are oblong-triangular and one-pinnate-pinnatifid. This species is native to Japan, Korea, Taiwan, southwestern China, the Himalayas, and Asian tropics.

var. *dispar* (Kunze) Hooker & Baker (*Pteris dispar* Kunze). A form with lobed upper pinna margins.

Pteris tremula R. Brown   FIGURE 13.105.18
Australian brake
Semi-hardy

A large fern with densely clustered fronds and clump-forming rhizomes. Grows well under low to high-medium light or full sun in some areas in moist-dry garden soil or potting mix. The plants grow rapidly and are easy to cultivate. They often volunteer from spores. This is one of the more finely divided species of *Pteris.*

Figure 13.105.18. *Pteris tremula:* frond, bar = 5 cm (2 in.).

The blades of *Pteris tremula* are triangular, membranous, and two- to four-pinnate-pinnatifid. The ultimate segments are narrowly oblong to more linear and serrate with blunt teeth. The fertile segments are narrower than the sterile ones. The veins are free, not netted. This species is native to Australia, Tasmania, New Zealand, and Fiji.

Pteris tripartita Swartz   FIGURE 13.105.19
Trisect brake
Tender, Zone 9

A large fern, to 2 m (6.5 ft.) tall, with clustered fronds and clump-forming rhizomes. Grows well under medium light in continually moist-wet garden soil or potting mix. The plants grow rapidly from spores but become too big for most gardens.

Pteris tripartita has broadly triangular blades divided into three parts: the central part is ovate-triangular and one-pinnate-pinnatifid, and the two lateral parts (the basal pinnae) are as long as the central part, and each forks twice on the lower side. The veins are netted. This species is native to the Old World but has become naturalized in tropical America.

Pteris vittata Linnaeus   FIGURES 13.105.2, 20
Chinese brake, rusty brake
Semi-hardy, Zone (7)8

A medium-large fern with short-creeping rhizomes and clustered fronds. Grows well under high-medium light to full sun in moist-dry garden soil or potting mix. The plants are easy to start from spore, but they tend to become weedy. They grow on old masonry and bricks, as can be seen in the French Quarter in New Orleans.

Pteris vittata is characterized by one-pinnate blades widest above the middle, with narrow pinnae and a terminal pinna that resembles the lateral ones. The stipes and rachises are sparsely scaly-hairy, and the pinnae are not jointed to the rachis. The veins are free, and the indusia have entire margins. This species greatly resembles *Pteris longifolia*. It is native to eastern Asia but has become widely naturalized throughout the tropics and subtropics of the world.

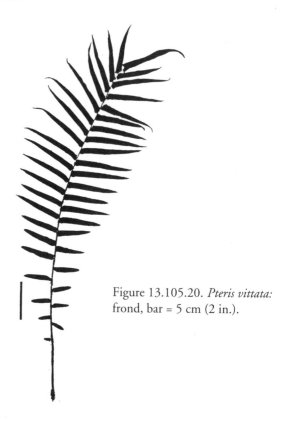

Figure 13.105.20. *Pteris vittata:* frond, bar = 5 cm (2 in.).

Figure 13.105.19. *Pteris tripartita:* a. small frond, bar = 5 cm (2 in.); b. large frond, bar = 15 cm (0.5 ft).

Pyrrosia   FIGURES 13.106.1–3
syn. *Cyclophorus, Drymoglossum, Niphobolus*
Felt fern

Most *Pyrrosia* species are small-medium-sized and have simple, entire blades (a few are deeply lobed) with star-shaped hairs. Be careful not to overwater pyrrosias. The epiphytic species in particular need a coarser soil mix and good drainage. The plants can be easily propagated by division of the rhizomes.

Figure 13.106.1. *Pyrrosia lingua:* habit.

Figure 13.106.2. *Pyrrosia lingua:* fronds.

Figure 13.106.3.
Pyrrosia lingua:
sori.

Pyrrosia is best known in cultivation by the Japanese felt fern or tongue fern (*Pyrrosia lingua*). Its tongue-shaped fronds are densely covered beneath with a felt-like mat of star-shaped hairs. This species is hardy outdoors in warm-temperate areas, where it is usually grown in the ground. If grown in pots, baskets, or on boards, it may need more protection during the winter. The fronds are dark green, leathery, and durable, tolerating low humidity. The plants grow moderately slowly, which is an advantage because they do not require frequent repotting. Some of the cultivars have an attractive crested habit.

Although less hardy, *Pyrrosia hastata* is also prized in cultivation. It has mostly hastate fronds borne in loose clusters. It can be grown outdoors in warm-temperate climates but also makes a good indoor plant.

Pyrrosia is distinguished by simple or lobed blades with star-shaped hairs on the surfaces, especially the lower surface. The rhizomes are scaly and vary from short- to long-creeping, bearing phyllopodia to which the fronds are attached and jointed. The fronds may be monomorphic or dimorphic, and they have a parchment-like to leathery or succulent texture. The veins are netted, and the areoles contain included veinlets, although the veins are often hard to see because of the thick blades. The sori vary from round to elongate, or sometimes merging. An indusium, as in all polypodiaceous ferns, is absent.

The fronds can vary tremendously within a species, due to cultural or genetic factors. Also, in those species with dimorphic fronds, the sterile and fertile fronds can intergrade with one another. For a technical treatment of the species of *Pyrrosia,* see Hovenkamp (1986).

Pyrrosia is native to the Old World tropics and temperate areas and contains about 50 mostly epiphytic or epilithic species. The genus name comes from the Greek *pyr,* fire, alluding to the dull reddish, scaly covering on the blade of the type species (*Pyrrosia chinensis* Mirbel).

Pyrrosia angustata (Swartz) Ching   FIGURE 13.106.4
Tender

A medium-sized fern with medium-creeping rhizomes. Grows well under medium light in moist-dry potting mix or uncut moss. This species is easy to grow.

Pyrrosia angustata has dimorphic sterile and fertile fronds, with the sterile blades oblong-lanceolate, 12–25 cm

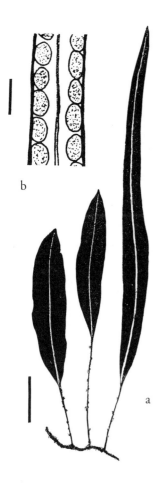

Figure 13.106.4.
Pyrrosia angustata:
a. habit, bar = 5 cm
(2 in.); b. sori, bar =
1 cm (0.4 in.).

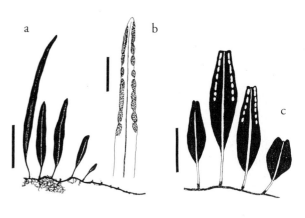

Figure 13.106.5. *Pyrrosia confluens:* a. var. *confluens* habit, bar = 5 cm (2 in.); b. var. *confluens* sori, bar = 1 cm (0.4 in.); c. var. *dielsii* habit, bar = 5 cm (2 in.).

(5–10 in.) long, and the fertile ones narrower and longer. Both kinds of fronds are covered with a loose, woolly deciduous down. The sori are 5–10 mm (0.2–0.4 in.) wide and vary from round to elongate, being deeply sunken in the lower surface of the blade and raised (embossed) on the upper surface. This species is native to Thailand, Sumatra, Malaya, Borneo, and the Moluccas.

Pyrrosia confluens (R. Brown) Ching   FIGURE 13.106.5
Tender to slightly hardier

A small fern with medium-creeping rhizomes. Grows well under medium light in moist-dry potting mix or uncut moss with good drainage.

The rhizome scales of *Pyrrosia confluens* are ciliate toward the apices. The sterile and fertile fronds vary from moderately to distinctly dimorphic. Both have narrowed apices (var. *confluens*), leathery texture, and hydathodes on or within the margin. The fertile fronds are longer. The sori are apical. If separate, the sori are oblong and in a single row; if confluent, they form a continuous band around the apex of the frond. This species is native to Australia, Norfolk Island, New Caledonia, Loyalty Islands, and Tahiti.

var. *confluens*. Fronds moderately dimorphic, leathery, apex narrow, hydathodes submarginal; sori separate or confluent.

var. *dielsii* (C. Christensen) Hovenkamp (*Pyrrosia dielsii* (C. Christensen) Tindale). Silvery felt fern. Fronds distinctly dimorphic, leathery and often brittle when dry, apex wide, often truncate or emarginate, hydathodes marginal; sori separate, round to oval, rarely confluent. Native to Australia. Though listed here, this variety is doubtfully cultivated in the United States. The fronds examined by the author were sterile, and the distinctness of the sori could not be confirmed.

Pyrrosia costata (Wallich ex C. Presl) Tagawa &
K. Iwatsuki   FIGURE 13.106.6
syn. *Pyrrosia beddomeana* (Giesenhagen) Ching
Tender

A medium-sized fern with short-creeping rhizomes. Grows under medium light in moist-dry potting mix or uncut moss with good drainage. The plants are slightly difficult to grow. This species requires higher temperatures than most species of *Pyrrosia*.

Pyrrosia costata has stout rhizomes over 5 mm (0.2 in.) thick. The stipes are absent or poorly developed, and the blades are crowded, widest above the middle, more than 30 cm (12 in.) long and 3 cm (1.2 in.) wide, dark green above, and rusty tan below. The sori are closely packed and usually apical on the blade. This species is native to southeastern Asia.

Pyrrosia costata might be confused with *P. stigmosa*. The latter has elongate rhizomes, long stipes, and costae and secondary veins narrowly grooved on the upper surface instead of flat or shallowly and broadly grooved. Broad frond forms of *P. costata* might be confused with *P. princeps* and *P. splendens*. *Pyrrosia princeps* has dentate or ciliate rhizome scales and a central bundle of dark support tissue in its stipe; in contrast, *P. costata* has entire rhizome scales and no central support tissue. *Pyrrosia splendens* has blade hairs with long erect spines; these are absent in *P. costata*.

Figure 13.106.6. *Pyrrosia costata:* a. habit and larger frond, bar = 5 cm (2 in.); b. stipe cross section, bar = 1 mm.

Pyrrosia eleagnifolia (Bory) Hovenkamp

FIGURE 13.106.7

syn. *Pyrrosia rupestris* of authors, not (R. Brown) Ching,
    P. serpens of authors, not (N. L. Forster) Ching
Semi-tender to hardier

A small fern with medium-creeping rhizomes. Grows under medium light in moist-dry potting mix or uncut moss with good drainage. The plants are difficult to establish but otherwise are tough and adaptable to drier conditions.

Pyrrosia eleagnifolia has entire to dentate rhizome scales, and the fronds are dimorphic, thick-leathery, and densely covered with tan hairs on the lower surfaces. Hydathodes are absent. The sterile fronds are almost rounded, rarely to 3 cm (1.2 in.) long, and the fertile ones are longer and narrower. The distinctly sunken sori are round, slightly spaced, and appear in two or three rows. Native to New Zealand.

This species was recently introduced from New Zealand and has shown promise in warm-temperate areas. Botanists have confused it with *Pyrrosia rupestris* (R. Brown) Ching of Australia and *P. serpens* (N. L. Forster) Ching of the South Pacific. *Pyrrosia rupestris* differs in having hydathodes. *Pyrrosia serpens* differs in having two rows of sori with the second row weakly developed. *Pyrrosia serpens* is doubtfully cultivated in the United States.

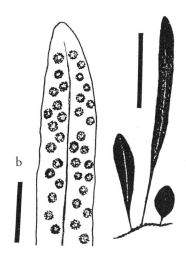

Figure 13.106.7. *Pyrrosia eleagnifolia:* a. habit, bar = 5 cm (2 in.); b. sori, bar = 1 cm (0.4 in.).

Pyrrosia fallax (Alderwerelt) M. G. Price

FIGURE 13.106.8

Tender (?)

A small fern with medium-creeping rhizomes. Grows well under medium light in moist-dry potting mix or uncut moss with good drainage.

Pyrrosia fallax has slender rhizomes covered by roundish, dark scales with pale erose-ciliate margins. The phyllopodia are about 1–1.5 cm (about 0.5 in.) apart, and lateral buds occurs on the rhizome about midway between phyllopodia. The fronds are dimorphic. The sterile ones are obovate or rounder, 1–4.5 cm (0.5–2 in.) long, and nearly glabrous above but with pale hairs below. The fertile fronds are narrowly linear, about 4–10 cm (1.5–4 in.) long. The sori are arranged in two or three irregular rows or are

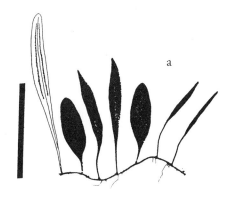

Figure 13.106.8. *Pyrrosia fallax:* a. habit, bar = 5 cm (2 in.); b. fertile frond with linear sori, bar = 1 cm (0.4 in.).

confluent along the distal margin of the frond. This species is native to Ambon eastward to Solomon Islands.

The cultivated plants named as this species are only tentatively identified as such. They are grown in scattered fern
collections in Florida and reportedly were collected in New
Guinea.

Pyrrosia hastata (Thunberg ex Houttuyn) Ching

FIGURE 13.106.9

syn. *Pyrrosia tricuspis* (Swartz) Tagawa
Semi-hardy to hardier, Zone 8

A small-medium fern with short-creeping rhizomes. Grows
well under medium light in moist-dry garden soil or potting mix with good drainage. This species is easy to grow in
baskets or in the ground.

The stipes of *Pyrrosia hastata* are less than 1 cm (0.5 in.)
apart, and the blades are typically hastately lobed—they
may have up to five lobes, with the outer lobes much
smaller—and have star-shaped hairs to only 0.5 mm in diameter. This species is native to South Korea and Japan.

Pyrrosia hastata plants with five-lobed fronds may be
confused with *P. polydactyla*. In cultivated plants the stipe
and main veins near the base of the blade are pale green in
P. hastata and black in *P. polydactyla*. The star-shaped hairs
of *P. polydactyla* are also slightly larger than those of *P. hastata*, up to 1 mm in diameter. A variant of *P. hastata* with
small hastate blades is in cultivation.

Pyrrosia lanceolata (Linnaeus) Farwell

FIGURE 13.106.10

syn. *Pyrrosia adnascens* (Swartz) Ching, *P. varia*
    (Kaulfuss) Farwell
Tender

A small fern with medium-creeping rhizomes. Grows well
under medium-high light in moist-dry potting mix or
uncut moss with good drainage. The plants are easy to
grow.

Pyrrosia lanceolata has slender rhizomes clothed by lanceolate scales with pale marginal hairs. The fronds are dimorphic: the sterile ones are oval to ovate-lanceolate, to 24
cm (10 in.) long, 4 cm (1.5 in.) wide, whereas the fertile
ones are narrower and longer. The sori are about 1 mm
wide in weakly defined, oblique rows. This species is native to tropics of the Old World east to Polynesia.

Pyrrosia linearifolia (Hooker) Ching

FIGURE 13.106.11

Hardy to semi-hardy, Zone 8

A small fern with medium-creeping rhizomes. Grows well
under low-medium light in moist-dry potting mix or uncut
moss with good drainage. The species can survive minimum winter temperatures of −7°C (20°F)

The blades of *Pyrrosia linearifolia* are widest above the
middle and up to 9 cm (3.5 in.) long. The sori are round,

Figure 13.106.9. *Pyrrosia hastata:* frond variations, bar =
5 cm (2 in.).

submarginal, usually in a row on each side of the frond on
the upper half. This species is native to southeastern China,
Taiwan, North and South Korea, and Japan.

Pyrrosia lingua (Thunberg) Farwell

FIGURES 13.106.1–3, 12

Japanese felt fern, tongue fern
Hardy, Zone 6

A small fern with medium- to long-creeping rhizomes.
Grows well under medium to high (indirect) light in moist-
dry potting mix or uncut moss with good drainage. The

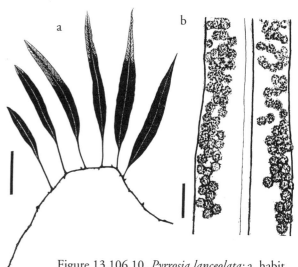

Figure 13.106.10. *Pyrrosia lanceolata:* a. habit,
bar = 5 cm (2 in.); b. sori, bar = 1 cm (0.4 in.).

Figure 13.106.11. *Pyrrosia linearifolia:* habit, bar = 5 cm (2 in.).

plants are easy to grow in pots, baskets, on boards, or in the ground. The fronds are an attractive dark green.

Pyrrosia lingua has moderately slender rhizomes 1.2–3.7 mm thick with phyllopodia spaced 2–8 cm (0.75–3 in.) apart. The blades vary from lanceolate to oblong to elliptic-lanceolate. They can grow up to 50 cm (20 in.) long and 5 cm (2 in.) wide but are usually only half this length. The sori are many, round, 1 mm in diameter, and closely placed between visible lateral veins. This species is native to China, southeastern Asia, and India.

There are two botanical varieties of *Pyrrosia lingua:*

var. *heteractis* (Mettenius ex Kuhn) Hovenkamp (*Pyrrosia heteractis* (Mettenius ex Kuhn) Ching). Figure 13.106.12b. Blades broader than the type variety, apices cuspidate, with star-shaped hairs of two types, those in the upper layer with boat-shaped rays, those in the lower layer with mainly woolly rays.

var. *lingua.* Figure 13.106.12a. Frond apices acute or subobtuse, lower layer of star-shaped hairs with woolly rays absent.

Many cultivars of *Pyrrosia lingua* var. *lingua* are grown, differing in such characteristics as amount of cresting, type of emargination, and blade width. Successive fronds can differ in shape. The fancy-foliage forms often grow more slowly than other forms. A few samples of the many cultivars include the following:

'Cristata'. Crested tongue fern, Obake pyrrosia. Figure 13.106.12c. Blade tips several times irregularly forked, the forks not greatly twisted.

'Monstrifera'. Lacerate pyrrosia. Figure 13.106.12d. Blade margins lacerate.

'Nankin-shishi'. Peacock pyrrosia. Figure 13.106.12e. Blade tips many times irregularly forked, the forks congested and twisted.

'Nokogiri-ba'. Figure 13.106.12f. Blades serrate-crenate.

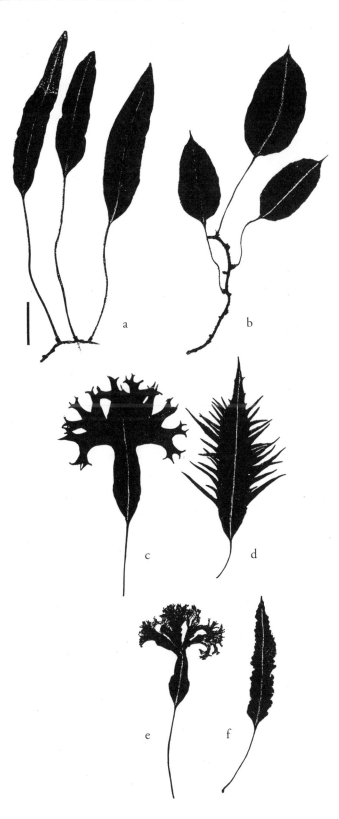

Figure 13.106.12. *Pyrrosia lingua:* a. var. *lingua* habit, with fertile frond on left; b. var. *heteractis* habit; c. 'Cristata'; d. 'Monstrifera'; e. 'Nankin-shishi'; f. 'Nokogiri-ba'. Bar = 5 cm (2 in.). After Hoshizaki (1981).

Pyrrosia longifolia (N. L. Burman) C. V. Morton

FIGURE 13.106.13

Tender to hardier (?)

A medium-sized fern with medium-creeping to sometimes longer creeping rhizomes. Grows well under high light in moist-dry to dry potting mix or uncut moss with good drainage. The plants are easy to grow and tolerate irregular watering. The long, strap-shaped, pale, leathery fronds are distinct features of this fern in cultivation.

Pyrrosia longifolia has entire rhizome scales. The fronds are long, leathery, and narrowly strap-shaped, to 60 cm (24 in.) long and 3.5 cm (1.5 in.) wide. This species is native from southern China to southeastern Asia, to Indonesia, Micronesia, the Philippines, and Australia.

A smaller, slightly thinner textured form is also found in cultivation. It reportedly was imported from New Guinea.

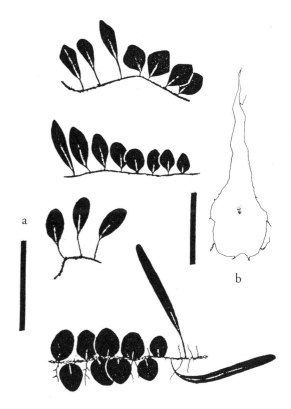

Figure 13.106.14. *Pyrrosia nummulariifolia*: a. habits of different plants, bar = 5 cm (2 in.); b. rhizome scale, bar = 0.5 mm, after Hoshizaki (1981).

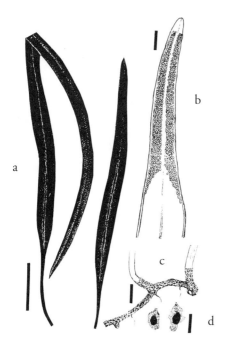

Figure 13.106.13. *Pyrrosia longifolia*: a. fronds, bar = 5 cm (2 in.); b. sori, bar = 1 cm (0.4 in.), after Hoshizaki (1981); c. rhizome and stipe bases, bar = 1 cm (0.4 in.), after Hoshizaki (1981); d. rhizome scales, bar = 1 mm.

Pyrrosia nummulariifolia (Swartz) Ching

FIGURE 13.106.14

syn. *Pyrrosia obovata* (Blume) Ching
Tender

A small fern with medium-creeping rhizomes. Grows well under medium light in moist-dry potting mix or uncut moss with good drainage. The plants are easy to grow and make an ideal terrarium plant.

Pyrrosia nummulariifolia has fleshy, dimorphic fronds. The sterile fronds are roundish, mostly to 2 cm (0.75 in.)

long, and the fertile ones are longer, narrower, and more erect. The sori are mostly 1 mm wide, three or four on each side of midrib, scattered, and sometimes fusing. This species is native to India, southeastern Asia to Indonesia, and the Philippines. The forms with longer fronds were formerly called *P. obovata*.

Pyrrosia piloselloides (Linnaeus) M. G. Price

FIGURE 13.106.15

syn. *Drymoglossum piloselloides* (Linnaeus) C. Presl
Tender

A small fern with medium-creeping rhizomes. Grows well under medium light in moist-dry potting mix or uncut moss with good drainage. The plants are easy to grow and suitable for terrariums.

The rhizome scales of *Pyrrosia piloselloides* are dark with pale margins and bear long hairs. The fronds are dimorphic, thick and fleshy, glossy green, and have deciduous hairs. The sterile fronds are roundish-oblong, sessile or nearly so, and to 6 cm (2.5 in.) long by 2 cm (0.75 in.) wide. The fertile fronds are short stalked, linear-oblong, and to 12 cm (4.75 in.) long by 1 cm (0.5 in.) wide. The sori occur in a marginal band around the apex. This species is native from India to Malaysia and China (Hainan).

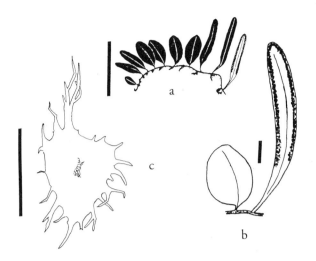

Figure 13.106.15. *Pyrrosia piloselloides:* a. habit, bar = 5 cm (2 in.); b. habit, with sterile frond (left) and fertile frond (right), bar = 1 cm (0.4 in.); c. rhizome scale, bar = 0.5 mm. After Hoshizaki (1981).

This species might be confused with *Pyrrosia nummulariifolia,* which has persistent instead of deciduous hairs on the fronds and different rhizome scales.

Pyrrosia polydactyla (Hance) Ching

FIGURE 13.106.16; PLATE 48

Semi-tender

A small-medium fern with short-creeping rhizomes. Grows well under medium light in moist-dry garden soil, potting mix, or uncut moss with good drainage. The plants are easy to grow and are suitable in baskets or the ground.

Pyrrosia polydactyla resembles *P. hastata,* but its blades have six to eight deep, pedately divided lobes and the stipe and main veins near the base of the blade are blackish. This species is native to Taiwan.

Pyrrosia porosa (C. Presl) Hovenkamp

FIGURE 13.106.17

syn. *Pyrrosia davidii* (Giesenhagen ex Diels) Ching, *P. pekinensis* (C. Christensen) Ching

Semi-tender or hardier

A small fern with medium-creeping rhizomes. Grows well under medium light in moist-dry potting mix or uncut moss with good drainage.

The rhizomes of *Pyrrosia porosa* are 1.6–3.1 mm wide, with the stipes spaced 3–7 mm (0.1–0.3 in.) apart. The lanceolate, entire blades are 9–31 cm (3.5–12.5 in.) long and 0.3–3.5 cm (0.1–1.5 in.) wide with scattered hydathodes. The sori are 1–2 mm wide and clustered toward the apex or spread all over the blade. This species is native from the Himalayan area to India, southeastern Asia, and the Philippines.

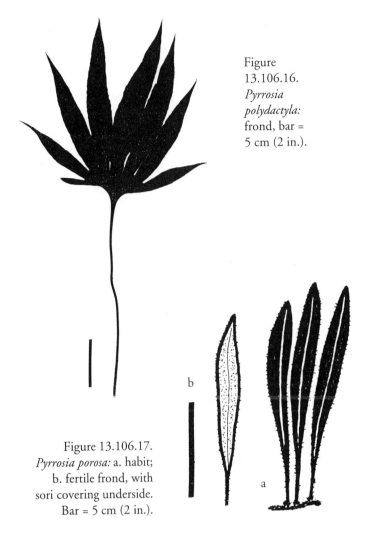

Figure 13.106.16. *Pyrrosia polydactyla:* frond, bar = 5 cm (2 in.).

Figure 13.106.17. *Pyrrosia porosa:* a. habit; b. fertile frond, with sori covering underside. Bar = 5 cm (2 in.).

The differences between *Pyrrosia porosa* and *P. davidii* are insufficient to recognize the latter (Hovenkamp 1986). In their extreme forms, *P. porosa* is larger and inconsistently has two kinds of star-shaped hairs, whereas *P. davidii* is smaller and consistently has two kinds of star-shaped hairs.

Pyrrosia princeps (Mettenius) C. V. Morton

FIGURE 13.106.18

Tender

A medium-large fern, to 1 m (3 ft.) by 10 cm (4 in.), with short-creeping rhizomes and tightly clustered fronds. Grows well under medium light in moist-dry potting mix or uncut moss with good drainage.

The rhizomes of *Pyrrosia princeps* are stout, compact, and covered by trough-like, dentate or ciliate scales. The fronds are close together and sessile. Narrowly oblanceolate blades are 24–125 cm (10–50 in.) long by 3.5–12 cm (1.5–4.75 in.) wide, gradually narrowed to the base, with mostly acuminate apices. The upper layer of stellate hairs has spreading needle-like rays. The hydathodes are distinct

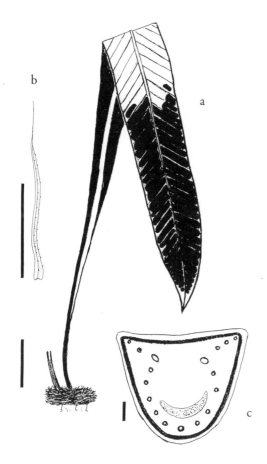

Figure 13.106.18. *Pyrrosia princeps:* a. habit, showing frond with fertile area, bar = 5 cm (2 in.); b. trough-like rhizome scale with marginal teeth, bar = 0.5 mm; c. stipe cross section, with the stippled area showing the dark, thick-walled cells (sclerenchyma) that strengthen the stipe, bar = 1 mm.

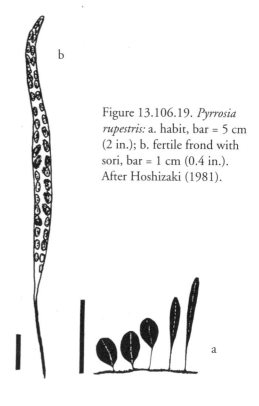

Figure 13.106.19. *Pyrrosia rupestris:* a. habit, bar = 5 cm (2 in.); b. fertile frond with sori, bar = 1 cm (0.4 in.). After Hoshizaki (1981).

and scattered. The round sori are 0.5 mm wide and densely packed between the main veins in the apical part of blade. This species is native to Sulawesi, the Moluccas, and New Guinea.

Pyrrosia princeps can be confused with *P. splendens,* a species that differs by having entire rhizome scales and blade hairs with a distinct, long, spine-like ray.

Pyrrosia rupestris (R. Brown) Ching

FIGURE 13.106.19

Rock felt fern
Semi-tender to hardier (?)

A small fern with medium- to long-creeping rhizomes. Grows well under medium light in moist-dry potting mix or uncut moss with good drainage.

Pyrrosia rupestris has entire rhizome scales without marginal hairs. The fronds are dimorphic, with the sterile ones to about 7 cm (3 in.) long, typically angular-rhomboid,

with conspicuous hydathodes in a row near the apex. The fertile fronds are longer and narrower than the sterile ones, mostly to 8–20 cm (3–8 in.) long. The sori are relatively large (1–2.5 mm wide) and slightly sunken, appearing in one to four rows on each side of the midrib. This species is native to Australia.

Pyrrosia samarensis (C. Presl) Ching

FIGURE 13.106.20

Tender

A small-medium fern with medium- to longer-creeping rhizomes. Grows well under medium-high light in moist-dry potting mix or uncut moss with good drainage. The plants are easy to grow.

Pyrrosia samarensis has dimorphic sterile and fertile fronds covered with loose white hairs that eventually fall off. The sterile fronds are narrowly lanceolate and tapered at both ends; the fertile ones are narrowed apically and covered beneath with roundish sori running together. This species is native to the Philippines.

Pyrrosia angustata also has loose, deciduous hairs but differs by a more erect habit, thicker and grooved stipes, acute blade apices, and discrete, sunken sori.

Pyrrosia sheareri (Baker) Ching

FIGURE 13.106.21

Semi-tender or hardier (?)

A medium-sized fern with short-creeping rhizomes. Grows well under medium-high light in moist-dry potting mix or uncut moss with good drainage. The plants grow slowly.

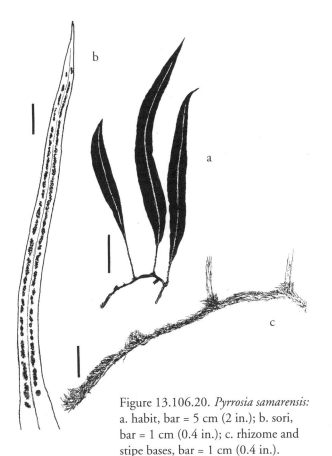

Figure 13.106.20. *Pyrrosia samarensis:* a. habit, bar = 5 cm (2 in.); b. sori, bar = 1 cm (0.4 in.); c. rhizome and stipe bases, bar = 1 cm (0.4 in.).

Figure 13.106.21. *Pyrrosia sheareri:* frond, bar = 5 cm (2 in.).

The rhizomes of *Pyrrosia sheareri* are up to 7 mm (0.3 in.) thick. The stipes are about half to as long as the blades, which are narrowly ovate, to 50 cm (20 in.) long, leathery, acuminate at the apex, and cordate-truncate to wedge-shaped at the base, often with lobes or teeth. Hydathodes are evident and scattered on the upper surface. The sori are round, small, and densely scattered to confluent. This species is native to China, Taiwan, and Vietnam.

Pyrrosia splendens (C. Presl) Ching   FIGURE 13.106.22
Tender

A medium-sized fern with short-creeping rhizomes. Grows well under medium light in moist-dry potting mix or uncut moss with good drainage.

Pyrrosia splendens has rhizomes up to 8 mm (0.3 in.) thick. The rhizome scales are somewhat shiny red-brown and entire. The fronds are close together, widest above the middle, and 33–100 cm (13–40 in.) long by 3.2–11.5 cm (1.2–4.5 in.) wide. The hairs on the upper surfaces of the blades have a distinct, long, more or less erect, spine-like ray about two to four times longer than the other appressed rays. This species is native to the Philippines. It resembles *P. princeps.*

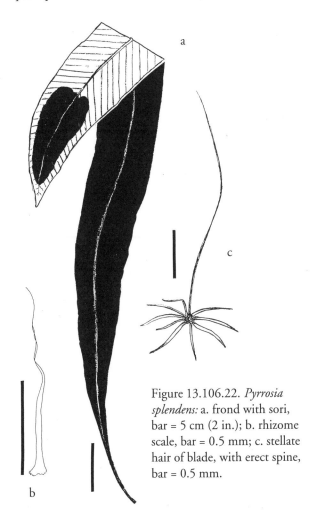

Figure 13.106.22. *Pyrrosia splendens:* a. frond with sori, bar = 5 cm (2 in.); b. rhizome scale, bar = 0.5 mm; c. stellate hair of blade, with erect spine, bar = 0.5 mm.

Pyrrosia stigmosa (Swartz) Ching   FIGURE 13.106.23
Tender

A medium-sized fern with short-medium-creeping rhizomes. Grows well under medium-high light in moist-dry potting mix or uncut moss with good drainage.

The rhizomes of *Pyrrosia stigmosa* are about 4.5 mm (0.2 in.) thick, with the stipes spaced 1–2 cm (0.5–0.75 in.) apart. The fronds are 11–48 cm (4.5–19 in.) long by 1.5–5.2 cm (0.6–2 in.) wide. They are wedge-shaped toward the base and acuminate to rounded at the apex. The hydathodes are distinct. The sori are about 0.5 mm wide and scattered. This species is native to southeastern Asia and Indonesia.

Pyrrosia stigmosa is similar to *P. costata,* but the latter species has a stouter rhizome and little or no stipe.

Regnellidium

Horticulturists interested in aquatic plants might consider growing *Regnellidium.* The genus is related to *Marsilea,* the clover fern, but differs by having two leaflets instead of four. The leaves are produced too far apart on the rhizome to make an attractive pot plant; the plants are mainly used as a novelty in aquariums.

Regnellidium roots in mud, although sometimes it is submerged and the fronds are floating. The rhizomes are

Figure 13.106.23. *Pyrrosia stigmosa:* habit, showing fertile area distal on frond, bar = 5 cm (2 in.).

creeping and bear fronds 1–3 cm (0.5–1.2 in.) apart. At the top of the stipe are two leaflets that have veins free or netted at their ends.

The genus has only one species, native to southern Brazil and adjacent Argentina. The genus name honors André Frederick Regnell (1807–1884), a Swedish botanist who collected and studied plants in Brazil.

Regnellidium diphyllum Lindman   FIGURE 13.107.1
Very tender

A small fern with medium-creeping rhizomes. Grows well under high light in moist-wet soil (a mixture of sand and peat) or fully submerged. The plants are typically grown in pots set in water or in an aquarium with plants partly submerged. *Regnellidium diphyllum* is easy to grow but apt to die if the temperature drops below 21°C (70°F). Further characteristics are described under the genus.

Rumohra
Leather fern

The genus *Rumohra* consists of medium-sized, terrestrial or epiphytic ferns with broad, dark green, coarsely divided, leathery fronds. The durable fronds are used extensively by florists in cut flower arrangements. The plants grow in beds or pots or baskets and require only moderate watering and humidity. Over the years, commercial growers, mainly located in Florida, have made many selections from their stock, and today's leather fern looks quite different from wild plants, though the wild plants vary considerably as well.

The rhizomes of *Rumohra* are medium-creeping, branched, and covered by peltately attached scales. The

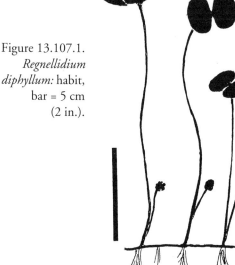

Figure 13.107.1. *Regnellidium diphyllum:* habit, bar = 5 cm (2 in.).

glabrous fronds are broadly triangular and three-pinnate, with the basal pinnae the largest. The sori are covered by a round, peltate indusium.

This genus is distinguished from the similar *Polystichum* by its peltately attached rhizome scales, large basal pinnae, and medium-creeping rhizomes. In contrast, *Polystichum* has basally attached rhizome scales, fronds narrowed at the base, and erect rhizomes. *Rumohra* is currently believed to be related to the dryopteroid ferns, not to the davallioids as previously thought.

Rumohra consists of seven species and is native to the tropics of the Southern Hemisphere. The genus name honors Karl F. von Rumohr (1785–1843), an art student from Dresden, Germany.

Rumohra adiantiformis (G. Forster) Ching

FIGURES 13.108.1, 2

syn. *Polystichum adiantiforme* (G. Forster) J. Smith, *P. capense* J. Smith, *P. coriaceum* Schott

Leather fern
Semi-hardy, Zone 8

A medium-sized fern with short- to medium-creeping rhizomes. Grows well under high-medium light in moist-dry garden soil or potting mix. The plants are easy to grow. When subjected to temperatures of $-7°C$ (19°F) for seven days, the fronds spot-burned or died, but the plants resumed growth afterward. Unconfirmed reports indicate that a skin rash may develop in response to contact with this fern.

The wild and cultivated plants of *Rumohra adiantiformis* are highly variable in the size and cutting of the fronds. The young indusium arches over the sorus, forming an upside-down cup, and is black when mature. The species is native to the Southern Hemisphere.

'Davis'. Pinnules slightly contracted.

Sadleria

Although *Sadleria* contains species with an arborescent growth form, it is related to *Blechnum* instead of such traditional tree-fern genera as *Cibotium, Cyathea,* or *Dicksonia. Sadleria* differs from these genera by having relatively little-divided blades and linear sori. Some *Sadleria* species are nonarborescent, although these are not cultivated. Commercial nurseries used to import living trunks of *Sadleria* from the Hawaiian Islands; later, plants were commercially grown from spores. *Sadleria* is grown outdoors as a tub or bedding plant in southern California, but the plants need protection from the occasional freezing temperatures. They may also be used as houseplants. Young fronds are often red. Since the genus is sensitive to root disturbance, extra care must be taken when transplanting.

Sadleria consists of tree ferns and smaller plants with creeping rhizomes. The trunk or rhizome is scaly and bears one-pinnate-pinnatifid or two-pinnate fronds. The veins

Figure 13.108.1. *Rumohra adiantiformis:* habit.

Figure 13.108.2. *Rumohra adiantiformis:* a. frond, bar = 5 cm (2 in.); b. sori and indusia, bar = 1 cm (0.4 in.); c. pinnae from different mature plants, bar = 5 cm (2 in.).

are netted along the midvein but free beyond. The sori are linear and continuous along both sides of the segment midribs. The indusium is shaped like the sorus and opens toward the midrib.

The genus contains six species, all endemic to the Hawaiian Islands. It is named for Joseph Sadler (1791–1849), a botany professor and student of the flora of Hungary. See the section on "Tree Ferns" in Chapter 10 for more information on *Sadleria;* for a technical treatment of the species, see Palmer (1997).

Sadleria cyatheoides Kaulfuss

Amaumau FIGURES 13.109.1–3

Semi-tender to tender

A large tree fern, often with reddish new foliage. Grows well under high light in moist garden soil or potting mix with good drainage. This species is sensitive to root disturbance; transplant with care. It will die at temperatures of about −2°C (30°F).

The stipe of *Sadleria cyatheoides* is scaly mostly at the base, not distally. The blades are one-pinnate-pinnatisect, with the veins stopping short of the margins and immersed (not visible) on the lower surface. The sori occupy more than half the length of the segment. This species is native to the Hawaiian Islands.

Sometimes small trunks are individually packaged and sold as novelties. Shipments of *Sadleria cyatheoides* trunks occasionally contain a few trunks of *S. pallida*. This latter species can be distinguished by scaly stipes throughout and by obvious veins on the lower surfaces of the blades running to the margin. Its culture is the same as that of *S. cyatheoides*.

Figure 13.109.2. *Sadleria cyatheoides:* sori and indusia.

Figure 13.109.1. *Sadleria cyatheoides:* habit.

Figure 13.109.3. *Sadleria cyatheoides:* a. frond, bar = 5 cm (2 in.); b. fertile segments, bar = 1 cm (0.4 in.).

Salvinia

FIGURE 13.110.1

Water spangle

The water spangles are small floating ferns, although they also grow in mud around the shores of ponds, lakes, or swamps. Their small, rounded leaves add interest to ponds, dish gardens, and aquariums. *Salvinia* does not tolerate much cool weather and dies during the winter in most parts of the United States. Culture is the same as for another aquatic fern, *Azolla*.

Salvinia minima is the only indigenous species in the United States. A small clump of plants can grow rapidly and carpet the water's surface in short time. *Salvinia molesta* also grows rapidly and is a terrible weed in waterways in the Old World tropics, and now in the United States, where it hampers navigation and fishing. For this reason, any member of the *S. auriculata* complex (species with egg-beater-like hairs) may not be imported into the United States; see *S. molesta* for more details.

The fronds of this genus are 1–2 cm (0.5–0.75 in.) long and vary from round to oblong. Three fronds occur at each node on the stem. Two of the fronds are green, floating, and leaf-like, and the third is whitish, submerged, finely divided, and root-like (true roots are lacking). The upper surfaces of the green fronds bear water-repellent hairs. The submerged, root-like fronds rarely produce sori, but when they do, the sori consist of sporangia enclosed by a globose indusium (the entire unit is called a sporocarp).

Salvinia is native to tropical and subtropical regions of the world. It consists of 10 species. The genus name honors Antonio Maria Salvini (1633–1729), an Italian professor of Greek.

Figure 13.110.1. *Salvinia molesta*: habit.

Salvinia auriculata Aublet

FIGURE 13.110.2

syn. *Salvinia rotundifolia* Willdenow
Semi-tender to tender

A small aquatic fern with short-creeping rhizomes. Grows well under direct sunlight. Possession of the plants is prohibited by governmental agencies; see *S. molesta* for details.

The roundish fronds of *Salvinia auriculata* bear hairs on the upper surfaces that have four branches uniting at their tips to form an egg-beater- or cage-like structure. The sori (sporocarps) are long-stalked, whitish, and spherical. Up to 30 are borne in a branched cluster. They all hang at about the same level. The spores are normal, not aborted. This species is native to tropical America.

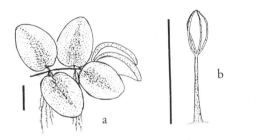

Figure 13.110.2. *Salvinia auriculata*: a. habit, bar = 1 cm (0.4 in.); b. hair from upper surface, bar = 1 mm; c. sporocarp, bar = 1 cm (0.4 in.), after Sota (1963).

Salvinia minima Baker

FIGURE 13.110.3

Semi-tender, Zone (8)9

A small aquatic fern with short-creeping rhizomes. Grows well under direct sunlight.

Salvinia minima is a generally smaller plant than *S. auriculata* and *S. molesta*. It can be distinguished from these two species by hairs that are free at the tip, not united into an egg-beater-like structure. The hairs are often sessile, not borne on a cone-like base as in the other two species, and they vary from one to four per group. The sori (sporocarps) are sessile and four to eight in a chain-like cluster. This spe-

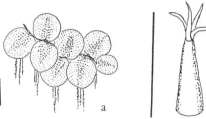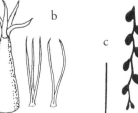

Figure 13.110.3. *Salvinia minima*: a. habit, bar = 1 cm (0.4 in.); b. hairs from upper surface, typical (left) and atypical (two on right), bar = 1 mm; c. sporocarps, bar = 1 cm (0.4 in.), after Sota (1963).

cies is native to the southeastern United States, West Indies, and Central and South America.

At different times of the year, cultivated material may have many atypical hairs. These hairs might be lacking, represented by a bump, or stoutly cone-shaped. The free branch-hairs borne at the tip of the cone-like hair may be poorly developed and number less than four. When sporocarps are not present, *Salvinia minima* might be confused with *S. natans* except for the roundish leaves of the former.

Salvinia molesta D. S. Mitchell   FIGURES 13.110.1, 4
Semi-tender to tender

A small aquatic fern with short-creeping rhizomes. Grows well under direct sunlight.

Salvinia molesta has rounded fronds, and the mature ones are often folded lengthwise along the midrib, especially in crowded conditions. As in *S. auriculata*, stiff hairs are present on the upper surfaces of the blades. These hairs consist of a stalk tipped by four hairs that unite at their apices to form an egg-beater- or cage-like structure. The fertile part of the frond is chain-like (unbranched) and toward the base has short-stalked sori (sporocarps) that are ovate with a slight beak at the tip. The sori gradually become sessile toward the apex of the fertile part. The spores are mostly aborted. *Salvinia auriculata* can be distinguished from this species by its branched, corymb-like fertile part. *Salvinia molesta* is native to southern South America (southern Brazil, Uruguay, and Paraguay) but has become naturalized in Africa, India, Sri Lanka, Indonesia, Australia, and New Zealand.

This species is a terrible weed in the Old World tropics and is becoming a serious pest in the southern United States from Texas to Florida. Although killed by hard frosts and prolonged subfreezing temperatures, it should not be cultivated anywhere in the United States because of its potential to escape. In the United States it has been declared a Federal Noxious Weed, which makes it illegal to import, own, cultivate, transport, or sell the species. In some states, laws also prohibit its possession. Check the World Wide Web site at http://nas.er.usgs.gov/ferns for more information. Moran (1992c) discusses the plant's weediness and the biological control methods that have been used to combat it.

Salvinia natans (Linnaeus) Allioni   FIGURE 13.110.5
Semi-tender to hardier

A small aquatic fern with short-creeping rhizomes. Grows well under direct sunlight.

Salvinia natans has oblong-truncate to ovate fronds. The hairs on the upper surfaces of the blades have four free branches, not united. The sori (sporocarps) are spherical, about six in a tight cluster. The species is native to Europe and Asia.

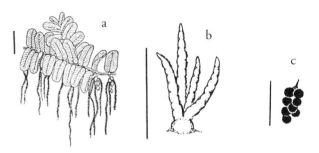

Figure 13.110.5. *Salvinia natans:* a. habit, bar = 1 cm (0.4 in.); b. hair from upper surface, bar = 1 mm; c. sporocarps, bar = 1 cm (0.4 in.).

Schaffneria

This small, charming fern bears clusters of rounded, diamond-shaped fronds. It grows on mossy rocks and ledges (usually limestone) in tropical areas and is well suited for terrarium culture.

The rhizomes are erect and bear small, clathrate scales. The clustered fronds are 2.5–15 cm (1–6 in.) tall, and the blades are entire, rhombic-obovate to fan-shaped, glabrous, and lacking a midrib. The veins spread and divide in a fan-shaped pattern, forming areoles without included veins. The sori are short to linear, with indusia shaped like the sori and attached on one side to a vein. Some pteridologists classify this genus in *Asplenium*.

Schaffneria consists of only one species native to Central America and Cuba. The genus is named for Wilhelm H. J. Schaffner (1830–1882), a German pharmacist who collected plants in Mexico.

Schaffneria nigripes Fée   FIGURE 13.111.1
syn. *Asplenium nigripes* (Fée) Hooker
Tender

A small fern with erect rhizomes. Grows well under low-medium to medium light in potting mix with good drain-

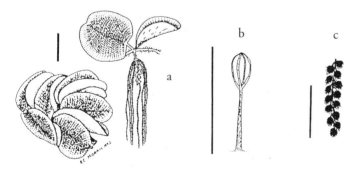

Figure 13.110.4. *Salvinia molesta:* a. habit, bar = 1 cm (0.4 in.), after Moran (1992c); b. hair from upper surface, bar = 1 mm, after Moran (1992c); c. sporocarps, bar = 1 cm (0.4 in.).

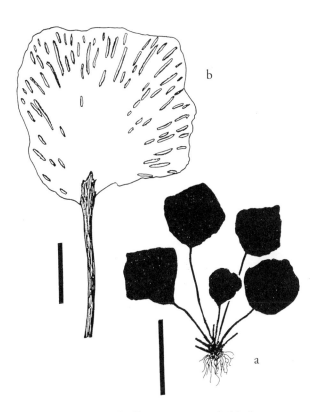

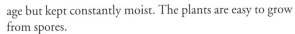

Figure 13.111.1. *Schaffneria nigripes:* a. habit, bar = 5 cm (2 in.); b. frond, bar = 1 cm (0.4 in.).

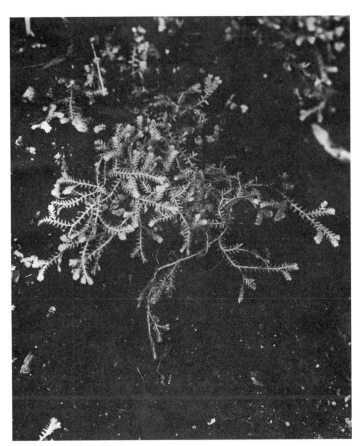

Figure 13.112.1. *Selaginella kraussiana:* mat-like growth habit.

age but kept constantly moist. The plants are easy to grow from spores.

See the characteristics of the genus for a description.

Selaginella
Spike moss

FIGURES 13.112.1–5

Selaginellas are mostly small- to medium-sized terrestrial plants. They are moss-like or fern-like with many branches bearing small, scaly leaves. They are used in rock gardens, as ground covers, or as accent plants. The tropical species are particularly eye-catching for their unusually colored leaves, such as red or bronze shades or iridescent blue-greens. A few tropical species are epiphytic, but they are rare and not cultivated.

Different regions of the United States are associated with certain species of native and cultivated *Selaginella*. In the northeastern United States the mat-forming meadow spike moss (*Selaginella apoda*) is often found in shady lawns, especially in moist depressions. In the southern United States *S. kraussiana,* a warm-temperate and sub-tropical species with mossy, mat-like growth, is widely available in the trade and grows easily outdoors. It can invade gardens and has become weedy in some areas. *Selaginella plana,* a taller plant with frond-like branches, is easily grown in more tropical areas and has also become widely

Figure 13.112.2. *Selaginella kraussiana:* branches with "cones."

Figure 13.112.3. *Selaginella umbrosa:* frond-like growth habit. Photo courtesy of B. Hoshizaki.

Figure 13.112.4. An example of a *Selaginella* with rosette growth habit. Shown are several plants of *S. tamariscina,* which are frequently grown in Japan, but are very rarely cultivated in the United States and not treated in this book. They are native to Asia, where they usually grow on exposed rocks or hillsides.

naturalized. The main requirements for promoting luxuriant growth of the ornamental tropical and subtropical species are ample humidity, soil moisture, and warm temperatures. In arid climates selaginellas are used mainly in rock gardens. The species adapted to such climates are generally more difficult to grow and do not have wide ornamental appeal. The resurrection plant (*S. lepidophylla*) is an exception: it uncurls from a ball of foliage to form an attractive spreading rosette. For more cultural information, see "Fern Allies" in Chapter 10.

In general, the plants of *Selaginella* are moss-like and produce small leaves less than 5 mm (0.2 in.) long. The leaves contain only a single vein or midrib. The main stems may be erect, prostrate, creeping, trailing, or scrambling, but they sooner or later fork into successively smaller branches. In some species, such as *Selaginella oregana,* the leaves are spirally arranged around the stem, but in most species they are arranged in four rows, with two lateral rows pointing outward (the lateral leaves) and two dorsal rows pointing more or less forward (the median leaves). Also, a single leaf, known as the axillary leaf, occurs on the lower surface of the stem at each fork (Figure 13.112.5). The leaves on the main part of the stem (the main-stem leaves) may differ from those on the branchlets. The leaves vary in such details as shape and type of margin or attachment. The fertile leaves usually form a spike or cone-like cluster at the tip of a branch, often appearing slightly or strongly angular. The lower leaves of the cone usually bear large female sporangia, and upper leaves bear smaller male sporangia, but this characteristic varies greatly among the species.

Selaginella might be confused with *Lycopodium,* though several technical differences separate the two genera. The most important distinction is the two kinds of sporangia and spores (male and female) in *Selaginella* versus only one kind in *Lycopodium.* This difference, however, is not easily observed. In aspect the cultivated species of *Selaginella* are more herbaceous and delicate than *Lycopodium* and have inconspicuous "cones."

Selaginella is a large genus, with about 750 species, and is extremely diverse in external form. It is cosmopolitan but primarily tropical. The genus name is derived from adding the Latin suffix *-ella,* indicating a diminutive, to *Selago,* the former name of a club moss in the genus *Huperzia;* thus, *Selaginella* means "like a small *Selago.*"

Identifying *Selaginella* species can be difficult due to their large number, the small size of the distinguishing characters, and (with cultivated plants) the lack of data about country of origin. For these reasons, selaginellas in horticulture are often misidentified. There are many more species in cultivation than those listed here, but they are uncommon and hard to obtain commercially. Native plants —such as *Selaginella densa,* native to midwestern states, *S. rupestris,* native to central and eastern states, and *S. wallacei,* native to northwestern states—are sometimes used in rock gardens and are well described in United States floras.

To facilitate identification, we have divided the cultivated species into three groups based on growth form. If a

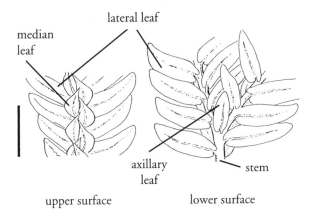

median leaf

lateral leaf

axillary leaf

stem

upper surface   lower surface

Figure 13.112.5. *Selaginella:* leaf arrangement (*Selaginella articulata*), bar = 5 mm (0.2 in.).

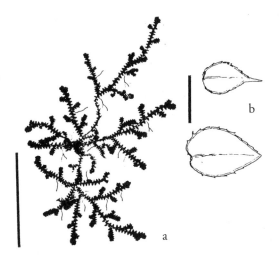

b

a

Figure 13.112.6. *Selaginella apoda:* a. habit, bar = 5 cm (2 in.); b. leaves, lateral (below) and median (above), bar = 1 mm.

species has two growth forms (for example, *Selaginella heterodonta*), it is listed under both groups.

Mat-like growth. These species resemble mosses. Their main stems and branches are leafy and creeping, with a mat-like or low-trailing habit. The growth is indefinite (that is, of unlimited growth), not determinate as in many upright species, and the roots are produced more or less all along the stem at the branch forkings. *Selaginella apoda, S. diffusa, S. douglassii, S. heterodonta, S. kraussiana, S. oregona, S. serpens, S. uncinata.*

Frond-like growth. These species have foliage that resembles fern fronds. The main stems are erect, resembling a stipe, and produce roots at the base. They branch repeatedly above to form a blade-like structure resembling a fern frond with numerous tiny, scale-like leaflets. This frond-like foliage arises from a long-creeping stem, or rarely scrambling as in *Selaginella willdenovii*. The species in this group are *S. braunii, S. erythropus, S. heterodonta, S. involvens, S. martensii, S. moellendorffii, S. oaxacana, S. plana, S. pulcherrima, S. umbrosa, S. viticulosa, S. vogelii,* and *S. willdenovii.*

Rosette growth. These species have frond-like branch systems (as in the preceding group), but the fronds are arranged in a rosette. They curl into a ball when dry. The species in this group are *Selaginella lepidophylla, S. harrisii,* and *S. pallescens* (in dense shade the latter two may be more irregularly clustered than rosette-like).

Selaginella apoda (Linnaeus) Spring   FIGURE 13.112.6
Meadow spike moss
Hardy, Zone 5

A small plant with mat-like growth from delicate, low, creeping, branched stems. Grows well under low to medium light in moist to moist-wet garden soil. This species is easy to cultivate. In the northeastern United States it can become weedy in lawns, especially around downspouts

from gutters and in shallow depressions. It makes a good terrarium plant.

The lateral leaves of *Selaginella apoda* are distant, ovate to ovate-lanceolate, slightly cordate at the base, green throughout but with one or two (rarely three) rows of transparent cells along the margins, and minutely serrate with acute apices. The medial leaves are ovate to ovate-lanceolate, either with an acute apex or attenuate without a midrib extension; the base is slightly oblique on the inner side but rounded and prominent on the outer side. This species is native to the eastern United States and Mexico.

Selaginella braunii Baker   FIGURE 13.112.7
Chinese lace fern
Hardy, Zone 7

A small-medium plant with erect, open, frond-like growth arising from medium-creeping horizontal stems. Grows well under medium light in moist garden soil or potting mix.

The lower, stalk-like part of the stem is somewhat stiff and firm with few leaves. The blade-like part of *Selaginella braunii* is triangular to ovate and horizontal with short, hairy branches. The lateral leaves of the ultimate branches are subdistant, spreading, and decurrent on the basiscopic side. This species is native to China but has become naturalized in many parts of the world.

Selaginella diffusa (C. Presl) Spring   FIGURE 13.112.8
Tender

A small plant with delicate, mat-like growth and long-creeping, branched stems. Grows well under low to medium light in moist-wet to moist garden soil or potting mix. The mat-like growth may also be trailing.

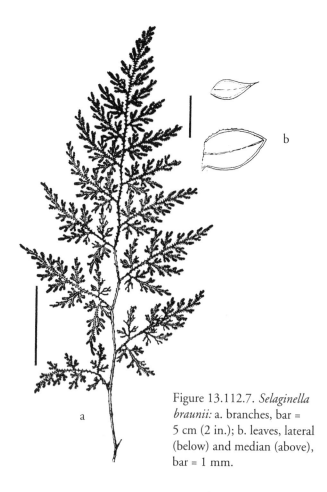

Figure 13.112.7. *Selaginella braunii:* a. branches, bar = 5 cm (2 in.); b. leaves, lateral (below) and median (above), bar = 1 mm.

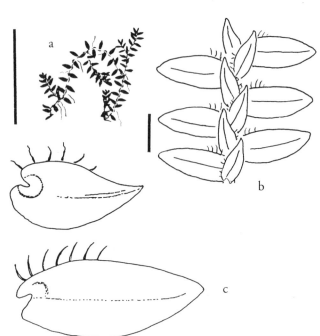

Figure 13.112.8. *Selaginella diffusa:* a. habit, bar = 5 cm (2 in.); b. leaf arrangement, bar = 2 mm; c. leaves, lateral (below) and median (above), bar = 1 mm.

Selaginella diffusa varies tremendously in shape, size, and amount of cilia on the leaves. The stems have a dark band or swelling below each fork. The lateral leaves are distant to close (but not overlapping), elliptical-lanceolate, acute, sometimes white-bordered, and sparsely ciliate to entire. The leaf has a prolonged ear with small cilia at the base on the acroscopic side. The median leaves are elongate-ovate and broadest near the middle, with long-acuminate apices; the base on the basiscopic side has a prolonged, tongue-shaped ear with or without a whitish border. The margins are finely denticulate and usually have multicellular cilia. This species is native to the American tropics.

Selaginella douglassii (Hooker & Greville) Spring
FIGURE 13.112.9

Douglas spike moss
Hardy, Zone 5

A small plant with delicate, mat-like growth and long-creeping, branched stems. Grows well under medium light in moist garden soil.

Selaginella douglassii has delicate leaves that resemble those of *S. apoda* in size but are firmer in texture. The lateral leaves are more or less spreading and distant. They are shiny green or turn brown with an orange to red spot at the base or are completely reddish. The apices are rounded, and the bases are eared and ciliate (elsewhere the leaf is entire). The median leaves are entire, pointed, and unevenly eared

Figure 13.112.9. *Selaginella douglassii:* a. habit, bar = 5 cm (2 in.); b. leaf arrangement, bar = 2 mm.

at the base, the ears ciliate. This species is native to the northwestern United States.

Selaginella erythropus (C. Martius) Spring
FIGURE 13.112.10

Tender

A small plant with erect, frond-like growth arising from short-creeping, horizontal stems. Grows well under medium light in moist potting mix. This species is often used in terrariums and bottle gardens because it likes humidity.

The lower surfaces of the leaves are burgundy and remain so with age, whereas the upper surfaces are dark green. The margins have numerous minute teeth. *Selaginella erythropus* is native to northern South America.

Figure 13.112.10. *Selaginella erythropus:* a. branches, bar = 5 cm (2 in.); b. leaf arrangement, bar = 2 mm; c. leaves, lateral (below) and median (above), bar = 1 mm.

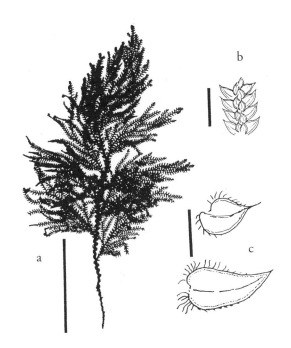

Figure 13.112.11. *Selaginella harrisii:* a. branches, bar = 5 cm (2 in.); b. leaf arrangement, bar = 2 mm; c. leaves, lateral (below) and median (above), bar = 1 mm.

Selaginella harrisii Underwood & Hieronymus

FIGURE 13.112.11

Tender

A small plant with erect, frond-like growth borne in a rosette or cluster; if the plants have clustered growth, they arise from a short-creeping horizontal stem. Grows well under medium light in moist garden soil or potting mix.

In *Selaginella harrisii,* the lower surfaces of the leaves are lighter colored than those of most selaginellas, often a silvery green. The lateral leaves are ovate and tightly imbricate near the stem tips, with the apex sharply acute and the base subauriculate with long cilia; the acroscopic margin is narrow, white, and short-ciliate to denticulate at the apex, and the basiscopic margin entire to denticulate. The older lateral leaves are green. The median leaves are ovate and aristate, with the base bearing a single short ear; the margin is short-ciliate and has a narrow white border. This species is native to Mexico, Belize, Honduras, and Jamaica.

Selaginella harrisii was formerly included with *S. pallescens,* which differs by the following characteristics: leaves on the unbranched part of the main stem are long-ciliate, not short-ciliate; the base of these leaves have long, almost overlapping ears, rather than a rounded base; the lateral leaves are short-ciliate, not long-ciliate; the basiscopic margin has a white border that is narrow to lacking, rather than a wider, white border; and the older lateral leaves are tan, not green.

Selaginella heterodonta (Desvaux ex Poiret)

Hieronymus   FIGURE 13.112.12
Tender

A small-medium plant with erect, frond-like or mat-forming growth from long-creeping horizontal stems. Grows well under medium light in moist garden soil or potting mix. This species is suitable as a ground cover in terrariums.

If mat-like in growth, *Selaginella heterodonta* has main stems that are usually long and whip-like at the tips; if frond-like in growth, the branches are erect-ascending or arched. The narrow branchlets are 3–4 mm (0.1–0.2 in.) wide. The lateral leaves vary from oblong-ovate to more elliptic and are acutish with subcordate bases; margins are strongly ciliate especially on the acroscopic side. The median leaves are ovate-falcate, aristate or not, usually eared on the basiscopic side, and have long-ciliate margins. This species is native to the Greater Antilles.

Selaginella involvens (Swartz) Spring

FIGURE 13.112.13

syn. *Selaginella caulescens* (Wallich ex Hooker & Greville) Spring
Tree spike moss
Semi-tender to hardier

A medium-sized plant with erect, frond-like growth arising from medium-creeping horizontal stems. Grows well under medium light in moist garden soil or potting mix. It likes humidity.

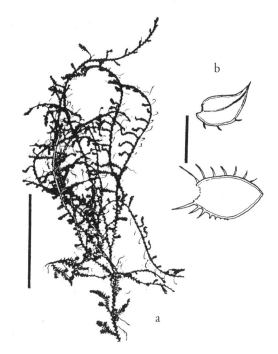

Figure 13.112.12. *Selaginella heterodonta:* a. habit, bar = 5 cm (2 in.); b. leaves, lateral (below) and median (above), bar = 1 mm.

The frond-like part of *Selaginella involvens* is triangular with overlapping leaves. The leaves on the main stem between the middle and lower lateral branches have very unevenly lobed bases and are extended on the basiscopic side and often lobed again, with erose-ciliate margins. The lateral leaves are ovate-triangular and ciliate-denticulate (less so toward the apex), and the midrib and two longitudinal grooves parallel to the midrib are indistinct. The median leaves are ovate and have a more or less keeled midrib and attenuate apices with two longitudinal grooves. This species is native to Japan, Korea, China, and Vietnam.

Selaginella kraussiana (Kunze) A. Braun
FIGURES 13.112.1, 2, 14

Spreading selaginella
Hardy, Zone (6)7

A small plant with mat-like growth and long-creeping (except for 'Brownii'), irregularly branching stems. Grows well under medium to low light in moist garden soil. The plants are used for ground cover but may become weedy. It is the most common species in the United States trade.

The lateral leaves of *Selaginella kraussiana* are ovate, finely dentate-serrate, and acute. The median leaves are ovate and acuminate, with bases slightly cordate on the basiscopic side. This species is native to Africa but has become widely naturalized in the tropics and subtropics, including parts of the southeastern United States.

Selaginella kraussiana is often misidentified in the trade as *S. denticulata* (Linnaeus) Spring, a species of central Europe and the Near East not cultivated in the United States.

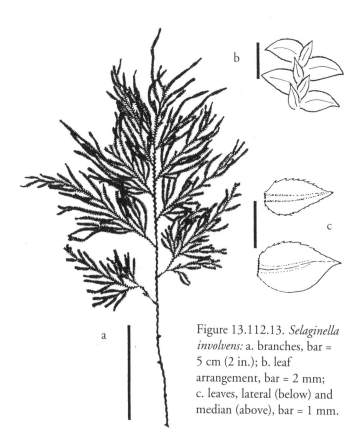

Figure 13.112.13. *Selaginella involvens:* a. branches, bar = 5 cm (2 in.); b. leaf arrangement, bar = 2 mm; c. leaves, lateral (below) and median (above), bar = 1 mm.

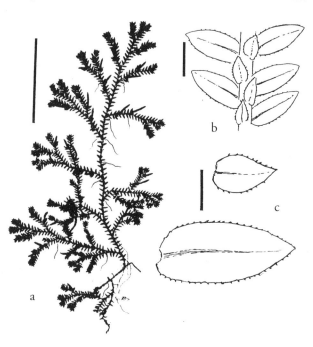

Figure 13.112.14. *Selaginella kraussiana:* a. habit, bar = 5 cm (2 in.); b. leaf arrangement, bar = 2 mm; c. leaves, lateral (below) and median (above), bar = 1 mm.

'Aurea'. Plants yellow green or chartreuse; slightly less robust growth form.

'Brownii'. Pin-cushion moss. Growth very compact, cushion-like.

'Gold-tips' ('Gold'). Branchlets lighter green at the tip.

Selaginella lepidophylla (Hooker & Greville) Spring
FIGURE 13.112.15

Resurrection plant
Semi-hardy, Zone 8

A small plant with a rosette growth form. Grows well under high light in basic, moist to moist-dry garden soil with sand and good drainage. The plants are popular because of their ability to curl into a ball when dry and uncurl into a flat rosette when watered. This uncurling is a mechanical action brought about by the absorption of water. It does not indicate that the plant is alive. If not too desiccated, the plants can be re-established by placing in a well-drained mix in a moderately humid environment.

All the leaves on *Selaginella lepidophylla* are imbricate, broadly ovate, and pubescent, with transparent margins. The lateral leaves are yellowish to reddish on the lower surface and green on the upper surface, cordate and ciliate at the base. The median leaves are cordate to truncate at the base and ciliate toward base to dentate-ciliate toward the apex. This species is native to the southwestern United States (New Mexico and Texas) and Mexico.

Selaginella martensii Spring
FIGURE 13.112.16
Semi-tender to hardier

A medium-sized plant with erect to suberect, frond-like growth arising from short-creeping horizontal stems. Grows well under medium light in moist to moist-wet garden soil or potting mix. This species likes humidity.

Selaginella martensii has leaves that are dark green, smooth, and shiny above but lighter green below. The lat-

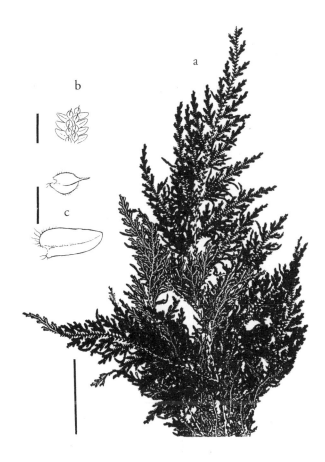

Figure 13.112.16. *Selaginella martensii:* a. branches, bar = 5 cm (2 in.); b. leaf arrangement, bar = 2 mm; c. leaves, lateral (below) and median (above), bar = 1 mm.

eral leaves are oblong, to 5 mm (0.2 in.) long. The apex is rounded, the base unequal, acroscopic side rounded, basiscopic side with a small ear, margins ciliate to denticulate at the base to more entire toward the apex. The median leaves are ovate, keeled, and usually long-aristate, the aristae to about half the blade length; the base has two uneven ears, and the leaf margins are ciliate, becoming more denticulate toward the apex, often with a white border. This species is native to Central America.

'Albolineata'. Snowy club moss. Leaves variegated with scattered creamy-white to white streaks.

Selaginella moellendorffii Hieronymus
FIGURE 13.112.17
Semi-tender

A medium-sized plant with erect to suberect, frond-like growth arising from creeping horizontal stems. Grows well under medium light in moist garden soil. It likes humidity.

The blade-like part of *Selaginella moellendorffii* is triangular to ovate. The leaves on the main stem between main branches have larger leaves that are triangular, acuminate,

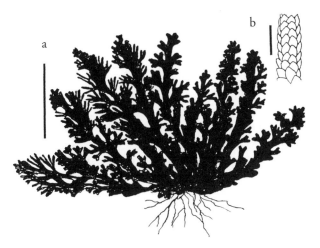

Figure 13.112.15. *Selaginella lepidophylla:* a. habit, bar = 5 cm (2 in.); b. leaf arrangement, bar = 2 mm.

Figure 13.112.17. *Selaginella moellendorffii:* a. habit, bar = 5 cm (2 in.); b. leaf arrangement, bar = 2 mm; c. leaves, lateral (below) and median (above), bar = 1 mm.

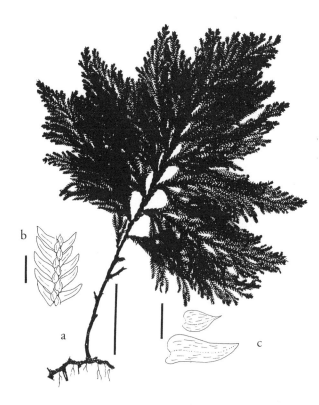

Figure 13.112.18. *Selaginella oaxacana:* a. habit, bar = 5 cm (2 in.); b. leaf arrangement, bar = 2 mm; c. leaves, lateral (below) and median (above), bar = 1 mm.

and outward-pointing. The lateral leaves are ovate-falcate, often with a faint false vein on either side of the midrib; the apex is acute, the margins minutely ciliate. The median leaves are appressed, ovate, unequal sided, short-toothed apically, and ciliate. This species is native to China, Taiwan, the Philippines, and Vietnam.

Selaginella moellendorffii reproduces vegetatively by gemmae produced at the branch tips. The gemmae resemble cones and tend to be slightly angular and redder than the rest of the branchlet. They fall off easily, and as a result this species can become weedy in greenhouses.

Selaginella oaxacana Spring   FIGURE 13.112.18
Oaxaca spike moss
Tender

A medium-sized plant with erect, frond-like growth arising from creeping horizontal stems. Grows well under medium light in moist garden soil or potting mix in humid environments.

The frond-like part of *Selaginella oaxacana* is flabellate, and the leaves on the main stem below the first branch are pressed to the stems and broadly ovate. The lateral and me-

dial leaves have fine streaks (idioblasts) on the upper surfaces, and their margins often curl upon drying. The lateral leaves are obliquely oblong-triangular, obtuse at the apex, truncate to rounded at the base, and serrulate. The medial leaves are smaller, ovate, acuminate, and also serrulate. This species is native to Central America.

Selaginella oaxacana is sometimes misidentified in the trade as *S. pulcherrima*.

Selaginella oregana D. C. Eaton   FIGURE 13.112.19
Oregon spike moss
Semi-hardy, Zone 8

A small-medium-sized plant with hanging or trailing stems. Grows well under medium light. The plants are cultivated as hanging epiphytes, either without soil or over moist soil and rocks in rock gardens. In the wild this species forms mats of hanging, stringy growth on trees, rarely on soil.

Selaginella oregana is distinctive by its spirally arranged leaves, all of one type, that are narrowly triangular to linear-lanceolate. The leaves are not four-ranked, and therefore the branchlets do not appear flattened. This species is native to western North America.

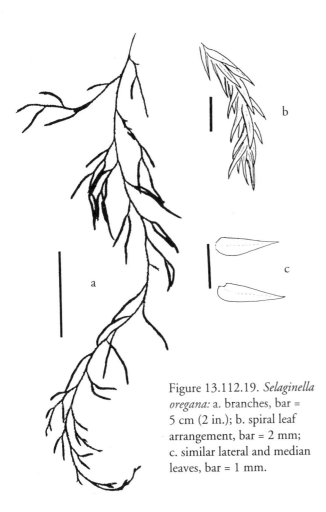

Figure 13.112.19. *Selaginella oregana*: a. branches, bar = 5 cm (2 in.); b. spiral leaf arrangement, bar = 2 mm; c. similar lateral and median leaves, bar = 1 mm.

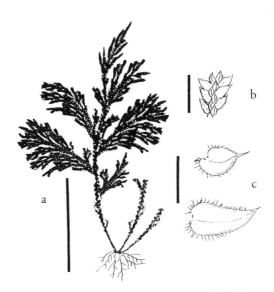

Figure 13.112.20. *Selaginella pallescens*: a. habit, bar = 5 cm (2 in.); b. leaf arrangement, bar = 2 mm; c. leaves, lateral (below) and median (above), bar = 1 mm.

Selaginella pallescens (C. Presl) Spring
FIGURE 13.112.20

syn. *Selaginella emmeliana* Van Geert
Sweat plant
Semi-hardy, Zone 8

A small plant with a rosette growth form, or if only loosely clustered, then arising from a short, horizontal stem. Grows well under medium light in moist garden soil or potting mix. The plants form flat rosettes when young but tend to become loosely clustered with more erect branches with age.

Most plants of *Selaginella pallescens* can be distinguished by their rosette growth form and (mostly) white-bordered leaves. The lateral leaves of the smaller branches closely overlap and are ovate-acuminate, mostly subfalcate at the apex and short-ciliate. Their basiscopic margins may lack the white narrow border. The median leaves are ovate and serrate, with a small tooth at the apex. Older leaves of both forms are tan. This species is native to Mexico, Central America, Colombia, and Venezuela.

Selaginella pallescens is often confused with *S. harrisii*. Another, unidentified species circulating in cultivation is also related to *S. pallescens*. It has sparsely ciliate leaves, and the median leaves are ovate and long-attenuate.

Selaginella plana (Desvaux ex Poiret) Hieronymus
FIGURE 13.112.21

Tender to semi-tender

A small to medium plant with a frond-like growth that is often sprawling, branched, and rooting on the underside. Grows well under medium light in moist garden soil. Mature plants may appear untidy because of their scrambling habit. They sometimes become invasive and weedy. The species is common in southern Florida fern gardens.

The erect stem of *Selaginella plana* is either greenish, straw-colored, or (in Florida specimens) reddish brown. All the leaves are entire, not ciliate. The lateral ones have an acute to rounded apex, and the base is unequal; the base of the acroscopic side has a narrow, often twisted ear, and the basiscopic side is truncate or rounded. The median leaves are narrowly ovate or oblong, eared or not. The axillary leaf is strongly eared on both sides, and the ears are often twisted. This species is native to southeastern Asia and Indonesia and has become widely naturalized elsewhere in the tropics.

Two unidentified species resembling *Selaginella plana* are also in cultivation.

Selaginella pulcherrima Liebmann ex E. Fournier
FIGURE 13.112.22

Tender

A small-medium plant with frond-like growth arising from long-creeping horizontal stems. Grows well under medium light in moist to moist-wet garden soil or potting soil. The plants like humidity.

All leaves of *Selaginella pulcherrima* are dark green above, lighter below, and more or less smooth. The oldest

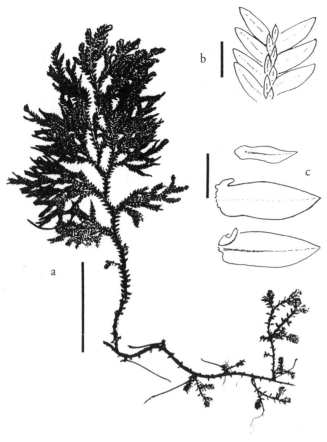

Figure 13.112.21. *Selaginella plana:* a. habit, bar = 5 cm (2 in.); b. leaf arrangement, bar = 2 mm; c. leaves, median leaf (above), upper surface of lateral leaf (center), under surface of lateral leaf (below), bar = 1 mm.

Figure 13.112.22. *Selaginella pulcherrima:* a. branches, bar = 5 cm (2 in.); b. leaf arrangement, bar = 2 mm; c. leaves, lateral (below) and median (above), bar = 1 mm.

ones turn buff. The lateral leaves are ovate, acute, and ciliate to denticulate. The medial leaves are ovate, acuminate at the apex, ciliate to denticulate, with or without an indistinct white border. The axillary leaves lack ears. This species is native to Mexico.

Selaginella oaxacana is sometimes misidentified in the trade as *S. pulcherrima.*

Selaginella serpens (Desvaux ex Poiret) Spring
FIGURE 13.112.23

Tender

A small plant with low, mat-like growth from branched, creeping stems. Grows well under low-medium light in moist garden soil or potting mix. The foliage undergoes a diurnal color change from bright green in the morning to pale silvery in the late afternoon. This change is caused by a contraction of the contents of the epidermal cells, allowing a layer of air to accumulate between the cuticle and the outer cell wall. This layer diffracts light, making the leaf appear pale silvery.

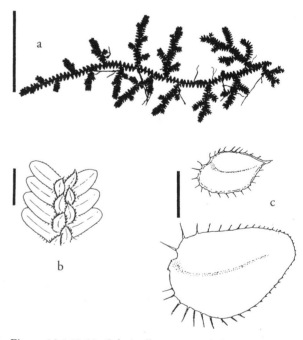

Figure 13.112.23. *Selaginella serpens:* a. habit, bar = 5 cm (2 in.); b. leaf arrangement, bar = 2 mm; c. leaves, lateral (below) and median (above), bar = 1 mm.

The lateral leaves of *Selaginella serpens* are ovate, obtuse, cordate at the base, and ciliate (less so toward the apex). The median leaves are ovate-acuminate, ciliate, and sometimes larger or broadly eared on the outer basiscopic side. This species is native to the West Indies.

Selaginella umbrosa Lemaire ex Hieronymus
FIGURES 13.112.3, 24

Red spike moss
Tender

A medium-sized plant with frond-like growth arising from long-creeping, branched horizontal stems. Grows well under medium light in moist-wet garden soil or potting mix. It likes humidity. The species is attractive because of its red stems.

The main, erect stems of *Selaginella umbrosa* are red, and the blade-like part is irregularly and densely flabellate, flat, and bright green. The lateral leaves of the main branches are ovate-lanceolate, unequally sided, and strongly ciliate at the base. The median leaves are ovate-acuminate and slightly keeled. This species is native to the American tropics and has become naturalized in many parts of the tropics throughout the world.

Selaginella uncinata (Desvaux ex Poiret) Spring
FIGURE 13.112.25; PLATE 49

Blue spike moss, peacock plant, rainbow moss
Hardy, Zone 6

A small to medium plant with mat-like growth from long-creeping or trailing, branched stems. Grows well under medium light in moist garden soil or potting mix. The plants reportedly overwinter well in coastal New York (Zone 6). This species is attractive for its blue-green, iridescent foliage. This color is best developed when the plants are grown in low light.

Selaginella uncinata has ovate or ovate-oblong lateral leaves with transparent and entire margins. Some are weakly stalked, and the leaf base is truncate to weakly cordate, with the acroscopic side often overlapping the stem. The median leaves are overlapping, ovate-lanceolate, the margins transparent and entire, the apex abruptly attenuate, and the base often oblique and weakly cordate. This species is native to southern China and has become naturalized in the southeastern United States.

Selaginella viticulosa Klotzsch
FIGURE 13.112.26
Tender

A small-medium plant with frond-like growth arising from creeping horizontal stems. Grows well under medium light in moist potting soil and in humidity. This species has softer and laxer foliage than other selaginellas.

Figure 13.112.24. *Selaginella umbrosa*: a. habit, bar = 5 cm (2 in.); b. leaf arrangement, bar = 2 mm; c. leaves, lateral (below) and median (above), bar = 1 mm.

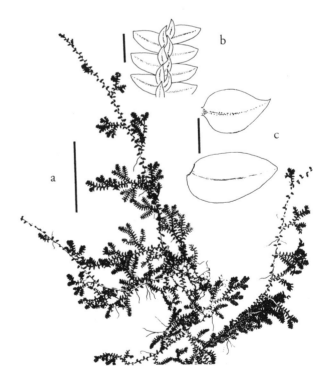

Figure 13.112.25. *Selaginella uncinata*: a. habit, bar = 5 cm (2 in.); b. leaf arrangement, bar = 2 mm; c. leaves, lateral (below) and median (above), bar = 1 mm.

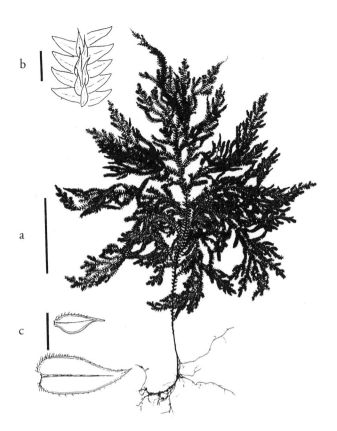

Figure 13.112.26. *Selaginella viticulosa:* a. habit, bar = 5 cm (2 in.); b. leaf arrangement, bar = 2 mm; c. leaves, lateral (below) and median (above), bar = 1 mm.

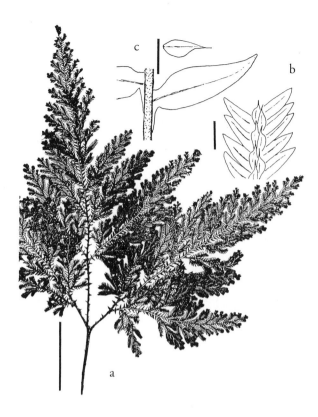

Figure 13.112.27. *Selaginella vogelii:* a. branches, bar = 5 cm (2 in.); b. leaf arrangement, bar = 2 mm; c. leaves, lateral broadly attached to stem (below) and median (above), bar = 1 mm.

The lateral leaves on the distal half of the main stem are oblong, two times longer than wide, spreading (not imbricate), and faintly streaked. The acroscopic margin is ciliate toward the base to denticulate toward the apex, and the basiscopic base is truncate. *Selaginella viticulosa* is native to Costa Rica, Panama, Colombia, and Venezuela.

Selaginella vogelii Spring   FIGURE 13.112.27
Tender

A small plant with frond-like growth arising from short-creeping horizontal stems. Grows well under medium light in moist garden soil or potting mix. This species likes humidity.

The main, erect stems of *Selaginella vogelii* are about as long as the blade-like part. The latter is broadly triangular and bears branches with many short, stiff hairs on the lower surface. The lateral leaves are narrowly triangular, constricted near the base then decurrent, and entire (not ciliate). The median leaves are long-acuminate, unequal at the base, and entire. This species is native to tropical Africa.

Selaginella willdenovii (Desvaux ex Poiret) Baker
FIGURE 13.112.28

Peacock fern, vine spike moss
Tender, Zone 9

A medium to large plant with sprawling to erect, frond-like growth. Grows well under medium-high light in moist garden soil. Give the plants a lot of space to grow. The scrambling stems may reach 6 m (20 ft.) long and typically bear small leaves with a strikingly beautiful sky-blue iridescence on their upper surface. The iridescence, however, develops only on plants grown in shade; those plants grown in full or partial sun are not iridescent. Iridescence in pteridophytes tends to occur in species that grow on deep-shaded forest floors, which suggests that this trait is an adaptation to low light. See Moran (1995a) for a popular account of iridescence in ferns.

All the leaves are entire on *Selaginella willdenovii*. The lateral leaves are whitish eared on the acroscopic side, and the axillary ones have two elongate-rounded ears. This species is native to tropical Asia and Indonesia and has occasionally become naturalized elsewhere in the tropics.

Figure 13.112.28. *Selaginella willdenovii:* a. branches, bar = 5 cm (2 in.); b. leaf arrangement, bar = 2 mm; c. leaves, lateral (below), median (middle), and axillary (above), bar = 1 mm.

Selliguea

syn. *Crypsinus*

The best-known cultivated species in this genus, *Selliguea feei,* is grown as a novelty in pots or baskets or, in subtropical climates, in the ground. *Selliguea* consists of small- to medium-sized epiphytic, epilithic, or terrestrial species. The rhizomes are relatively long-creeping and contain conspicuous black fibers (seen in cross section). The rhizome scales are peltately attached, lanceolate, attenuate or with hair-like tips, and opaque or with a membranous margin; if the margins are toothed or ciliate, the projections are glandular. The fronds are distant along the rhizome and jointed to it. The sterile and fertile fronds are dimorphic or not; if dimorphic, the fertile fronds are narrowed or skeletonized and taller than the sterile ones. The glabrous sterile fronds are simple, pinnatifid, hastate, or subpinnate, with cartilaginous margins usually sinuate or minutely notched. The veins are netted and form irregular areoles with free, included veinlets pointing in all directions. The main veins are conspicuous and nearly reach the margin. The sori are elongate or linear, and indusia are absent, as in all polypodiaceous ferns.

Because the distinguishing characters are inconsistent, the genus *Crypsinus* is now included in *Selliguea* (the older name, which has priority). Species formerly placed in *Crypsinus* are rarely grown or offered in the trade and therefore are not treated here. Although the plants are attractive, resembling small polypodiums, reports differ on their ease of culture.

Selliguea contains about 50 species or more and is native to Africa, India, Malaysia to Australia, New Guinea, the Pacific Islands, the Philippines, and Japan. The genus is named for M. Selligue, a French optician and instrument maker.

Selliguea feei Bory   FIGURE 13.113.1
Semi-tender

A small fern with medium- to long-creeping rhizomes. Grows well under high-medium light in moist to moist-dry potting mix or garden soil. The plants are easy to cultivate in pots or in the ground, but the fronds tend to become brittle with age.

Selliguea feei is characterized by broadly ovate rhizome scales, broadly lanceolate sterile fronds, often narrower and taller fertile fronds, and linear sori oblique to the costa. The fronds have a slightly brittle, leathery texture, and the lateral veins are conspicuous. The species is native to Java.

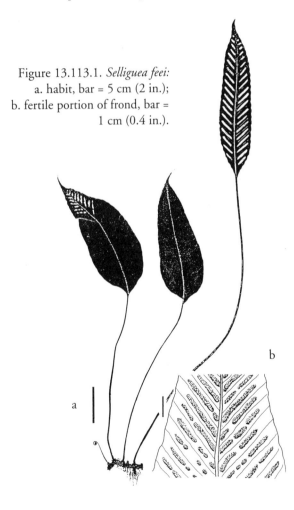

Figure 13.113.1. *Selliguea feei:* a. habit, bar = 5 cm (2 in.); b. fertile portion of frond, bar = 1 cm (0.4 in.).

Solanopteris

Potato fern

Comprising small epiphytes, the genus *Solanopteris* is grown as a novelty for its globose tubers (modified stems), which in nature are inhabited by ants. Growers report that the plants often do well for a while then suddenly die, although plants at the Marie Selby Botanical Garden in Florida have been flourishing for a long time. *Solanopteris* grows high in trees in its native, wet-forest habitat.

This genus and *Lecanopteris* are the only ferns that have stems inhabited by ants. The ants fiercely attack anything that disturbs the plant. In *Solanopteris,* they eventually fill the tuber with organic debris and frass, at which point the ants seek another tuber in which to live. The plant's roots then grow inside the tuber and extract water and mineral nutrients from the organic matter left behind by the ants. Thus, the plant receives two benefits from the ants' activities: protection and nutrients. The plants seem to grow better when inhabited by ants; however, the tubers will form even if ants are absent. For more about the natural history of this fern, see Moran (1992b).

In addition to the tubers, *Solanopteris* is characterized by long-creeping rhizomes covered by minute, circular scales. The sterile and fertile fronds are dimorphic, with the sterile fronds entire to pinnately lobed, and the fertile ones longer and narrower. The sori vary from round to elongate and, like in all polypodiaceous ferns, they lack indusia.

Some pteridologists consider *Solanopteris* close enough to *Microgramma* to be placed in that genus. It is kept distinct here because the name has been used in many floras and is well established in horticulture.

The genus is native to the American tropics and consists of four species. The name is derived from the potato genus, *Solanum,* and the Greek *pteris,* fern, in reference to the potato-like tubers.

Solanopteris bifrons (Hooker) Copeland

FIGURE 13.114.1

Tender

A small fern with medium-creeping rhizomes. Grows under high-medium light in moist to moist-wet potting mix or uncut moss with good drainage. This species is usually planted in a pad of uncut moss and fastened to a hanging board. It is difficult to grow.

The sterile fronds of *Solanopteris bifrons* are pinnately lobed, and the tubers are covered by a glaucous bloom. This species is native to the Amazonian lowlands of Colombia, Ecuador, and Peru.

Solanopteris brunei (Wercklé ex H. Christ)

W. H. Wagner   FIGURE 13.114.2

Tender

A small fern with medium-creeping rhizomes. Grows under high-medium light in moist to moist-dry(?) potting

Figure 13.114.1. *Solanopteris bifrons:* habit, bar = 5 cm (2 in.).

Figure 13.114.2. *Solanopteris brunei:* habit, bar = 5 cm (2 in.).

mix or uncut moss with good drainage. Usually planted in a pad of uncut moss and fastened to a hanging board. This species is difficult to grow.

The sterile fronds of *Solanopteris brunei* are entire or have slightly wavy margins. The tubers bear long, narrow scales. This species is native from Costa Rica to Ecuador.

Sphaeropteris   FIGURES 13.115.1–6
Tree fern

This genus belongs to the Cyatheaceae, which is *the* major family of tree ferns. The family also includes *Alsophila, Cnemidaria,* and *Cyathea* (which see for a comparison of these genera). *Sphaeropteris* can be distinguished from these others by its stipe scales, which are typically white or brown, not purplish or black, and are composed of cells that have the same shape (narrowly rectangular) throughout the scale, as compared to the differentiated border of diverging, irregularly shaped cells in the other tree-fern genera. Such scales are said to be "conform" or "nonmarginate." In many species of *Sphaeropteris* the scale margins bear short, dark teeth (a hand lens is needed to see these).

The Australian *Sphaeropteris cooperi* is probably the most common tree fern in the trade and is readily available from nurseries in California and Florida. It grows rapidly in many gardens, reaching 5 m (16 ft.) tall. The blond tree fern (*S. horrida*), which has stipes neatly and densely covered with blond scales, has been reintroduced into United States cultivation. New introductions and reintroductions of other species continue.

The trunks and stipe bases of *Sphaeropteris* plants are scaly (not hairy as in the dicksoniaceous tree ferns), and the blades are two- to three-pinnate-pinnatifid. Sori are located on the lower surfaces of the blades (not the margins) and are either naked or protected by a globose indusium.

Sphaeropteris, which contains about 110 species, is native to the American tropics, India, southeastern Asia, New Zealand, and the islands of the Pacific. The genus name

Figure 13.115.2. *Sphaeropteris cooperi:* scales on stipes and trunk.

Figure 13.115.3. *Sphaeropteris cooperi:* sori.

Figure 13.115.1. *Sphaeropteris cooperi:* habit.

Figure 13.115.4. *Sphaeropteris cooperi:* frond.

comes from the Greek *sphaera,* sphere, and *pteris,* fern, alluding to the globose sori.

Sphaeropteris aramaganensis (Kanehira) R. M. Tryon

FIGURE 13.115.7

syn. *Cyathea aramaganensis* Kanehira
Mariana Island tree fern
Semi-tender or hardier

A large tree fern. Grows well under medium or higher light in moist-dry garden soil or potting mix. The plants are robust growers and occasionally form offsets on the sides of the trunks. The offsets should be removed to maintain the symmetry of the plant and to avoid crowding the main crown. The removed offsets sometimes take root.

The stipes of *Sphaeropteris aramaganensis* are prickly on the lower surfaces and covered by pale brown, slightly shiny, narrowly triangular scales that are long-tapered and

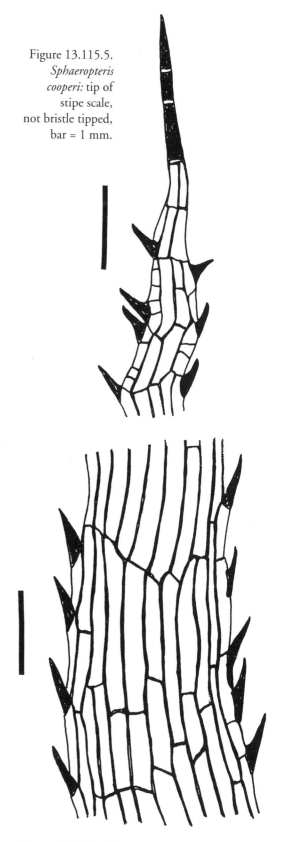

Figure 13.115.5. *Sphaeropteris cooperi:* tip of stipe scale, not bristle tipped, bar = 1 mm.

Figure 13.115.6. *Sphaeropteris cooperi:* central part of stipe scale, with the marginal cells same as the central cells, bar = 1 mm.

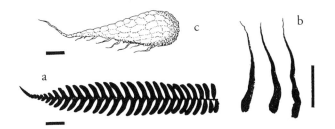

Figure 13.115.7. *Sphaeropteris aramaganensis*: a. pinnule, bar = 1 cm (0.4 in.); b. stipe scales, bar = 1 cm (0.4 in.); c. scale from underside of segment midrib (side view), bar = 0.1 mm.

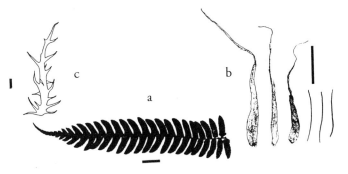

Figure 13.115.8. *Sphaeropteris cooperi*: a. pinnule, bar = 1 cm (0.4 in.); b. large stipe scales (left) and small stipe scales (right), bar = 1 cm (0.4 in.); c. scale from underside of minor leaf axis, bar = 0.1 mm.

twisted at the apex. The segment midribs on the lower surface near the base have small, whitish, puffy scales. The sori have many hair-like paraphyses mixed among the sporangia (magnification needed) and lack an indusia. The species is native to the Mariana Islands.

Sphaeropteris cooperi (F. V. Müller) R. M. Tryon

FIGURES 13.115.1–6, 8; PLATES 2, 3

syn. *Cyathea cooperi* (F. V. Müller) Domin

Australian tree fern, Cooper's tree fern, coin-spot tree fern

Semi-tender

A large tree fern. Grows well under medium to high light and may tolerate nearly full sun. The plants prefer moist-dry garden soil or potting mix, but they are relatively tolerant of aridity. This species survives occasional cold weather to near −5°C (20°F) for 4–6 hours; plants die completely at temperatures of −7°C (19°F) lasting one week. Cold weather can kill fronds, but the plants usually produce new ones. These plants grow rapidly. Mature plants shed their old fronds, leaving numerous rounded to oval leaf scars on the trunks. The scars resemble coins, hence the name coin-spot tree fern. This species has become naturalized in the wet tropics. It is the most common tree fern cultivated in the United States. It is often confused with the seldom cultivated *Alsophila australis*.

The stipes of *Sphaeropteris cooperi* vary from greenish to tan and are more or less smooth beneath (not spiny). The stipe scales are mostly of two types: one is long, linear-triangular, to 4 cm (1.5 in.) long, mostly smoky white, with margins irregularly dark bordered or not and bearing minute, dark teeth; the other is short, to 2 cm (0.75 in.), linear, dark, and tending to be straight and bearing minute teeth. The costules and midribs have very small, narrow-triangular, spiny scales. The sori are surrounded beneath by small, fringed scales, and a few hair-like paraphyses occur among the sporangia. An indusium is absent. The species is native to Australia.

'Brentwood'. Plants more massive than the typical form cultivated in the United States. The fronds are fuller and

trunks thicker; the growth is more rapid and robust. It is said to withstand *Rhizoctonia* disease better than the usual trade form.

'Robusta'. Tall and rapid growing, otherwise not distinct. It was difficult to propagate and no longer in the trade.

Sphaeropteris excelsa (Endlicher) R. M. Tryon

FIGURE 13.115.9

syn. *Cyathea brownii* Domin

Norfolk Island tree fern

Semi-hardy to semi-tender

A large tree fern, up to 12 m (40 ft.) tall. Thrives under medium light in moist garden soil or potting mix. This species seems to grow more rapidly and robustly than *Sphaeropteris cooperi*.

Sphaeropteris excelsa has a dark brown trunk, and the stipe bases are typically dark brownish and prickly on the lower surfaces. The stipes are covered by nonmarginate (conform) scales of two types: one is longer and wider,

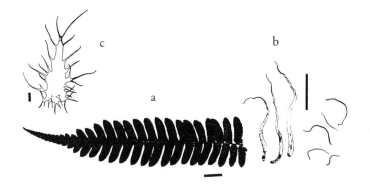

Figure 13.115.9. *Sphaeropteris excelsa*: a. pinnule, bar = 1 cm (0.4 in.); b. large stipe scales (left) and small stipe scales (right), bar = 1 cm (0.4 in.); c. spiny, ovate scale from underside of minor leaf axis, bar = 0.1 mm.

whitish, long-linear triangular, and has a narrow, trim, dark margin bearing small, dark teeth; the other is short, dark, linear, often twisted, and bears minute spines (magnification needed). The lower surfaces of the pinnules and segment midribs bear a mat of tangled, whitish, fringed, variously shaped small scales that fall early. The sori have paraphyses but lack indusia. This species is endemic to Norfolk Island.

Sphaeropteris excelsa closely resembles *S. cooperi* but differs by more foliaceous fronds, prickly stipes, whiter stipe scales, and the mat of whitish scales on the lower surfaces of the pinnules and segment midribs.

Sphaeropteris horrida (Liebmann) R. M. Tryon
FIGURE 13.115.10

syn. *Cyathea princeps* E. Mayer
Blond tree fern, monkey-tail fern
Semi-tender

A large tree fern. Best grown under medium or higher light in moist garden soil or potting mix. This handsome fern is conspicuous for its trim, blond scales covering the stipes and rachises.

The stipes of *Sphaeropteris horrida* bear a dense layer of pale, nonmarginate (conform) scales. The pinna midribs are roundish in cross section and bear tubercles at the bases on the lower surfaces. The midribs of the pinnules and segments have fine, pale, jointed hairs on the lower surfaces. The sori are completely enclosed by globose indusia. This species is native to Mexico and Central America.

Sphaeropteris medullaris (G. Forster) Bernhardi
FIGURE 13.115.11; PLATE 1

syn. *Cyathea medullaris* (G. Forster) Swartz
Black tree fern, sago tree fern
Semi-hardy

A large tree fern. Best grown under medium or higher light. This species grows well in moist garden soil or potting mix and should be planted in areas sheltered from the wind. The plants do especially well in cool, humid coastal climates. They are conspicuous by their (usually) black trunks. The rachises and blade scales are also black to vary-

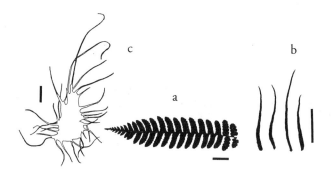

Figure 13.115.11. *Sphaeropteris medullaris:* a. pinnule, bar = 1 cm (0.4 in.); b. stipe scales, bar = 1 cm (0.4 in.); c. scale from underside of minor leaf axis, bar = 0.1 mm.

ing degrees. The species is found only occasionally in the trade.

A distinctive feature of *Sphaeropteris medullaris* is its black trunk with patterned, hexagonal leaf scars left by the fallen fronds. The stipes are black and covered by nonmarginate (conform), linear, black scales. The pinna midribs on the lower frond surfaces are typically blackened, and the scales of costae and costules are ovate with spiny margins, the spines often black or black-tipped. The indusia are globose and completely surround the sporangia. The species occurs from New Zealand to the Pitcairns.

Stenochlaena

This fern has scandent rhizomes that climb trees. The fronds are large, coarse, and somewhat far apart. The plants are best displayed by allowing them to climb trees or by planting them in big tubs provided with a moss-covered pole. When planted in baskets or pots, *Stenochlaena* usually becomes too scandent in growth to maintain a neat appearance.

The long-creeping, climbing rhizomes are green and covered by peltate scales that fall away early. The fronds are distant and dimorphic. The sterile fronds are one-pinnate with veins forming a single row of narrow areoles next to the costa; the veins are otherwise free and forked. The fertile fronds are one- or two-pinnate with contracted pinnae and pinnules that are completely covered beneath with sporangia. Indusia are absent.

Stenochlaena contains six species and occurs mostly in the tropical regions of Africa and Malaysia. The genus name comes from the Greek *stenos,* narrow, and *chlaena,* cloak, referring to the enrolled margins of the narrow fertile pinnae.

Stenochlaena tenuifolia (Desvaux) T. Moore
FIGURES 13.116.1, 2

Semi-hardy to semi-tender

A medium-large fern with long-creeping, climbing rhizomes. Grows well under high light in moist garden

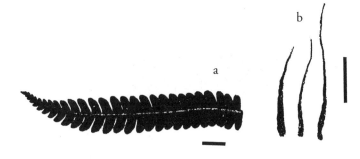

Figure 13.115.10. *Sphaeropteris horrida:* a. pinnule, bar = 1 cm (0.4 in.); b. stipe scales, bar = 1 cm (0.4 in.).

Figure 13.116.1. *Stenochlaena tenuifolia:* habit.

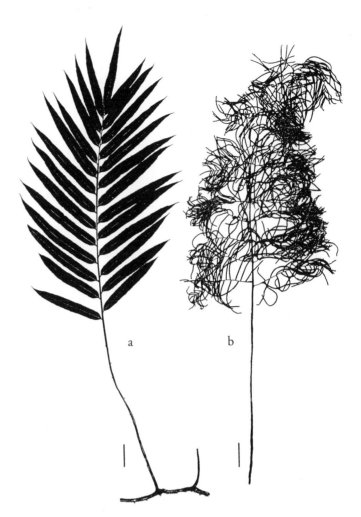

Figure 13.116.2. *Stenochlaena tenuifolia:* a. habit with sterile frond, bar = 5 cm (2 in.); b. fertile frond, bar = 5 cm (2 in.).

soil. Use care in transplanting. Plants may be propagated from apical sections of the rhizome but are slow to establish. This species is able to survive three days of −8°C (18°F) temperatures.

The sterile and fertile fronds of *Stenochlaena tenuifolia* are strongly dimorphic: the sterile fronds are one-pinnate with numerous pairs of close-set, serrulate pinnae, and the fertile fronds are two-pinnate with greatly contracted pinnae. This species is native to tropical Africa.

Stenochlaena tenuifolia is often misidentified in cultivation as *S. palustris* (N. L. Burman) Beddome, a closely related species that might be cultivated in the Hawaiian Islands. *Stenochlaena palustris* has sterile pinnae set far apart on the rachis, inconspicuous marginal teeth, and one-pinnate fertile fronds. It is native to Asia, Australia, and Polynesia.

Tectaria   FIGURES 13.117.1, 2

syn. *Cionidium, Hemigramma, Quercifilix*

Most cultivated species of *Tectaria* are terrestrial, small- to medium-sized ferns grown in pots as house or greenhouse plants. Some of the coarsely cut or trilobed species are at-

tractive as accent plants. Most species must be protected during the winter (except in southern Florida) and seem to need frequent watering and high humidity to grow well. They are generally easy to grow from spores. The often soft foliage of *Tectaria* is frequently attacked by scale insects and leaf-spot diseases—a situation that is exacerbated in some species by additional damage from insecticides and fungicides.

Tectaria is a large and diverse genus, with more than 150 species. It is difficult to characterize, but nearly all the species have netted veins, basal pinnae that are broader on the lower half than the upper, and minutely hairy upper surfaces of the rachises and costae. The juvenile fronds typically differ greatly from the mature ones. Other characteristics of the genus include scaly rhizomes that vary from creeping to erect, more than three vascular bundles in the stipes, blades sinuate to lobed to three-pinnate-pinnatifid, and apices reduced to shallow lobes or hastate. The sori vary from small dots to elongate or (rarely) linear. The indusia can be either present or absent. If present, the indu-

Figure 13.117.1. *Tectaria gemmifera:* habit.

sia may be kidney-shaped, peltate, horseshoe-shaped, or rarely linear.

Tectaria has not been thoroughly studied, and its species are sometimes difficult to identify. It can be distinguished from related ferns, such as *Arachniodes, Dryopteris,* and *Polystichum,* by the pinna midribs, which have ungrooved upper surfaces and are minutely pubescent; the other genera have grooved pinna midribs, with the groove decurrent into the main rachis, and are rarely pubescent.

Tectaria is widespread in the tropics and subtropics of the world. The genus name comes from the Latin *tectum,*

Figure 13.117.2. *Tectaria gemmifera:* veins and sori, the indusia shed.

roof, and *-aria,* a substantive suffix, alluding to the roof-like indusium of certain species.

Tectaria beccariana (Cesati) C. Christensen
FIGURE 13.117.3

Tender or perhaps slightly hardier

A medium-large fern with erect rhizomes. Grows well under low-medium to medium light in moist potting mix. This species is best used as an accent plant.

The upper part of stipe has a narrow, ruffled wing, and the blades are coarsely trilobed or more deeply lobed, with the lower pinna pair free. The veins are netted, not free, and the sori are elongate, numerous, scattered, and non-indusiate. *Tectaria beccariana* is native to the Philippines and New Guinea.

Tectaria decurrens (C. Presl) Copeland
FIGURE 13.117.4

Tender

A medium-large fern with erect rhizomes. Grows well under medium light in moist potting mix. This species is best used as an accent plant.

The stipes of *Tectaria decurrens* are winged nearly to the base, and the blades are deeply pinnatilobed. The veins are

Figure 13.117.3. *Tectaria beccariana:* juvenile frond, bar = 8 cm (3 in.).

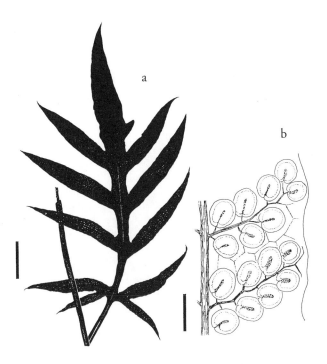

Figure 13.117.4. *Tectaria decurrens:* a. frond, bar = 8 cm (3 in.); b. sori and indusia, bar = 5 mm (0.2 in.).

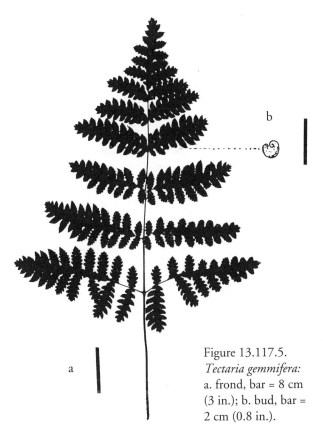

Figure 13.117.5. *Tectaria gemmifera:* a. frond, bar = 8 cm (3 in.); b. bud, bar = 2 cm (0.8 in.).

netted, not free. The indusia are horseshoe-shaped. This species is native to the Asian tropics, the Himalayas, Taiwan, and Polynesia.

Tectaria gemmifera (Fée) Alston

FIGURES 13.117.1, 2, 5

Button fern
Semi-tender

A medium-sized fern with erect rhizomes. Grows well under medium light in moist to moist-dry garden soil or potting mix. *Tectaria gemmifera* is the most commonly cultivated species in the genus. The plants volunteer readily from buds and tolerate subtropical temperatures with less humidity.

The fronds of this species are two-pinnate-pinnatilobed and bud-bearing. The indusia are round-kidney-shaped and minutely ciliate. *Tectaria gemmifera* is native to African tropics.

In the trade *Tectaria gemmifera* is often misidentified as *T. cicutaria* (Linnaeus) Copeland.

Tectaria heracleifolia (Willdenow) Underwood

FIGURE 13.117.6

Halberd fern
Tender

A medium-large fern with erect rhizomes. Grows well under medium light in moist garden soil or potting mix. In greenhouses the plants readily volunteer from spores. The coarsely cut foliage is visually striking because of its broad pentagonal outline.

Tectaria heracleifolia has one-pinnate fronds with three to five pairs of pinnae on mature plants. The lateral pinnae are slightly cordate, the basal pinnae each with one large lobe and other shallower lobes. The indusia are peltate.

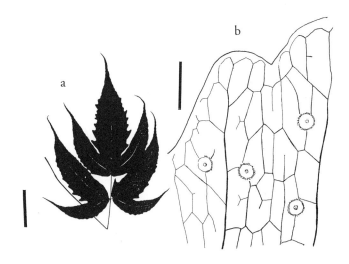

Figure 13.117.6. *Tectaria heracleifolia:* a. juvenile frond, bar = 8 cm (3 in.); b. indusia and veins, bar = 5 mm (0.2 in.).

This species is native to the United States (Florida and Texas), Mexico, Central and South America, and the West Indies.

Young plants may be distinguished from the similar *Tectaria incisa* by the absence of hairs in the rachis and costa grooves.

Tectaria hilocarpa (Fée) M. G. Price   FIGURE 13.117.7
syn. *Hemigramma latifolia* (Mejen) Copeland, *Tectaria latifolia* (G. Forster) Copeland
Tender

A small fern with erect rhizomes. Grows well under low-medium to medium light in moist potting mix. The plants are grown as novelty items for their small size, mottled fronds, and rosette arrangement. They respond well to frequent applications of fertilizer.

The sterile fronds of *Tectaria hilocarpa* have light green blotches, although plain green variants are also known; the fertile fronds are contracted and linear and have irregular, elongate sori. Indusia are absent. This species is native to Java and the Philippines.

Tectaria incisa Cavanilles   FIGURE 13.117.8
Tender

A medium to large fern with erect rhizomes. Grows well under medium light in moist soil or potting mix.

Tectaria incisa is a coarse fern with one-pinnate blades and three to six pairs of pinnae with oblique bases and mostly subentire or undulate margins. Minute hairs are present in the grooves of the rachises and costae. The main

Figure 13.117.8. *Tectaria incisa:* a. frond, bar = 8 cm (3 in.); b. indusia, bar = 5 mm (0.2 in.).

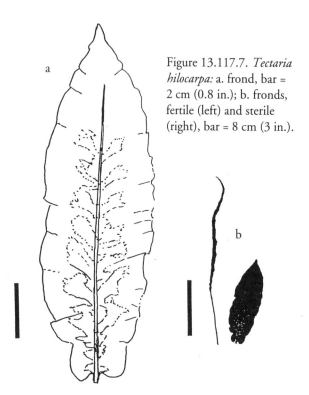

Figure 13.117.7. *Tectaria hilocarpa:* a. frond, bar = 2 cm (0.8 in.); b. fronds, fertile (left) and sterile (right), bar = 8 cm (3 in.).

lateral veins are conspicuous and parallel. The indusium is false-peltate. This species is native to the United States (Florida), Mexico to South America, and the West Indies.

Tectaria incisa is highly variable in blade cutting and pubescence. As presently defined, it probably represents a complex of several undescribed species.

Tectaria vivipara Jermy & T. G. Walker
FIGURE 13.117.9
syn. *Tectaria incisa* forma *vivipara* (Jenman) C. V. Morton
Tender

Medium-sized fern with erect rhizomes. Grows well under low to medium light in moist soil.

Tectaria vivipara resembles *T. incisa,* but it can be distinguished by the buds produced in the axils of the medial and distal pinnae. This species also tends to have slightly more pinna pairs than *T. incisa* (8–12 vs. 3–6), and both surfaces of the blade are glabrous. The species is widespread in the American tropics.

Figure 13.117.9. *Tectaria vivipara:* a. frond, bar = 8 cm (3 in.); b. bud at base of pinna, bar = 5 cm (2 in.); c. indusium, bar = 5 mm (0.2 in.).

Tectaria zeylanica (Houttuyn) Sledge

FIGURE 13.117.10

syn. *Quercifilix zeylanica* (Houttuyn) Copeland

Tender

A small fern with branching, short-creeping to ascending rhizomes. Grows well under medium light in moist potting mix. Because of its small but attractive fronds, this species makes an excellent terrarium or pot plant.

The sterile and fertile leaves of *Tectaria zeylanica* are strongly dimorphic. The sterile fronds are shaped like small oak leaves. The fertile fronds stand erect and are taller than

Figure 13.117.10. *Tectaria zeylanica:* habit, with contracted fertile frond, bar = 8 cm (3 in.).

the sterile. The stipes are elongate and the blades greatly contracted, with the sporangia acrostichoid, spreading across the lower surface and lacking indusia. This species is native to Sri Lanka, India, southern China, Vietnam, and Taiwan.

Thelypteris

FIGURES 13.118.1, 2

syn. *Amauropelta, Christella, Cyclosorus, Goniopteris, Lastrea, Meniscium, Oreopteris, Parathelypteris, Stegnogramma*

Thelypteris is a large genus of mostly medium-sized, terrestrial ferns. They are useful in borders, beds, backgrounds, and natural plantings. Some species are adapted to wet areas. Species with erect or semi-erect rhizomes are handsome in pots. Those with long-creeping rhizomes can become weedy if planted in the ground. A wide choice of species is available for use in warm-temperate and subtropical

Figure 13.118.1. *Thelypteris puberula:* habit.

Figure 13.118.2. *Thelypteris puberula:* sori and indusia.

climates. Generally, the species of *Thelypteris* are easy to grow and establish rapidly from spore. Some species (such as *Thelypteris dentata* and *T. parasitica*) frequently volunteer in greenhouses or appear as contaminants in spore pans.

For a long time *Thelypteris* was included in *Dryopteris,* but it differs by typically having one-pinnate-pinnatifid blades, sharp-pointed hairs, and two vascular bundles in the stipes. Other characteristics of the genus are scaly rhizomes that vary from erect to creeping and rachises and costae that are usually rounded, not grooved, on the upper surface, but if grooved, the grooves are interrupted at the rachis-costa junctures, not continuous. Whitish or yellowish bumps or peg-like structures known as aerophores are usually present at the base of the rachis-costa junctures on the lower surface. Depending on the subgroup, the veins are free or netted. Sori are borne on the lower surfaces of the blades (not the margins) and are almost always round. Indusia may be present or absent. If present, they are mostly kidney-shaped.

Thelypteris is cosmopolitan and contains about 1000 species. Its name comes from the Greek *thelys,* female, and *pteris,* fern.

Various authors have divided *Thelypteris* into as many as 30 genera, most of which are difficult to identify and are based on obscure or microscopic characteristics such as chromosome number, spores, and hair type. The nine genera listed in the synonymy above are only those that pertain to the commonly cultivated species of *Thelypteris.* Two segregate genera are treated as distinct in this book: *Macrothelypteris* and *Phegopteris.*

Because there are so many cultivated species of *Thelypteris,* the following key to species-groups is provided to facilitate identification.

1.   Veins free, meeting the margin above the sinus; blades one-pinnate-pinnatifid.
    2.   Blades widest or nearly so at the base (*Thelypteris palustris* and *T. simulata*).

    2.   Blades narrowed toward the base (*Thelypteris limbosperma, T. nevadensis, T. noveboracensis, T. resinifera, T. rudis,* and *T. quelpaertensis*).
1.   Veins meeting the margin at the bottom of the sinus; blades simple to one-pinnate-pinnatifid.
    3.   Blades with a terminal pinna resembling the lateral ones (*Thelypteris poiteana, T. reticulata,* and *T. serrata*).
    3.   Blades tapered to the tip, pinnatifid toward the apex, the apical part unlike the lateral pinnae (*Thelypteris acuminata, T. augescens, T. dentata, T. guadalupensis, T. kunthii, T. ovata, T. parasitica, T. patens, T. puberula,* and *T. reptans*).

Thelypteris acuminata (Panz) C. V. Morton

FIGURE 13.118.3

syn. *Cyclosorus acuminatus* (Houttuyn) Nakai, *Thelypteris* 'K. O. Sessions'
Semi-hardy

A medium-sized, deciduous or semi-deciduous fern with long-creeping rhizomes. Grows well under high light in moist to moist-dry garden soil. The plants can tolerate short periods of drought.

Thelypteris acuminata is characterized by long-creeping rhizomes, abruptly narrowed and long-tapered blade

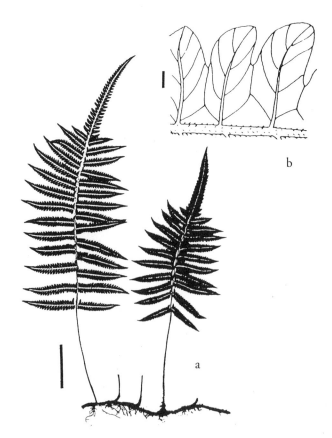

Figure 13.118.3. *Thelypteris acuminata:* a. habit, bar = 5 cm (2 in.); b. segments, bar = 1 mm.

apices, elongate pinnae, and veins of each segment united with the vein of an adjacent segment and forming an excurrent vein running to the sinus. Native to eastern Asia.

Thelypteris augescens (Link) Munz & I. M. Johnston
FIGURE 13.118.4

Abrupt-tipped maiden fern
Tender, Zone 10

A large fern, up to 120 cm (4 ft.) tall, with medium-creeping rhizomes. Grows well under high light in moist, basic garden soil or potting mix.

The abruptly narrowed frond tip and long, narrow pinnae are distinct features of *Thelypteris augescens*. The apical portions of the leathery blades are about five times longer than they are broad, and the lateral pinnae are less than 1.5 cm (0.6 in.) wide. On the undersurfaces of the pinnae the costae, costules, and veins are sparsely covered with hairs and scales. This species is native to Florida, Cuba, the Bahamas, and Central America.

Much of the cultivated material by this name is actually *Thelypteris puberula*, which differs by having less abruptly narrowed frond apices and irregularly crimped hairs on the lower pinna surfaces.

Thelypteris dentata (Forsskål) E. St. John
FIGURE 13.118.5

syn. *Christella dentata* (Forsskål) Brownsey & Jermy, *Cyclosorus dentatus* (Forsskål) Ching

Downy thelypteris
Semi-tender, Zone (7)8

A medium-sized fern with short-creeping to suberect rhizomes. Grows well under medium light in moist garden soil or potting mix. The plants are easy to grow but do poorly in areas with cool nights. They often become weedy in greenhouses.

Thelypteris dentata can be identified by the combination of one-pinnate-pinnatifid blades, basal pinnae that are usually reduced and bent forward and downward, and basal veins that unite and form an excurrent vein that runs to the base of the sinus. Other helpful characteristics are the often

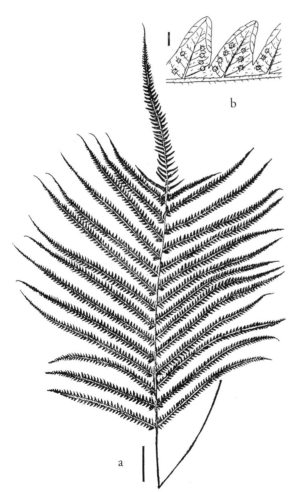

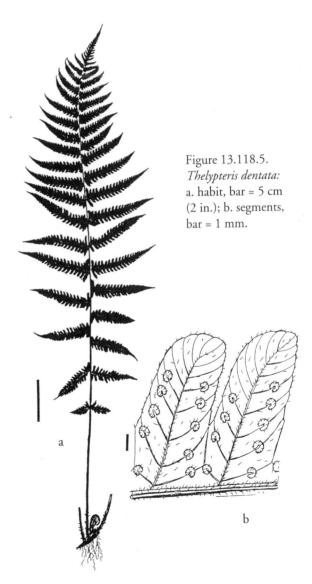

Figure 13.118.5. *Thelypteris dentata:* a. habit, bar = 5 cm (2 in.); b. segments, bar = 1 mm.

Figure 13.118.4. *Thelypteris augescens:* a. frond, bar = 5 cm (2 in.); b. segments, bar = 1 mm.

purplish stipes and rachises, and the lower surfaces of the blades and costae are minutely but evenly hairy, without glands. The species is native to the tropics of Africa and Asia but has become widely naturalized in the American tropics.

Thelypteris guadalupensis (Wikström) Proctor

FIGURE 13.118.6

syn. *Cyclosorus guadalupensis* (Wikström) Ching
Tender

A small fern with short-creeping to nearly erect rhizomes. Grows well under medium light in moist garden soil or potting mix.

The stipes and rachises of *Thelypteris guadalupensis* are minutely hairy with star-shaped hairs. The lanceolate blades are mostly lobed or pinnatifid, except pinnate toward the narrowed base, with the margins entire to crenate or lobed. The fertile fronds are erect and long-stalked. This species is native to the West Indies.

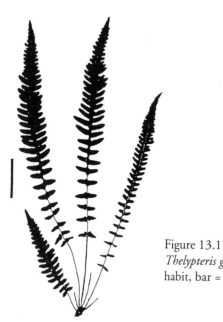

Figure 13.118.6.
Thelypteris guadalupensis:
habit, bar = 5 cm (2 in.).

Thelypteris kunthii (Desvaux) C. V. Morton

FIGURE 13.118.7

syn. *Thelypteris normalis* (C. Christensen) Moxley
Widespread maiden fern, southern shield fern, southern wood fern
Semi-tender to hardier, Zone (7)8

A medium-sized fern with short- to medium-creeping rhizomes. Grows well under medium light in moist garden soil or potting mix. The plants are easy to grow.

The basal veins of *Thelypteris kunthii* are free (not uniting with that of the adjacent segment) and run to the bases of the sinuses. The lower surfaces of the blades are hairy

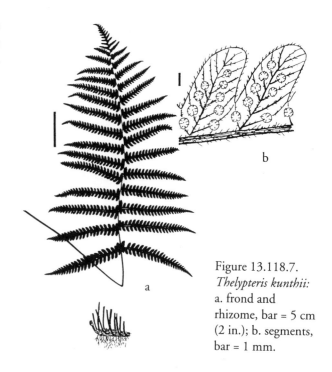

Figure 13.118.7.
Thelypteris kunthii:
a. frond and
rhizome, bar = 5 cm
(2 in.); b. segments,
bar = 1 mm.

with even-length, long hairs. Hairs are also present on the upper surfaces. The species is native to tropical and subtropical America.

Thelypteris limbosperma (Allioni) H. P. Fuchs

FIGURE 13.118.8

syn. *Oreopteris limbosperma* (Allioni) Holub
Hardy, Zone 5(6)

A medium-sized fern with short-creeping to suberect rhizomes and deciduous fronds. Grows well under medium light in moist, acidic garden soil or potting mix.

The rhizomes of *Thelypteris limbosperma* are hidden by old stipe bases that have persistent scales. The blades are tapered toward the base and on the lower surfaces usually have abundant yellow glands. Needle-like hairs (not scales) occur on the lower surfaces of the costae. The veins meet above the sinus base. This species is native to Europe.

A *Thelypteris* along the northwestern coast of North America has been called this species but is actually *Thelypteris quelpaertensis* (H. Christ) Ching, a species of eastern Asia. It differs by having few, small, colorless glands on the lower surfaces of the blades and narrow, pale scales on the lower surfaces of the costae (rarely with needle-like hairs).

Thelypteris nevadensis (Baker) Clute ex C. V. Morton

FIGURE 13.118.9

syn. *Parathelypteris nevadensis* (Baker) Holttum
Sierra water fern
Semi-hardy, Zone 8

A medium-sized fern with short-creeping to suberect rhizomes and fronds that wither and persist. Grows well under

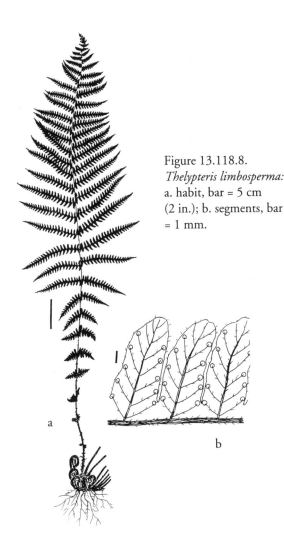

Figure 13.118.8. *Thelypteris limbosperma:* a. habit, bar = 5 cm (2 in.); b. segments, bar = 1 mm.

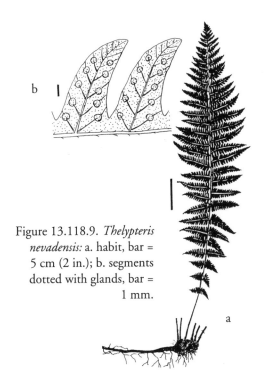

Figure 13.118.9. *Thelypteris nevadensis:* a. habit, bar = 5 cm (2 in.); b. segments dotted with glands, bar = 1 mm.

medium light in moist-wet garden soil or potting mix. This species does poorly in warm climates.

Thelypteris nevadensis has slender rhizomes 1–3 mm wide. The blades are tapered toward the base and bear stalked, yellow-orange glands on their lower surfaces. The costae are glabrous or sparsely hairy beneath. The veins are simple, free, and end above the sinus base. This species is native to northwestern North America.

The commercial plants labeled as *Thelypteris nevadensis* are often *T. noveboracensis,* which differs by lacking glands on the blades, or if present, then sessile and sparse, and the hairs on the costae are longer.

Thelypteris noveboracensis (Linnaeus) Nieuwland
FIGURE 13.118.10

syn. *Dryopteris noveboracensis* (Linnaeus) Nieuwland,
   Parathelypteris noveboracensis (Linnaeus) Ching
New York fern
Very hardy, Zone (3)4

A medium-sized fern with long-creeping rhizomes and deciduous, herbaceous leaves. Grows well under high light in moist garden soil or potting mix. The plants are easy to grow and may become invasive, tending to spread irregularly throughout the garden if not contained. They are not adapted to subtropical climates.

Thelypteris noveboracensis is characterized by one-pinnate-pinnatifid blades gradually tapered toward the base, with the lowest pinnae appearing as mere stubs or nubbins.

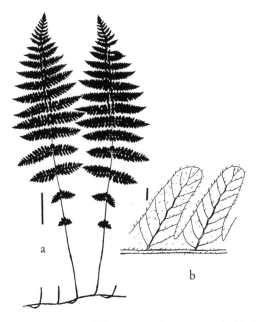

Figure 13.118.10. *Thelypteris noveboracensis:* a. habit, bar = 5 cm (2 in.); b. segments, bar = 1 mm.

The rhizomes are long-creeping, and the blades either lack or are sparsely beset with sessile glands. The costae are conspicuously hairy on the lower surface. The veins are unbranched and meet the margin above the sinus. This species is native to eastern North America.

Thelypteris ovata R. St. John   FIGURE 13.118.11
Semi-hardy, Zone 8

A medium-sized fern with medium-creeping rhizomes. Grows well under medium light in moist to moist-dry garden soil or potting mix. The plants are easy to grow.

   Thelypteris ovata is characterized by blade apices less than five times long as wide, more or less attenuate and different from the lateral pinnae, and sessile pinnae with the basal segment slightly longer than the other segments and often toothed. Unlike in similar species, the costules and veins on the upper surface are glabrous and the sori are submarginal. The species is native to the southeastern United States, Central America, and the West Indies.

Figure 13.118.11. *Thelypteris ovata:* a. habit, bar = 5 cm (2 in.); b. segments, with elongate basal segments, bar = 1 cm (0.4 in.).

Thelypteris palustris Schott   FIGURE 13.118.12
syn. *Thelypteris thelypteroides* (Michaux) Holub
Marsh fern
Very hardy, Zone (2)3

A medium-sized fern with long-creeping rhizomes and deciduous fronds. Grows well under medium-high light in moist-wet garden soil or potting mix.

   Thelypteris palustris can be identified by long-creeping rhizomes, one-pinnate-pinnatifid blades tapered toward the apex and widest (or nearly so) at the base, and fertile pinnae narrower and more contracted than the sterile ones. The veins are free, once-forked, and meet the margin above the sinus. The lower surfaces of the costae bear scattered scales. The species is native to North America, Mexico, the West Indies, and Europe.

   A crested variant (forma *pufferae* A. A. Eaton) is reported in cultivation.

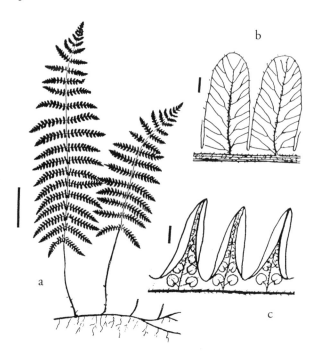

Figure 13.118.12. *Thelypteris palustris:* a. habit, bar = 5 cm (2 in.); b. sterile segments, bar = 1 mm; c. fertile segments, bar = 1 mm.

Thelypteris parasitica (Linnaeus) Fosberg
                                    FIGURE 13.118.13
syn. *Christella parasitica* (Linnaeus) H. Léveillé,
    Cyclosorus parasiticus (Linnaeus) Farwell
Semi-tender to slightly hardier

A medium-sized fern with medium-creeping rhizomes. Grows well under medium light in moist garden soil or potting mix. The plants volunteer readily from spores.

   In *Thelypteris parasitica,* the basal veins on a segment unite with those of adjacent segments to form an excurrent vein that runs to the base of the sinus. Both surfaces of the blade–particularly the veins on the lower one–have hairs and stalked, orange glands. The indusia are long-ciliate. The species is native to tropical Asia and the islands of the Pacific.

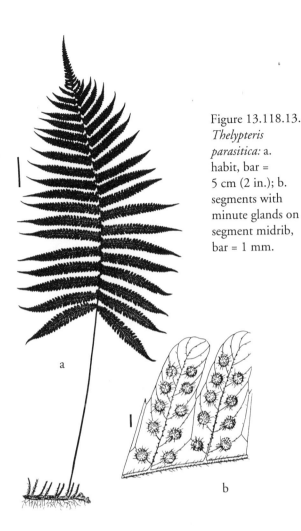

Figure 13.118.13. *Thelypteris parasitica:* a. habit, bar = 5 cm (2 in.); b. segments with minute glands on segment midrib, bar = 1 mm.

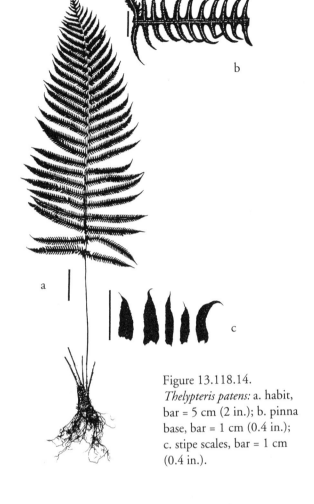

Figure 13.118.14. *Thelypteris patens:* a. habit, bar = 5 cm (2 in.); b. pinna base, bar = 1 cm (0.4 in.); c. stipe scales, bar = 1 cm (0.4 in.).

Thelypteris patens (Swartz) Small   FIGURE 13.118.14
Grid-scale maiden fern
Tender, Zone 10

A medium-large fern with stout, suberect to erect rhizomes. Grows well under medium light in moist garden soil or potting mix.

The scales at the base of the stipe are distinctive in *Thelypteris patens:* they are tan, broadly ovate, and persistent. Also distinctive are the pinna bases, which are sessile and have the basal segments slightly more elongate and toothed than the adjacent ones. The species is native to Florida, Central and South America, and the West Indies.

'Lepida'. Blades skeletonized.

Thelypteris poiteana (Bory) Proctor   FIGURE 13.118.15
syn. *Goniopteris poiteana* (Bory) Ching
Tender

A medium-sized fern with hard, medium-creeping rhizomes and few fronds. Grows well under medium light in moist garden soil or potting mix.

Thelypteris poiteana is characterized by netted veins and one-pinnate blades with a terminal pinna that resembles the

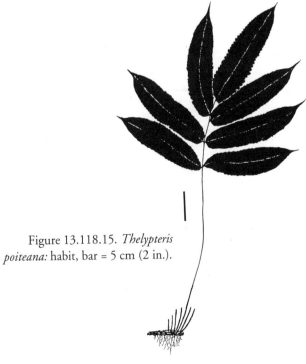

Figure 13.118.15. *Thelypteris poiteana:* habit, bar = 5 cm (2 in.).

two to five lateral ones. The pinnae are elliptic with suben-tire to coarsely serrate-crenate margins. Minute, forked, or star-shaped hairs are present only on the rachis near the junctions with the costae. The sori lack indusia and form a double row between the main lateral veins. This species is native to, and widespread in, the American tropics.

Thelypteris puberula (Baker) C. V. Morton

FIGURES 13.118.1, 2, 16

Semi-tender, Zone (8)9

A medium-sized fern with medium- to long-creeping rhizomes. Grows well under high-medium light in moist-dry garden soil or potting mix.

The blades of *Thelypteris puberula* are broadest at or near the base, gradually or somewhat abruptly tapered toward the apex, and glabrous on the upper surface except for crimped hairs on the costae. The basal veins of each segment end at or above the sinus. The indusia are densely hairy. This species is native to the southwestern United States, Mexico, and Central America.

Thelypteris reptans (J. F. Gmelin) C. V. Morton

FIGURE 13.118.17

syn. *Goniopteris reptans* (J. F. Gmelin) C. Presl
Creeping woodfern, creeping star-hair fern
Tender, Zone 9, with warm nights

A small fern with short-creeping to suberect rhizomes and evergreen fronds. Grows well under medium light in basic,

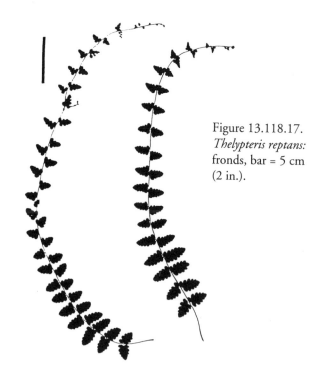

Figure 13.118.17.
Thelypteris reptans:
fronds, bar = 5 cm
(2 in.).

moist-dry garden soil or potting mix. The plants are easy to grow.

Thelypteris reptans is characterized by its small size and elongate blade apices that bear buds. If you look along the rachis with a hand lens, you will see minute star-shaped, forked, or needle-like hairs. The indusium is absent or, if present, minute and conspicuously ciliate. The fertile fronds are erect, whereas the sterile ones are spreading. The species is native to tropical America.

Thelypteris resinifera (Desvaux) Proctor

FIGURE 13.118.18

syn. *Amauropelta resinifera* (Desvaux) Pichi-Sermolli
Wax-dot maiden fern, glandular wood fern
Tender, Zone 9

A medium-sized fern with short-creeping to erect rhizomes and evergreen, erect fronds. Grows well under medium light in moist-wet garden soil or potting mix.

Thelypteris resinifera is characterized by sessile pinnae, blades gradually narrowed toward the base, and resinous, red, sessile glands on the lower surfaces of the blades. Other characteristics include rhizomes hidden by old stipe bases; erect, rigid, blades; and veins free and reaching the margin above the base of the sinus. The species is native to tropical America.

This species is sometimes mislabeled in gardens as *Thelypteris sancta* (Linnaeus) Ching, a species unknown in cultivation.

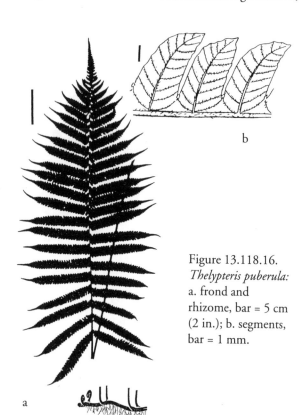

Figure 13.118.16.
Thelypteris puberula:
a. frond and
rhizome, bar = 5 cm
(2 in.); b. segments,
bar = 1 mm.

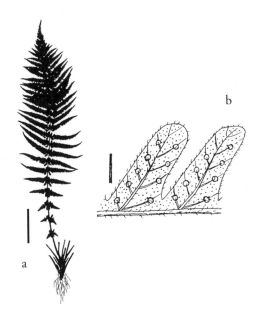

Figure 13.118.18. *Thelypteris resinifera:* a. habit, bar = 5 cm (2 in.); b. segments dotted with glands, bar = 1 mm.

Thelypteris reticulata (Linnaeus) Proctor

FIGURE 13.118.19

syn. *Meniscium reticulatum* (Linnaeus) Swartz
Lattice-vein fern
Tender, Zone 10

A medium-large fern with short-creeping to nearly erect rhizomes. Grows well under low light in moist, slightly acidic garden soil or potting mix with good drainage.

Thelypteris reticulata has red-brown rhizome scales, and the stipes of the fertile fronds are slightly longer than those of the sterile ones. The sterile blades vary from triangular-oblong to lance-oblong and are one-pinnate. The pinnae are oblong-attenuate to lanceolate-triangular, 2–6 cm (0.6–2.5 in.) wide, and tailed at the apex, with margins wavy to slightly crenate or entire and without hairs. The veins form several parallel rows of areoles between costae and margins. Curved-elliptic sori are borne at the middle of transverse veins and lack indusia. This species is native to tropical and subtropical America.

Thelypteris rudis (Kunze) Proctor   FIGURE 13.118.20

syn. *Amauropelta rudis* (Kunze) Pichi-Sermolli
Tender, Zone (9)10

A medium-sized fern with short-creeping to suberect rhizomes. Grows well under medium light in moist-wet garden soil or potting mix.

Thelypteris rudis has one-pinnate-pinnatifid blades abruptly reduced toward the base to tiny, wart-like pinnae. The lower surfaces of the costae and rachises are hairy and sparsely scaly, the hairs stiff, short, forward-pointing, and

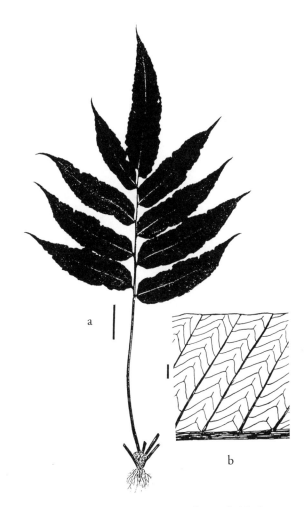

Figure 13.118.19. *Thelypteris reticulata:* a. habit, bar = 5 cm (2 in.); b. margin and veins of pinna, bar = 1 mm.

the scales slightly clathrate. The veins are simple and meet the margin above the base of the sinus. The sori are round and lack an indusium. This species is native from Mexico to Bolivia.

Thelypteris serrata (Cavanilles) Alston

FIGURE 13.118.21

syn. *Meniscium serratum* Cavanilles
Serrate lattice-vein fern
Tender, Zone (9)10

A medium to large fern with short-creeping rhizomes. Grows well under medium-high light in moist to moist-wet garden soil or potting mix.

The blades of *Thelypteris serrata* are gradually reduced toward the apex, the terminal pinna usually smaller than the lateral ones. The pinnae are hooked-serrate, at least toward the tips. In mature plants, the veins form 10–18 areoles between the costae and margins. Indusia are lacking. This species is native to Florida, Central and South America, and the West Indies.

Figure 13.118.20.
Thelypteris rudis: a.
habit, bar = 5 cm
(2 in.); b. reduced
lower pinnae, bar =
5 cm (2 in.).

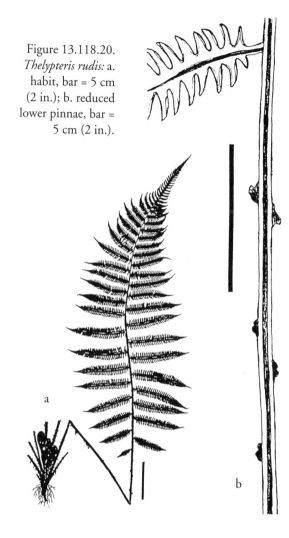

A similar species, *Thelypteris reticulata,* differs by having nearly entire pinna margins.

Thelypteris simulata (Davenport) Nieuwland

FIGURE 13.118.22

syn. *Parathelypteris simulata* (Davenport) Holttum
Massachusetts fern, bog fern
Very hardy, Zone 4

A medium-sized fern with medium- to long-creeping, slender rhizomes and deciduous fronds. Grows well under medium light in wet, acidic garden soil or potting mix. This species is excellent for bog gardens but is more difficult to grow than *Thelypteris palustris,* a similar species that grows in wet soils.

   Thelypteris simulata has lanceolate blades with yellowish, short-stalked glands on the lower surfaces and numerous shiny, sessile, reddish to orangish, hemispherical glands (use a hand lens). The veins are simple, ending above the sinus. The fertile fronds are slightly longer than the sterile ones due to longer stipes. The indusia are often glandular, the glands reddish or orangish. The species is native to eastern North America.

Todea

A handsome accent or pot plant, *Todea* forms a large, erect funnel of bright green foliage. In their native habitat these terrestrial ferns can become large plants with stout trunks to 1 m (3 ft.) tall and fronds to 1.2 m (4 ft.) long. The trunks

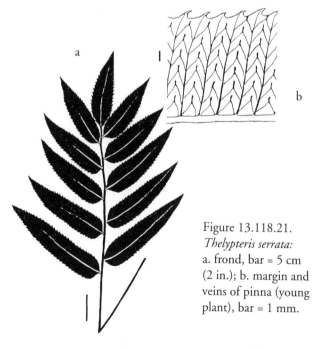

Figure 13.118.21.
Thelypteris serrata:
a. frond, bar = 5 cm
(2 in.); b. margin and
veins of pinna (young
plant), bar = 1 mm.

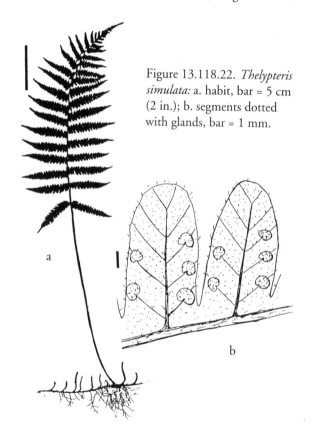

Figure 13.118.22. *Thelypteris simulata:* a. habit, bar = 5 cm (2 in.); b. segments dotted with glands, bar = 1 mm.

can be massive and bear multiple crowns. The cultivated plants in the United States, however, maintain moderate growth and size.

The rhizomes are erect and, when old, become trunk-like. The fronds are oblong, two-pinnate, and leathery. The fertile pinnae are slightly contracted or not, and on their lower surfaces they bear scattered, large sporangia. An indusium is lacking. The spores are green and short-lived.

This genus, which contains only one species, is native to southern Africa, Australia, and New Zealand. The name *Todea* honors the German botanist Henrrich Julius Tode (1733–1797).

Todea barbara (Linnaeus) T. Moore

FIGURES 13.119.1–3

Semi-hardy to semi-tender; tolerates light frost

A medium to large fern with erect rhizomes capable of forming offshoots and fronds borne in a spiral. Grows well under medium to high light in moist garden soil or potting mix. *Todea barbara* is easy to grow from spores and usually does well once established. The spores ripen nearly simultaneously and are shed when the sporangia are green. See the characteristics listed for the genus.

Trachypteris

This genus of small, terrestrial or rock-inhabiting ferns has short-creeping rhizomes, densely scaly leaves (at least on the undersurface), and netted veins. The sori lack an indusium. The genus name comes from the Greek word *trachys,* rough, and *pteris,* fern, referring to the rough texture imparted by the scales to the fronds.

Figure 13.119.2. *Todea barbara:* sporangia scattered on pinnules.

Figure 13.119.3. *Todea barbara:* frond, bar = 5 cm (2 in.).

Figure 13.119.1. *Todea barbara:* habit.

Trachypteris pinnata (Hooker f.) C. Christensen

FIGURE 13.120.1

Tender

A small fern, about 30 cm (12 in.) tall, that bears a rosette of fronds from an erect or nearly erect rhizome. Seems to do best in airy environments with well-drained soil and medium light. Avoid overwatering and overpotting. This species is an attractive fern recently introduced from Peru.

The sterile fronds of *Trachypteris pinnata* are widest above the middle, blunt-tipped, and arranged in a rosette. Their upper surfaces bear narrow, whitish scales, whereas the lower surfaces are densely covered with rusty-red lanceolate scales. When dry, the fronds curl and expose their scaly lower surfaces. The fertile fronds are erect and pinnate or pinnatifid. They bear sporangia on their undersides along the veins. The species is native to Ecuador, Peru, Bolivia, Argentina, Paraguay, and Brazil.

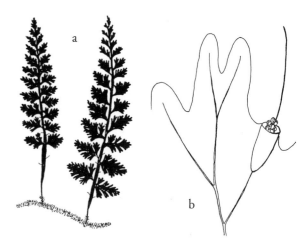

Figure 13.121.1. *Trichomanes radicans:* a. habit; b. indusium and sorus with extended receptacle.

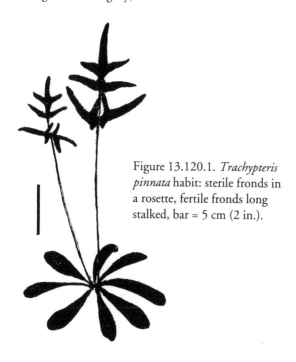

Figure 13.120.1. *Trachypteris pinnata* habit: sterile fronds in a rosette, fertile fronds long stalked, bar = 5 cm (2 in.).

Trichomanes

FIGURE 13.121.1

syn. *Cardiomanes, Crepidomanes, Vandenboschia*
Filmy fern, bristle fern

Filmy ferns are mostly small, terrestrial or epiphytic ferns with fronds one-cell-layer thick between the veins. This thinness imparts a filmy texture to the blades–hence the common name. The other common name, bristle fern, refers to the bristle-like receptacle that protrudes beyond the mouth of the indusium. Because of the thin blades, the plants need high humidity and should be grown in terrariums. Species seem to come and go in the United States trade, with old introductions often lost and replaced by new ones.

Most *Trichomanes* species grow from slender, long-creeping rhizomes, although the rhizome is erect in *Trichomanes holopterum* and a few others. The fronds vary tremendously in shape and size but are mostly small and membranous. The sori are borne at the margin of the blade, not on the lower surface as in many other ferns. Each sorus has an elongated tissue (the receptacle) that protrudes as a bristle above the trumpet- or tubular-shaped indusium. The mouth of the indusium is dilated or sometimes two-lipped. The spores are green and short-lived.

Trichomanes and *Hymenophyllum* are the traditionally recognized genera of filmy ferns. They have been split into as many as 34 segregate genera, and although these largely represent natural groups, pteridologists generally recognize only two genera. *Hymenophyllum* differs from *Trichomanes* by the indusium, which in the former consists of two broad lips and includes the receptacle within it, not protruding out from the indusium.

Trichomanes occurs mostly in the tropics worldwide, with a few species in the subtropics and temperate regions. If defined in the broad sense, as is done here, the genus contains about 300 species. The genus name comes from the Greek *thrix,* hair, and *manes,* cup, alluding to the receptacles protruding from the cup-like indusium. For more information, see "Filmy Ferns" in Chapter 10.

Trichomanes auriculatum Blume   FIGURE 13.121.2

syn. *Crepidomanes auriculatum* (Blume) K. Iwatsuki,
    Vandenboschia auriculata (Blume) Copeland
Semi-tender (?)

A small to small-medium fern with hairy-tipped, medium-creeping rhizomes and distant fronds. Grows well under low light in moist to moist-wet potting mix or uncut moss with good drainage. This species does well in terrariums but may go semi-dormant during the winter.

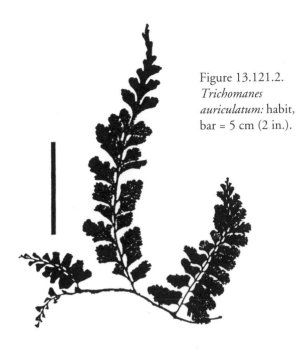

Figure 13.121.2. *Trichomanes auriculatum:* habit, bar = 5 cm (2 in.).

cies is native to Europe, Madeira, and the Canary Islands.

Trichomanes speciosum is sometimes confused in the literature with *T. radicans* Swartz, a pantropical species with ovate to lanceolate blades.

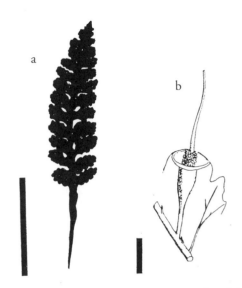

Figure 13.121.3. *Trichomanes holopterum:* a. frond, bar = 5 cm (2 in.); b. indusium and sorus with extended receptacle, bar = 1 mm.

The fronds of *Trichomanes auriculatum* are sessile or have stipes to 4 mm (0.2 in.) long. The blades are linear-oblong, 10–40 cm (4–16 in.) long, and one-pinnate, with the sterile pinnae lobed and crenate; the fertile pinnae are deeply and sharply incised. This species is native from India to southeastern Asia, Japan, Malaysia to Indonesia and Micronesia.

Trichomanes holopterum Kunze   FIGURE 13.121.3
Tender

A small fern with short, erect rhizomes. Grows well under low light in moist to moist-wet potting mix or uncut moss with good drainage. The plants reliably produce fertile fronds and are easy to grow; however, they need fresh media every now and then.

Trichomanes holopterum has tightly clustered, erect fronds 4–13 cm (1.5–5 in.) long with broadly winged stipes. The blades are oblong or lanceolate-oblong, stiff, translucent, and deeply pinnatifid into 5–10 pairs of oblong lobes with coarsely sinuate margins. This species is native to southern Florida, southern Mexico, and the West Indies.

Trichomanes speciosum Willdenow   FIGURE 13.121.4
syn. *Vandenboschia speciosa* (Willdenow) Copeland
Killarney bristle fern
Semi-hardy

A small fern with creeping rhizomes. Grows under low light in moist to moist-wet potting mix with good drainage.

The rhizomes of *Trichomanes speciosum* are black and wiry, with bristly hair-like scales. The fronds are generally 5–18 cm (2–7 in.) long with the stipes winged nearly to the base, the blades triangular and to four-pinnatifid. This spe-

Figure 13.121.4. *Trichomanes speciosum:* frond, bar = 5 cm (2 in.).

Vittaria

FIGURES 13.122.1, 2

Shoestring fern

The genus *Vittaria* derives its common name from the long, narrow, shoestring-like fronds of most species. These infrequently cultivated epiphytes are usually grown on boards or in baskets or pots to display their pendent foliage and maintain good drainage. The fronds are close together and make a handsome plant. Young fronds are sometimes reddish. The genus is characterized by the usually grass-like, linear fronds and sori that appear in one long line on either side of the midrib, with the indusium absent. The rhizome has clathrate scales.

Crane (1997) showed that the Old World species of *Vittaria* form a group distinct from the New World ones. They differ in technical characteristics, such as rhizome symmetry, type of gemmae on the gametophytes, and paraphyses. Accordingly, the Old World species have now been transferred to *Haplopteris*.

Vittaria is native to the tropics and subtropics worldwide and contains about 50 species. The genus name comes from the Latin *vitta*, ribbon or stripe, and *-aris,* resembling, referring to the long, linear leaves of the type species.

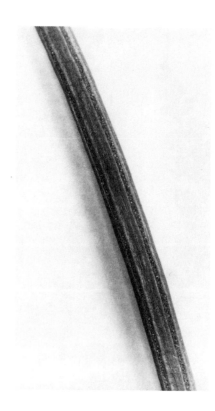

Figure 13.122.2. *Vittaria lineata:* immersed linear sori.

Figure 13.122.1. *Vittaria lineata:* habit.

Vittaria elongata Swartz

FIGURE 13.122.3

syn. *Haplopteris elongata* (Swartz) E. H. Crane
Tender

A medium-sized fern with short-creeping rhizomes and pendent, grass-like leaves. Grows well under medium light in moist potting mix or uncut moss with good drainage.

Vittaria elongata is distinguished by sori in a marginal groove, not submarginal as in most other species. Other characteristics include reddish brown to nearly black rhizome scales, to 1 cm (0.5 in.) long; stipes present; blades to 70 cm (28 in.) by 3–10 mm (0.1–0.4 in.) wide, widest in the middle; midribs distinct on the upper blade surfaces; and paraphyses with tips enlarged to an inverted cone-shape. This species is native to the tropics and subtropics from Africa to Polynesia.

Vittaria lineata (Linnaeus) J. E. Smith

FIGURES 13.122.1, 2, 4

Grass fern, shoestring fern
Tender

A medium-sized fern with short-creeping rhizomes and pendent, grass-like leaves. Grows under medium light in moist potting mix or uncut moss with good drainage; seems to do best with high humidity. This species grows readily from spores, and the prothalli (gametophytes) proliferate copiously from minute, several-celled gemmae borne along the margins. The prothalli can form thick mats in terrariums and remain green for many years. Mature plants are difficult to transplant.

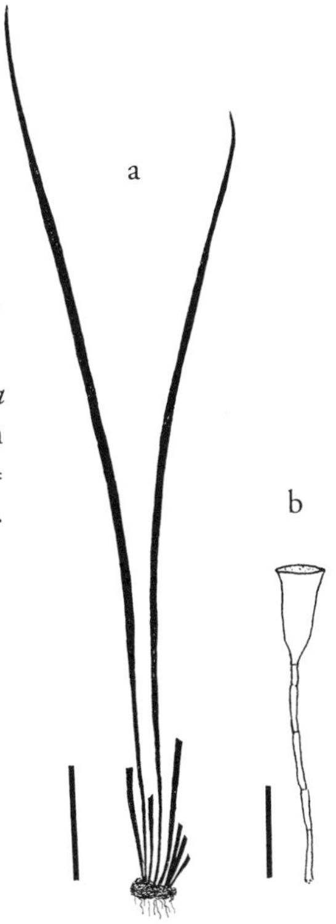

Figure 13.122.3. *Vittaria elongata:* a. habit, bar = 5 cm (2 in.); b. paraphysis, bar = 0.2 mm.

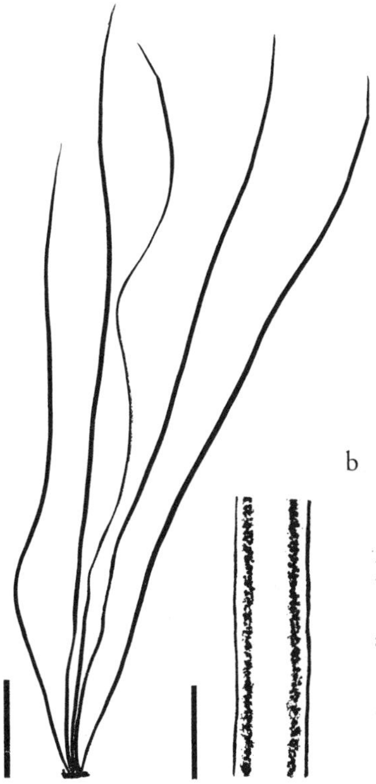

Figure 13.122.4. *Vittaria lineata:* a. habit, bar = 5 cm (2 in.); b. sori, bar = 3 mm (0.1 in.).

Vittaria lineata has sori in grooves on the lower surfaces of the blades, not on the margins. The rhizome scales are particularly distinctive by their elongate, thread-like tips. The fronds are up to 60 cm (24 in.) long and 3 mm (0.1 in.) wide. The paraphyses are slender, without expanded obconic tips (a strong hand lens or microscope is needed to see this). The species is native to tropical and subtropical America.

Woodsia
Cliff fern

FIGURES 13.123.1–3

The plants of the genus *Woodsia* are known as cliff ferns because of their tendency to grow on or among rocks. They are mostly small, delicate ferns used in rock gardens in cold- to cool-temperate climates. Most cliff ferns adapt poorly to warmer climates.

The rhizomes are mostly short-creeping and scaly, producing dense tufts of persistent stipes that may or may not be jointed (articulate) in the middle. The stipes contain two vascular bundles. The blades are one-pinnate-pinnatifid to two-pinnate, usually ovate to linear-lanceolate, herbaceous to firm, and deciduous. The lower pinnae are shorter and increasingly placed further apart toward the base of the frond. The sori are round, not elongate or linear. The indusium is attached beneath the sporangia and comes up around them, cup-like, to form a protective cover. They vary considerably in shape at maturity, being either entire and globose or splitting into several lobes or fragile filaments.

Woodsia resembles *Cystopteris* and can be distinguished from it by the persistent stipe bases and the indusia attached completely beneath the sori (instead of only on one side). The persistent stipe bases may be all fairly even in length or uneven, and this trait is helpful in identifying the species.

Figure 13.123.1. *Woodsia scopulina:* habit.

Figure 13.123.2. *Woodsia ilvensis:* fertile pinnae.

The stipe bases of even length break at a joint that may be seen as a slight ridge or bump on the stipe. Stipe bases that are uneven lack joints.

The genus *Woodsia* contains about 25 species and is native to alpine, boreal, and temperate regions, mostly in the Northern Hemisphere. The genus is named for Joseph Woods (1776–1864), a British architect and author of *A Tourist's Flora.*

Woodsia alpina (Bolton) Gray   FIGURE 13.123.4

Northern woodsia
Very hardy, Zone (1)2

A small fern with erect to ascending rhizomes and deciduous fronds. Grows well under medium light in moist garden soil or potting mix.

A fertile hybrid, *Woodsia alpina* originated from a cross of *W. glabella* and *W. ilvensis.* It resembles *W. ilvensis,* but the hairs and scales on the blades are few or absent, and the largest pinnae have one to three pairs of pinnules. The species is native to northern North America, Greenland, and northern Europe and Asia.

Woodsia ilvensis (Linnaeus) R. Brown

FIGURES 13.123.2, 5

Rusty woodsia
Very hardy, Zone (1)2

A small fern with ascending to erect rhizomes and deciduous fronds. Grows under medium light in moist-wet, acidic garden soil or potting mix. This species is attractive because of the rusty color of the scales covering the lower surfaces of the blades, but it may be difficult to grow.

The stipes of *Woodsia ilvensis* break at a swollen joint near the base and, along with the blades, are copiously covered with many hairs and scales, especially on the lower surface. The largest pinnae have four to nine pairs of pinnules, and the indusium consists of slender hairs. This species is native to northern regions of North America, Europe, and Asia.

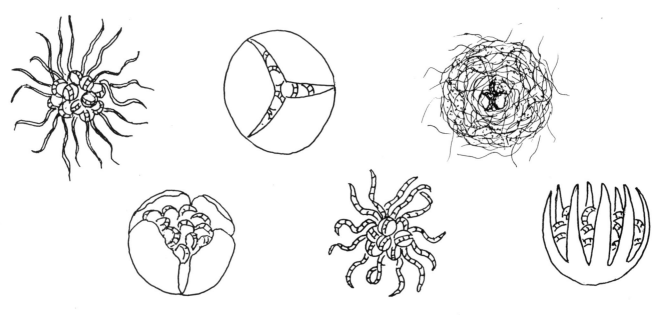

Figure 13.123.3. *Woodsia:* sori from different species.

Figure 13.123.4. *Woodsia alpina:* a. frond, bar = 2.5 cm (1 in.); b. sorus and indusium, bar = 1 mm.

a

b

Woodsia manchuriensis Hooker   FIGURE 13.123.6
Manchurian woodsia
Very hardy, Zone 4

A small fern with short, erect rhizomes and deciduous fronds. Grows well under medium light in moist garden soil or potting mix.

Woodsia manchuriensis has shiny red-brown, minutely hairy to glabrous stipes that are not jointed and hence break unevenly. The blades are narrowly elliptic, one-pinnate-pinnatifid, and whitish beneath. The indusia are globose, thin, and shallowly and irregularly lobed, with the lobes not ciliate. The species is native to northeastern Asia.

a

b

Figure 13.123.6. *Woodsia manchuriensis:* a. frond, bar = 2.5 cm (1 in.); b. sorus and indusium, bar = 1 mm.

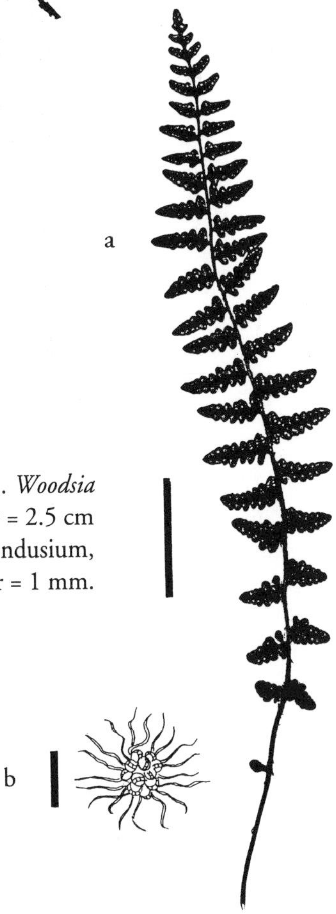

Figure 13.123.5. *Woodsia ilvensis:* a. frond, bar = 2.5 cm (1 in.); b. sorus and indusium, bar = 1 mm.

a

b

Woodsia obtusa (Sprengel) Torrey   FIGURE 13.123.7
Blunt-lobed woodsia
Very hardy, Zone 3

A small fern with short-creeping or ascending rhizomes and deciduous fronds. Grows well under medium light in basic to neutral, moist-wet garden soil or potting mix. The plants are easy to cultivate in rock gardens or open woods.

The stipes of *Woodsia obtusa* are not jointed and break unevenly. They bear scattered scales or are nearly naked.

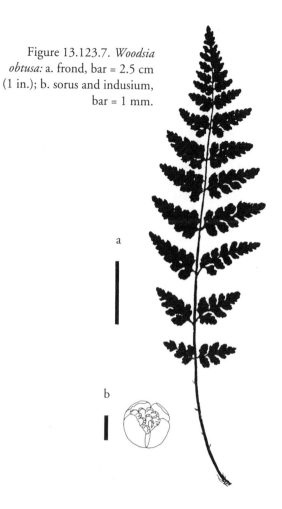

Figure 13.123.7. *Woodsia obtusa:* a. frond, bar = 2.5 cm (1 in.); b. sorus and indusium, bar = 1 mm.

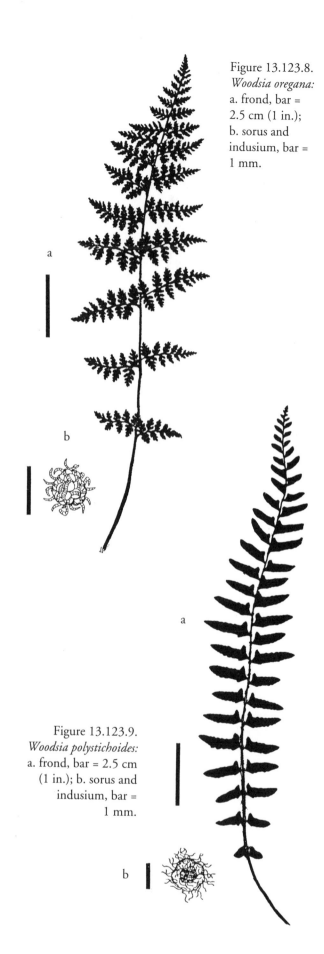

Figure 13.123.8. *Woodsia oregana:* a. frond, bar = 2.5 cm (1 in.); b. sorus and indusium, bar = 1 mm.

Figure 13.123.9. *Woodsia polystichoides:* a. frond, bar = 2.5 cm (1 in.); b. sorus and indusium, bar = 1 mm.

The blades are glandular, with the glands appearing as minute hairs with swollen heads (magnification is needed to see this), and the indusia consist of about four strap-shaped lobes. This species is native to eastern North America.

Woodsia oregana D. C. Eaton   FIGURE 13.123.8
Oregon woodsia, western cliff fern
Very hardy, Zone 4

A small fern with ascending to erect rhizomes and deciduous fronds. Grows well under medium light in moist garden soil or potting mix with good drainage.

The stipes are not jointed and therefore break unevenly, their surfaces smooth or bearing a few scattered scales. The blades of *Woodsia oregana* are naked or have minute glands, and the indusia consist of short hairs about the length of the sporangia. The species is native to western North America.

Woodsia polystichoides D. C. Eaton   FIGURE 13.123.9
Very hardy, Zone (3)4

A small fern with short, erect rhizomes and deciduous fronds. Grows well under medium light in moist garden soil or potting mix.

Woodsia polystichoides has stipes jointed near the top that break to form an even stubble. The blades are one-pinnate, and the pinnae are eared (thus making the plant resemble *Polystichum*), entire to dentate, and sessile but not decurrent on the rachis. The rachis scales are lanceolate, and the indusia are subglobose, shallowly lobed, and ciliate. The species is native to China, Korea, and Japan.

Woodsia scopulina D. C. Eaton   FIGURES 13.123.1, 10
Mountain woodsia
Hardy, Zone 5

A small fern with erect to ascending rhizomes and deciduous fronds. Grows under medium light in moist-wet garden soil or potting mix with good drainage. It is reportedly difficult to grow.

The stipes of *Woodsia scopulina* lack joints and therefore break unevenly. The stipes and blades have white hairs and minute, short-stalked glands (use magnification). The indusium consists of narrow, strap-like lobes that fray at the tips. The species is native to North America.

Woodsia subcordata Turczaninow   FIGURE 13.123.11
Hardy, Zone (5)6

A small fern with short-creeping to ascending rhizomes and deciduous fronds. Grows well under medium light in moist garden soil or potting mix.

Although often inconspicuous, the joints of *Woodsia subcordata* occur near the middle of the stipe. The stipe scales are ovate-lanceolate and sparsely ciliate. The one-pinnate blades are scaly and hairy on both surfaces, and the pinnae are lobed and eared at the base. The rachis scales are linear, and the indusia are lobed, with the margins of the lobes densely long-ciliate. The species is native to Korea, Japan, eastern China, and eastern Russia.

The identification of this species is tentative. It is one of the few *Woodsia* species that grows well in subtropical climates.

Woodwardia   FIGURES 13.124.1–3
syn. *Anchistea, Lorinseria*
Chain fern

Woodwardia is a genus of medium- to large-sized, coarse, mostly terrestrial ferns of cool-temperate and warmer areas. Those species with cascading fronds can be used to cover banks. Others do well in beds or pots, and some are favored as accent plants. The commonly grown species are easy to culture and are adapted to a wide variety of soil types. The young fronds are reddish.

The rhizomes are scaly and in most species short-creeping or ascending, but a few species have slender, long-creeping ones. The sterile and fertile fronds are monomorphic, except for those of *Woodwardia areolata,* which are strongly dimorphic. The stipes contain more than three vascular bundles. The blades vary from pinnatifid to one-pinnate-

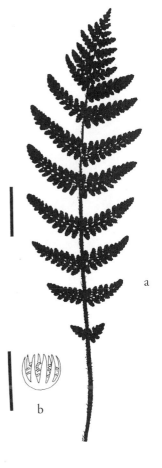

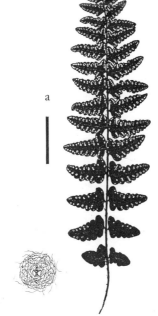

Figure 13.123.10. *Woodsia scopulina:* a. frond, bar = 2.5 cm (1 in.); b. sorus and indusium, bar = 1 mm.

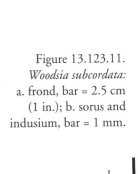

Figure 13.123.11. *Woodsia subcordata:* a. frond, bar = 2.5 cm (1 in.); b. sorus and indusium, bar = 1 mm.

pinnatifid and from firm to subleathery. The margins are minutely to coarsely serrate-dentate. The veins are netted, but the areoles lack included veinlets. The sori are mostly oblong and dorsal, appearing in a row on each side of the midribs. The indusia open toward the midribs, not the margins.

Woodwardia consists of 14 species and is native to North America, Central America, Mediterranean Europe, and eastern Asia. The genus is named for Thomas Jenkinson Woodward (1745–1820), a British phycologist.

Figure 13.124.1. *Woodwardia radicans:* habit.

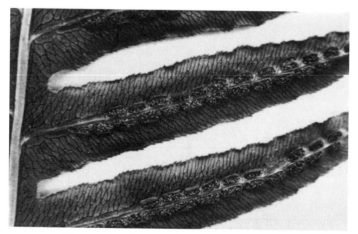

Figure 13.124.2. *Woodwardia radicans:* veins, sori, and indusia.

Figure 13.124.3. *Woodwardia orientalis:* leaf buds.

Woodwardia areolata (Linnaeus) T. Moore
FIGURE 13.124.4

syn. *Lorinseria areolata* (Linnaeus) C. Presl
Swamp fern, narrow-leaved chain fern, net-veined chain fern
Very hardy, Zone 3

A medium-sized fern with slender, long-creeping rhizomes and erect, deciduous fronds. Grows well under low to medium light in wet, acidic garden soil or potting mix.

Woodwardia areolata differs from the other cultivated chain ferns by its strongly dimorphic sterile and fertile fronds. The sterile blades are lanceolate and deeply lobed to a narrow wing along the rachis, and they lack buds. The fertile blades are one-pinnate with highly contracted pinnae and soon wither after the spores are shed. The species is native to southeastern Canada and the eastern United States.

Figure 13.124.4. *Woodwardia areolata*: a. habit with fertile frond (right), sterile frond (left), bar = 10 cm (4 in.); b. fertile pinnae, bar = 1 cm (0.4 in.).

Figure 13.124.5. *Woodwardia fimbriata*: a. frond, bar = 10 cm (4 in.); b. lowest pinna, bar = 5 cm (2 in.).

Woodwardia fimbriata J. E. Smith   FIGURE 13.124.5
syn. *Woodwardia chamissoi* Brackenridge
Giant chain fern
Semi-hardy to slightly hardier, Zone (7)8

A large fern with short-creeping rhizomes and evergreen fronds. Grows well under medium light in moist garden soil or potting mix.

Woodwardia fimbriata has erect-spreading fronds with broadly oblanceolate blades, without buds, glabrous on the lower surfaces. This species is native to southern Arizona and the Pacific Coast from Oregon to Baja California.

Woodwardia orientalis Swartz   FIGURES 13.124.3, 6
Oriental chain fern
Semi-hardy to hardier, Zone 8

A large fern with short-creeping rhizomes and evergreen fronds. Grows well under high or medium light in moist garden soil or potting mix. The plants are easy to grow and can be propagated by detaching the buds and planting their basal ends in a fine soil mix kept in humid conditions.

Once established, the plants need a lot of room because the fronds tend to spread horizontally.

The emerging fiddleheads of *Woodwardia orientalis* are densely scaly. The blades are triangular to ovate, flat, glossy, and can have many buds developed on the upper surface. These buds bear small, obovate fronds while still attached to the main fronds. This species is native to the Himalayas, Japan, and China through Taiwan to the Philippines.

Woodwardia radicans (Linnaeus) Smith
FIGURES 13.124.1, 2, 7; PLATE 50

European chain fern
Semi-hardy, Zone 8

A large fern with short-creeping rhizomes and evergreen fronds. Grows well under high or medium light in moist garden soil. Established plants need a lot of space for their arching or cascading fronds. They are easy to grow. The bud on the underside of the frond tip roots easily by itself when left on the plant, or it may be removed and rooted.

Woodwardia radicans has oblong-ovate blades that bear a scaly, large, well-developed bud below the tip. On the basal pinnae, the basiscopic segment next to the rachis is reduced in size. This species is native to southern Europe.

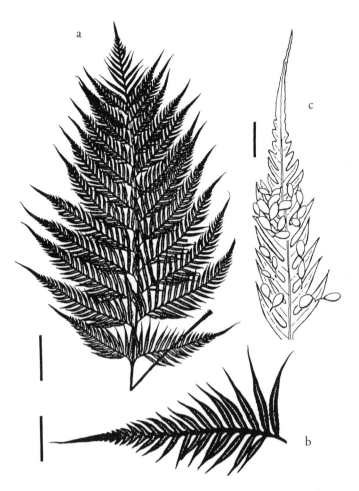

Figure 13.124.6. *Woodwardia orientalis:* a. frond, bar = 10 cm (4 in.); b. lowest pinna, bar = 5 cm (2 in.); c. leaf buds, bar = 2 cm (0.8 in.).

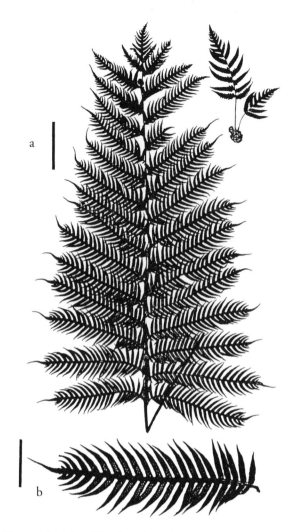

Figure 13.124.7. *Woodwardia radicans:* a. frond (left) and leaf bud (right), bar = 10 cm (4 in.); b. lowest pinna, bar = 5 cm (2 in.).

Woodwardia ×semicordata Mickel & Beitel

FIGURE 13.124.8

Semi-tender, Zone 9

The general culture of this fern is similar to that for *Woodwardia spinulosa* except that it might be more cold tolerant. According to Mickel and Beitel (1988), *W. ×semicordata* resulted from a cross between *W. martinezii* and *W. spinulosa,* but further research is needed to determine whether it is actually of hybrid origin. At least some spores appear to be normal and well formed, and the plants might be apogamous.

In cultivation, *Woodwardia ×semicordata* has been confused with both of its putative parents. It resembles *W. spinulosa* by having sori distributed along the costules (the midribs of the pinnules) but differs by having sori also distributed in the distal half or less of the costae (the midribs of the pinnae). Beneath the pinnatifid apex, only one pair of free pinnae with decurrent bases is present (all other pinnae are nondecurrent), whereas *W. spinulosa* has two or

more pairs of decurrent pinnae. *Woodwardia martinezii* Maxon ex Weatherby, native to Mexico, is unknown in cultivation. It differs from *W. ×semicordata* by long-creeping rhizomes and sori along the costules and entire length of the costae and rachis. *Woodwardia ×semicordata* is native to Mexico.

Woodwardia spinulosa M. Martens & Galeotti

FIGURE 13.124.9

Mexican chain fern
Semi-tender, Zone (9)10

A large fern with short-creeping rhizomes and evergreen fronds. Grows well under high light in moist garden soil. The plants are easy to grow.

Woodwardia spinulosa can be distinguished from *W. fimbriata* by the triangular blades with fimbriate scales on the lower surfaces. The lower pinnae have basal segments

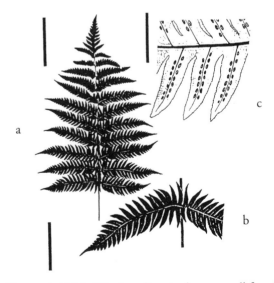

Figure 13.124.8. *Woodwardia × semicordata*: a. frond, bar = 10 cm (4 in.); b. lowest pinna, bar = 5 cm (2 in.); c. sori along costules and costae, bar = 2.5 cm (1 in.).

Figure 13.124.9. *Woodwardia spinulosa*: a. small frond, bar = 10 cm (4 in.); b. lowest pinnae with basal pinnules overlaying the rachis, bar = 5 cm (2 in.); c. sori along costules only, bar = 2.5 cm (1 in.).

that tend to overlap the rachis. It can be distinguished from *W. radicans* by the absence of buds on the fronds. This species is native to Mexico and Central America.

Woodwardia unigemmata (Makino) Nakai

FIGURE 13.124.10

Semi hardy or hardier, Zone 8

A large, semi-deciduous to deciduous fern with short-creeping rhizomes. Grows in medium light in moist garden soil or potting mix. The plants may be propagated from the bud near the frond tip.

Woodwardia unigemmata is similar to *W. radicans* except it lacks the lowest downward-pointing (basiscopic) segment immediately next to the rachis. It is native to eastern Asia.

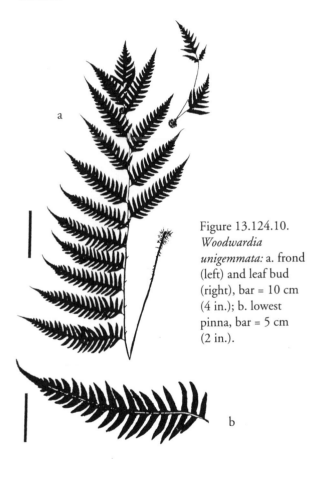

Figure 13.124.10. *Woodwardia unigemmata*: a. frond (left) and leaf bud (right), bar = 10 cm (4 in.); b. lowest pinna, bar = 5 cm (2 in.).

Woodwardia virginica (Linnaeus) Smith

FIGURE 13.124.11

syn. *Anchistea virginica* (Linnaeus) C. Presl
Virginia chain fern
Very hardy, Zone 3

A large, deciduous fern with long-creeping rhizomes up to 1 cm (0.5 in.) thick. Grows in medium to high light in wet, acidic garden soil. This species is considered invasive in some areas.

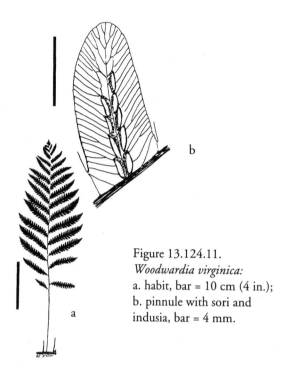

Figure 13.124.11.
Woodwardia virginica:
a. habit, bar = 10 cm (4 in.);
b. pinnule with sori and
indusia, bar = 4 mm.

The stipes of *Woodwardia virginica* are blackish at the base. The fronds are one-pinnate-pinnatifid with narrow, linear pinnae deeply pinnatifid and jointed (articulate) to the rachis. The sori are elongate, borne along the costae and costules, and covered by membranous indusia. It is native to southeastern Canada and the eastern United States.

APPENDIX I
Measuring Light

The human eye often has difficulty judging light intensity. For this reason, special light meters can be purchased to measure light intensity in foot-candle units. Photographic light meters can also be used, and the readings can be converted to foot-candle units. The formula is as follows:

foot-candles = $20f^2 / TS$

where f is the aperture in f-stop, T the shutter speed in seconds, and S the film speed in ASA units.

To measure light intensity using a photographic light meter, place a large sheet of white paper on the surface to be measured. Set an appropriate ASA film speed on the meter and read the shutter speed required for proper exposure at a given f-stop. Read the meter at about 30 cm (12 in.) from the paper, and use the preceding formula to calculate the equivalent foot-candle measurement. For example, if the ASA film speed setting is set at 100 and the proper exposure is ½ second at an f-stop of 16, the foot-candle value is 102:

$20 \times (16)^2 / ½ \times 100 = 102$ foot-candles

This formula provides a workable approximation. Results will vary according to the accuracy of the light meter and the cone of light measured by the meter.

For scientific work, precise light intensities need to be measured. A quantum meter accurately measures the blue and red part of the spectrum (the photosynthetically active radiation, or PAR). Plants use the blue and red light but not yellow and green light. With quantum meters, the intensity is measured in units known as micromoles, instead of foot-candles. A reading of 200 micromoles (μmol m^{-2} sec^{-1}) is equivalent to about 1000 foot-candles. Quantum meters are specifically designed for plants, but the average fern grower will find photometers sufficiently accurate for monitoring the light needs of ferns.

Other light-measuring units that may be encountered, and their approximate equivalency to foot-candles, are as follows:

1 lumen/cm^2 = 1000 foot-candles
1 lux = $^1/_{10}$ foot-candle
1 micromole = 5 foot-candles

APPENDIX II
Fern Societies

Updated information and addresses for various fern societies in the United States and abroad can be obtained from the American Fern Society. Contact the secretary of the American Fern Society:

Dr. W. Carl Taylor
Botany Department
Milwaukee Public Museum
800 W. Wells Street
Milwaukee, Wisconsin 53233-1478

The information is also available from the American Fern Society's World Wide Web page:

http://www.amerfernsoc.org

Membership information for the American Fern Society can be obtained from the membership secretary:

Dr. David B. Lellinger
Botany Department, MRC-166
Smithsonian Institution
Washington, D.C. 20560

A highly informative Web site about ferns is maintained by the San Diego Fern Society. It has links to nearly all other fern Web sites and is an excellent way to search for current information about the fern society nearest you.

http://www.inetworld.net/sdfern/society.htm

Another helpful Web site for growers is that maintained by the British Pteridological Society.

http://www.nhm.ac.uk/hosted_sites/bps/

An e-mail exchange for fern information is available and called Fernet. Inquire about the service at

koning@escu.ctstateu.edu

APPENDIX III
Importing Ferns

The following information will be helpful for importing plants to the United States and knowing what to expect as your plants pass through customs. When plants are carried through as personal luggage and they comply with all regulations, a United States Department of Agriculture (USDA) Plant Import Permit is not required for one-time or infrequent importers (though see the regulations and restrictions applicable to ferns). Frequent importers need a plant-import permit. This permit also allows you to send plants to the United States by mail or separate carrier to an inspection station. If the plants pass the inspection, they are forwarded to you.

You must pay attention to the regulations and directions that come with the import permit. These rules are not given here, except in a general way applicable to ferns. Because regulations and procedures are subject to change, always check with the agencies involved for the latest information.

Obtaining Permits for Collecting and Importing

The United States Department of Agriculture's Plant Import Permit is free. To obtain one, you should contact the USDA well before you travel. The address is

USDA, APHIS, PPQ Unit 136
4700 River Road
Riverdale, Maryland 20737-1235
telephone: (301) 734-7885; (301) 734-5948
fax: (301) 734-3560
e-mail: cbare@aphis.usda.gov
Web site: www.aphis.usda.gov

Your permit will come with the latest information on how plants must be prepared for entry into the United States and which plants are forbidden or have special restrictions. Ferns currently forbidden entry into the United States because of their potential to be serious weeds include the mosquito fern (*Azolla pinnata*) and water spangles (*Salvinia auriculata, S. biloba, S. herzogii,* and *S. molesta*). Some genera of tree ferns require special documents because of their endangered status, and this also applies to herbarium specimens (see the section "Convention on International Trade in Endangered Species of Wild Fauna and Flora"). Import permits are not required for fern spores or dried herbarium specimens of non-CITES species.

Each country has its own laws about collecting and exporting plants. Before you leave home, check with the embassy, consulate, or tourist information office of countries you plan to visit for any plant collecting or export requirements. Also check with the CITES office for updated information and the address of the CITES office abroad. Once at your destination, the local customs or plant protection or regulating agency should be able to inform you of their regulations.

Preparing Plants for Import into the United States

Plants may be brought into the United States by various kinds of mail, freight, or in your luggage. In all cases they must be prepared and packaged as directed in the papers that arrive with your import permit (also see the section "Packing Ferns," in Chapter 3). At minimum, the import permit requires that plants be free of soil, pests, disease, and seeds. The plants must be packed in approved packing material, meet the size-age factor, be labeled, and have certification papers from the proper plant quarantine officials in the country of origin. They must not be on the forbidden list.

The size-age factor ruling applies only to tree ferns, not herbaceous plants. Tree ferns need to be less than 45 cm (18 in.) long, as measured from the soil line to the terminal growing point. Plants should be labeled, preferably with their scientific name and where they were collected. Phytosanitary certificates are issued by local agricultural or quarantine officials. Although importing fern spores into the United States is not restricted, they must be free of soil, pests, disease, and seed contaminants. Fragments of leaves in the spore packet do not ordinarily present a problem if they are clean. When spores or herbarium specimens are carried in your luggage, the plant inspectors may ask to see them. Green spores should be airmailed to their destination and sown as soon as possible because they are short-lived.

Entry by Mail or Freight

You can mail or freight plants to the United States only if you have an import permit and have met all the requirements. When plants are mailed using the yellow and green address labels issued with the permit, the package will go directly to United States customs and a plant inspection station. If all is in order, the package is sent by mail under the original postage to the address on your permit. Air-freight arrivals valued above a certain price require the service and fee of a customs broker. The broker's function is to meet the shipment, complete the formalities at customs (pay the custom fee on your behalf), and convey the shipment to the plant inspector. If the shipment is valued at less than a certain amount, you may process the shipment yourself. Ask your local customs bureau for information on procedures.

Using the mail or freight has both advantages and disadvantages as compared to carrying the plants in your luggage. A plant sent by mail can be lost or subjected to slow service, rough handling, and/or extreme temperatures. Sending the plants by mail or freight, however, avoids the possible delays that can result from inspection of the plants upon arrival at the airport and, perhaps, also avoids unexpected broker's fees. If you do not live near a plant inspection station, or if your point-of-entry into the United States does not have a plant inspector on duty, it may be more convenient and economical to mail the plants. If stopovers in other countries are necessary, it is best to send the plants directly to the United States before you leave the country where the plants originated. If you carry plants to subsequent countries, they may be barred from entry. In New Zealand, facilities are available to hold a small number of plants at the plant inspection station until you can retrieve them when you leave the country. There is a small charge for holding fern plants (including spores) for more than than 48 hours. You also must enter and leave the country through the same airport. It is difficult, however, to determine in advance if such services are available.

ENTRY WITH YOUR LUGGAGE

If you enter the United States with plants in your luggage, you will be asked to declare them on your customs form. After passing customs, you will be directed to an inspector who will see that the plants meet the legal requirements. It is helpful but not necessary to have your import permit in hand. Generally, if there are 12 or fewer plants, if there are no special restrictions, and if all plants are properly identified and free of pests, then the inspector can clear them on the customs floor. Plants protected by CITES, more than 12 plants, or identification problems will require that the plants be sent to a plant inspection station. Expect problems even if you have followed all procedures correctly. Inspectors frequently cannot identify the plant, or regulations may have changed. The inspector may assist you (but is not required to) in getting the plants to the plant inspection station. You may have to hire a bonded carrier to bring the plants to an inspection station. If the cargo is large, it may be delivered to the airline's cargo station, and the airline may assist in getting the ferns to the station. Before your plants leave for the plant inspection station, be certain that the invoice papers issued by customs indicating customs' clearance (Post-entry papers or Manifest) are securely attached to the plants or their wrappings. The entire inspection process can take anywhere from a few hours to a few days. Unless arrangements are made to forward them to you, the plants will have to be retrieved at the inspection station, which is not necessarily located near the airport.

Delays and inconveniences are also possible if the inspection station is closed (the hours are generally 8:00 A.M. to 4:30 P.M.), or if the plants arrive just before the weekend. Not all entry points into the United States have plant inspection stations, and this can complicate carrying the plants in your luggage. In such cases, the plants are sent to the closest plant inspection station. If possible, plan your entry at a customs facility that has a plant inspection station. A list of the plant inspection stations (called Ports of Quarantine Clearance) is usually sent with your import permit.

Convention on International Trade in Endangered Species of Wild Fauna and Flora

The permits required by the Convention on International Trade in Endangered Species (CITES) are a separate entity from the United States Department of Agriculture's Plant Import Permit. If the plants you collect are listed by CITES, you must get CITES permits, which often requires a fee. Presently, the only ferns on the CITES list are tree ferns in the Cyatheaceae and Dicksoniaceae. To import these restricted ferns you must obtain export permits from the country of origin, even if the plants are from cultivation or are dried specimens for herbarium sheets. Tree fern spores are exempt from CITES permits. Approval for the export permit is dependant on the species, where the plant was collected, and whether it is cultivated. The United States Fish and Wildlife Service handles all CITES inquiries and will send you the addresses of foreign CITES offices that issue export permits. Their address is

United States Fish and Wildlife Service
Office of Management Authority, CITES Permits
4401 N. Fairfax Drive
Arlington, Virginia 22203
telephone: (703) 358-2104

You can also contact any office of the USDA Animal and Plant Health Inspection Service, Plant Protection and Quarantine (USDA, APHIS, PPQ). They are located nationwide.

CITES regulations are subject to change, and therefore it is a good idea to contact CITES officials early. When entering the United States with a CITES plant, be sure to pack the plant and its export permit separately from non-CITES plants. The plant inspector will routinely send any CITES plants to the inspection station before release. Before relinquishing the plant, be certain that the CITES permit and the plant are securely together, preferably in their own bag. Also make sure that the customs invoice (Post-entry papers or Manifest) indicates that the plant passed customs. In addition to the usual USDA plant import requirements, tree-fern trunks may not be more than 45 cm (18 in.) long measured from the soil level to the tip of the stem (apical bud). The latest CITES regulations indicate that all tree ferns on the CITES list, with or without trunks, are subject to the CITES regulations (formerly, those without trunks were exempt).

Avoid traveling to a second country with a CITES plant even if you have an export permit issued from the first country you visited. You will need to get a second export permit (re-export) from the second country, and this can take several days. It may be better to change your itinerary or mail the ferns along with their CITES export permit from the original country directly to the United States. CITES regulations specify that CITES export permits must come from the country of origin, and that may be interpreted to mean the last country visited. That last country may refuse to issue an export permit.

The preceding procedures and restrictions are meant to protect the United States from introduced pests and diseases, and to prevent the extinction of threatened or endangered species. The restrictions may be inconvenient and complicated, but they are imposed for the well being of agriculture, the environment, and ultimately all of us.

APPENDIX IV
Names of Pest and Disease Control Substances

The active ingredients of common pest and disease control products are given in the following charts. The trade names appear in upper case. Some products are available to commercial applicators only. Formulations vary, and no attempt has been made to account for these variations. The Federal and State Environmental Protection Agencies (EPA) regulate the label content and use of pesticides, fungicides, bactericides, disinfectants, and other substances. Their directions are the law. EPA regulations may change, and new products continue to be produced, so check with county agricultural services or other reputable sources for the latest information. Always test a product on one plant before wider application. The reader acts on his or her own responsibility. *No endorsement is intended in the use of trade names, nor is criticism implied of similar products not mentioned.*

Pesticides

Alphabetical listing	Corresponding names	Applications
acephate	ORTHENE	broad spectrum, systemic, some formulations for indoor use; aphids, mealybugs, millipedes, psocids, mites, scales, sowbugs, pillbugs, thrips, whiteflies, others
Bacillus thuringiensis	BT KURSTAKI, DIPEL	bacterial formulation for larvae of moths, butterflies
Bacillus thuringiensis H-14	GNATROL	bacterial formulation for fungus gnats only
BAYGON	*see* propoxur	
bendiocarb	DYCARB, TURCAM	ants and others
BLACK-LEAF 40	*see* nicotine alkaloid	
BT KURSTAKI	see *Bacillus thuringiensis*	
carbaryl	SEVIN	broad spectrum, easily available to home growers, some formulations for indoor use; ants, some aphids, earwigs, fungus gnats, millipedes, mites, sowbugs, pillbugs, psocids, others

Alphabetical listing	Corresponding names	Applications
chlorpyrifos	DURSBAN	some formulations for indoor use, easily available to home growers; earwigs, fungus gnats, millipedes, mites, sowbugs, pillbugs, psocids, thrips, root mealybugs, ground-crawling pests
CYGON 2E	*see* dimethoate	
diazinon	DIAZINON, KNOX-OUT	broad spectrum, easily available to home growers; aphids, earwigs, fungus gnats, mealybugs, psocids, mites, scale crawlers, thrips, whiteflies, others
dicofol	KELTHANE	mites only
dienochlor	PENTAC	mites only
dimethoate	CYGON 2E	broad spectrum, systemic; aphids, fungus gnats, scales, thrips, whiteflies, others; law limits use to injection equipment only in California (1993)
DIPEL	see *Bacillus thuringiensis*	
disulfoton	DI-SYSTON	systemic, easily available to home growers, some formulations for indoor use; aphids, mites, scales, thrips, others
DI-SYSTON	*see* disulfoton	
DURSBAN	*see* chlorpyrifos	
DYCARB	*see* bendiocarb	
ENSTAR 5E	*see* kinoprene	
ethoprop	MOCAP	nematodes only; use restricted to commercial applicators
fluvalinate	MAVRIK AQUAFLOW	synthetic type of pyrethrin; aphids, fungus gnats, mites, thrips, whiteflies, others
GNATROL	see *Bacillus thuringiensis* H-14	
imidacloprid	MARATHON	broad spectrum, systemic for greenhouse and nursery use; aphids, mealybugs, scales, thrips, whiteflies, others; not available to home growers
KELTHANE	*see* dicofol	
kinoprene	ENSTAR 5E	insect growth regulator; aphids, fungus gnats, mealybugs, scales, whiteflies
KNOX-OUT	*see* diazinon	an encapsulated diazinon
MARATHON	*see* imidacloprid	
malathion (maldison)	MALATHION	broad spectrum, easily available to home growers; aphids, fungus gnats, mealybugs, scales, whiteflies, others
MARGOSAN	*see* neem	
MAVRIK AQUAFLOW	*see* fluvalinate	
MESUROL	*see* methiocarb	
META-SYSTOX R	*see* oxydemetron-methyl	
methyl methaldehyde	SNAROL	slugs, snails
methiocarb	MESUROL	slugs, snails, others

Alphabetical listing	Corresponding names	Applications
mexacarbate	ZECTRAN	slugs, snails
MOCAP	*see* ethoprop	
neem (azadirachtin)	MARGOSAN	general insecticide with some fungicidal qualities; insect growth regulator
NEMACUR	*see* phenamiphos	
nicotine alkaloid	NICOTINE SMOKE GENERATOR	very toxic, restricted use; aphids, thrips, adult whiteflies, others; nicotine sulfate is no longer available in the United States
NICOTINE SMOKE GENERATOR	*see* nicotine alkaloid	
ORTHENE	*see* acephate	
oxamyl	VYDATE	broad spectrum, more or less systemic; fungus gnat larvae, nematodes, others; no longer labeled for ornamental plants
oxydemetron-methyl	META-SYSTOX R	broad spectrum, systemic; aphids, mealybugs, others
PENTAC	*see* dienochlor	
PERMETHRIN		synthetic type of pyrethrin (pyrethroid); sowbugs, pillbugs, others
phenamiphos	NEMACUR	nematodes; restricted to commercial use
propoxur	BAYGON	ground-crawling pests
pyrethrin (pyrethreum)	PYRETHRIN	short residual effect, easily available to home growers; ants, aphids, earwigs, thrips, whiteflies, others
pyrethroid	*see* PERMETHRIN, RESMETHRIN, or fluvalinate	synthetic types of pyrethrin
resmethrin	RESMETHRIN	synthetic type of pyrethrin (pyrethroid), some formulations for indoor use; mainly fungus gnats, whiteflies, also aphids
rotenone	ROTENONE	broad spectrum, short residual effect; beetles, true bugs (Hemiptera), mites, scales, thrips, others
SAFERSOAP	*see* soap	
SEVIN	*see* carbaryl	
SNAROL	*see* methyl methaldehyde	
soap	IVORY LIQUID, SAFERSOAP	soft-bodied insects, mealybugs, not thrips
TURCAM	*see* bendiocarb	
VYDATE	*see* oxamyl	
ZECTRAN	*see* mexacarbate	

Fungicides, Bactericides, and Disinfectants

Alphabetical listing	Corresponding names	Applications
AGRI-STREP	*see* streptomycin	
ALIETTE	*see* fosetyl-Al	
ARASAN	*see* thiram	
BANNER	*see* propiconazole	
BANROT	*see* etridiazole and thiophanate-methyl	very broad spectrum, mix of two fungicides
BENLATE	*see* benomyl	
benomyl	BENLATE	no longer labeled for ornamental plant use; *see* thiophanate-methyl
BLUESTONE	*see* copper sulfate	
captan	CAPTAN	broad spectrum; some blights, damping-off, leaf spots, rots, water molds
carbolic acid (phenol)	LYSOL	general disinfectant
CHIPCO 26019	*see* iprodione	
chloramphenical		algaecide, but also bactericide
chlorothalonil	DACONIL 2787	broad spectrum, easily available to home growers; some blights and damping-off, gray molds, some leaf spots, *Rhizoctonia,* rusts, some algae
CLEARY'S 2226	*see* dimethyl 4,4'-*O*-phenylenebis (3-thioallophanate)	
CLOROX	*see* sodium hypochlorite	
CONSAN	*see* quaternary ammonium compounds	
copper sulfate	BLUESTONE	algaecide
copper sulfate pentahydrate	PHYTON 27	bactericide and fungicide, systemic, leaves no residue; some leaf spots, *Botrytis*
DACONIL 2787	*see* chlorothalonil	
DEXON	*see* fenaminosulf	
dimethyl 4,4'-*O*-phenylenebis (3-thioallophanate)	CLEARY'S 2226	some blights, damping-off, leaf spots and rots, gray molds, *Rhizoctonia*
DITHANE M-22	*see* maneb	
DITHANE M-45	*see* mancozeb	
DITHANE Z-78	*see* zineb	
etridiazole (ethazol)	TRUBAN, TERRAZOLE, BANROT in part	blights, damping-off, and rots caused by water molds; best mixed in soil before planting
fenaminosulf (diazoben)	DEXON, LESAN	blights, damping-off, and rots caused by water molds; use drench at once, light sensitive
folpet	PHALTAN	similar to captan; rusts, some leaf spots
fosetyl-Al	ALIETTE	some blights, damping-off, and rots, water molds; burns ferns

Alphabetical listing	Corresponding names	Applications
GREEN SHIELD	*see* quaternary ammonium compounds	
iprodione	CHIPCO 26019	somewhat systemic; some blights, damping-off, and leaf spots, gray mold, *Rhizoctonia*
LESAN	*see* fenaminosulf	
LYSOL	*see* carbolic acid	
mancozeb	DITHANE M-45	some blights, damping-off, and leaf spots, gray mold, rusts, some algae; leaves a residue
maneb	DITHANE M-22	some blights, damping-off, and leaf spots, gray mold, rust
metalaxyl	SUBDUE	systemic; blights, damping-off, and rots caused by water molds; use as spray, drench, or granules
PCNB	*see* pentachloronitro-benzene	
pentachloronitro-benzene	PCNB, TERRACLOR	some blights, damping-off, and rots, gray molds, *Rhizoctonia;* may burn ferns when used as a soil fungicide, can persist in soil and cause plant toxicity
PHALTAN	*see* folpet	
PHYSAN 20	*see* quaternary ammonium compounds	
PHYTON 27	*see* copper sulfate pentahydrate	
potassium permanganate		general disinfectant
propiconazole	BANNER	general fungicide, some systemic action; leaf spots, rusts
quaternary ammonium compounds	CONSAN, PHYSAN 20, GREEN SHIELD	general disinfectant
quintozene	*see* pentachloronitro-benzene	
sodium hypochlorite (bleach)	CLOROX	general disinfectant
streptomycin	AGRI-STREP	systemic; leaf spots, rots, and diseases caused by bacteria
SUBDUE	*see* metalaxyl	
TERRACLOR	*see* pentachloronitro-benzene	
TERRAZOLE	*see* etridiazole	
thiophanate-methyl	ZYBAN, BANROT in part	systemic, acts like benomyl; some blights, damping off, and leaf spots, *Rhizoctonia;* use as a drench

Alphabetical listing	Corresponding names	Applications
thiram	ARASAN	*Rhizoctonia*
TRUBAN	*see* etridiazole	
zineb	DITHANE Z-78	some blights, damping-off, and leaf spots, gray molds, rusts
ZYBAN	*see* mancozeb and thiophanate-methyl	very broad spectrum, mix of two fungicides

APPENDIX V
Family Classification of Fern Genera Treated in the Text

Aspleniaceae (spleenwort family)

Asplenium   *Phyllitis*
Camptosorus   *Schaffneria*
Ceterach

Blechnaceae (blechnum family; chain fern, hacksaw fern, and relatives)

Blechnum   *Stenochlaena*
Doodia   *Woodwardia*
Sadleria

Cyatheaceae (cyathea family)

Alsophila   *Sphaeropteris*
Cyathea

Davalliaceae (davallia family; bear's-foot fern and relatives)

Davallia   *Leucostegia*
Davallodes

Dennstaedtiaceae (cup fern family)

Dennstaedtia   *Microlepia*
Histiopteris   *Odontosoria*
Hypolepis   *Paesia*
Lindsaea   *Pteridium*
Lonchitis

Dicksoniaceae (dicksonia family)

Cibotium   *Dicksonia*

Dryopteridaceae (wood fern family)

Arachniodes	*Hypoderris*
Athyrium	*Lastreopsis*
Ctenitis	*Matteuccia*
Cyclopeltis	*Megalastrum*
Cyrtomium	*Olfersia*
Cystopteris	*Onoclea*
Deparia	*Polybotrya*
Didymochlaena	*Polystichum*
Diplazium	*Rumohra*
Dryopteris	*Tectaria*
Gymnocarpium	*Woodsia*

Equisetaceae (horsetail or scouring-rush family)

Equisetum

Gleicheniaceae (gleichenia family)

Grammitidaceae (grammitid family)

Hymenophyllaceae (filmy fern family)

Hymenophyllum	*Trichomanes*

Lomariopsidaceae (elephant-ear family)

Bolbitis	*Elaphoglossum*

Lycopodiaceae (ground pine family)

Lycopodium

Marattiaceae (mule's-foot fern family)

Angiopteris	*Marattia*

Marsileaceae (water-clover family)

Marsilea	*Regnellidium*
Pilularia	

Nephrolepidiaceae

Nephrolepis

Oleandraceae (oleandra family)

Arthropteris	*Oleandra*

Ophioglossaceae (adder's-tongue and grape-fern family)

Botrychium　　　　　　　　　　　*Ophioglossum*

Osmundaceae (cinnamon fern family)

Leptopteris　　　　　　　　　　　*Todea*
Osmunda

Polypodiaceae (polypody family)

Aglaomorpha　　　　　　　　　　*Microgramma*
Belvisia　　　　　　　　　　　　*Microsorum*
Campyloneurum　　　　　　　　*Niphidium*
Dictymia　　　　　　　　　　　　*Pecluma*
Drynaria　　　　　　　　　　　　*Phlebodium*
Goniophlebium　　　　　　　　　*Platycerium*
Lecanopteris　　　　　　　　　　*Polypodium*
Lemmaphyllum　　　　　　　　　*Pyrrosia*
Lepisorus　　　　　　　　　　　*Selliguea*
Leptochilus　　　　　　　　　　*Solanopteris*

Psilotaceae (whisk fern family)

Psilotum

Pteridaceae (pteris family)

Acrostichum　　　　　　　　　　*Cryptogramma*
Actiniopteris　　　　　　　　　　*Doryopteris*
Adiantopsis　　　　　　　　　　*Hemionitis*
Adiantum　　　　　　　　　　　*Llavea*
Anogramma　　　　　　　　　　*Mildella*
Argyrochosma　　　　　　　　　*Notholaena*
Aspidotis　　　　　　　　　　　*Onychium*
Astrolepis　　　　　　　　　　　*Pellaea*
Bommeria　　　　　　　　　　　*Pentagramma*
Ceratopteris　　　　　　　　　　*Pityrogramma*
Cheilanthes　　　　　　　　　　*Pteris*
Coniogramme　　　　　　　　　*Trachypteris*

Salviniaceae (floating-fern family)

Azolla　　　　　　　　　　　　　*Salvinia*

Schizaeaceae (climbing fern family)

Anemia　　　　　　　　　　　　*Lygodium*

Selaginellaceae (spike moss family)

    Selaginella

Thelypteridaceae (marsh fern, maiden fern family)

    Macrothelypteris   *Thelypteris*
    Phegopteris

Vittariaceae (shoestring fern family)

    Vittaria

Evolutionary Tree for Vascular Plants

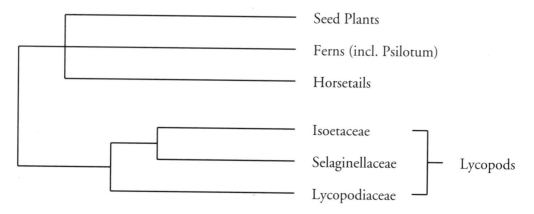

An evolutionary tree (cladogram) showing the current ideas about the relationships of major groups of vascular plants. The lycopod line of evolution has been distinct from other plants since the early Devonian, about 395 million years ago. It is based on evidence from morphology, anatomy, and DNA sequences of living and fossil plants.

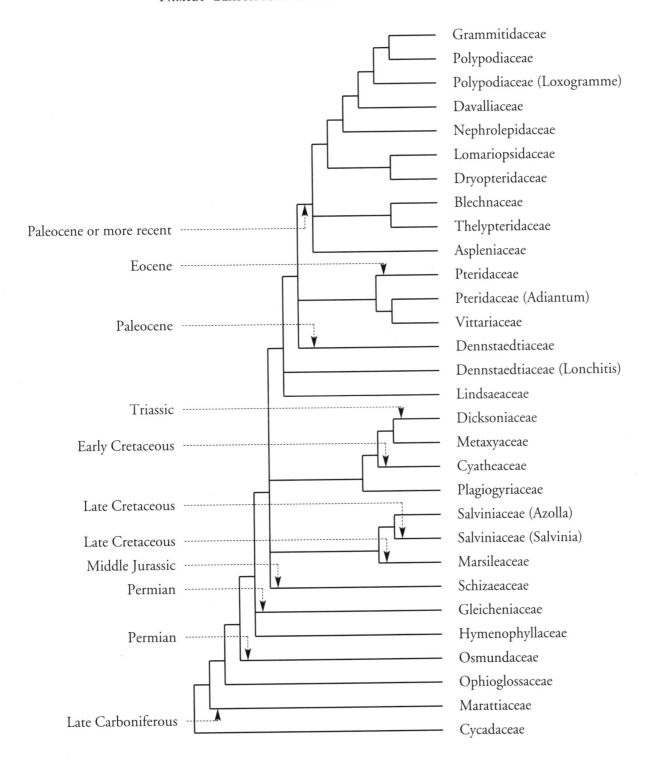

An evolutionary tree (cladogram) showing the current ideas about the relationships of major families of ferns. The tree is based on a combined analysis of data from morphology and DNA and is modified from Pryer et al. (1995). The geologic periods given for some of the branches of the tree are times of earliest origin based on fossil evidence (Collinson 1996).

Glossary

acroscopic: the side facing the apex. The acroscopic margin of a pinna is that which faces the apex of the leaf. The acroscopic margin of a pinnule is that which faces the apex of the pinna. Compare to basiscopic.

acrostichoid: with the sporangia spread throughout the surface, not in discrete lines or dots.

acuminate: tapering to a long point with the margins pinched or concave just before the tip.

acute: short-tapering to a point, the margins not pinched or concave just before the tip.

adnate: grown to or united with an unlike part.

aerophore: the aerating tissue of the leaf, usually in the form of a light-colored line running lengthwise along the leaf stalk and sometimes down into the stem. In genera such as *Blechnum* and *Thelypteris,* aerophores may occur as short white or yellowish pegs at the bases of the pinnae where they join the rachis. Stomata are abundant in aerophores, and thus these structures allow air to diffuse into the leaf. Aerophores are characteristic of fern leaves, being absent from leaves of other plants.

anadromic (anadromous): with the first basal branch or vein (as on a pinna) arising from the side toward the frond tip. Compare to catadromic.

anastomosed: said of veins that unite to form areoles; net-veined.

annulus: a complete or partial ring or cluster of thick-walled cells on the spore case functioning to open the spore case.

antheridium: the male sex organ containing the sperm. Borne on the underside of the prothallus.

apogamy: a form of asexual reproduction in which new sporophytes are produced directly from the prothallus tissue instead of from the fertilized egg cell (zygote).

apospory: a form of asexual reproduction in which prothalli are produced directly from young sporophyte tissue instead of from spores.

appressed: pressed close to the surface, not spreading.

archegonium: the female sex organ containing the egg.

areolate: having netted veins.

areole: the area enclosed by netted veins.

aristate: having stiff, bristle-like appendages.

articulate: having nodes or joints that naturally separate at maturity; jointed.

attenuate: gradually tapering to a very narrow, slender point.

axes: a collective term referring to the petiole, rachis, costae, costules, and midrib of a leaf.

basiscopic: the side facing the base. The basiscopic margin of a pinna is that which faces the base of the leaf. The basiscopic margin of a pinnule is that which faces the base of the pinna. Compare to acroscopic.

bicolorous: having two colors, usually referring to scales in which the central part is darker than the margins. Compare to concolorous.

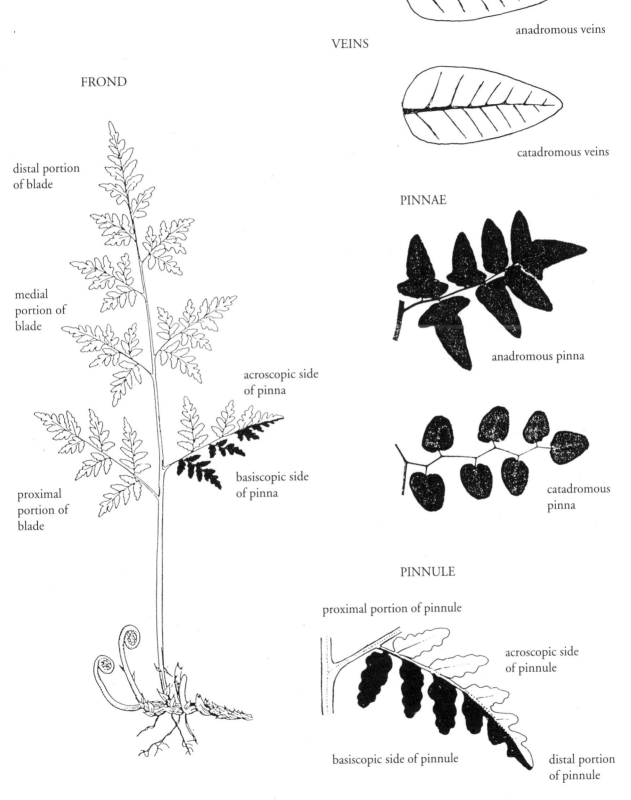

VEINS

anadromous veins

catadromous veins

FROND

distal portion
of blade

medial
portion of
blade

proximal
portion of
blade

acroscopic side
of pinna

basiscopic side
of pinna

PINNAE

anadromous pinna

catadromous
pinna

PINNULE

proximal portion of pinnule

acroscopic side
of pinnule

basiscopic side of pinnule

distal portion
of pinnule

Location of plant parts. Courtesy of Carl Taylor, Paul Nelson, and the Milwaukee Public Museum.

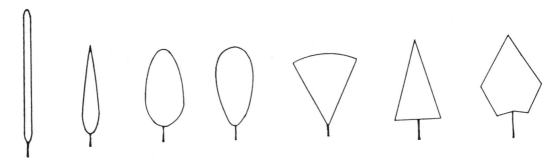

Leaf shapes (left to right): linear, lanceolate, ovate, obovate, cuneate, triangular, pentagonal.

binomial: the species name, which is the two words consisting of the genus name and the specific epithet.

bipinnate: twice pinnate (two-pinnate). Both primary and secondary divisions of the frond are pinnate.

bipinnatifid: twice pinnatifid. The divisions of a pinnatifid frond are again pinnatifid.

blade: the thin, broad part of a leaf or frond. Also called the lamina.

bud: in ferns the term usually applies to a proliferous bud or lump of tissue that grows into a new fern plant.

bulbil or **bulblet:** a small bulb-like body borne upon a stem or leaf and serving to vegetatively reproduce the plant.

bullate: puffy or inflated, humped. Usually refers to the base of a scale, especially in tree ferns.

catadromic (catadromous): with the first basal branch or vein (as on a pinna) arising from the side toward the frond base. Compare to anadromic.

caudate: having a slender, tail-like appendage.

ciliate: having short hairs (cilia) along the margin.

clathrate: refers to scales composed of cells that have dark side cell walls and broad, clear central portions (the "body" of the cell); thus the scale resembles leaded glass. A hand lens or microscope is needed to see this characteristic.

compound: said of a leaf having two or more leaflets.

concolorous: having one uniform color throughout, usually referring to scales. Compare to bicolorous.

cone: a tight cluster of highly modified, spore-bearing leaves borne at the branch tips.

confluent: running together.

cordate: heart-shaped.

costa (plural, costae): the midrib of a simple frond, or of the pinna (secondary rachis) or pinnules of a compound frond.

costule: the midrib of a pinnule.

crenate: having low, rounded teeth.

crested: having forked tips, usually many. Usually refers to the frond, pinnae, or segments.

crown: the tip of the stem where the leaves arise. Usually this term is applied to thick, upright stems.

crozier: a young coiled fern frond; the fiddlehead.

cultivar: a cultivated variety of plant, originating in cultivation or selected from among wild plants, generally chosen for a desirable trait(s).

decurrent: having the base of a blade or blade division extending down the petiole, rachis, or costa as a winged expansion or ridge. A decurrent base is winged downward, at least for a short distance.

deltate: triangular.

dentate: toothed, usually with broad teeth directed outward.

denticulate: minutely dentate.

dichotomous: forked regularly into pairs.

dimorphic: having two forms. In ferns the term usually refers to differences in size or shape of the sterile and fertile leaves (or segments). Compare to monomorphic.

distal: the part farthest away from the main body or leaf axis. Compare to proximal.

dorsal: relating to the back or lower side of a leaf.

emarginate: having a shallow notch in the margin.

entire: having an unmodified margin (not divided, lobed, or toothed).

epilithic: growing on rocks; also epipetric, saxicolous, or rupestral.

epiphyte (epiphytic): a plant that grows upon another plant. An epiphyte uses its host plant only for support; it is not parasitic.

erose: appearing as if gnawed. Usually refers to an irregular margin.

excurrent vein: a vein running toward the margin, not the midrib.

falcate: scythe-shaped, curved and flat, tapering gradually.

false indusium: an indusium formed by the enrolled margin of the leaf. Characteristic of many genera in the Pteridaceae, such as *Adiantum, Cheilanthes,* and *Pellaea.*

false peltate: appearing peltate but with a narrow, inconspicuous sinus running to the centrally attached stalk; also referred to as pseudopeltate. *See* peltate.

family: a group of related genera. Plant family names end with the suffix *-aceae.*

farina: a meal-like powder, usually white or yellow and found on the lower surfaces of fronds. Characteristic of such fern genera as *Argyrochosma, Pentagramma,* and *Pityrogramma.*

farinose: covered with a meal-like powder (farina).

fern allies: vascular plants that reproduce by spores and have a life cycle similar to that of true ferns, but differ by how they bear their sporangia and by having small leaves and usually simple, unbranched veins. Most of the fern allies are not closely related to the true ferns. The living families of fern allies are the Equisetaceae, Isoëtaceae, Lycopodiaceae, Psilotaceae, and Selaginellaceae.

fertile: in ferns usually referring to leaves that bear sori.

fiddlehead: a fern leaf, young or in bud, that is coiled in a spiral pattern. *Also see* crozier.

fimbriate: having a fringed margin, the fringe often consisting of numerous hairs or narrow segments.

flora: a list of all the species growing in a region, or a collective term for all the species growing in a region. It also refers to books that identify the plants within a certain geographical area.

foot-candle: a unit of measuring light intensity. One foot-candle is equal to the amount of light cast by a standard candle one foot away from the flame.

friable: describing soil that is moist and loose.

frond: the leaf of a fern, typically consisting of the petiole and blade.

fused: grown to or united with a similar part.

gametophyte: a small, usually flat plant bearing the sex organs (archegonia and antheridia) that in turn produce the gametes. Each cell in the body of the gametophyte has one set of chromosomes ($1n$). Gametophytes grow from spores.

gene: a unit on a chromosome that determines the inheritance of a particular trait.

genus: a group of related species.

glabrous: lacking hairs or scales, smooth.

glaucous: having a whitish, waxy bloom.

hardened plants: plants that have adjusted physiologically to harsher growing conditions.

hastate: arrowhead-shaped, but with the basal lobes pointing outward at wide angles.

heterosporous: having two kinds of spores, male and female, the males being smaller than the females and produced in separate sporangia.

homosporous: having one kind of spore.

hybrid: an offspring of two different species.

hydathode: an enlarged vein tip on the upper surface of a blade. It often secretes water and minerals. In some ferns, such as *Nephrolepis,* the minerals may accumulate as a white deposit over the hydathode.

imbricate: overlapping.

immersed: sunken into the surrounding tissue.

incised: cut sharply and irregularly, more or less deeply.

included veinlet: a vein within an areole or mesh formed by other veins.

indusium: the structure covering the sorus. *Also see* false indusium.

internode: the portion of a stem between two successive nodes.

jointed: able to separate naturally at a certain point, leaving a scar; articulate.

laciniate: slashed or cut into narrow-pointed lobes.

lanceolate: lance-shaped.

leaflet: one of the divisions in a compound leaf.

linear: long and narrow, usually 10 times longer than wide, the sides parallel or nearly so.

lunate: shaped like a crescent or half-moon.

marcescent: withering (senescing) without falling off; in contrast to jointed or articulate, which indicate withering and falling off at a joint.

marginal: at or relating to the margin or edge of a leaf.

meiosis: the type of cell division that gives rise to spores. During meiosis, the cell replicates its chromosomes once and divides twice; the result is four cells with only half the chromosome number of the original cell.

mesh: refers to netted veins.

monomorphic: having only one form. In ferns the term usually refers to sterile and fertile leaves that are not differentiated. Compare to dimorphic.

mucronate: tipped with a short, abrupt point or mucro.

mutation: a sudden heritable change appearing in animals or plants due to changes in the genes or chromosomes.

node: the point on a stem where a leaf emerges.

nonclathrate: refers to scales in which the cells lack dark, easily visible cell walls outlining the body of the cell. Compare to clathrate.

oblanceolate: lanceolate with the broadest part near the tip.

obovate: ovate or egg-shaped with the broader end apical.

obtuse: blunt or rounded at the tip.

ovate: egg-shaped in outline.

palmate: having main veins, segments, or lobes radiating from a common point.

paraphysis (plural, paraphyses): a sterile hair that is mixed among the sporangia.

pedate: palmate with the side lobes cleft into two or more segments.

peltate: having the stalk attached centrally rather than at the edge (like the handle on an open umbrella). *See* false peltate.

petiole: a leaf stalk; also known as a stipe.

phyllopodium (plural, phyllopodia): a stump-like extension from the rhizome to which the fronds are attached, usually by a distinct abscission layer.

pinna (plural, pinnae): the primary division of a pinnately divided frond; a leaflet.

pinnate: having a feather-like arrangement, with a single mid-vein from which leaflets arise.

pinnate-pinnatifid: referring to a blade that is once-pinnate and with the pinnae deeply lobed or cut, but not to their midrib.

pinnatifid: cut half to three-fourths to the rachis.

pinnatisect: cut almost all the way to the rachis.

pinnule: a secondary pinna.

prothallus (plural, **prothalli**): the gametophyte (which see).

proximal: the part nearest or toward the base or point of attachment. Compare to distal.

pteridologist: a student of pteridophytes.

pteridophytes: the ferns and fern allies. These plants have a life cycle in which the sporophyte and gametophyte generations grow independently of one another (that is, they are not attached). The sporophyte is the large and conspicuous generation, the gametophyte is inconspicuous and ephemeral. (See Chapter 8.)

puberulent: minutely hairy.

pubescent: hairy.

pups: a colloquial term referring to the young plants arising from older plants of *Platycerium* usually by root proliferation.

rachis: the midrib of a compound frond.

receptacle: the tissue upon which the sporangia are borne. The receptacle is bristle-like in *Hymenophyllum* and *Trichomanes;* in most other ferns it is flush with the leaf surface or slightly elevated.

reflexed: abruptly bent downward or backward.

reniform: kidney-shaped.

revolute: rolled backward from the margins or apex. In ferns the term usually refers to a leaf margin rolled back to protect the sori.

rhizome: a stem that grows horizontally and is anchored to the soil by its roots.

rootstock: a short, erect stem.

rosette: a cluster of leaves arranged circularly.

rupestral: growing on rocks; epilithic.

saxicolous: growing on rocks; epilithic.

scale: an outgrowth of the epidermal layer that appears as a small, flat, usually dry structure two or more cells wide. Hairs (trichomes) are similar but only one cell wide.

segment: the ultimate division into which a blade is divided.

serrate: having sharp, forward-pointing teeth, like the blade of a saw.

sessile: without a stalk.

seta (plural, **setae**): a sharp, stiff, bristle-like hair. In ferns these tend to be brown or black.

simple: not divided; not compound. Usually refers to blades that are not divided to the midrib, but can also refer to unbranched veins.

sinus: a space or recess between two lobes of a frond or other expanded structure.

sorus (plural, **sori**): a cluster of spore cases (sporangia).

species: a category of individuals that usually interbreed freely and have many characteristics in common. The word is used for both the singular and plural.

spinulose: having small spines or spine-like processes along the margin.

sporangium (plural, **sporangia**): the specialized structure within which the spores are produced; the spore case.

spore: a reproductive cell produced in a sporangium, germinating and developing into a prothallus.

sporeling: a young fern plant (sporophyte) that arises from the prothallus.

sporocarp: a round structure that contains sporangia within. Characteristic of two fern families: the Salviniaceae and Marsileaceae. Sporocarps are globose and delicate in the Salviniaceae but bean-like and hard in the Marsileaceae.

sporophyte: the familiar plant that bears roots, stems, and leaves (as opposed to a gametophyte or prothallus). So-called because it is the phase of the life cycle that produces spores. Each cell in the body of a sporophyte has two sets of chromosomes (that is, is $2n$).

stellate: star-like; having arms or hairs that radiate from a central point. Usually refers to hairs or scales.

sterile: refers to leaves that do not produce sori and to hybrids in which spores are aborted.

stipe: the leaf stalk or petiole.

stipule: a basal appendage of a stipe or petiole, usually two. In ferns the term is applied to the Marattiaceae and sometimes to the flared leaf bases in *Osmunda*.

stolon: a long, slender stem capable of producing a new plant at its tip or along its length.

strigose: having curved, sharp, forward-pointing hairs.

synonym: an alternative scientific name, but not the one currently accepted by taxonomists.

terrestrial: growing in the ground, not on trees.

tomentum: a dense covering of woolly hair.

ultimate segment: the final division of a frond.

undulate: having a wavy surface or margin.

vascular: pertaining to specialized tissue (xylem and phloem) that conducts water, mineral nutrients, and sugars.

vascular bundle: a bundle or strand of vascular tissue.

veins: the strands of vascular tissue in a leaf. "Free veins" are those unconnected to other veins; "netted veins" are those so connected.

wing: a thin expansion or flat extension of an organ or structure.

xerophyte: a plant adapted to dry habitats.

zygote: a fertilized egg cell. The first cell in the development of a sporophyte.

Literature Cited

ABRS/CSIRO Australia. 1998. Flora of Australia. Vol. 48, Ferns, Gymnosperms and Allied Groups. Melbourne.

Andrews, S. B. 1990. Ferns of Queensland: A handbook to the ferns and fern allies. Queensland Department of Primary Industries Information series Z189008. Queensland Herbarium, Brisbane.

Anonymous. 1986. Guidelines for the control of plant diseases and nematodes. Agricultural Handbook No. 656. United States Department of Agriculture, Washington, D.C.

Basile, D. A. 1973. A simple method of initiating axenic cultures of pteridophytes from spores. American Fern Journal 63: 147–151.

Beddome, R. H. 1864. Ferns of Southern India, Being Descriptions and Plates of the Ferns of the Madras Presidency. Madras.

Beitel, J. M. 1979. The clubmosses *Lycopodium sitchense* and *L. sabinaefolium* in the upper Great Lakes area. Michigan Botanist 18: 3–13.

Beitel, J. M., W. H. Wagner Jr., and K. S. Walter. 1981. Unusual frond development in sensitive fern *Onoclea sensibilis* L. American Midland Naturalist 105: 396–400.

Best, R. 1980? Growing Ferns. Bay Books Australian Gardening Library, Bay Books, Sydney.

Boodley, J. W. 1972. Soilless mixes. Horticulture 50: 38–39.

Bosman, M. T. M. 1991. A monograph of the fern genus *Microsorum* (Polypodiaceae). Leiden Botanical Series 14: i–ix, 1–161.

Brown, E. D. W. 1920. The value of nutrient solutions as culture media for fern prothallia. Torreya 20: 76–83.

Brownsey, P. J., and J. C. Smith-Dodsworth. 1989. New Zealand Ferns and Allied Plants. David Bateman, Aukland.

Burrows, J. E. 1990. Southern African Ferns and Fern Allies. Frandsen Publishers, Sandton, Republic of South Africa.

Ching, R. C., and Hsen Hsu Hu. 1930. Icones Filicum Sinicarum. Bishen Singh Mahendra Pal, Singh, India.

Cody, W. J., and D. M. Britton. 1989. Ferns and Fern Allies of Canada. Canadian Government Publishing Center, Ottawa.

Collinson, M. E. 1996. "What use are fossil ferns?"—20 years on: With a review of the fossil history of extant pteridophyte families and genera. Pages 349–394. In: Pteridology in Perspective, edited by J. M. Camus, M. Gibby, and R. J. Johns. Royal Botanic Gardens, Kew.

Crane, E. H. 1997. A revised circumscription of the genera of the fern family Vittariaceae. Systematic Botany 32: 509–517.

Curtwright, D. 1995. *Ceratopteris thalactroides* and its relatives. Journal of the Los Angeles International Fern Society, Inc. 22: 28–33.

Dittmer, H. J., E. F. Castetter, and O. M. Clark. 1954. The ferns and fern allies of New Mexico. University of New Mexico Publications in Biology 6: 1–139.

Druery, C. T. 1912. British Ferns and Their Varieties. Routledge, London.

Dyce, J. W. 1963. Variation in *Polystichum* in the British Isles. British Fern Gazette 9: 97–109.

———. 1972. British fern varieties: The Scolopendriums. Newsletter No. 10 (November). British Pteridological Society, London.

———. 1985. New fern varieties—wild and cultivated. Pteridologist 1: 78–80.

———. 1987. Classification of fern variations in Britain. Pteridologist 1: 154–155.

———. 1991. The variation and propagation of British ferns. Special Publication No. 3. British Pteridological Society, London.

Dyer, A. F. 1979. The culture of fern gametophytes for experimental investigation. In: The Experimental Biology of Ferns, edited by A. F. Dyer. Academic Press, London.

Edie, H. H. 1978. Ferns of Hong Kong. Hong Kong University Press, Hong Kong.

Evans, A. M. 1969. Interspecific relationships in the *Polypodium pectinatum–plumula* complex. Annals of the Missouri Botanical Garden 55: 193–293.

Farrar, D. R. 1968. A culture chamber for tropical rain forest plants. American Fern Journal 58: 97–102.

Flora of North America Editorial Committee. 1993. Flora of North America North of Mexico. Vol. 2, Pteridophytes and Gymnosperms. Oxford University Press, Oxford.

Ford, M. V., and M. F. Fay. 1990. Growth of ferns from spores in axenic culture. Methods in Molecular Biology 6: 171–180.

Foster, F. G. 1984. Ferns to Know and Grow. 3rd ed. Timber Press, Portland, Oregon.

Franks, W. 1969. *Platycerium*-Fern Facts. Published privately, Los Angeles, California.

Fraser-Jenkins, C. R. 1986. A classification of the genus *Dryopteris* (Pteridophyta: Dryopteridaceae). Bulletin of the British Museum (Natural History), Botany Series 14: 183–218.

Goudey, C. J. 1985. Maidenhair Ferns in Cultivation. Lothian Publishing Co., Melbourne, Australia.

Grounds, R. 1974. Ferns. Pelham Books, London.

Hennipman, E. 1977. A monograph of the fern genus *Bolbitis* (Lomariopsidaceae). Leiden Botanical Series 2: i–xiii, 1–331.

Hennipman, E., and M. C. Roos. 1982. A monograph of the fern genus *Platycerium* (Polypodiaceae). Verhandelingen der Koninklijke Nederlandse Akademie van Wetenschappen, Afdeeling Natuurkunde, Tweede Reeks 80: 1–126.

Hickey, R. J. 1977. The *Lycopodium obscurum* complex in North America. American Fern Journal 67: 45–49.

Hickman, J. C., ed. 1993. The Jepson Manual: Higher Plants of California. University of California Press, Berkeley.

Hill, R. H. 1976. Cold requirements of several ferns in southeastern Michigan. American Fern Journal 66: 83–88.

Hill, R. S. 1984. Propagation of Marattiaceae. Australian Fern Journal 74: 11–15.

Hoagland, D. R., and D. I. Arnon. 1950. The water-culture method for growing plants without soil. California Agricultural Experiment Station, Circular 347. College of Agriculture, University of California, Berkeley.

Hoshizaki, B. J. 1970a. The genus *Adiantum* in cultivation (Polypodiaceae). Baileya 17: 97–196.

———. 1970b. Rhizome scales of *Platycerium*. American Fern Journal 60: 144–160.

———. 1972. Morphology phylogeny of *Platycerium* species. Biotropica 4: 93–117.

———. 1975. The Fern Growers Manual. Alfred A. Knopf, New York.

————. 1975. A staghorn fern (*Platycerium*) hybrid. American Fern Journal 65: 99–101.

————. 1981. The fern genus *Davallia* in cultivation (Davalliaceae). Baileya 21: 1–50.

————. 1982. The genus *Polypodium* in cultivation (Polypodiaceae). Baileya 22: 1–98.

————. 1991. An "intergeneric" hybrid: *Aglaomorpha* × *Drynaria*. American Fern Journal 81: 37–43.

Hoshizaki, B. J., and M. G. Price. 1990. *Platycerium* update. American Fern Journal 80: 58–69.

Hoshizaki, B. J., and K. A. Wilson. 1999. The cultivated species of the fern genus *Dryopteris* in the United States. American Fern Journal 89: 1–100.

Hovenkamp, P. H. 1986. A monograph of the fern genus *Pyrrosia*. Leiden Botanical Series 9: i–xiii, 1–310.

Hovenkamp, P. H., and N. A. P. Franken. 1993. An account of the fern genus *Belvisia* Mirbel (Polypodiaceae). Blumea 37: 511–527.

Hu, I. H., and R. C. Ching. 1930. Icones Filicum Sinicarum. Fascicle 1.

Huang, Tsen-Chieng, ed. 1994. Flora of Taiwan. 2nd ed. Vol. 1, Pteridophyta and Gymnospermae. Editorial Committee of the Flora of Taiwan, Ta'an Taipei, Taiwan.

Iwatsuki, K., T. Yamazaki, D. Boufford, and H. Ohba. 1995. Pteridophyta and Gymnospermae. Vol. 1 of Flora of Japan. Kodansha, Tokyo, Japan.

Jacobsen, W. B. G. 1983. The Ferns and Fern Allies of Southern Africa. Butterworth Publishers, Durban, South Africa.

Joe, B. 1958. *Pteris* species cultivated in California. Lasca Leaves 8: 26–29.

————. 1964. A review of the species of *Platycerium* (Polypodiaceae). Baileya 12: 69–126.

Johns, R. J. 1995. *Lecanopteris lomarioides,* Polypodiaceae. Curtis's Botanical Magazine 12: 89–95.

Johnson, D. M. 1986. Systematics of the New World species of *Marsilea* (Marsileaceae). Systematic Botany Monographs 11: 1–87.

Jones, D. L. 1987. Encyclopaedia of Ferns. Timber Press, Portland, Oregon.

Jones, D. L., and S. C. Clemesha. 1981. Australian Ferns and Fern Allies. A. H. and A. W. Reed, Sydney, Australia.

Kato, M. 1984. A taxonomic study of the athyrioid fern genus *Deparia* with main reference to the Pacific species. Journal of the Faculty of Science, University of Tokyo, section 3, 13: 375–429.

————. 1985. A systematic study of the genera of the fern family Davalliaceae. Journal of the Faculty of Science, University of Tokyo, section 3, 13: 553–573.

Kaye, R. 1965. Variations in *Athyrium* in the British Isles. British Fern Gazette 9: 197–204.

————. 1968. Hardy Ferns. Faber and Faber, London.

Khullar, S. P. 1994. An Illustrated Fern Flora of West Himalaya. International Book Distributor, Dehra Dun, India.

Knobloch, I. W., and D. S. Correll. 1962. Ferns and Fern Allies of Chihuahua, Mexico. Texas Research Foundation, Renner, Texas.

Knudson, L. 1946. A new nutrient solution for the germination of orchid seed. American Orchid Society Bulletin 15: 214–217.

Kramer, K. U., and P. S. Green, eds. 1990. Pteridophytes and Gymnosperms. Vol. 1 of The Families and Genera of Vascular Plants, edited by K. Kubitzki. Springer-Verlag, Berlin.

Krusberg, L. R. 1992. Best nematode control. Flower and Garden 36 (2): 8.

Kurata, S. 1963. On Japanese ferns belonging to the genus *Cyrtomium*. Science Report of the Yokosuka City Museum 8: 23–47.

Kurata, S., and T. Nakaike. 1964–1997. Illustrations of Pteridophytes of Japan. Vols. 1–8. University of Tokyo Press, Tokyo.

Langsdorff, G. H., and F. Fischer. 1810. Plantes recueillies pendant le voyage des Russes autour du monde. Published privately by the authors, Tübingen.

Launert, E. 1968. A monographic survey of the genus *Marsilea* Linnaeus. I: The species of Africa and Madagascar. Senckenbergiana Biologica 49: 273–315.

Lee, H. 1887. The vegetable lamb of Tartary, a curious fable of the cotton plant. Sampson, Low, Marston, Searle, and Rivington, London.

Lellinger, D. B. 1972. A revision of the fern genus *Niphidium*. American Fern Journal 62: 101–120.

———. 1985. A Field Manual of the Ferns and Fern Allies of the United States and Canada. Smithsonian Institution Press, Washington, D.C.

———. 1988. Some new species of *Campyloneurum* and a provisional key to the genus. American Fern Journal 78: 14–35.

———. 1989. The ferns and fern allies of Costa Rica, Panama, and the Chocó. Part 1: Psilotaceae through Dicksoniaceae. Pteridologia 2A: 5–364.

———. 1994. Useful fern books in print: 1993–1994. Fiddlehead Forum 21: 19–21.

Little, E. L., Jr., and F. H. Wadsworth. 1964. Common trees of Puerto Rico and the Virgin Islands. Agricultural Handbook No. 249. United States Department of Agriculture, Forest Service, Washington, D.C.

Lloyd, R. M. 1974. Systematics of the genus *Ceratopteris* Brongn. (Parkeriaceae). II: Taxonomy. Brittonia 26: 139–160.

Lloyd, R. M., and E. J. Klekowski Jr. 1970. Spore germination and viability in Pteridophyta: Evolutionary significance of chlorophyllous spores. Biotropica 2: 129–137.

Lovis, J. D. 1968. Fern hybridists and fern hybridising. II: Fern hybridising at the University of Leeds. British Fern Gazette 10: 13–20.

Lovis, J. D., and G. Vida. 1969. The resynthesis and cytogenetic investigation of ×*Asplenophyllitis microdon* and ×*A. jacksonii*. British Fern Gazette 10: 53–67.

Lowe, E. J. 1890. British Ferns and Where Found. Swan Sonnenschein, London.

Lumpkin, T. A., and D. L. Plucknett. 1980. *Azolla:* Botany, physiology, and use as a green manure. Economic Botany 34: 111–153.

MacPhail, J. 1990. Trough gardening. Pacific Horticulture (spring): 31–39.

Marticorena, C., and R. Rodríguez. 1995. Pteridophyta–Gymnospermae. Vol. 1 of Flora de Chile. Universidad de Concepción, Concepción, Chile.

Matkin, O. A., and P. A. Chandler. 1957. The U.C.-type soil mixes. In: U.C. System for Producing Healthy Container-Grown Plants, edited by K. F. Baker. Extension Service Manual No. 23, California Agricultural Experiment Station.

Maxon, W. R. 1912. Studies of tropical American ferns. Contributions to the United States National Herbarium 16: 54–58.

Mickel, J. T. 1979. How to Know the Ferns and Fern Allies. W. C. Brown, Dubuque, Iowa.

———. 1992. Pteridophytes. In: Gymnosperms and Pteridophytes, Vol. 17 of Flora Novo-Galiciana, edited by R. McVaugh. University of Michigan, Ann Arbor.

———. 1994. Ferns for American Gardens. MacMillan Publishing Company, New York.

Mickel, J. T., and J. M. Beitel. 1988. Pteridophyte flora of Oaxaca, Mexico. Memoirs of the New York Botanical Garden 46: 1–568.

Moore, A. W. 1969. *Azolla:* Biology and agronomic significance. The Botanical Review 35: 17–35.

Moran, R. C. 1982. The *Asplenium trichomanes* complex in the United States and adjacent Canada. American Fern Journal 72: 5–11.

———. 1986. The neotropical fern genus *Olfersia*. American Fern Journal 76: 161–178.

———. 1987. Monograph of the neotropical fern genus *Polybotrya* (Dryopteridaceae). Illinois Natural History Survey Bulletin 34 (1): i–v, 1–138.

———. 1992a. The vegetable lamb of Tartary—A pteridological tale. Fiddlehead Forum 19: 2, 7, 8.

————. 1992b. The potato fern. Fiddlehead Forum 19: 18–20.

————. 1992c. The story of the molesting *Salvinia*. Fiddlehead Forum 19: 26–28.

————. 1993. Bracken, the poisoner. Fiddlehead Forum 20: 18–19, 22.

————. 1995a. Iridescent ferns and their shady behavior. Fiddlehead Forum 22: 2–4, 8.

————. 1995b. Nardoo. Fiddlehead Forum 22: 20–22.

————. 1997. The little nitrogen factories. Fiddlehead Forum 24: 9, 12–14.

————. 1998. Palea-botany. Fiddlehead Forum 25: 19–23.

Moran, R. C., and R. Riba, eds. 1995. Psilotaceae a Salviniaceae. In: Flora Mesoamericana, Vol. 1, edited by G. Davidse, M. Sousa S., and S. Knapp. Universidad Nacional Autónoma de México, Ciudad de México.

Morton, C. V. 1967. The fern herbarium of André Michaux. American Fern Journal 57: 166–182.

Moteetee, A., J. G. Duckett, and A. J. Russell. 1996. Mycorrhizas in ferns of Lesotho. In: Pteridology in Perspective: Proceedings of the Holttum Memorial Pteridophyte Symposium, Kew, edited by J. M. Camus, M. Gibby, and R. E. Johns.

Nooteboom, H. P. 1994. Notes on Davalliaceae. II: A revision of the genus *Davallia*. Blumea 39: 151–214.

————. 1997. The microsoroid ferns. Blumea 42: 261–395.

Palmer, D. D. 1994. The Hawaiian species of *Cibotium*. American Fern Journal 84: 73–85.

————. 1997. A revision of the genus *Sadleria* (Blechnaceae). Pacific Science 51: 288–305.

Panigrahi, G. 1993. *Parahemionitis,* a new genus of Pteridaceae. American Fern Journal 83: 90–92.

Parrella, M. P., K. L. Robb, and P. Morishita. 1985. Snails and slugs in ornamentals. California Agriculture (January–February): 6–88.

Patterson, P. M., and A. S. Freeman. 1963. The effect of photoperiodism on certain ferns. American Fern Journal 53: 126–128.

Pichi-Sermolli, R. E. G. 1962. On the fern genus *Actiniopteris* Link. Webbia 17: 1–32.

Piggott, A. G. 1988. Ferns of Malaysia in Colour. Tropical Press, Kuala Lumpur SDN.BHD, Malaysia.

Proctor, G. R. 1977. Flora of The Lesser Antilles: Pteridophyta. Arnold Arboretum, Harvard University, Jamaica Plain, Massachusetts.

————. 1985. Ferns of Jamaica. British Museum (Natural History), London.

————. 1989. Ferns of Puerto Rico and the Virgin Islands. New York Botanical Garden, Bronx, New York.

Pryer, K. M., A. R. Smith, and J. E. Skog. 1995. Phylogenetic relationships of extant ferns based on evidence from morphology and *rbcL* sequences. American Fern Journal 85: 205–282.

Rasbach, H., T. Reichstein, and R. L. Viane. 1994. *Asplenium chiuahuenge* (Aspleniaceae, Pteridophyta): An allohexaploid species and the description of a simplified hybridization technique. American Fern Journal 84: 11–40.

Reasoner, S. 1982. Play "Misty" for me. Greenhouse Manager (September): 39–42.

Rickard, M. 1981. Survey of variations in British polypodiums. British Pteridological Society Bulletin 1: 138–140.

————. 1986. Vegetative reproduction in ferns. Pteridologist 1: 112–115.

————. 2000. The Plantfinder's Guide to Garden Ferns. Timber Press, Portland, Oregon.

Rogers, G. 1998. The history and classification of the Farley fern, *Adiantum tenerum* 'Farleyense'. American Fern Journal 88: 32–46.

Roos, M. C. 1985. Phylogenetic systematics of the Drynarioideae (Polypodiaceae). Verhandelingen der Koninklijke Nederlandse Akademie van Wetenschappen, Afdeeling Natuurkunde, Tweede Reeks 85: 1–138.

Rothwell, G. W., and R. A. Stockey. 1991. *Onoclea sensibilis* in the Paleocene of North America: A dramatic example of structural and ecological stasis. Review of Palaeobotany and Palynology 709: 113–24.

Rush, R. 1983. A hardy hybrid *Adiantum.* British Pteridological Society Bulletin 2: 261–262.

———. 1984a. A guide to hardy ferns. Special Publication No. 1. British Pteridological Society, London.

———. 1984b. Raising pteridophytes from spores: The special cases. Pteridologist 1: 3–5.

Scamman, E. 1960. The maidenhair ferns (*Adiantum*) of Costa Rica. Contributions of the Gray Herbarium of Harvard University 187: 3–22.

Sessions, A. 1978. Key to the cultivars of *Nephrolepis exaltata* 'Bostoniensis'. Privately published.

Shivas, M. G. 1962. The *Polypodium vulgare* complex. British Fern Gazette 9: 65–70.

Smith, A. R. 1981. Pteridophytes. In: Flora of Chiapas, Part 2, edited by D. E. Breedlove. California Academy of Sciences, San Francisco.

———. 1995. Pteridophytes. In: Flora of the Venezuelan Guayana, Vol. 2, edited by J. Steyermark, P. E. Berry, and B. K. Holst. Timber Press, Portland, Oregon.

Snyder, L. H., Jr., and J. G. Bruce. 1986. Field Guide to the Ferns and Other Pteridophytes of Georgia. University of Georgia Press, Athens.

de la Sota, E. R. 1963. Contribución al conocimiento de las "Salviniaceae" neotropicales. IV. Darwiniana 12: 612–623.

———. 1966. Revisión de las especies Americanas del grupo "*Polypodium squamatum*" L. "Polypodiaceae" (s. str.). Revista del Museo de La Plata, Sección Botânica 10: 69–186, t. I–VII.

Sowerby, J. E., and C. Johnson. 1855. The Ferns of Great Britain. Self-published, London.

Tagawa, M., and K. Iwatsuki. 1979–1989. Flora of Thailand. Vol. 3, Pteridophytes. Chutima Press, Bangkok.

Taylor, W. C. 1984. Arkansas Ferns and Fern Allies. Milwaukee Public Museum, Milwaukee, Wisconsin.

Thurston, S. H. 1939. Forcing a collection of native ferns of New England and the middle Atlantic states for exhibition. American Fern Journal 29: 85–94.

Tindale, M. 1965. A monograph of the genus *Lastreopsis* Ching. Contributions to the New South Wales National Herbarium 3: 249–339, t. 1–23.

Trehane, P., ed. 1995. International Code of Nomenclature for Cultivated Plants. Regnum Vegetabile 133: 1–175.

Tryon, A. F. 1957. A revision of the fern genus *Pellaea* section *Pellaea.* Annals of the Missouri Botanical Garden 44: 125–193.

Tryon, R. M. 1956. A revision of the American species of *Notholaena.* Contributions of the Gray Herbarium of Harvard University 179: 1–106.

———. 1962. Taxonomic fern notes. II: *Pityrogramma* and *Anogramma.* Contributions of the Gray Herbarium of Harvard University 189: 5–76.

Tryon, R. M., and R. G. Stolze. 1989. Pteridophyta of Peru. Part I: 1. Ophioglossaceae–12. Cyatheaceae. Fieldiana, Botany, new series 20: 1–145.

———. 1989. Pteridophyta of Peru. Part II: 13. Pteridaceae–15. Dennstaedtiaceae. Fieldiana, Botany, new series 22: 1–128.

———. 1991. Pteridophyta of Peru. Part IV: 17. Dryopteridaceae. Fieldiana, Botany, new series 27: 1–176.

———. 1993. Pteridophyta of Peru. Part V: 18. Aspleniaceae–21. Polypodiaceae. Fieldiana, Botany, new series 27: 1–176.

———. 1994. Pteridophyta of Peru. Part VI: 22. Marsileaceae–28. Isoëtaceae. Fieldiana, Botany, new series 32: 1–190.

Tryon, R. M., and A. F. Tryon. 1982. Ferns and Allied Plants, with Special Reference to Tropical America. Springer-Verlag, Berlin.

Tutin, T. G., V. H. Heywood, N. A. Burges, D. H. Valentine, S. M. Walters, D. A. Webb. 1964. Flora Europaea. Vol. 1, Lycopodiaceae to Platanaceae. Cambridge University Press, Cambridge.

Vail, R. 1984. *Platycerium* Hobbyist's Handbook. Desert Biological Publications, Mena, Arkansas.

van Hove, C. 1989. *Azolla* and its multiple uses, with emphasis on Africa. Food and Agriculture Organization of the United Nations, Rome.

Vareschi, V. 1968. Helechos. In: Flora de Venezuela, Vol. 1, parts 1 and 2. Edición Especial del Instituto Botânico, Caracas.

Wagner, D. H. 1979. Systematics of *Polystichum* in western North America north of Mexico. Pteridologia 1: 1–64.

Wagner, G. M. 1997. *Azolla:* A review of its biology and utilization. Botanical Review 63: 1–26.

Wagner, W. H., Jr. 1942. Bipinnate Christmas fern. American Fern Journal 32: 27–29.

Wagner, W. H., Jr., and F. S. Wagner. 1975. A hybrid polypody from the New World tropics. Fern Gazette 11: 125–135.

Walker, T. G. 1970. Species of *Pteris* commonly in cultivation. British Fern Gazette 10: 143–151.

Weatherby, C. A. 1939. The group of *Polypodium polypodioides.* Contributions of the Gray Herbarium of Harvard University 124: 22–35.

Webster, T. R. 1979. An artificial crossing technique for *Selaginella.* American Fern Journal 69: 9–13.

Wherry, E. T. 1972. The Southern Fern Guide. Doubleday, Garden City, New York.

Windham, M. D. 1987. *Argyrochosma,* a new genus of cheilanthoid ferns. American Fern Journal 77: 37–41.

Yatskievych, G. 1996. A revision of the fern genus *Phanerophlebia* (Dryopteridaceae). Annals of the Missouri Botanical Garden 83: 168–199.

Subject Index

Please see page 581 for the Plant Name Index.

Plant Name Index

Plants listed in boldface have entries in Chapter 13, "Ferns and Fern Allies in Cultivation." Cultivars and common names are cross-referenced to species or genus. Cultivars are listed at the end of the genus.